International cat

scientific literature Eleventh

Annual Issue C. Physics

Unknown

Alpha Editions

This edition published in 2020

ISBN : 9789354048173 (Hardback)

ISBN : 9789354048678 (Paperback)

Design and Setting By
Alpha Editions
www.alphaedis.com
email - alphaedis@gmail.com

INTERNATIONAL CATALOGUE OF SCIENTIFIC LITERATURE.

GOVERNMENTS AND INSTITUTIONS CO-OPERATING IN THE PRODUCTION OF THE CATALOGUE.

The Government of Austria.
The Government of Belgium.
The Government of Canada.
The Government of Cuba.
The Government of Denmark.
The Government of Egypt.
The Society of Sciences, Helsingfors, Finland.
The Government of France.
The Government of Germany.
The Royal Society of London, Great Britain.
The Government of Greece.
The Government of Holland.
The Government of Hungary.
The Asiatic Society of Bengal, India.
The Government of Italy.
The Government of Japan.
The Government of Mexico.
The Government of New South Wales.
The Government of New Zealand.
The Government of Norway.
The Academy of Sciences, Cracow
The Polytechnic Academy, Oporto, Portugal.
The Government of Queensland.
The Government of Russia.
The Government of the Cape of Good Hope.
The Government of South Australia.
The Government of Spain.
The Government of Sweden.
The Government of Switzerland.
The Smithsonian Institution, United States of America.
The Government of Victoria.
The Government of Western Australia.

INTERNATIONAL CATALOGUE OF SCIENTIFIC LITERATURE.

CENTRAL BUREAU.

34 AND 35, SOUTHAMPTON STREET.

STRAND,

LONDON, W.C.

Director.—H. FORSTER MORLEY, M.A., D.Sc.

REGIONAL BUREAUS.

All communications for the several Regional Bureaus are to be sent to the addresses here given.

Argentine Republic.—Prof. Felix F. Outes, Universidad de Buenos-Aires.

Austria.—Herr Hofrat Dr. Josef v. Karabacek, Direktor. K. K. Hofbibliothek, Vienna.

Belgium.—Monsieur Louis Masure, Secrétaire-Général de l'Office International de Bibliographie, Brussels.

Canada.—Prof. J. G. Adami, McGill College, Montreal.

Cuba.—Prof. Santiago de la Huerta, Havana.

Denmark.—Dr. Martin Knudsen, Polytekmsk Læreanstalt, Copenhagen. O.

Egypt.—E. M. Dowson, Esq., A.I.C.E., Director-General, Survey Department, Cairo.

Finland.—Herr Dr. G. Schauman, Bibliothekar der Societät der Wissenschaften, Helsingfors.

France.—Monsieur le Dr. J. Deniker, 8, Rue de Buffon, Paris.

Germany.—Herr Prof. Dr. O. Uhlworm, Enckeplatz, 3A, Berlin, S.W.

Greece.—Monsieur P. Calogeropoulos, Boulé tōn Ellēnōn, 20 Homer Street, Athens.

Holland.—Heer Prof. D. J. Korteweg, Universität, Amsterdam.

Hungary.—Herr Prof. Gustav Rados, viii, Muzeumkörut, Müegyetem, Buda-Pest.

India and Ceylon.—The Hon. Sec., Asiatic Society of Bengal, 1, Park Street, Calcutta.

Italy.—Cav. E. Mancini, Accademia dei Lincei. Palazzo Corsini, Lungara, Rome.

Japan.—Prof. J. Sakurai, Imperial University, Tokyo.

Mexico.—Señor Don José M. Vigil, Presidente del Instituto Bibliografico Mexicano, Biblioteca Nacional, Mexico City.

New South Wales.—The Hon. Sec., Royal Society of New South Wales, Sydney.

New Zealand.—The Director, New Zealand Institute, Wellington, N.Z.

Norway.—Mr. A. Kjær, Universitetet, Kristiania.

Poland (Austrian, Russian and Prussian).—Dr. T. Estreicher. Sekretarz, Komisya Bibliograficzna. Akademii Umiejętności, Cracow.

Portugal.—Senhor F. Gomez Teixeira, Faculté de Sciences, Universidade do Pôrto, Oporto.

Queensland.—John Shirley, Esq., B.Sc., Cordelia Street, South Brisbane.

Russia.—Monsieur E. Heintz, l'Observatoire Physique Central Nicolas, Vass. Ostr. 23-me ligne, 2, St. Petersburg.

South Africa.—Dr. L. Péringuey, South African Museum, Cape Town, Cape of Good Hope.

South Australia.—The Librarian, Public Library of South Australia, Adelaide.

Spain.—Señor Don José Rodriguez Carracido, Real Academia de Ciencias, Valverde 26, Madrid.

Straits Settlements.—The Director, Raffles Museum, Singapore.

Sweden.—Dr. E. W. Dahlgren, Royal Academy of Sciences, Stockholm.

Switzerland.—Herr Prof. Dr. J. H. Graf, Schweizerische Landesbibliothek, Berne.

The United States of America.—Leonard C. Gunnell, Esq., Smithsonian Institution, Washington.

Victoria and Tasmania.—Thomas S. Hall, Esq., Hon. Sec. Royal Society of Victoria, Victoria Street, Melbourne.

Western Australia.—J. S. Battye, Esq., Victoria Public Library, Perth.

INSTRUCTIONS.

The present volume contains (a) Schedules and Indexes in four languages; (b) An Author Catalogue; (c) A Subject Catalogue.

The Schedules have been revised in accordance with the decisions of the International Convention of 1905.

The Subject Catalogue is divided into sections, each of which is denoted by a four-figure number between 0000 and 9999 called a Registration number. These numbers follow one another in numerical order.

In each section the final arrangement of papers is in the alphabetical order of authors' names.

To find the papers dealing with a particular subject the reader may consult either the Schedule or the Index to the Schedule. The numbers given in the Index are Registration numbers, and can be used at once for turning to the proper page of the Subject Index. This is done by looking at the numbers at the right-hand top corners of the pages.

In the Author Catalogue the numbers placed within square brackets at the end of each entry are Registration numbers, and serve to indicate the scope of each paper indexed. The meaning of these numbers will at once be found by reference to the Schedule.

In case the abbreviated titles of Journals are not understood, a key to these is provided at the end of the volume.

The literature indexed is mainly that of 1911, but includes those portions of the literature of 1901-1910 in regard to which the index slips were received by the Central Bureau too late for inclusion in the previous volumes. There are also entries dated 1912.

CONTENTS.

International Catalogue of Scientific Literature

SCHEDULE

OF

CLASSIFICATION

(C) PHYSICS

PRIMARY DIVISIONS

GENERAL	0000
GENERAL MOLECULAR PHYSICS..	0100
HEAT	0900
LIGHT AND INVISIBLE RADIATION	2990
ELECTRICITY AND MAGNETISM..	4900
VIBRATION AND SOUND	8990

(C) PHYSICS.

The Subject THEORETICAL AND APPLIED MECHANICS including Statics, Dynamics, Elasticity and Strength of Materials, is indexed separately as Volume B.

[Papers on the relation of Chemical Constitution to Physical Properties will be indexed under (D) Chemistry.]

0000 Philosophy.
0010 History. Biography.
0020 Periodicals. Reports of Institutions, Societies, Congresses, etc.
0030 General Treatises, Text Books. Dictionaries, Collected Works. Tables.*
0032 Bibliographies.
0040 Addresses, Lectures, etc., of a general character.*
0050 Pedagogy. Lecture Apparatus and Experiments.
0060 Institutions, Museums, Collections.
0070 Nomenclature.
0090 Methods of Research. Instruments and Apparatus.

GENERAL MOLECULAR PHYSICS.

0100 General.
0150 Estimates and Calculations of Molecular Magnitudes.
0200 The Molecular Theory of Gases and Liquids (General Mathematical Theories).
0250 Absorption and Adsorption of Gases.

* In sections 0030 and 0040 entries will be grouped under headings corresponding with the main divisions of Physics, viz., General, Heat, Light, Electricity, Sound.

(C) PHYSIK.

THEORETISCHE UND ANGE-WANDTE MECHANIK, einschl. Statik, Dynamik, Elastizität und Festigkeit der Materialien, wird separat katalogisiert und bildet den Band B.

[Arbeiten, welche die Wechselbeziehungen chemischer Constitution und physikalischer Eigenschaften behandeln, kommen unter (D) Chemie.]

Philosophie.
Geschichte, Biographien.
Periodica. Berichte von Instituten, Gesellschaften, Kongressen etc.
Allgemeine Abhandlungen. Lehrbücher, Wörterbücher, Sammelwerke, Tabellen.*
Bibliographien.
Festreden, Vorträge u.s.w., allgemeiner Art.*
Pädagogik. Vorlesungsapparate und -versuche.
Institute, Museen, Sammlungen.
Nomenklatur.
Untersuchungsmethoden, Instrumente und Apparate.

ALLGEMEINE MOLECULARPHYSIK.

Allgemeines.
Abschätzung und Berechnung molecularer Grössen.
Moleculare Theorie der Gase und Flüssigkeiten (allgemeine mathematische Theorien).
Absorption und Adsorption von Gasen.

* In den Abschnitten 0030 und 0040 werden die Eintragungen nach Rubriken geordnet, welche mit den Hauptabteilungen der Physik—Allgemeines, Wärme, Licht, Elektrizität, Schall—übereinstimmen.

(C) PHYSIQUE.

(C) FISICA.

LA MÉCANIQUE THÉORIQUE ET APPLIQUÉE, y compris la Statique, la Dynamique, l'Elasticité et la Résistance des Matériaux, est cataloguée séparément et constitue le volume B.

[Les travaux ayant trait au rapport de la composition chimique avec les propriétés physiques seront inscrits sous la Chimie (D).]

LA MECCANICA TEORETICA ED APPLICATA, compresovi la Statica, la Dinamica, l'Elasticità e la Resistenza dei Materiali, viene catalogata separatamente e costituisce il tomo B.

[I lavori sulle relazioni fra la costituzione chimica e le proprietà fisiche verranno catalogati sotto (D) Chimica.]

0000	Philosophie.	Filosofia.
0010	Histoire. Biographies.	Storia. Biografie.
0020	Périodiques. Rapports d'Institutions, de Sociétés, de Congrès, etc.	Periodici. Rapporti di Istituti, Società, Congressi, ecc.
0030	Traités généraux. Manuels, Dictionnaires. Recueils, Tables.*	Trattati generali, Libri di testo, Dizionari, Raccolte, Tavole.*
0032	Bibliographies.	Bibliografie.
0040	Discours, Cours, etc., d'un caractère général.*	Discorsi, Lezioni, ecc., aventi un carattere generale.*
0050	Pédagogie. Appareils et expériences de cours.	Pedagogia. Apparecchi ed esperimenti da lezione.
0060	Institutions, Musées, Collections.	Istituti, Musei, Collezioni.
0070	Nomenclature.	Nomenclatura.
0090	Méthodes de recherche, Instruments et Appareils.	Metodi di ricerca, Istrumenti ed Apparecchi.

PHYSIQUE MOLÉCULAIRE GÉNÉRALE.

FISICA MOLECOLARE GENERALE.

0100	Généralités.	Generalità.
0150	Évaluations et calculs des grandeurs moléculaires.	Valutazioni e calcoli della grandezza delle molecole.
0200	La théorie moléculaire des gaz et des liquides (théories mathématiques générales).	Teoria molecolare dei gas e dei liquidi (teorie matematiche generali).
0250	Absorption et adsorption des gaz.	Assorbimento e adsorbimento dei gas.

* Dans les sections 0030 et 0040 les titres seront disposés sous des rubriques qui correspondent aux divisions principles de la physique, c. à d., Généralités, Chaleur, Lumière, Electricité, Acoustique.

* Nelle sezioni 0030 e 0040 i lavori verranno aggruppati sotto intestazioni che corrispondano alle divisioni principali della Fisica, cioè : Generalità, Calore, Luce, Elettricità, Acustica.

4

0300	Capillarity. (See also D 7165.)	Kapillarität. (Siehe auch D 7165.)
0310	Osmosis. Osmotic Pressure. (See also D 7155.)	Osmose. Osmotischer Druck. (Siehe auch D 7155.)
0320	Diffusion of Gases, Liquids, and Solids. Effusion. Transpiration. (See also D 7155.)	Diffusion von Gasen, Flüssigkeiten und festen Körpern. Effusion. Transpiration. (Siehe auch D 7155.)
0325	Viscosity of fluids (internal friction). (See also D 7170.)	Viskosität der Flüssigkeiten (innere Reibung). (Siehe auch D 7170.)
0340	Colloidal Substances.	Kolloidalkörper.
0400	Molecular Theories of Crystals and other Solids. (See also Elasticity, B 3210 and G 140.)	Moleculare Theorie der Krystalle und sonstiger fester Körper. (Siehe auch Elastizität, B 3210 und G 140.)

Ultimate Physical Theories.
Grundtheorien der Physik.

0500	Theories of the Constitution of Matter. (See Vortex-Motion. B 2450, and Physical Chemistry, D 7000.)	Theorien der Konstitution der Materie. (Siehe auch Wirbelbewegung, B 2450, und Physikalische Chemie, D 7000.)
0600	Theories of the Ether. (See also E 1830.)	Theorien des Aethers. (Siehe auch E 1830.)
0700	Dynamical Theories of Gravitation.	Dynamische Theorien der Gravitation.

Measurement of Mechanical Quantities. Elasticity. [Only such papers as are of interest to physicists are to be indexed here.]
Messung Mechanischer Quantitäten. Elastizität. [Nur solche Abhandlungen sind hier aufzunehmen, die für Physiker Interesse haben.]

0800	General.	Allgemeines.
0805	Theory of Measurement (combination of observations). Harmonic Analysis. Units and Dimensions.	Theorie der Messung (Kombination von Beobachtungen). Harmonische Analyse. Einheiten und Dimensionen.
0807	Measurement of Length (mechanical and optical).	Längenmessung (mechanische und optische).
0809	Measurement of Time (mechanical and electrical).	Zeitmessung (mechanische und elektrische).
0810	Measurement of Mass and Density. Balance. (See also D 7115.)	Massen- und Dichtigkeitsmessung. Wage. (Siehe auch D 7115.)
0820	Measurement of Velocity, Acceleration, Energy of Visible Motion.	Messung von Geschwindigkeit, Beschleunigung, Energie sichtbarer Bewegung.
0825	Measurement of Force: Pendulum, Spring-balance, Torsion-balance.	Messung von Kräften: Pendel, Federwage, Torsionswage.
0835	Measurement of Fluid Pressure and Fluid Velocity.	Messung von Druck und Geschwindigkeit der Flüssigkeiten.
0840	Elastic Deformation of Solids. Compressibility and Rigidity. Elongation, Torsion, Flexure, Young's Modulus.	Elastische Deformation fester Körper. Kompressibilität und Druckfestigkeit. Ausdehnung, Torsion, Biegung, Young's Modul.
0842	Compressibility of liquids.	Kompressibilität der Flüssigkeiten.
0845	Numerical Values of Mechanical Quantities (Density, Gravitation, etc.).	Numerische Werte mechanischer Quantitäten (Dichtigkeit, Schwere etc.).

0300 Capillarité. (*Voy. aussi* D 7165.)	Capillarità. (*Vedi anche* D 7165.)
0310 Osmose. Pression osmotique. (*Voy. aussi* D 7155.)	Osmosi. Pressione osmotica. (*Vedi anche* D 7155.)
0320 Diffusion des gaz, des liquides et des solides. Effusion. Transpiration. (*Voy. aussi* D 7155.)	Diffusione dei gas, dei liquidi e dei solidi. Effusione. Traspirazione. (*Vedi anche* D 7155.)
0325 Viscosité des fluides (frottement intérieur). (*Voy. aussi* D 7170.)	Viscosità dei fluidi (attrito interno). (*Vedi anche* D 7170.)
0340 Substances colloïdales.	Sostanze colloidali.
0400 Théories moléculaires des cristaux et des autres solides. (*Voy. aussi* Elasticité, B 3210 et G 140.)	Teorie molecolari dei cristalli ed altri solidi. (*Vedi anche* Elasticità, B 3210 e G 140.)

Théories physiques fondamentales.   **Teorie Fisiche Fondamentali.**

0500 Théories de la constitution de la matière. (*Voy.* mouvement tourbillonnaire, B 2450, et Chimie physique, D 7000.)	Teorie della costituzione della materia. (*Vedi* movimenti vorticosi, B 2450, e Chimica fisica, D 7000.)
0600 Théories de l'éther. (*Voy. aussi* E 1830.)	Teorie dell'etere. (*Vedi anche* E 1830.)
0700 Théories dynamiques de la gravitation.	Teorie dinamiche della gravità.

Mesure des quantités mécaniques Elasticité. [On ne devra cataloguer ici que les mémoires qui sont intéressants pour les physiciens.]   **Misura delle Quantità Meccaniche. Elasticità.** [Verranno qui registrati solamente quelli articoli che possono avere dell'interesse per i fisici.]

0800 Généralités.	Generalità.
0805 Théorie de la mesure (combinaison d'observations). Analyse harmonique. Unités et dimensions.	Teoria della misura (combinazione di osservazioni). Analisi armonica. Unità e dimensioni.
0807 Mesure des longueurs (mécanique et optique).	Misura di lunghezze (meccanica ed ottica).
0809 Mesure du temps (mécanique et électrique).	Misura del tempo (meccanica ed elettrica).
0810 Mesure des masses et de la densité. Balance. (*Voy. aussi* D 7115.)	Misura di masse e densità. Bilancia. (*Vedi anche* D 7115.)
0820 Mesure de la vitesse, de l'accélération, de l'énergie du mouvement visible.	Misura di velocità, accelerazione, energia di un moto visibile.
0825 Mesure des forces : pendule, balance à ressort, balance de torsion.	Misura di forze : pendolo, bilancia a molla, bilancia di torsione.
0835 Mesure de la pression et de la vitesse d'un fluide.	Misura della pressione e velocità dei fluidi.
0840 Déformation élastique des solides. Compressibilité et rigidité. Elongation, torsion, flexion, module de Young.	Deformazione elastica dei solidi. Compressibilità e rigidità. Elongazione, torsione, flessione, modulo di Young.
0842 Compressibilité des liquides.	Compressibilità dei liquidi.
0845 Valeurs numériques des quantités mécaniques (densité, gravitation, etc.).	Valori numerici delle quantità meccaniche (densità, gravitazione, ecc.).

HEAT.

WARMELEHRE.

0900 General.

Allgemeines.

Sources of Heat and Cold.

1000 General.

1010 Methods of Producing High Temperatures.
1012 Methods of Producing Low Temperatures.
1014 Methods of Producing Constant Temperatures. Thermostats.

Thermometry.

1200 General.

1210 Expansion and Pressure Thermometry.
1230 Electrical Thermometry.

1240 Temperature Measurement by Calorimeter, Vapour Density, Transpiration, Viscosity, etc.
1250 Special Thermometers (Maximum, Minimum, Self-recording, etc.). (See also Meteorology, F 0250.)

1255 Radiation Thermometry, Optical Pyrometry, etc.
1260 Comparison of Thermometers. Thermometric Scales. Reduction to Thermodynamic Scale. (See also Thermodynamics, 2400, etc.)

Relations involving Expansion and Stress.

1400 General. (See also D 7245.)

1410 Expansion of Solids by Heat. (For Compressibility of Solids, see Elasticity, B 3200, etc.)
1420 Permanent Deformation and Thermal Hysteresis. Annealing.
1430 Expansion of Liquids: Pressure-Volume-Temperature Relations.

1450 Expansion of Gases and Unsaturated Vapours: Pressure-Volume-Temperature Relations. (See also D 7160.)

Wärme- und Kälte-Quellen.

Allgemeines.

Methoden zum Erzeugen hoher Temperaturen.
Methoden zum Erzeugen niedriger Temperaturen.
Methoden zum Erzeugen konstanter Temperaturen. Thermostaten.

Thermometrie.

Allgemeines.

Ausdehnungs -und Druckthermometrie.
Elektrische Thermometrie.

Temperaturmessung mittels Kalorimetrie, Dampfdichte, Transpiration, Viskosität etc.).
Thermometer für spezielle Zwecke (Maximum-, Minimum-Thermometer, selbstregistrierende Thermometer etc.). (Siehe auch Meteorologie, F 0250.)

Strahlungsthermometrie, optische Pyrometrie etc.
Vergleichung von Thermometern. Thermometrische Skalen. Reduction auf thermodynamische Skala. (Siehe auch Thermodynamik, 2400 etc.)

Bedingungen, unter denen Ausdehnung und Deformation stattfinden.

Allgemeines. (Siehe auch D 7245.)

Ausdehnung fester Körper durch die Wärme. (Kompressibilität fester Körper siehe unter Elastizität, B 3200 etc.)
Dauernde Deformation und thermische Hysteresis. Anlassen.
Ausdehnung der Flüssigkeiten: Beziehungen zwischen Druck-Volumen und Temperatur.
Ausdehnung der Gase und ungesättigten Dämpfe: Beziehungen zwischen Druck - Volumen und Temperatur. (Siehe auch D 7160.)

CHALEUR.   CALORE.

0900 Généralités.   Generalità.

Sources de chaleur et de froid.   Sorgenti di caldo e freddo.

1000 Généralités.   Generalità.

1010 Méthodes de production des températures hautes.   Metodi per produrre temperature alte.

1012 Méthodes de production des températures basses.   Metodi per produrre temperature basse.

1014 Méthodes de production des températures constantes. Thermostats.   Metodi per produrre temperature costanti. Termostati.

Thermométrie.   Termometria.

1200 Généralités.   Generalità.

1210 Thermométrie à dilatation et à pression.   Termometria a dilatazione ed a pressione.

1230 Thermométrie électrique.   Termometria elettrica.

1240 Mesure des températures par la calorimétrie, la densité de vapeur, la transpiration, la viscosité, etc.   Misura delle temperature per mezzo della calorimetria, densità dei vapori, traspirazione, viscosità, ecc.

1250 Thermomètres à destinations spéciales (à maxima, à minima, enregistreurs, etc.). (*Voy. aussi* Météorologie, F 0250.)   Termometri a scopi speciali (a massima, a minima, registratori, ecc.). (*Vedi anche* Meteorologia, F 0250.)

1255 Thermométrie des radiations, pyrométrie optique, etc.   Termometria delle radiazioni, pirometria ottica, ecc.

1260 Comparaison des thermomètres. Echelles thermométriques. Réduction à l'échelle thermodynamique. (*Voy. aussi* Thermodynamique, 2400, etc.)   Confronto di termometri. Scale termometriche. Riduzione alla scala termodinamica. (*Vedi anche* Termodinamica, 2400, ecc.)

Relations qui se rattachent à la dilatation et à la déformation.   Relazioni che producono la dilatazione e la deformazione.

1400 Généralités. (*Voy. aussi* D 7245.)   Generalità. (*Vedi anche* D 7245.)

1410 Dilatation des solides par la chaleur. (Pour la compressibilité des solides *voy.* Élasticité, B 3200, etc.)   Dilatazione dei solidi pel calore. (Per la compressibilità dei solidi *vedi* Elasticità, B 3200, ecc.)

1420 Déformation permanente et hystérésis thermique. Recuit.   Deformazione permanente ed isteresi termale. Tempera

1430 Dilatation des liquides : Relations entre la pression, la température et le volume.   Dilatazione dei liquidi : relazioni tra la pressione, temperatura e volume.

1450 Dilatation des gaz et des vapeurs non saturantes : Relations entre la pression, la température et le volume. (*Voy. aussi* D 7160.)   Dilatazione dei gas e dei vapori non saturi : relazioni tra la pressione, temperatura e volume. (*Vide anche* D 7160.)

Calorimetry and Specific Heat.	Kalorimetrie und spezifische Wärme.
1600 General. Units of Heat.	Allgemeines. Wärme-Einheiten.
1610 Calorimetric Methods.	Kalorimetrische Methoden.
1620 Specific Heats of Solids and Liquids. (*See also* D 7220.)	Spezifische Wärmen fester und flüssiger Körper. (*Siehe auch* D 7220.)
1640 Specific Heats of Gases and Vapours. (*See also* D 7220.)	Spezifische Wärmen von Gasen und Dämpfen. (*Siehe auch* D 7220.)
1660 Chemical Constitution and Specific Heat (Dulong and Petit Law, etc.). (*See also* D 7220.)	Spezifische Wärme und chemische Konstitution (Dulong-Petit'sches Gesetz etc.). (*Siehe auch* D 7220.
1670 Heats of Fusion.	Schmelzwärmen.
1680 Heats of Vaporisation.	Verdunstungswärmen.
1690 Heats of Dissolution. (*See also* D 7230.)	Auflösungswärmen. (*Siehe auch* D 7230.)
1695 Heats of Transformation.	Umwandlungswärmen.

Phenomena of Change of State.	Phänomene der Zustandsänderung.
1800 General.	Allgemeines.
1810 Fusion and Solidification (General). (*See also* D 7205.)	Schmelzen und Erstarren (Allgemeines). (*Siehe auch* D 7205.)
1840 Saturated Vapours. Pressure; Boiling - Points. Evaporation. (*See also* D 7210; F 1050.)	Gesättigte Dämpfe. Druck; Siedepunkte. Verdampfung. (*Siehe auch* D 7210; F 1050.)
1850 Vapour Densities. (*See also* B 0140; D 7115.)	Dampfdichten. (*Siehe auch* B 0140; D 7115.)
1860 Ebullition.	Sieden.
1870 Liquefaction of Gases and Gaseous Mixtures	Verflüssigung von Gasen und Gasgemischen.
1880 Continuity of State. Critical State, Critical Point, etc. Characteristic Equations. (*See also* D 7000, 7212.)	Kontinuirliche Zustandsänderung. Kritischer Zustand, kritischer Punkt etc. Characteristische Gleichungen. (*Siehe auch* D 7000, 7212.)
1885 Corresponding States.	Korrespondierende Zustände.
1887 Equilibrium in coexistent phases. Phase Rule (General).	Gleichgewicht bei coexistierenden Phasen. Phasenlehre (Allgemeines).
1890 Hygroscopy and Hygrometry. (*See also* F 0270, 1000-1060.)	Hygroskopie und Hygrometrie. (*Siehe auch* F 0270, 1000-1060.)
1900 Vaporization of Solids. Sublimation.	Verdunstung fester Körper. Sublimation.
1920 Solutions and Liquid Mixtures Melting-Point, Boiling-Point, Vapour Pressure, etc.	Lösungen und flüssige Mischungen: Schmelzpunkt, Siedepunkt, Dampfdruck etc.
1925 Solutions: Other Thermal Properties (Latent Heat). (*See* 1690.)	Lösungen: sonstige thermische Eigenschaften (latente Wärme). (*Siehe* 1690.)
1930 Dissociation. Allotropic Transformations.	Dissociation. Allotropische Umwandlungen.
1940 Retardation Phenomena (Superfusion, Superheating, Supersaturation).	Verzugsphänomene (Ueberschmelzen, Ueberhitzen, Uebersättigung).

Calorimetrie et Chaleur Spécifique.　　　Calorimetria e calore specifico.

	French	Italian
1600	Généralités. Unités de chaleur.	Generalità. Unità di calore.
1610	Méthodes calorimétriques.	Metodi calorimetrici.
1620	Chaleurs spécifiques des solides et des liquides. (Voy. aussi D 7220.)	Calori specifici dei solidi e dei liquidi. (Vedi anche D 7220.)
1640	Chaleurs spécifiques des gaz et des vapeurs. (Voy. aussi D 7220.)	Calori specifici dei gas e dei vapori. (Vedi anche D 7220.)
1660	Constitution chimique et chaleur spécifique (loi de Dulong et de Petit, etc.). (Voy. aussi D 7220.)	Costituzione chimica e calore specifico (legge di Dulong e Petit, ecc.). (Vedi anche D 7220.)
1670	Chaleurs de fusion.	Calori di fusione.
1680	Chaleurs de vaporisation.	Calori di vaporizzazione.
1690	Chaleurs de dissolution. (Voy. aussi D 7230.)	Calori di soluzione. (Vedi anche D 7230.)
1695	Chaleurs de transformation.	Calori di trasformazione.

Phénomènes de Changements d'état.　　　Fenomeni del cangiamento di stato d'aggregazione.

1800	Généralités.	Generalità.
1810	Fusion et solidification (généralités). (Voy. aussi D 7205.)	Fusione e solidificazione (generalità). (Vedi anche D 7205.)
1840	Vapeurs saturantes. Pression ; Points d'ébullition. Evaporation. (Voy. aussi D 7210 ; F 1050.)	Vapori saturi. Pressione ; Punti di ebollizione. Evaporazione. (Vedi anche D 7210 ; F 1050.)
1850	Densités des vapeurs. (Voy. aussi B 0140 ; D 7115.)	Densità dei vapori. (Vedi anche B 0140 ; D 7115.)
1860	Ebullition.	Ebollizione.
1870	Liquéfaction des gaz et des mélanges gazeux.	Liquefazione dei gas e delle mescolanze gasose.
1880	Continuité de l'état physique. Etat critique, point critique, etc. Equations caractéristiques. (Voy. aussi D 7000, 7212.)	Continuità degli stati, stato critico, punto critico, ecc. Equazioni caratteristiche. (Vedi anche D 7000, 7212.)
1885	Etats correspondants.	Stati corrispondenti.
1887	Equilibre dans les phases co-existantes. Règle des phases (généralités).	Equilibrio nelle fasi coesistenti. Regola delle fasi (generalità).
1890	Hygroscopie et Hygrométrie. Voy. aussi F 0270, 1000-1060.)	Igroscopia ed Igrometria. (Vedi anche F 0270, 1000-1060.)
1900	Vaporisation des solides. Sublimation.	Vaporizzazione dei solidi. Sublimazione.
1920	Dissolutions et mélanges liquides : Point de fusion, point d'ébullition, pression de vapeur, etc.	Soluzioni e mescolanze liquide : Punto di fusione, punto di ebollizione, pressione dei vapori, ecc.
1925	Dissolutions : Autres propriétés thermiques (chaleur latente). (Voy. 1690.)	Soluzioni : Altre proprietà termali (calore latente). (Vedi 1690.)
1930	Dissociation. Transformations allotropiques.	Dissociazione. Trasformazioni allotropiche.
1940	Phénomènes de retardation (surfusion, surchauffe, sursaturation).	Fenomeni di ritardamento (surfusione, sovrariscaldamento, sursaturazione).

Thermal Conduction and Convection.		**Wärmeleitung und Konvektion.**
2000	General. (*See also* D 7240.)	Allgemeines. (*Siehe auch* D 7240.)
2010	Mathematical Analysis and Applications (Fourier).	Mathematische Analyse und Anwendungen (Fourier).
2020	Solids, Conductance of.	Leitfähigkeit fester Körper.
2030	Liquids, Conductance of.	Leitfähigkeit der Flüssigkeiten.
2035	Gases, Conductance of.	Leitfähigkeit der Gase.
2040	Convection. Laws of Cooling. (*See* 4210.)	Konvektion. Gesetze der Abkühlung. (*Siehe* 4210.)

	Thermodynamics.	**Thermodynamik.**
2400	General.	Allgemeines.
2405	The First Law. Conservation of Energy. Different Forms of Energy.	Der erste Hauptsatz. Erhaltung der Energie. Verschiedene Energieformen.
2410	Mechanical Equivalent of Heat.	Das mechanische Wärmeäquivalent.
2415	The Second Law. Carnot Cycles. Entropy and Available Energy. Irreversible Phenomena. Free Energy and Thermodynamic Potentials.	Der zweite Hauptsatz. Carnot'scher Zyklus. Entropie und nutzbare Energie. Irreversibele Phänomene. Freie Energie und thermodynamische Potentiale.
2425	Absolute Temperature and its determination.	Absolute Temperatur und deren Bestimmung.
2435	Special Thermodynamic Relations.	Spezielle thermodynamische Beziehungen.
2445	Thermodynamic Surfaces, Models, etc.	Thermodynamische Flächen, Modelle etc.
2455	Thermodynamics of Single Substances.	Thermodynamik einzelner Substanzen.
2457	Thermodynamics of Solutions and Mixtures.	Thermodynamik der Lösungen und Mischungen.
2465	Thermodynamics of Systems with External and Capillary Forces.	Thermodynamik von Systemen mit äusseren Kräften und Kapillarkräften.
2472	Thermodynamics of Chemical Processes.	Thermodynamik chemischer Prozesse.
2475	Thermodynamics of Electro-Chemical Processes.	Thermodynamik elektrochemischer Prozesse.
2490	Theory of Heat Engines.	Theorie der Wärmemaschinen.
2495	Refrigerators.	Kühlmaschinen.

	LIGHT AND INVISIBLE RADIATION.	**LICHT UND UNSICHTBARE STRAHLUNG.**
2990	General.	Allgemeines.

	Geometrical Optics.	**Geometrische Optik.**
3000	General.	Allgemeines.
3010	Photometry. Units of Light. Brightness. Optical pyrometry. (*See also* 1255.)	Photometrie. Einheiten der Lichtstärke. Helligkeit. Optische Pyrometrie. (*Siehe auch* 1255.)
3020	Reflexion and Refraction. Refractometers. (*See also* 3800; D 7310.) Refractive Indices.	Reflexion und Brechung. Refraktometer. (*Siehe auch* 3800; D 7310.) Brechungsindices.

Conductibilité et Convection thermiques.

2000 Généralités. (*Voy. aussi* D 7240.)
2010 Analyse mathématique et ses applications (Fourier).
2020 Conductivité des solides.
2030 Conductivité des fluides.
2035 Conductivité des gaz.
2040 Convection. Lois du refroidissement. (*Voy.* 4210.)

Conducibilità termica e Trasporto (convezione).

Generalità. (*Vedi anche* D 7240).
Analisi matematica ed applicazioni (Fourier).
Conducibilità dei solidi.
Conducibilità dei liquidi.
Conducibilità dei gas.
Trasporto. Leggi del raffreddamento. (*Vedi* 4210.)

Thermodynamique

2400 Généralités.
2405 La première loi. Conservation de l'énergie. Diverses formes de l'énergie.
2410 L'équivalent mécanique de la chaleur.
2415 La seconde loi. Cycles de Carnot. Entropie et énergie utilisable. Phénomènes irréversibles. Energie libre et potentiels thermodynamiques.
2425 Température absolue et sa détermination.
2435 Relations thermodynamiques spéciales.
2445 Surfaces thermodynamiques, modèles, etc.
2455 Thermodynamique de substances isolées.
2457 Thermodynamique des dissolutions et des mélanges.
2465 Thermodynamique des systèmes à forces externes et capillaires.
2472 Thermodynamique des phénomènes chimiques.
2475 Thermodynamique des phénomènes électrochimiques.
2490 Théorie des machines thermiques.
2495 Réfrigérateurs.

Termodinamica.

Generalità.
La prima legge. Conservazione dell'energia. Diverse forme dell'energia.
Equivalente dinamico del calore.
La seconda legge. Cicli di Carnot. Entropia ed energia utilizzabile. Fenomeni non reversibili. Energia libera e potenziali termodinamici.
Temperatura assoluta e la sua determinazione.
Relazioni termodinamiche speciali.
Superfici termodinamiche, modelli, ecc.
Termodinamica di singole sostanze.
Termodinamica delle soluzioni e mescolanze.
Termodinamica di sistemi a forze esterne e capillari.
Termodinamica dei processi chimici.
Termodinamica dei processi chimico-elettrici.
Teoria delle macchine a calore.
Refrigeratori.

LUMIÈRE ET RADIATIONS INVISIBLES.

2990 Généralités.

LUCE E L'IRRADIAZIONE INVISIBILE.

Generalità.

Optique géométrique.

3000 Généralités.
3010 Photométrie. Unités lumineuses. Eclat. Pyrométrie optique. (*Voy. aussi* 1255.)
3020 Réflexion et réfraction. Réfractomètres. (*Voy. aussi* 3800 ; D 7310.) Indices de réfraction.

Ottica geometrica.

Generalità.
Fotometria. Unità di luce. Splendore. Pirometria ottica. (*Vedi anche* 1255.)
Riflessione e rifrazione. Rifrattometri. (*Vedi anche* 3800 ; D 7310.) Indici di rifrazione.

3030	Spectrometry. Dispersion. (See also 3800; D 7310.)	Spektrometrie. Dispersion. (Siehe auch 3800; D 7310.)
3040	Rays, General Theory of.	Allgemeine Theorie von Strahlensystemen.
3050	Optical Systems. Cardinal Points. Theory of Images.	Optische Systeme. Kardinalpunkte. Theorie der Bilderzeugungen.
3060	Mirrors and Lenses. (See also E 2040.)	Spiegel und Linsen. (Siehe auch E 2040.)
3070	Aberrations. Spherical and Chromatic. Distortion, etc. Achromatism.	Sphärische und chromatische Abweichungen. Verdrehung etc. Achromasie.
3080	Telescopes. Field-glasses. (See also E 2040–2600.)	Teleskope. Feldsucher. (Siehe auch E 2040–2600.)
3082	Microscopes. (See also L 0110; O 0140.)	Mikroskope. (Siehe auch L 0110; O 0140.)
3084	Eye-pieces.	Okulare.
3085	Photographic Lenses and Systems.	Photographische Linsen und Systeme.
3090	Optical Apparatus not scheduled elsewhere. Stereoscope.	Sonstige, an anderen Stellen nicht verzeichnete, optische Apparate. Stereoskop.
3100	Transmission through Heterogeneous Media. (See 3210.)	Transmission durch heterogene Medien. (Siehe 3210.)

Spectrum Analysis, Apparatus for.

Apparat für Spektralanalyse.

3150	General.	Allgemeines.
3155	Prisms.	Prismen.
3160	Gratings.	Gitter.
3165	Special Spectroscopic Apparatus.	Spezielle spektroskopische Apparate.

Optics of the Atmosphere. (Duplicate entries will, as far as possible, be avoided.)

Meteorologische Optik. (Doppeleintragungen sind so weit als möglich zu vermeiden.)

3200	General.	Allgemeines.
3210	Atmospheric Refraction. Scintillation. (See also 3100; E 5400; F 0520.)	Atmosphärische Refraktion. Funkeln. (Siehe auch 3100; E 5400; F 0520.)
3220	Rainbows, Halos, etc. Colours of Clouds. (See also 3640.) (For observations see Meteorology, F 0540–0570.)	Regenbögen, Höfe etc. Färbung der Wolken. (Siehe auch 3640.) (Beobachtungen siehe unter Meteorologie, F 0540–0570.)
3230	Colour and Polarisation of the Sky. (See also 3640, 4010, F 0510, 0520.)	Färbung und Polarisation des Himmels. (Siehe auch 3640, 4010; F 0510, 0520.)
3240	Atmospheric Absorption. (See also 3850; E 5400.)	Absorption in der Atmosphäre. (Siehe auch 3850; E 5400.)
3260	Energy of Sun-light. (See also Astronomy.)	Energie des Sonnenlichtes. (Siehe auch Astronomie.)

Velocity, Wave-Length, etc., of Radiation.

Fortpflanzungsgeschwindigkeit, Wellenlänge etc. der Strahlung.

3400	General.	Allgemeines.
3405	Radiation-pressure. Mechanical Equivalent of Light. (See 4210; 4215.)	Strahlungsdruck. Mechanisches Lichtäquivalent. (Siehe 4210; 4215.)
3410	Velocity of Light, Measurements of.	Messung der Fortpflanzungsgeschwindigkeit des Lichtes.

3030	Spectrométrie. Dispersion. (*Voy. aussi* 3800; D 7310.)	Spettrometria. Dispersione. (*Vedi anche* 3800; D 7310.)
3040	Théorie générale des rayons.	Teoria generale dei raggi.
3050	Systèmes optiques. Points cardinaux. Théorie des images.	Sistemi ottici. Punti cardinali. Teoria delle immagini.
3060	Miroirs et lentilles. (*Voy. aussi* E 2040.)	Specchi e lenti. (*Vedi anche* E 2040).
3070	Aberrations sphérique et chromatique. Distorsion, etc. Achromatisme.	Aberrazione sferica e cromatica. Storcimento, ecc. Acromatismo.
3080	Télescopes. Jumelles. (*Voy. aussi* E 2040-2600.)	Telescopi. Canocchiali. (*Vedi anche* E 2040-2600.)
3082	Microscopes. (*Voy. aussi* L 0110; O 0140.)	Microscopi. (*Vedi anche* L 0110; O 0140.)
3084	Oculaires.	Oculari.
3085	Lentilles et systèmes photographiques.	Lenti e sistemi fotografici.
3090	Appareils optiques non catalogués ailleurs. Stéréoscope.	Apparecchi di ottica non specificati altrove. Stereoscopio.
3100	Transmission à travers les milieux hétérogènes. (*Voy.* 3210.)	Trasmissione attraverso mezzi eterogenei. (*Vedi* 3210.)

Appareils d'analyse spectrale. / **Apparecchi da Analisi spettrale.**

3150	Généralités.	Generalità.
3155	Prismes.	Prismi.
3160	Réseaux.	Reticoli.
3165	Appareils spectroscopiques spéciaux.	Apparecchi spettroscopici speciali.

Optique de l'atmosphère. (Les doubles entrées seront autant que possible évitées.) / **Ottica meteorologica.** (Schede duplicate saranno il più possibile evitate.)

3200	Généralités.	Generalità.
3210	Réfraction atmosphérique. Scintillation. (*Voy. aussi* 3100; E 5400; F 0520.)	Rifrazione atmosferica. Scintillazione. (*Vedi anche* 3100; E 5400; F 0520.)
3220	Arcs-en-ciel, halos, etc. Couleurs des nuages. (*Voy. aussi* 3640.) (Pour les observations *voy.* Météorologie, F 0540-0570.)	Arcobaleni, aloni, ecc. Colori delle nubi. (*Vedi anche* 3640.) (Per le osservazioni *vedi* Meteorologia. F 0540-0570.)
3230	Couleur et polarisation du ciel. (*Voy. aussi* 3640, 4010; F 0510, 0520.)	Colore e polarizzazione del cielo. (*Vedi anche* 3640, 4010; F 0510, 0520.)
3240	Absorption atmosphérique. (*Voy. aussi* 3850; E 5400.)	Assorbimento dell' atmosfera. (*Vedi anche* 3850; E 5400.)
3260	Energie de la radiation solaire. (*Voy. aussi* Astronomie.)	Energia della radiazione solare. (*Vedi anche* Astronomia.)

Vitesse, longueur d'onde, etc., des radiations. / **Velocità, lunghezza d'onda, ecc., delle radiazioni.**

3400	Généralités.	Generalità.
3405	Pression des radiations. Equivalent mécanique de la lumière. (*Voy.* 4210, 4215.)	Pressione delle radiazioni. Equivalente dinamico della luce. (*Vedi* 4210, 4215.)
3410	Mesures de la vitesse de la lumière.	Misure della velocità della luce.

3420	Aberration and Moving Media. Doppler's Principle.
3430	Wave - Length of Rays in the Luminous Spectrum, Measurement of. (See also 3030.)
3435	Wave-Length of Infra-Red Rays, Measurement of.
3440	Wave-Length of Ultra-Violet Rays, Measurement of.

Aberration und bewegte Mittel. Doppler's Prinzip.
Messung der Wellenlänge der Strahlen im sichtbaren Spektrum. (Siehe auch 3030.)
Messung der Wellenlänge der ultraroten Strahlen.
Messung der Wellenlänge der ultravioletten Strahlen.

Interference and Diffraction.

3600	General.
3610	Interference. Interferential Refractometers. Colours of Thin Sheets.
3620	Diffraction.
3630	Spectra formed by Diffraction and by Gratings.
3640	Diffraction by Small Particles. Theory of Rainbow, Optical Resonance, etc. (See also 3220 ; F 0550.)
3650	Definition of Optical Instruments, General Theory.

Interferenz und Beugung.

Allgemeines.
Interferenz. Interferenz-Refraktometer. Farben dünner Plättchen.

Beugung.
Beugungsspektra und durch Beugungsgitter gebildete Spektra.
Beugung durch kleine Teilchen. Theorie des Regenbogens, der optischen Resonanz etc. (Siehe auch 3220 ; F 0550.)
Trennungsvermögen optischer Instrumente, allgemeine Theorie.

Reflexion, Refraction and Absorption of Radiation. (See also 3020, 3030.)

3800	General.
3810	Reflecting and Absorbing Powers of Materials. Irregular Reflexion.
3820	Dynamical Theory of Reflexion and Refraction in Transparent Media. Polarization by Reflexion.
3822	Refraction : Influence of Temperature, Density and Change of State.
3824	Total Reflexion.
3830	Crystalline Media, Refraction in.
3835	Strained Media, Refraction in.
3840	Metallic Reflexion.
3850	Selective Reflexion and Absorption, including Objective Colours. Dichroism. Anomalous Dispersion.
3855	Heat Rays, Reflexion, Refraction and Absorption of.
3860	Chemical Constitution, Relation of Refraction, Dispersion and Absorption to. Optical Glass.
3875	Reflexion, Refraction and Absorption of Electric Radiation.

Reflexion, Refraktion und Absorption der Strahlung. (Siehe auch 3020, 3030).

Allgemeines.
Reflexions- und Absorptionsvermögen von Substanzen. Diffuse Reflexion.
Dynamische Theorie der Reflexion und Brechung in durchsichtigen Medien. Polarisation durch Reflexion.
Brechung : Einfluss von Temperatur, Dichtigkeit und Zustandsänderung.
Totalreflexion.
Brechung in krystallinischen Medien.
Brechung in deformirten Medien.
Metallreflexion.
Selektive Reflexion und Absorption, einschl. objektive Farben. Dichroismus. Anomale Dispersion.
Reflexion, Refraktion und Absorption von Wärmestrahlen.
Beziehung von Brechung, Reflexion und Absorption zur chemischen Zusammensetzung. Optische Gläser.
Reflexion, Refraktion und Absorption elektrischer Strahlungen.

3420	Aberration et mouvement des milieux. Principe de Doppler.	Aberrazione e mezzi in moto. Principio di Doppler.
3430	Mesure des longueurs d'onde du spectre lumineux. (*Voy. aussi* 3030.)	Misura della lunghezza d'onda delle radiazioni nello spettro luminoso. (*Vedi anche* 3030.)
3435	Mesure des longueurs d'onde des rayons infra-rouges.	Misura della lunghezza d'onda delle radiazioni infra-rosse.
3440	Mesure des longueurs d'onde des rayons ultra-violets.	Misura della lunghezza d'onda delle radiazioni ultra-violette.

Interférence et diffraction. — Interferenza e diffrazione.

3600	Généralités.	Generalità.
3610	Interférence. Réfractomètres interférentiels. Couleurs des lames minces.	Interferenza. Rifrattometri interferenziali. Colori delle lamine sottili.
3620	Diffraction.	Diffrazione.
3630	Spectres de diffraction et spectres formés par les réseaux.	Spettri di diffrazione e spettri prodotti da reticoli.
3640	Diffraction par de petites particules. Théories de l'arc-en-ciel, de la résonance optique, etc. (*Voy. aussi* 3220 ; F 0550.)	Diffrazione prodotta da piccole particelle. Teoria dell' arcobaleno, della risonanza ottica, ecc. (*Vedi anche* 3220 ; F 0550).
3650	Pouvoir définissant des instruments d'optique, théorie générale.	Potere risolutivo di strumenti ottici, teoria generale.

Réflexion, Réfraction et Absorption des radiations. (*Voy. aussi* 3020, 3030.) — Riflessione, rifrazione ed assorbimento delle radiazioni. (*Vedi anche* 3020, 3030.)

3800	Généralités.	Generalità.
3810	Pouvoirs réflecteurs et absorbants des corps. Réflexion irrégulière.	Potere riflettente ed assorbente dei materiali. Riflessione irregolare.
3820	Théorie dynamique de la réflexion et de la réfraction dans les milieux transparents. Polarisation par réflexion.	Teoria dinamica della riflessione e rifrazione in mezzi trasparenti. Polarizzazione per riflessione.
3822	Réfraction : influence de la température, de la densité et des changements d'état.	Rifrazione : Influenza della temperatura, densità e cangiamento di stato.
3824	Réflexion totale.	Riflessione totale.
3830	Réfraction dans les milieux cristallins.	Rifrazione in mezzi cristallini.
3835	Réfraction dans les milieux déformés.	Rifrazione in mezzi deformati.
3840	Réflexion métallique.	Riflessione metallica.
3850	Réflexion élective et absorption, comprenant les couleurs objectives. Dichroïsme. Dispersion anomale.	Riflessione selettiva e assorbimento, inclusi i colori obbiettivi. Dicroismo. Dispersione anomala.
3855	Réflexion, réfraction et absorption des rayons calorifiques.	Riflessione, rifrazione ed assorbimento dei raggi calorifici.
3860	Relation de la réfraction, de la dispersion et de l'absorption, avec la constitution chimique. Verres d'optique.	Relazione della rifrazione, dispersione ed assorbimento colla costituzione chimica. Vetri ottici.
3875	Réflexion, réfraction et absorption des radiations électriques.	Riflessione, rifrazione ed assorbimento delle radiazioni elettriche.

Polarization.	Polarisation.
4000 General. Instruments and Methods.	Allgemeines. Instrumente und Methoden.
4005 Elliptic and Circular Polarization. General.	Elliptische und zirkulare Polarisation. Allgemeines.
4010 Production of Polarized Radiation.	Erzeugung polarisierter Strahlung.
4020 Measurement of Polarized Radiation.	Messung polarisierter Strahlung.
4030 Rings and Brushes of Crystals.	Ringe und Büschel in Krystallen.
4040 Rotatory Polarization and Dispersion, Structural and Magnetic. General. (See also 6650, 6655; D 7315.)	Rotationspolarisation und -dispersion, strukturelle und magnetische. Allgemeines. (Siehe auch 6650, 6655; D 7315.)
4050 Rotatory Powers of Substances.	Rotationsvermögen von Substanzen.

The Emission and Analysis of Radiation, Phosphorescence, Radioactivity, Spectra, etc.	Emission und Analyse der Strahlung, Phosphorescenz, Radioaktivität, Spektren etc.
4200 General.	Allgemeines.
4202 Sources: Lamps, Arcs. Vacuum Tubes.	Quellen: Lampen, Bögen, Vakuumröhren.
4205 Spectra. Distribution of Spectral Lines.	Spektren: Verteilung von Spektrallinien.
4206 Influence of Pressure, Temperature, etc., on Spectra.	Wirkung von Druck, Temperatur etc. auf Spektren.
4207 Structure of Spectral Lines.	Bau von Spektrallinien.
4208 Influence of Magnetic Field on Spectra. (See also 6660.)	Wirkung des magnetischen Feldes auf Spektren. (Siehe auch 6660.)
4210 Intensity and Distribution of Energy. Temperature and Radiation. Temperature Law of Radiation. Radiation of Black Bodies.	Intensität und Verteilung der Energie. Temperatur und Strahlung. Temperaturgesetz der Strahlung. Strahlung schwarzer Körper.
4215 Radiation-Pressure. (See also 3405.)	Strahlungsdruck. (Siehe auch 3405.)
4220 Chemical Luminescence. (See also 6840.)	Chemische Luminescenz. (Siehe auch 6840.)
4225 Photochemistry and Photography.	
4230 Phosphorescence produced by Impact of Radiation, Heat, Electric Discharge, etc. Fluorescence. (See also 6840; D 7305.)	Phosphorescenz hervorgerufen durch Auftreffen von Strahlen, durch Wärme, elektrische Entladung, etc. Fluorescenz. (Siehe auch 6840; D 7305.)
4240 Röntgen and allied Radiations. (See also 6840, 6850.)	Röntgenstrahlen und verwandte Strahlungen. (Siehe auch 6840, 6850.)
4250 Electric Radiations. General.	Elektrische Strahlungen. Allgemeines.
4270 Various Radiations.	Verschiedene Strahlungen.
4275 Radioactivity (radium, etc.).	Radioaktivität (Radium etc.)

Polarisation.	Polarizzazione.
4000	Généralités. Instruments et méthodes.	Generalità. Istrumenti e metodi.

4000   Généralités. Instruments et méthodes.
        Generalità. Istrumenti e metodi.

4005   Polarisation circulaire et elliptique. Généralités.
        Polarizzazione ellittica e circolare. Generalità.

4010   Production des rayons polarisés.
        Produzione di radiazioni polarizzate. Generalità.

4020   Mesure des radiations polarisées.
        Misura delle radiazioni polarizzate.

4030   Anneaux et franges des cristaux.
        Anelli e frangie dei cristalli.

4040   Polarisation et dispersion rotatoires, moléculaire et magnétique. Généralités. (Voy. aussi 6650, 6655; D 7315.)
        Polarizzazione e dispersione rotatoria, di struttura e magnetica. Generalità. (Vedi anche 6650, 6655; D 7315.)

4050   Pouvoirs rotatoires des substances.
        Poteri rotatori delle sostanze.

Emission et analyse des radiations, phosphorescence, radioactivité, spectres, etc.

Emissione ed analisi delle radiazioni, fosforescenza, radioattività, spettri, ecc.

4200   Généralités.
        Generalità.

4202   Sources : lampes, arcs, tubes à vide.
        Sorgenti : Lampe, archi, tubi a vuoto.

4205   Spectres. Distribution des lignes spectrales.
        Spettri. Distribuzione delle linee spettrali.

4206   Influence de la pression, de la température, etc., sur les spectres.
        Influenza della pressione, temperatura, ecc., sugli spettri.

4207   Structure des lignes spectrales.
        Struttura delle linee spettrali.

4208   Influence du champ magnétique sur les spectres. (Voy. aussi 6660.)
        Influenza del campo magnetico sugli spettri. (Vedi anche 6660.)

4210   Intensité et distribution de l'énergie Radiation et température. Loi de la température des radiations. Radiation des corps noirs.
        Intensità e distribuzione dell'energia. Temperatura e radiazione. Legge della temperatura delle radiazioni. Radiazione dei corpi neri.

4215   Pression des radiations. (Voy. aussi 3405.)
        Pressione delle radiazioni. (V. di anche 3405.)

4220   Luminescence chimique. (Voy. aussi 6840; D 7305.)
        Luminescenza chimica. (Vedi anche 6840; D 7305.)

4225   Photochimie et photographie.
        Fotochimica e fotografia.

4230   Phosphorescence due à la rencontre d'une radiation, à chaleur, à la décharge électrique. Fluorescence. (Voy. aussi 6840; D 7305.)
        Fosforescenza dovuta all' urto delle radiazioni, al calore, alle scariche elettriche, ecc. Fluorescenza. (Vedi anche 6840; D 7305.)

4240   Radiations de Röntgen et radiations analogues. (Voy. aussi 6840, 6850.)
        Radiazioni di Röntgen e affini. (Vedi anche 6840, 6850.)

4250   Radiations électriques. Généralités.
        Radiazioni elettriche. Generalità.

4270   Radiations diverses.
        Radiazioni diverse.

4275   Radioactivité (radium, etc.).
        Radioattività (radium, ecc.).

(c–4388)

Physiological Optics.

(*See also* Physiology. Such papers only will be entered here as are likely to be of interest to Physicists.)

4400 General.
4410 Construction and Dioptrics of the Eye. (*See also* Q 3711.)
4420 Movements of the Eye. Accommodation. (*See also* Q 3715, 3740.)
4430 Defects of the Eye and their correction. Short Sight, Astigmatism, Irradiation, etc.
4440 Binocular Vision (Magnitude and Distance of Objects. Relief). (*See also* Q 3745.)
4450 Colour Vision. Subjective Colours. Colour Blindness. (*See also* Q 3735.)
4455 Visual Acuity.
4460 Phenomena within the Eye.

4470 Instruments connected with Physiological Optics.

ELECTRICITY AND MAGNETISM.
4900 General.

General Dynamical Theory and Relations. Units.

4940 Equations of the Electrodynamic Field. (*See also* 6410.)
4960 Electrons. Moving Media.
4970 Tubes and Lines of Force.
4980 Transfer of Energy, Momentum, etc.

5000 Units, Electric and Magnetic.

Electrostatics.
5200 General.
5210 Electrification by Contact or Friction. Various Sources of Electrification.
5220 Electric Charge and Distribution; Quantity; Density; Induction; Condensers.
5240 Potential Difference.
5250 Theory of the Dielectric. Stress; Energy, etc.
5252 Measurement of Dielectric Constants. Dielectric Hysteresis. (*See also* D 7280.)

Physiologische Optik.

(*Siehe auch* Physiologie. Nur solche Abhandlungen sind hier aufzunehmen, für die bei den Physikern ein Interesse erwartet werden kann.)

Allgemeines.
Aufbau und Dioptrik des Auges. (*Siehe auch* Q 3711.)
Bewegungen des Auges. Akkommodation. (*Siehe auch* Q 3715, 3740.)
Fehler des Auges und ihre Verbesserung. Kurzsichtigkeit, Astigmatismus, Irradiation etc.
Binokulares Sehen (Grösse und Entfernung von Objekten. Relief). (*Siehe auch* Q 3745.)
Farbenwahrnehmung. Subjektive Farben. Farbenblindheit. (*Siehe auch* Q 3735.)
Sehschärfe.
Erscheinungen im Innern des Auges.

Instrumente für physiologischoptische Untersuchungen.

ELEKTRIZITÄT UND MAGNETISMUS.
Allgemeines.

Allgemeine dynamische Theorie und deren Beziehungen. Einheiten.

Gleichungen des elektrodynamischen Feldes. (*Siehe auch* 6410.)
Elektronen. Bewegte Mittel.
Kraftröhren und -linien.
Uebertragung der Energie, des Moments etc.

Elektrische und Magnetische Einheiten.

Elektrostatik.
Allgemeines.
Elektrisierung durch Berührung oder Reibung. Verschiedene Elektrisierungsquellen.
Elektrische Ladung und Verteilung; Menge; Dichte; Induktion; Kondensatoren.
Potential-Differenz.
Theorie des Dielektrikums. Spannungen, Energie etc.
Messung dielektrischer Konstanten. Dielektrische Hysteresis. (*Siehe auch* D 7280.)

Optique Physiologique.

(*Voy. aussi* Physiologie. On ne devra cataloguer ici que les mémoires qui paraîtront intéressants pour les physiciens.)

4400 Généralités.
4410 Construction et dioptrique de l'œil. (*Voy. aussi* Q 3711.)
4420 Mouvements de l'œil. Accommodation. (*Voy. aussi* Q 3715, 3740.)
4430 Défauts de l'œil et leur correction. Myopie, astigmatisme, irradiation, etc.
4440 Vision binoculaire. (Grandeur et distance des objets. Relief.) (*Voy. aussi* Q 3745.)
4450 Vision des couleurs. Couleurs subjectives. Cécité des couleurs. (*Voy. aussi* Q 3735.)
4455 Acuité visuelle.
4460 Les divers phénomènes qui se produisent dans l'œil.
4470 Instruments concernant l'optique physiologique.

ÉLECTRICITÉ ET MAGNÉTISME.

4900 Généralités.

Théorie dynamique et relations générales. Unités.

4940 Équations du champ électrodynamique. (*Voy. aussi* 6410.)
4960 Électrons. Milieux en mouvement.
4970 Tubes et lignes de force.
4980 Transport de l'énergie, du moment, etc.
5000 Unités électriques et magnétiques.

Electrostatique.

5200 Généralités.
5210 Électrisation par contact ou par frottement. Diverses sources d'électrisation.
5220 Charge électrique et sa distribution ; quantité ; densité ; induction ; condensateurs.
5240 Différence de potentiel.
5250 Théorie des diélectriques. Déplacement électrique. Énergie, etc.
5252 Mesure des constantes diélectriques. Hystérésis diélectrique. (*Voy. aussi* D 7280.)

(c-1388)

Ottica Fisiologica.

(*Vedi* pure Fisiologia. Verranno qui registrati solamente quegli articoli che possano avere dell' interesse per il fisico.)

Generalità.
Costruzione e diottrica dell' occhio. (*Vedi anche* Q 3711.)
Movimenti dell' occhio. Accomodamento. (*Vedi anche* Q 3715, 3740.)
Difetti dell' occhio e loro correzione Miopia, astigmatismo, irradiazione, ecc.
Visione binoculare. (Grandezza e distanza degli oggetti. Rilievo.) (*Vedi anche* Q 3745.)
Visione dei colori. Colori soggettivi. Cecità pei colori. (*Vedi anche* Q 3735.)
Acutezza visiva.
Fenomeni prodotti entro l'occhio.
Istrumenti che si riferiscono all' ottica fisiologica.

ELETTRICITÀ E MAGNETISMO.

Generalità.

Teoria dinamica e relazioni generali. Unità.

Equazioni del campo elettrodinamico. (*Vedi anche* 6410.)
Elettroni. Mezzi in moto.
Tubi e linee di forza.
Trasporto dell' energia, del momento, ecc.
Unità elettriche e magnetiche.

Elettrostatica.

Generalità.
Elettrizzazione per contatto o strofinio. Diverse sorgenti di elettrizzazione.
Carica elettrica e distribuzione quantità ; densità ; induzione condensatori.
Differenza di potenziale.
Teoria del dielettrico. Tensione ; energia, ecc.
Misura delle costanti dielettriche. Isteresi dielettrica. (*Vedi anche* D 7280.)

Magnetism.

Magnetismus.

The Electric Current and Conduction.

Der elektrische Strom und die elektrische Leitung.

5253	Electrostriction.	Elettrostrizione.
5260	Pyro- et Piézo-électricité. Autres sources.	Piro- e piezoelettricità. Altre sorgenti.
5270	Électricité atmosphérique. (*Voy. aussi* F 1600.)	Elettricità atmosferica. (*Vedi anche* F 1600.)

Magnétisme.   Magnetismo.

5400	Généralités.	Generalità.
5410	Aimants naturels et artificiels. (*Voy. aussi* 6030.)	Calamite naturali ed artificiali. (*Vedi anche* 6030.)
5420	Théorie du champ magnétique. Circuit magnétique.	Teoria del campo magnetico. Circuito magnetico.
5430	Théorie de l'induction magnétique et de l'hystérèsis.	Teoria dell' induzione magnetica e dell' isteresi.
5435	Épreuves magnétiques. Instruments.	Istrumenti per lo studio delle proprietà magnetiche.
5440	Mesure de la force magnétique, de la susceptibilité, de l'induction, etc.	Misura della forza magnetica, suscettività, induzione, ecc.
5450	Mesure de l'hystérésis. Pertes d'énergie.	Misura dell' isteresi. Perdite di energia.
5460	Relations entre les propriétés thermiques, élastiques et magnétiques des corps. Effet de la température.	Relazioni tra le proprietà termiche, elastiche e magnetiche dei corpi. Effetto della temperatura.
5462	Magnétostriction.	Magnetostrizione.
5465	Pyro- et Piézo-magnétisme.	Piro- e piezomagnetismo.
5466	Propriétés magnétiques des alliages de fer et d'autres substances ferromagnétiques.	Proprietà magnetiche delle leghe di ferro e di altre sostanze ferromagnetiche.
5467	Propriétés magnétiques des sels et des dissolutions.	Proprietà magnetiche dei sali e delle soluzioni.
5470	Diamagnétisme.	Diamagnetismo.
5480	Théories physiques de la nature du magnétisme.	Teorie fisiche sulla natura del magnetismo.
5490	Théories concernant le champ magnétique terrestre.	Teorie relative al campo magnetico terrestre.

Le courant électrique et la conduction.   Corrente elettrica e conduzione.

5600	Généralités.	Generalità.
5610	Théorie et construction des piles primaires.	Teoria e costruzione di pile primarie.
5620	Théorie et construction des piles secondaires.	Teoria e costruzione di pile secondarie.
5630	Loi d'Ohm. Courants dérivés et circuits linéaires complexes.	Legge di Ohm. Correnti derivate e reti di conduttori lineari.
5640	Méthodes de comparaison des résistances.	Metodi di confronto delle resistenze.
5650	Etalons de résistance. Mesures absolues.	Campioni di resistenza. Misura assoluta.
5660	Résistance spécifique. Relation avec la température, la torsion, le magnétisme, la lumière, etc.	Resistenza specifica. Relazione colla temperatura, torsione, magnetismo, luce, ecc.
5675	Nature de la conduction métallique. Électrons libres.	Natura della conduzione metallica. Elettroni libri.

Electrical Instruments and Apparatus.

Elektrische Instrumente und Apparate

5680	Conduction dans les milieux continus à deux, à trois dimensions.
	Conduzione in mezzi continui da due e tre dimensioni.
5685	Conduction dans les gaz et dans les vapeurs. (*Voy. aussi* 6805.)
	Conduzione nei gas e nei vapori. (*Vedi anche* 6805.)
5695	Mesure de la force électromotrice.
	Misura della forza elettromotrice.
5700	Mesure des courants continus (intensité, consommation d'énergie, etc.). (*Voy. aussi* 6010.)
	Misura delle correnti continue (forza, consumo di energia, ecc.). (*Vedi anche* 6010).
5705	Mesure des courants alternatifs (périodicité, amplitude, consommation d'énergie, travail. etc.). (*Voy. aussi* 6015.)
	Misura di correnti alternanti (periodicità, ampiezza, consumo di energia, lavoro, ecc.) (*Vedi anche* 6015.)
5707	Mesure des courants discontinus.
	Misura di correnti discontinue.
5710	Thermo-électricité. Effet Peltier et Thomson.
	Termoelettricità. Effetto Peltier e Thomson.
5720	Mesures relatives à l'énergie du courant. Effet calorifique.
	Misure relative all'energia della corrente. Effetto calorifico.
5740	Mesure de la capacité. (*Voy.* 6005.)
	Misura della capacità. (*Vedi* 6005.)
5770	Isolation : détermination de sa résistance. Localisation des défauts dans les conducteurs.
	Determinazione della resistenza dell'isolamento. Localizzazione dei guasti nei conduttori.
5900	Electricité physiologique.
	Elettricità fisiologica.

Instruments et appareils électriques.

Istrumenti ed apparecchi elettrici.

6000	Généralités.
	Generalità.
6005	Electrometres.
	Elettrometri.
6010	Galvanomètres, rhéostats, voltmètres, wattmètres, etc. Instruments enregistreurs. (*Voy.* 5700.)
	Galvanometri, comparatori di resistenza, voltmetri, wattmetri, ecc. Istrumenti registratori. (*Vedi* 5700.)
6015	Appareils pour déterminer le caractère des courants variables. (*Voy.* 5705.)
	Apparecchi per determinare il carattere delle correnti variabili. (*Vedi* 5705.)
6020	Appareils destinés à l'établissement et au réglage des courants.
	Apparecchi per chiudere e regolare le correnti.
6025	Machines électrostatiques à frottement.
	Macchine elettrostatiche a strofinio.
6027	Machines électrostatiques à induction.
	Macchine elettrostatiche d'induzione.
6030	Electroaimants. (*Voy. aussi* 5410.)
	Elettromagneti. (*Vedi anche* 5410.)
6040	Bobines d'induction. Transformateurs. Interrupteurs pour les bobines d'induction.
	Rocchetti d' induzione. Trasformatori. Interruttori per rocchetti d'induzione.
6043	Appareils de télégraphie sans fil. Cohéreurs.
	Apparecchi di telegrafia senza fili. Coerer.
6045	Alternateurs.
	Alternatori.
6047	Convertisseurs et rectificateurs.
	Convertitori e rettificatori.
6050	Machines magnéto-électriques.
	Macchine magnetelettriche.
6060	Dynamos.
	Dinamo.
6070	Moteurs.
	Motori.
6080	Lampes électriques.
	Lampade elettriche.
6090	Fours et appareils de chauffage électriques.
	Forni ed apparecchi di riscaldamento elettrici.

Electrolysis.	Elektrolyse.

Electrodynamics, Special Phenomena.	Elektrodynamik, besondere Phänomene.

Electrolyse.		**Elettrolisi.**

6200 Généralités. (*Voy. aussi* Chimie physique, D 7255, etc.)

6210 Séries électro-chimiques et équivalents électro-chimiques. Différences de potentiel voltaïque.

6220 Mélanges d'électrolytes et actions secondaires.

6230 Polarisation et passivité.

6235 Phénomènes électro-capillaires.

6240 Conductivité. Migration des ions.

6242 Propriétés des dépôts électrolytiques.

6245 Osmose électrique. Courants dans les diaphragmes.

6250 Théories de l'électrolyse. Décomposition des électrolytes.

6255 Piles à concentration. Théories relatives à la diffusion.

Generalità. (*Vedi anche* Fisico-chimica, D 7255, ecc.)

Serie elettrochimiche ed equivalenti elettrochimici. Differenze di potenziale voltaico.

Elettroliti misti ed azioni secondarie.

Polarizzazione e passività.

Fenomeni elettrocapillari.

Conduttività. Trasporto degli ioni.

Proprietà dei depositi elettrolitici.

Osmosi elettrica. Correnti nei diaframmi.

Teorie dell' elettrolisi. Dissociazione degli elettroliti.

Pile a concentrazione. Teorie relative alla diffusione.

Electrodynamique, Phénomènes speciaux.		**Elettrodinamica, Fenomeni speciali.**

6400 Généralités.

6410 Théories de l'électrodynamique. (*Voy.* 4940.)

6420 Actions réciproques des courants constants. Actions réciproques des courants et des aimants.

6430 Théories spéciales dynamiques des courants électriques.

6435 Convection électrique. Effet Rowland.

6440 Self-induction et induction mutuelle. Courants tourbillonnaires. Coefficients d'induction. Mesure de l'induction.

6450 Effets de l'induction et de la capacité sur le flux des courants.

6455 Effets d'un champ magnétique sur le flux des courants. Effet Hall.

6460 Courants alternatifs et polyphasés dans les fils.

6470 Courants de haute fréquence.

6480 Télégraphie. (Pour la télégraphie sans fil *voy.* 6615.)

6485 Téléphonie.

6490 Energie dans les phénomènes spéciaux de l'électrodynamique.

Generalità.

Teorie dell' elettrodinamica. (*Vedi* 4940.)

Mutue azioni di correnti continue e di correnti e calamite.

Teorie dinamiche speciali delle correnti elettriche.

Convezione elettrica. Effetto Rowland.

Auto-induzione ed induzione mutua. Correnti vorticose. Coefficienti d'induzione. Misura dell' induzione.

Effetti dell' induzione e della capacità sul flusso delle correnti.

Effetti d'un campo magnetico sul flusso delle correnti. Effetto Hall.

Correnti alternanti e polifasi nei fili.

Correnti ad alta frequenza.

Telegrafia. (Per la telegrafia senza fili *vedi* 6615.)

Telefonia.

L'energia nei fenomeni elettrodinamici.

	Electromagnetic Waves. General Electromagnetic Theory of Light.	Elektromagnetische Wellen. Allgemeine elektromagnetische Theorie des Lichtes.
6600	General.	Allgemeines.
6610	Production and Properties of Electromagnetic Waves.	Erzeugung und Eigenschaften der elektromagnetischen Wellen.
6615	Wireless Telegraphy and Telephony.	Drahtlose Telegraphie und Telephonie.
6620	General Theory of Electromagnetic Radiations.	Allgemeine Theorie der elektromagnetischen Strahlungen.
6625	Transparent Media in the Electromagnetic Theory of Light.	Durchsichtige Medien in der elektromagnetischen Theorie des Lichtes.
6627	Metallic Media in the Electromagnetic Theory of Light.	Metallene Medien in der elektromagnetischen Theorie des Lichts.
6630	Aberration and Moving Media.	Aberration und bewegte Medien.

Influence of Electric and Magnetic Fields on Light. / Einfluss elektrischer und magnetischer Felder auf das Licht.

6635	General.	Allgemeines.
6640	Double Refraction due to Electro- and Magneto-striction.	Doppelbrechung in Folge von Elektro- und Magnetostriktion.
6650	Magnetic Action on Polarized Light. (See also 4040; D 7285.)	Wirkung des Magnetismus auf polarisiertes Licht. (Siehe auch 4040; D 7285.)
6655	Magnetic Rotation of Special Substances.	Magnetische Drehung besonderer Substanzen.
6660	Influence of Magnetism on the Emission and Absorption of Light. (See also 4208.)	Einfluss des Magnetismus auf Emission und Absorption des Lichtes. (Siehe auch 4208.)

Electric Discharge. / Elektrische Entladung.

6800	General.	Allgemeines.
6805	Ionisation of Gases. (See also 5685.)	Ionisation von Gasen. (Siehe auch 5685.)
6810	Convective Loss. Points. Leakage.	Verluste durch Konvektion. Spitzenwirkung. Zerstreuung.
6820	Disruptive Discharge. The Electric Spark. Oscillatory Discharge.	Disruptive Entladung. Der elektrische Funke. Oscillatorische Entladung.
6825	Mechanical Action of the Discharge (Disintegration of Metals. etc.).	Mechanische Wirkung der Entladung (Zerstäubung von Metallen etc.).
6830	The Voltaic Arc.	Der Lichtbogen.
6840	Discharge in Rarefied Gases.	Entladung in verdünnten Gasen.
6845	Cathode. Becquerel and other projected discharges (Velocity, Charge, Effect of Magnetism, etc.).	Kathoden-, Becquerel- etc. Strahlen als Emanation geladener Teilchen (Geschwindigkeit, Grösse der Ladung, magnetische Ablenkbarkeit etc.).
6850	Effects of Light, Röntgen Rays, etc., on the Discharge.	Wirkung von Licht, Röntgenstrahlen etc., auf die Entladung.

Ondes électromagnétiques. Théorie générale électromagnétique de la lumière.

6600	Généralités.
6610	Production et propriétés des ondes électro-magnétiques.
6615	Télégraphie et téléphonie sans fil.
6620	Théorie générale des radiations électromagnétiques.
6625	Milieux transparents dans la théorie électromagnétique de la lumière.
6627	Milieux métalliques dans la théorie électromagnétique de la lumière.
6630	Aberration et mouvements des milieux.

Ondulazioni elettromagnetiche. Teoria elettromagnetica generale della luce.

Generalità.
Produzione e proprietà delle ondulazioni elettromagnetiche.
Telegrafia e telefonia senza fili.
Teoria generale delle ondulazioni elettromagnetiche.
Mezzi trasparenti nella teoria elettromagnetica della luce.
Mezzi metallici nella teoria elettromagnetica della luce.
Aberrazione e mezzi in moto.

Influence des champs électrique et magnétique sur la lumière.

6635	Généralités.
6640	Double réfraction due à l'électro- et à la magnéto-striction.
6650	Actions magnétiques sur la lumière polarisée. (*Voy. aussi* 4040; D 7285.)
6655	Rotation magnétique de substances spéciales.
6660	Influence du magnétisme sur l'émission et l'absorption de la lumière (*Voy. aussi* 4208.)

Influenza del campo elettrico e magnetico su fenomeni della luce.

Generalità.
Birifrangenza dovuta all' elettro- ed alla magneto-trizione.
Azione magnetica sulla luce polarizzata. (*Vedi anche* 4040; D 7285.)
Rotazione magnetica di sostanze particolari.
Influenza del magnetismo sull'emissione ed assorbimento della luce. (*Vedi anche* 4208.)

Décharge électrique.

6800	Généralités.
6805	Ionisation des gaz. (*Voy. aussi* 5685.)
6810	Perte par convection. Pointes. Déperdition.
6820	Décharge disruptive. L'étincelle électrique. Décharge oscillatoire.
6825	Action mécanique de la décharge (désintégration des métaux, etc.).
6830	L'arc voltaïque.
6840	Décharge dans les gaz raréfiés.
6845	Rayons cathodiques. rayons Becquerel et autres décharges projetées (vitesse, charge, effets du magnetisme, etc.).
6850	Action de la lumière, des rayons Röntgen, etc., sur la décharge.

Scarica elettrica.

Generalità.
Ionizzazione dei gas. (*Vedi anche* 5685.)
Perdita per convezione. Punte. Dispersione.
Scarica disruptiva. Scintilla elettrica. Scarica oscillatoria.
Effetto meccanico della scarica (disintegrazione di metalli, ecc.).
Arco voltaico.
Scarica nei gas rarefatti.
Raggi catodici, *raggi* Becquerel ed altre scariche projettili (velocità, carica, effetto del magnetismo. ecc.).
Effetti della luce, raggi Röntgen, ecc., sulla scarica.

VIBRATION AND SOUND.	SCHALL.

8990 General.

Allgemeines.

Kinematics of Vibrations and Wave-motions

Kinematik der Schwingungen und Wellenbewegungen.

9000 General.

Allgemeines.

9010 Analysis and Synthesis of Periodic Motions.

Analyse und Synthese periodischer Bewegungen.

9020 Methods of Maintaining, Observing, and Measuring Vibrations.

Methoden zur Unterhaltung, zur Beobachtung und zur Messung von Schwingungen.

9030 Methods of Exhibiting and Illustrating the Phenomena of Wave-Motion.

Methoden zur Demonstration und Erläuterung der Phänomene bei der Wellenbewegung.

9040 Reflexion and Refraction of Waves.

Reflexion und Brechung von Wellen.

9050 Interference, Diffraction, and Scattering of Waves. Huygens' Principle.

Interferenz, Beugung und Zerstreuung von Wellen. Huygens'sches Prinzip.

Vibrations.

Schwingungen.

9100 General. (*See also* B 3220.)

Allgemeines. (*Siehe auch* B 3220.)

9105 Mechanical Action of Vibrations (Acoustic Attraction).

Mechanische Wirkung der Schwingungen (akustische Anziehung).

9110 Vibrations of Strings and Rods. Curved Rods.

Schwingungen von Saiten und Stäben. Gekrümmte Stäbe.

9120 Vibrations of Membranes and Plates. Curved Plates. Bells.

Schwingungen von Membranen und Platten. Gekrümmte Platten. Glocken.

9130 Vibrations of Gases in Tubes and other Cavities. Effects of Apertures.

Schwingungen von Gasen in Röhren und andern Hohlräumen. Wirkung von Oeffnungen.

9135 Forced Vibrations.

Erzwungene Schwingungen.

9140 Resonance. Resonators. Objective Combination-tones. (*See also* Q 3545.)

Resonanz. Resonatoren. Objective Kombinationstöne. (*Siehe auch* Q 3545.)

Propagation of Sound.

Fortpflanzung des Schalles.

9200 General.

Allgemeines.

9210 Velocity of Sound.

Fortpflanzungsgeschwindigkeit des Schalles.

9220 Reflexion and Refraction of Sound.

Reflexion und Brechung des Schalles.

9230 Interference and Diffraction of Sound. Beats.

Interferenz und Beugung des Schalles. Schwebungen.

9240 Damping of Sound-waves by viscosity and heat-conduction.

Dämpfung von Schallwellen durch innere Reibung und Wärmeleitung.

9250 Acoustic Transparency.

Akustische Transparenz.

9255 Acoustics of Buildings.

Akustik der Gebäude.

VIBRATION ET ACOUSTIQUE.	VIBRAZIONE E SUONO.

8990   Généralités.   Generalità.

Cinématique des vibrations et des mouvements ondulatoires. / Cinematica dei movimenti vibratori ed ondulatori.

9000   Généralités. — Generalità.

9010   Analyse et synthèse des mouvements périodiques. — Analisi e sintesi dei movimenti periodici.

9020   Méthodes propres à entretenir, observer et mesurer les vibrations. — Metodi per produrre, osservare e misurare le vibrazioni.

9030   Méthodes propres à montrer et à étudier les phénomènes des mouvements ondulatoires. — Metodi per mostrare e studiare i fenomeni dei movimenti ondulatori.

9040   Réflexion et réfraction des ondes. — Riflessione e rifrazione delle onde.

9050   Interférence, diffraction et dispersion des ondes. Principe de Huygens. — Interferenza, diffrazione e diffusione delle onde. Principio di Huygens.

Vibrations. / Vibrazioni.

9100   Généralités. (Voy. aussi B 3220.) — Generalità. (Vedi anche B 3220.)

9105   Action mécanique des vibrations (attraction acoustique). — Azione meccanica delle vibrazioni (attrazione acustica).

9110   Vibrations des cordes et des verges. Verges courbes. — Vibrazioni delle corde e delle verghe. Verghe curve.

9120   Vibrations des membranes et des plaques. Lames gauches. Cloches. — Vibrazioni delle membrane e delle lamine. Lamine curve. Campane.

9130   Vibrations des gaz dans les tuyaux et autres cavités. Influence des ouvertures. — Vibrazioni dei gas in tubi ed altre cavità. Effetti delle aperture.

9135   Vibrations forcées. — Vibrazioni forzate.

9140   Résonance. Résonnateurs. Tons combinés. (Voy. aussi Q 3545.) — Risonanza. Risonatori. Toni di combinazione. (Vedi anche Q 3545.)

Propagation du son. / Propagazione del suono.

9200   Généralités. — Generalità.

9210   Vitesse du son. — Velocità del suono.

9220   Réflexion et réfraction du son. — Riflessione e rifrazione del suono.

9230   Interférence et diffraction du son. Battements. — Interferenza e diffrazione del suono. Battimenti.

9240   Amortissement des ondes sonores par la viscosité et la conductibilité calorifique. — Smorzamento delle onde sonore per la viscosità e la conducibilità calorifica.

9250   Transparence acoustique. — Trasparenza acustica.

9255   Acoustique des bâtiments. — Acustica degl' edifizi.

Methods of Analysis and Measurement.	**Methoden zur Analyse und Messung von Schallwellen.**
9300 General.	Allgemeines.
9310 Methods of Illustrating and Observing Air-Waves.	Methoden zur Erläuterung und Beobachtung von Luftwellen.
9320 Measurement of the Velocity, Amplitude, Energy and Frequency of Sound-Waves.	Messung der Fortpflanzungsgeschwindigkeit, der Amplitude, der Energie und der Schwingungszahl von Schallwellen.
9340 Analysis of Compound Sound-Waves.	Analyse zusammengesetzter Schallwellen.

The Physical Basis of Music and the Sensation of Sound.	**Die physikalischen Grundlagen der Musik und die Tonempfindung.**
9400 General.	Allgemeines.
9410 Musical Instruments.	Musikalische Instrumente.
9420 The Voice. Speaking Machines.	Die Stimme. Sprechmaschinen.
9430 Limits of Audition as Dependent on Intensity and Pitch. (*See also* Q 3533.)	Grenzen des Gehörs in ihrer Abhängigkeit von Intensität und Tonhöhe. (*Siehe auch* Q 3533.)
9440 Modification of Vibrations in Transit through the Ear.	Modification der Schwingungen beim Durchgang durch das Ohr.
9450 Quality of Musical Tones. Consonance and Dissonance. Chords. Physical Explanation of Harmony. (*See also* Q 3540–3555.)	Qualität musikalischer Töne. Konsonanz und Dissonanz. Akkorde. Physikalische Erklärung der Harmonie. (*Siehe auch* Q 3540–3555.)
9460 Absolute Pitch. Standards of Pitch.	Absolute Tonhöhe. Normaltonmasse.
9470 Scales. Temperament.	Tonleitern. Musikalische Temperatur.
Physiological Acoustics. (*See also* Physiology, Q 2753, 4141, 3500–3590.) Such papers only will be entered here as are likely to be of interest to physicists.	**Physiologische Akustik.** (*Siehe auch* Physiologie, Q 2753, 4141, 3500–3590.) Nur solche Abhandlungen sind hier aufzunehmen, für die bei den Physikern ein Interesse erwartet werden kann.
9500 General.	Allgemeines.
9510 Arrangement and Action of the Vocal Organs. (*See* 9420.)	Anordnung und Wirkungsweise der Stimmorgane. (*Siehe auch* 9420.)
9520 Arrangement and Action of the Ear.	Anordnung und Wirkungsweise der Gehörsorgane.

	Methodes d'analyse et mesures.	Metodi di analisi e misure.
9300	Généralités.	Generalità.
9310	Méthodes pour étudier et observer les ondes aériennes.	Metodi per istudiare ed osservare le ondulazioni nell' aria.
9320	Mesure de la vitesse, de l'amplitude, de l'énergie et de la fréquence des ondes sonores.	Misura della velocità, ampiezza, energia e frequenza delle onde sonore.
9340	Analyse des ondes sonores complexes.	Analisi delle onde sonore complesse.

La base physique de la musique et la sensation du son.

Base fisica della musica e la sensazione del suono.

9400	Généralités.	Generalità.
9410	Instruments de musique.	Istrumenti musicali.
9420	La voix. Machines parlantes.	La voce. Macchine parlanti.
9430	Limites de perceptibilité des sons dans leur dépendance de l'intensité et de la hauteur. (*Voy. aussi* Q 3533.)	Limiti dell' audizione dipendenti dall' intensità ed altezza. (*Vedi anche* Q 3533.)
9440	Modification des vibrations dans leur passage à travers l'oreille.	Modificazione delle vibrazioni nel passaggio attraverso l'orecchio.
9450	Qualité des notes musicales. Consonnance et dissonnance. Accords. Explication physique de l'harmonie. (*Voy. aussi* Q 3540-3555.)	Qualità dei toni musicali. Consonanza e dissonanza. Accordi. Spiegazione fisica dell' armonia. (*Vedi anche* Q 3540-3555.)
9460	Hauteur absolue. Etalons de hauteur.	Altezza assoluta. Campioni di altezza.
9470	Gammes. Tempérament.	Scale. Temperamento.

	Acoustique physiologique. (*Voy. aussi* Physiologie, Q 2753, 4141, 3500-3590.) Les mémoires de cette catégorie ne doivent figurer ici qu'autant qu'ils sont intéressants pour les physiciens.	**Acustica fisiologica.** (*Vedi anche* Fisiologia, Q 2753, 4141, 3500-3590.) Verranno qui registrati solamente quelli articoli che possono avere dell' interesse per il fisico.
9500	Généralités.	Generalità.
9510	Disposition et action des organes vocaux. (*Voy.* 9420.)	Disposizione ed azione degli organi vocali. (*Vedi* 9420.)
9520	Disposition et action des organes de l'oreille.	Disposizione ed azione dell' orecchio.

INDEX

TO

(C) PHYSICS.

TABLE DES MATIÈRES

POUR LA

PHYSIQUE (C).

44

INDEX

zu

(C) PHYSIK.

48

INDICE

PER LA

(C) FISICA

AUTHOR CATALOGUE.

Abbot, C[harles] G[reeley]. The silver disk pyrheliometer. Washington D.C. Smithsonian Inst. Misc. Collect **56** No. 19 (Pub. 2008) 1911 (1-10 with pl. table). [4200]. 38881

———— The sun. New York and London (Appleton) 1911 (i-xxv 1-448 with ff. pls. tables). 20 cm. [4200]. 38882

———— and **Aldrich,** L. B. The pyrheliometric scale. Astroph. J. Chicago Ill. **33** 1911 (125-129). [4200]. 38883

———— and **Fowle,** F[rederick] E[ugene], *jun.* Note on the reflecting power of clouds. (Addenda to Ann. Astroph. Obs. Smithsonian Inst. Vol. 2.) Washington D.C. 1908 (3 with fig.). 23 cm. [4210]. 38884

Abegg, R[ichard]†, **Auerbach,** Fr., **Luther,** R. Messungen elektromotorischer Kräfte galvanischer Ketten mit wässerigen Elektrolyten. Gesammelt und bearb. im Auftrage der Deutschen Bunsen-Gesellschaft. (Abhandlungen der Deutschen Bunsen-Gesellschaft für angew. physikalische Chemie. Nr. 5.) Halle a. S. (W. Knapp) 1911 (IX — 213). 25 cm. 8,40 M. [5610 6210]. 38885

Abetti, Antonio. Sul modo di illuminare il campo oppure il reticolo di un refrattore. Catania Mem. Soc. spettroscop. ital. **40** 1911 (49-54). [3080]. 38886

Abney, W. de W. Colour-blindness and the trichromatic theory of colour vision. Part II. London Proc. R. Soc. (Ser. A) **84** 1910 (449-464). [4450]. 38887

Abraham, Henri. Principe de nouveaux appareils pour courants alternatifs. J. phys. Paris (sér. 5) **1** 1911 (264-274 av. fig.). [6070]. 38888

Abraham, Henri. Sur les relais et les servo-moteurs électriques. Paris C. R. Acad. sci. **152** 1911 (513-515). [6070]. 38889

———— et **Villard,** P. Voltmètre électrostatique à lecture directe pour très haute tension. J. phys. Paris (sér. 5) **1** 1911 (525-529 av. fig.) [6010]. 38890

———— r. Villard, P.

Abraham, Max. Sulla velocità di gruppo in un mezzo dispersivo. Nuovo Cimento Pisa (Ser. 6) **2** 1911 (443-454). [6620]. 38891

———— Sulla teoria della gravitazione. Roma Rend. Acc. Lincei (Ser. 5) **20** 2. sem. 1911 (678-682). [0700]. 38892

———— Zur Theorie der Gravitation. (Übers.) Physik. Zs. Leipzig **13** 1912 (1-4). [0700]. 38893

———— Das Elementargesetz der Gravitation. (Übers.) Physik. Zs. Leipzig **13** 1912 (4-5). [0700]. 38894

Accolla, Giuseppe. Sulla rotazione magnetica delle scariche elettriche del rocchetto d'induzione. Catania Bull. Acc. Gioenia (Ser. 2) **7** 1909 (2-4). [6400]. 38895

———— Dispersione elettrica e potenziale dell'atmosfera in Tunisi durante il passagio della cometa di Halley. Nuovo Cimento Pisa (Ser. 6) **1** 1911 (132-138). [6810]. 38896

Achalme, Pierre. Du rôle des électrons intra-atomiques dans la catalyse. Paris C. R. Acad. sci. **154** 1912 (352-355). [5675]. 38897

Acquino (D'), L. Le emanazioni radioattive esistenti nell'aria di Napoli. Riv. fis. mat. sc. nat. Pavia **22** 1910

(110-114); Rend. Soc. chim. ital.
Roma (Ser. 2) 2 1910 (129-133). [4275].
38898
Acquino (D'), L. Le conoscenze moderne sulle dimensioni molecolari.
Napoli (Tip. M. D'Auria) 1909 (15).
24 cm. [0150]. 38898A

Adams, L. H. v. Johnston, J.

Adams, Walter S[ydney] v. Gale, H. G.

Adda (D'), Lorenzo. Un importante contributo alla radiotelegrafia. Trasmissione delle immagini senza fili.
Lega navale 7 1911 (60-61). [6615].
38899
Adams, E[dwin] P[limpton]. The propagation of long electric waves along wires. Philadelphia Proc. Amer. Phil.
Soc. 49 (1910) 1911 (364-369). [6440].
38900
Addenbrooke, G. L. The electrical properties of celluloid. Elect. London
66 1911 (629-630). [5252]. 38901

———— On selenium. Elect.
London 67 1911 (591-592). [5660].
38902
Ageno, F. v. Nasini, R.

Agnew, P[aul] G[ough]. A tubular electrodynamometer for very heavy currents. [Abstract.] Physic. Rev.
Ithaca N.Y. 32 1911 (629-630). [6010].
38903

———— A device for measuring the torque of electrical instruments. Washington D.C. Dept. Comm. Lab. Bull.
Bur. Stand. 7 1911 (45-48 with fig.).
[0825 6000]. 38904

Agulhon, H. Action des rayons ultraviolets sur les diastases. Paris
C. R. Acad. sci. 152 1911 (398-401).
[4225]. 38907

Aimonetti, Cesare. Una modificazione all' apparato pendolare di Sterneck o nuova determinazione della gravità relativa a Torino e Genova. Torino
Atti Acc. sc. 46 1911 (605-622). [0845].
38908
Airey, H. M. v. Eccles, W. H.

Alasia, C. Per una nuova ipotesi cosmogonica. Riv. fis. mat. sc. nat.
Pavia 21 1910 (337-356). [0500].
38909
Albaret, John. Nouvelle formule usuelle d'émission de la chaleur. Genève
Bul. Inst. Nat. 38 1909 (235-238).
[1600]. 38910

Albers-Schönberg, H. Röntgenstrahlenwirkung auf Gartenerde. Fortschr. Röntgenstr. Hamburg 16 1911
(284-286). [4210]. 38911

Albert, Armando. Sull' astigmatismo e sulle costruzioni ottiche anastigmatiche. Prog. fotogr. Milano 17 1910
(163-168 203-209). [3085]. 38912

———— Il diaframma e la limitazione dei raggi negli obbiettivi fotografici. Prog. fotogr. Milano 17 1910
(229-234 265-271). [3085]. 38913

———— Proiezioni ordinarie e cinematografiche a luce fredda. Prog. fotogr. Milano 18 1911 (166-170).
[4225]. 38914

Albertotti, Giuseppe. L'opera scientifica del prof. Reymond nel campo della oftalmologia. Clin. ocul. Roma 13
1911 (537-564). [0010 2990]. 38915

Albrecht. Über eine neue Methode zur Untersuchung elektrischer Vorgänge am menschlichen Körper. Ber.
Kongr. exp. Psych. Leipzig 4 1911
(191-196). [5900]. 38916

Aldis, A. C. W. v. Scarle.

Aldrich, L. B. v. Abbot, C. G.

[Aleksějev, A. et Malikov, M[ichail]
Feodosějevič.] Алексѣевъ, А. и
Маликовъ, М[ихаилъ] Ѳеодосѣевичъ].
Зарядъ газового іона. [La charge du gaz-ion.] St. Peterburg Žurn. russ.
fiz.-chim. Obšč. Fiz. otd. 41 1909 (247-257). [6845]. 38917

Alessio, Alberto. Determinazione della gravità relativa fra Padova e Potsdam: E valori delle durate d'oscillazione dei pendoli dell' apparato tripendolare. Ann. idrogr. Genova 6 1909
(1-148). [0845]. 38918

———— Osservazioni gravimetriche eseguite a Genova nel 1910. Ann. idrogr. Genova 7 1910 (405-415).
[0845]. 38919

———— Come si determina l'accelerazione della gravità. Riv. astr. sc. affini Torino 4 1910 (435-449
528-552). [0845]. 38920

———— e Silva, G. Esperienze comparative sopra alcuni apparati gravimetrici e nuova determinazione della gravità relativa fra Genova e Padova. Ann. idrogr. Genova 7 1910
(309-403). [0845]. 38921

Alexander, Béla. Ueber das Verhalten der X-Strahlen bei Durchstrahlung geometrischer Glaskörper. Arch. physik. Med. Leipzig 4 1909 (263–281). [4240]. 38922

Alexanderson, Ernst F. W. Mehrphasenmotoren im Anschluss an Einphasennetze. [Phasenumformung.] Elektrot. Zs. Berlin 32 1911 (705–707). [6047]. 38923

————— Die magnetischen Eigenschaften des Eisens bei Hochfrequenz bis zu 200,000 Per Sek. Elektrot. Zs. Berlin 32 1911 (1078–1081). [6140 5450 5466 5720]. 38924

Alïthan-Klotz, Marie Czeslava. La compressibilité des récipients en verre de quartz et les constantes élastiques du quartz fondu. Thèse Genève 1909 (VI + 32 av. 1 fig.). 24 cm. [0840]. 38925

Algeri, Marino. Di alcuni metodi nella trasmissione della parola per la modulazione delle onde elettriche. Elettricista Roma (Ser. 2) 10 1911 (246–247). [6185]. 38926

Allara, Giacomo. Trasformazione grafica del diagramma dinamico di una motrice a vapore nel diagramma entropico. Mon. tecn. Milano 17 1911 (272–274). [2490]. 38927

Allen, F. A new method of measuring the luminosity of the spectrum. Phil. Mag. London (Ser. 6) 21 1911 (604–607). [3040]. 38928

Allen, H. Stanley. The path of an electron in combined radial magnetic and electric fields. London Proc. R. Soc. (Ser. A) 85 1911 (257–262). [4960]. 38929

Allen, S[amuel] J[ames] McIntosh. On the secondary β radiation from solids and liquids. Physic. Rev. Ithaca N.Y. 32 1911 (201–210) with tables. [4275]. 38930

————— On the absorption of the γ rays of radium by solids. [Abstract.] Physic. Rev. Ithaca N.Y. 32 1911 (222–224 with tables text fig.). [4275]. 38931

————— On the absorption of the γ rays of radium by liquids. [Abstract.] Physic. Rev. Ithaca N.Y. 32 1911 (225–226 with table). [4275]. 38932

Almansi, E. Sul concetto di deformazione derivata applicato allo studio delle deformazioni dei solidi cilindrici. Nuovo Cimento Pisa (Ser. 6) 1 1911 (269–282); 2 1911 (93–100). [0840]. 38933

————— Sulla distribuzione dell'elettricità in equilibrio nei conduttori. Roma Rend. Acc. Lincei (Ser. 5) 20 1. sem. 1911 (150–154). [5220]. 38934

Altenkirch, Edmund. Elektrothermische Kälteerzeugung und reversible elektrische Heizung. Physik. Zs. Leipzig 12 1911 (920–924); Zs. Kälteind. München 19 1912 (1–9). [5710]. 38935

Amadori, M. e **Pampanini**, G. Sulla capacità degli alogenuri potassici di dare soluzioni solide, in rapporto colla temperatura. Roma Rend. Acc. Lincei (Ser. 5) 20 2. sem. 1911 (473–480 572–577). [1840]. 38936

Amaduzzi, Lavoro. Distribuzione del potenziale e potenziale totale in scariche ad effluvio. Bologna Rend. Acc. sc. (N. Ser.) 13 1909 (112–121 con 3 tav.). [6810]. 38938

————— L'effetto Hallwachs nel selenio cristallino. Bologna Rend. Acc. sc. (N. Ser.) 14 1910 (39–47); [sunto] Riv. fis. mat. sc. nat. Pavia 24 1911 (269–270). [6350 5660]. 38940

————— Über den inneren Hallwachs-Effekt im Selen. Physik. Zs. Leipzig 13 1912 (165). [5660]. 38941

Amagat, E. H. Sur la pression intérieure des fluides et la détermination du zéro absolu. Paris C. R. Acad. sci. 153 1911 (851–857). [1880 2425]. 38942

Amann, J. Ultramikroskopische Beobachtungen. Zs. Kolloide Dresden 8 1911 (11–15). [0340 0100]. 38943

Ambronn, H. Ueber anomale Doppelbrechung beim Zelluloid. Leipzig Ber. Ges. Wiss. math.-phys. Kl. 63 1911 (240–257 402–406). [3822 3830 3850 3860]. 38944

————— Ueber die Dispersion der Doppelbrechung in zweiphasigen Systemen. Zs. Kolloide Dresden 9 1911 (147–153). [3835 3822 3860]. 38946

Ambrosius, F. Die Stromverhältnisse in Gegensprech - Brückensystemen. Arch. Post Berlin **39** 1911 (353–367). [6485]. 38947

―――― Neuere Simultanschaltungen. Helios Leipzig **17** 1911 Fach-Zs. (101–102). [6480]. 38948

―――― Beeinflussung von Telegraphenleitungen durch eine Hochspannungsanlage. Helios Leipzig **17** 1911 Fach-Zs. (257–258). [6480]. 38949

―――― Einzelanruf in Ruhestromleitungen. Helios Leipzig **17** 1911 Fach-Zs. (413–415). [6480]. 38950

Amerio, Alessandro. Un'esperienza da lezione sulla ricomposizione della luce. Nuovo Cimento Pisa (Ser. 6) **2** 1911 (80–82). [0050 2990]. 38951

―――― Recenti progressi nello studio delle radiazioni di temperatura. Nuovo Cimento Pisa (Ser. 6) **2** 1911 (397–403). [2040]. 38952

Ames, Joseph S. An introduction to the theory of optics. By Arthur Schuster. [Review.] Astroph. J. Chicago **34** 1911 (410–412). [3000]. 38953

―――― r. Kayser, H.

Ammon, Ludwig von. Ueber radioaktive Substanzen in Bayern. Geogn. Jahreshefte München **23** (1910) 1911 (191–209). [4275]. 38954

Anderson, A. On the comparison of two self-inductions. Phil. Mag. London (Ser. 6) **21** 1911 (608–610). [6440]. 38955

―――― and **Bowen, J. E.** On the measurement of contact differences of potential. London Proc. Physic. Soc. **23** 1911 (346–350). [6210]. 38956

Anderson, J. A. and **Sparrow, C. M.** On the effect of the groove form on the distribution of light by a grating. Astroph. J. Chicago Ill. **33** 1911 (338–352 with text fig. tables). [3160]. 38957

Anderson, J. S. r. Houstoun, R. A.

Andrade, E. N. da C. Über eine neue Methode, die Flammengeschwindigkeit zu bestimmen. Ann. Physik Leipzig (4. Folge) **37** 1912 (380 385). [0090 5685]. 38960

Andrade, Jules. Sur un nouvel organe régulateur des chronomètres. Paris C. R. Acad. sci. **153** 1911 (496–497). [0809]. 38958

―――― Le mouvement : mesures de l'étendue et mesures du temps. Paris 1911 (328 av. fig.). 22 cm. [0807 0809]. 38959

André, Ch. Rapport sur les observations faites à Roquetas (Espagne), à l'occasion de l'éclipse totale de Soleil du 30 août 1905. Ann. bur. longit. Paris **8** 1911 (f. 1 à f.28). [4205]. 38961

Andreae, J. L. Die Methode des Schwebens zur Dichtebestimmung homogener fester Körper. Zs. physik. Chem. Leipzig **76** 1911 (491–496). [4810]. 38962

Andreen-Svedberg, Andrea r. Svedberg, T.

[**Andreini, Corrado.**] Nuovo sistema di telegrafia multipla armonica. Elettricista Roma (Ser. 2) **9** 1910 (329–331). [6480]. 38963

[**Andrejev, N. N.**] Андреевъ, Н. Н. Къ дисперсіи затухающихъ волнъ. [Zur Theorie der Dispersion gedämpfter Wellen.] St. Peterburg. Žurn. russ. fiz.-chim. Obšč. Fiz. Otd. **41** 1909 (46–55 deutsch. Res. 56). [6625 3875]. 38964

―――― Объ одномъ примѣненіи термостата. [Eine Anwendung des Thermostaten.] Vopr. fiziki St. Peterburg **3** 1909 (186–187). [1014]. 38965

Andrews, F[rank] M[arion]. Apparatus for illustrating Boyle's law. Indianapolis Ind. Proc. Acad. Sci. **1909** 1910 (369 371 with fig.). [0090]. 38966

Angelini, Oreste. A proposito della "Microtelegrafia." Elettricista Roma (Ser. 2) **10** 1911 (258). [6480]. 38968

Angenheister, G. Ergebnisse der Arbeiten des Samoa-Observatoriums der kgl. Ges. Wiss. zu Göttingen. VI. Die luftelektrischen Beobachtungen am Samoa-Observatorium 1906, 1907, 1908. Göttingen Abh. Ges. Wiss. math.-phys. Kl. **9** 1911 No. 2 (III 43 mit 3 Taf.). [5270]. 38969

Angermann. Über Schlupfmessung. Elektrot. Zs. Berlin **33** 1912 (60–61). [6015]. 38970

Antonoff, G. N. The disintegration
products of uranium. Phil. Mag.
London (Ser. 6) 22 1911 (419-432).
[4275]. 38971

———— v. Evans, E. J.

Antony, Ubaldo. I colloidi inorganici. Rend. Soc. chim. ital. Roma
(Ser. 2) 2 1910 (45-47). [0310]. 38972

———— La costituzione degli
atomi. Rend. Soc. chim. ital. Roma
(Ser. 2) 2 1910 (225-227). [0500].
38973

———— e Bianchi, Michelina.
Contributo allo studio dello stato colloidale. Milano Rend. Ist. lomb. (Ser. 2)
42 1909 (929-931). [0310]. 38974

Antropoff, A. von. Die Dynamik
osmotischer Zellen. I. Vorl. Mitt.
Zs. physik. Chem. Leipzig 76 1911 (721-
731). [0310]. 38975

Appleby, M. P. v. Berkeley.

Apt, R. Über den gegenwärtigen
Stand und die nächsten Aufgaben der
Hochspannungs-Kabeltechnik. [Nebst
Erwiderung von L. Lichtenstein.] Elek-
trot. Zs. Berlin 32 1911 (356). [6000].
38976

Archbutt, Sydney L. v. Rosenhain, W.

Arco, Graf Georg von. Der heutige Stand der drahtlosen Telegraphie.
Zs. Schwachstromtechn. München 6
1912 (67-74). [6615]. 38977

Aretz, Matthias. Über den lang-
welligen Teil des Kupferfunken- und
Kupferbogenspektrums. Zs. wiss.
Phot. Leipzig 9 1911 (256-269); Diss.
Bonn. Leipzig (J. A. Barth) 1911 (19),
24 cm. [4205]. 38978

Argangeli, Giovanni. Sulla scoperta
delle macchie solari e delle facole.
Ann. Univ. tosc. Pisa 29 1910 (1-15).
[0010]. 38980

Arlitewicz, Tomasz. Skrócony sposób
obliczenia rozdziału prądów w sieciach
zamkniętych. [Sur une méthode qui
peut servir au calcul simplifié de la
distribution des courants dans les
circuits fermés complexes.] Przegl.
techn. Warszawa 49 1911 (644-647).
[5630]. 38981

Arndt, Siegfried. Einige Methoden
zur Bestimmung von Dielektrizitätskonstanten und ein neues Verfahren zur
Erzeugung schwach gedämpfter Schwingungen. Diss. Leipzig. Braunschweig

(Druck v. J. H. Meyer) 1911 (VII + 79),
23 cm. [5252-6610-3875]. 38982

Arnò, Riccardo. Nuovi metodi di
misura industriale. Atti Assoc. elettrotecn. Milano 14 1910 (191-196). [5705].
38983

———— Rappresentazione grafica
e verifica sperimentale dei nuovi
metodi di misura industriale per la
tariffeazione dell' energia elettrica nei
sistemi di distribuzione a corrente
alternata. Atti Assoc. elettrotecn.
Milano 14 1910 (583-613). [5720].
38984

———— Galvanometro telefonico a
campo Ferraris. Suo impiego come
frequenziometro. Milano Rend. Ist.
lomb. (Ser. 2) 43 1910 (161-165 con
4 tav.). [6010]. 38985

———— Considerazioni pratiche su:
Voltamperometro, volteculombometro,
fasometro. [Sunto.] Mon. tecn. Milano
16 1910 (461-464 con 1 tav.; 507-513).
[5705]. 38986

———— Watt-voltamperometri
elettrodinamici e ad induzione. Atti
Assoc. elettrotecn. Milano 15 1911
(979-980). [6010]. 38987

Arnold, E. Das magnetische Dreh-
feld und seine neuesten Anwendungen.
Verh. Ges. D. Natf. Leipzig 83 I 1911
(206-211). [6045]. 38988

Arnold, H. D. Limitations imposed
by slip and inertia terms upon Stoke's
law for the motion of spheres through
liquids. [Abstract.] Physic. Rev.
Ithaca N.Y. 32 1911 (233). [0325].
38989

Arons, Leo. Das Chromoskop.
Elektrot. Zs. Berlin 32 1911 (729-738).
[0090-3610-4000]. 38990

Arrhénius, Svante. L'énergie libre.
Rev. gén. sci. Paris 22 1911 (266-275).
[0500]. 38991

———— Über die Energieverhältnisse der Dampfbildung und der
elektrolytischen Dissoziation. Stockholm Medd. Vet.-Ak. Nobelinst 2 No. 8
1911 (34). [2457-2472-2475]. 38992

———— Das Hauptgesetz der
Adsorptionserscheinungen. Stockholm
Medd. Vet.-Ak. Nobelinst. 2 No. 7
1911 (44). [0250-0842]. 38993

———— Les conditions physiques
de la planète Mars. J. phys. Paris
(sér. 5) 2 1912 (81-97). [3850]. 38994

Arrhénius, Svante. Il divenire dei mondi. [Trad.] Milano (Soc. ed. libraria) 1909 (XV + 192). 26 cm. [0700].
38995

Arsem, W. C. Electric vacuum furnace installations in the research laboratory of the General Electric Company. J. Ind. Engin. Chem. Easton Pa. 2 1910 (3–9 with ff.). [6090].
38996

Artmann, P. Radioaktivität des Meerwassers. Ber. intern. Kongr. Thalassother. Berlin 5 1911 (311–321). [4275].
38997

Artom, Alessandro. Sopra alcuni problemi di radiotelegrafia. Torino (V. Bona) 1909 (16 con 4 tav.). 25 cm. [6610].
38998

Artom, Camillo. La successione dei suoni spiegata col fenomeno del-l'attrazione melodica tetracordale. Riv. music. Torino 17 1910 (433–449). [9450].
38999

Artoos, Louis. Une étude de la boussole. Ouvrier mineur 1908 (121). [5435].
39000

Aschoff, Karl. Die Radioaktivität der Kreuznacher Solquellen. Allgemein verständliche Abhandlung. Kreuznach (K. Scheffel) [1911] (16). 22 cm. 0.30 M. [4275].
39001

Askenasy, Paul. Ein Ersatz für Diapositive für Projektionszwecke. Zs. Elektroch. Halle 18 1912 (64). [0050].
39002

Aspestrand, T. H. Die gebräuchlichsten Wechselstromwicklungen. Strelitz i. M. (M. Hittenkofer) [1912] (41). 27 cm. 2 M. [6945].
39003

Aston, F. W. The distribution of electric force in the Crookes dark space. London Proc. R. Soc. (Ser. A) 84 1911 (526–535). [6840].
39004

Aten, A. H. W. Die spezifische Leitfähigkeit des geschmolzenen Kaliumnitrats. Zs. physik. Chem. Leipzig 78 1911 (1–23). [5660 6240]. 39005

Atzler, E. r. Wilke, E.

Aubel, Edm. van. Sur le phénomène de Hall et l'effet thermomagnétique transversal dans le graphite. Paris C. R. Acad. sci. 153 1911 (331–333 568–569). [6455].
39006

Aue, Jul. Bestimmung der allgemeinen Konstanten eines photographischen Objektives. Phot. Ind. Berlin 1911 (689–690 723–724). [3085].
39008

Auerbach, Erich. Einfache Formel für die Überlastbarkeit des Asynchronmotors. Elektrot. Zs. Berlin 32 1911 (738–739). [6070].
39009

Auerbach, Felix. Die Grundlagen der Musik. (Wissen und Können. 18.) Leipzig (J. A. Barth) 1911 (VI + 209). 23 cm. Geb. 5 M. [9400 9500]. 39010

Auerbach, Friedrich. Die Potentiale der wichtigsten Bezugselektroden. Zs. Elektroch. Halle 18 1912 (13–18). [5610].
39011

—— r. Abegg, R.

Auer von Welsbach, Carl. Ueber die chemische Untersuchung der Aktinium enthaltenden Rückstände der Radiumgewinnung. Zs. anorg. Chem. Hamburg 69 1911 (353–391). [4275].
39012

Aust, Franz A. The electrical discharge between a pointed conductor and a hemispherical surface in gases at different pressures. [Abstract.] Physic. Rev. Ithaca N.Y. 32 1911 (254–255). [6820].
39013

—— A variable high resistance of India ink on paper. [Abstract.] Physic. Rev. Ithaca N.Y. 32 1911 (256); (Übers.) Physik. Zs. Leipzig 12 1911 (732 733). [6010 5660].
39014

Austerweil, G. Sur le passage de l'hydrogène à travers le tissu caoutchouté des aérostats. Paris C. R. Acad. sci. 154 1912 (196–198). [0320]. 39016

Austin, L[ouis] W[inslow]. Quantitative Versuche über drahtlose Telegraphie auf lange Strecken. [Quantitative experiments in long distance radiotelegraphy.] (Übers.) Physik. Zs. Leipzig 12 1911 (863–869). 39017

—— Der Gleichrichterdetektor mit Schleifkontakt. [The sliding contact rectifying detector.] (Übers.) Physik. Zs. Leipzig 12 1911 (867–868). [6043].
39018

—— Vorläufige Mitteilung über den Widerstand von Antennen für drahtlose Telegraphie. [A preliminary note on the resistance of radio-telegraphic antennas.] (Übers.) Physik. Zs. Leipzig 12 1911 (924–926). [6615 6043].
39019

Austin, L.[ouis] W[inslow]. Hohe Funkenfrequenz in der drahtlosen Telegraphie. [High spark frequency in radiotelegraphy.] (Übers.) Physik. Zs. Leipzig 12 1911 (1131–1133). [6615]. 39020

——— Die Messung elektrischer Schwingungen in der Empfangsantenne. [The measurement of electrical oscillations in the receiving antenna.] (Übers.) Physik. Zs. Leipzig 12 1911 (1133–1135); Washington D.C. Dept. Comm. Lab. Bull. Bur. Stand. 7 1911 (295–299 with fig. table). [6615]. 39021

——— Thermoelemente für Versuche mit Hochfrequenzströmen. [Thermo-elements for experiments with high frequency currents.] (Übers.) Physik. Zs. Leipzig 12 1911 (1226–1227). [6043]. 39022

——— Some experiments with coupled high frequency circuits. Washington D.C. Dept. Comm. Lab. Bull. Bur. Stand. 7 1911 (301–314 with fig. tables). [6615]. 39024

Auwers, K[arl]. Über die Spektrochemie der Enole und Enol-Derivate. Berlin Ber. D. chem. Ges. 44 1911 (3514–3524). [3850]. 39025

——— Über spektrochemisches Verhalten und Konstitution des Acetessigesters. Berlin Ber. D. chem. Ges. 44 1911 (3525–3542). [3850]. 39026

——— Zur Spektrochemie ungesättigter Verbindungen. Berlin Ber. D. chem. Ges. 44 1911 (3679–3692). [3850]. 39027

——— Spektrochemische Untersuchungen. Liebigs Ann. Chem. Leipzig 387 1912 (165–253). [3850]. 39028

——— und Eisenlohr, F. Spektrochemische Untersuchungen. (2. Mitt.) J. prakt. Chem. Leipzig (N.F.) 84 1911 (1–121). [3860 3030). 39029

Ayres, T. r. Barkla.

Azambuja, L. d' r. Deslandres, H.

Babcock, Harold D. The Zeeman effect for vanadium. Astroph. J. Chicago Ill. 34 1911 (209–224 with tables). [4208]. 39030

——— The Zeeman effect for chromium. Astroph. J. Chicago Ill. 33 1911 (217–233 with tables pls.). [4208]. 39031

Babcock, Harold D. Note on the grouping of triplet separations produced by a magnetic field. Astroph. J. Chicago Ill. 34 1911 (288–293 with fig. tables). [4960 4208]. 39032

Babini, V. r. Mascarelli, L.

Baborovský, Jiří. Friedrich Kohlrausch. (Czechisch.) Listy Chem. Prag 1910 (128–130). [0010]. 39033

——— Elektrochemický potenciál kovového magnesia v ethylalkoholových roztocích chloridu hořečnatého. [Elektrochemischer Potential des Metallmagnesiums in Aethylalkohollösungen von Magnesiumchlorid.] Prag Rozpr. České Ak. Frant. Jos. 19 1910 No. 47 (34). [5240 6200]. 39034

——— Přehled pokroků fysiky za rok 1907. 6. Chemie fysikální. [Fortschritte in der physikalischen Chemie im Jahre 1907.] Prag Věstn. České Ak. Frant. Jos. 1910 (1–38 81–125). [0030]. 39035

——— Přehled pokroků fysiky za rok 1908. Radioaktivita. [Uebersicht der physikalischen Fortschritte im Jahre 1908. Radioaktivitaet.] Prag Věstn. České Ak. Frant. Jos. 1911 (235–252 290–307). [0030 4275]. 39036

——— i Kužma, Bohumil. Studie o tak zvaném elektrolytickém superoxydu stříbra. Pokračování. [Studie über den sog. elektrolytischen Silbersuperoxyd.] [Forts.] Listy Chem. Prag 1910 (156–159); Prag Rozpr. České Ak. Frant. Jos. 1910 (5). [6242]. 39038

——— et Voženílek, Jindřich. Převodná čísla chloridu hořečnatého v jeho roztocích ethylalkoholových. [Ueberführungszahlen von Magnesiumchlorid in seinen Aethylalkohollösungen.] Prag Rozpr. České Ak. Frant. Jos. 20 1911 No. 28 (12). [6240]. 39039

Bachmann, Wilhelm. Untersuchungen über die ultramikroskopische Struktur von Gallerten mit Hilfe des Spalt- und Kardioid-Ultramikroskops. Zs. anorg. Chem. Leipzig 73 1911 (125–172 mit 1 Taf.). [0340]. 39040

Backus, Cecil F. r. Comey, A. M.

Bacon, F. Sulla conduttività per il calore di alcuni coibenti. [Trad.] Industria Milano 25 1911 (205). [2020]. 39041

Bacon, R. F. *v.* Hulbert, C. H.

Baedeker, K. Zur Elektronentheorie der Thermoelektrizität. Ann. Physik Leipzig (4. Folge) **35** 1911 (75–89). [5710 5675]. 39042

Baerwald, H. Untersuchung der Einwirkung des Magnetfeldes auf den Dopplereffekt der Kanalstrahlen. Ann. Physik Leipzig (4. Folge) **34** 1911 (883–906). [6845 4208]. 39043

——— Erwiderung auf die Bemerkung des Hrn. Stark zu meiner Mitteilung über die Untersuchung der Einwirkung des Magnetfeldes auf den Dopplereffekt der Kanalstrahlen. Ann. Physik Leipzig (4. Folge) **36** 1911 (293–296). [6845 4208]. 39043A

Baeyer, O. v. und **Fool**, A. Die Anfangsgeschwindigkeit lichtelektrisch ausgelöster Elektronen. Berlin Verh. D. physik. Ges. **13** 1911 (569–572). [6845 6850]. 39044

——— **Hahn**, Otto und **Meitner**, Lise. Ueber die β-Strahlen des aktiven Niederschlags des Thoriums. Physik. Zs. Leipzig **12** 1911 (273–279). [4275]. 39045

——— ——— ——— Nachweis von β-Strahlen bei Radium D. Physik. Zs. Leipzig **12** 1911 (378–379 mit 1 Taf.). [4275]. 39046

——— ——— ——— Magnetische Spektren der β-Strahlen des Radiums. Physik. Zs. Leipzig **12** 1911 (1099–1101 mit 1 Taf.). [6845 4275]. 39047

——— *v.* Rubens, H.

Bagyon *v.* Szabó.

Bahr, Eva von. Über die Veränderung von Absorptionslinien durch fremde Gase. (Bemerkung zu Mitteilungen von Chr. Füchtbauer und G. Hertz.) Physik. Zs. Leipzig **12** 1911 (1167–1169). [3850]. 39048

——— und **Koenigsberger**, J[ohannes]. Ueber die Farbe anorganischer Salze und die Berechnung der schwingenden Teile. Heidelberg SitzBer. Ak. Wiss. math.-natw. Kl. **1911** Abh. 26 (26). 25 cm. [3800 3860 5467]. 39049

Bahrdt, Wilhelm. Wellenmaschine zur Demonstration der Interferenz zweier gegeneinander laufender Wellen. Zs. physik. Unterr. Berlin **24** 1911 (27–28). [9030]. 39050

——— Ein neuer Apparat zur Untersuchung der Gesetze des freien Falls. Zs. physik. Unterr. Berlin **24** 1911 (205–209). [0820 0050]. 39051

Baillaud, B. Précision de la connaissance de l'heure à l'Observatoire de Paris dans les derniers mois de 1911 et le commencement de janvier 1912. Paris C. R. Acad. sci. **154** 1912 (157–159). [0809]. 39052

Baillehache, de. Détermination de la force électromotrice de l'élément Weston normal, par MM. Haga et Bœrema. J. phys. Paris (sér. 5) **2** 1912 (112–120). [5695]. 39053

Baillehache (**De**), R. Analisi critica dell'opera: Battelli, Occhialini e Chella "La radio-activité et la constitution de la matière." Scientia Bologna **9** 1911 (440–445). [4275]. 39054

Baisch, Erich. Versuche zur Prüfung des Wien-Planckschen Strahlungsgesetzes im Bereich kurzer Wellenlängen. Ann. Physik Leipzig (4. Folge) **35** 1911 (543–590). [4210 4202]. 39055

Baker, Robert H. The spectroscopic binary β Aurigae. Pittsburg Pa. Pub. Allegheny Obs. Univ. Pittsburg **1** [1910] (163–190 with tables ff.). [3410]. 39056

Bakunin, Marussia. Reazioni fotochimiche. Rend. Soc. chim. ital. Roma (Ser. 2 **2** 1910 (231–233). [4225]. 39057

——— Sull'azione dei raggi ultravioletti sugli stereoisomeri della serie cinnamica. Napoli Rend. Soc sc. (Ser. 3) **17** 1911 (372–375). [4225]. 39058

——— Sulla esplosività dei residui delle soluzioni eteree dei fenilnitroindoni esposti alla luce. Napoli Rend. Soc. sc. (Ser. 3) **17** 1911 (375–378). [4225]. 39059

——— Gli indoni ed i loro prodotti di trasformazione al sole. Napoli Rend. Soc. sc. (Ser. 3) **17** 1911 (379–386). [4225]. 39060

——— e **Lanis**, E. Reazioni fotochimiche dei nitrofenilindoni. Gazz. chim. ital. Roma **41** 2. sem. 1911 (155–184). [4225]. 39061

Baldet, F. *v.* La Baume Pluvinel, A.

Baldit, A. Les mesures récentes d'électricité atmosphérique en ballon libre. Bruxelles Bul. Soc. astron. **1907** (269–281 290–302). [5270]. 39062

——— Observations sur les charges électriques de la pluie en 1910, au Puy-en-Velay. Paris C. R. Acad. sci. 152 1911 (807-810). [5270]. 39063

Bancelin. La viscosité des émulsions. Paris C. R. Acad. sci. 152 1911 (1382-1384). [0325]. 39064

———— Über die Viskosität von Suspensionen und die Bestimmung der Avogadroschen Zahl. Zs. Kolloide Dresden **9** 1910 (154-156). [0340 0325 0150]. 39065

Baraldi, Coriolano. Genesi del moto universale e formazione della materia. Milano Tip. moderna) 1910 (15 con 18 tav.). 35 cm. [0790]. 39066

Barassi, Vittorio. La protezione degli impianti elettrici contro le sopratensioni pericolose per il pubblico. Industria Milano **24** 1910 (82-84 101-103 120-122). [6450]. 39067

Barbagelata, Angelo. Prova indiretta dei trasformatori di misura per forti intensità di corrente. Atti Assoc. elettrotecn. Milano **14** 1910 (639-654); [sunto] Mon. tecn. Milano **16** 1910 (308-310). [5705]. 39068

———— Sulla prova indiretta degli alternatori mediante la prova come motore sincrono a vuoto. Elettricità Milano **35** 1910 (388-392). [6945]. 39069

———— e **Emanueli,** L. I metodi di opposizione colle correnti alternate e la loro applicazione industriale. Atti Assoc. elettrotecn. Milano **15** 1911 (987-999). [6040]. 39070

Bardeloni, C. La radiotelegrafia all'estero. Riv. Artig. Genio Roma **2.** trim. 1910 (428-412 con 1 tav.). [6615]. 39072

Barduzzi, Domenico. Sulla radioattività delle sorgenti minerali ed in particolare maniera in quelle di S. Giuliano (Pisa). Atti del X Congresso nazionale di idrologia, climatologia e terapia fisica. Perugia (Un. tip. coop.) 1910 6 (158-164). 25 cm. [4275]. 39073

Barkhausen, H. Die Probleme der Schwachstromtechnik. Dinglers polyt. J. Berlin **326** 1911 (513-517 531-534). [6480 6485]. 39074

———— Theorie der gleichzeitigen Messung vom Sende- und Empfangsstrom. Jahrb. drahtlos. Telegr. Leipzig **5** 1912 (261-269). [6615]. 39075

Barkla, Charles G. Note on the energy of scattered X-radiation. Phil. Mag. London (Ser. 6) **21** 1911 (648-652). [4240]. 39076

———— The spectra of the fluorescent Röntgen radiations. Phil. Mag. London (Ser. 6) **22** 1911 (396-412); (Übers.) Jahrb. Radioakt. Leipzig **8** (1911) 1912 (471-488). [4205 4230 4240 3875]. 39077

———— and **Ayres,** T. The distribution of secondary X-rays and the electromagnetic pulse theory. Phil. Mag. London (Ser. 6) **21** 1911 (270-278). [4240]. 39079

Barnes, James. An enclosed arc for spectroscopic work. Astroph. J. Chicago Ill. **34** 1911 (154-158 with text fig.); [abstract] Physic. Rev. Ithaca N.Y. **32** 1911 (617-618). [6080 4202]. 39080

———— The spectra of aluminium, copper, and magnesium in the arc under reduced pressure. Astroph. J. Chicago Ill. **34** 1911 (159-163 with pl. table); Physic. Rev. Ithaca N.Y. **32** 1911 (618-619). [4205 4206]. 39081

Barni, Edoardo. Il montatore elettricista. Ed. 10. Milano (Lodi, Succ. Wilmant) 1909 (562). 19 cm. [0030 4900]. 39082

Baroncz, Z. Versuche über den sogenannten Metakontrast. Arch. ges. Physiol. Bonn **140** 1911 (491-508). [4450]. 39083

Baroni, Mario. Studi sugli scambi di calore. Milano Rend. Ist. lomb. (Ser. 2) **44** 1911 (99-132). [2015]. 39084

Barr, J. Parallel working of alternators. London J. Inst. Electr. Engin. **47** 1911 (276-310). [6945]. 39085

Barratt, T. s. Marsden.

Barreca, Pasquale. Secondo contributo circa le facoltà radiative delle antenne. Atti Assoc. elettrotecn. Milano **14** 1910 (757-764). [6610]. 39086

———— Circa una maggiore precisazione della legge di degradazione universale e circa una possibile disponibilità indefinita di energia degradabile. Nuovo Cimento Pisa (Ser. 6) **2** 1911 (85-92). [2415 0500]. 39087

———— Zweiter Beitrag zur Frage nach den Strahlungsfähigkeiten der Antennen. (Secondo contributo circa le facoltà radiative delle antenne.) (Übers.) Jahrb. drahtlos. Telegr. Leipzig **5** 1912 (285–293). [6615]. 39088

Barreca, Pasquale. Lezioni elementari di correnti alternate. Ed. 2. Livorno (R. Giusti) 1910 (XII + 250). 16 cm. [0030 4900]. 39089

———— Elementi di telegrafia e telefonia senza fili. Livorno (Giusti) 1910 (XII + 265). 16 cm. [0030 4900]. 39090

Barschall, Hermann. Über spezifische Wärmen fester Stoffe bei tiefen Temperaturen. Zs. Elektroch. Halle **17** 1911 (341–345). [1620]. 39091

———— Über die Verdampfungswärme des Sauerstoffes. Zs. Elektroch. Halle **17** 1911 (345–348). [1680]. 39092

Barth, Ernst. Einführung in die Physiologie. Pathologie und Hygiene der menschlichen Stimme. Leipzig (G. Thieme) 1911 (XIV + 507 mit 2 Taf.). 26 cm. 15 M. [9510]. 39093

Barth, Friedrich. Die Dampfmaschinen. Kurzgefasstes Lehrbuch . . . 2., verb. u. verm. Aufl. I. Wärmetheoretische und dampftechnische Grundlagen. II. Bau und Betrieb der Dampfmaschinen. (Sammlung Göschen 8, 572.) Leipzig (G. J. Göschen) 1912 (152 168). 16 cm. Je 0,80 M. [2490]. 39094

Bartoli, G. Alternatore per telegrafia senza fili. Riv. marit. Roma 1910 2. trim. (425–429). [6043]. 39095

Bartoševič, A. M. v. Korolikov, A. L.

Barus, C. Elliptic and other interference with reflecting gratings. Phil. Mag. London (Ser. 6) **22** 1911 (118 129); Science New York (N. Ser.) **33** 1911 (113). [3610]. 39096

———— A continuous record of atmospheric nucleation. Washington D.C. Smithsonian Inst. Cont. Knowl. **34** (No. 1651) 1905 (i–xvi 1–226 with text ff. charts tables). [1800]. 39097

———— Ueber die Sedimentation. Zs. Kolloide Dresden **9** 1911 (14–16). [0100]. 39098

———— Ueber den Gang der Luft durch eine Wasserwand. Zs. Kolloide Dresden **8** 1911 (288–291). [0320]. 39099

———— [and] Barus, M. I. The production of elliptic interferences

in relation to interferometry. Washington (Carnegie Inst. Pub. No. 149) 1911 (vi + 77 with fl. pl. tables). 25.5 cm. [3610]. 39100

Barus, M. v. Barus, C.

Bary, Paul. Sur le mode de dissolution des matières colloïdales. Paris C. R. Acad. sci. **152** 1911 (1386–1387). [0340]. 39101

———— Sur les phénomènes osmotiques dans les milieux non conducteurs. Paris C. R. Acad. sci. **152** 1911 (1766–1767). [0310]. 39102

Baslini, Carlo. Occhiali con astuccio del secolo XVII. Clinica ocul. Roma **13** 1911 (521–523). [0010 2990]. 39103

Bateman, Harry. The transformation of a particular type of electromagnetic field, and its physical interpretation. London Proc. Math. Soc. (Ser. 2) **10** 1911 (7–14). [4940 6410]. 39104

———— On certain vectors associated with an electromagnetic field, and the reflexion of a disturbance at the surface of a perfect conductor. London Proc. Math. Soc. (Ser. 2) **10** 1911 (96–115). [4940 6410]. 39105

Bates, F. W. Effet de la lumière sur l'isolement par le soufre. Radium Paris **8** 1911 (312–313). [5252 5660]. 39106

Batschinski, A. On the equation of continuity of the liquid and gaseous states of matter. Phil. Mag. London (Ser. 6) **22** 1911 (221). [1880]. 39107

———— Ueber die Ermittlung des Grades der molekularen Association von Flüssigkeiten. Zs. physik. Chem. Leipzig **75** 1911 (665–673). [1880 2457]. 39108

———— Bemerkung über die Empfindlichkeit der Wage. Zs. physik. Unterr. Berlin **24** 1911 (24–25). [0810]. 39109

Battaglia, A. Telegrafia duplice. Elettricista Roma (Ser. 2) **10** 1911 (35–38). [6480]. 39110

———— Arco voltaico in globo chiuso. Elettricista Roma (Ser. 2) **10** 1911 (113–115). [6830]. 39111

———— Nuovo scatto meccanico per il controllo del telegrafo Hughes. Elettricista Roma (Ser. 2) **10** 1911 (249–251). [6480]. 39112

Battelli, Angelo. **Occhialini,** Augusto. **Chella,** Silvio. La radioattività. Milano Atti fondar. Cagnola 22 1909 (XII + 438). [0030 2900 4275].
39113

— — — — La radioattività. Bari (G. Laterra e figli) 1909 (XII + 438). 24 cm. [0030 2900 4275].
39114

Baud, E. Sur la chaleur moléculaire de fusion. Paris C. R. Acad. sci. 152 1911 (1480-1483). [1670].
39115

— — — — Sur une loi générale de la dissolution. Paris C. R. Acad. sci. 154 1912 (198-201 351-352). [2457].
39116

Bauer, Edmond. Sur la théorie du rayonnement. Paris C. R. Acad. sci. 153 1911 (1466-1469). [4210].
39118

Bauer, Heinz. Das Oudimeter. Verh. D. Röntgenges. Hamburg 7 1911 (137-139). [6800].
39119

Bauer, L. A. Zur Theorie der Säkularvariation des Erdmagnetismus. Physik. Zs. Leipzig 12 1911 (445-448). [5490].
39120

— — — — The broader aspects of research in terrestrial magnetism. [Address as retiring vice-president and chairman of Section B (Physics), American Association for the Advancement of Science, given at Minneapolis, Minn., December 29 1910.] Science New York (N. Ser.) 33 1911 (41-54). [5490].
39121

— — — — Általános nézőpontok a földmágnességi vizsgálatokban. (Allgemeine Gesichtspunkte für die erdmagnetischen Untersuchungen.) Termt. Közl. Budapest 43 1911 (577-595). [5490].
39122

Bauer, O. v. Heyn, E.

Baum, F. Demonstration seines Ophthalmo-Fundoskops. Verh. Ges. D. Natf. Leipzig 81 (1909) II 2 1910 (219-222). [4470].
39123

— — — — Ein neues Corneal-Mikroskop für grösste Vergrösserungen. Verh. Ges. D. Natf. Leipzig 81 (1909) II 2 1910 (222-223). [4470].
39124

Baume, Georges et **Germann,** Albert F. O. Courbes de fusibilité des mélanges gazeux : systèmes oxoniens formés par l'acétylène, l'éthylène, l'oxyde azotique et l'oxyde de méthyle. Paris C. R. Acad. sci. 153 1911 (569-571). [1920].
39125

— — — — et **Perrot,** F. Louis. Courbes de fusibilité des mélanges gazeux : systèmes formés par l'anhydride carbonique et l'anhydride sulfurique avec l'alcool méthylique et l'oxyde de méthyle. Paris C. R. Acad. sci. 152 1911 (1763-1766). [1920].
39126

Baumhauer, Heinrich. Krystallographisch-optische Untersuchungen. (Forts. v. 47 1.) Zs. Krystallogr. Leipzig 49 1911 (113-132). [3830].
39127

Baumhauer, H. F. I filamenti di wolframio per le lampade elettriche ad incandescenza. [Trad.] Industria chim. Torino 10 1910 (359-360); [sunto] Riv. fis. mat. sc. nat. Pavia 23 1911 (70-71). [6080].
39128

— — — — Sulla fabbricazione dei filamenti per lampadine elettriche. [Trad.] Industria Milano 25 1911 (165-167). [6080].
39129

Baur, Emil. Ueber kolloide und molekulardisperse Lösungen. Natw. Rdsch. Braunschweig 27 1912 (3-5 17-18).
39130

Baxmann, Alfred. Absorption und Geschwindigkeitsverlust der β-Strahlen des Radiums. (Mitteilungen des Laboratoriums für theoretische Physik, Halle. No. 1.) Diss. Halle a. S. (Druck v. C. A. Kaemmerer & Co.) 1911 (50 mit Taf.). 29 cm. [6845 4275 3875].
39131

Bayeux, Raoul. Sur un appareil de précision pour l'emploi de l'oxygène gazeux en physiologie et en thérapeutique. Paris C. R. Acad. sci. 153 1911 (999-1002 av. fig.). [0835].
39132

Beattie, R. e **Gerrard,** H. L'isteresi magnetica alla temperatura dell' aria liquida. [Sunto. Trad.] Atti Assoc. elettrotecn. Milano 15 1911 (121-122). [5450].
39133

Beatty, R. T. The ionisation of heavy gases by X-rays. Cambridge Proc. Phil. Soc. 16 1911 (46-47); London Proc. R. Soc. (Ser. A) 85 1911 (230-239). [5685].
39135

Bechterew, P. Untersuchung einiger galvanischer Elemente mit Kohlenanoden. Zs. Elektroch. Halle 17 1911 (851-877). [5610 6230 6210].
39136

Beck, C. The pupil of an optical system with regard to perspective. London Proc. R. Soc. (Ser. A) 85 1911 (462-470). [3050].
39137

Beck, Emil. Absolute Messungen über den Peltier-Effekt. Zürich Vierteljahrschr. Natf. Ges. **55** 1910 (103–155 470–482). [5710]. 39138

Beck, K. Über ein Verfahren zur Bestimmung der Erweichungspunkte von Silikatgläsern. Zs. Elektroch. Halle **17** 1911 (848–849). [1810]. 39140

Beck, Wilhelm. Die neuesten Fortschritte auf dem Gebiete der Elektrotechnik. ErgBd zu „Die Elektrizität und ihre Technik." Leipzig (E. Wiest Nachf.) 1911 (III + 110). 24 cm. Geb. 2 M. [6000]. 39141

Beckenhaupt, C. Ueber das Verhältnis der chemischen Elemente zu den Massen und Bewegungen der Himmelskörper und die ursprüngliche Art der Energie. N. Weltanschaug Leipzig **4** 1911 (93–107). [0000]. 39142

———— Sprechen die in Königsberg durch Planck besprochenen Untersuchungen für oder gegen die Existenz des Aethers und die mechanische Theorie ? Wie weit sind Relativität und Vierdimensionalität begründet ? Strassburg Monatsber. Ges. Wiss. **45** 1911 (119–137). [0000 0600]. 39143

Becker, A. Über die Elektrizitätsträger in Gasen. Ann. Physik Leipzig (4. Folge) **36** 1911 (209–280). [5685 6805 0150]. 39144

Becker, A[ugust]. Ueber die Diffusion leuchtender Metalldämpfe in Flammen und über die Lichtemissionszentren dieser Dämpfe. Tl 1 : Messmethode und deren Theorie. Heidelberg SitzBer. Ak. Wiss. math.-natw. Kl. **1911** Abh. 7 (20). [4202 0320]. 39145

———— Über die Absorption der Kathodenstrahlen. Physik. Zs. Leipzig **12** 1911 (1020–1023). [6845 3875]. 39146

Becker, Felix. Über Kondensation von Dämpfen. Zs. physik. Chem. Leipzig **78** 1911 (39–70). [1840]. 39147

Becker, Hans. Physik und Chemie. [Photographische Methoden.] [In : Angewandte Photographie in Wissenschaft und Technik. Hrsg. von K. W. Wolf-Czapek. Tl 1.] Berlin (Union) 1911 (3–26 mit 13 Taf.). [0090 4225 3085]. 39148

Beckman, Bengt. Über den Einfluss des Druckes auf die elektrische Leitfähigkeit bei Pyrit, Eisenglanz und Metallegierungen. Upsala Univ. Arsskr. 1911 (109) ; Diss. Upsala 1911. [5660]. 39149

Beckmann, H. Stato attuale della tecnica degli accumulatori stazionari e trasportabili. Atti Assoc. elettrotecn. Milano **15** 1911 (1155–1158). [5620]. 39150

———— Stato attuale della tecnica degli accumulatori fissi e portabili. Industria Milano **25** 1911 (790–791). [5620]. 39151

Becquerel, Henri. Liste des Ouvrages et Mémoires publiés de 1875 à 1908 par M. Becquerel. Nouv. arch. Muséum Paris (sér. 5) **1** 1909 (iii–x av. 1 portr.). [0032]. 39152

———— **Becquerel**, Jean et **Kamerlingh-Onnes**, H. Phosphorescence des sels d'uranyle aux très basses températures. Ann. chim. phys. Paris (sér. 8) **20** 1910 (145–166 av. fig.). [4230]. 39152A

Becquerel, Jean. Les idées modernes sur la constitution de la matière. Rev. sci. Paris **48** 1910 (417–425). [0500]. 39153

———— Sur l'effet magnéto-optique de sens positif présenté par les bandes de phosphorescence du rubis et de l'émeraude et sur les relations entre l'émission et l'absorption dans un champ magnétique. Paris C. R. Acad. sci. **151** 1910 (1344–1347). [4230 6660]. 39154

———— Sur les modifications magnétiques des bandes de phosphorescence et d'absorption du rubis et sur une question fondamentale de magnéto-optique. Paris C. R. Acad. sci. **152** 1911 (183–186). [4230 6660]. 39155

———— Sur la durée de la phosphorescence des sels d'uranyle. Paris C. R. Acad. sci. **152** 1911 (511–513). [4230]. 39156

———— Sur la propagation de la lumière dans les corps fluorescents. Paris C. R. Acad. sci. **153** 1911 (936–938). [4230]. 39157

———— Modern ideas on the constitution of matter. [Translated from Rev. sci. Paris, **48**, No. 14, Oct. 1, 1910.] Washington D.C. Smithsonian Inst. Rep. **1910** 1911 (275–290). [0500]. 39158

———— c. Becquerel, H.

Bedeau. Etude de la variation de force électromotrice des piles avec la température. Ann. chim. phys. Paris (sér. 8) 24 1911 (553–563 av. fig.). [6210]. 39159

Beez, Carl. Über ein direkt zeigendes elektrisches Röntgenstrahlen-Energiemeter. Verh. D. Röntgenges. Hamburg 7 1911 (118–120). [6080]. 39160

Behne, E. Die Temperaturkompensation bei Millivoltmetern. [Nebst Erwiderung von D. Bercovitz.] Elektrot. Zs. Berlin 32 1911 (482 700). [6010]. 39161

Behnsen, Feodor. Der Einfluss von Oxydbildung und thermischer Behandlung auf den Magnetismus des Kupfers. Physik. Zs. Leipzig 12 1911 (1157–1160); Diss. Halle a. S. (Druck v. H. John) 1911 (41). 22 cm. [5460 5466 5470]. 39162

Behrendsen, O. und **Gotting,** E. Demonstrationsapparat zur Erläuterung des Ohm'schen Gesetzes. Zs. physik. Unterr. Berlin 24 1911 (29–31). [6035]. 39163

Bell, Louis. On the opacity of certain glasses for the ultra violet. Boston Proc. Amer. Acad. Arts Sci. 46 1911 (669–680 with pl.). [3810 3860]. 39164

Bellati, Manfredo e **Finazzi,** L. Metodo idrostatico a compensazione per lo studio della dilatazione termica dei corpi. Venezia Atti Ist. ven. 68 parte 2 1909 (917–923). [1410]. 39165

———— Ricerche dilatometriche su alcuni azotati alcalini polimorfi e sull'azotato talloso. Venezia Atti Ist. ven. 69 parte 2 1910 (1151–1168). [1410]. 39166

Bellini, E. and **Tosi,** A. Wireless telegraph working in relation to interferences and perturbations. Elect. London 67 1911 (66). [6615]. 39167

Belluzzo, G. Le centrali termoelettriche ed il consumo di carbone per KW-ora. Atti Assoc. elettrotecn. Milano 14 1910 (237–251). [4980]. 39168

Belopolsky. Durée de rotation de la planète Vénus sur elle-même. Paris C. R. Acad. sci. 153 1911 (15–16). [3420]. 39169

Belot, Emile. Expériences de M. Ch. Weyher sur les tourbillons. J. Ec. polytech. Paris (sér. 2) 1911 (255–271 av. fig.). [5480]. 39170

———— Essai de cosmogonie tourbillonnaire. L'origine dualiste des mondes. Paris (Gauthier-Villars) 1911 (XI + 280 av. fig.). 8vo. [0590]. 39171

Bemmelen, J[akob] M[aarten] van. Sur la plasticité des terres argileuses. Haarlem Arch. Néerl. Sci. Soc. Holl. (Sér. 3 A) 1 1911 (1–14). [Traduit de: Amsterdam Chem. Weekbl. 7 1910 (793–805).] [0840]. 39172

Bemporad, Angelo. La teoria della rifrazione astronomica direttamente fondata sui risultati della fisica dell'atmosfera. Catania Atti Acc. Gioenia (Ser 5) 3 1910 (Mem 5 1–11). [3210]. 39173

Bénard, H. Sur les tourbillons cellulaires. Ann. chim. phys. Paris (sér. 8) 24 1911 (563–566 av. fig.). [0300 0325]. 39174

———— Sur la formation des cirques lunaires d'après les expériences de C. Danzere. Paris C. R. Acad. sci. 154 1912 (260–263 av. fig.). [1810]. 39175

Benasso, L. Le turbine a vapore marine. Milano (H. O. Sperling) 1910 (222 con 18 tav.). 21 cm. [2490]. 39176

Benischke, Gustav. Über den Leistungssprung asynchroner Drehfeldmotoren beim Durchgang durch den Synchronismus. [Nebst Erwiderung von Th. Lehmann.] Elektrot. Zs. Berlin 32 1911 (147–148). [6070]. 39177

———— Experimentelle Ermittlung des Hysteresedrehmoments. [Nebst Erwiderung von Zipp.] Elektrot. Zs. Berlin 32 1911 (890). [6045]. 39178

———— Die experimentelle Bestimmung des Streufaktors von Transformatoren und Drehstrommotoren. Elektr. Kraftbetriebe München 10 1912 (83–85). [6040 6070]. 39179

———— Die Schutzvorrichtungen der Starkstromtechnik gegen atmosphärische Entladungen und Überspannungen. 2. erweit. Aufl. (Elektrotechnik in Einzeldarstellungen. Hrsg. von G. Benischke. H. 1.) Braun-

schweig (F. Vieweg & S.) 1911 (VIII + 123). 22 cm. 3.50 M. [6000 6820].
39180

Benndorf, H. Über die Bestimmung der Geschwindigkeit transversaler Wellen in der äussersten Erdkruste. Physik. Zs. Leipzig 13 1912 (83–84). [9040].
39181

Bennewitz. Messmethoden der Radioaktivität und ihre Anwendung in der Radiotherapie. Radium Leipzig 1 1911 (121–131 153–162). [4275]. 39182

Benoist, L. Application de l'harmonica chimique à la chronophotographie. Paris C. R. Acad. sci. 153 1911 (196–197). [4225]. 39183

Benrath, A[lfred] und **Wainoff,** J. Über die elektrische Leitfähigkeit von Salzen und Salzgemischen. Zs. physik. Chem. Leipzig 77 1911 (257–268). [6240]. 39184

Bercovitz, D. Die Temperaturkompensation bei Millivoltmetern. [Nebst Erwiderung von J. **Kollert.**] Elektrot. Zs. Berlin 32 1911 (299–300). [6010]. 39185

—— Gegenkraft und Ampèrewindungszahl bei direkt zeigenden elektrischen Messinstrumenten. Helios Leipzig 17 1911 Fach-Zs. (241–244 258–261). [6010]. 39186

—— *v.* Behne, E.

Bergansius, F. L. Een nieuwe formule om den coëfficient van zelfinductie voor lange solenoiden met vele draadlagen met groote nauwkeurigheid te berekenen. [Formule nouvelle pour le calcul exact du coëfficient de self-induction dans le cas de longs solénoides à nombreuses couches de fil.] Handl. Ned. Nat. Geneesk. Congres 13 1911 (173–176). [6440]. 39187

—— Methoden ter berekening van de zelfinductie voor lange solenoiden. [Méthodes pour le calcul de l'auto-induction de longs solénoides.] 's Gravenhage (Gebr. J. & A. van Langenhuyzen) 1912 (87). 29 cm. [6440]. 39188

Berger. Der Telegraphenbetrieb bei starken Erdströmen. Elektrot. Zs. Berlin 32 1911 (213–214). [6480]. 39189

Berger, R. Versuche über die Durchlässigkeit gegen Luftschall. Gesundhts-Ing. München 34 1911 (925–932). [9250 9320]. 39190

—— Ueber die Schalldurchlässigkeit. Diss. München (Druck v. R. Oldenbourg) 1911 (42). 33 cm. [9250 9320 9210]. 39191

Berget, Alphonse. Détermination précise de la salinité des eaux de mer par la mesure de l'indice de réfraction. Paris C. R. Acad. sci. 152 1911 (984–986). [3860]. 39192

Bergter, F. Der zeitliche Verlauf der Absorption von Gasen durch Holzkohle. Ann. Physik Leipzig (4. Folge) 37 1912 (472–510); Diss. Rostock. Leipzig (J. A. Barth) 1911 (55). 23 cm. [0250]. 39193

Bergwitz, K. Ueber den Ioniumkollektor. Physik. Zs. Leipzig 12 1911 (83–85). [6095]. 39194

Berkeley and **Appleby,** M. P. On the boiling point of water. London Proc. R. Soc. (Ser. A) 85 1911 (477–489). [1840]. 39195

—— —— On the boiling point of some saturated solutions. London Proc. R. Soc. (Ser. A) 85 1911 (489–505). [1840]. 39196

Berliner, Arnold. Lehrbuch der Experimentalphysik in elementarer Darstellung. 2. Aufl. Jena (G. Fischer) 1911 (XVI + 720 mit Taf.). 26 cm. 18 M. [0030]. 39197

Bermbach. Ohm, der grosse Physiker. [In: Das Marzellen-Gymnasium in Köln 1450–1911. Festschrift . . .] Köln (P. Neubner) 1911 (165–172). [0010]. 39198

Berndt, O. u. **Wirtz,** [Karl]. Versuche über den elektrischen Widerstand von unbewehrtem Beton . . . Unter Mitwirkung von W. **Müller.** (Deutscher Ausschuss für Eisenbeton. H. 6.) Berlin (W. Ernst & S.) 1911 (III + 69). 28 cm. 3.60 M. [5660 6240]. 39200

Bernini, Arciero. Magnetoskope für Unterrichtszwecke. (Übers.) D. MechZtg Berlin 1911 (215–216). [0050 5435]. 39201

—— Sul magnetismo susseguente del ferro. Nuovo Cimento Pisa (Ser. 6) 2 1911 (291–322). [5440]. 39203

Bernini, Arciero. Sulla macchina idroelettrica ad influenza di R. W. Thomson. Nuovo Cimento Pisa (Ser. 6) 1 1911 (348-374). [5220]. 39204

———— Sulla radioattività dei gas emananti dalle sorgenti termali di S. Saturnino. Nuovo Cimento Pisa (Ser. 6) 1 1911 (455-461). [4275]. 39205

———— Contributo allo studio della velocità degli ioni di fiamma. Roma Mem. Acc. Lincei (Ser. 5) 8 1911 (Mem. 11 (506-526)); Nuovo Cimento Pisa (Ser. 6) 2 1911 (101-130). [6805]. 39206

Bernoulli, A. L. Zur Elektronentheorie der metallischen Mischkristalle. Ann. Physik Leipzig (4. Folge) 35 1911 (162-170). [5710 5675]. 39207

———— Das Gesetz von Babo und die Elektronentheorie der metallischen Mischkristalle. Berlin Verh. D. physik. Ges. 13 1911 (213-218). [5710 5675]. 39208

———— Das Nernstsche Wärmetheorem und die Thermodynamik der thermoelektrischen Erscheinungen. (Vortrag . . .) Berlin Verh. D. physik. Ges. 13 1911 (573-583) : Zs. Elektroch. Halle 17 1911 (689-694). [5710 5675]. 39209

Berry, Arthur John r. Soddy, F.

Berry, C. H. Pianoforte bridges. Phil. Mag. London (Ser. 6) 22 1911 (113-118). [9410]. 39210

Bertarelli, E. L'evoluzione dell'illuminazione elettrica. Riv. ing. san. Torino 7 1911 (137-138 151-154). [6080]. 39211

Berthelot, Daniel. Les effets chimiques des rayons ultraviolets. Rev. gén. sci. Paris 22 1911 (322-332). [4225]. 39212

———— et Gaudechon, Henry. Principaux types de photolyse des composés organiques par les rayons ultraviolets. Paris C. R. Acad. sci 151 1910 (1349-1352). [4225]. 39213

———— ———— Photolyse des acides à fonction complexe par les rayons ultraviolets. Action des sels d'uranium comme catalyseurs lumineux. Paris C. R. Acad. sci. 152 1911 (262-265). [4225]. 39214

———— ———— Action comparée des rayons ultraviolets sur les composés organiques à structure linéaire et à structure cyclique. Étude des sels minéraux en solution aqueuse. Paris C. R. Acad. sci. 152 1911 (376-378). [4225]. 39215

Berthelot, Daniel et Gaudechon, Henry. Sur la photolyse des alcools, des anhydrides d'acides, des éthers-oxydes et des éthers-sels par les rayons ultraviolets. Paris C. R. Acad. sci. 153 1911 (383-386). [4225]. 39216

———— ———— Sur la stabilité de divers types de poudre sans fumée vis-à-vis des rayons ultraviolets. Paris C. R. Acad. sci. 153 1911 (1220-1223). [4225]. 39217

———— ———— Décomposition photolytique des poudres sans fumée par les rayons ultraviolets. Influence des stabilisants. Étude des poudres avariées. Paris C. R. Acad. sci. 154 1912 (201-203). [4225]. 39218

Berthier, A. Lampade elettriche a filamento metallico. [Trad.] Industria Milano 24 1910 (200-201 250-251 390-394). [6080]. 39219

Berthoud, A. Sur l'impossibilité de surchauffer un solide. Journ. Chim. Phys. Genève 8 1910 (337-339) ; Neuchâtel Bul. Soc. Sci. Nat. 37 1910 (144-146). [1410 1940]. 39220

———— Théorie cinétique des gaz et thermodynamique. Journ. Chim. Phys. Genève 9 1911 (352-381). [2400 2455]. 39221

Berti, C. A. Esperienze con tubi di Wehnelt ad ossido di calcio. Elettricista Roma (Ser. 2) 10 1911 (241-243). [6845]. 39222

Bertolini, Giulio. I proiettori elettrici per la difesa delle coste. Riv. maritt. Roma 1910 1. trim. (451-500). [3010]. 39223

Besig, Karl. Die Dampfturbine als Schiffsmotor. Vergleichsrechnung für verschiedene Systeme . . . Diss. Berlin. Stettin (Druck v. Herrcke & Lebeling) [1911] (75 mit Taf.). 24 cm. [2490]. 39224

Besson, A. Action de l'effluve sur le gaz ammoniac sec et humide. Paris C. R. Acad. sci. 152 1911 (1850-1852). [6820]. 39225

———— Sur la formation d'eau oxygénée sous l'effluve électrique. Paris

C. R. Acad. sci. 153 1911 (877–879).
[6820]. 39225A

Besson, E. Sur la dissymétrie des ions positifs et négatifs relativement à la condensation de la vapeur d'eau. Paris C. R. Acad. sci. 153 1911 (250–254). [6805]. 39226

—————— Sur la condensation de la vapeur d'eau par détente dans une atmosphère de gaz carbonique. Paris C. R. Acad. sci. 154 1912 (342–345). [6805]. 39227

Bestelmeyer, A. Die Bahn der von einer Wehneltkathode ausgehenden Kathodenstrahlen im homogenen Magnetfeld. Ann. Physik Leipzig (4. Folge) 35 1911 (909–930); (Vorl. Mitt.) Göttingen Nachr. Ges. Wiss. math.-phys. Kl. 1911 (429–430). [6845]. 39228

—————— Über die spezifische Ladung langsamer Kathodenstrahlen. Physik. Zs. Leipzig 12 1911 (972–975); Berlin Verh. D. physik. Ges. 13 1911 (984–989). [6845]. 39229

—————— Berechnung, Herstellung und Messung eines homogenen Magnetfeldes. (Vorl. Mitt.) Physik. Zs. Leipzig 12 1911 (1107–1111). [6030 5410 5440]. 39230

Bettineschi, P. G. Osservazioni sul comportamento del coherer a limatura metallica. Riv. fis. mat. sc. nat. Pavia 22 1910 (295–300). [6043]. 39231

Beuss, Wilhelm. Untersuchungen über die spezifische Wärme von binären Flüssigkeitsgemischen. Diss. Münster i. W. Neumünster (Druck v. R. Hieronymus) 1911 (59). 23 cm. [1920 1620]. 39232

Beutell, A. Vorführung der neuesten Modelle seiner automatischen Quecksilberluftpumpe mit Luftpolster D. R.P. Breslau Jahresber. Ges. vaterl. Cultur 88 (1910) 1911 natw. Sekt. (1–7). [0090]. 39233

—————— Neue automatische Quecksilberluftpumpe und Destillation von Arsenkies, Glaukodot und Kobaltglanz im Vakuum der Kathodenstrahlen. Centralbl. Min. Stuttgart 1911 (491–495). [0090]. 39234

Beutner, R. Einige Versuche mit Gaselementen unter Strom bei hohen Temperaturen. Zs. Elektroch. Halle 17 1911 (91–93). [5610]. 39235

Bevan, P. V. The absorption spectra of lithium and caesium. London Proc. R. Soc. (Ser. A) 85 1911 (54–58). [3850]. 39236

—————— Dispersion in vapours of the alkali metals. London Proc. R. Soc. (Ser. A) 85 1911 (58–76). [3860]. 39237

Bialobjeski v. Bialobrzeski.

Bialobrzeski, Czeslaw. Zasada względności i niektóre jej zastosowania. [Le principe du relativisme et ses applications.] Wektor Warszawa 1 1911 (1–19). [0000 2990 4900]. 39239

—————— Jonizacya dielektryków. [Sur l'ionisation des diélectriques.] Wektor Warszawa 1 1911 (201–214). [5250 6805]. 39240

—————— L'ionisation des carbures d'hydrogène liquides. Radium Paris 8 1911 (293–299 av. fig.). [5250]. 39238

Bianchi, Michelina v. Antony, U.

Bianco, Alfredo. Telegrafo stampante Baudot, sistema automatico "Bianco." Elettricista Roma (Ser. 2) 10 1911 (115–123). [6480]. 39241

Bidlingmaier, Fr[iedrich]. Zur säkularen Variation des Erdmagnetismus. Physik. Zs. Leipzig 12 1911 (449–459); Herrn L. A. Bauer zur Entgegnung. l.c. (926–927). [5490]. 39242

Bidwell, Shelford. Magnetism. Encycl. Brit. (ed. 11) 15 1911. [5400]. 39242A

Bieber, Willie. Untersuchungen über die Kondensation von Wasserdampf in Gegenwart von Ozon, Stickstoffoxyden und Wasserstoffsuperoxyd. Insbesondere über die Kerne des blauen Nebels. Diss. Marburg (Druck v. Enz & Rudolph) 1911 (48 mit Taf.). 23 cm. [1840 6805]. 39243

Biedenkapp, Georg. James Watt und die Erfindung der Dampfmaschine. Eine biographische Skizze. Stuttgart (Franckh) 1911 (54). 27 cm. [0010]. 39244

Biehle, Johannes. Theorie der pneumatischen Orgeltraktur und die Stellung des Spieltisches. Sammelbde intern. Musikges. Leipzig 13 1911 (1–33 mit 2 Taf.). [9410]. 39245

Bielschowsky, Karl W. Die objektive Wertung von Dissonanz und Geräusch. Monatshefte natw. Unterr. Leipzig 4 1911 (451–452). [9450]. 39246

Bieringer, Emil. Telephonie. D. Mus. Vortr. München II. 8 [1911] (25). [6485]. 39247

——— Telegraphie. D. Mus. Vortr. München II. 7 [1911] (30). [6480]. 39248

Bierlein, Wilhelm. Studien über elektrische gekoppelte Schwingungssysteme. (Mitteilungen der physikalischen Versuchs-Station Halle-Cröllwitz.) (No. 26.) Diss. Halle a. S. (Druck v. O. A. Kaemmerer & Co.) 1911 (28 mit Tab.). 29 cm. [6615 6460]. 39249

Biernacki, Wiktor. W sprawie cisnienia energii promienistej. [Über den Strahlungsdruck.] Warszawa Spraw. Tow. Nauk. 4 1911 (442 446). [4215]. 39250

Bierry, Henri. **Henri,** Victor et **Rane,** Albert. Action des rayons ultraviolets sur la glycérine. Paris C. R. Acad. sci. 152 1911 (535 536). [4225]. 39250A

——— et **Larguier des Bancels,** J. Action de la lumière émise par la lampe à mercure sur les solutions de chlorophylle. Paris C. R. Acad. sci. 153 1911 (124 125). [4225]. 39251

Biffi, Emilio. La mostra dell'elettricità all'esposizione internazionale di Torino 1911. Mon. tecn. Milano 17 1911 (468 470 611 615 692 698). [6090 4900]. 39252

Bignami, L. Macchine marine a vapore soprariscaldato con distribuzione a valvole. Riv. maritt. Roma 2. trim. 1911 (564 569). [2490]. 39253

——— Le macchine Stumpf. Riv. maritt. Roma 1. trim. 1911 (570 582). [2490]. 39254

Bigourdan, G. Rapport sur les observations faites à Sfax (Tunisie) à l'occasion de l'éclipse totale de Soleil du 29 30 août 1905. Ann. bur. longit. Paris 8 1911 (A. 1 A. 75 av. pl.). [4205]. 39255

——— "Grandeur et figure de la terre." Ouvrage jusqu'ici inédit de Delambre. Paris C. R. Acad. sci. 154 1912 (250). [0807]. 39256

Billiter, J[ean]. Die Atomtheorie im Lichte der neueren Forschungsergebnisse. Oesterr. ChemZtg Wien 15 1912 (72 78). [0150 4960]. 39257

(c–1388)

Biltz, Wilhelm. Über den Schmelzpunkt und die Atomschwingungszahl des Germaniums. Zs. anorg. Chem. Leipzig 72 1911 (313 318). [1810]. 39258

——— Das System der Elemente auf Grund der periodischen Abhängigkeit von Schwingungszahl und Gewicht der Atome. Zs. Elektroch. Halle 17 1911 (670 674). [0500]. 39259

——— Ueber den osmotischen Druck der Kolloide. 3. Mitt.: Weitere Beiträge zur Dialyse und Osmose von Farbstofflösungen. (Nach Versuchen von F. Pfenning.) Zs. physik. Chem. Leipzig 77 1911 (91 116). [0310 0340]. 39260

Binaghi, Rinaldo. Il fenomeno di Tyndall nell'acqua potabile di Cagliari e la presenza dell'idrato di ferro colloidale. Ann. Igiene Roma 19 1909 (313 342). [0340]. 39261

Binder, Ludwig. Ueber äussere Wärmeleitung und Erwärmung elektrischer Maschinen. Diss. München. Halle a. S. (W. Knapp) 1911 (V + 112). 24 cm. [2000 2040 6060]. 39262

——— Über Wärmeübergang auf ruhige oder bewegte Luft sowie Lüftung und Kühlung elektrischer Maschinen. Halle a. S. (W. Knapp) 1911 [1912] (V + 112). 25 cm. 5,70 M. [2000 6000]. 39263

Bingham, Eugene C. Viscosity and fluidity. [Ninth communication bearing on this subject.] Amer. Chem. J. Baltimore 45 1910 (287 309) with text fig. tables). [0325]. 39264

Binghinotto, Maria v. Gnesotto, T.

Birkeland, Kr. Les anneaux de Saturne sont-ils dus à une radiation électrique de la planète ? Paris C. R. Acad. sci. 153 1911 (375 379). [4960]. 39265

——— Le Soleil et ses taches. Paris C. R. Acad. sci. 153 1911 (456 459). [4960]. 39266

——— Sur la constitution électrique du Soleil. Paris C. R. Acad. sci. 153 1911 (513 516). [6805 6845]. 39267

——— Phénomènes célestes et analogies expérimentales. Paris C. R. Acad. sci. 153 1911 (938 941). [6840 6810]. 39268

Biscan, Wilh. Die Dynamomaschine. Zum Selbststudium für Mechaniker ... leicht fasslich dargestellt. 12. verm. Aufl. Leipzig (O. Leiner) 1911 (IV + 104 mit 2 Taf.). 22 cm. 2 M. [6060]. 39269

Bishop, Edwin S. Eine absolute Bestimmung der kleinsten Ionisierungsenergie eines Elektrons und die Anwendung der Theorie der Ionisierung durch Stoss auf Gasgemische. [An absolute determination of the minimum ionizing energy of an electron, and the application of the theory of ionization by collision to mixtures of gases.] (Übers.) Physik. Zs. Leipzig 12 1911 (1148–1157). [6805 6840]. 39270

Biske, Felix. Die Krümmung der Spektrallinien beim Plangitter. Ann. Physik Leipzig (4. Folge) 34 1911 (971–978). [3639 3160 4207]. 39271

Bjerknes, V[ilhelm]. Über die einfachsten hydrodynamischen Kraftfelderscheinungen. Physik. Zs. Leipzig 13 1912 (21–28). [4940]. 39272

Bjerrum, Niels. Ueber die Gültigkeit der Planckschen Formel für das Diffusionspotential. Zs. Elektroch. Halle 17 1911 (58–61). [6255]. 39273

————— Über die Elimination des Flüssigkeitspotentials bei Messungen von Elektrodenpotentialen. Zs. Elektroch. Halle 17 1911 (389–393). [5640 6255]. 39274

————— Über die spezifische Wärme der Gase. Zs. Elektroch. Halle 17 1911 (731–735); II. op. cit. 18 1912 (101–104). [1640]. 39275

————— v. Perrin, J.

Björnbo, Axel Anthon† und Vogl. Seb. Alkindi, Tideus und Pseudo-Euklid. Drei optische Werke. Mit einem Gedächtniswort auf A. A. Björnbo von G. H. Zeuthen ... Abh. Gesch. math. Wiss. Leipzig H. 26 1912 3 (176). [4040 3900]. 39276

Blackman, A. E. Weighing the earth. [Abstract.] Papers and Proc. R. Soc. Tasmania 1910 (376–379). [0840]. 39277

Blake, F[rederic] C[olumbus] and **Ruppersberg,** E. A. On the free vibrations of a Lecher system using a Blondlot oscillator. Physic. Rev. Ithaca N.Y. 32 1911 (449–475 with text fig. tables); [abstract] l.c. (233–234). [6610]. 39278

Blake, F[rederic] C[olumbus] and **Sheard,** Charles. On the free vibrations of a Lecher system using a Lecher oscillator. Physic. Rev. Ithaca N.Y. 32 1911 (533–560 with fig. tables); [abstract] l.c. (235 236). [6610]. 39279

Blake, Lucien I. Is energy atomic in structure? Denver Proc. Colo. Sci. Soc. 9 1910 (425–429). [4960 4200]. 39280

Blein, Jean. Aberrations d'un miroir parabolique. J. phys. Paris (sér. 5) 1 1911 (996–1003 av. fig.). [3070]. 39281

Blessing, P. J. Über den Klang der Kirchenglocken. Physik. Zs. Leipzig 12 1911 (597–600). [9120 9410]. 39282

Bloch, Eugène. Sur le potentiel de décharge dans le champ magnétique. Paris C. R. Acad. sci. 152 1910 (191–194). [6840]. 39283

————— Le potentiel disruptif dans un champ magnétique. Radium Paris 8 1911 (51–59 av. fig.); [sunto. trad.] Riv. fis. mat. sc. nat. Pavia 23 1911 (463–466). [6840 6820]. 39284

Bloch, F. L. v. Grossmann, H.

Bloch, Léon. Recherche sur les actions chimiques et l'ionisation par barbotage. Ann. chim. phys. Paris (sér. 8) 22 1911 (370–417 441–495); 23 1911 (28–114). [6805 5685]. 39285

————— Sur quelques théorèmes généraux de Mécanique et de Thermodynamique. Paris C. R. Acad. sci. 152 1911 (1843–1846); J. phys. Paris (sér. 5) 1 1911 (820–830 912–922 988–996). [2445]. 39286

Bloch, O. Über die magnetischen Eigenschaften der Nickel-Kobalt-Legierungen. Verh. Schweiz. Natf. Ges. Aarau 94 1912 (213–217). [5466]. 39287

————— v. Weiss, P.

Block, Heinrich. Über die Volumenänderung beim Schmelzen von Kristallen und die Wärmeausdehnung der Kristalle unter ihrer Schmelzen. Zs. physik. Chem. Leipzig 78 1912 (385–425). [1800 2445 1400]. 39288

Blondel, André. Application de la syntonie acoustique et électrique a l'hydrotélégraphie ; méthode pour la réaliser. Paris C. R. Acad. sci. 152 1911 (1571–1574). [6480]. 39289

—————— Sur les diverses méthodes de mesure de l'orientation en radiotélégraphie dans le cas d'ondes entretenues. Paris C. R. Acad. sci. 153 1911 (544–547). [6615]. 39289A

—————— Influence de l'amortissement des ondes dans l'emploi des cadres d'orientation en radiotélégraphie. Paris C. R. Acad. sci. 153 1911 (593–597). [6615]. 39290

—————— Utilisation des cadres d'orientation en radiotélégraphie pour la réception des trains périodiques d'ondes amorties. Paris C. R. Acad. sci. 153 1911 (661–664). [6615]. 39291

—————— et Rey, J. Application aux signaux de la loi de perception des lumières brèves à la limite de leur portée. J. phys. Paris (sér. 5) 1 1911 (643–655). [4440–4455]. 39292

—————— Sur la perception des lumières brèves à la limite de leur portée. J. phys. Paris (sér. 5) 1 1911 (530–550 av. fig.) ; Paris C. R. Acad. sci. 153 1911 (54–56). [4455–4450]. 39293

Boas, Hans. Löschfunkenstrecke für enge Koppelung. Berlin Verh. D. physik. Ges. 13 1911 (527–539). [6820]. 39294

—————— Maschine und Methode zur Erzeugung hochgespannter, gleichgerichteter Stromstösse mit besonderer Berücksichtigung der Röntgentechnik. Berlin Verh. D. physik. Ges. 13 1911 (651–664). [6040]. 39295

Boccara, Vittorio. Antonio Pacinotti. Cenni biografici. Cronache agrarie Firenze 1 1911 (209–213). [0010]. 39296

Bocci, Baldoino. Il meccanismo dell'accomodazione oculare per la distanza. Prove subiettive nell'uomo e obiettive nell'animale. Siena Atti Acc. Fisiocritici (Ser. 5) 3 1911 (39–47). [4420]. 39297

—————— La teoria dell'audizione più consentanea alla complessa morfologia dell'organo del Corti. Siena Atti Acc. Fisiocritici (Ser. 5) 3 1911 (201–217). [9520]. 39298

(c-1388)

Bock, F. Einige neue Apparate der Cambridge Scientific Instrument Company. Physik. Zs. Leipzig 12 1911 (729–732). [0090]. 39299

—————— Instrument zum Messen kleiner Widerstände. Elektrot. Zs. Berlin 33 1912 (43–44). [6040]. 39300

Boeseken, J[akob] et Rossem, A[driaan] van. Etudes sur la configuration des systèmes annulaires. Rec. Trav. chim. Leiden 30 1911 (392–406 avec 2 pl.). [6220]. 39301

Böhi, Paul. Eine neue Methode der Bestimmung der Avogadroschen Zahl N. Zürich Vierteljahrschr. Natf. Ges. 56 1911 (183–212 mit 2 Taf.). [0150]. 39302

Böhm, Paul. Untersuchungen über die Dielektrizitätskonstante von Isomeren. Diss. Halle a. S. (Druck v. C. A. Kaemmerer & Co.) 1911 (47 mit 5 Taf.). 22 cm. [5252]. 39303

Bolling, F. Widerstandsmaterial für elektrische Oefen. Elektroch. Zs. Berlin 18 1911 (62–63) ; [Nebst Entgegnung von W. Schuen] t.c. (331–333) ; 18 1911 (5). [6090]. 39304

Börnstein, R[ichard]. Das neuerbaute physikalische Institut der landwirtschaftlichen Hochschule in Berlin. Physik. Zs. Leipzig 12 1911 (551–558 mit 2 Taf.) ; Berlin Verh. D. physik. Ges. 13 1911 (206–208). [0060]. 39305

—————— Beleuchtung und Lichtmessung. [In : Chemische Technologie der Neuzeit. Hrsg. von O. Dammer. Bd 2.) Stuttgart (F. Enke) 1910 [1911] (243–301). [3010–6080]. 39306

—————— Heizung und Wärmemessung. [In : Chemische Technologie der Neuzeit. Hrsg. von O. Dammer. Bd 2.] Stuttgart (F. Enke) 1910 [1911] (302–351). [1200]. 39307

Boguski, J. J. Pirometrya (Techniczne mierzenie wysokich temperatur). Ciąg dalszy. [La pyrométrie. Mesure industrielle des températures élevées.] Przegl. techn. Warszawa 49 1911 (28–30). [1255]. 39308

Bohle, H. Effects of uniformity and contrast on light. Cape Town Trans. R. Soc. S. Afric. 2 pt. 2 1911 (127–135). [3800]. 39309

Bohr, N. On the determination of the tension of a recently formed water-surface. London Proc. R. Soc. (Ser. A) **84** 1910 (395–403). [0300]. 39310

—————— Studier over Metallernes Elektrontheori. [Researches on the theory of electrons for the metals.] København Doktordisputatser **1911** (1–120 with 1 pl.) V. Thaning & Appel. [5675]. 39311

Bois, H[enri] du. L'effet Zeeman généralisé dans les absorbants sélectifs. Haarlem Arch. Néerl. Sci. Soc. Holl. (Sér. 3 A) **1** 1912 (209–230). [4208 6650]. 39312

Boissoudy (de), T. Le problème de la constitution de l'atome. Scientia Bologna **10** 1911 (250–277). [0500]. 39313

Boll, Marcel. Application de l'élec-tromètre à l'étude des réactions chimi-ques dans les électrolytes. Paris C. R. Acad. sci. **154** 1912 (349–351). [5660 4225]. 39314

Boltwood, B. B. Report on the separation of ionium and actinium from certain residues and on the production of helium by ionium. London Proc. R. Soc. (Ser. A) **85** 1911 (77–81); [trad.] Radium Paris **8** 1911 (104–106) [4275]. 39315

—————— et **Rutherford,** E. Sur la production de l'hélium par le radium. Radium Paris **8** 1911 (381–388 av. fig.); Phil. Mag. London (Ser. 6) **22** 1911 (586–604). [4275]. 39316

Bolza, Oskar. Bemerkungen zu der Arbeit von Herrn H. Weber: Ueber den Satz von Malus für krummlinige Lichtstrahlen. Palermo Rend. Circ. mat. **32** 1911 (263–266). [3040]. 39317

Bonacini, Carlo. Il trionfo odierno della tricromia. Firenze Boll. Soc. fot. **22** 1911 (305–315). [3860]. 39318

—————— e **Nicolis,** U. Ricerche sulla conducibilità elettrica nell' aria. Modena Mem. Acc. (Ser. 3) **9** 1910 (3–20). [5685]. 39319

Bonazzi, Ottavio. L'induttanza per correnti alternate di un circuito com-prendente ferro. Roma Rend. Acc. Lincei (Ser. 5) **19** 2. sem. 1910 (633–637). [6460]. 39320

—————— Misura della permeabilità del ferro nel campo magnetico delle scariche oscillatorie. Nuovo Cimento

Pisa (Ser. 5) **20** 1910 (361–383); [sunto] Atti Assoc. elettrotecn. Milano **15** 1911 (532–533). [5440]. 39321

Bonnerot, S. v. Charpy, G.

Borchardt, Bruno. Das Aronssche Chromoskop. Chem. Ind. Berlin **34** 1911 (500–504); Mechaniker Berlin **19** 1911 (193–195). [0090]. 39323

Borchers, W. Elektrischer Tiegelofen zum Schmelzen und Vergiessen von Metallen. Metallurgie Halle **8** 1911 (209–211). [6090]. 39324

Borck, H. v. Byk, A.

Borda v. Méchain.

Bordoni, Ugo. Le basi sperimentali della teoria degli elettroni. Roma Ann. Soc. ing. **25** 1910 (2–10 29–44). [4960]. 39325

—————— Contributo allo studio dell'influenza dello stato magnetico sopra i fenomeni termoelettrici. Nuovo Cimento Pisa (Ser. 6) **2** 1911 (245–290). [5710]. 39326

—————— Sull'impiego dei comuni obbiettivi fotografici per riproduzioni alla luce artificiale. Roma Ann. Soc. ing. **26** 1911 (173–185). [3085]. 39327

Borelli, Jacques. Résistance au mouvement dans un fluide de petits corps non sphériques. Paris C. R. Acad. sci. **152** 1911 (133–136). [0325]. 39328

Borino, Domenico. Lezioni di tele-grafia elementare. Bologna (N. Zanichelli) 1910 (230). 19 cm. [0030 4900]. 39329

Borletti, Francesco. Metodi pratici per determinare l'ingrandimento di un cannocchiale astronomico. Politecn. Milano **59** 1911 (394–397). [3080]. 39331

Born, Max. Elastizitätstheorie und Relativitätsprinzip. Physik. Zs. Leip-zig **12** 1911 (569–575). 39332

—————— und **Ladenburg,** Rudolf. Ueber das Verhältnis von Emissions-und Absorptionsvermögen bei stark absorbierenden Körpern. Physik. Zs. Leipzig **12** 1911 (198–202). [4210]. 39333

Borns, H. Die Elektrochemie im Jahre 1910. Chem. Ind. Berlin **34** 1911 (648–660 705–717 739–751 776–786). [6200]. 39334

Bosch, Franz. Robert Wilhelm Bun-sen, der Begründer der Spektralanalyse.

Hochland München **8** 1911 (684 695). [0010]. 39335

Bose, E[mil]. Experimentalbeitrag zur Schwarmtheorie der anisotropen Flüssigkeiten. [Klärung durch magnetische Kräfte.] Physik. Zs. Leipzig **12** 1911 (60 62). [5467]. 39336

———— und **Bose,** Margrete. Ueber die Turbulenzreibung verschiedener Flüssigkeiten. Physik. Zs. Leipzig **12** 1911 (126 135). [0325]. 39337

Bose, Margrete. Das physikalische Institut der Universität La Plata. Physik. Zs. Leipzig **12** 1911 (1230-1243). [0060]. 39338

———— r. Bose, E.

Boselli, J. Vitesses de réactions dans les systèmes gaz-liquides. Paris C. R. Acad. sci. **152** 1911 (374 375 602 603). [0320]. 39339

Bosler, J. Sur les relations des courants telluriques avec les perturbations magnétiques. Paris C. R. Acad. sci. **152** 1911 (342 345). [5490]. 39340

———— Sur le spectre de la comète de Brooks (1911 c). Paris C. R. Acad. sci. **153** 1911 (756-757). [4205]. 39341

Bottazzi, Filippo. Su una più precisa definizione dei sistemi colloidali e sulla sistematica dei colloidi in generale. Atti Soc. ital. prog. sci. Roma **4** 1911 (353-373); [Übers. von Felix Fraenckel nebst Bemerkungen von Wolfgang Ostwald] Kolloidchem. Beih. Dresden **3** 1912 (161 184 185 190). [0340]. 39342

———— e Buglia, G. Ricerche dilatometriche. Nuova forma di dilatometro per miscele di liquidi. Roma Rend. Acc. Lincei (Ser. 5) **20** 2. sem. 1911 (623 627). [1430]. 39343

———— Ricerche dilatometriche. Primi risultati riguardanti soluzioni non colloidali. Nota 2. Roma Rend. Acc. Lincei (Ser. 5) **20** 2. sem. 1911 (627-633). [1430]. 39344

Bottlinger, C. F. Zur Theorie der Lotschwankungen. Astr. Nachr. Kiel **190** 1912 (241-244). [0700]. 39345

Botti, Luigi. Ricerche sperimentali sulle illusioni ottico-geometriche. Torino Mem. Acc. sc. (Ser. 2) **60** 1910 (139-191). [4490]. 39346

Bouasse, H. et alii. De la méthode dans les sciences. 2. éd. Paris (Alcan) 1910 (412). 18.5 cm. [0000]. 39347

Boucherot, G. Fenomeni elettromagnetici che risultano dalla brusca chiusura di un alternatore in corto circuito. [Sunto.] Atti Ass. elettrotecn. Milano **15** 1911 (901 905). [6440]. 39348

Boudouard, O. Essais des métaux pour l'amortissement des mouvements vibratoires. Paris C. R. Acad. sci. **152** 1911 (45 47). [0840]. 39349

———— Résistivité électrique des aciers spéciaux. Paris C. R. Acad. sci. **153** 1911 (1475-1478). [5660]. 39350

Boudry. Sur une nouvelle méthode d'utilisation à distance des eaux minérales thermales. Paris C. R. Acad. sci. **152** 1911 (1535-1538). [2040]. 39351

Bouju, G. Lo stato presente della telegrafia senza fili. [Trad.] Industria Milano **25** 1911 (146-148 246-248). [6615]. 39352

Boulouch, R. La loi des phases. Bordeaux Proc.-verb. soc. sci. nat. **1909-1910** (6 11); Journ. Chim. Phys. Genève **8** 1910 (113-118). [1887]. 39353

———— Sur une démonstration de la loi des phases. Bordeaux Proc.-verb. soc. sci. phys. nat. **1909-1910** (18-22). [1887]. 39354

———— Images stigmatiques des points d'un petit volume situé autour de l'axe d'un système centré. Bordeaux Proc.-verb. soc. sci. phys. nat. **1909-1910** (83-85). [3070]. 39355

———— La relation des sinus de Abbe est une condition de stigmatisme. Condition de l'aplanétisme vrai. Paris C. R. Acad. sci. **153** 1911 (99-102). 39356

Bourcart, Paul. Optique physiologique. Nouvel appareil rotatif pour observer les nuances données par un mélange de couleurs. Mülhausen Bull. Soc. ind. **81** 1911 (288-289 mit 1 Taf.). [4470 2990]. 39357

Bourgeois, R. Sur une cause d'erreur instrumentale des appareils de mesure de base. Paris C. R. Acad. sci. **152** 1911 (246-249). [0807]. 39358

———— Détermination des coordonnées géographiques aux colonies en employant la télégraphie sans fil. Essai de la méthode entre Paris (Observatoire) et Bruxelles (Palais de Laeken). Paris C. R. Acad. sci. **153** 1911 (497-500). [6615]. 39359

———— Résultats des observations faites pour la détermination par la télégraphie sans fil de la différence de longitude entre Paris et Bizerte, obtenus par MM. Noirel et Bellot. Paris C. R. Acad. sci. **154** 1912 (181–184). [6615]. 39360

Bourget, Henry. Rapport de la Mission de l'Observatoire de Toulouse envoyée à Guelma par le Bureau des Longitudes pour l'observation de l'éclipse totale du 30 août 1905. Ann. bur. longit. Paris 8 1911 (N. 1 à N. 24 av. pl.). [4205]. 39361

Bourquin, Hans. Mittel und Wege der elektrischen Bildübertragung. Zs. Elektrot. Potsdam **14** 1911 (417–419). 39362

Boussinesq. Aperçu théorique sur les oscillations d'une colonne de liquide dans un tube en V. J. phys. Paris (sér. 5) **1** 1911 (173–177). [0325]. 39363

———— Calcul de l'absorption dans les cristaux translucides. pour un pinceau de lumière parallèle. Paris C. R. Acad. sci. **153** 1911 (16–21). [3850]. 39364

———— Vibrations spontanées d'une barre à bouts fixes et imperméables à la chaleur, qui se met en équilibre thermique avec une atmosphère à température constante. Paris C. R. Acad. sci. **153** 1911 (409–414). [2040]. 39365

———— Vibrations spontanées d'une barre libre, se refroidissant par contact à ses extrémités et par rayonnement ou convection à sa surface latérale. Paris C. R. Acad. sci. **153** 1911 (452–456). [2040]. 39366

———— Construction simple (en recourant seulement aux deux ellipsoïdes inverse et direct) de la vibration, du rayon lumineux et de la vitesse de ce rayon, pour chacun des deux systèmes d'ondes planes de direction donnée propagés dans un cristal transparent. Paris C. R. Acad. sci. **152** 1911 (1721–1726). [3830]. 39367

———— Calcul de l'absorption dans les cristaux translucides, pour les systèmes d'ondes planes latéralement indéfinies. Paris C. R. Acad. sci. **152** 1911 (1808–1813). [3850]. 39368

Boutaric, A. Sur les phénomènes présentés par les grains d'amidon en lumière polarisée. J. phys. Paris (sér. 5) **1** 1911 (891–896 av. fig.). [4030]. 39369

Boutaric, A. Cryoscopie dans l'hyposulfite de sodium fondu. Paris C. R. Acad. sci. **153** 1911 (876–877). [1920]. 39370

———— r. Leenhardt, C.

Bouty, E. Cohésion diélectrique des gaz monoatomiques. Ann. chim. phys. Paris (sér. 8) **23** 1911 (5–28). [6805 5685]. 39371

———— Potentiel d'effluve et potentiel en décharge dans les gaz très raréfiés. Ann. chim. phys. Paris (sér. 8) **25** 1912 (430–437). [6840 6820]. 39372

Bovini, F. r. Padoa, M.

Bowen, J. E. r. Anderson, A.

Bcyer, Carl and Wherry, Edgar T[heodore]. A comparative study of the radioactive minerals in the collection of the Wagner Free Institute of Science. [With bibliography.] Philadelphia Trans. Wagner Free Inst. Sci. **7** 1910 (31–34 with pls. table). [4275]. 39373

Boyle, R. W. The behaviour of radium emanation at low temperatures. Phil. Mag. London (Ser. 6) **21** 1911 (722–732). [4275]. 39374

Bracchi, Guido. Corso preparatorio per gli aspiranti telegrafisti. Ed. 2. Firenze (Succ. Le Monnier) 1909 (243). 18 cm. [0030 4900]. 39375

Bradhering, Friedrich. Zur Geschichte des Schiffskompasses. [In : Festschrift dem König Wilhelms-Gymnasium zu Magdeburg . . . dargebracht.] Magdeburg (K. Peters) 1911 (121–142). [5435]. 39376

Bradley, W. P., Browne, A. W. und Hale, C. F. Wirkung von mechanischer Erschütterung auf Kohlensäure in der Nähe der kritischen Temperatur. Zs. komprim. Gase Weimar **13** 1911 (101–109). [1880 1840]. 39377

Bragg, William H. Radio-activity as a kinetic theory of a fourth state of matter. Nature London **85** 1911 (491–494). [4275]. 39378

———— The mode of ionization by X-rays. Phil. Mag. London (Ser. 6) **22** 1911 (222–223). [5685]. 39379

———— Studies in radio-activity. London (Macmillan) 1912 (X + 196). 23 cm. 5s. [4275]. 39380

———— and Porter, H. L. Energy transformations of X-rays. London

Proc. R. Soc. (Ser. A) 85 1911 (349–365). [4240]. 39381

Bragstad, O. S. und Liska, J. Die magnetische Prüfung von Eisenblech. [Nebst Erwiderung von J. Epstein.] Elektrot. Zs. Berlin 32 1911 (866). [5435]. 39382

Brandt, A. Über die innere latente Verdampfungswärme. Ann. Physik Leipzig (4. Folge) 37 1912 (847–848). [1680 0200]. 39383

Brandt, Otto. Beitrag zur Herstellung von Kohlenelektroden für galvanische Elemente. Elektrot. Zs. Berlin 32 1911 (1183 1185). [5610]. 39384

Branly, Edouard. Les deux étapes de la télégraphie sans fil. Roma Mem. Acc. Nuovi Lincei 29 1911 (163–164). [6615]. 39385

Brauer, Geo. Die harmonischen Obertöne und ihre Bedeutung für Harmonie und Stimmkunst. Zs. InstrBau Leipzig 31 1911 (494 496 540 541 1143 1144 1179 1181). [9450]. 39386

Braun, F. Electrische Schwingungen und drahtlose Telegraphie. Nobel-Vortrag. Les prix Nobel en 1909 1910 (18 mit 2 Taf. 15 Textfigg.). [6043 6615]. 39387

Brauns, R[einhard]. Die Aenderung des optischen Achsenwinkels in Gips bei höherer Temperatur. Centralbl. Min. Stuttgart 1911 (401–405). (3830 3822]. 39388

——— Die Ursachen der Färbung dilut gefärbter Mineralien und der Einfluss von Radiumstrahlen auf die Färbung. Fortschr. Min. Jena 1 1911 (129–140). [4275]. 39389

——— r. Goldschmidt, V.

Breda, Stefano r. Gnesotto, T.

Bredow, H. Drahtlose Telegraphie mit besonderer Berücksichtigung von Schiffsinstallationen. Jahrb. schiffbaut. Ges. Berlin 13 1912 (105 172). [6615]. 39390

Breisig, F. Über die Energieverteilung in Fernsprechkreisen. Elektrot. Zs. Berlin 32 1911 (558 561 590–593). [6485]. 39391

Breitfeld, C. Berechnung von Wechselstrom-Fernleitungen. (Elektrotechnik in Einzeldarstellungen. Hrsg. von C. Benischke. H. 17.) Braun-

schweig (F. Vieweg & S.) 1912 (VIII 89). 22 cm. [6460]. 39392

Brenken, E. Elektrostatischer Dynen- und Voltmesser. (Zugleich Apparat zum Nachweis des Coulombschen Gesetzes.) Monatshefte natw. Unterr. Leipzig 4 1911 (35–38). [0050]. 39393

Briggs, C. A. r. Wolff, F. A.

Brillouin, Marcel. Éléments cristallins et orientations moléculaires. Paris C. R. Acad. sci. 153 1911 (380–383). [0400]. 39394

——— Méthode interférentielle pour la détermination des modules de torsion des cristaux. Paris C. R. Acad. sci. 153 1911 (710–713). [0840]. 39395

Brion, G. Überspannungen in elektrischen Anlagen. Helios Leipzig 17 1911 Fach-Zs. (53 58 73 77 145–150 157 162 173–177 185–190 201–206). [6000 6450]. 39396

Brisset, D. La matière et les forces de la nature. Paris (Dunod) 1910 (70). 18.5 cm. [0600]. 39397

Brizard, L. r. Broglie, M.

Broca, André. Sur la constitution d'axes de rotation assez stables pour permettre la mesure des angles géodésiques par la méthode de la répétition. Paris C. R. Acad. sci. 152 1911 (847–849). [0890]. 39398

——— Mercadier. Rev. gén. sci. Paris 22 1911 (709–710). [0010]. 39399

Brochet, Charles. Sur la figuration des lignes équipotentielles dans un électrolyseur. Paris C. R. Acad. sci. 153 1911 (1150–1152 av. fig.). [6240]. 39400

Broemser, Ph. Zur Theorie der registrierenden Apparate. Erzwungene Schwingungen graphisch dargestellt. Zs. Biol. München 57 1911 (81–89). [0090 9135]. 39401

Broglie (De), Maurizio. Studio sulle sospensioni nei gas. Riv. fis. mat. sc. nat. Pavia 20 1909 (461–473). [0100]. 39402

——— Sur l'abaissement des différences de potentiel de contact apparent entre métaux par suite de l'enlèvement des couches d'humidité adhérentes. Paris C. R. Acad. sci. 152 1911 (696–698). [5240]. 39403

Broglie (De), Maurizio. Sur un cas particulier de distribution de l'ionisation dans un gaz. Couche superficielle très mince contenant des ions des deux signes. Paris C. R. Acad. sci. 152 1911 (1298-1299). [6805 5685]. 39404

———— Les petits ions dans les gaz issus des flammes. Radium Paris 8 1911 (106-108 av. fig.). [6805 5685]. 39405

———— Sur les observations du mouvement brownien dans les gaz à basse pression. Paris C. R. Acad. sci. 154 1912 (112 113). [0200]. 39406

———— et Brizard, L. Sur la radiation du sulfate de quinine, ionisation et luminescence. Paris C. R. Acad. sci. 152 1911 (136-138). [4220 6840]. 39407

———— ———— Sur la mobilité des ions produits dans l'air par le sulfate de quinine en voie d'hydratation. Paris C. R. Acad. sci. 152 1911 (855-856). [6805]. 39408

———— ———— Sur certains effets d'ionisation des gaz observés en présence de corps non radioactifs. Activité et luminescence du sulfate de quinine. Radium Paris 8 1911 (181-186 273-279). [6805 5685]. 39409

Broniewski, Witold. Sur les propriétés électriques des alliages aluminium-magnésium. Paris C. R. Acad. sci. 152 1911 (83-85). [5660 5710]. 39410

———— O zredukowaniu liczby jednostek zasadniczych. [Sur la réduction du nombre d'unités fondamentales.] Wiad. mat. Warszawa. 15 1911 (121-124). [0805]. 39411

———— Recherches sur les propriétés électriques des alliages d'aluminium. Ann. chim. phys. Paris (sér. 8) 25 1912 (5-125 av. fig.). [5710 5680 6210]. 39412

———— et Hackspill. Sur les propriétés électriques des métaux alcalins, du rhodium et de l'iridium. Paris C. R. Acad. sci. 153 1911 (814-817 av. fig.). [5660 5710]. 39413

———— v. Guntz, A.

Bronson, H. L. and Shaw, A. N. Clark and Weston standard cells. Elect. London 66 1911 (698-702). [5610]. 39414

Brooks, H. B. The deflection potentiometer considered as a genera-

lized null instrument. [Abstract.] Physic. Rev. Ithaca N.Y. 32 1911 (625). [5700]. 39415

Brotherus, Hj. Photometrische Untersuchung der Struktur einiger Spektrallinien. Physik. Zs. Leipzig 12 1911 (193-196 mit 1 Taf.). [4207]. 39416

Brown, F[ay] C[luff]. The electric properties of light-positive and light-negative selenium. [Abstract.] Rev. Ithaca N.Y. 32 1911 (237-239). [5660]. 39417

———— The nature of the recovery of light-positive and light-negative selenium. [Abstract.] Physic. Rev. Ithaca N.Y. 32 1911 (252-254). [5660]. 39418

———— The nature of light action in selenium. Physic. Rev. Ithaca N.Y. 33 1911 (1-26 with fig. tables). [5660]. 39419

———— and Clark, W. H. The method of measuring the fluctuations in a rapidly varying resistance. [Abstract.] Physic. Rev. Ithaca N.Y. 32 1911 (251-252); 33 1911 (53-59 with fig. table). [5640]. 39420

Brown, R. A. v. Houstoun, R. A.

Brown, William. Mechanical stress and magnetisation of nickel (Part II.), and the subsidence of torsional oscillations in nickel and iron wires when subjected to the influence of longitudinal magnetic fields. Dublin Proc. R. Soc. 13 1911 (28-48). [5460]. 39421

Browne, A. W. v. Bradley, W. P.

Brücke, E[rnst] Th. von und Inouye, N. Über die Anordnung der homogenen Lichter auf der Mischlinie des Rotgrünblinden mit unverkürztem Spektrum. Arch. ges Physiol. Bonn 145 1911 (573-590). [4450]. 39421A

Brückmann, A. Stroboskopischer Schlüpfungsmesser. Elektrot. Zs. Berlin 32 1911 (219 220). [6070]. 39422

———— Wechselstrom-Kollektormotoren. Helios Leipzig 17 1911 Fach-Zs. (345 350 363-366). [6070]. 39423

Brüninghaus, L. Sur la loi de Stokes et sur une relation générale entre l'absorption et la phosphorescence. Paris C. R. Acad. sci. 152 1911 (1578-1580); Radium Paris 8 1911 (411-415 av. fig.). [4230]. 39424

Bruninghaus, L. Une relation entre l'absorption et la phosphorescence. Radium Paris 8 1911 (147–153). [4230]. 39425

Bruger, Th. Über einige neuere Messapparate der Hartmann und Braun A. G. Elektrot. Zs. Berlin 32 1911 (519–522). [5640 6010]. 39426

Bruhat, G. Étude du dichroïsme rotatoire d'un composé organique défini (diphényl-ε-bornyldithiouréthane). Paris C. R. Acad. sci. 153 1911 (248 250). [4040 3850]. 39427

Brunelli, L. M. Considerazioni sui moti pendolari delle macchine sincrone. Mon. tecn. Milano 17 1911 (188–193 209–211 249–252). [6400]. 39428

Brani, Giuseppe. Soluzioni solide e colloidi. Padova Atti Mem. Acc. 27 1911 (137–140). [1925]. 39429

——— Su alcune applicazioni della crioscopia. Padova (Soc. coop. tip.) 1909 (20). 24 cm. [1920]. 39430

——— Sul congelamento di soluzioni colloidali e di gelatina. Rend. soc. chim. ital. Roma (Ser. 2) 1 1909 (36). [1920]. 39431

——— und **Meneghini, D.** Bildung metallischer fester Lösungen durch Diffusion im festen Zustande. 1 Mitt. Intern. Zs. Metallogr. Berlin 2 1911 (26–35). [0320]. 39432

——— ——— Formazione di soluzioni solide per diffusione allo stato solido. Roma Rend. Acc. Lincei (Ser. 5) 20 1. sem. 1911 (671–674) 927–931). [0320]. 39433

Brunn, E. Petroleum bei Kondensatorplatten. Zs. physik. Unterr. Berlin 24 1911 (98). [0090]. 39434

Brush, Charles F[rancis]. A kinetic theory of gravitation. [Abstract.] Physic. Rev. Ithaca N.Y. 32 1911 (633–635); Science New York (N. Ser.) 33 1911 (384–386). [0700]. 39435

Bryant, E. G. Curious thermal phenomenon. Chem. News London 104 1911 (96); l.c. (118). [2040 2060]. 39436

Bucherer, A[lfred] H. Die neuesten Bestimmungen der spezifischen Ladung des Elektrons. Ann. Physik Leipzig (4. Folge) 37 1912 (597–598). [6845]. 39437

Buchwald, Eberhard. Untersuchungen von Flammenspektren mit dem Vakuumbolometer. Diss. Breslau (Druck v. H. Fleischmann) 1910 (46). 21 cm. [1202 4210 4205]. 39438

Budd, L. C. v. Wilson.

Budde, E. Zur Theorie des Mitschwingens. Berlin Verh. D. physik. Ges. 13 1911 (121 137 224). [9100 9140 9135]. 39439

——— Kilogramm-Kraft und Kilogramm-Masse, ein Vorschlag zur Einigung. Elektrot. Zs. Berlin 32 1911 (53 54). [0805]. 39440

——— Das Dopplersche Prinzip für bewegte Spiegel und ein Versuch von Klinkerfues. Physik. Zs. Leipzig 12 1911 (725–729). [3420]. 39441

——— Zur Theorie des Michelsonschen Versuches. Physik. Zs. Leipzig 12 1911 (979–994). [3420 3610]. 39442

Budig, W. Messungen der Radioaktivität der atmosphärischen Luft auf dem Brocken. Berlin Veröff. met. Inst. No. 229 1911 (66–71). [4275]. 39443

Büchner, E[rnst] H[endrik]. Het radiumgehalte der aardkorst. [Der Radiumgehalt der Erdrinde.] Ned. Nat. Geneesk. Congres 13 1911 (374–380). [4275]. 39444

——— Onderzoekingen over het radiumgehalte van gesteenten. III. [Investigations on the radium content of rocks. III.] Amsterdam Versl. Wis. Nat. Afd. K. Akad. Wet. 20 1912 (1045–1048) (Dutch); Amsterdam Proc. Sci. K. Akad. Wet. 14 1912 (1063–1066). (English). [4275]. 39445

Büeler-de Florin, H. Verfahren zum Erschmelzen von Quarz. Elektroch. Zs. Berlin 18 1912 (271–274). [0090]. 39446

Bürger, W. Die Messung hoher Temperaturen. [Segerkegel.] Elektroch. Zs. Berlin 17 1911 (309 311 337–340). [1240]. 39447

Buglia, G. v. Bottazzi, F.

Buisson, H. et **Fabry, Ch.** Sur la mesure des intensités des diverses radiations d'un rayonnement complexe. Paris C. R. Acad. sci. 152 1911 (1838–1841). [4210]. 39448

——— ——— Sur la dépense d'énergie nécessaire pour produire l'unité d'intensité lumineuse. Paris C. R. Acad. sci. 153 1911 (254 255). [3405]. 39449

Buisson, H. et Fabry, Ch. La lumière ultraviolette. Rev. gén. sci. Paris 22 1911 (309–322 av. 1 g.). [4200].
39450

—— r. Fabry, Ch

Bunet, Paul. Il problema della trasformazione della frequenza. [Sunto.] Atti Assoc. elettrotecn. Milano 15 1911 (892–896). [6040].
39451

Burbidge P. r. Laby, T. H.

Burgess, G[eorge] K[imball] r. Waidner, C. W.

Burmeister, Frerik r. Wiegner, G.

Burson, N. r. Deslandres, H.

Burstall, F. W. The energy-diagram for gas. London Proc. Inst. Mech. Engin. 1 1911 (171–194). [2415 2490].
39452

Busch, Friedr[ich] und Jensen, Chr[istian]. Tatsachen und Theorien der atmosphärischen Polarisation nebst Anleitung zu Beobachtungen verschiedener Art. Hamburg Jahrb. wiss. Anst. 28 (1910) Beih. 5 1911 (1–532). [3230 3640 4000].
39453

Buschmann, Gustav Adolf. Glasmaterial für Musikinstrumente und physikalisch-akustisches Studium. Zs. InstrBau Lepizig 32 1911 (272–274). [9410].
39454

Bush, George C. The value and limitations of quantitative work in physics and chemistry. [In: National Education Association of the United States. Journal of proceedings and addresses, 1907, (684–686).] [0050].
39455

Butavand, F. Note au sujet de l'absorption et du rayonnement secondaire des rayons cathodiques. Ann. chim. phys. Paris (sér. 8) 24 1911 (421–432). [6845].
39456

Butterfield, W. J. A., Haldane, J. S. and Trotter, A. P. Corrections for the effects of atmospheric conditions of photometric flame standards. Elect. London 67 1911 (711–713). [3010].
39457

Byk, A[lfred]. Fortschritte der Photochemie in den Jahren 1909 und 1910. Zs. Elektroch. Halle 17 1911 (581–592). [4225].
39458

—— und Borck, H. Einfluss des Lichtes auf das Leitvermögen von Anthracenlösungen. Jahrb. Phot. Halle 25 1911 (58–60). [5660]. 39459

Caan, Albert. Ueber Radioaktivität menschlicher Organe. Heidelberg SitzBer. Ak. Wiss. math.-natw. Kl. 1911 Abh. 5 (44 mit 1 Taf.). [4275].
39460

Cady, W[alter] G[uyton]. Isolierte Doppelklemmen. (Insulated double connectors.) (Übers.) Physik. Zs. Leipzig 12 1911 (1254–1255). [0050].
39461

—— Color dispersion in the astigmatic eye. Science New York (N. Ser.) 34 1911 (26–28 with fig.). [4430 4450].
39462

Cajori, Floriano. Storia della fisica elementare. [Trad. con appendici.] Bologna (N. Zanichelli) 1909 (VIII + 430). 23 cm. [0010].
39463

Caldonazzo, Bruto. Forze ponderomotrici esercitate da un campo magnetico omogeneo su una corrente continua rettilinea indefinita. Nuovo Cimento Pisa (Ser. 6) 2 1911 (63–79). [6450].
39464

Callendar, H. L. The radio-balance. A thermoelectric balance for the absolute measurement of radiation, with applications to radium and its emanation. London Proc. Physic. Soc. 23 1910 (1–34). [4275 1230]. 39465

—— The caloric theory of heat and Carnot's principle. London Proc. Physic. Soc. 23 1911 (153–189). [2400].
39466

—— and Moss, Herbert. On the absolute expansion of mercury. London Phil. Trans. R. Soc. 211 1911 (1–32). [1430].
39467

Calzecchi, Temistocle. Di un modo semplice di caricare l'elettroscopio protetto dalla camera di Faraday. Milano Rend. Ist. lomb. (Ser. 2) 43 1910 (340–341). [5210].
39468

Calzecchi Onesti, Temistocle. Le mie esperienze e quelle di Edoardo Branly sulla conduttività elettrica delle limature metalliche. Milano Rend. Ist. lomb. (Ser. 2) 44 1911 (497–505); Nuovo Cimento Pisa (Ser. 6) 2 1911 (387–396): [sunto] Riv. fis. mat. sc. nat. Pavia 24 1911 (172–173). [6600 4900].
39469

Calzolari, F. Solubilità ed elettroaffinità. Ferrara Atti Acc. med. nat. 85 1911 (147–154). [1920].
39470

Campbell, A. and Dye, D. W. On very high sound vibrations produced

by electric sparks. Elect. London 66
1911 (862 863). [9130 6820]. 39471

Campbell, Leslie | L[yle] v. Hall, E. H.

Campbell, Norman. A note on a
method of determining capacities in
measurements of ionization. Phil. Mag.
London (Ser. 6) 21 1911 (42 45).
[5740]. 39472

———— Delta rays. Phil. Mag.
London (Ser. 6) 22 1911 (276 302).
[4275]. 39473

———— Bemerkungen zu der
Arbeit des Herrn Hauser: Über die
Selbstaufladung von Polonium. [Re-
marks on the work of Herr Hauser
" Die Selbstaufladung von Polonium."]
Physik. Zs. Leipzig 12 1911 (870 871).
(Übers.) [1275 6845]. 39474

———— Relativitätsprinzip und
Äther. Eine Entgegnung an Herrn
Wiechert. (Übers.) Physik. Zs.
Leipzig 13 1912 (120 128). [6600].
39475

Campetti, Adolfo. Misure e nuovi
apparecchi relativi ai fenomeni termici.
Nuovo Cimento Pisa (Ser. 5) 20 1910
(155-162). [0900]. 39476

———— Studi recenti intorno alle
leghe. Nuovo Cimento Pisa (Ser. 6)
2 1911 (323-328). [2060]. 39477

———— Sulla mobilità degli ioni
positivi prodotti nell'ossidazione del
rame. Torino Atti Acc. sc. 46 1911
(242-254). [6805]. 39478

———— e Delgrosso, C. Sul-
l'equilibrio di coppie di liquidi parzialmente miscibili. Equilibrio tra le fasi
liquide. Torino Mem. Acc. sc. (Ser. 2)
61 1911 (187-197 con 1 tav.). [1887].
39479

Campos, Gino. La propagazione e
lo smorzamento delle sovratensioni.
Nuovi dispositivi di protezione. Atti
Assoc. elettrotecn. Milano 15 1911
(549-609). [6460]. 39480

———— La propagazione delle
sovratensioni oscillatorie. Atti Assoc.
elettrotecn. Milano 15 1911 (1014
1015). [6440]. 39481

Cannegieter, H. G. Ionisatie van
gassen door licht, uitgestraald door
Geissler'sche buizen. Onderzoek naar
eventueel hierbij zich voordoende
selectieverschijnselen. [Ionisation of
gases by light emitted from Geissler
tubes. Research after the existence of

selective effects on the ionisation.]
Amsterdam Versl. Wis. Nat. Afd. K.
Akad. Wet. 19 1911 (1331-1336)
(Dutch); Amsterdam Proc. Sci. K.
Akad. Wet. 13 1911 (1114-1119)
(English); Handl. Ned. Nat. Geneesk.
Congres 13 1911 (169 172). [6805].
39482

Cannegieter, H. G. Waarnemingen
betreffende ionisatie van gassen door licht
van stralende gassen afkomstig. [Obser-
vations sur l'ionisation des gaz par la
lumière émise par des gaz rayonnants.]
Utrecht (J. van Druten) 1911 (98 avec
6 pl.). 23 cm. [6805]. 39483

Cantani, C. Guida del telegrafista.
Ed. 2. Milano (U. Hoepli) 1909 (X +
218). 15 cm. [0030 4900]. 39485

Cantone, Michele. Relazione sulla
Nota del dott. Paolo Rossi: La doppia
rifrazione accidentale del caucciù studiata in rapporto al comportamento
elastico. Napoli Rend. Soc. sc. (Ser. 3)
16 1910 (121-125). [3835]. 39486

Capart, R. Les caractéristiques des
piles. Bruxelles Bul. Soc. belge électr.
Juin 1910 (295-300). [5610]. 39487

Caprotti, Arturo. Scappamento ed
ammissione nei motori a due tempi.
Pisa (Succ. flli Nistri) 1909 (26 con 2
tav.). 26 cm. [2490]. 39488

Carbonelli, C. Emilio. Coibenti
industriali specialmente per uso di
bordo. Atti Coll. ing. nav. mecc. Genova
8 1910 (39-54). [2620]. 39489

Carcano, F. E. La situazione attuale
del forno elettrico quale produttore di
ghise. Politecn. Milano 58 1910 (129-
143). [6090]. 39490

Cardani, Pietro. Sul rapporto
esistente tra l'energia spesa in un tubo
sorgente di raggi X e la jonizzazione
prodotta dai raggi emessi. Nuovo
Cimento Pisa (Ser. 6) 2 1911 (453-478).
[6490]. 39491

Cardoso, Ettore. Sur les densités
des phases coexistantes (densités ortho-
bares) et le diamètre de l'anhydride
sulfureux au voisinage du point critique.
Paris C. R. Acad. sci. 153 1911 (257-
259); Genève C. R. Soc. Phys. Hist.
Nat. 28 1912 (54). [1880]. 39493

Cardot, H. et Laugier, H. Localisation des excitations de fermeture dans
la méthode unipolaire. Paris C. R.
Acad. sci. 154 1912 (375-377). [5900].
39494

Carhart, Henry S. The Bureau of standards. Pop. Sci. Mon. New York 79 1911 (209-219 with illus.). [0060]. 39495

Carlier, J. Les méthodes et appareils de mesures du temps, des distances, des vitesses et des accélérations. Bruxelles Bul. Soc. belge électr. 1904 (329-414 439-506 551-594 668-706 766-783 811-864); 1905 (31-58 73-133 156-222 245-276). [0809 0820]. 39496

Carlson, Tor. Sur la vitesse de solution dans le système gaz-fluide. Stockholm Medd. Vet.-Ak. Nobelinst. 2 No. 5 1911 (17 avec 3 figs.). [0250 2457]. 39497

——— On the diffusion of oxygen and carbon dioxide in water. Stockholm Medd. Vet.-Ak. Nobelinst. 2 No. 6 1911 (8). [0320]. 39498

Carnevale Arella, A. L'azione dei raggi X a dosi minime. Idrol. climatol. Ter. fis. Firenze 22 1911 (382-386). [5900]. 39499

——— Azione dei raggi Röntgen sul timo. Firenze (Soc. tip. fiorentina) 1910 (11). 24 cm. [5900]. 39500

Carnot, Jean v. Damour, E.

Caro, N. und Schück, B. Untersuchungen über die Veränderung von Wasserstoff in Gasballons. ChemZtg Cöthen 35 1911 (405-407). [0820]. 39501

Carpentier, J. [présente à l'Académie des Sciences] un sphéromètre modifié par M. Nugues. Paris C. R. Acad. sci. 152 1911 (421-423). [0807]. 39502

Carpini, Camillo. Su di una forma di barometro a peso. Riv. fis. mat. sc. nat. Pavia 19 1909 (25-36). [0090]. 39503

Carus-Wilson, C. Musical sands of Eigg. Nature London 86 1911 (518). [9100]. 39504

Carvallo, E. Goniomètre universel de haute précision et à miroirs. J. Ec. polytech. Paris (sér. 2) 1910 (71-81 av. fig.). [3030 5070]. 39507

——— Théorie des moteurs à gaz et à pétrole. J. Ec. polytech. Paris (sér. 2) 1911 (211-254 av. fig.). [2490]. 39508

Carvallo, J. Sur la conductibilité de l'éther pur. Paris C. R. Acad. sci. 153 1911 (1144-1145). [5660]. 39509

Casaccio, Enrico. Moto e materia o metamorfosi eterne universali. Caltanisetta (S. Petrantoni) 1910 (30). 21 cm. [0000]. 39510

Cassebaum, Hans. Ueber das Verhalten von weichem Flussstahl jenseits der Proportionalitätsgrenze. Ann. Physik Leipzig (4. Folge) 34 1911 (106-130 mit 3 Taf.). [0840]. 39511

Cassini v. Méchain.

Castelnuovo, Guido. Le principe de relativité et les phénomènes optiques. Scientia Bologna 9 1911 suppl. (51-75 64-86). [3000]. 39513

Cataldi, P. La meccanica nelle scuole e nell'industria. Generatori di vapore, macchine termiche. Ed. 2, vol. 2. Milano (Hoepli) 1909 (XV + 735). 15 cm. [0030 0900]. 39514

——— Forni elettrici ad induzione. Industria Milano 24 1910 (769-771 787-790 812-814); Elettricità Milano 36 1911 (250-252 262-267 301-304); Roma Ann. Soc. ing. 26 1911 (69-80). [6090]. 39515

——— Forni elettrici industriali. Atti Assoc. elettrotecn. Milano 15 1911 (293-316). [6090]. 39516

Caudrelier, E. Recherches sur la constitution de l'étincelle électrique. Paris C. R. Acad. sci. 152 1911 (762-763). [6820]. 39517

Caudrelier, C. Fréquence des oscillations électriques qui prennent naissance dans l'étincelle. Paris C. R. Acad. sci. 152 1911 (1758-1759). [6820]. 39518

Cavazzani, Emilio. Intorno alla viscosità dell'umor acqueo. Ferrara Atti Acc. med. nat. 83 1909 (131-133). [0325]. 39519

Cederberg, Ivar W. Ueber eine allgemeine Beziehung zwischen Verdampfungswärme, Dampfdruck und Temperatur. Zs. physik. Chem. Leipzig 77 1911 (498-509). [1840 1680]. 39520

——— Zur Kenntnis der Dampfdruckfunktion. Zs. physik. Chem. Leipzig 77 1911 (707-718). [1840]. 39521

Cegielskij, Roman. Über das Sieden von Elektrolyten bei Stromdurchgang. Berlin Verh. D. physik. Ges. 13 1911 (227-248). [6200 1860 5720]. 39522

Cei, Leonioro. La caldaia multitubulare. Come funziona e come é costituita. Torino (Tip. Eredi Botta) 1909 (53 con tav.). 32 cm. [0030 0900]. 39523

Cermak, Paul. Ueber die Theorien der Thermoelektrizität und ihre Erfüllung durch neuere experimentelle Ergebnisse. Jahrb. Radioakt. Leipzig 8 1911 (241–275). [5710 5675]. 39524

————— und **Schmidt**, Hans. Die thermoelektrischen Kräfte beim Übergang vom festen zum flüssigen Aggregatzustande. Ann. Physik Leipzig (4. Folge) 36 1911 (575–588). [5710]. 39525

Ceruti, Giuliano. Sul potenziale esplosivo nell' aria compressa. Milano Rend. Ist. lomb. (Ser. 2) 42 1909 (476–495). [6820]. 39526

————— Sulla scarica elettrica nell'ossigeno a pressioni elevate. Milano Rend. Ist. lomb. (Ser. 2) 43 1910 (42–47 con 1 tav.). [6820]. 39527

Ceruti, Ivanhoe. Acido solforico per accumulatori. Industria chim. Torino 10 1910 (305–307). [5620]. 39528

Chambers, F. J. Experiments in impact excitation. Elect. London 67 1911 (553). [6615]. 39529

Chanoz, M. Développement physique d'une image radiographique après fixage par l'hyposulfite de soude et lavage prolongé de la plaque sensible irradiée. Paris C. R. Acad. sci. 152 1911 (1576–1578). [4240 4225]. 39530

————— Des images révélées physiquement après fixage de la plaque au gélatinobromure d'argent irradiée. Actions isolées ou successives de la lumière et des rayons X. Paris C. R. Acad. sci. 152 1911 (1832–1834). [4225 4240]. 39531

Chapman, Edgar K. A comparison of theoretical and observed equilibrium temperatures in fog chambers. Physic. Rev. Ithaca N.Y. 32 1911 (561–564 with tables). [1840]. 39532

Chapman, H. G. and **Petrie**, J. M. On the action of the latex of *Euphorbia peplus* on a photographic plate. Nature London 86 1911 (517–518). [4225]. 39533

Chapman, J. Crosby. Attempt to detect a fatigue effect in the production of secondary Röntgen radiations. Cambridge Proc. Phil. Soc. 16 1911 (142–147). [4240]. 39534

————— Homogeneous Röntgen radiation from vapours. Phil. Mag. London (Ser. 6) 21 1911 (446–454). [4240]. 39535

————— and **Guest**, E. D. The intensity of secondary homogeneous Röntgen radiation from compounds. Cambridge Proc. Phil. Soc. 16 1911 (136–141). [4240]. 39536

Charpy, G. et **Bonnerot**, S. Sur les gaz contenus dans les aciers. Paris C. R. Acad. sci. 152 1910 (1247 1250). [0250]. 39537

Charron, F. Influence de l'air dans le frottement des solides. Ann. chim. phys. Paris (sér. 8) 24 1911 (5–86 av. fig.). [0250]. 39538

Chaspoul et **Jaubert de Beaujeu**. Recherches sur la radioactivité des eaux de Vals-les-Bains. Paris C. R. Acad. sci. 153 1911 (944–946). [4275]. 39539

Chassy, A. Conductibilité des gaz sous la pression atmosphérique sous l'influence d'une haute tension alternative. J. phys. Paris (sér. 5) 1 1911 (737–744 av. fig.). [5685]. 39540

Chauveau, A. Sur un spectre météorique de la Tour Eiffel observé en 1900. Paris C. R. Acad. sci. 153 1911 (1048–1053 av. fig.). [3210]. 39542

————— Sur quelques données actuelles relatives à l'électricité de la pluie. (A propos des observations récentes de M. Baldit.) Radium Paris 8 1911 (153–157). [5270]. 39543

————— Sur les mesures récentes du courant vertical de conductibilité entre l'atmosphère et le sol. Radium Paris 8 1911 (187–196 av. fig.). [5270]. 39544

Chauvenet, Ed. Dissociation de ThCl⁴18NH³. Ann. chim. phys. Paris (sér. 8) 23 1911 (275–280). [1930]. 39545

Chella, Silvio v. Battelli, A.

Chéneveau, C. Sur un goniomètre réfractomètre auto-collimateur. J. phys. Paris (sér. 4) 9 1910 (823–829 av. fig.). [3020]. 39546

————— et **Heim**. Sur l'extensibilité du caoutchouc vulcanisé. Paris

C. R. Acad. sci. 152 1911 (320 322). [0849]. 39547

Chevallier, H. Sur le fonctionnement des lampes à incandescence à filament de carbone et filament métallique. Bordeaux Proc.-verb. soc. sci. phys. nat. 1909-1910 (13-18). [6080]. 39548

Chiari, Richard. Untersuchungen über physikalische Zustandsänderungen der Kolloide. II. Mitt. Die Glutinquellung in Säuren und Laugen. Biochem. Zs. Berlin 33 1911 (167-181). [0340]. 39549

Chieffi, Generoso r. Paternò, E.

Child, Clement] D[exter]. Discharge from hot CaO. Physic. Rev. Ithaca N.Y. 32 1911 (492-511 with fig. tables). [6845]. 39550

Chistoni, Ciro. Necrologia di Eugenio Semmola. Nuovo Cimento Pisa (Ser. 6) 1 1911 (139-142). [0010]. 39551

Chofardet, P. r. Lebeuf, A.

Chopin, Marcel. La mesure absolue des courants de grande intensité. Paris C. R. Acad. sci. 151 1910 (1037-1040). [5700]. 39552

Choppé, L. Notice sur M. Aimé Schuster. Metz Mém. de l'ac. (sér. 3.) 39 (1909-10) 1911 (81-92). [0010]. 39553

Chree, C. Terrestrial Magnetism. Encycl. Brit. (ed. 11) 17 1911. [5490]. 39553A

Chrétien, H. r. Lagrula, J.

Christen, Th. Zur Arbeitsberechnung am Quecksilbermanometer. [Bemerkung hierzu v. Otto Frank.] Zs. Biol. München 55 1911 (460-462 463-465). [0835]. 39554

Christiansen, C. Experimental-undersøgelser om Gnidningselektricitetens Oprindelse III. [Experimental investigations as to the origin of electricity produced by friction III.] Kobenhavn Vid. Selsk. Overs. 1911 (209-244 with 1 pl.) [5210]. 39555

Christlein, Paul. Untersuchungen über das allgemeine Verhalten des Geschwindigkeitskoeffizienten von Leitvorrichtungen des praktischen Dampfturbinenbaues. Berlin Zs. Ver. D. Ing. 55 1911 (2084-2089); Zs. Turbinenwesen München 9 1912 (1-6 21-24 33-38 52-57); Diss. Berlin. München (Druck v. R. Oldenbourg) 1911 (36). 32 cm. [2490]. 39557

**Chwolson, O[rest] D[anilovic].] Хвольсонъ, О[рестъ].] Цанилович1.] Усп±хи физики въ 1908 году. [Der Fortschritt in der Physik im Jahre 1908.] Vopr. fiziki St. Peterburg 3 1909 (119-143). [0040]. 39559

Ciamician, Giacomo. La coopération des sciences. Rev. sci. Paris 49 (2. semest.) 1911 (612-619). [0040]. 39560

—— e **Silber, Paolo.** Azioni chimiche della luce. Memoria 6. Bologna Mem. Acc. sc. (Ser. 6) 6 1909 (11-46); Nota XIX. Roma Rend. Acc. Lincei (Ser. 5) 20 1. sem. 1911 (721-724); Nota XX. t.c. (881-885); op. cit. 20 2. sem. 1911 (673-677). [4225]. 39561

Cicali, Giovanni. Note relative ad alcuni fenomeni osservati nel funzionamento delle motrici termiche. Politecn. Milano 59 1911 (535-539). [2490]. 39562

—— Sui potenziali e diagrammi termodinamici con applicazioni alle motrici termiche. Politecn. Milano 59 1911 (641-661). [2490]. 39563

Cicconetti, G. Determinazioni di gravità relativa eseguite a Napoli e dintorni nel 1908. Ann. R. Ist. tecn. Napoli 26 (1908) 1910 (43-76). [0845]. 39564

Cintolesi, Filippo r. Mantovani, Pio.

Cisotti, Umberto. La ereditarietà lineare e i fenomeni dispersivi. Milano Rend. Ist. lomb. (Ser. 2) 44 1911 (667-675); Nuovo Cimento Pisa (Ser. 6) 2 1911 (234-244). [6620]. 39566

—— Sulla dispersività in relazione ad una assegnata frequenza. Milano Rend. Ist. lomb. (Ser. 2) 44 1911 (676-688); Nuovo Cimento Pisa (Ser. 6) 2 1911 (360-374). [6610 6620]. 39567

—— Deformazione di una sfera elastica dovuta al suo moto in seno ad un liquido. (Modello meccanico di un elettrone.) Nuovo Cimento Pisa (Ser. 6) 2 1911 (375-386). [4960]. 39568

Clark, Herbert A. The selective reflection of salts of chromium acids. Physic. Rev. Ithaca N.Y. 32 1911 (442-443). [3850]. 39569

Clark, W. H. r. Brown, F. C.

Classen, J[ohannes]. Kleine Universalbogenlampe mit festem Lichtpunkt für optische Versuche. Zs.

physik. Unterr. Leipzig 24 1911 (283–284). [6080 0050]. 39570

Claude, A., Ferrié, G. et Driencourt, L. L'emploi de la télégraphie sans fil pour la détermination des longitudes. Rev. gén. sci. Paris 22 1911 (518–525, 562–570). [6615 0809]. 39571

Claude, Georges. Sur les tubes luminescents au néon. Paris C. R. Acad. sci. 151 1910 (1122–1124); 152 1911 (1377–1380). [4202 6840]. 39572

——— L'illuminazione al néon. Atti Assoc. elettrotecn. Milano 15 1911 (1223–1225). [6080]. 39573

——— Sur la volatilisation des électrodes dans les tubes à néon. Paris C. R. Acad. sci. 153 1911 (713–715). [6840]. 39574

——— Sur la fabrication industrielle de l'azote pur. Paris C. R. Acad. sci. 153 1911 (764–767). [1870]. 39575

Clausen, Heinr. Temperatureinfluss auf Dichte und elektrische Leitfähigkeit wässeriger Salzlösungen. Ann. Physik Leipzig (4. Folge) 37 1912 (51–67). [6240 0845]. 39576

Clay, J[acob]. On the change with temperature of the electrical resistance of alloys at very low temperatures. Leiden Comm. Physic. Lab. No. 107d 1909 (1–5 with 1 pl.). [5660]. 39577

——— Invloed van electrische trillingen op platina-spiegels (Cohererwerking). [On the influence of electric waves upon platinum mirrors (Cohereraction).] Amsterdam Versl. Wis. Nat. Afd. K. Akad. Wet. 19 [1910] (718–720) (Dutch); Amsterdam Proc. Sci. K. Acad. Wet. 14 [1911] (126–128) (English). [5660 6043]. 39578

——— Der galvanische Widerstand von Metallen und Legierungen bei tiefen Temperaturen. Jahrb. Radioakt. Leipzig 8 1911 (383–406 mit 1 Taf.). [5660 5675]. 39579

Clay, Reginald S. Treatise on practical light. London (Macmillan) 1911 (XV + 519). 20 cm. 10s. 6d. [0030 2990]. 39580

Clemens, H. G. J. F. Schrader und seine Spiegelteleskope. Weltall Berlin 11 1911 (193–202). [0040]. 39581

Clerici, Enrico. Sulla viscosità dei liquidi per la separazione meccanica dei minerali. Roma Rend. Acc. Lincei (Ser. 5) 20 1 sem. 1911 (45–50). [0325]. 39582

Clo, J. Harry. The effects of temperature on the ionization of a gas. Astroph. J. Chicago Ill. 33 1911 (115–124 with text fig. tables); Radium Paris 8 1911 (108–112 avec fig.). [6805 5685 4275]. 39583

Coblentz, W[illiam] W[eber]. Eine Eigentümlichkeit spektraler Energiekurven. (Übers.) Jahrb. Radioakt. Leipzig 8 1911 (1–5). [4210]. 39585

——— Further data on water of crystallization. [Abstract.] Physic. Rev. Ithaca N.Y. 32 1911 (444). [3860]. 39586

——— A characteristic of spectral energy curves. A correction. Physic. Rev. Ithaca N.Y. 32 1911 (591–592). [4210]. 39587

——— Recent determinations of the elementary electrical charge. [Abstract.] Physic. Rev. Ithaca N.Y. 32 1911 (613). [4960 4210]. 39588

——— Die Farbe des von Feuerfliegen und Leuchtkäfern (Lampyridae) ausgesandten Lichtes. [The color of the light emitted by fire-flies.] Physik. Zs. Leipzig 12 1911 (917–920). [Übers.] [4200 4210]. 39589

——— The reflecting power of various metals. Washington D.C. Dept. Comm. Lab. Bull. Bur. Stand. 7 1911 (197–225 with fig. tables). [3060 3840 4210 5710]. 39590

——— Selective radiation from various substances. 3. Washington D.C. Dept. Comm. Lab. Bull. Bur. Stand. 7 1911 (243–294 with fig. table). [4202 4210]. 39591

——— Vorläufige Mitteilung über die selektive Strahlung der Azetylenflamme. Zs. Beleuchtungsw. Berlin 17 1911 (71–73). [4202 4210]. 39592

Coe, H. J. Mangan in Gusseisen und die Volumenveränderungen während der Abkühlung. Metallurgie Halle 8 1911 (102–118 mit Taf.). [1410]. 39593

Cohen, Ernst. Honderd jaren in de molekulaire wereld (1811–1911). [Hundert Jahre in der Welt der Moleküle (1811–1911).] Amsterdam Chem. Weekbl. 8 1911 (421–442); Handl. Ned. Nat. Geneesk. Congres 13 1911 (93–118). [0010 0200]. 3959

Cohen, Ernst. Die Berechnung elektromotorischer Kräfte aus thermischen Grössen. Zs. Elektroch. Halle 17 1911 (143–145). [5610]. 39596

———— Zur Thermodynamik der Normalelemente. (5. Mitt.) Zs. physik. Chem. Leipzig 76 1911 (75–78). [5610]. 39597

Cohn. Kraftübertragung mittels Wechselstroms auf weite Entfernungen. Elektrot. Zs. Berlin 32 1911 (114–115). [6460]. 39598

Coker, E. G. Photo-elasticity. Engineering London 91 1911 (1–4). [3835 4000]. 39599

Colard, Osc. Les efforts mécaniques dans les champs électriques ou magnétiques. Liége Bul. Ass. ing. électr. 6 1906 (277–313). [5220 5420]. 39600

Cole, A. D. A spectrometer for electromagnetic radiation. Granville Ohio Bull. Sci. Lab. Denison Univ. 14 1909 (189–198 with text fig.). [3030]. 39601

Colin, G. r. Recoura, A.

Collis, A. G. L'influenza dell' apertura di corti circuiti sulla tensione. [Trad.] Industria Milano 25 1911 (357–359). [6440]. 39602

Collodi, T. La scarica intermittente attraverso i gas rarefatti posti nel campo magnetico. Roma Rend. Acc. Lincei (Ser. 5) 19 2. sem. 1910 (637–641). [6840]. 39603

———— Misura della carica portata dai raggi magnetici. Roma Rend. Acc. Lincei (Ser. 5) 20 1. sem. 1911 (27–30). [4960]. 39604

Colombo, Giuseppe. Trasporto dell'energia. Cinquanta anni di storia italiana. Milano (Hoepli) 1911 (1–45). [6400]. 39605

Colson, Alb. Sur la particule dissoute. J. phys. Paris (sér. 5) 1 1911 (721–726). [1925 1690]. 39607

———— Sur la théorie des solutions. Paris C. R. Acad. sci. 153 1911 (719–721). [1920 6250]. 39608

———— La théorie des solutions et les chaleurs de dissolution. Paris C. R. Acad. sci. 153 1911 (812–814). [1920 6250]. 39609

———— La dissolécule et la formule de Van't Hoff. Paris C. R. Acad. sci. 153 1911 (1074–1076). [1920 1925]. 39610

Colson, Abh. La théorie des dissolutions vis-à-vis de l'expérience (cas du peroxyde d'azote). Paris C. R. Acad. sci. 154 1912 (276–279). [2457]. 39611

Colver-Glauert, E. r. Hilpert, S.

Comanducci, Ezio. Influenza delle scariche elettriche oscure sovra alcuni miscugli di gas e vapori. Rend. Soc. chim. ital. Roma (Ser. 2) 1 1909 (102–104); Gazz. chim. ital. Palermo 40 1. sem 1910 (660–602). [6845]. 39612

Combebiac, G. Les actions à distance. Paris (Gauthier-Villars) 1910 (90). 22 cm. [0700]. 39613

Comey, Arthur M[essinger] and **Backus,** Cecil F. The coefficient of expansion of glycerine. J. Ind. Engin. Chem. Easton Pa. 2 1910 (11–16 with tables). [1430]. 39614

Contarino, Francesco. Effetto della deformazione che subisce la sezione di un fascio di luce parallela traversante l'atmosfera terrestre sulle misure fotometriche che si fanno su di esso. Napoli (Tip. R. Acc. sci. 1910 (58 con 1 tav.). 25 cm. [3010]. 39615

Contino, A. Sulla misura della profondità della camera anteriore [occhio]. Clinica ocul. Roma 12 1910 (377–401). [4410]. 39616

———— Sulla determinazione del diametro della pupilla. Clinica ocul. Roma 13 1911 (761–776). [4410]. 39617

Conway, A. W. On the application of quaternions to some recent developments of electrical theory. Dublin Proc. R. Irish Acad. 29 (sec. A) 1911 (1–9). [6620 4940]. 39618

Cook, S. S. r. Parsons, C. A.

Cooke, H. L. r. Richardson, O. W.

Cooper, W. R. The Benkö primary battery and its applications. London J. Inst. Electr. Engin. 46 1911 (741–760); London Proc. Physic. Soc. 23 1911 (374–375). [5610]. 39619

Coppadoro, Angelo. L'accumulatore Edison 1910. Industria Milano 25 1911 (196–198 230–232 263–266). [5620]. 39620

Corbino, Orso Mario. La massa del-l'energia. Nuovo Cimento Pisa (Ser. 5) 20 1910 (462-469); [sunto] Riv. fis. mat. sc. nat. Pavia 23 1911 (466-469). [0500]. 39621

——— Dopo cinquant' anni dalla scoperta dell'anello di Pacinotti. Atti Soc. ital. prog. sci. Roma 4 1911 (131-138). [6400]. 39622

——— Variazioni periodiche di resistenza dei filamenti sottili percorsi da correnti alternate, e deduzione delle loro proprietà termiche a temperatura elevata. Nuovo Cimento Pisa (Ser. 6) 1 1911 (123-131); Roma Rend. Acc. Lincei (Ser. 5) 20 1. sem. 1911 (222-228); (d. Uebers.) Physik. Zs. Leipzig 12 1911 (292-295). [5660 5705 5720]. 39623

——— Azioni elettromagnetiche dovute agli ioni dei metalli deviati dalla traiettoria normale per effetto di un campo. Nuovo Cimento Pisa (Ser. 6) 1 1911 (397-420); [sunto] Riv. fis. mat. sc. nat. Pavia 24 1911 (270-272); Roma Rend. Acc. Lincei (Ser. 5) 20 1. sem. 1911 (342-344); [sunto] Riv. fis. mat. sc. nat. Pavia 23 1911 (371-372). [6455]. 39624

——— Lo studio sperimentale del fenomeno di Hall e la teoria elettronica dei metalli. Nuovo Cimento Pisa (Ser. 6) 2 1911 (39-46); Roma Rend. Acc. Lincei (Ser. 5) 20 1. sem. 1911 (914-920); (d. Übers.) Physik. Zs. Leipzig 12 1911 (842-845). [6455 5675]. 39625

——— Elektromagnetische Effekte, die von der Verzerrung herrühren, welche ein Feld an der Bahn der Ionen in Metallen hervorbringt. (Effetti elettromagnetici dovuti alla distorsione che un campo produce sulla traiettoria degli ioni nei metalli.) (Übers.) Physik. Zs. Leipzig 12 1911 (561-568). [6400 5675]. 39627

——— Azione elettromagnetica di un disco percorso da corrente radiale e disposto in un campo. Roma Rend. Acc. Lincei (Ser. 5) 20 1. sem. 1911 (416-423). [6420]. 39632

——— Forze elettromotrici radiali indotte in un disco metallico da un campo magnetico variabile. Roma Rend. Acc. Lincei (Ser. 5) 20 1. sem. 1911 (424-428). [6455]. 39633

(c-1388)

Corbino, Orso Mario. Rotazione nel campo magnetico di un disco di bismuto, riscaldato al centro o alla periferia. Roma Rend. Acc. Lincei (Ser. 5) 20 1. sem. 1911 (569-574). [6455]. 39634

——— Rotazione in un campo di un disco metallico percorso da una corrente elettrica radiale. Roma Rend. Acc. Lincei (Ser. 5) 20 1. sem. 1911 (746-749). [6455]. 39635

——— I fondamenti sperimentali delle nuove teorie fisiche. Annuario della R. Università Roma (Tip. Feli Pallotta) 1910 (3-29). 26 cm. [0040 0406 0500]. 39637

——— Nozioni di fisica per le scuole secondarie. Ed.3,vol.1. Palermo (R. Sandron) 1910 (144). 22 cm. [0030 0050]. 39638

Cornec, Eugène. Étude cryoscopique de quelques acides minéraux et de quelques phénols. Paris C. R. Acad. sci. 153 1911 (341-343). [1920]. 39639

Costantino, A. v. Mascarelli, L.

Costanzi, Giulio. La distribuzione della gravità in Europa specialmente in relazione coi sollevamenti montuosi. Riv. fis. mat. sc. nat. Pavia 22 1910 (23-39 115-130 237-259); 21 1910 (113-150 274-291 371-387 con 1 tav.). [0845]. 39640

Costanzo, Giovanni. Misure di radioattività sull'acqua di Fiuggi. Roma Atti Acc. Nuovi Lincei 63 1910 (53-62). [4275]. 39641

——— Effetti fotoelettrici con i raggi β. Roma Atti Acc. Nuovi Lincei 63 1910 (92-96). [4225 6850]. 39642

Cotton, A. On Doppler's principle, in connection with the study of the radial velocities on the sun. Astroph. J. Chicago Ill. 33 1911 (375-384 with text fig.). [3420]. 39643

——— Sur la sensibilité des mesures interférentielles et les moyens de l'accroître; appareils interférentiels à pénombre. Paris C. R. Acad. sci. 152 1911 (131-133). [3610]. 39645

——— Dichroïsme circulaire et polarisation rotatoire. Paris C. R. Acad. sci. 153 1911 (245-248). [4040 3850]. 39646

——— Remarques sur l'effet Doppler-Fizeau, à propos de l'étude des vitesses radiales du Soleil. Radium Paris 8 1911 (9-13). [3420]. 39647

II

Cotton, A. La théorie de Ritz du phénomène de Zeeman. Radium Paris 8 1911 (363–373) ; Rev. gén. sci. Paris 22 1911 (597–602). [4208 6660]. 39648

—————— Sur la pureté des raies spectrales lorsque l'intensité varie rapidement. Note au travail " La théorie de Ritz du phénomène de Zeeman." Radium Paris 8 1911 (404–405 av. fig.). [4208 6660]. 39649

—————— Sur les mesures du phénomène de Zeeman. J. phys. Paris (sér. 5) 2 1912 (97–105) ; Changements magnétiques des raies d'émission des corps gazeux. Radium Paris 8 1911 (33–43 av. fig.). [6660 4208]. 39650

—————— et **Mouton, H.** Sur la biréfringence magnétique des liquides purs. Comparaison avec le phénomène électro-optique de Kerr. Ann. chim. phys. Paris (sér. 8) 19 1910 (154–186) ; 20 1910 (194–275) ; J. phys. Paris (sér. 5) 1 1911 (5–52 av. fig.) ; Berlin Verh. D. physik. Ges. 13 1911 (766–770) ; Physik. Zs. Leipzig 12 1911 (953–955). [6640]. 39651

Cottrell, F[rederick] G[ardner]. The electrical precipitation of suspended particles. J. Ind. Engin. Chem. Easton Pa. 3 1911 (542–550 with ff.). [6890]. 39652

Cotty, André. Chaleur spécifique de l'eau. Ann. chim. phys. Paris (sér. 8) 24 1911 (282–288 av. fig.). [1620]. 39653

Courmont, Jules. La stérilisation de l'eau potable par les rayons ultraviolets. Rev. gén. sci. Paris 22 1911 (332–338 av. fig.). [4225]. 39654

—————— et **Nogier, Ch.** Diminution progressive du rendement en ultraviolet des lampes en quartz à vapeur de mercure, fonctionnant à haute température. Paris C. R. Acad. sci. 152 1911 (1746–1748). [4202]. 39655

Courty, F. r. Rayet, G.

Crain, R. Maschinenbau nach dem Austauschverfahren. [Forts.] Werkstattstechnik Berlin 5 1911 (626–633 712–722). [0807]. 39656

Crandall, S. B. r. Trowbridge, A.

Crehore, Albert C. r. Squier, G. O.

Creighton, E. E. F. Condizioni per la protezione di apparecchi elettrici in America. Atti Ass. elettrotecn. Milano 15 1911 (1006–1012). [6410]. 39657

Cremer, Friedrich. Das Absorptionsspektrum des Toluols im Ultravioletten. Zs. wiss. Phot. Leipzig 10 1912 (349–367). [2850 3860]. 39658

Crémieu, V. r. Danne, J.

Crew, Henry. Handbuch der Spectroscopie, Band V. Von H. Kayser. [Review.] Astroph. J. Chicago Ill. 33 1911 (87–89). [4205]. 39659

Crismer, L. Détermination exacte de la densité des alcools absolus à l'aide de leur température critique de dissolution. Bruxelles Bul. Soc. chim. 1906 (294–305). [1880]. 39660

Crittenden, E. C. r. Rosa, E. B.

Crommelin, C[laude] A[ugust] r. Kamerlingh Onnes, H.

Crowther, J. A. On the distribution of the secondary Röntgen radiations round the radiator. Cambridge Proc. Phil. Soc. 16 1911 (112–120). [4240]. 39661

—————— On an attempt to detect diffusion in a pencil of Röntgen rays. Cambridge Proc. Phil. Soc. 16 1911 (177–188). [4240]. 39662

—————— Further experiments on scattered Röntgen radiation. Cambridge Proc. Phil. Soc. 16 1911 (188). [4240]. 39663

—————— On the energy and distribution of scattered Röntgen radiation. London Proc. R. Soc. (Ser. A) 85 1911 (29–43). [4240]. 39664

Croze, F. Sur le second spectre de l'hydrogène dans l'extrême rouge. Paris C. R. Acad. sci. 152 1911 (1574–1576). [4205]. 39665

—————— Sur le spectre du pôle négatif de l'oxygène. Paris C. R. Acad. sci. 153 1911 (664–665). [4025]. 39666

Crudeli, Umberto. Su la teoria dei fluidi rotanti. Nuovo Cimento Pisa (Ser. 6) 1 1911 (437–442). [0700]. 39667

Cunningham, Ebenezer. The application of the mathematical theory of relativity to the electron theory of matter. London Proc. Math. Soc. (Ser. 2) 10 1911 (116–127). [4940 6410]. 39668

Curie, *Mme*. P. La radioactivité.
Rev. sci. Paris 48 1910 (577-580).
[1275]. 39669

——— Sur la variation avec le
temps de l'activité de quelques substances radioactives. Radium Paris
8 1911 (353-354). [1275]. 39670

——— Sur la distribution des
intervalles d'émission des particules α
du polonium. Radium Paris 8 1911
(354-356). [1275]. 39671

——— Traité de Radioactivité.
Paris (Gauthier-Villars) 1910 t. 1 (126
av. fig. et pl.), II (548 p. av. fig. et pl.).
24 cm.; Autoris. deutsche Ausg. von
B. Finkelstein. Mit einem Bd. der
deutsche Ausg. verf. Nachtrag von P.
Curie. 2 Bde. Bd. 1. 2. Leipzig
(Akademische Verlagsges. 1912 [1911]
(XV + 420 mit Portr. u. 2 Taf. VI +
583 mit 5 Taf.). 24 cm. 28 M. [1275,
6845-5270]. 39673

——— e Debierne, A. Sul radio
metallico. [Trad. Sunto.] Riv. fis. mat.
sc. nat. Pavia 22 1910 (470-472).
[1275]. 39674

Curtis, H. L. and Grover, F[rederick]
W[arren]. Resistance coils for alternating current work. [Abstract.]
Physic. Rev. Ithaca N.Y. 32 1911 (612).
[5650-5705]. 39675

——— v. Grover.

Cuthoertson, Clive and Cuthbertson,
Maude. An optical method of measuring vapour pressures: vapour pressure
and apparent superheating of solid
bromine. London Proc. R. Soc. Ser. A
85 1911 (306-308). [1920]. 39676

Cuthbertson, Maude v. Cuthbertson, C.

Czapski, A. v. Fresenius. H.

Czepek, R. v. Niethammer. F.

Czudnochowski, W. Bogen von.
Ueber einige neuere physikalische Projektions-Demonstrationen. Physik.
Zs. Leipzig 12 1911 (32-39). [0050].
39677

——— Eine einfache Quecksilber-
Elektrisiermaschine. Zs. physik. Unterr. Berlin 25 1912 (40). [5210].
39678

Daghlian, G. R. v. Morgan, J. L. R.

Dam, W[illem] van en Donk,
A[drianus] D[ouwe]. Evenwichten in
het stelsel: zilverjodide, kaliumjodide
en water. [Équilibres dans le système:
(c. 4388)

iodure d'argent iodure de potassium et
eau.] Amsterdam Chem. Weekbl. 8
1911 (846-855). [1887]. 39679

Damour, Émilio. Carnot, Jean, Rengade, Étienne. Les sources de l'énergie
calorifique. Paris (Béranger) 1912
(XXVI + 501). 24 cm. [1040]. 39680

Dangeard, P. A. Action de la
lumière sur la chlorophylle. Paris
C. R. Acad. sci. 151 1910 (1386-1388).
[4225]. 39681

——— Sur la détermination des
rayons actifs dans la synthèse chloro-
phyllienne. Paris C. R. Acad. sci. 152
1911 (277-279). [4225]. 39682

Daniele, E. Sul problema dell'equilibrio elastico nello spazio esterno ad
un ellissoide per dati spostamenti in
superficie. Nuovo Cimento Pisa
(Ser. 6) 1 1911 (211-229). [0840].
39683

——— Sul problema dell'induzione magnetica di un ellissoide a tre
assi. Nuovo Cimento Pisa (Ser. 6) 1
1911 (421-430). [5430]. 39684

——— Sull' induzione mag-
netica di un involucro ellissoidico.
Nuovo Cimento Pisa (Ser. 6) 2 1911
(131-140). [6440-4940]. 39685

Danne, Jacques et Crémieu, Victor.
Sur la quantité d'émanation du radium
dégagée par l'une des sources de
Colombières-sur-Orb (Hérault). Paris
C. R. Acad. sci. 153 1911 (870-871).
[4275]. 39686

Danneel, Heinrich. Elektrochemie.
I. Theoretische Elektrochemie und ihre
physikalisch-chemischen Grundlagen.
2. Aufl. (Sammlung Göschen. 252.)
Leipzig (G. J. Göschen) 1911 (189).
16 cm. 0.80 M. [6200]. 39687

Danysz, Sur les rayons β de la
famille du radium. Paris C. R. Acad.
sci. 153 1911 (339-341 1066-1068).
[4275]. 39688

Darling, C. R. Heat-insulating
materials: the relation between surface
temperature and efficiency. Engineering London 92 1911 (395-396). [2020].
39689

——— Pirometri industriali.
[Trad.] Industria Milano 25 1911 (100-
102). [1210]. 39690

——— The formation of spheres
of liquids. Nature London 85 1911
(512). [0100]. 39691

H 2

Darling, C. R. The formation of stable columns of liquids. Nature London **86** 1911 (555). [0300]. 39692

Darmois, E. Recherches sur la polarisation rotatoire naturelle et la polarisation rotatoire magnétique. Ann. chim. phys. Paris (sér. 8) **22** 1911 (247–281 495 590). [4050]. 39693

—————— e Leblanc, M. L'arco a mercurio a luce bianca. [Sunto. Trad.] Atti Assoc. elettrotecn. Milano **15** 1911 (941 943). [6080]. 39694

David, Ludw. Photographisches Praktikum. Lehrbuch der Photographie. 2., völlig neu bearb. Aufl. Halle a. S. (W. Knapp) 1911 (IX + 642 mit 26 Taf.). 21 cm. Geb. 10 M. [4225]. 39695

David, W. T. Radiation in explosions of coal-gas and air. London Phil. Trans. R. Soc. **211** 1911 (375–410). [2040 4210]. 39696

Davisson, C. J. Positive thermions from salts of alkali earths. [Abstract.] Physic. Rev. Ithaca N.Y. **32** 1911 (620). [6800 4960]. 39697

—————— The rôle played by gases in the emission of positive thermions from salts. [Abstract.] Physic. Rev. Ithaca N.Y. **32** 1911 (620). [6800 4960]. 39698

Day, Arthur L. and **Sosman, Robert B.** High temperature gas thermometry. [With an investigation of the metals by E. T. Allen.] Washington (Carnegie Inst. Pub. No. 157) 1911 (vi + 129 with ff. front. tables). 25 cm. [1200 1810 2425 1450 1410]. 39699

Debierne, A. v. Curie, P.

Debye, P. Die Frage nach der atomistischen Struktur der Energie. Zürich Vierteljahrschr. Natf. Ges. **56** 1911 (156–167). [0100]. 39700

—————— Einige Resultate einer kinetischen Theorie der Isolatoren. (Vorl. Mitt.) Physik. Zs. Leipzig **13** 1912 (97 100). [5250]. 39701

Dechend, H. v. und **Hammer, W.** Bemerkung zu der Mitteilung der Herren E. Gehrcke und O. Reichenheim : Über das Dopplerspektrum der Wasserstoffkanalstrahlen. Berlin Verh. D. physik. Ges. **13** 1911 (203 205 312). [6845]. 39702

Dechend, H. v. und **Hammer, W.** Ueber positive Strahlen. (Vorl. Mitt.) Freiburg i. B. Ber. natf. Ges. **18** 1911 (67 71). [6840]. 39703

—————— Spezifische chemische Wirkungen von Kanalstrahlen verschiedener Elemente. Freiburg i. B. Ber. natf. Ges. **18** 1911 (127–132); Zs. Elektroch. Halle **17** 1911 (235 238). [6840 6845]. 39704

—————— Bericht über die Kanalstrahlen im elektrischen und magnetischen Feld. Jahrb. Radioakt. Leipzig **8** 1911 (31 91 mit 1 Taf.). [6845]. 39705

Deckert, A. A. Temperaturmessung mittelst eines Widerstandsthermometers. Elektroch. Zs. Berlin **18** 1911 (91 97 126 131 160 163); Diss. Tübingen. Berlin (Druck v. S. Scholem) 1911 (35 mit Taf.). 22 cm. [1230 1840]. 39707

Décombe, L. Sur la nature de la chaleur non compensée. J. phys. Paris (sér. 5) **1** 1911 (359 372). [2415]. 39708

—————— Sur l'interprétation mécanique du principe de Carnot-Clausius. Paris C. R. Acad. sci. **151** 1910 (1044–1047). [2415]. 39709

—————— Sur la définition de l'entropie et de la température. Les systèmes monocycliques. Paris C. R. Acad. sci. **152** 1911 (81 83). [2415]. 39710

—————— Sur une interprétation mécanique de la chaleur non compensée. Paris C. R. Acad. sci. **152** 1911 (315–318). [2415]. 39711

—————— Sur une interprétation physique de la chaleur non compensée. Paris C. R. Acad. sci. **152** 1911 (1300–1302). [2415]. 39712

—————— Sur la chaleur de Siemens. Paris C. R. Acad. sci. **152** 1911 (1755–1758). [2415]. 39713

—————— La chaleur de Siemens et la notion de capacité. Paris C. R. Acad. sci. **153** 1911 (1469–1472). [5250]. 39714

—————— Théorie électronique des phénomènes diélectriques résiduels. Application à la chaleur de Siemens. J. phys. Paris (sér. 5) **2** 1912 (181–196 av. pl.). [5252 4960]. 39715

—————— Sur la théorie des diélectriques. Paris C. R. Acad. sci. **154** 1912 (191 193). [5250]. 39716

Dele, L. Ueber den Einfluss von Rohrzuckerzusatz auf die Genauigkeit des Kupfervoltameters. Zs. Elektroch. Halle **17** 1911 (238–239). [6010]. 39717

Defregger, Robert. Neue Untersuchungsmethode orthochromatischer Platten. Phot. Rdsch. Halle **1912** (69–73). [4225]. 39718

Deguisne, C. Messmethoden in Stationen für drahtlose Telegraphie. Frankfurt a. M. Jahresber. physik. Ver. **1909-1910** 1911 (53–55). [6615]. 39719

De Heen, P. La succession des étapes de l'élévation des sciences physiques et les théories hybrides modernes. Bruxelles Bul. Acad. roy. **1905** (678–699). [0010]. 39720

————— Contribution à l'analyse du phénomène de l'induction électrostatique. Bruxelles Bul. Acad. roy. **1906** (139–167). [5220]. 39721

————— Coup d'œil rétrospectif sur la science de l'électricité. Bruxelles Bul. Acad. roy. **1908** (650–661). [0010]. 39722

————— Considérations sur la signification physique du potentiel électrique. Bruxelles Bul. Acad. roy. **1909** (1066–1076 1910 426–511); **1910** (209–224 306–331). [5240]. 39723

Dehn, Frank B. Ueber die Abhängigkeit der Umlagerungsgeschwindigkeit des β-Dimethensteinsäureesters von der Dissoziationskraft der Lösungsmittel. Diss. Jena (Druck v. A. Kämpfe); Physik. Zs. Leipzig **12** 1911 (285–291). [2000]. 39724

De Keyser, Ch. Note sur l'exposé des principes élémentaires de la thermodynamique par la notion de l'entropie. Bruxelles Bul. Techn. Ass. ing. **1909** (281–305). [2415]. 39725

Delambre, J. B. J. Grandeur et figure de la Terre, ouvrage augmenté de notes, de cartes et publié par les soins de G. Bigourdan. Paris (Gauthier-Villars) 1912 (viii + 402). 24 cm. [0807]. 39726

————— v. Méchain.

Delbet, P. v. Bouasse, H.

Delépine, Marcel. Nouveaux cas d'oxydabilité spontanée avec phosphorescence. Paris C. R. Acad. sci. **150** 1910 (1607–1608). [4220]. 39727

Delgrosso, C. v. Campetti, A.

Dellinger, T. H. The temperature coefficient of resistance of copper. Washington D.C. Dept. Comm. Lab. Bull. Bur. Stand. **7** 1911 (71–101 with tables); [sunto trad.] Atti Ass. elettrotecn. Milano **15** 1911 (456–458). [5660]. 39728

————— The expression of resistivity of electrical conductors. Elect. London **67** 1911 (708–709). [5660]. 39729

————— Note on a variable low resistance. Physic. Rev. Ithaca N.Y. **33** 1911 (215–216). [5660]. 39730

————— v. Wolff. F. A.

Delvalez, J. Sur la figuration des lignes équipotentielles dans un électrolyseur. Réclamation de priorité. Paris C. R. Acad. sci. **153** 1911 (1474–1475). [6240]. 39732

Dember, H. Ueber den Einfluss von Radiumstrahlen auf die lichtelektrische Empfindlichkeit der Metalle. Berlin Verh. D. physik. Ges. **13** 1911 (313–327). [6850 4275]. 39733

————— Über eine Methode zur Erzeugung sehr weicher Röntgenstrahlen im äussersten Vakuum. Berlin Verh. D. physik. Ges. **13** 1911 (601–606). [6850 6840 4240]. 39734

Delemer. Sulla corrispondente delle impressioni sulla retina prodotte sui due occhi nell' atto della visione. [Sunto.] Riv. fis. mat. sc. nat. Pavia **20** 1909 (266–267). [4440]. 39735

————— La vibration pendulaire, son rôle véritable en acoustique. Bruxelles Ann. Soc. sci. **1910** (149–163). [9000]. 39736

————— Über das „Weiss" auf Autochromplatten. Zs. wiss. Phot. Leipzig **10** 1911 (68). [4225]. 39737

Deslandres, H. Recherches sur les mouvements des couches atmosphériques solaires par le déplacement des raies spectrales. Dissymétrie et particularités du phénomène. Paris C. R. Acad. sci. **152** 1911 (233–139 av. fig.). [3420]. 39738

————— Explication simple des protubérances solaires et d'autres phénomènes par des champs magnétiques très faibles. Paris C. R. Acad. sci. **152** 1911 (1433–1439 av. fig.). [3420 4960]. 39739

Deslandres, H. Remarques complémentaires sur les champs magnétiques faibles de l'atmosphère solaire. Paris C. R. Acad. sci. **152** 1911 (1541–1544). [3420 4960]. 39740

———— Ionisation des gaz solaires. Relations entre le rayonnement et la rotation des corps célestes. Paris C. R. Acad. sci. **153** 1911 (10–15). [3420 6805]. 39741

———— Remarques sur les mouvements des protubérances solaires. Paris C. R. Acad. sci. **153** 1911 (221–225). [3420 6805]. 39742

———— et d'Azambuja, L. Vitesse de rotation des filaments noirs dans la couche supérieure de l'atmosphère solaire. Paris C. R. Acad. sci. **153** 1911 (442–451). [3420]. 39743

———— et Burson, V. Lois relatives aux mouvements des protubérances solaires. Paris C. R. Acad. sci. **152** 1911 (1281–1284). [3420]. 39744

Dessauer, Friedrich. Versuche mit Funkeninduktoren und Röntgenröhren. Physik. Zs. Leipzig **12** 1911 (14–17). [6040 4275]. 39745

———— Einige technische Neuerungen. Verh. D. Röntgenges. Hamburg **7** 1911 (145–147). [6080]. 39746

Dettmar, Geo[rg]. Erläuterungen zu den Normalien für Bewertung und Prüfung von elektrischen Maschinen und Transformatoren . . . Im Auftr. des Verbandes deutscher Elektrotechniker hrsg. 3 Aufl. Berlin (J. Springer) 1911 (116). 21 c.m. Geb. 2,40 M. [6000]. 39747

Deuss, Elsa. Bestimmung des Wärmeausdehnungskoeffizienten der spezifischen Wärme und der Schmelzwärme des Rubidiums und der spezifischen Wärme des Cadmiums. Zürich Vierteljahrschr. Natf. Ges. **56** 1911 (15–41). [1410 1620 1670]. 39748

Deuss, J[oseph] J[ohan] B[althasar] c. Schreinemakers. F. A. H.

Deutsch, W. Über das Blondel-Le Roysche Annäherungsverfahren zur Berechnung von Hochspannungs-Kraftübertragung. Elektrot. Zs. Berlin **32** 1911 (56 58 83 86). [6460]. 39749

———— Die elektrische Festigkeit der Kabel. Elektrot. Zs. Berlin **32** 1911 (1175–1179). [6460]. 39750

Deutschmann, W[alter]. Die Volumänderung binärer Gemische. Diss. Berlin (Druck v. G. Schade) 1911 (55). 22 cm. 39751

Devaux-Charbonnel. Mesure directe de l'affaiblissement et de la caractéristique des lignes téléphoniques. Paris C. R. Acad. sci. **152** 1911 (951–952). [6485]. 39752

Deventer, Ch[arles] M[arius] van. Over de zelfveredeling met een semiisolator in betrekking tot concentratiecellen. [Ueber Selbstveredlung mit einem Semi-Isolator in Bezug auf Konzentrationszellen.] Amsterdam Chem. Weekbl. **8** 1911 (168 472). [6210]. 39753

Devoto, A. Forni elettrici industriali. Riv. maritt. Roma 3. trim. 1911 (191–193). [6090]. 39754

Dexheimer, Arthur. Ueber die Darstellung anorganischer Kolloide in kolloidalen organischen Medien. Diss. Erlangen (Druck v. E. Th. Jacob) 1910 (58). 22 cm [0340]. 39755

Dibbern, E. Über Empfindlichkeitserhöhung der Drehspulgalvanometer. Zs. Instrumentenk. Berlin **31** 1911 (105–112). [6010]. 39756

Dick, J. R. Abnormal pressure rises on H. T. alternating circuits. Elect. London **67** 1911 (629–631). [6450 6460]. 39757

Dickson, Ernest. Über die ultraviolette Fluoreszenz des Benzols und einiger seiner Derivate. Zs. wiss. Phot. Leipzig **10** 1911 (166–189 181–199); Diss. Bonn. Leipzig (J. A. Barth) 1911 (37). 24 cm. [3860 4205]. 39758

Dickson, J. D. Hamilton. Thermoelectric diagram from —200°C to 100°C deduced from the observations of Professors Dewar and Fleming. Edinburgh Trans. R. Soc. **47** 1911 (737–791). [5710]. 39759

Dieckmann, Max. Thermischer Indikator zur Resonanzbestimmung nach der Nullmethode. (Bemerkung zu der Mitteilung von L. Isakow.) Physik. Zs. Leipzig **13** 1912 (165). [6643]. 39760

———— Drahtlos telegraphischer Orientierungs- und meteorologischer Beratungsdienst für die Luftschiffahrt. Zs. Flugtechnik München **2** 1911 (184–187 196–197). [6615]. 39761

Dieckmann, Max. Drahtlos-telegraphische Luftschiflorienterung. Zs. Flugtechnik München 2 1911 (293–295). [6615]. 39762

—— —— Das Elektrometerwehr. Physik. Zs. Leipzig 13 1912 (108–112). [6905]. 39763

Dieckmann, Theodor r. Hilpert, S.

Diesselhorst, H. Über die Berechnung von Drehspulgalvanometern und die Beschreibung einer Neukonstruktion. Zs. Instrumentenk. Berlin 31 1911 (247–255 276–288). [6010]. 39764

Dieterici, C. Zur Theorie der Zustandsgleichung. Ann. Physik Leipzig (4. Folge) 35 1911 (220–242). [1800 1450 0200]. 39765

Dike, Paul H[arrison]. Photoelectric potentials of thin cathode films. Physic. Rev. Ithaca N.Y. 32 1911 (631–632). [5260]. 39766

Dina, Alberto. La risonanza in circuiti contenenti ferro. Atti Ass. elettrotecn. Milano 15 1911 (15 30). [6610]. 39767

—— —— —— Misura delle resistenze di isolamento in un impianto a corrente alternativa durante l'esercizio. Atti Ass. elettrotecn. Milano 15 1911 (983–987); Industria Milano 25 1911 (625–627 650–651 666–667 764–765 777–779). [5770]. 39768

—— —— —— Sopra alcuni metodi di prevenzione delle sovratensioni interne. Atti Ass. elettrotecn. Milano 15 1911 (1015–1016); Elettricista Roma (Ser. 2) 10 1911 (309–311). [6440 6450]. 39769

Dittmann, Ernst. Berechnung elektrischer Leitungsnetze. Strelitz i. M. (M. Hittenkofer) [1911] (108). 28 cm. 5 M. [5630]. 39772

Dixon, Henry H. A thermo-electric method of cryoscopy. Dublin Proc. R. Soc. 13 1911 (49–62). [1230]. 39773

Dobson, G. M. B. r. Searle, G. F. C.

Dochmann, Abraham. F. W. Ostwalds Energetik. 1. Teil. Diss. Bern 1908 (IV + 59). 22 cm. [0000]. 39774

Dodonow, Jacob r. Meisenheimer, J.

Doelter, Cornelio. Allgemeines über Gleichgewichte in Silikatschmelzen. Zs. Elektroch. Halle 17 1911 (795 800). [1810]. 39775

—— —— Ueber den amorphen und den kristallinen Zustand. Gedenkboek van Bemmelen. Helder (C. de Boer) 1910 (232 239). 10 [0400 0340]. 35818

—— —— und Sirk, H. Beitrag zur Radioactivität der Minerale. (1. Mitt.) Wien SitzBer. Ak. Wiss. 119 1910 (181–190). 10 [4275]. 35819

—— —— —— Die Bestimmung des Absolutwertes der Viskosität bei Silikatschmelzen. Wien SitzBer. Ak. Wiss. Abt. 1. 120 1911 (659–669). [0325]. 39776

Dorge, O. Schulversuche aus der Akustik. Zs. physik. Unterr. Berlin 24 1911 (11–17). [9030 9310 9050]. 39777

—— —— Siedepunktserhöhung bei erhöhtem Druck. Zs. physik. Unterr. Berlin 25 1912 (39). [0050]. 39778

Dokulil, Th. Neue Ablesevorrichtungen für Teilkreise. Mechaniker Berlin 19 1911 (85–88). [0807]. 39779

Dolch, Moritz. Das Verhalten von Zinnano len in Natronlauge. Diss. Dresden. Borna-Leipzig (Druck v. R. Noske) 1911 (VI + 111). 23 cm. [6230]. 39780

Domke, J[ohannes] und **Reimerdes, E[rnst].** Handbuch der Aräometrie nebst einer Darstellung der gebräuchlichsten Methoden zur Bestimmung der Dichte von Flüssigkeiten . . . Berlin (J. Springer) 1912 (XII + 235 + 115). 24 cm. 12 M. [0810 0845 0300]. 39781

Donati, Luigi. Sulla distribuzione del potenziale nelle reti di fili conduttori. Bologna Rend. Acc. sc. (N. Ser.) 14 1910 (136–144). [5630]. 39782

—— —— Sul coordinamento dei fatti e delle relazioni fondamentali dell'elettromagnetismo. Bologna Mem. Acc. sc. (Ser. 6) 6 1909 (391–413). [6400]. 39783

—— —— Sugli effetti delle alte frequenze nelle trasmissioni di correnti alternate. [Sunto.] Atti Ass. elettrotecn. Milano 14 1910 (735–756). [6460]. 39784

Donau, Julius. Ueber die Herstellung kolloider Färbungen des Glases und anderer Stoffe durch elektrische Zerstäubung im 18. Jahrhundert. Zs. Kolloide Dresden 9 1911 (146–147). [6825]. 39785

Donk, A[drianus] D[ouwe] r. Dam, W. van.

Donle, Wilh[elm]. Lehrbuch der Experimentalphysik für den Unterricht an höheren Lehranstalten. 5. u. 6. verb. Aufl. Stuttgart (Fr. Grub) 1911 (VIII + 397 mit 4 Taf.). 23 cm. Geb. 3.60 M. [0030]. 39786

Donnan, F. G. Theorie der Membrangleichgewichte und Membrampotentiale bei Vorhandensein von nicht dialysierenden Elektrolyten. Ein Beitrag zur physikalisch-chemischen Physiologie. Zs. Elektroch. Halle. 17 1911 (572–581). [6245]. 39787

Dorn, E[rnst]. Die Erzeugung kathodenstrahlartiger Sekundärstrahlen durch Röntgenstrahlen. (Eine kurze Darlegung der Geschichte der Entdeckung.) Physik. Zs. Leipzig 13 1912 (31–32). [6810 4240]. 39788

Dorsey, N. E. r. Rosa, E. B.

Dosne, Paul. Optique physiologique. Complémentaire d'une couleur donnée, sa détermination par le calcul. Mülhausen Bull. Soc. ind. 81 1911 (173–179 mit 1 Taf.). [2990 4400]. 39789

Douglas, J. F. H. A simple proof of Poynting's theorem. Physic. Rev. Ithaca N.Y. 33 1911 (322–324 with fig.). [4980]. 39790

Doumer, E[manuel]. Weitere Studien über die Arsonvalisation. Zs. med. Elektrol. Leipzig 13 1911 (11–13). [5900]. 39791

Drago, Ernesto. Influenza delle scariche oscillatorie sulla rapidità di smorzamento delle oscillazioni torsionali di fili di ferro. Roma Rend. Acc. Lincei (Ser. 5) 20 2. sem. 1911 (160–167 369–376). [6825]. 39792

Drecq, M. r. Féry, C.

Driencourt, L. r. Claude, G.

Dreisbach. Die Telegraphiergeschwindigkeit in Kabelleitungen. Arch. Post Berlin 39 1911 (65–78). [6480]. 39794

Drexnowski, K. Kondensatory elektryczne Mościckiego i ich zastoso-

wanie. [Les condensateurs de M. Mościcki et leur application.] Przegl. techn. Warszawa 49 1911 (48–52 95–99). [5220]. 39795

Dreyfus, L. Das Vektordiagramm der mehrphasigen Einankerumformer und Doppelmaschinen. Elektrot. Zs. Berlin 32 1911 (5–10 12–13). [6047]. 39796

Drož, Bedřich. O therapeutickém významu negativních ionův (anionův) a elektronu v atmosféře a radioaktivních pramenech. [Ueber die therapeutische Bedeutung von negativen Ionen (Anionen) und Elektronen in der Atmosphäre und radioaktiven Quellen.] Čas. Lékař. Česk. Prag 1911 (7–14). [4275]. 39797

——— O racionálním zacházení rourami Roentgenovými. [Ueber rationelles Verfahren mit Roentgenröhren.] Čas. Lékař. Česk. Prag 1911 (297–300). [4249]. 39798

——— O léčbě emanací radiouvou. [Ueber die Radiumemanationstherapie.] Čas. Lékař. Česk. Prag 1911 (327–331 363 366 395–400). [4275]. 39799

Dracker, K[arl]. Das Dissoziationsschema der Schwefelsäure und die Beweglichkeit des Hydrosulfations. Zs. Elektroch. Halle 17 1911 (398–403). [6250]. 39800

——— Ueber die spezifischen Wärmen der Gase. Zs. Elektroch. Halle 17 1911 (466–472); Discussion. l.c. (849). [1640]. 39801

——— und Kassel, R. Fluidität von binären Gemischen. Zs. physik. Chem. Leipzig 76 1911 (367–384). [0842]. 39802

Drumaux, Paul. La théorie corpusculaire de l'électricité. Liége Bul. Ass. ing. électr. 1910 (193–264 269–304). [5200]. 39803

Drysdale, C. V. The propagation of magnetic waves in an iron bar. Elect. London 67 1911 (95–96). [5420]. 39804

Duane, William. Sur la masse des ions gazeux. Paris C. R. Acad. sci. 153 1911 (336–339). [6805]. 39805

Dubilier, W. An improved wireless telegraph transmitter. Elect. London 67 1911 (931–932). [6615]. 39806 du **Bois**, H. Geradsichtiger lichtstarker Monochromator. Zs. Instrumentenk. Berlin 31 1911 (1–6). [0090 3165]. 39807

———— Neue Halbring-Elektromagnete. Zs. Instrumentenk. Berlin 31 1911 (362–378). [6030]. 39808

———— Der verallgemeinerte Zeemaneffekt in selektiv absorbierenden Körpern. (L'effet Zeeman généralisé dans les absorbants sélectifs.) (Übers.) Physik. Zs. Leipzig 13 1912 (128–136). [4208 6660 6640 4230 4040 5167 3850]. 39809

———— und **Elias**, G. J. Der Einfluss von Temperatur und Magnetisierung bei selektiven Absorptions- und Fluoreszenzspektren. (2. Mitt.) Ann. Physik Leipzig (4. Folge) 35 1911 (617–678 mit 1 Taf.); Berlin Verh. D. physik. Ges. 13 1911 (345–352). [4208 3850]. 39810

———— ———— Hochdispergierender lichtstarker Monochromator und Spektralapparat. Zs. Instrumentenk. Berlin 31 1911 (79–87). [3165]. 39811

———— und **Rubens**, H[einrich]. Polarisation ungebeugter langwelliger Wärmestrahlen durch Drahtgitter. Ann. Physik Leipzig (4. Folge) 35 1911 (243–276). [3855 4010 4020]. 39812

———— ———— On polarization of undiffracted long-waved heat rays by wire gratings. Phil. Mag. London (Ser. 6) 22 1911 (322–342). [4020 4010]. 39813

———— ———— Polarisation langwelliger Wärmestrahlung durch Hertzsche Drahtgitter. Berlin Verh. D. physik. Ges. 13 1911 (434–444). [3855 4010 4020]. 39814

Dubrisay, René. Sur les équilibres chimiques en solution. Paris C. R. Acad. sci. 153 1911 (1076–1078). [2457]. 39815

Ducelliez, F. Étude sur les alliages de cobalt et d'argent. Bordeaux Proc.-verb. soc. sci. phys. nat. 1909–1910 (46–48). [6210]. 39816

———— Forces électromotrices des alliages de cobalt et de zinc. Bordeaux Proc.-verb. soc. sci. phys. nat. 1909–1910 (108–109). [6210]. 39817

Duclaux, Jacques. La dilatation et l'état physique de l'eau. J. phys. Paris (sér. 5) 1 1911 (105–109). [1430]. 39818

———— Absorption des gaz par les corps poreux. Paris C. R. Acad. sci. 153 1911 (1217–1220). [0250]. 39819

———— La constitution de l'eau. Paris C. R. Acad. sci. 152 1911 (1387–1390). [0500]. 39820

———— et **Wollmann**, Mme E. Pression osmotique des colloïdes. Paris C. R. Acad. sci. 152 1911 (1580–1583). [0340]. 39821

Ducretet, E. v. Licret, H., Paillat, J.

Duculot, Henri. Propriétés des rayons X. Liège Bul. Ass. ing. électr. 1909 (251–282). [4240]. 39822

Duffield, W. Geoffrey. The effect of pressure upon arc spectra. No. 3.—Silver, λ 4000 to λ 4600. No. 4.—Gold. London Phil. Trans. R. Soc. 211 1911 (33–73). [4206]. 39823

Dufour, A. Nouvelles mesures du phénomène de Zeeman présenté par quelques bandes d'émission de molécules de corps à l'état gazeux. Ann. chim. phys. Paris (sér. 8) 21 1910 (568–573). [6660 4208]. 39824

———— Rotation spontanée et rotation dans un champ magnétique de l'arc à mercure. Observation du phénomène de Doppler. Ann. chim. phys. Paris (sér. 8) 22 1911 (282–296 av. fig.); J. phys. Paris (sér. 5) 1 1911 (109–116 av. fig.). [3420]. 39825

———— Sur le phénomène de Zeeman présenté par les groupes de raies des spectres du type H. Radium Paris 8 1911 (97–101). [6660 4208]. 39826

Duhem, M. P. Les origines de la statique. Rev. quest. sci. Bruxelles 4 1904 (463–516); 5 (560–596); 6 (9–66); 7 (394–473 508–558); 1905 (463–524); 9 1906 (115–148 383–441); 10 (65–109). [0360]. 39827

Duhem, Pierre. Traité d'Énergétique ou de Thermodynamique générale. 2 vol. Paris (Gauthier-Villars) 1911 (IV + 528) (IV + 504). 25 cm. [2400]. 39828

———— Die Wandlungen der Mechanik und der mechanischen Naturerklärung. Autoris. Übers. von Philipp **Frank** unter Mitwirkung von

Emma Stiasny. Leipzig (J. A. Barth)
1912 (VIII + 242). 22 cm. 6.40 M.
[0000 0100 2400]. 39829

Dumas, Léon. Une nouvelle échelle
thermométrique. Ann. de Gembloux
1906 (650–658). [1260]. 39830

Dunoyer, L. La théorie cinétique
des gaz et la réalisation d'un rayonnement matériel d'origine thermique.
Paris C. R. Acad. sci. 152 1911 (592–
595). [0200]. 39831

—— Recherches sur la fluorescence des vapeurs des métaux alcalins.
Paris C. R. Acad. sci. 153 1911 (333–
336). [1230]. 39832

—— Sur la réalisation d'un
rayonnement matériel d'origine purement thermique. Cinétique expéri-
mentale. Radium Paris 8 1911 (142
146 av. fig.). [0500]. 39833

Dunstan, A. E. v. Hildisch, T. P.

Dunz, Berthold. Bearbeitung un-
serer Kenntnis von den Serien. Diss.
Tübingen (Druck v. H. Laupp jr.) 1911
(III + 69). 23 cm. [1205]. 39834

Durand, A. Il contatore elettrico.
Influenza della natura e dei valori del
carico. Errori. Irregolarità del funzionamento. Atti Assoc. elettrotecn.
Milano 15 1911 (971–979). [6010].
39835

Durkheim, E. v. Bonasse, H.

Dussaud. Nouvelles applications des
ampoules à bas voltage. Paris C. R.
Acad. sci. 152 1911 (689–699 1054–
1055). [6080]. 39836

—— Éclairage à incandescence
réalisant une économie très notable sur
les lampes à filaments de charbon.
Paris C. R. Acad. sci. 152 1911 (1849–
1850). [1202]. 39838

Dutoit, Paul. Volumétrie physico-
chimique. Précipitations suivies par
les conductibilités électriques. Journ.
Chim. Phys. Genève 8 1910 (12–26).
[6210]. 39839

—— — et Mojoiu, Pierre. Volumétrie physico-chimique. Dosage et
séparation des métaux alcalino-terreux.
Journ. Chim. Phys. Genève 8 1910
(27–41). [1260]. 39840

Duval, H. Réfraction moléculaire
de composés azoïques. Paris C. R.
Acad. sci. 153 1911 (871–875). [3860].
39841

Dvořak, V. Bemerkungen zur
Entdeckung der Fallgesetze und über
das verkehrte Pendel. Zs. physik.
Unterr. Berlin 25 1912 (7–11). [0010].
39842

Dwelshauvers-Dery, V. L'évolution
des forces. Alliance indust. Brux elles
1909 (217–226). [0010]. 39843

Dye, D. W. v. Campbell, A.

Dyk, J. W. van. Über die Messung
der Voreilung parallel arbeitender
Wechselstrommaschinen. Elektrot.
Zs. Berlin 32 1911 (99–101). [6060].
39844

Dyke, C. B. v. Fleming, J. A.

Dzierzbicki, J. de v. Kowalski, J. de.

Eagle, Albert. On the curvature of
the spectrum lines in a concave grating.
London Proc. Physic. Soc. 23 1911
(233–236). [3630 3160]. 39845

—— Über eine neue Konkav-
gitter-Anordnung. (Übers. von L.
Glaser.) Zs. wiss. Phot. Leipzig 10
1911 (137–148 149–165 mit 1 Taf.).
[3160]. 39846

Eales, H. Patentschau. Jahrb.
drahtlos. Telegr. Leipzig 4 1911 (326–
333 438–443 551–556 653–658); 5 1911
(112–119 243–249). [6043]. 39847

Earhart, Robert F[rancis] and Pote,
F. W. Distribution of discharge
between a point and plane under
varying pressures. [Abstract.] Physic.
Rev. Ithaca N.Y. 32 1911 (230).
[6820]. 39848

Eberhard, G[ustav]. Ueber die
Verwendung des Spurgeschen Röhrenphotometers für exakte photometrische
Messungen. Jahrb. Phot. Halle 25
1911 (109–111). [3010]. 39849

Eberlein, L. Elektrische Messungen
und Rechnungen. Beitrag zum Un-
terrichte in der Elektrizitätslehre. Ber.
Lehrersem. Frankenberg i. S. 1 (1901–
06) 1906 (VIII + 64). [0050]. 39850

Ebert, Erich. Optische Untersuchungen ungesättigter organischer Verbindungen. Diss. Leipzig. Weida i. Th.
(Druck v. Thomas & Hubert) 1910 (99).
23 cm. [3860]. 39851

—— v. Stobbe, H.

Ebert, H[ermann]. Lehrbuch der
Physik. Nach Vorlesungen an der
technischen Hochschule zu München.

Bd 1: Mechanik. Wärmelehre. (Naturwissenschaft u. Technik in Lehre u. Forschung. Hrsg. v. F. Dolfein u. K. T. Fischer.) Leipzig u. Berlin (B. G. Teubner) 1912 [1911] (XX + 661). 24 cm. Geb. 14 M. [0030 0900 0100]. 39852

Ebler, Erich. Ueber die Adsorption radioaktiver Stoffe durch kolloide Kieselsäure. Vortrag . . . Zs. Kolloide Dresden 9 1911 (158 159). [1275]. 39852A

———— und **Fellner, M.** Über die Anreicherung und Isolierung radioaktiver Substanzen durch „fraktionierte Adsorption". Berlin Ber. D. chem. Ges. 44 1911 (2332 2338). [4275]. 39853

———— Über die Adsorption radioaktiver Substanzen durch Kolloide. (Methoden zur Anreicherung und Isolierung radioaktiver Substanzen.) Zs. anorg. Chem. Leipzig 73 1911 (1 30). 39854

———— Zur Kenntnis der Radioaktivität der Mineralquellen. Zs. anorg. Chem. Leipzig 72 1911 (233 301). [4275]. 39855

Eccles, W. H. Note on an electrical Trevelyan rocker. London Proc. Physic. Soc. 23 1911 (204 208). [6900]. 39856

———— and **Airey, H. M.** Note on the electrical waves occurring in nature. London Proc. R. Soc. (Ser. A) 85 1911 (145 150). [6600]. 39857

———— and **Makower, A. J.** Syntony of a quenched spark. Elect. London 66 1911 (673). [6615]. 39858

———— Ueber den Wirkungsgrad der Löschfunkenmethoden zur Erzeugung elektrischer Schwingungen. (Uebers.) Jahrb. drahtlos. Telegr. Leipzig 4 1911 (253 259). [6820 6615]. 39859

Eck, P[ieter] N[oach] van. Triboluminescentie. [Luminescence par pression.] Pharm. Weekbl. Amsterdam 48 1911 (581 588 611 614 654 665). [4220]. 39860

Edelmann, M[ax] Th[om.]. Leitfaden der Akustik für Ohrenärzte. Berlin (S. Karger) 1911 (118 mit 1 Portr.). 26 cm. [9500]. 39861

Eder, J[osef] M[aria]. Relative Aktinität. Jahrb. Phot. Halle 25 1911 (56 57). 39862

———— Ausführliches Handbuch der Photographie. Bd 1. Tl 1: Die photographischen Objektive. 3. gänzlich umgearb. und verm. Aufl. Halle a. S. (W. Knapp) 1911 (VII + 329). 25 cm. 12 M. [3085]. 39863

———— und **Valenta, E.** Photographie. Jahrb. Chem. Braunschweig 20 (1910) 1911 (501 522). [1225]. 39864

Edler, Robert. Ein Beitrag zur Schaltungstheorie . . . Helios Leipzig 17 1911 Fach-Zs. (138 141). [6020]. 39865

———— Ein Wattmeter-Umschalter für Drehstrom-Leistungs-Messungen nach der Zweiwattmeter-Methode. Helios Leipzig 17 1911 Fach-Zs. (446 448). [5705]. 39866

———— Die spezifische elektrische Leitfähigkeit und ihre Abhängigkeit vom Widerstands-Temperatur-Koeffizienten und vom Wärme-Ausdehnungs-Koeffizienten. Zs. Elektrot. Potsdam 14 1911 (385 386). [5660]. 39867

Edwards, Hiram Wheeler. The distribution of current and the variation of resistance in linear conductors of square and rectangular cross-section when carrying alternating currents of high frequency. Physic. Rev. Ithaca N.Y. 33 1911 (184 202 with fig. table). [5660 5705 6460]. 39868

Edwards, Preston Hampton. A method for the quantitative analysis of musical tone. Physic. Rev. Ithaca N.Y. 32 1911 (23 37 with text fig. table). [9340 9450]. 39869

Eginitis, D. Sur les phénomènes physiques présentés par la comète de Halley. Paris C. R. Acad. sci. 151 1910 (291 293). [4200]. 39870

Ehrenfest, Paul. Welche Züge der Lichtquantenhypothese spielen in der Theorie der Wärmestrahlung eine wesentliche Rolle? Ann. Physik Leipzig (4. Folge) 36 1911 (91 118). [4200]. 39871

———— Zu Herrn v. Ignatowskys Behandlung der Bornschen Starrheitsdefinition II. Nebst einer Erwiderung von W. v. Ignatowsky. Physik. Zs. Leipzig 12 1911 (412 413 606 607). [1960]. 39872

Ehrenfest, Paul. Das Prinzip von Le Chatelier-Braun und die Reziprozitätssätze der Thermodynamik. Zs. physik. Chem. Leipzig 77 1911 (227–244). [2435 2400]. 39873

— und Ehrenfest, T. Begriffliche Grundlagen der statistischen Auffassung in der Mechanik. [Encyclopädie d. mathem. Wissenschaften. Bd 4, Abt. 2. H.) Leipzig (B. G. Teubner) 1911 (3–9). [0200 2400]. 39874

Ehrenfest, T. v. Ehrenfest, P.

Ehrenhaft, Felix. Ueber die Frage nach der atomistischen Konstitution der Elektrizität. Physik. Zs. Leipzig 12 1911 (94 104). [6545 0150 4960]. 39875

— Ueber die Frage des Elementarquantums der Elektrizität. (Zum Teil Erwiderung an die Herren E. Regener, R. A. Millikan und H. Fletcher.) Physik. Zs. Leipzig 12 1911 (261–268). [4960 0150]. 39876

Ehrhardt, Erwin. Neuerungen auf dem Gebiete der automatischen Morsetelegraphie. Elektrot. Zs. Berlin 32 1911 (922–924). [6480]. 39877

— Ein Versuch aus dem Gebiete der magnetischen Kraftlinien. Zs. physik. Unterr. Berlin 24 1911 (271–272). [0050 6420]. 39878

— Ein hydromechanischer Apparat zur Erläuterung einiger beim galvanischen Element auftretenden Erscheinungen. Zs. physik. Unterr. Berlin 24 1911 (268–271). [0050 5610]. 39879

Eichberg, Francesco. Nuovo apparecchio per la fotografia metrica. Roma Boll. Soc. fot. 22 1911 (326 330). [3085]. 39880

Eichelberger, C. Zusammenstellung und Ableitung der wichtigsten Formeln der mechanischen Wärmetheorie der Gase in elementarer Abhandlung. Uhlands Wochenschr. Ind. Leipzig 25 1911 (360 362 395 397). [0200 1450]. 39881

[Eichenwald, A[leksandr] A[leksandrovič].] Эйхенвальдъ, А[лександръ] А[лександровичъ]. О движении энергіи при полномъ внутреннемъ отраженіи свѣта. [Ueber die Bewegung der Energie bei Totalreflexion.] St. Peterburg Žurn. russ. fiz.-chim. Obšč. Fiz. otd. 41 1909 (131–153 deutsch. Res.

154); Ann. Physik Leipzig (4. Folge) 35 1911 (1037 1040). [3824]. 39882

[Eichenwald, A[leksandr] A[leksandrovič].] Эйхенвальдъ, А[лександръ] А[лександровичъ]. О магнитномъ дѣйствіи электрической конвекціи. [Die magnetische Wirkung der elektrischen Konvektion.] Vopr. fiziki St. Peterburg 3 1909 (235–250). [6435]. 39883

Eichhorn, Gustav. Der heutige Stand der drahtlosen Telegraphie und Telephonie. Fortschr. natw. Forschg Berlin 3 1911 (137–212). [6615]. 39884

— Über einige Versuche mit Radiotelegraphie auf grosse Entfernungen. Jahrb. drahtl. Telegr. Leipzig 5 1911 (75 106). [6615]. 39885

— Automatische Telephonie. Fortschr. natw. Forschg Berlin 4 1912 (273–299). [6485]. 39886

Eijkman, P. H. Neue Anwendungen der Stereoskopie. Fortschr. Röntgenstr. Hamburg 13 1909 (382–391 mit 2 Taf.). 39886A

— Die Symphanometrie in der Parallaxaufnahme. Vortrag . . . Zs. wiss. Phot. Leipzig 9 1911 (195–200). [3090]. 39887

Einstein, A[lbert]. Bemerkung zu dem Gesetz von Eötvös [für Flüssigkeiten]. Ann. Physik Leipzig (4. Folge) 34 1911 (165–169). [2457 0200 1885]. 39888

— Eine Beziehung zwischen dem elastischen Verhalten und der spezifischen Wärme bei festen Körpern mit einatomigem Molekül. Ann. Physik Leipzig (4. Folge) 34 1911 (170–174). [0400 0840 1620 1600]. 39889

— Bemerkungen zu den P. Hertzschen Arbeiten: „Ueber die mechanischen Grundlagen der Thermodynamik". Ann. Physik Leipzig (4. Folge) 34 1911 (175 176). [2400]. 39890

— Bemerkung zu meiner Arbeit: „Eine Beziehung zwischen dem elastischen Verhalten . . ." Ann. Physik Leipzig (4. Folge) 34 1911 (590). [0400 0840]. 39891

— Berichtigung zu meiner Arbeit: Eine neue Bestimmung der Moleküldimensionen". [Viskosität von Suspensionen.] Ann. Physik Leipzig

(4. Folge) 34 1911 (591–592). [0325 0150]. 39892

Einstein, A[lbert]. Elementare Betrachtungen über die thermische Molekularbewegung in festen Körpern. Ann. Physik Leipzig (4. Folge) 35 1911 (679–694). [0100 1600 1400 4200]. 39893

——— Über den Einfluss der Schwerkraft auf die Ausbreitung des Lichtes. Ann. Physik Leipzig (4. Folge) 35 1911 (898–908). [3490]. 39894

——— Thermodynamische Begründung des photochemischen Äquivalentgesetzes. Ann. Physik Leipzig (4. Folge) 37 1912 (832–838). [4200]. 39895

——— Die Relativitäts-Theorie. Zürich Vierteljahrschr. Natf. Ges. 56 1911 (1–14). [0000]. 39896

Eisenlohr, Fritz. Die Anwendbarkeit der Molekular-Refraktion und Dispersion zur Ermittelung der chemischen Konstitution. HabSchr. Greifswald. Leipzig (J. A. Barth) 1910 (127). 22 cm. [3860]. 39897

——— v. Auwers, K., Roth, D. A.

Eisenreich, Kurt. Ueber die Verwendung von Silberfluoridlösungen im Silbercoulometer. (Mit einer Einleitung von F. Foerster.) Zs. physik. Chem. Leipzig 76 1911 (643–712). [6010 6210]. 39898

Eitner, [Paul]. Die in Deutschland gebräuchlichen photometrischen Methoden. Bericht an den III. Kongress der internationalen Lichtmesskommission in Zürich 1911. J. Gasbeleucht München 54 1911 (1049–1051). [3010]. 39899

Elias, G. J. Anomale magnetische Drehungsdispersion und selektive Absorption. Ann. Physik Leipzig (4. Folge) 35 1911 (299–346). [4040 3850 4050]. 39900

——— Zur Theorie lichtstarker Monochromatoren. Zs. Instrumentenk. Berlin 31 1911 (137–145). [3165 3090]. 39901

——— v. du Bois, H.

Ellinger, Philipp. Untersuchungen an einfach ungesättigten Kohlenwasserstoffen, Säuren und Estern mit semicyclischer Doppelbindung. Diss. Greifswald. Heidelberg (Druck v. J. Hörning) 1911 (65 mit Taf.). 22 cm. [3860]. 39902

——— v. Auwers, K.

Ellis, Ridsdale. Die Eigenschaften der Ölemulsionen. I. Die elektrische Ladung. (Übers. von W. Neumann.) Zs. physik. Chem. Leipzig 78 1911 (321–352). [0340 5220 6240]. 39903

[Elliot, Giulio.] 4 brevetti Jacoviello. Elettricista Roma (Ser. 2) 9 1910 (318–320). [6615]. 39904

——— Contributo allo studio dell'arco Duddell alimentato da corrente alternativa. Elettricista Roma (Ser. 2) 10 1911 (33–35). [6830]. 39905

——— Protezione degli impianti elettrici contro le sovratensioni. Elettricista Roma (Ser. 2) 10 1911 (109–110). [6450]. 39906

——— La Microtelegrafia sistema "Ballerini e Santoni." Elettricista Roma (Ser. 2) 10 1911 (227–229). [6480]. 39907

Elliott, J. W. and Parsons, O. S. Experiments on a mercury arc converter. Elect. London 67 1911 (534–538). [6830]. 39908

Elsässer, Wilh. Zur Bestimmung der Schwingungszahl eines Tones mit der Sirene. Zs. physik. Unterr. Berlin 25 1912 (22–23). 39909

Elster, J[ulius] und Geitel, H[ans]. Über den lichtelektrischen Effekt im Ultrarot und einige Anwendungen hochempfindlicher Kaliumzellen. Physik. Zs. Leipzig 12 1911 (758–761). [6850]. 39910

——— Weitere Untersuchungen an photoelektrischen Zellen mit gefärbten Kaliumkathoden. Physik. Zs. Leipzig 12 1911 (609–614). [6850]. 39911

Ely, Owen. Newton's law and the cause of gravitation. Philadelphia J. Franklin Inst. 168 1909 (121–129 with fig.). [0700]. 39912

Emanaud, M. Fonctionnement interne des générateurs de vapeur. Technique moderne Paris 3 1911 (152–155 355 357). [2490]. 39913

Emde, Fritz et alii. „Feld" und „Fluss". Elektrot. Zs. Berlin 32 1911 (811–812). [0070]. 39914

Emanueli, L. L'autoinduzione e le perdite di energia nei cavi trifasi. Atti Ass. elettrotecn. Milano 14 1910 (513–534). [6440]. 39915

——— v. Barbagelata, A.

Emerson, Cha[rles] J. A new bomb calorimeter. J. ind. eng. chem. Easton Pa. 1 1909 (17–18 with ill. table). |1660|.
39916

Engelhardt. Beitrag zum „Luftwiderstand der Geschosse nach der kinetischen Theorie der Gase". Artill. Monatshefte Berlin 1911 (215–266). |6200|.
39917

Enklaar, C[ornelis] J[acobus]. Het verband tusschen moleculaire refractie en structuur bij koolwaterstoffen met meerdere aethenoïde groepen. |La relation entre la réfraction moléculaire et la structure des hydrocarbures à plusieurs groupes éthénoïdes.] Handl. Ned. Nat. Geneesk. Congres 13 1911 (205–209). |3860|.
39918

Enklaar, J[ohannes] E[liza]. De dissociatie-constante K van het zwavelzuur en het oxaalzuur. |Die Dissoziations-Konstante K der Schwefelsäure und der Oxalsäure.] Amsterdam Chem. Weekbl. 8 1911 (824–829). |1930|.
39919

————— De neutralisatie-curve van het zwavelzuur. [La courbe de neutralisation de l'acide sulfurique.] Amsterdam Chem. Weekbl. 9 1912 (28–31). |6220|.
39920

Enskog, D. Ueber eine Verallgemeinerung der zweiten Maxwellschen Theorie der Gase. Physik. Zs. Leipzig 12 1911 (56–60). |6200|.
39921

————— Bemerkungen zu einer Fundamentalgleichung in der kinetischen Gastheorie. Physik. Zs. Leipzig 12 1911 (533–539). |6200|.
39922

Epstein, T. Die magnetische Prüfung von Eisenblech. Elektrot. Zs. Berlin 32 1911 (334–339 363–368); [nebst Erwiderung von E. Gumlich, W. Rogowski] l.c. (1218–1219 1314–1317); [sunto, trad.] Atti Ass. elettroteen. Milano 15 1911 (459–460). |5435 5440 5450 5466|.
39924

————— r. Bragstadt, O. T.

Ercolini, Guido. Sulle variazioni magnetiche prodotte nel ferro dalle deformazioni. Nuovo Cimento Pisa (Ser. 5) 20 1910 (317 340). |5460|.
39925

————— Sulle variazioni magnetiche prodotte nel nichel dalle deformazioni. Nuovo Cimento Pisa (Ser. 6) 1 1911 (237 268). |5460|.
39926

Ercolini, Guido. Sulla magnetizzazione del ferro per effetto di due campi ortogonali. Nuovo Cimento Pisa (Ser. 6) 1 1911 (375 393). |5430|.
39927

————— Alcuni fenomeni magnetoelastici del ferro e del nichel. Nuovo Cimento Pisa (Ser. 6) 2 1911 (213–222). |5460|.
39928

Erikson, Henry A[nton]. The coefficient of recombination of ions in carbon-dioxid and hydrogen. |Abstract.| Physic. Rev. Ithaca N.Y. 32 1911 (247). |4960 6805|.
39929

Ermen, W. F. A. and Gamble, C. W. Modification in the sulphide toning of bromide tints. London J. Soc. Chem. Indust. 30 1911 (657–659). |4225|.
39930

Erskine-Murray, T. Diluizione del rendimento pratico di un apparecchio di radiotelegrafia. Atti Ass. elettroteen. Milano 15 1911 (1151–1152). |6600|.
39931

————— Der Ursprung der atmosphärischen Störungen in der Radiotelegraphie. Jahrb. drahtlos. Telegr. Leipzig 5 1911 (108–112). |6615|.
39932

Esau, A. Widerstand und Selbstinduktion von Spulen für Wechselstrom. I. Spulen mit einer Wickelungslage. Ann. Physik Leipzig (4. Folge) 34 1911 (57 80); Jahrb. drahtlos. Telegr. Leipzig 4 1911 (490–501); II. Mehrphasige Spulen. Ann. Physik Leipzig (4. Folge) 34 1911 (81–94); III. Einfluss der Dämpfung auf Widerstand und Selbstinduktion. l.c. (547–564). |6460 6440|.
39933

————— Über den Selbstinduktionskoeffizienten von Flachspulen. Jahrb. drahtlos. Telegr. Leipzig 5 1911 (212–217). |6440|.
39936

————— Über den Einfluss der Atmosphäre auf die Dämpfung funkentelegraphischer Sender und Empfänger. Vorl. Mitt. Physik. Zs. Leipzig 12 1911 (798–800). |6615|.
39937

|Escard, Jean.| Metodi di preparazione dei filamenti metallici per lampade ad incandescenza. [Trad.] Industria chim. Torino 11 1911 (377–382). |6080|.
39938

————— Les lampes électriques à arc, à incandescence et à luminescence. Paris (Dunod et Pinat) 1912 (445 av. fig.). 24 cm.
39939

Eschenburg, Behn. Caratteristiche elettriche e meccaniche dei generatori elettrici moderni, avuto speciale riguardo a quelli di altissima velocità. [Sunto.] Atti Assoc. elettrotecn. Milano **15** 1911 (883 888). [6060]. 39940

Esclangon, Ernest. Sur un système de synchronisation fixe ou différentielle. Paris C. R. Acad. sci. **152** 1911 (170–173 av. fig.). [0820]. 39941

———— Sur un régulateur rotatif à vitesse fixe ou variable. Paris C. R. Acad. sci. **152** 1911 (32 35 av. fig.). [0820]. 39942

———— Sur un régulateur thermique de précision. Paris C. R. Acad. sci. **154** 1912 (178 181 av. fig.). [1011]. 39943

Estanave, E. Synthèse des couleurs complémentaires par les réseaux lignés. Paris C. R. Acad. sci. **153** 1911 (1464 1466). [4410]. 39944

Estreicher, Tad. und Schneer, Al. Über die Verdampfungswärme einiger verflüssigter Gase. [Schwefeldioxyd ; Jodwasserstoff ; Bromwasserstoff ; Chlorwasserstoff ; Chlor ; Ammoniak ; Schwefelwasserstoff.] Zs. komprim. Gase Weimar **13** 1911 (133 139 149–153). [1680]. 39945

Estrup, Knud s. Svedberg, T.

Eucken, A. Ueber die Temperaturabhängigkeit der Wärmeleitfähigkeit fester Nichtmetalle. Ann. Physik Leipzig (4. Folge) **34** 1911 (185 221). [2020]. 39946

———— Die Wärmeleitfähigkeit einiger Kristalle bei tiefen Temperaturen. Berlin Verh. D. physik. Ges. **13** 1911 (829–835) ; Physik. Zs. Leipzig **12** 1911 (1005 1008). [2020]. 39946A

———— Die Molekularwärme des Wasserstoffs bei tiefen Temperaturen. Berlin SitzBer. Ak. Wiss. **1912** (141 151). [1640 1660 1610 2455]. 39947

———— Neuere Untersuchungen über den Temperaturverlauf der spezifischen Wärme. Jahrb. Radioakt. Leipzig **8** (1911) 1912 (489 534). [1600]. 39948

———— Über die Temperaturabhängigkeit der Wärmeleitfähigkeit einiger Gase. Physik. Zs. Leipzig **12** 1911 (1101 1107). [2035]. 39949

———— und **Gehlhoff, Georg.** Elektrisches, thermisches Leitvermögen und Wiedemann-Franzsche Zahl der Antimon-Cadmiumlegierungen zwischen 0 und 190 C. Berlin Verh. D. physik. Ges. **14** 1912 (169 182). [5060 5710 2020]. 39950

Euler, K. Untersuchung eines Zugmagneten für Gleichstrom. Kraftbetriebe München **9** 1911 (701 709 726 733) ; Diss. Berlin (J. Springer) 1911 (92). 23 cm. [6030]. 39951

Euler, Leonhard. Dioptrica. Edidit Emil **Cherbuliez.** Vol. prius. (Leonhardi Euleri opera omnia. Ser. III. Vol. III.) Lipsiae et Berolini (B. G. Teubneri) 1911 (VII + 510). 29 cm. Geb. 24 M. [3000 0010]. 39951A

Evans, Evan. Über ein neues, einfaches Zahlenprüfverfahren Elektrot. Anz. Berlin **28** 1911 (998 1000). [6010]. 39953

Evans, E. J. and Antonoff, G. N. The absorption spectrum of selenium vapor and the effect of temperature upon it. Astroph. J. Chicago Ill. **34** 1911 (277–287). [3850 3860]. 39954

Eve, A. S. On the coefficient of absorption by air of the Beta rays from radium C. Phil. Mag. London (Ser. 6) **22** 1911 (8 17). [4275]. 39955

———— On the ionization of the atmosphere due to radio-active matter. Phil. Mag. London (Ser. 6) **21** 1911 (26 40) ; Radium Paris **8** 1911 (63 67). [6805 4275]. 39956

———— On the number of ions produced by the beta rays and the gamma rays from radium C. Phil. Mag. London (Ser. 6) **22** 1911 (551–562). [6805 4275]. 39957

Evesheim, Paul. Weitere Messungen über Wellenlängennormale im Eisenspektrum. Ann. Physik Leipzig (4. Folge) **36** 1911 (1071–1076). [3430 4205]. 39958

Everts, Hermann. Bestimmung der spezifischen Wärme von Luft sowie von chemisch-reinem Stickstoff und Berechnung des mechanischen Wärmeäquivalentes. Diss. (Druck v. M. Strucken) 1911 (52 mit 1 Taf.). 23 cm. [1640 2410]. 39959

Ewell, Arthur W. Rotationspolarisation durch Torsion. (Torsional rotatory polarization.) (Übers.) Physik. Zs. Leipzig **13** 1912 (100 114). [4040]. 39960

Exner, Franz und **Haschek**, Eduard. Die Spektren der Elemente bei normalem Druck. Zugleich 2. wesentl. verm. Aufl. der Wellenlängentabellen für spektralanalytische Untersuchungen. Bd 1. 2. Leipzig u. Wien (F. Deuticke) 1911 (VI + 216 347). 26 cm. Bd. 3. op. cit. 1912 (332). 26 cm. 28 M. [4205 3430 3435 3440]. 39961

Exner, Sigm. Berichtigung. [Betr. : Z. Baronez. Versuche über den sogenannten Metakontrast, Dieses Arch. 140 491.] Arch. ges. Physiol. Bonn 141 1911 (617). [4450]. 39962

Eykman, J. F. Refractometrische onderzoekingen. [Recherches réfractométriques.] Amsterdam Chem. Weekbl. 8 1911 (651-677). [3822]. 39963

Faasch, Heinrich. Ueber die spezifische Wärme von wässerigen Salzlösungen. Diss. Rostock (Druck v. Eichemeyer & Fett) 1911 (59). 22 cm. [1620]. 39964

Fabinyi, Rudolf. A szénképelemzés és alkalmazásai. [Die Spektralanalyse und ihre Anwendung.] Termt. Közl. Budapest 43 1911 (241-255). [3450 4200]. 39965

Fabris, Cesare v. Gnesotto, T.

Fabry, Ch. et **Buisson**, H. Études de quelques propriétés spectroscopiques et électriques de l'arc entre métaux. J. phys. Paris (sér. 4) 9 1910 (929 961 av. fig.). [6830 4205]. 39966

——— Sur le rayonnement des lampes à vapeur de mercure. Paris C. R. Acad. sci. 153 1911 (93 96). [4205]. 39967

——— v. Buisson, H., Kayser, H.

Faccioli, G. La misura delle perdite nelle linee ad alta tensione. [Trad.] Industria Milano 25 1911 (324 326). [6460]. 39968

Faiella, Pasquale. Sistema di telegrafia elettrica con pile opposte e sdoppiamento del circuito. Elettricista Roma (Ser. 2) 9 1910 (225 226). [6480]. 39969

Fajans, Kasimir. Über die komplexe Natur von Radium C. Physik. Zs. Leipzig 12 1911 (369 377). [1275]. 39970

——— und **Makower**, Walter. Über den Rückstoss des Ra C im Vakuum. (Anhang.) Physik. Zs. Leipzig 12 1911 (378). [1275]. 39971

——— v. Moseley, H. A.

Falciola, Pietro. L'acido ortofosforico idrato come solvente in crioscopia. Atti Soc. ital. prog. sci. Roma 4 1911 (767-769). [1920]. 39972

Farkas, Gyula. Alapvetés az elektromosság és mágnesség folytonossági elméletéhez. [Grundlegung zur Kontinuitätstheorie der Elektrizität und des Magnetismus.] II. Mitt. Math. Termt. Ért. Budapest 29 1911 (771-809). [4900 4970 4910]. 39973

Farrow, F. D. Depression of the freezing-point of water by carbondioxide in solution. Wellington Trans. N. Zeal. Inst. 43 1911 (29 33). [1920]. 39974

Faucon, A. Recherches sur les mélanges d'eau et d'acides gras. Ann. chim. phys. Paris (sér. 8) 19 1910 (70 153 av. fig.). [1887]. 39975

——— v. Massol, G.

Favaro, Antonio. Serie decimottava di scampoli Galileiani. Padova Atti Mem. Acc. (N. Ser.) 24 1908 (5 32) ; id. ser. 19. op. cit. 25 1909 (5-25) ; id. ser. 20. op. cit. 26 1910 (5-28). [0010] 39978

Fedotieff, P[avel] P[avlovic]. Ein besonderer Fall des heterogenen Gleichwichts. (Übers. von J. Pinsker.) Zs. anorg. Chem. Leipzig 73 1911 (173 199). [6255]. 39986

Fehrmann, Karl. Maschinen-Kontrolle und Maschinen-Betriebsführung in den Gärungsgewerben. Berlin (P. Parey) 1911 (X + 261). 23 cm. Geb. 10 M. [2490]. 39981

Feige, A. v. Urbain, E.

Fellner, M. v. Ebler, E.

Ferrari, Carlo v. Pizzuti, M.

Ferrara, Gerardo. Su di un sistema di cannocchiale a due obbiettivi, ovvero cannocchiale composto. Riv. Astr. sci. affini Torino 3 1909 (157-166). [3080]. 39982

Ferrero, Michele. La locomotiva, come funziona e come è costruita. Ed. 2. Torino (S. Lattes e C.) 1910 (19 con tav.). 31 cm. [0030 0900]. 39983

Ferri, Francesco. Lo spostamento dell' asse di rotazione terrestre nella massa della terra, in rapporto colle variazioni di latitudine e con i grandi terremoti mondiali. Riv. fis. mat. sc.

nat. Pavia 19 1909 (321 349); 20 1909
(245-261). [0815 0840]. 39984

Ferrié. Sur la mesure des longueurs
d'ondes hertziennes. Paris C. R. Acad.
sci. **152** 1911 (515 518). [6610]. 39985

———— v. Claude, A.

Ferroux, G. Les applications
récentes des condensateurs industriels.
Techn. mod. Paris **3** 1911 (147 150
216 218). [6460 5220]. 39986

Fery, Ch. A prism with curved faces,
for spectrograph or spectroscope. Astroph. J. Chicago Ill. **34** 1911 (79 87
with text fig.). [3155]. 39987

———— Spectrophotomètre à ab-
sorption. J. phys. Paris (sér. 4) **9** 1910
(819 822 av. fig.). [3860 3910]. 39988

———— Nouveau chronomètre
électrique. J. phys. Paris (sér. 5) **1**
1911 (815 820 av. fig.). [0809]. 39989

———— et **Drecq, M.** Sur la
constante de la loi du rayonnement.
J. phys. Paris (sér. 5) **1** 1911 (551 559);
Paris C. R. Acad. sci. **152** 1911 (590
592 av. fig.). [1210]. 39990

Fesch, L. Nouvelles démonstrations
des deux formules fondamentales de
l'électromagnétisme. Liége Bul. Ass.
ing. électr. **1909** (336 340). [6410].
 39991

Feussner, K. Neuer Kompensationsapparat. Elektrot. Zs. Berlin **32** 1911
(187 190 215 218). [6010 5640].
 39992

Feytis, Mlle E. Magnétisme de
quelques sels complexes. Paris C. R.
Acad. sci. **152** 1911 (708 711). [5467].
 39993

———— Étude magnétique du rôle
de l'eau dans la constitution de quelques
hydrates solides. Paris C. R. Acad. sci.
153 1911 (666 671). [5467]. 39995

Fichter, Friedrich. Ueber die
kapillarelektrische Fällung positiver
Kolloide. Zs. Kolloide Dresden **8** 1911
(1 2). [0340 6235]. 39996

Figee, Th. v. Schreinemakers. F. A. H.

Filippi, Eduardo. Sui rapporti tra i
tramutamenti della viscosità della
tensione superficiale del sangue vivente
sotto l'influenza dei vari farmaci. Lo
Sperimentale Firenze **63** 1909 (373 407).
[0325]. 39997

Finazzi, L. v. Bellati, M.

Firth, W. W. Measurement of
relative angular displacement in syn-
(c-1388)

chronous machines. London J. Inst.
Electr. Engin. **46** 1911 (728 740).
[6060 6070]. 39998

Fischer, C. Strahlung von Antennen.
Physik. Zs. Leipzig **12** 1911 (295 303).
[6615]. 39999

Fischer, Emil. Ueber Mikropolarisation Berlin Ber. D. chem. Ges. **44** 1911
(129 132); [In: Handbuch der biochem. Arbeitsmeth. hrsg. v. E. Abderhalden. Bd 5. Tl 1.] Berlin (Urban
& Schwarzenberg) 1911 (572 574).
[1000]. 40000

———— **Holzapfel,** Julius und
Gwinner, Hans v. Über optisch-aktive
Dialkyl-essigsäuren. Berlin Ber. D.
chem. Ges. **45** 1912 (247 257). [4050].
 40001

Fischer, Franz und **Tiede, Erich.**
Ein für chemische Zwecke geeigneter
elektrischer Wolfram-Widerstandsofen.
Berlin Ber. D. chem. Ges. **44** 1911 (1717
1720). [6090]. 40002

Fischer, K. Über die Verwendung
von Kondensatoren in Starkstromanlagen. Helios Leipzig **17** 1911 Fach-Zs.
(213 218). [5220]. 40003

———— Elektro-optische Aufnahme von physikalischen Vorgängen
mit dem Oszillographen. Zs. physik.
Unterr. Berlin **24** 1911 (74 80). [6050].
 40004

Fischer, Kuno. Über die Wahrscheinlichkeit eines Einflusses meteorologischer Verhältnisse auf funkentelegraphische Reichweiten unter besonderer Berücksichtigung einer drahtlosen
Verbindung des Reiches mit seinen
westafrikanischen Kolonien. Elektrot.
Zs. Berlin **32** 1911 (339 341). [6615].
 40005

Fisher, Willard James. The kinetic
pressure-drop correction in the transpiration method for gas-viscosity. Physic Rev. Ithaca N.Y. **32** 1911 (216 218).
[0325]. 40006

———— The flow of a gas in
capillary tube when Boyle's law is not
obeyed. Physic. Rev. Ithaca N.Y. **32**
1911 (433 436). [0325]. 40007

Flade, Fr. Beiträge zur Kenntnis
der Passivität. Zs. physik. Chem.
Leipzig **76** 1911 (513 559). [6230].
 40008

———— Ueber die Passivität bei
Eisen. Nickel und Chrom. Habschr.

Marburg (Druck v. R. Friedrich) 1910
(84 mit Taf.). 21 cm. [6230]. 40009

Fleiss, Christof. Untersuchungen
über die Reibung beim Schreiben in
Russ. Physik. Zs. Leipzig **12** 1911
(391–398). [0090 0800] 40010

Fleissner, Hans. Trübe Medien.
Umschau Frankfurt a. M. **15** 1911 (226–
228). [3800]. 40011

Fleming, J. A. A note on the
experimental measurement of the high-
frequency resistance of wires. London
Proc. Physic. Soc. **23** 1911 (103–116).
[6470]. 40012

——— Thermodynamics. Encycl.
Brit. (ed. 11) **26** 1911. [2400]. 40013

——— and **Dyke,** G. B. The
measurement of energy losses in condensers traversed by high-frequency
electric oscillations. Elect. London
66 1911 (658–660) ; London Proc.
Physic. Soc. **23** 1911 (117–135). [6470].
40014

——— ——— Some resonance curves
taken with impact and spark ball-
dischargers. London Proc. Physic.
Soc. **23** 1911 (136–146). [6470]. 40015

Fletcher, Arnold L. The radio-
activity of the Leinster granite. Phil.
Mag. London (Ser. 6) **21** 1911 (102–111).
[4275]. 40016

——— The radio-activity of some
igneous rocks from Antarctic regions.
Phil. Mag. London (Ser. 6) **21** 1911
(770–773). [4275]. 40017

Fletcher, Harvey. A verification of
the theory of Brownian movements and
a direct determination of the value of
Ne for gaseous ionization. Physic. Rev.
Ithaca N.Y. **33** 1911 (81–110 with fig.
tables) ; Radium Paris **8** 1911 (279–
286). [4900 0150 0200 0500]. 40018

——— Einige Beiträge zur
Theorie der Brownschen Bewegung mit
experimentellen Anwendungen. (Some
contributions to the theory of Brownian
movements with experimental applications.) (Uebers.) Physik. Zs. Leipzig
12 1911 (202 208). [0200]. 40019

——— v. Millikan, R. A.

Florian, Ch. v. Violette, H.

Foch, A. Mesure du parcours des
particules α de l'uranium par la méthode
des scintillations. Radium Paris **8** 1911
(101 104 av. fig.). [1275]. 40020

Föppl, A[ugust]. Einführung in die
Maxwellsche Theorie der Elektrizität.
Mit einem einleitenden Abschnitte über
das Rechnen mit Vektorgrössen in der
Physik. 4., umgearb. Aufl. hrsg. von
M. Abraham. (Theorie der Elek-
trizität von M. Abraham. Bd 1.)
Leipzig u. Berlin (B. G. Teubner) 1912
(XVIII + 410). 32 cm. Geb. 11 M.
[4900 0030]. 40021

Foerster, F[ritz]. Allgemeines elek-
trochemisches Verhalten der Metalle.
(Sammelreferat über die Zeit von
Anfang 1909 bis Ende 1910.) Zs.
Elektroch. Halle **17** 1911 (877–889).
[6230]. 40022

Förster, Gustav. Beitrag zur Theorie
der Seitenrefraktion. Diss. Berlin.
Leipzig (W. Engelmann) 1911 (V + 58).
22 cm. [3210]. 40023

Försterling, K. Formeln zur Berechnung der optischen Konstanten
einer Metallschicht von beliebiger Dicke
aus den Polarisationszuständen des
reflektierten und des durchgegangenen
Lichts. (Mit Beobachtungen von N.
Galli.) Göttingen Nachr. Ges. Wiss.
math.-phys. Kl. **1911** (449–454). [3840
3820]. 40024

Foex, G. v. Weiss, P.

Foix, A. Sur le rayonnement du
manchon Auer et des corps amorphes
en général. Ann. chim. phys. Paris
(sér. 8) **23** 1911 (281–347). [4210].
40025

——— Construction de rayons
marginaux dans les systèmes centrés
aplanétiques. J. phys. Paris (sér. 5)
1 1911 (896–900 av. fig.). [3070].
40026

Foley, Arthur L[ee]. Recent developments in physical science. Indianapolis
Ind. Proc. Acad. Sci. **1909** 1910 (89–100).
[0040]. 40027

Fontenay, Guillaume de. Sur la
reproduction photographique des documents par réflexion (cataphotographie).
Paris C. R. Acad. sci. **152** 1911 (1055–
1057) ; t.c. (1298). [4225]. 40028

Fool, A. v. Bayer, O. v.

Forcrand, de. Recherches sur les
sels haloïdes et les oxydes métaux
alcalins et alcalino-terreux. Ann.
chim. phys. Paris (sér. 8) **24** 1911 (256–
282). [1695]. 40030

——— Sur quelques propriétés
chimiques probables du radium et de

ses combinaisons. Paris C. R. Acad. sci. **152** 1911 (66–69). [4275]. 40031

Forcrand, de. Sur les hydrates des fluorures de rubidium et de cæsium. Paris C. R. Acad. sci. **152** 1911 (1208–1212). [1930]. 40032

Forel, F. A. La Fata-morgana. Paris C. R. Acad. sci. **153** 1911 (1054–1057). [3210]. 40033

———— *v.* Veillon.

Forli Forti, G. *v.* Paternò, E.

Forssbla4, Nils. Ein graphisches Verfahren zur Berechnung des Spannungsabfalles in Freileitungen. Elektrot. Zs. Berlin **32** 1911 (1185–1186). [5705]. 40035

Forster, A. Wie entsteht das „Weiss" auf Dr. Lumières Autochromplatten ? Zs. wiss. Phot. Leipzig **9** 1911 (291–301 mit 1 Taf.). [4225]. 40036

Forsterling, Karl *v.* Galli, N.

Forsythe, William E. A determination of the melting-points of tantalum and tungsten. Astroph. J. Chicago **34** 1911 (353–370 with tables fig.). [1810]. 40037

Fouard, Eugène. Sur une méthode de préparation des membranes semiperméables et son application à la mesure du poids moléculaire au moyen de la pression osmotique. J. phys. Paris (sér. 5) **1** 1911 (627–643). [0310]. 40038

———— Sur un procédé pratique de préparation des membranes semiperméables, applicable à la mesure des poids moléculaires. Paris C. R. Acad. sci. **152** 1911 (519–521). [0310]. 40039

———— L'osmométrie des solutions salines et la théorie des ions d'Arrhenius. Paris C. R. Acad. sci. **153** 1911 (769–772). [6250]. 40040

———— Sur le mécanisme de l'osmose. Paris C. R. Acad. sci. **153** 1911 (1152–1155). [0310]. 40041

Foveau de Courmelles. Identification par les rayons X de cadavres carbonisés. Paris C. R. Acad. sci. **153** 1911 (693). [4240]. 40042

———— L'année électrique, électrothérapique et radiographique. Revue annuelle des progrès électriques en 1909. Dixième année. Paris (Béranger) 1910 (200). 19 cm.; Revue annuelle des progrès électriques en 1911. Douzième

(c-4388)

année. *ibid.* 1912 (384). 19 cm. [0030–4900[. 40043

Fowle, F[rederick] E[ugene]. Smithsonian physical tables. 5th rev. ed. Washington D.C. Smithsonian Inst. Misc. Collect. **58** No. 1 (Pub. 1914) 1910 [1911] (i–xxxiv 1–318 with 335 tables). [0030]. 40044

———— *v.* Abbot, C. G.

Fowler, A. and **Strutt,** R. J. Spectroscopic investigations in connection with the active modification of nitrogen. I. Spectrum of the afterglow. London Proc. R. Soc. (Ser. A) **85** 1911 (377–388). [4205]. 40045

Fraenkel, F[ritz]. Über binokulare Ophthalmoskopie. Verh. Ges. D. Natf. Leipzig **81** (1909) II 2 1910 (223–224). [4470]. 40046

Franck, J. und **Hertz,** G. Über einen Zusammenhang zwischen Quantenhypothese und Ionisierungsspannung. Berlin Verh. D. physik. Ges. **13** 1911 (967–971). [6895–6850–6800]. 40047

———— und **Meitner,** Lise. Über radioaktive Ionen. Berlin Verh. D. physik. Ges. **13** 1911 (671–675). [6845]. 40048

———— und **Pohl,** R[obert]. Bemerkung zu den Versuchen des Hrn. Marx über die Geschwindigkeit der Röntgenstrahlen. Ann. Physik Leipzig (4. Folge) **34** 1911 (936–940). [4240–6845]. 40049

———— und **Pringsheim,** P. Ueber das elektrische und optische Verhalten der Chlorflamme. Berlin Verh. D. physik. Ges. **13** 1911 (328–334). [6805–5685–4207]. 40050

———— and **Westphal,** W. On the question of valency in gaseous ionization. Phil. Mag. London (Ser. 6) **22** 1911 (547–551). [6895]. 40051

———— ———— Über eine Beeinflussung der Stossionisation durch Fluorescenz. Berlin Verh. D. physik. Ges. **14** 1912 (159–166). [6850–6895]. 40052

———— und **Wood,** R. W. Ueber die Beeinflussung der Fluoreszenz von Jod- und Quecksilberdampf durch Beimengungen von Gasen mit verschiedener Affinität zum Elektron. Berlin Verh. D. physik. Ges. **13** 1911 (78–83) ; Phil. Mag. London (Ser. 6) **21** 1911 (314–318). [4230]. 40053

———— *v.* Wood.

Frank, Jos. Über die Schmelzwärme von Kolloiden. Berlin Verh. D. physik. Ges. **13** 1911 (890–898). [0340]. 40055

————— Kontraktionen und Ausdehnungskoeffizienten kolloidaler Lösungen. Diss. Erlangen (Druck v. Junge & S.) 1911 (61). 22 cm. [1430 0340 1920]. 40056

Frank, Otto. Über die „kritischen Randglossen" von Clemens Schäfer zu meinen theoretischen Untersuchungen [über Manometer]. Zs. Biol. München **55** 1911 (537–546). [9100 0835]. 40057

————— Zu den Angriffen K. Hürthles auf meine „Kritik der elastischen Manometer". Zs. Biol. München **55** 1911 (547–561). [0835]. 40058

————— Zur Lehre von der erzwungenen Schwingung. Zs. Biol. München **56** 1911 (398–400). [9135]. 40059

————— Die Theorie des Transmissionsmanometers. Zs. Biol. München **57** 1911 (171–175). [0835]. 40060

————— Die Theorie des Lufttonographen. Zs. Biol. München **57** 1911 (176–178). [0835]. 40061

————— Kymographien. Schreibhebel, Registrierspiegel. Prinzipien der Registrierung. [In: Handbuch d. physiologischen Methodik, hrsg. v. R. Tigerstedt, Bd 1. Abt. 4. Leipzig (S. Hirzel) 1911 (1–50). [0090]. 40062

————— Hämodynamik. [In: Handbuch d. physiologischen Methodik, hrsg. v. R. Tigerstedt, Bd 2. Abt. 4.] Leipzig (S. Hirzel) 1911 (1–378). [0835]. 40063

Frank, Philipp. Das Verhalten der elektromagnetischen Feldgleichungen gegenüber linearen Transformationen der Raumzeitkoordinaten. Ann. Physik Leipzig (4. Folge) **35** 1911 (599–607). [4940]. 40064

————— Über den Zusammenhang von kinetischer Energie und transversaler Masse. Physik. Zs. Leipzig **12** 1911 (1112–1113). [4960]. 40065

————— Gibt es eine absolute Bewegung? Vortrag . . . (Wiss. Beilage z. 23. Jahresber. (1910) d. Philos. Ges. zu Wien.) Leipzig (J. A. Barth) 1911 (1–19). [0090]. 40066

Franz, K. Vergleichende Untersuchungen über neuere Methoden der Lichtprüfung in Schulen. Zs. Hyg. Leipzig **68** 1911 (477–505). [3010]. 40067

Fredenhagen, Karl. Neuere Fortschritte im Akkumulatorenbau mit besonderer Berücksichtigung des Edison-Akkumulators. (Vortrag . . .) Helios Leipzig **17** 1911 FachZs. (577–582 597–599). [5620]. 40068

————— Die Abgabe negativer Elektronen von erhitztem Kalium und Natrium und die Leitfähigkeit der Dämpfe dieser Metalle. Physik. Zs. Leipzig **12** 1911 (398–408). [5685 6805]. 40069

————— Über die Beeinflussung der Absorption des Natriumdampfes durch neutrale Gase. Physik. Zs. Leipzig **12** 1911 (909–911). [3860]. 40070

Frederking, H. Naturfarbige mikrophotographische Aufnahmen auf „Autochromplatten" bei künstlichem Licht. Berlin Mitt. Materialprüfgsamt **29** 1911 (55–56). [4225]. 40071

Freedericksz, Vsévolod. Dispersion und Absorption in Chrom und Mangan für das sichtbare und ultraviolette Spektrum. Ann. Physik Leipzig (4. Folge) **34** 1911 (780–796). [3840 3810]. 40072

————— Einige Zahlen zu den neuen von Herrn Bernoulli aufgestellten Beziehungen zwischen den optischen Konstanten und dem Eigenpotential der Metalle. Physik. Zs. Leipzig **12** 1911 (346–347). [3840 6210]. 40073

————— Sur le frottement intérieur des solides aux basses températures. Thèse. Genève 1910 (IV + 61 av. 10 fig. et 2 pl.). 23 cm. [0325 0840]. 40074

Freimann, Hans. Über Kolloide und deren Bedeutung. Nach dem Vortrag . . . Zs. angew. Chem. Leipzig **24** 1911 (2420–2426). [0340]. 40075

Fresenius, H[einrich]. Chemische und physikalisch-chemische Untersuchung der König-Ludwig-Quelle zu Fürth bei Nürnberg, sowie Untersuchung derselben auf Radioaktivität. Balneol. Ztg Berlin **22** 1911 wiss.-techn. Tl (57–59). [4275]. 40076

————— und **Czapski,** A. Die neue Quelle zu Brambach i. V., die stärkste überhaupt bekannte radioaktive Mineralquelle. Balneol. Ztg Berlin **22** 1911 wiss.-techn. Tl (49). [4275]. 40077

————— Über die neue radioaktive Mineralquelle zu Brambach i. V.

ChemZtg Cöthen 35 1911 (722 723). [4275]. 40078

Fresenius, W[ilhelm] und **Grünhut**, L[eo]. Tafel der spezifischen Gewichte von Alkohol-Wassermischungen bei 17,5° C. Zs. anal. Chem. Wiesbaden 51 1912 (123 124). [0845]. 40079

Freund, Leopold. Fortschritte auf dem Gebiete der Röntgenstrahlen. Wien Schr. Ver.Verbr.Naturw. Kenntn. 51 1910–11 1911 (457–475). [1240]. 40080

Frey, G. Die Prüfung photographischer Objektive. Centralztg Opt. Berlin 32 1911 (32 33). [3085]. 40081

Frey, Hugo. Die physiologische Bedeutung der Hammer-Ambossverbindung. Arch. ges. Physiol. Bonn 139 1911 (548–561 mit Taf.). [9520]. 40082

Fric, R. Sur les modifications subies par les nitrocelluloses et les poudres qui en dérivent sous l'influence de la chaleur. Paris C. R. Acad. sci. 154 1912 (31–32). [0325]. 40083

Friedel, G. et **Grandjean**, F. Structure des liquides à coniques focales. Paris C. R. Acad. sci. 152 1911 (322–325). [4000]. 40084

Friedrich, Kurt. Die kubische Kompressibilität vom Kadmium und ihre Abhängigkeit von der Temperatur. Diss. Marburg i. H. (Druck v. C. Schaaf) 1911 (47 mit 2 Taf.). 22 cm. [0840]. 40085

Friedrich, Walter v. Koch, Peter P.

Froboese, Victor. Versuche über die fraktionierte Kristallisation von Argon. Diss. Berlin (Druck v. E. Ebering) 1911 (51 mit Taf.). 23 cm. [4205]. 40086

Froschels, Emil v. Handek, M.

Froelich, H. Zur Rettung Isaak Newtons. N. Weltanschaug Leipzig 3 1910 (372 378). [9700]. 40087

——— Energie und Entropie. N. Weltanschaug Leipzig 5 1912 (1 17). [0000]. 40088

Frommel, Wilhelm. Radioaktivität. 2. Aufl. (Sammlung Göschen. 317.) Leipzig (G. J. Göschen) 1911 (115). 16 cm. 0,80 M. [4275]. 40089

Frossard v. Melchissédec.

Früh, Jean. Ueber die Abscheidung von Eisen und Nickel aus komplexen Oxalat- und Laktatlösungen. Diss.

Dresden. Weida i. Th. (Druck v. Thomas & Hubert) 1911 (84). 23 cm. [6210]. 40090

Fry, Harry Shipley. Die Konstitution des Benzols vom Standpunkte des korpuskular-atomistischen Begriffs der positiven und negativen Wertigkeit. I. Eine Interpretation der Regel von Crum Brown und Gibson. II. Dynamische Interpretation des Ultraviolettabsorptionsspektrum des Benzols. (Uebers. von W. **Neumann**.) Zs. physik. Chem. Leipzig 76 1911 (385–412). 40091

——— Einige Anwendungen des Elektronenbegriffs der positiven und negativen Wertigkeit. III. Dynamische Formeln und das Ultraviolettabsorptionsspektrum des Naphtalins. (Uebers. von W. **Neumann**.) Zs. physik. Chem. Leipzig 76 1911 (591–600); Druckfehlerberichtigung 77 1911 (128). [3860]. 40092

Füchtbauer, Christian. Ueber Elektrizitätsleitung in gesättigtem Alkalimetalldampf. Physik. Zs. Leipzig 12 1911 (225–228). [5685]. 40093

——— Über eine Methode zur Untersuchung von Absorptionslinien mit dem Stufengitter und über die Veränderung von Absorptionslinien durch fremde Gase. Vortrag ... Physik. Zs. Leipzig 12 1911 (722–725). [3850 3165 0090]. 40094

Furstenau, R. Über Röntgenstrahlendosierung. Verh. D. Röntgenges. Hamburg 7 1911 (132–137). [6080 4240]. 40095

Fujiwara, S[akuhei]. Note on the problem of ice-formation. Tokyo Bull. Cent. Met. Obs. 3 1910 (9–18). [1810]. 40096

——— On the anomalous propagation of sound rays in the atmosphere. Tokyo Su. Buts. Kw. K. (Ser. 2) 6 1911 (132–142 with pl.). [9210]. 40097

——— and **Miyazawa**, T[orao]. On the linear flow of heat in snow on the ground. Tokyo Bull. Cent. Met. Obs. 4 1910 (1–19). [2010]. 40098

Fulcher, Gordon Scott. The production of light by canal rays. Astroph. J. Chicago Ill. 33 1911 (28–57 with table text if.); [abstract] Physic. Rev. Ithaca N.Y. 32 1911 (234). [6845 4270]. 40099

——— The production of light by cathode rays. Astroph. J. Chicago

34 1911 (388 396 with pls. II.). [4270 6845]. 40100

Gabelli, Lucio. Nuove ricerche sperimentali sul sistema di rottura di lamine vitree per squilibrio termico. Roma Mem. Acc. Nouvi Lincei 27 1909 (181–207). [2000]. 40102

Gaede, Wolfgang. Die äussere Reibung der Gase. Habschr. Freiburg i. Br.; Freiburg i. B. Ber. natf. Ges. 18 1911 (133–197). [0325 0320 0200 0835]. 40103

Gaedicke, Johannes. Intermittierende Entwicklung. Jahrb. Phot. Halle 25 1911 (60–63). [4225]. 40104

Gaehr, Paul Frederick. On the relation between the density and concentration of aqueous solutions. Physic. Rev. Ithaca N.Y. 32 1911 (476–491 with fig. tables). [0810]. 40105

Gage, H. P. A heterochromatic photometer. [Abstract.] Physic. Rev. Ithaca N.Y. 32 1911 (627–628 with fig.). [3010]. 40106

———— Ultra-violet from the arc [Abstract.] Physic. Rev. Ithaca N.Y 32 1911 (628). [4202]. 40107

———— The radiant efficiency of arc lamps. Physic. Rev. Ithaca N.Y. 33 1911 (111–127 with fig. tables). [3010 6080]. 40108

Gaglio, G. Il telefono. Milano (Soc. ed. milanese) 1909 (62). 17 cm. [0030 4900]. 40109

Gaillard, Gaston. Recherches sur l'influence de la vitesse sur le compas. Paris C. R. Acad. sci. 152 1911 (309–310). [5440]. 40110

Gaisberg (von), S. F. Manuale del montatore elettricista. [Trad.] Bari (G. Laterza e figli) 1909 (XVI + 314). 17 cm. [0030 4900]. 40111

Gale, Henry G[ordon] and Adams. Walter S[ydney]. The spectrum of the spark under pressure and an application of the results to the spectrum of the chromosphere. [Abstract.] Physic. Rev. Ithaca N.Y. 32 1911 (229–230). [4206]. 40112

———— The pressure shift of the arc and spark lines of titanium. [Abstract.] Physic. Rev. Ithaca N.Y. 32 1911 (438–440). [4206]. 40113

Galeotti, Gino. Ricerche dilatometriche nei processi fermentativi. Rend. Soc. chim. ital. Roma (Ser. 2) 2 1910 (234–235). [1400]. 40114

———— e Porcelli, F. Ricerche di elettrofisiologia secondo i criteri dell'elettro-chimica. VI. Influenza della temperatura sulle correnti di demarcazione dei nervi. Zs. allg. Physiol. Jena 11 1910 (317–338). [5900]. 40115

Galilei, Galileo. Le opere. Vol. 20. Firenze (Tip. Barbera) 1909 (589). 28 cm. [0030]. 40116

Galissot, Ch. Sur l'absorption sélective de l'atmosphère. Paris C. R. Acad. sci. 152 1911 (569–571). [3860]. 40117

G[allé] P[eter] H[elbert]. Echo van geluidseinen bij mist, buiging en terugkaatsing van geluidsgolven. [Echo of sound-signals in mist, diffraction and reflection of sound waves.] Zee Tijdschr. Ned. Stoomv. Rotterdam 33 1911 (982–983). [9220]. 40118

Gallenga, C. Stereoscopio a corsoio per esercizii di visione binoculare. Clinica Ocul. Roma 13 1911 (633–638). [4470]. 40119

Galletti, R. C. Syntony of a quenched spark. Elect. London 66 1911 (570–573); 67 1911 (26–27). [6615 6820]. 40120

———— Eccles, W. H. and Makower, A. J. Syntony of a quenched spark. Elect. London 66 1911 (957–959). [6615 6820]. 40121

Galli, Ignazio. Come si svolse il primo concetto del termoscopio ad aria. Roma Mem. Acc. Nuovi Lincei 27 1909 (59–111). [0010]. 40122

———— Come il termoscopio ad aria fu trasformato in termoscopio a liquido. Roma Mem. Acc. Nuovi Lincei 27 1909 (209–264). [0010]. 40123

Galli, Nadjeschda und Försterling, Karl. Theoretische und experimentelle Untersuchungen über das optische Verhalten dünnster Metallschichten. Göttingen Nachr. Ges. Wiss. math.-phys. Kl. 1911 (58–70). [3840 3820]. 40124

Galt, R. H. v. Wood, R. W.

Gambèra, Pietro Alcune conseguenze dedotte dalla ipotesi moderna sulla entità del calorico e della temperatura. Torino Atti Acc. sc. 45 1910 (563–568). [2400]. 40125

Gamble, C. W. v. Ermen, W. F. A.

Gaus, R[ichard]. Zur Elektronen-theorie des Ferromagnetismus. (2. Mitt.) Göttingen Nachr. Ges. Wiss. math.-phys. Kl. 1911 (118–164). [5480].
40126

————— Wie fallen Stäbe und Scheiben in einer reibenden Flüssigkeit? München SitzBer. Ak. Wiss. 41 1911 (191–203). [0325 6845 4960]. 40127

————— Über das Biot-Savartsche Gesetz. Physik. Zs. Leipzig 12 1911 (806–811). [6410 6420]. 40128

————— Bemerkung zu den Untersuchungen der Herren W. Kaufmann und W. Meier über „Magnetische Eigenschaften elektrolytischer Eisenschichten". Physik. Zs. Leipzig 12 1911 (811–812). [5480]. 40129

————— Das magnetische Verhalten im Magnetfeld hergestellter elektrolytischer Eisenschichten. Physik. Zs. Leipzig 12 1911 (911–917). [5466]. 40130

————— Die Gleichung der Kurve der reversiblen Suszeptibilität. Physik. Zs. Leipzig 12 1911 (1053–1054). [5440]. 40131

Ganzlin, Karl. Untersuchungen über den Bleiglanz-Graphitdetektor. Diss. Kiel (Druck v. H. Fiencke) 1911 (52). 23 cm. [6043]. 40132

Garbasso, Antonio. L'emissione della luce. Atti Soc. ital. prog. Sci. Roma 4 1911 (139–151). [4200]. 40133

————— Sopra un particolare fenomeno di diffusione. Roma Rend. Acc. Lincei (Ser. 5) 20 1. sem. 1911 (197–201). [0320]. 40134

————— L'aereo Artom e la dirigibilità delle onde elettriche. Torino (V. Bona) 1909 (14). 24 cm. [6610]. 40135

————— Fisica d'oggi, filosofia di domani. Milano (Libreria ed. milanese) 1910 (XVI + 192). 25 cm. [2405]. 40136

————— Über die Strahlung einer geneigten Antenne. (Übers.) Jahrb. drahtlos. Telegr. Leipzig 5 1912 (280–285). [6615]. 40137

————— e Vacca, Giovanni. Sopra una vecchia esperienza di Bennet e Volta. Roma Rend. Acc. Lincei (Ser. 5) 20 2. sem. 1911 (239–245). [0010 4900]. 40138

————— Su la diffusione del potenziale elettrostatico nell'aria.

Roma Rend. Acc. Lincei (Ser. 5) 20 2. sem. 1911 (296–302). [6805]. 40139

Gardner, J. Appareil de réception téléphonique de signaux sous-marins. Paris C. R. Acad. sci. 152 1911 (1834–1835). [6485]. 40140

Garten, S[iegfried]. Über die Verwendung der Seifenmembran zur Schallregistrierung. Zs. Biol. München 56 1911 (41–74 mit 2 Taf.). [9120 9020 9140]. 40141

Garuffa, E. Motori a scoppio e loro applicazione. Milano (Hoepli) 1910 (X + 450). 15 cm. [0030 0900]. 40142

Gaubert, P. Sur les indices de réfraction des cristaux liquides. Paris C. R. Acad. sci. 153 1911 (573–576 1158–1160). [3020 3822 4000]. 40143

Gaudechon, H. v. Berthelot, D.

Gauterio, G. e Loria, L. Macchinista e fuochista. Ed. 12. Milano (Hoepli) 1910 (XVI + 271). 15 cm. [0030 0900]. 40144

Gautier, A. Remarques au sujet d'une Note de M. Grenet intitulée "Etude sur la porosité des bougies filtrantes". Paris C. R. Acad. sci. 151 1910 (1016–1017). [0300]. 40145

Gay, L. Sur les mélanges d'acide acétique avec les liquides normaux. Paris C. R. Acad. sci. 152 1911 (518–519). [1887]. 40146

————— Sur la notion de tension d'expansibilité. Paris C. R. Acad. sci. 153 1911 (262–265). [2435]. 40147

————— Sur la tension d'expansibilité d'un fluide normal. Paris C. R. Acad. sci. 153 1911 (522–724). [2435]. 40148

Gebb, Heinrich v. Löhlein, W.

Gehlhoff, Georg. Über die Glimmentladung und Emission der Alkalimetalldämpfe. 2. Mitt. Berlin Verh. D. physik. Ges. 13 1911 (183–192). [6840 4206 4202]. 40149

————— Ueber eine einfache Methode zur Erzeugung von Metallspektren in der Glimmentladung. Berlin Verh. D. physik. Ges. 12 1911 (266–270). [3165 4202]. 40150

————— Ueber eine einfache Methode zur Reindarstellung von Edelgasen, Wasserstoff und Stickstoff. Berlin Verh. D. physik. Ges. 13 1911 (271–277). [0090]. 40151

————— v. Eucken, A.

Gehrcke, E. Bemerkungen über die Grenzen des Relativitätsprinzips. Berlin Verh. D. physik. Ges. 13 1911 (665–669). [4940]. 40152

————— Über die Anwendung der Zylinderlinse in Spektralapparaten. Zs. Instrumentenk. Berlin 31 1911 (87–89). [3165]. 40153

————— und **Reichenheim**, O[tto]. Über das Dopplerspektrum der Wasserstoffkanalstrahlen. Berlin Verh. D. physik. Ges. 13 1911 (111–118). [4205 6845]. 40154

————— und **Wogau**, M. v. Über die absolute Messung des Ampère. Berlin Verh. D. physik. Ges. 13 1911 (470–473). [5000]. 40155

————— ——— Magnetische Messungen II. Berlin Verh. D. physik. Ges. 13 1911 (448–469). [5435 6010 6420]. 40156

Gehrts, A. Reflexion und Sekundärstrahlung lichtelektrisch ausgelöster Kathodenstrahlen. Ann. Physik Leipzig (4. Folge) 36 1911 (995–1026); Diss. Berlin. Leipzig (J. A. Barth) 1911 (64). 23 cm. [6845 6850]. 40157

Geibel, Wilhelm. Über einige elektrische und mechanische Eigenschaften von Edelmetall-Legierungen. II. Zs. anorg. Chem. Hamburg 70 1911 (240–254). [5660 5710]. 40158

Geigel, Robert. Über das Elektron. Arch. physik. Med. Leipzig 5 1911 (99–109). [6845 4960]. 40159

————— Die Wärme. (Bücher der Naturwissenschaft, hrsg. von Siegmund Günther. Bd 10.) Leipzig (P. Reclam jun.) [1911] (191 mit 4 Taf.). 14 cm. Geb. 1 M. [0900 0030]. 40160

Geiger, H. The transformation of the actinium emanation. Phil. Mag. London (Ser. 6) 22 1911 (201–204). [4275]. 40161

————— and **Kovarik**, A. F. On the relative number of ions produced by the β particles from the various radio-active substances. Phil. Mag. London (Ser. 6) 22 1911 (604–613). [4275]. 40162

————— and **Nuttall**, J. M. The ranges of the α particles from various radio-active substances and a relation between range and period of transformation. Phil. Mag. London (Ser. 6) 22 1911 (613–621). [4275]. 40163

————— v. Rutherford, E.

Geiger. Bestimmung der Kapazität eines Elektrometers. Bl. GymnSchulw. München 47 1911 (307–309). [6005 5740]. 40164

————— Steigerung der Empfindlichkeit bei der Gauss-Poggendorfischen Spiegelmethode. (Vorl. Mitt.) Physik. Zs. Leipzig 12 1911 (66–70). [0090 0800]. 40165

————— Über die Schwärzung und Photometrie photographischer Platten. Ann. Physik Leipzig (4. Folge) 37 1912 (68–78). [3010 4225]. 40166

Geissler, J. E. A. Konzentrationsketten mit ternären Elektrolyten. Zs. Elektroch. Halle 18 1912 (131–137). [6255]. 40167

Geitel, Hans v. Elster, J.

Geitel, Max. Entlegene Spuren Goethes. Goethes Beziehungen zu der Mathematik, Physik, Chemie und zu deren Anwendung in der Technik, zum technischen Unterricht und zum Patentwesen. München u. Berlin (R. Oldenbourg) 1911 (VIII + 215). 24 cm. Geb. 6 M. [0010]. 40168

Geller, Walter. Ueber Dampfspannung von Salzlösungen. Diss. Bonn. Düren (Rhld.) (Druck v. Hamel) 1911 (27). 22 cm. [1920]. 40169

Gentsch, Wilhelm. Über Verbrennungsturbinen. Berlin Verh. Ver. Gewerbfl. 90 1911 (194–208). [2490]. 40170

Gerber, Paul †. Gravitation und Elektrizität. (Progr. [der städt. Oberrealschule i. E. Ostern 1910].) Stargard (Druck v. Hendess) 1910 (17). 25 cm. [4940 0700]. 40171

German, T. und **Hills**, M. Ueber die Verwendung und Prüfung von Isoliermitteln. Elektrot. Anz. Berlin 27 1910 (1114–1116 1128–1130 1141–1143). [5252]. 40172

Germann, Albert v. Baume, G.

Gernez, D. Sur un moyen de restituer aux sulfures alcalino-terreux leurs propriétés phosphorescentes. Ann. chim. phys. Paris (sér. 8) 20 1910 (166–173). [4230]. 40173

Geronimi, Ferdinando. Telegrafo Hughes. Milano (Tip. Indipendenza) 1909 (68). 24 cm. [6043]. 40174

Gerrard, H. v. Beattie, R.

Gerstmeyer, M. Versuche über das Ausschalten von Wechselstrom. Elektr. Kraftbetriebe München **9** 1911 (141–148). [6020]. 40175

——— Beiträge zur Kenntnis der Wechselstrom-Kommutatormotoren. Elektr. Kraftbetriebe München **9** 1911 (287–293). [6070]. 40176

Gewecke r. Möllinger.

Gherardi, Bancroft. Die Belastung von Fernleitungen. Zs. Schwachstromtechn. München **5** 1911 (564 566 597 601 620–622 655 657). [6485]. 40177

Ghersi, T. Galvanotegia. Ed. 2. Milano (Hoepli) 1909 (XII + 383 con 5 ritratti). 15 cm. [0030 4900]. 40178

Ghilarducci, Francesco. Azione biologica e curativa della folgorazione. Roma Bull. Acc. med. **35** 1909 (251–259). [5900]. 40179

Ghione, Anacleto. Luce naturale e luci artificiali. N. Ed. Torino (Tip. salesiana) 1910 (59). 19 cm. [4200]. 40180

Gianfranceschi, Giuseppe. Necrologia di Giulio Lambiasi. [Sunto.] Riv. fis. mat. sc. nat. Pavia **20** 1909 (438–440). [6010]. 40181

Giard, A. r. Bouasse, H.

Gibson, Charles R. Was ist Elektrizität ? Erzählungen eines Elektrons. Autoris. deutsche Bearb. von Hanns **Günther**. Stuttgart (Franckh) [1912] (102). 20 cm. 1 M. [4900]. 40182

Gibson, C. E. Bemerkungen zum Planckschen Wirkungsquantum. Berlin Verh. D. physik. Ges. **14** 1912 (104–112). [4200 4960]. 40183

——— Über eine monochromatische Temperaturstrahlung des Thalliumdampfes. Physik. Zs. Leipzig **12** 1911 (1145–1148). [4210]. 40184

Giebe, E. Präzisionsmessungen an Selbstinduktionsnormalen (T) 1. 2.). Zs. Instrumentenk. Berlin **31** 1911 (6–20 33–52). [6440]. 40185

Giersing, E. Fehlerortsbestimmung in Fernsprechkabeln ohne gute Rückleitung. Elektrot. Zs. Berlin **33** 1912 (189). [5770]. 40186

Giesswein, Max. Ueber die „Resonanz" der Mundhöhle und der Nasenräume im besonderen der Nebenhöhlen der Nase. Berlin Anat. Ohr. Berlin **4** 1911 (305–353). [9140]. 40187

Gildemeister, Martin. Theoretisches und Praktisches aus der neueren Elektrophysiologie. Münchener med. Wochenschr. **58** 1911 (1113 1119). [5900]. 40189

Gill, E. W. B. The intensity of the ultra-violet light emitted by an electrical discharge at low pressures. Phil. Mag. London (Ser. 6) **22** 1911 (412–418). [6840]. 40190

Ginneken, P. J. H. van. Das Merkurosulfat als Depolarisator im Weston- und Clarkschen Normalelement. Zs. physik. Chem. Leipzig **75** 1911 (687 709). 40191

——— und **Kruyt**, H. R. Zur Theorie der Normalelemente. Zs. physik. Chem. Leipzig **77** 1911 (744–760). [5610]. 40192

Giovanetti, T. La natura elettrica della materia. Boll. Soc. Ticinese Sci. Nat. **5** 1909 (5–12). [0500]. 40193

Girard, P. L'osmose aux points de vue physique et biologique. J. physiol. path. gén. Paris **13** 1911 (359–371) ; Rev. gén. sci. Paris **22** 1911 (234–240). [0310]. 40195

——— Sur le rôle prépondérant de deux facteurs électrostatiques dans l'osmose des solutions d'électrolytes. Mouvements osmotiques normaux. Paris C. R. Acad. sci. **153** 1911 (401–404). [0310]. 40196

——— et **Henri**, Victor. Au sujet de nouvelles hypothèses sur l'état moléculaire des corps en solution. Paris C. R. Acad. sci. **153** 1911 (946–948). [0310]. 40197

Girardeau, Emile. Conférence sur les progrès des applications de la télégraphie sans fil. Mülhausen Bull. Soc. ind. **81** 1911 (267–287). [6615]. 40198

Girousse, Sur un moyen de supprimer les troubles causés aux lignes télégraphiques par les lignes d'énergie. Paris C. R. Acad. sci. **153** 1911 (97–99). [6480]. 40199

——— Sur la protection des installations à courant faible contre les perturbations provoquées par les courants alternatifs. Paris C. R. Acad. sci. **153** 1911 (1135–1137). [6460]. 40200

Giudice (Del), Italo. Evangelista Torricelli e l'opera sua. Riv. astron. sci. affini Torino **3** 1909 (31–37). [0010]. 40201

Giuganino, Luigi. Action de la translation terrestre sur les phénomènes lumineux. Paris C. R. Acad. sci. 152 1911 (1662–1664 1829–1832). [3420]. 40202

Giulietti, Giulio. Studio sul comportamento del materiale magnetico nel galvanometro del prof. Riccardo Arnò. Milano Rend. 1st. lomb. (Ser. 2) 43 1910 (820–824). [5430]. 40203

Giurgea, Émile. Recherches sur le phénomène de Kerr dans les vapeurs et les gaz. Paris C. R. Acad. sci. 153 1911 (1461–1464). [5250 6640]. 40204

Giuseppe, Ovio. L'image cyclopique dans le miroir plan. Arch. ophtalm. Paris 1911 (710–716). [3050]. 40205

Glaser, F. v. Henrich, F.

Glasson, J. L. The variation of ionizing power with the velocity of cathode rays. Phil. Mag. London (Ser. 6) 22 1911 (647–656). [6845]. 40206

Glatzel, Br. Nouvelles expériences sur l'excitation par chocs dans la télégraphie sans fil. Paris C. R. Acad. sci. 151 1910 (1049–1052 av. fig.). [6043]. 40207

———— Eine neue Methode zur Erzeugung von Hochfrequenzströmen nach dem Prinzip der Stosserregung. Ann. Physik Leipzig (4. Folge) 34 1911 (711–738). [6470 6820]. 40208

———— Die Trägheit von Selenzellen. Berlin Verh. D. physik. Ges. 13 1911 (778–792) : Physik. Zs. Leipzig 12 1911 (1169–1175). [5660]. 40209

———— Eine Maschine zur Demonstration von Wechselstromvorgängen. Berlin Verh. D. physik. Ges. 13 1911 (821–828) : Physik. Zs. Leipzig 12 1911 (1069–1073 mit 1 Taf.). [0050 6045]. 40210

———— Neuere Fortschritte auf dem Gebiete der Bildtelegraphie. D. MechZtg Berlin 1911 (153–158). [6480]. 40211

———— Die neuere Entwicklung der Phototelegraphie. Helios Leipzig 17 1911 Fach-Zs. (473–476). [6480]. 40212

———— Demonstrationsversuch über die Energieaufnahme in Wechselstromkreisen. Physik. Zs. Leipzig 12 1911 (30). [0050 5705]. 40213

———— v. Korn, A.

Glazebrook, R. T. The electromotive force of standard cells. Nature London 85 1911 (508). [5610]. 40214

———— **Bousfield,** W. R. and **Smith,** F. E. The heating effect of the currents in precise measurements of electrical resistance. London Proc. R. Soc. (Ser. A) 85 1911 (541–556). [5650]. 40215

Gleditsch, Ellen. Sur le rapport entre l'uranium et le radium dans les minéraux radioactifs. Radium Paris 8 1911 (256–273). [4275]. 40216

Gleichen, A[lexander]. Über die Helligkeit photographischer Objektive. Mechaniker Berlin 19 1911 (97–98). [3085]. 40217

———— Ueber Helligkeit, Tiefe und richtigen Betrachtungsabstand bei photographischen Aufnahmen. Mechaniker Berlin 19 1911 (217–219 232–234 242–245 255–258 266–268 278–280). [3085]. 40218

———— Über den richtigen Betrachtungsabstand und über perspektivische Übertreibung. Phot. Rdsch. Halle 25 1911 (209–214 223–229). [3085]. 40219

———— Ueber eine bekannte scheinbare perspektivische Anomalie. Phot. Rdsch. Halle 25 1911 (272–275). [3085]. 40220

———— Über Helligkeit und Tiefe insbesondere bei der naturgetreuen photographischen Abbildung. Zs. wiss. Phot. Leipzig 9 1911 (241–255 273–290). [3085]. 40221

———— Die Optik in der Photographie in gemeinverständlicher Darstellung. Stuttgart (F. Enke) 1911 (XII + 223). 23 cm. 6 M. [3085 3000 4225 4400]. 40222

———— Die Theorie der modernen optischen Instrumente. Ein Hilfs- und Uebungsbuch für Physiker . . . Stuttgart (F. Enke) 1911 (XII + 332). 25 cm. 10.80 M. [3000 4000]. 40223

Glikin, W. Kalorimetrie organischer Verbindungen. [In : Die Methoden der organischen Chemie. Hrsg. v. Th. Weyl. Bd 2.] Leipzig (G. Thieme) 1911 (1330–1356). [1610]. 40224

Glinzer. Ein neuer Luftverflüssigungsapparat. Autoreferat. Zs. angew. Chem. Leipzig 24 1911 (447–448). [1870 0050]. 40225

Gnesotto, Tullio e **Binghinotto**, Maria. Costanti magnetiche di leghe debolmente magnetiche. Nuovo Cimento Pisa (Ser. 5) 20 1910 (384–441); Venezia Atti Ist. ven. 69 parte 2 1910 (1313–1401). [5460]. 40348

—————— e **Breda**, Stefano. Il fenomeno Wiedemann in fili sottili di acciaio al silicio. Venezia Atti Ist. ven. 70 parte 2 1911 (1255–1274 con 2 tav.). [5460]. 40349

—————— e **Fabris**, Cesare. Ricerche sperimentali su alcune costanti termiche dell'acetato sodico idrato. Venezia Atti Ist. ven. 70 parte 2 1911 (471–482). [1620]. 40350

Gockel, Albert. Messungen der durchdringenden Strahlung bei Ballonfahrten. Physik. Zs. Leipzig 12 1911 (595–597). [4275 5270]. 40231

Goebel, [Arthur]. Ueber die tonverstärkende Wirkung des über den Stimmlippen befindlichen Ansatzrohres, über den Toncharakter der Vokale und die Verstärkung dieser Töne durch das Ansatzrohr. Arch. Laryng. Berlin 24 1911 (225–230). [9510]. 40232

—————— Über die Ursache der Einklangsempfindung bei Einwirkung von Tönen, die im Oktavenverhältnis zueinander stehen. Zs. Psychol. Leipzig Abt. 2 45 1911 (109–116). [9450]. 40233

Göcke, Curt. Ueber die Schwankungen der Erfolge untermaximaler Reize. Diss. Freiburg i. B. Dresden (o. Dr.) 1910 (38). 22 cm. [5900]. 40234

Goecke, Otto. Der elektrische Vakuumofen und seine Verwendung. Metallurgie Halle 8 1911 (667–676 mit 1 Taf.). [6090]. 40235

Görges, H., **Weidig**, P., **Jaenich**, A. Über Versuche zur Bestimmung der Koronaverluste auf Freileitungen. Elektrot. Zs. Berlin 32 1911 (1071–1072). [6460 6810 5705]. 40236

Görner, J. Neue Ferraris-Messgeräte der Firma Hartmann und Braun A.-G. Helios Leipzig 17 1911 Fach-Zs. (269–271). [6015]. 40237

Götting, E. e. Behrendsen, O.

Gola, Giovanni. Su un nuovo modello di resistenze ohmiche per

scaricatori. Atti Ass. elettrotecn. Milano 15 1911 (427–430). [6000]. 40238

Goldberg, E. La preparazione di prismi o di schermi di tono grigio neutro per usi fotometrici. Boll. Soc. fot. Firenze 22 1910 (315–317). [3085]. 40239

—————— Die Herstellung neutral grauer Keile und verlaufender Filter für Photometrie und Photographie. Jahrb. Phot. Halle 25 1911 (149–155); Zs. wiss. Phot. Leipzig 10 1911 (238–244). [3010 3165 4225]. 40240

—————— Studien über die Detailwiedergabe in der Photographie. Zs. wiss. Phot. Leipzig 9 1911 (313–323). [4225]. 40241

—————— **Luther**, R. und **Weigert**, F. Ueber die automatische Herstellung der charakteristischen Kurve. Zs. wiss. Phot. Leipzig 9 1911 (323–331). [4225]. 40242

Goldmann, A. u. **Kalandyk**, S. Lichtelektrische Untersuchungen an festen Dielektriken. Ann. Physik Leipzig (4. Folge) 36 1911 (589–623). [5660 6850]. 40243

Goldschmidt, Robert. Ueber Wärmeleitfähigkeit von Flüssigkeiten. Physik. Zs. Leipzig 12 1911 (417–424). [2030]. 40245

—————— Un baromètre électrique. Bruxelles Bul. Soc. belge électr. 1908 (661–664); Bruxelles Bul. Soc. roy. sci. méd. nat. 1908 (125–129). [6000]. 40246

—————— La photographie des couleurs. Bruxelles Bul. Soc. chim. 1908 (29–37). [4225]. 40247

—————— Recherches sur un accumulateur léger. Bruxelles Bul. Soc. chim. 1908 (317–327). [5620]. 40248

Goldschmidt, Rud. Maschinelle Erzeugung von elektrischen Wellen für die drahtlose Telegraphie. Elektrot. Zs. Berlin 32 1911 (54–56). [6043]. 40251

—————— Hochfrequenzmaschine für die direkte Erzeugung von elektrischen Wellen für die drahtlose Telegraphie. Jahrb. drahtlos. Telegr. Leipzig 4 1911 (341–347). [6043]. 40252

Goldschmidt, Karl. Drahtlose Telegraphie. Berlin Verh. kol.-techn. Komm. 1911 (23–33 mit 3 Taf.). [6615].
40244

—————— An alternator for direct production of electric waves for wireless telegraphy. Elect. London 66 1911 (744–746). 40249

Goldschmidt, V[ictor]. Ueber Lichtkreis und Lichtknoten an Kristallkugeln. [Almandin; Beryll; Rosenquarz.] Mit Zusatz v. R. Brauns. N. Jahrb. Min. Stuttgart Beilagebd 31 1911 (220–242 mit 1 Taf.). [3830].
40253

Goldstein, E. Über die Untersuchung der Emissionsspektra fester aromatischer Substanzen mit dem Ultraviolettfilter. Berlin Verh. D. physik. Ges. 13 1911 (378–392); Physik. Zs. Leipzig 12 1911 (614–620). [4205 4230 6050].
40254

—————— Zur Orientierung an Spektrogrammen. Berlin Verh. D. physik. Ges. 13 1911 (419–422). [3165].
40255

—————— Notiz über farbige Projektion ungefärbter Spektrogramme. Berlin Verh. D. physik. Ges. 13 1911 (423–425). [6050]. 40256

—————— Über Erzeugung von Kanalstrahlen in Kalium, Rubidium und Cäsium. Berlin Verh. D. physik. Ges. 13 1911 (972–973); Physik. Zs. Leipzig 13 1912 (6). [6840]. 40257

—————— Über die Emissionsspektra aromatischer Verbindungen in ultraviolettem Licht, in Kathodenstrahlen, Radiumstrahlen und Kanalstrahlen. Berlin Verh. D. physik. Ges. 14 1912 (33–42). [4205 4230]. 40258

Golowin, S[ergej] S[elivan]. Ein Ophthalmoskop ohne Zentralöffnung. Klin. Monatsbl. Augenheilk. Stuttgart (49) N.F. 12 1911 (325–327). [4470].
40259

Goos, F. Ein Toepferscher Messapparat für Spektrogramme. Zs. Instrumentenk. Berlin 31 1911 (52–55). [3165]. 40260

—————— Über die Dispersion und die Ausmessung von Konkavgitterspektrogrammen. Zs. wiss. Phot. Leipzig 10 1911 (200–208). [3430 3160].
40261

Gordon, J. W. The Vernier arc. Engineering London 92 1911 (419). [0807]. 40262

Gossen. Über ein neues Drehspul-Messinstrument für Gleich- und Wechselstrom. Vortrag . . . Elektrot. Zs. Berlin 33 1912 (73–74 94–96). [6010 6015]. 40263

Gouy. Sur la tension de vapeur d'un liquide électrisé. J. phys. Paris (sér. 5) 1 1911 (85–88). [6235]. 40264

—————— Sur la structure périodique des rayons magnéto-cathodiques. Paris C. R. Acad. sci. 152 1911 (353–356). [6845]. 40265

—————— Sur un cas particulier de l'action intercathodique. Paris C. R. Acad. sci. 153 1911 (438–441). [6845]. 40266

—————— Sur la structure et les propriétés des rayons magnéto-cathodiques dans un champ uniforme. Radium Paris 8 1911 (129–134 av. fig.). [6845]. 40267

Grablovitz, Giulio. Sulla velocità della propagazione sismica. [Sunto.] Riv. fis. mat. sc. nat. Pavia 20 1909 (268–270). [0840]. 40268

Gradenwitz, Alfredo. Ondometro a lettura diretta. Elettricista Roma (Ser. 2) 10 1911 (317). [6015]. 40269

Grattdijk, I[mmina] M[aria]. Magnetische splitsing van het nikkel- en kobalt-spectrum en van het ijzerspectrum λ 4400–λ 6500. [Le phénomène de Zeeman dans les spectres du nickel, du cobalt et du fer de λ = 4400 jusqu'à λ = 6500.] Amsterdam (N.V. Electrische drukkerij „Volharding") 1911 (45). 23 cm. [6660 4208]. 40270

Graham, Th. Abhandlungen über Dialyse (Kolloide). Drei Abhandlungen. Hrsg. von E. Jordis. (Ostwald's Klassiker der exakten Wissenschaften. Nr. 179.) Leipzig (W. Engelmann) 1911 (179). 19 cm. Geb. 3 M. [0340 0010]. 40271

Graham, W. v. Roe, E. D., junr.

Gramatzki, H. J. Lamellar-Elektrizität. Bericht über ein neues Gebiet elektrischer Erscheinungen. Umschau Frankfurt a. M. 15 1911 (963–965). [5210]. 40272

Grande, Corrado Paolo. Le lampade da 10 candele nell' illuminazione pubblica a luce elettrica. Elettricista Roma (Ser. 2) 10 1911 (170–171). [6080]. 40273

Grandjean, F. v. Friedel, G.

117

Grassi, Guido. Raddoppiamento della frequenza di una corrente per mezzo di lampade a filo metallico. Torino Atti Acc. Sc. **45** 1910 (614–617 685–688); Elettricista Roma (Ser. 2) **10** 1911 (57–59). [6460].   40274

———— Oscillazioni prodotte in una corrente alternata per mezzo di lampade a filamento metallico. Atti Ass. elettrotecn. Milano **15** 1911 (3–8). [6460].   40275

———— Corso di Elettrotecnica. Ed. 2, vol. 2. Torino (Soc. tip. ed. nazionale) 1910 (559). 26 cm. [0030 4900].   40276

Grassi, Ugo. Osservazioni alla nota: Sulla viscosimetria e tensimetria clinica, del dott. Luciano Luziani. Lo sperimentale Firenze **64** 1910 (736). [0325].   40277

———— Su un problema e su alcune esperienze di diffusione. Nuovo Cimento Pisa (Ser. 6) **1** 1911 (120–122), **2** 1911 (229–233). [0320].   40278

Grassmann, Hermann. Gesammelte mathematische und physikalische Werke . . . Unter Mitwirkung der Herren Jacob Lüroth [u. a.] hrsg. von Friedrich **Engel.** Bd 3. Tl 1: Theorie der Ebbe und Flut. Prüfungsarbeit 1840 und Abhandlungen zur mathematischen Physik. [Analytische Optik; Undulationstheorie; Schall — Ätheratome.] Aus dem Nachlasse hrsg. von Justus **Grassmann** und Friedrich **Engel.** Leipzig (B. G. Teubner) 1911 (V + 353). 25 cm. 18 M. [0030].   40280

Grave, Ernst. Die Passivität der Metalle . . . Kritische Betrachtung und neue Untersuchungen . . . Jahrb. Radioakt. Leipzig **8** 1911 (94–174). [6230].   40281

———— Neue Untersuchungen über die Passivität von Metallen. Zs. physik. Chem. Leipzig **77** 1911 (513–576). [6230].   40282

Gray, J. A. Secondary γ-rays produced by β-rays. London Proc. R. Soc. (Ser. A) **85** 1911 (131–139). [4275].   40283

Gray, James G. and **Ross,** Alexander D. On magnetic testing. Phil. Mag. London (Ser. 6) **21** 1911 (1–11). [5435].   40284

Gray, Robert C. v. Ross, A. D.

Gray, R. Whytlaw und **Ramsay,** Sir William. The density of niton (radium emanation) and the disintegration theory. London Proc. R. Soc. (Ser. A) **84** 1911 (536–550); [Übers.] Jahrb. Radioakt. Leipzig **8** 1911 (5–23). [0810 4275].   40285

Gray, Thomas. Smithsonian physical tables. 4th rev. ed. Washington D.C. Smithsonian Inst. Misc. Collect. **1038** 1908 (i–xxxiv 1–301 incl. 315 tables). [0030].   40286

Graziani, F. v. Padoa, M.

Grebe, Leonhard]. Die Strahlung der Quecksilberbogenlampe. Ann. Physik Leipzig (4. Folge) **36** 1911 (834–840). [4202 4210].   40287

———— Die Ladung des Elektrons. Math.-naturw. Bl. Berlin **8** 1911 (36–38). [6845].   40288

Greeff. Elektrizitätszähler. Elektrotomotor Berlin **1** 1911 (4–11 21–26 37–42 53–58 69–72). [6040].   40289

Green, George. Illustration of the modus operandi of the prism. Edinburgh Proc. R. Soc. **31** 1911 (290–295). [3020].   40290

Greenwood, H. C. The specific heats at high temperatures and the latent heats of fusion of metals. Engineering London **92** 1911 (419). [1620].   40291

———— Notiz über die Dampfdruckkurve und die Verdampfungswärme einiger schwerflüchtiger Metalle. Zs. physik. Chem. Leipzig **76** 1911 (484–490). [1840 1680].   40292

Grégoire, Ant. Conseils pratiques sur l'emploi des machines parlantes dans l'enseignement des langues vivantes. Rev. instr. pub. Belg. 1910 (348–361). [9420].   40293

Grégoire de Bollemont, E. v. Reboule, C.

Greift, de v. Guntz, A.

Greinacher, H. Ein neues Radium perpetuum mobile. Berlin Verh. D. physik. Ges. **13** 1911 (398–404); D. MechZtg Berlin 1911 (101–104). [4275].   40294

———— Ein Ionisierungsgefäss zur Messung von Radium- und Röntgenstrahlen. Physik. Zs. Leipzig **12** 1911 (209–214). [6805].   40296

Greinacher. H. Radioaktivität.
Taschenbuch Math. Leipzig 2 1911
(434–446). [4275].   40297

————— Über die Stromkurve für
gleichförmig ionisierte Luft. Ann.
Physik Leipzig (4. Folge) 37 1912 (561–
568). [5685 6805].   40298

Grenet, L. La trempe des bronzes.
Paris C. R. Acad. sci. 151 1910 (870–
871). [1930].   40299

Grész, Leó. A luminografia. [Die
Luminographie.] Termt. Közl. Budapest 43 1911 (147–148). [4225]. 40300

Griffith, O. W. A note on the
measurement of the refractive index
of liquids. Phil. Mag. London (Ser. 6)
21 1911 (301–309). [3020].   40301

Griffiths, Albert. On the movement
of a coloured index along a capillary
tube, and its application to the measurement of the circulation of water in a
closed circuit. London Proc. Physic.
Soc. 23 1911 (190–197). [0320]. 40302

Griffiths, E. The magnetic properties of some manganese steels of definite
composition. London J. Inst. Electr.
Engin. 47 1911 (771–778). [5466].
                                 40303

Grimsehl, E. Lehrbuch der Physik.
Zum Gebrauche beim Unterricht . . .
2., verm. u. verb. Aufl. Leipzig u. Berlin
(B. G. Teubner) 1912 [1911] (XVI +
1262 mit 2 Taf.). 24 cm. 15 M.
[0030].   40304

Gripenberg, W. S. Über die Kristallisation dünner Selenplatten. (Nachtrag und Berichtigung zu meiner frü-
heren Arbeit.) Physik. Zs. Leipzig 13
1912 (161). [5660].   40305

Grisolia, G. La protezione delle
telecomunicazione elettriche militari.
Riv. Artig. Genio Roma 4. trim. 1911
(64–101 con 1 tav.). [6480].   40306

Griveau, Maurice. Le pendule et
l'oscillation mélodique. Riv. music.
Torino 17 1910 (179–194). [9100].
                                 40307

Grix, W. Geschweisstes Spezial-
Kompensationsmetall in besonderer
Anordnung zur Hervorbringung relativ
grosser Bewegungen bei Temperaturänderungen. Physik. Zs. Leipzig 12 1911
(72–75). [1410 0050 0090]. 40308

Grober, Max Karl. Zur Theorie
der Dämpfung bei Hertzschen Wellen.
Physik. Zs. Leipzig 12 1911 (121–124).
[6610 9135].   40309

————— Verwendung von Bar-
retter und Thermoelement zu Messzwecken. Physik. Zs. Leipzig 12 1911
(239–241). [6043 5710].   40310

————— und Zöllich, H. Zur
Theorie der thermischen Messgeräte.
I. Theorie des Barretters. (Vorl.
Mitt.) Physik. Zs. Leipzig 12 1911
(1048–1053). [6943 5720].   40311

Gröber, Heinrich. Wärmeleit-
fähigkeit von Isolier- und Baustoffen.
Mitt. ForschArb. Ingenieurw. Berlin
H. 104 1911 (49–59). [2020].   40312

Groedel, Theo und Meyer-Lierheim.
Vergleich des Saitengalvanometers und
des Oscillographen-Elektrocardio-
gramms. Berliner klin. Wochenschr.
48 1911 (1082–1085). [5900].   40313

Gross, Gustav. Zur Kenntnis des
Lambertschen Kosinusgesetzes. Diss.
Breslau (Druck v. Grass Barth &
Comp.) 1911 (39). 24 cm. [3010
4210].   40314

Grossmann, H[ermann] und Bloch,
F. L. Studien über Rotationsdispersion und Mutarotation der Zuckerarten
in Wasser, Pyridin und Ameisensäure.
Berlin Zs. Ver. D. Zuckerind. 62 (N.F.
49) 1912 Techn. Tl (19–74). [4050].
                                 40315

Grotowski, Maryan. Miroslaw Kernbaum. (Wspomnienie pośmiertne.)
[Miroslav Kernbaum. Notice nécro-
logique.] Wektor Warszawa 1 1911
(266–267). [0010].   40316

————— L'effet photoélectrique
et la phosphorescence. Diss. Freiburg
i. Schw. Paris 1910 (VI + 103).
25 cm. [4230 4250].   40317

Grotrian, O[tto]. Der Eisenzylinder
im homogenen Magnetfelde. Ann.
Physik Leipzig (4. Folge) 34 1911
(1–56); 36 1911 (929–957). [5440
5410].   40318

————— Magnetizzazione di un
cilindro di ferro in un campo magnetico
uniforme. [Trad. Sunto.] Atti Ass.
elettrotecn. Milano 15 1911 (363–364).
[5440].   40319

Grover, F[rederick] W[arren]. The capacity and phase difference of paraffined paper condensers as functions of temperature and frequency. [Abstract.] Physic. Rev. Ithaca N.Y. 32 1911 (607–609). [5220]. 40320

—————— Ueber die Wirbelströme in einem Blech oder Zylinder mit Rücksicht auf die Theorie der Induktionswage untersucht. Diss. München. Leipzig (Druck v. B. B. Teubner) 1909 (71). 23 cm. [6440 6410]. 40321

—————— and **Curtis,** H. L. The measurement of inductances with very small time constant. [Abstract.] Physic. Rev. Ithaca N.Y. 32 1911 (609–611). [6440]. 40322

—————— v. Curtis.

Grünbaum, F. Zur Darstellung des Michelsonschen Interferenzversuches. Berlin Verh. D. physik. Ges. 13 1911 (584–589). [3610 3420]. 40323

Grüneisen, E. Das Verhältnis der thermischen Ausdehnung zur spezifischen Wärme fester Elemente. Berlin Verh. D. physik. Ges. 13 1911 (426–430); Zs. Elektroch. Halle 17 1911 (737–739). [1400 1600 1620]. 40324

—————— Die Beziehungen zwischen Atomwärme, Ausdehnungskoeffizient und Kompressibilität fester Elemente. Berlin Verh. D. physik. Ges. 13 1911 (491–503). [1410 0840 1660 0460]. 40325

—————— Zur Theorie einatomiger fester Körper. Berlin Verh. D. physik. Ges. 13 1911 (836–847); Physik. Zs. Leipzig 12 1911 (1023–1028). [0100 1800 1600 1810 0840]. 40326

Grünfeld, E. Schülerübung zur Bestimmung des spezifischen Gewichts der Luft. Zs. physik. Unterr. Berlin 25 1912 (32). [0050]. 40327

Grünhut, L[ev] v. Fresenius, W., Hintz, E.

Grünzweig, C. Korkstein-Blätterholzkohle. Eine Entgegnung. Zs. Kälteind. München 18 1911 (171–174). [2020]. 40328

Grünzweig, Max. Der Kork als Wärmeisolator. Vortrag . . . Kälteind. Hamburg 8 1911 (113–118). [2020]. 40329

Grumbach, A. Contribution a l'étude de l'électricité de contact. Ann. chim. phys. Paris (sér. 8) 24 1911 (433–452 av. fig.). [5250]. 40330

Gruner, P. Ueber ein paradox scheinendes Resultat aus der kinetischen Gastheorie. Ann. Physik Leipzig (4. Folge) 35 1911 (381–388). [0200]. 40331

—————— Ueber einige Fortschritte im Gebiete der Radioaktivität. Monatshefte natw. Unterr. Leipzig 4 1911 (391–405). [4275]. 40332

—————— Die neueren Anschauungen über die Strahlungserscheinungen. [Ref.] Bern Mitt. Natf. Ges. 1911 1912 (XVI–XVII). [4210]. 40333

—————— Die neueren Vorstellungen über das Wesen der Elektrizität. Verh. Schweiz. Natf. Ges. Aarau 94 1912 (129–161). [4900]. 40334

Grunwald, Max. Juden als Erfinder und Entdecker. Emil Berliner, der Erfinder des Grammophons und des „Berliners". Allg. Ztg Judentum Berlin 75 1911 (148–150). [0010]. 40335

Gruschke, Georg. Die Brechung und Dispersion des Lichtes in einigen Gasen. Ann. Physik Leipzig (4. Folge) 34 1911 (801–816); Breslau Jahresber. Ges. vaterl. Cultur 88 (1910) 1911 natw. Sect. (67–92); Diss. Breslau (Druck v. Grass Barth & Comp.) 1910 (29). 23 cm. [3020 3030 3860]. 40336

Guadet, J. Sur une méthode d'observation et d'étude du phénomène de Zeemann. Ann. chim. phys. Paris (sér. 8) 21 1910 (283–289 av. fig). [4208 6660]. 40339

Guareschi, Icilio. Die Pseudosolutionen oder Scheinlösungen nach Francesco Selmi. [Uebers. von O. Kuhn.] Zs. Kolloide Dresden 8 1911 (113–123). [0340]. 40340

Guarini, Emile. Appareils de mesures électriques avec en registreurs. Industrie Bruxelles 1905 (43). [6010]. 40341

—————— Sur l'électricité atmosphérique. Bruxelles Bul. Soc. astron. 1906 (13–23). [5270]. 40342

Güldenpfennig, Otto. Beiträge zur Kenntnis eines Empfangssystems mit abgestimmtem Indikatorkreise und Untersuchungen über den Einfluss der Atmosphäre auf die Intensität und Dämpfung der sie durchlaufenden

elektrischen Wellen. (Mitteilungen
der physikalischen Versuchs-Station
Halle-Cröllwitz.) (No. 25.) Diss.
Halle a. S. (Druck v. C. A. Kaemmerer & Co.) 1911 (V + 14 mit Taf.).
29 cm. [6645].   40343

Gülich. Die Bestimmung des spezifischen Gewichts und Molekulargewichts von Gasen. Wasser u. Gas
Oldenburg **1** 1911 (535–536). [0810].
                                   40344

Günther, Erich. Energie von
Oeffnungs- und Schliessungsfunken besonders bei einer zur Funkenstrecke
parallel liegenden Kapazität. Leipzig
Ber. Ges. Wiss. math.-phys. Kl. **63**
1911 (258–263). [6820 5720]. 40345

Günther, Hanns. Der elektrische
Strom. Bd 1: Elemente und Elektrochemie. Technische Plaudereien.
Stuttgart (Franckh) [1911] (88). 21 cm.
1 M. [5600].   40346

Guertler, W. M. The electrical
conductivity and constitution of alloys.
Engineering London **92** 1911 (544–547).
[5660].   40347

Guest, E. D. v. Chapman.

|**Guglielmo,** Giovanni.] Sulla sede
della forza elettromotrice delle coppie
voltaiche. Nuovo Cimento Pisa (Ser. 6)
2 1911 (47–51); [sunti] Elettricista
Roma (Ser. 2) **10** 1911 (109); Riv. fis.
mat. sc. nat. Pavia **23** 1911 (71–72).
[5695].   40348

———— Sul valore delle componenti la forza elettromotrice della
coppia Daniell. Nuovo Cimento Pisa
(Ser. 6) **2** 1911 (55–62). [5695]. 40349

Guidi, Ciro. Fenomeni ottenuti con
correnti ad alta frequenza e ad alto
potenziale. Cagliari (Tip. Meloni e
Altelli) 1909 (30). 24 cm. [6470].
                                   40350

Guillaume, Ch. Ed. Sur la définition des unités électriques pratiques.
Paris C. R. Acad. sci. **152** 1911 (47–49). [5600].   40351

———— L'anomalie de dilatation
de aciers au nickel. Paris C. R. Acad.
sci. **152** 1911 (189 191). [1410]. 40352

———— Coefficient du terme
quadratique dans la formule de dilatation des aciers au nickel. Paris C. R.
Acad. sci. **152** 1911 (1150 1158).
[1410].   40353

Guilleminot, H. Sur les rayons de
Sagnac. Paris C. R. Acad. sci. **152**
1911 (595–598 av. fig.). [4240]. 40354

———— Sur le rendement en
rayons secondaires des rayons X de
qualité différente. Paris C. R. Acad.
sci. **152** 1911 (763 766). [4240]. 40355

Guillet, A. Courant continu et
courant alternatif de convection. Ann.
chim. phys. Paris (sér. 8) **20** 1910 (131–138). [6435].   40356

———— Trieur par synchronisation. Paris C. R. Acad. sci. **152** 1911
(1749–1752). [6040].   40357

———— Interrupteur de la bobine
d'induction constitué par l'arc primaire.
Paris C. R. Acad. sci. **153** 1911 (866–867). [6040].   40358

———— Machine à plan de
référence électrique, propre à répéter
une même translation donnée. Paris
C. R. Acad. sci. **153** 1911 (1137–1140).
[6440 0807].   40359

Guillet, Léon. Sur le revenu des
produits écrouis. Paris C. R. Acad. sci.
151 1910 (1127 1128). [1930]. 40360

Guillot, A. Application du polygone
de Fresnel à la composition des forces
électromotrices d'induction. J. phys.
Paris (sér. 5) **2** 1912 (205–213 av. fig.).
[5705].   40361

Gullstrand, Allvar. Die optische
Abbildung in heterogenen Medien und
die Dioptrik der Kristallinse des
Menschen. Stockholm Vet.-Ak. Handl.
43 No. 2 1908 (58 + Textfig.). [3050
4410].   40362

Gumlich, E. und **Rogowski,** W. Die
Messung der Permeabilität des Eisens
bei sehr kleinen Feldstärken („Anfangspermeabilität"). Ann. Physik Leipzig (4. Folge) **34** 1911 (235–257); Elektrot. Zs. Berlin **32** 1911 (180–184).
[5440].   40363

———— Misura della permeabilità
del ferro per campi molto deboli.
[Sunto. Trad.] Atti Ass. elettrotecn.
Milano **15** 1911 (372 373). [5440].
                                   40364

———— Die magnetische Prüfung von Eisenblech. Bemerkungen
zu dem Aufsatz des Herrn Epstein.
Elektrot. Zs. Berlin **32** 1911 (613–614).
[5440].   40365

———— v. Epstein, T., Kummer,
W.

Guntz, A. i Broniewski, W. Opór elektryczny metali alkalicznych, galu i telluru. [Sur la résistance électrique des métaux alcalins, du gallium et du tellure.] Prace mat.-fiz. Warszawa 21 1910 (21–36). [5666]. . 40366

———— et Greift, de. Sur l'amalgame de cuivre. Paris C. R. Acad. sci. 154 1912 (357–358). [1920]. 40367

———— et Minguin, J. Contribution à l'étude des radiations ultraviolettes Paris C. R. Acad. sci. 152 1911 (372–373). [4225]. 40368

Guthe, K[arl] E[ugene] and Harris, J. E. Elastic properties of bismuth wires. [Abstract.] Physic. Rev. Ithaca N.Y. 32 1911 (228–229 with table). [0840]. 40369

———— and Worthing, A. G. A new formula for the vapor tension of water between 0° and 200° C. [Abstract.] Physic. Rev. Ithaca N.Y. 32 1911 (226–228 with tables). [1840]. 40370

Gutton, C. Expériences sur la vitesse de la lumière dans les milieux réfringents. J. phys. Paris (sér. 5) 2 1911 (196–203 av. fig.); Paris C. R. Acad. sci. 152 1911 (1089–1092). [3410 3822]. 40371

———— Comparaison des vitesses de propagation de la lumière et des ondes électromagnétiques dans les fils. Paris C. R. Acad. sci. 152 1911 (685–688); 153 1911 (1002–1005 av. fig.); J. phys. Paris (sér. 5) 2 1912 (41–52). [6610 6625]. 40372

Gutzmann, H[ermann]. Die Analyse künstlicher Vokale. Verh. Ver. D. Laryng. Würzburg 1911 (44–56 mit 6 Taf.). [9420]. 40374

Guyot, J. Sur les différences de potentiel de contact apparentes entre un métal et des solutions électrolytiques. Paris C. R. Acad. sci. 153 1911 (867–869). [6210]. 40375

Gwinner, Hans v. r. Fischer, E.

Gwyer, A. G. C. r. Travers, M. W.

Haas, W. J. de. Isotherms of diatomic gases and their binary mixtures. VIII. Control measurements with the volumenometer. Leiden Comm. Physic. Lab. No. 121a 1911 (1–17 with 3 pl.) (English); Amsterdam Versl. Wis. Nat. Afd. K. Akad. Wet. 19 1911 (1468–1479 with (c–1588)

3 pl.) (Dutch); Amsterdam Proc. Sci. K. Akad. Wet. 14 [1911] (101–113 with 3 pl.) (English). 40376

Haber, F[ritz]. Über den festen Körper sowie über den Zusammenhang ultravioletter und ultraroter Eigenwellenlängen im Absorptionsspektrum fester Stoffe und seine Benutzung zur Verknüpfung der Bildungswärme mit der Quantentheorie. Berlin Verh. D. physik. Ges. 13 1911 (1117–1136). [0100 4200]. 40377

———— Elektronenmission bei chemischen Reaktionen. ChemZtg Cöthen 35 1911 (1073–1076); Physik. Zs. Leipzig 12 1911 (1035–1044); Verh. Ges. D. Natf. Leipzig 83 I 1911 (215–229). [0100 6800 4270]. 40378

———— und Just, G. Über die Aussendung von Elektronenstrahlen bei chemischen Reaktionen. Ann. Physik Leipzig (4. Folge) 36 1911 (308–340). [4270 0100 6800]. 40379

———— und Zawadzki, J. Über die Polarisierbarkeit fester Elektrolyte. (Ein Beitrag zu den Grundlagen der Passivitätslehre.) Zs. physik. Chem. Leipzig 78 1911 (228–243). [6230]. 40380

Hack, Karl. Eine neue Aetherhypothese. Südd. ApothZtg Stuttgart 51 1911 (700–702). [0600]. 40381

———— Das Rätsel der Schwerkraft. Südd. ApothZtg Stuttgart 51 1911 (820–821). [0700]. 40382

Hacker, Carl. Ueber die Aenderung der Dampfspannung von wässerigen Schwefelsäurelösungen mit der Temperatur. Diss. Kiel (Druck v. Lüdtke & Martens) 1912 (28). 23 cm. [1920]. 40383

Hackspill, Louis. Densité, coefficient de dilatation et variation de volume à la fusion des métaux alcalins. Paris C. R. Acad. sci. 152 1911 (259–262). [1410 1440 1810]. 40384

———— r. Broniewski.

Hadamard. Sur une question relative aux liquides visqueux. Paris C. R. Acad. sci. 154 1912 (109). [0325]. 40385

Hadfield, Robert and Hopkinson, B. The magnetic properties of iron and its alloys in intense fields. London J. Inst. Electr. Engin. 46 1911 (235–306). [5466]. 40386

K

122

Hanert, Ludwig. Der reduzierte Raumwinkel und die Lichtgüte von Fenstern. Diss. Kiel (Druck v. L. Handorff) 1911 (47). 23 cm. [3010]. 40387

Härdén, J. A curious coherer phenomenon. Elect. London 67 1911 (22–23). [5680 6043]. 40388

Häussler, A. Wegweiser für die Gravitationsforschung. Berlin (R. Friedländer & S. i. Komm.) 1912 (99). 22 cm. 2 M. [0700]. 40389

Häussler, E. P. Beschreibung eines Thermometers aus dem Jahre 1636. ChemZtg Cöthen 35 1911 (436). [1210]. 40390

Hagelstein, Otto. Ueber Dekrementsbestimmungen von Kondensatorkreisen mittels des Helmholtzschen Pendelunterbrechers. Diss. Kiel. Neumünster (Druck v. R. Hieronymus) 1911 (47). 23 cm. [6820 6450]. 40391

Hagenbach, August. Über die verschiedenen Formen des Kupfer- und Eisenbogens. Physik. Zs. Leipzig 12 1911 (1015–1020); Berlin Verh. D. physik. Ges. 13 1911 (1047–1057). [6830]. 40392

Hahn, Otto. Über die Eigenschaften des technisch hergestellten Mesothoriums und seine Dosierung. ChemZtg Cöthen 35 1911 (845–846). [4275]. 40393

——— Nomenklatur und Radiumstandard. Physik. Zs. Leipzig 12 1911 (141–143). [4275]. 40394

——— Der Brüsseler Kongress für Radiologie und Elektrizität vom 13. bis 15. September 1910, Nomenklatur und Radiumstandard. Berlin Verh. D. physik. Ges. 13 1911 (154–158). [4275]. 40395

——— Mesothor und Radiothor. Umschau Frankfurt a. M. 15 1911 (323–326). [4275]. 40396

——— r. Baeyer, O. von.

Haken, W. Das Aronsche Chromoskop. Weltall Berlin 11 1911 (182–185). [4000 0090]. 40397

——— Über die Entwicklung des Baues der optischen Instrumente. Weltall Berlin 11 1911 (329–337). [3000]. 40398

Haldane, J. S. r. Butterfield, W. J. A.

Hale, C. F. r. Bradley, W. P.

Hall, Edwin H[erbert] and Campbell, L[eslie] L[yle]. On the electromagnetic and the thermomagnetic transverse and longitudinal effects in soft iron. Boston Proc. Amer. Acad. Arts Sci. 46 1911 (623–668 with fig. table). [6455]. 40399

Halla, Franz. Zur thermodynamischen Berechnung elektromotorischer Kräfte. II. Zs. Elektroch. Halle 17 1911 (179–182). [5610 6210]. 40400

Hallo, H. S. Il convertitore in cascata. [Sunto.] Atti Ass. elettrotecn. Milano 15 1911 (897–899). [6047]. 40401

——— Kommutation bei Einankerumformern. Elektrot. Zs. Berlin 32 1911 (880–883). [6047]. 40402

——— Die Eigenschaften des Kaskadenumformers und seine Anwendung. — Die Spaltpolumformer. Karlsruhe Arb. elektrot. Inst. 2 (1910–1911) 1911 (1–131). [6047]. 40403

Hamacher, Jakob. Elektrolytische Leitfähigkeit und Hydratation in ihrer Beziehung zur Temperatur. Diss. Bonn (Druck v. E. Eisele) 1910 (37 mit Taf.). 22 cm. [6248]. 40404

Hamburger, H[artog] J[acob]. 25 Jahre „Osmotischer Druck" in den medizinischen Wissenschaften. Janus Leyde 15 1910 (787–796 mit Porträts). [0010]. 40405

Hamley, H. R. and Rossiter, A. L. The magnetic properties of stalloy. Elect. London 68 1911 (150–151); Melbourne Proc. R. Soc. Vict. N.S. 23 Pt. 2 1911 (325–341 pls. LXII–LXV). [5466]. 40406

Hammer, Max. Untersuchungen über Hertzsche stehende Schwingungen in Luft. Berlin Verh. D. physik. Ges. 13 1911 (27–52). [6610]. 40407

Hammer, W. Über eine direkte Messung der Geschwindigkeit von Wasserstoffkanalstrahlen und über die Verwendung derselben zur Bestimmung ihrer spezifischen Ladung. Physik. Zs. Leipzig 12 1911 (1077–1080); Berlin Verh. D. physik. Ges. 13 1911 (955–960). [6845]. 40408

——— r. Dechend, H. v.

Handek, Martin und Fröschels, Emil. Röntgenaufnahmen der Form des Ansatzrohres bei den Sprachlauten. Arch. Laryng. Berlin 24 1911 (319–328 mit 3 Taf.). [9510]. 40409

Handovsky, Hans. Fortschritte in der Kolloidchemie der Eiweisskörper. Dresden (Th. Steinkopff) 1911 (56). 22 cm. 1,50 M. 40410

Handy, James O[tis]. A convenient method of refrigeration for analytical and industrial investigations at low temperatures (− 75° C.). J. Ind. Engin. Chem. Easton Pa. 2 1910 (92–94). [1012]. 40411

Hanriot. Sur l'adhésivité. Paris C. R. Acad. sci. 152 1911 (369–372 704–706). [0500 1810]. 40412

———— et Raoult, F. Sur les coefficients d'aimantation de l'or. Paris C. R. Acad. sci. 153 1911 (182–185). 40413

Hansen, Christian Johannes. Schlusswort zu der Erwiderung von C. von Rechenberg auf meine Arbeit: „Ueber die Temperaturabnahmen hochmolekularer Dämpfe bei kleinen Drucken". Zs. physik. Chem. Leipzig 76 1911 (753–756). [1840]. 40414

———— Siedepunkt. [Nachträge.] [In: Die Methoden der organischen Chemie. Hrsg. v. Th. Weyl. Bd 2.] Leipzig (G. Thieme) 1911 (1375–1376). 40415

Hansing, Siegfried. Kombinationstöne und ihre hohe Bedeutung für die Musik. Zs. InstrBau Leipzig 32 1911 (6–7). [9450 9140]. 40416

Hanszel, Hubert. Versuche an einer Dreifach-Expansions-Dampfmaschine. Mitt. ForschArb. Ingenieurw. Berlin H. 101 1911 (78 mit 1 Tab.): Beitrag zur Frage der Heizung der Dampfmaschine. Berlin Zs. Ver. D. Ing. 56 1912 (58–63 102–107). [2490]. 40417

Hantschel, Oskar. Das Linzer „Museum physicum". Geschichte des physikalischen Kabinetts am Linzer Staatsgymnasium und seiner Kustoden vom Jahre 1754 bis zur Gegenwart. JahrBer. StaatsGymnasium zu Linz 59 1910 Linz 1910 (1–27). [0060]. 40418

Hantzsch, A. Über das colorimetrische Verdünnungsgesetz. Liebigs Ann. Chem. Leipzig 384 1911 (135–142). [3810 3860]. 40419

(c–1388)

Hantzsch, A. und Shibata, Yuji. Über Rhodankobaltverbindungen — ein Beitrag zur Ursache des Farbenwechsels der Kobaltsalze. Zs. anorg. Chem. Leipzig 73 1912 (309–324). [3860]. 40420

———— und Voigt, Kurt. Über konjugierte aci-Nitrokörper. Berlin Ber. D. chem. Ges. 45 1912 (85–117 mit Taf.). [3860]. 40421

Harbich, Johannes. Glimmverluste paralleler Leiter. Diss. Darmstadt. Stuttgart (Union) 1911 (27). 24 cm. [6810] 40422

Harekmae. Le magnétisme et l'électricité d'après la conception de M. le professeur De Heen. Bruxelles Bul. Soc. belge électr. (81–86). [5480]. 40423

Haret. Les mesures en radiologie. Arch. physik. Med. Leipzig 4 1909 (308–317). [4240]. 40424

Hargreaves, R. A kinematical theorem in radiation. Cambridge Proc. Phil. Soc. 16 1911 (331–335). [2400]. 40425

Harkányi, B. von. Strahlung und Temperatur der Sterne. Umschau Frankfurt a. M. 15 1911 (756–760). [4210]. 40426

Harkins, M. R. v. McGinnis, C. S.

Harnack, Alfred. Vergleichende Untersuchungen über Spektren in der Sauerstoff-Wasserstoff- und in der Chlor-Wasserstoff-Knallgasflamme. Zs. wiss. Phot. Leipzig 10 1911 (281–312 mit 5 Taf.); 1912 (313–346 mit 5 Taf.). [4205]. 40427

Harris, J. E. v. Guthe, K. E.

Harrison, Leonard Hubert. Diffusion in Systemen von geschmolzenen Salzen. Diss. München. Freiburg i. B. (Speyer & Kaerner) 1911 (57). 22 cm. [0320]. 40428

Harrison, William. Ueber Farbe und Dispersitätsgrad kolloider Lösungen. Zs. Kolloide Dresden 10 1912 (45–49). [0340 3860]. 40429

Harting, H. Zur Theorie des sekundären Spektrums. Zs. Instrumentenk. Berlin 31 1911 (72–79). [3070]. 40430

Hartman, L[eon] W[ilson]. A laboratory manual of experiments in physics, for the students of the sophomore year in the University of Utah.

K 2

Rev., enl. Salt Lake City (University of Utah) 1907 (1 + 170 with text fig. tables). 23 cm. [0030]. 40431

Hartmann, A. Herkunft und Chemismus der Thermen von Baden und Schinznach. Schweiz. Wochenschr. Chem. Pharm. Zürich **47** 1909 (3–5 17–21). [4275]. 40432

Hartmann, Christian. Zur physikalischen Technik. [Herstellung von Schulapparaten.] Programm des k. humanistischen Gymnasiums Schweinfurt für d. Schuljahr 1910–11. Schweinfurt (Druck d. Reichardt'schen Buchdruckerei) 1911 (29). 22 cm. [0050]. 40433

Hartmann, J. Bemerkung zu dem Aufsatze des Herrn Erich Lehmann über „Eine neue Photometerkonstruktion". Berlin Verh. D. physik. Ges. **13** 1911 (444–446). [3010]. 40434

——— Berichtigung zu der Erwiderung des Herrn E. Lehmann [betr. Mikrophotometer]. Berlin Verh. D. physik. Ges. **13** 1911 (670). [3010]. 40435

Hartmann, Jul. En simpel Generator for Lydsvingninger. [A simple generator for waves of sound.] København Fysisk Tids. **9** 1911 (106–113 with 1 pl.). [9020]. 40436

Hartmann, L. Sur le mécanisme de la déformation permanente dans les métaux soumis à l'extension. Paris C. R. Acad. sci. **152** 1911 (1233–1237). [0840]. 40437

Hartmann, Otto. Bemerkungen [zu der Arbeit von A. Batschinski] über die Empfindlichkeit der Wage. Zs. physik. Unterr. Berlin **24** 1911 (93–94). [0810]. 40438

Hartmann-Kempf, R. Neuere Untersuchungen über den Resonanzverlauf abgestimmter Klangkörper. Ann. Physik Leipzig (4. Folge) **36** 1911 (74–90). [9140 9110]. 40439

——— Hitzdrahtamperemeter ohne Nebenschluss für drahtlose Telegraphie. Elektrot. Zs. Berlin **32** 1911 (1134–1135). [6043]. 40440

——— Über wichtigere Resonanzerscheinungen und deren experimentelle Vorführung. Zs. physik. Unterr. Berlin **24** 1911 (325–341). [9140 9030]. 40441

Hasenöhrl, F[ritz]. Über die Grundlagen der mechanischen Theorie der Wärme. Berlin Verh. D. physik. Ges. **13** 1911 (756–765); Physik. Zs. Leipzig **12** 1911 (931–935). [2400 4200]. 40442

Haschek, Eduard r. Esener, F.

Hatschek, Emil. Die Viskosität der Dispersoide. II. Zs. Kolloide Dresden **8** 1911 (34–39). [0340 0325]. 40443

——— Die Bildung von Schichten in heterogenen Systemen. Zs. Kolloide Dresden **9** 1911 (97–100). [0340]. 40444

Haubold, Edwin. Der perfekte Optiker. Sein Ausbildungsgang in Theorie und Praxis für alle Zweige seines Berufes. Lfg 9 (Schluss). Berlin (Verl. d. Centralztg f. Optik u. Mechanik) 1911 (111 + 385–439). 24 cm. 1 M. [3000]. 40445

Hauser, Fr. Wirkung von elektrischen und magnetischen Feldern auf die Selbstaufladung von Polonium und über die Durchdringungsfähigkeit der δ-Strahlen. Physik. Zs. Leipzig **12** 1911 (466–476). [4275 6845]. 40446

——— Untersuchung von Bronsonwiderständen. Physik. Zs. Leipzig **12** 1911 (785–791); Diss. München. Erlangen (Druck v. Junge & S.) 1911 (59 mit 4 Kart. u. 7 Tab.). 22 cm. [5685 6010 6805]. 40447

Hauser, O. Elektrische Fernthermometer mit direkter Anzeige ohne Spannungsregulierung. Gesundhtsing. München **34** 1911 (514–520). [1250]. 40449

Hausrath, H[erbert]. Über die Daten, die zur vollständigen Beurteilung elektrischer Messinstrumente erforderlich sind. Vortrag. D. MechZtg Berlin **1911** (209–215 222–226); Elektrot. Zs. Berlin **33** 1912 (79–82). [6010]. 40450

——— Die Saitengalvanometer, ihre optischen Hilfsmittel und ihre Anwendungen. Helios Leipzig **17** 1911 Fach-Zs. (117–123 133–138). [6010]. 40451

——— Verfahren zur Darstellung periodischer Hochfrequenzkurven mit der Braunschen Röhre. Physik. Zs. Leipzig **12** 1911 (1044–1046). [6015 5705]. 40452

Hausser, W. r. Ramsauer, C.

Havelock, T. H. Optical dispersion : an analysis of its actual dependence upon physical conditions. London Proc. R. Soc. (Ser. A) **84** 1911 (492–523). [3860]. 40453

Hawkesworth, Alan S[pencer]. A formula for optical instruments. Science New York (N. Ser.) **33** 1911 (249–250). [3020]. 40454

Hawkins, C. C. The principle of the static balancer. Elect. London **67** 1911 (342–345 380–383). [6060]. 40455

Hay, Alfred. A graphical treatment of the skin effect. London J. Inst. Electr. Engin. **46** 1911 (487–496). [6460]. 40456

Hayes, Hammond Vinton. Notes on the electrical conductivity of argentic sulphide. Boston Proc. Amer. Acad. Arts Sci. **46** 1911 (613–621 with tables). [5660]. 40457

Hayes, Harvey C. An investigation of the errors in cooling curves and methods for avoiding these errors ; also a new form of crucible. Boston Proc. Amer. Acad. Arts Sci. **47** 1911 (1–22 with text fig. pl.). [1610]. 40458

Heather, H. J. S. A new method of determining the efficiency of slip-ring induction motors. Elect. London **67** 1911 (575). [6070]. 40459

———— The Heyland diagram for induction motors and reverse current operation. Elect. London **68** 1911 (98–100). [6070]. 40460

Hebe, P. v. Wiebe, H. F.

Hecht, Leopold. Ueber die Natur des Sulfammoniums und eine Beitrag zur spektrometrischen Untersuchung eines Gemisches mehrerer lichtabsorbierender Stoffe. Diss. Danzig. Berlin (Druck v. A. W. Schade) 1910 (58). 24 cm. [3860 3810]. 40461

———— v. Ruff, O.

Hecker, O[skar]. Bemerkungen zu dem Aufsatze L. A. Bauers : " On gravity determinations at sea " in Amer. J. Sci. **31** January 1911. Beitr. Geophysik Leipzig **11** 1911 (200–205). [0825]. 40462

Heffter, L[othar]. Zur Einführung der vierdimensionalen Welt Minkowskis. Jahresber. D. MathVer. Leipzig **21** 1912 (1–8). [0000]. 40463

Heger, Richard. Zur Theorie und Praxis der Raumakustik. Zs. Archit. Wiesbaden **57** 1911 (309–322). [9255]. 40464

Heiberg, J. L. und **Wiedemann**, E[ilhard]. Eine arabische Schrift über die Parabel und parabolische Hohlspiegel. Bibl. math. Leipzig (3. Folge) **11** 1911 (193–208). [0010 3060]. 40465

Heidenreich, Karl. Photo-elektromotorische Untersuchungen von Chlorsilber und Bromsilber. Diss. München. Hildesheim (Druck v. A. Lax) 1911 (108). 22 cm. [6850 5610 6200]. 40466

Heilmann, K. Die Wärmeausnutzung der heutigen Kolbendampfmaschine. Berlin Zs. Ver. D. Ing. **55** 1911 (921–927 984–992 1026–1031). [2490]. 40467

Heim v. Chéneveau.

Heimstädt, Oskar. Spiegelreflexkamera für mikrophotographische Zwecke. Metallurgie Halle **8** 1911 (137–138). [3085]. 40468

———— Satzanastigmate aus drei miteinander verkitteten Linsen. Erwiderung an Herrn W. Zschokke. Zs. wiss. Phot. Leipzig **9** 1911 (193–195). [3085]. 40469

Heindlhofer, Kálmán. Eine absolute Messung der Schallintensität und die Bestimmung der Wärmeleitungsfähigkeit der Gase. Ann. Physik Leipzig (4. Folge) **37** 1912 (247–256). [9320 2035]. 40470

Henrich, Ferd[inand]. Neuere Forschungen auf dem Gebiete der Radioaktivität. Zs. angew. Chem. Leipzig **24** 1911 (1011–1020) ; [trad.] Ind. chim. Torino **10** 1910 (241–244). [4275]. 40471

Heissner, Conrad. Ueber Elektrizitätserregung durch Reibung. Diss. Erlangen (Druck v. Junge & S.) 1911 (58). 22 cm. [5210]. 40472

Hellenschmidt, G. Die Gemischbildungen der Gasmaschinen. Diss. Aachen. Berlin (J. Springer) 1911 (IV + 59 mit einer Taf.). 21 cm. [2490]. 40473

Heller, H. v. Stenger, E.

Helm, Georg. Das Relativitätsprinzip in der Ätherhypothese. Physik. Zs. Leipzig **13** 1912 (157–158). [0600]. 40474

Helmholtz, H. v. Handbuch der physiologischen Optik, ergänzt und hrsg. in Gemeinschaft mit A. Gullstrand und J. v. Kries von W. Nagel †. Bd 2 : Die Lehre von den Gesichtsempfindungen, hrsg. v. W. Nagel und J. v. Kries. Leipzig (L. Voss) 1911 (VIII + 392 mit 3 Taf.). 28 cm. Geb. 18 M. 4400]. 40475

———— *v.* Koenigsberger, L.

Hemsalech, G. A. Sur le spectre de l'air donné par la décharge initiale de l'étincelle de self-induction. Paris C. R. Acad. sci. 152 1911 (1471–1474). [4205]. 40476

Henk, O. Zur Methode und Philosophie des französischen Physikers Poincaré. (Wiss. Beil. zum Jahresber. der Realschule in Barmbeck.) Hamburg (Druck v. Lütcke & Wulff) 1910 (32). 25 cm. [0000]. 40477

Henning, F. Über Temperaturmessung mit Hilfe der Clapeyron-Clausiusschen Gleichung. Berlin Verh. D. physik. Ges. 13 1911 (645–650). [2425]. 40478

———— *v.* Holborn, L.

Henri, Victor. Étude du rayonnement ultraviolet des lampes à vapeur de mercure en quartz. Paris C. R. Acad. sci. 153 1911 (265–267). [4205]. 40479

———— Influence de diverses conditions physiques sur le rayonnement ultraviolet des lampes à vapeur de mercure en quartz. Paris C. R. Acad. sci. 153 1911 (426–429). [4206]. 40480

———— et **Lifchitz,** Samuel. Étude cinématographique de l'écartement des particules ultramiscroscopiques produit par des chocs sonores très rapides. Paris C. R. Acad. sci. 152 1911 (953–955). [0200]. 40481

———— *v.* Bierry, H., Girard, P.

Henrich, F[erdinand] und **Glaser,** F. Ueber die gebräuchlichen Apparate zur Bestimmung der Radioaktivität von Quellen. Zs. angew. Chem. Leipzig 25 1912 (16–19). [4275]. 40483

Henriot, E. Étude des rayons émis par les métaux alcalins. Ann. chim. phys. Paris (sér. 8) 25 1912 (377–404 av. fig.). [4275]. 40484

Henry et **Disdez.** Lumière et couleurs. Pet. rev. sci. 1908 (30–33). [2990]. 40485

Heraeus, W. C. Elektrische Laboratoriumsöfen mit Wicklung aus unedlem Metall. [Nebst Erwiderung von [Leo] **Ubbelohde.**] ChemZtg Cöthen 36 1912 (167) ; Zs. Elektroch. Halle 18 1912 (143–144). [6090]. 40486

Herbst, Carl. Über Schwingungsbewegungen. Unterrichtsbl. Math. Berlin 17 1911 (151–152). [9110]. 40487

Herglotz, G. Über die Mechanik des deformierbaren Körpers vom Standpunkte der Relativitätstheorie. Ann. Physik Leipzig (4. Folge) 36 1911 (493–533). [4940]. 40488

Hermann, L[udimar]. Der Einfluss der Drehgeschwindigkeit auf die Vokale bei der Reproduktion derselben am Edison'schen Phonographen. Arch. ges. Physiol. Bonn 139 1911 (1–9). [9420]. 40489

———— Zur Theorie der Kombinationstöne. Ann. Physik Leipzig (4. Folge) 37 1912 (425–434). [9140]. 40490

Herrmann, I[mmanuel]. Elektrotechnik. Einführung in die Starkstromtechnik. Tl 1. Die physikalischen Grundlagen. 3., erweit. Aufl. (Sammlung Göschen. 196.) Leipzig (G. J. Göschen) 1911 (128 mit Taf.). 16 cm. 0,80 M. ; Tl 2 : Die Gleichstromtechnik . . . 3., erweit. Aufl. (Sammlung Göschen. 197.) ibid. 1912 (144 mit 16 Taf.). 16 cm. 0,80 M. [6070 6400 5620]. 40491

Herrmann, Karl. Über die Widerstandszunahme von Spulen bei Wechselstrom. Berlin Verh. D. physik. Ges. 13 1911 (978–983). [6460]. 40492

Herschfinkel. Action de l'émanation du radium sur les sels de thorium. Paris C. R. Acad. sci. 153 1911 (255–257) ; Radium Paris 8 1911 (417–419 av. fig.). [4275]. 40493

———— Essais de préparation du radium métallique. Radium Paris 8 1911 (299–301). [4275]. 40494

Hertz, G[ustav]. Über das ultrarote Absorptionsspektrum der Kohlensäure in seiner Abhängigkeit von Druck und Partialdruck. Diss. Berlin. Braunschweig (Druck v. F. Vieweg & S.) 1911 (41). 23 cm. ; [Auszug] Berlin Verh. D. physik. Ges. 13 1911 (617–644). [3855]. 40495

Hertz, G[ustav]. Über die Absorption ultraroter Strahlung durch Gase. Natw. Rdsch. Braunschweig **26** 1911 (417–420). [3800 3850]. 40496

—————— *r.* Franck, J.

Hertz, Paul. Über die Abhängigkeit des Leitvermögens binärer normaler Elektrolyte von der Konzentration. Ann. Physik Leipzig (4. Folge) **37** 1912 (1–28 mit 2 Taf.). [6420 6200]. 40497

Herweg, Otto. Ein Knallgasvoltameter für den Unterricht. (Bericht über das k. Gymnasium zu Neustadt in Wpr. für die Zeit von Ostern 1909 bis Ostern 1910.) Neustadt Wpr. (Druck v. H. Brandenburg) 1910 (12 mit 1 Taf.). 26 cm. [6010 0050]. 40498

Herz, W[alter]. Die Fortschritte der physikalischen Chemie im Jahre 1910. ChemZtg Cöthen **35** 1911 (49–50 78–79 86–88); *id.* 1911. *op. cit.* **36** 1912 (77–78 84–86 111–112). [0030]. 40499

Herzog, R[eginald] O. Über die Lösungen der Farbstoffe. (Diffusion der Kolloide. III. Nach Versuchen von R[eginald] O. **Herzog** und A. **Polotsky.**) Zs. Elektroch. Halle **17** 1911 (679–684). [0320 0340]. 40501

—————— Ueber die negative Adsorption. Zs. Kolloide Dresden **8** 1911 (209–210). [0300]. 40502

—————— Bemerkungen über die Viskosität kolloider Lösungen. Zs. Kolloide Dresden **8** 1911 (210–211). [0340]. 40503

Herzog, S. I recenti progressi nella costruzione e nelle applicazioni degli apparecchi elettrici per riscaldamento e per cucina. Industria Milano **24** 1910 (233–236 246–250 261–263 275–277). [6090]. 40504

Hess, A. Radiotelegrafia „Goldschmidt". Elettricità Milano **36** 1911 (73–74). [6615]. 40505

Hess, Hans. Über die Plastizität des Eises. Ann. Physik Leipzig (4. Folge) **36** 1911 (449–492). [1810]. 40506

Hess, V[iktor] F. Ueber die Absorption der γ-Strahlen in der Atmosphäre. Wien VierteljBer. Ver. Förd. Phys.-Chem. Unt. **16** 1911 (123–128). [4210 4275 0250]. 40507

Hesselberg, Th. La physique des mers polaires. Rev. gén. sci. Paris **22** 1911 (7–14 av. fig.). [0845 1250]. 40508

Heurung, A. Untersuchungen über die magneto-optischen Effekte bei Chlor und Jod. Ann. Physik Leipzig (4. Folge) **36** 1911 (153–176 mit 2 Taf.). [6650 6060]. 40509

Heuse, Wilhelm *r.* Scheel, K.

Hevesy, G. v. Über den Nachweis der Aktiniumemanation in aktiniumhaltigen Mineralien. Physik. Zs. Leipzig **12** 1911 (1213–1214). [4275]. 40510

—————— Über die Löslichkeit von Aktiniumemanation in Flüssigkeiten und Kohle. Physik. Zs. Leipzig **12** 1911 (1214–1224). [4275]. 40511

Heydweiller, A[dolf]. Zur Magnetoneutheorie. [Lösungen paramagnetischer Salze.] Berlin Verh. D. physik. Ges. **13** 1911 (1063–1064). [5480 5467]. 40512

—————— Über physikalische Eigenschaften von Lösungen in ihrem Zusammenhang. III. Die Ionenmoduln der Dichte im Wasser. Ann. Physik Leipzig (4. Folge) **37** 1912 (739–771). [6250 0845]. 40513

Heyl, Paul R[enno]. The conversion of the energy of carbon into electrical energy on solution in iron. Philadelphia Proc. Amer. Phil. Soc. **49** 1910 (49–51). [5610]. 40514

Heym, W. Die Strahlungen bei Gasexplosionen [in bezug auf Gasmaschinen]. Ann. Gew. Berlin **69** 1911 (60–62). [2490]. 40515

Heyn, E[mil] und Bauer, O. Ueber Spannungen in kaltgereckten Metallen. Intern. Zs. Metallogr. Berlin **1** 1911 (16–50). [0810 0845]. 40516

—————— Über Spannungen in Kesselblechen. Stahl u. Eisen Düsseldorf **31** 1911 (760–765). [1400 0840]. 40517

—————— *r.* Martens, A.

Hilditch, Thomas Percy. Die Wirkung molekularer Symmetrie auf die optische Aktivität und das relative Rotationsvermögen von aromatischen Stellungsisomeren. (Uebers. von W. **Neumann.**) Zs. physik. Chem. Leipzig **77** 1911 (482–497). [4040]. 40518

—————— und Dunstan, A. E. Die Beziehung der Viskosität u anderen

physikalischen Eigenschaften. I.
Athen- und Äthinverbindungen.
(Übers. von Clara Haber.) Zs. Elektroch. Halle 17 1911 (929–934). [0325].
40519

Hills, M. v. German, T.

Hilpert, Siegfrid und Colver-Glauezt, Edward. Über die magnetischen Eigenschaften von Nickelstahlen. (1. Mitt.) Zs. Elektroch. Halle 17 1911 (750–761). [5466 5435 D 7285].
40520

——— und Mathesius, W|alter]. Ueber die magnetischen Eigenschaften von Nickel- und Manganstählen. Stahl u. Eisen Düsseldorf 32 1912 (96–104 mit 1 Taf.). [5466]. 40521

——— und Dieckmann, Theodor. Über Arsenide. 1. (Eisen- und Manganarsenide.) Berlin Ber. D. chem. Ges. 44 1911 (2378–2385). [5466].
40522

——— ——— Zur Kenntnis der ferromagnetischen Verbindungen des Mangans mit Phosphor, Arsen, Antimon und Wismut. Berlin Ber. D. chem. Ges. 44 1911 (2831–2835). [5466].
40523

——— und Mathesius, Walter. Über die magnetischen Eigenschaften von Mangan- und Nickelstahlen. (Zugleich 2. Mitteilung über die magnetischen Eigenschaften von Nickelstahlen.) Zs. Elektroch. Halle 18 1912 (54–64 mit 1 Taf.). [5466 5460]. 40524

Hinlein, Erwin. Ein Beitrag zur Frage der Erwärmung der elektrischen Maschinen. Mitt. ForschArb. Ingenieurw. Berlin H. 98-99 1911 (85–119). [6060 2000]. 40525

Hinrichs, W. Einführung in die geometrische Optik. (Sammlung Göschen. 532.) Leipzig (G. J. Göschen) 1911 (144). 16 cm. 0,80 M. [3000].
40526

——— Beitrag zur Theorie der natürlichen Blende optischer Instrumente. Diss. Rostock. Berlin (Druck v. E. Ebering) 1910 (131). 22 cm. [3050 3070]. 40527

Hintz, Ernst. Die neue Heilquelle zu Wiessee am Tegernsee. Chemische Untersuchung ausgeführt im chemischen Laboratorium Fresenius. Untersuchung auf Radioaktivität von Karl Kurz. Wiesbaden (C. W. Kreidel) 1911 (42). 22 cm. 1,20 M. [4275].
40528

Hintz, Ernst und Grünhut, L. Wiesbadener Kochbrunnen [Radioaktivität]. Zs. angew. Chem. 23 (1308). [4275].
40529

Hirsch, M. Vorschläge zur Verbesserung des Arbeitsvorganges der Kompressionskühlmaschinenanlagen. Zs. KältInd. München 18 1911 (166–171 193–196 203–205). [2495]. 40530

Hirsch, Richard. Ein direkt zeigender Wellenmesser. Jahrb. drahtlos. Telegr. Leipzig 4 1911 (250–253). [6043]. 40531

Hirshfeld, Clarence Floyd. Engineering thermodynamics. (Van Nostrand science series, No. 45.) New York (Van Nostrand) 1907 (v + 157 with diagrs.). 15 cm. [2400].
40532

Hnatek, Adolf. Bestimmung einiger effektiver Sterntemperaturen und relativer Sterndurchmesser auf spektralphotographischem Wage. Astr. Nachr. Kiel 187 1911 (369–382). [4210].
40533

——— Untersuchungen über das 38 cm-Objektiv des Rothschild-Coudé der Universitätssternwarte Wien. Astr. Nachr. Kiel 189 1911 (213–224). [3080]. 40534

Hobel, H. Volumenänderungen von Sammlerelektroden. Elektrot. Anz. Berlin 29 1912 (79–80). [5620 6220].
40535

Höfler, Alois. Zwei Modelle schematischer Farbenkörper und die vermutliche Gestalt des psychologischen Farbenkörpers. Zs. Psychol. Leipzig Abt. 1 58 1911 (356–371 mit 1 Taf.). [4450]. 40536

Hoerschelmann, Harald von. Über die Wirkungsweise des geknickten Marconischen Senders in der drahtlosen Telegraphie. Jahrb. drahtlos. Telegr. Leipzig 5 1911 (14–34 188–211); Diss. München. Leipzig (J. A. Barth) 1911 (79). 23 cm. [6615 6600 6043].
40537

Hoesslin, Hermann von. Die Schallgeschwindigkeit als Funktion der Verteilung der molekularen Geschwindigkeiten. München (H. Lukaschik) 1911 (V + 70). 25 cm. 2,80 M. [9210 9200 0200]. 40538

Hofe, Chr. von. Fernoptik. (Wissen und Können. 21.) Leipzig (J. A. Barth) 1911 (VI + 158). 23 cm. Geb. 5 M. [3080 3090]. 40539

Hoffheinz, Martha *v.* Meisenheimer, J.

Hoffmann. Untersuchung der Segerkegel durch die kaiserliche physikalisch-technische Reichsanstalt. Ber. Ver. D. Fabr. feuerfester Produkte Berlin 29 1909 (45–53). [1240]. 40540

———— [Erweichungstempera turen der Segerkegel.] Ber. Ver. D. Fabr. feuerfester Produkte Berlin 30 1910 (47–57). [1240]. 40541

———— Bericht der physikalisch-technischen Reichsanstalt . . . . (Untersuchungen der Segerkegel.) Ber. Ver. D. Fabr. feuerfester Produkte Berlin 31 1911 (53–58). [1240]. 40542

Hoffmann, G. Ein einfacher Demonstrationsapparat für Wechselstromversuche. Physik. Zs. Leipzig 13 1912 (30–31 mit 1 Taf.). [0050]. 40543

Hoffmann, Karl. Experimentelle Prüfung der durch verschiedene Messungsanordnungen in einem homogenen elektrischen Felde hervorgerufenen Störungen (Deformationen) der Niveauflächen. Diss. München (Druck v. C. Wolf & S.) 1911 (67 mit 12 Taf.). 22 cm. [5200 6800 0090 5685]. 40544

Hoke, Edmund. Ueber das Elektrokardiogramm eines Falles von Situs viscerum inversus totalis. Münchener med. Wochenschr. 58 1911 (802). 40545

Holborn, L. und **Henning**, F. Vergleichung von Platinthermometern mit dem Stickstoff-Wasserstoff- und Heliumthermometer und die Bestimmung einiger Fixpunkte zwischen 200 und 450°. Ann. Physik Leipzig (4. Folge) 35 1911 (761–774). [1230 1260]. 40546

Holl, E. Verschlussgeschwindigkeit und Lichtverlust. Phot. Mitt. Berlin 48 1911 (105–109 119–121). [3085]. 40547

Holland, Carl. Untersuchungen mit dem Quarzmanometer, die Dissoziation der gasförmigen Essigsäure und des Phosphorpentachlorids. Diss. Berlin (Druck v. E. Ebering) 1911 (35). 23 cm. [0835]. 40548

Holle, G. Neuer Apparat zur Demonstration des Boyle-Mariotteschen Gesetzes. Zs. physik. Unterr. Berlin 24 1911 (223–224). [0070 1450]. 40549

Holmes, A. The association of lead with uranium in rock-minerals, and its application to the measurement of geological time. London Proc. R. Soc. (Ser. A) 85 1911 (248–256). [4275]. 40550

Holtz, Adolf. Ueber den Einfluss von Fremdstoffen auf Elektrolyteisen und seine magnetischen Eigenschaften. Diss. Berlin (Druck v. E. Ebering) 1911 (80 mit Taf.). 23 cm. [5460]. 40551

Holzknecht, G. Ein neues Dosimeter für Röntgen-Strahlen. Wr. Med. WochSchr. Wien 61 1911 (2185–2188). [0090 4240]. 40552

Holzt, Alfred. Die Schule des Elektrotechnikers. Lehrbuch der angewandten Elektrizitätslehre. 2. vollst. neubearb. Aufl. Hrsg. im Verein mit E. Körner. Bd 3. Leipzig (M. Schäfer) [1911] (VIII + 435 mit 4 Taf.). 28 cm. 11,50 M. [5620 5630]. 40553

Holzwarth, H. Die Gasturbine. Jahrb. schiffbaut. Ges. Berlin 13 1912 (491–535); Theorie, Konstruktion und Betriebsergebnisse von zwei ausgeführten Maschinen. München u. Berlin (R. Oldenbourg) 1911 (VI + 159). 24 cm. Geb. 6,40 M. [2490]. 40554

Hoock, Theodore. Der maximale Leistungsfaktor und die Baulänge der Induktionsmotoren. Elektrot. Zs. Berlin 32 1911 (1300–1303). [6070]. 40555

Hoogenboom, C. M. *v.* Zeeman, P.

Hoorweg, J. L. Sur la perception des lumières brèves. J. phys. Paris (sér. 5) 2 1912 (177–181). [4450 3010 5900]. 40556

Hopkinson, B. *v.* Hadfield, R. A.

Horák, V. i Šebor, Jan. O aluminiu jakožto materialu kathodovém. [Ueber das Aluminium als Kathodenmaterial.] Listy Chem. Prag 1910 (253–255 297–301). [6242]. 40557

Horiba, S[hinkichi]. On the equilibrium in the system : water, ethyl alcohol and ethyl ether. Kyoto Mem. Coll. Sci. Eng. 3 1911 (63–78). [1887]. 40558

Horst, C. *v.* Wedekind, E.

Horst, Ludwig. Verbesserte CO-Expansions-Kältemaschine für ungünstige Kühlwasserverhältnisse (Tropen, Schiffe, im Sommer etc.). Zs. Sauerstoffind. Leipzig 3 1911 (241–246). [2495]. 40559

Hort, Hermann. Untersuchung von Flüssigkeiten, die als vermittelnde Körper im oberen Prozess einer Mehrstoffdampfmaschine Verwendung finden können. [Dampfspannungskurven von Nitrobenzol und Erdöldestillat.] Berlin Zs. Ver. D. Ing. 55 1911 (943–946). [1840 2490]. 40560

Horton, Frank. A spectroscopic investigation of the nature of the carriers of positive electricity from heated aluminium. London Proc. R. Soc. (Ser. A) 84 1910 (433–449). [4250 6845]. 40561

————— The vacuum tube spectra of mercury. London Proc. R. Soc. (Ser. A) 85 1911 (288–302). [4205]. 40562

————— On the origin of spectra. Phil. Mag. London (Ser. 6) 22 1911 (214–219). [4205]. 40563

Houllevigue, L. Préparation de lames minces par volatilisation dans le vide. Ann. chim. phys. Paris (sér. 8) 20 1910 (131–138). [6845]. 40564

————— Sur un rayonnement émis à l'intérieur des lampes à incandescence. Paris C. R. Acad. sci. 152 1911 (1240). [6845]. 40565

————— Sur les rayons cathodiques produits à l'intérieur des lampes à incandescence. Paris C. R. Acad. sci. 152 1911 (1846–1849 av. fig.). [6845]. 40566

————— Revue annuelle d'optique. Rev. gén. sci. Paris 22 1911 (650–655 av. fig.). 40567

Houstoun, R. A. The absorption of light by inorganic salts. No. I. Aqueous solutions of cobalt salts in the infra-red. Edinburgh Proc. R. Soc. 31 1911 (521–529). [3855 3860]. 40568

————— The absorption of light by inorganic salts. No. III. Aqueous solutions of nickel salts in the visible spectrum and the infra-red. Edinburgh Proc. R. Soc. 31 1911 (538–546). [3850 3855 3860]. 40569

————— On the absolute measurement of light : a proposal for an ultimate light standard. London Proc. R. Soc. (Ser. A) 85 1911 (275–284). 3010]. 40570

————— Über absolute Lichtmessung. Ein Vorschlag zur Aufstellung einer endgültigen Lichtnormale. (Übers.) Physik. Zs. Leipzig 12 1911 (800–806). [3010]. 40572

Houstoun, R. A. On magnetostriction. Phil. Mag. London (Ser. 6) 21 1911 (78–83). [5462]. 40571

————— and Anderson, J. S. The absorption of light by inorganic salts. No. IV. Aqueous solutions of cobalt and nickel salts in the ultraviolet. Edinburgh Proc. R. Soc. 31 1911 (547–558). [3850 3860]. 40573

————— and Brown, R. A. The absorption of light by inorganic salts. No. II. Aqueous solutions of cobalt salts in the visible spectrum. Edinburgh Proc. R. Soc. 31 1911 (530–537). [3850 3860]. 40574

Hovda, O. The effect of distance upon the electrical discharge between a point and a plane. [Abstract.] Physic. Rev. Ithaca N.Y. 32 1911 (255). [6820 5252]. 40575

Howe, G. W. O. Oscillatory currents in coupled circuits. Elect. London 67 1911 (8–9) : London Proc. Physic. Soc. 23 1911 (237–245). [6615 6820 6470]. 40576

————— The Brown telephone relay in wireless telegraphy. Elect. London 66 1911 (632). [6615 6043]. 40577

————— Recent developments in radio-telegraphy. Elect. London 67 1911 (854–857). [6615]. 40578

Hoyer, N. G. B. Die Tiefenschärfe bei konstantem Abbildungsmassstab. Phot. Rdsch. Halle 25 1911 (65–66). [3085]. 40579

Hubbard, J[ohn] C[harles]. Spark length, potential and frequency of oscillation : The "lag effect" in electric discharge. Physic. Rev. Ithaca N.Y. 32 1911 (565–580 with fig. tables). [6820]. 40580

Huber-Bonifacius. Einfluss der Selbstinduktion auf die Spektren von Metallen und besonders von Legierungen. Diss. Freiburg i. Schw. Altdorf 1909 (41 mit 10 Taf.). 24 cm. [4206 6440]. 40581

Huber-Stockar, E. L'alluminio per le condutture elettriche. Atti Ass. elettrotecn. Milano 15 1911 (932–936). [5680 5660]. 40582

Hübl, A[rthur] Freiherr von. Ist eine farblose Dunkelkammerbeleuchtung möglich ? Atel. Phot. Halle 18 1911 (35–36). [4225 3860]. 40583

Hürthle, K[arl]. Erwiderung an O[tto] Frank. Arch. ges. Physiol. Bonn 141 1911 (389–409). [0835].
40584

Hughes, A. L. On the velocities of the electrons produced by ultra-violet light. Cambridge Proc. Phil. Soc. 16 1911 (167–174). [6845]. 40585

——— On the ultra-violet light from the mercury arc. Phil. Mag. London (Ser. 6) 21 1911 (393–404). [4205]. 40586

Hulbert, Clinton H. and Bacon, R. F. A liquid concave mirror. Philippine J. Sci. Manila A. Chem. Geol. Sci. 5 1910 (19–20 with pls.). [3060]. 40587

Hulett, G[eorge] A[ugustus]. The construction of standard cells and a constant temperature bath. Physic. Rev. Ithaca N.Y. 32 1911 (257–280 with tables text fig.). [5610]. 40588

——— Merkurosulfat als Depolarisator in Normalelementen. (Uebers. von W. Neumann.) Zs. physik. Chem. Leipzig 77 1911 (411–419). [5610]. 40589

Humphreys, W[illiam] J[ackson]. Certain laws of radiation and absorption and a few of their applications. [With bibliography.] Washington D.C. U. S. Dept. Agric. Bull. Mt. Weather Obs. 2 1909 (109–132 with text ff.). [0960 3800 4200]. 40590

——— Bemerkung über die Anwendung von Zylinderlinsen für spektrographische Zwecke. [Nebst] Bemerkung von E. Gehrcke. Zs. Instrumentenk. Berlin 31 1911 (217–218). [3165]. 40591

Hunzinger, Richard. Die Bestimmung des Spannungsabfalles bei verschiedenen Phasenverschiebungen an Transformatoren. Elektrot. Zs. Berlin 33 1912 (131). [6040]. 40592

Hupka, E. Einfluss der geerdeten Umgebung auf die Höhe des Funkenpotentials zwischen Kugeln. Ann. Physik Leipzig (4. Folge) 36 1911 (440–448). [6820]. 40593

Hutb, E[rich] F. Ein direkt zeigender Wellenmesser etc. Physik. Zs. Leipzig 13 1912 (36–39 mit 3 Taf.). [6043]. 40594

Huygens, Christiaan. Treatise on Light. Trl. by Silvanus P. Th mpson.

London (Macmillan) 1912 (129). 23 cm. 10s. [0010]. 40595

Hýbl, Jac. Neue Tabellen für Ammoniakdampf. Zs. Kältelnd. München 18 1911 (161–166). [1840 1800]. 40596

Hybl, Jar. Zustandsgleichung der Dämpfe. Dinglers polyt. J. Berlin 327 1912 (135–138 154–157). [1450]. 40597

Hyde, Edw[ard] P[echin]. A new determination of the selective radiation from tantalum. [Abstract.] Physic. Rev. Ithaca N.Y. 32 1911 (632–633 with table). [6080 4210]. 40598

Hylla, E. Vom binokularen Sehen. Eine psycho-physiologische Untersuchung. Bl. Fortbildg Lehrer Berlin 4 1911 (449–455). [4440]. 40599

Ichinohe, R[yujiro]. On canal and cathode rays. Kyoto Mem. Coll. Sci. Eng. 3 1911 (193–195 with pls.). [6845]. 40604

——— and Kinoshita, M[asao]. Unilateral electric conductivity in a vacuum bulb containing an incandescent metallic filament. Kyoto Mem. Coll. Sci. Eng. 2 1910 (107–119). [5655 6047]. 40605

——— and Kimura, M[asamichi]. Observations of the electrical conductivity of the air. Kyoto Mem. Coll. Sci. Eng. 3 1911 (155–169 with pl.). [5685]. 40606

——— v. Kimura, M.

Icole. Détermination à différentes températures de la conductibilité calorifique du graphite et du sulfure cuivreux. Ann. chim. phys. Paris (sér. 8) 25 1912 (137–144). [2020]. 40607

Idrac. Premières observations sur le spectre de la nouvelle étoile du Lézard. Paris C. R. Acad. sci. 152 1911 (173–174). [4205]. 40608

——— Nouvelles observations sur le spectre de la Nova Lacertae. Paris C. R. Acad. sci. 152 1911 (302–303). [4205]. 40609

Ignatowsky, W. v. Bemerkung zu der Arbeit „Der starre Körper und das Relativitätsprinzip". Ann. Physik Leipzig (4. Folge) 34 1911 (373–375). [4960]. 40610

——— Das Relativitätsprinzip. [Forts. u. Schluss.] Arch. Math.

Leipzig (3. Reihe) 18 1911 (17–49).
[4940 4980]. 40611

Ignatowsky, W. v. Zur Elastizitätstheorie vom Standpunkte des Relativitätsprinzips. Physik. Zs. Leipzig 12
1911 (164–169). [4960]. 40612

——— Über Überlichtge-
schwindigkeiten in der Relativtheorie.
Physik. Zs. Leipzig 12 1911 (776–778).
[3400]. 40613

——— Zur Geschichte des
Kardioidkondensors. Zs. wiss. Mikrosk. Leipzig 28 1911 (52–55). [3082].
40614

——— r. Ehrenfest, P.

Ihde, Karl. Untersuchungen über
die Magnetisierbarkeit von Mangan,
Mangankupfer und Chrom. Diss.
Marburg i. H. (Druck v. C. Schaaf)
1912 (58 mit 1 Taf.). 22 cm. [5466].
40615

Illies. Erinnerungen an die Zeit
der ersten Dampfmaschinen. Vortrag.
Kattowitz Mitt. BezVer. D. Ing. 3 1911
(135–143 153–159). [2490]. 40616

Immisch, W. Ueber die Leitfähigkeit der Selenpräparate im Lichte.
Natw. Wochenschr. Jena 26 1911
(632–635). [5660]. 40617

——— Über Elektrizitätsträger
an der Grenze von Gasen und Flüssigkeiten. Natw. Wochenschr. Jena 26
1911 (721–729). [5210 6805]. 40618

Inchley, W. The calorific value of
solid and liquid fuels. Engineer London
111 1911 (155–156). [1610]. 40619

Inghilleri, G. Sintesi fotochimica
degli idrati di carbonio. Formazione
del sorbosio. Siena Atti Acc. Fisiocritici (Ser. 5) 1 1909 (461–472). [4225].
40620

——— Azione della luce sulle
soluzioni di formaldeide. Nota 2.
Siena Atti Acc. Fisiocritici (Ser. 5) 2
1910 (325). [4225]. 40621

——— Azione chimica della
luce. Nota 2. Siena Atti Acc. Fisiocritici (Ser. 5) 3 1911 (163–169).
[4225]. 40622

Inouye, Katsuji r. Svedberg, T.

Inouye, Nobuo und Oinuma, Soroku.
Untersuchung der Dunkeladaptation
des einen Auges mit Hilfe des belladap-
tierten andern. Graefes Arch. Ophthalm. Leipzig 79 1911 (145–159).
[4470]. 40623

——— r. Brücke, E. Th. von.

Isaachsen, J. Innere Vorgänge in
strömenden Flüssigkeiten und Gasen.
Berlin Zs. Ver. D. Ing. 55 1911 (215–
221 263–267 428–435). [0200]. 40624

Isakow, L. Thermischer Indikator
zur Resonanzabstimmung nach der
Nullmethode. (Vorl. Mitt.) (Übers.)
Physik. Zs. Leipzig 12 1911 (1224–
1226). [6043]. 40625

Isenkrahe, Kaspar. Energie, Entropie, Weltanfang, Weltende. (Kgl.
Kaiser Wilhelms-Gymnasiums mit Real-
gymnasium in Trier. Wiss. Beil.
zum Jahresber. 1909–10.) Trier
(Druck v. J. Lintz) 1910 (80). 22 cm.
[0000]. 40626

Ishiwara, J[un]. Über das thermodynamische Verhalten einer Strahlung
in einem bewegten diathermanen
Medium. Tokyo Su. Buts. Kw. K.
(Ser. 2) 5 1910 (214–221). [4210].
40627

——— Zur Theorie der elektro-
magnetischen Vorgänge in bewegten
Körpern. Tokyo Su. Buts. Kw. K.
(Ser. 2) 5 1910 (310–327). [4960]. 40628

——— Bemerkung über die
Fortpflanzung des Lichtes in bewegten
Medien. Tokyo Su. Buts. Kw. K.
(Ser. 2) 5 1910 (327–333). [6630]. 40629

——— Nachtrag zu meiner
Untersuchung „Zur Optik der bewegten
ponderablen Medien". Tokyo Su.
Buts. Kw. K. (Ser. 2) 6 1911 (2–8).
[6630]. 40630

——— Zur Theorie der Elektronenbewegung in Metallen. Tokyo
Su. Buts. Kw. K. (Ser. 2) 6 1911 (15–
34 36–46). [5675]. 40631

——— Berechnung der elek-
trischen Leitfähigkeit für oszillirende
elektrische Kraft aus der Elektronentheorie. Tokyo Su. Buts. Kw. K.
(Ser. 2) 6 1911 (56–65 72–81). [4960
5675]. 40632

——— Über die electromagnetischen Impulsgleichungen in der Relativitätstheorie. Tokyo Su. Buts. Kw.
K. (Ser. 2) 6 1911 (164–176). [4940].
40634

Isitani, D[enichiro]. A method of
slowly charging leaf-electrometers with
Zamboni's pile. Tokyo Su. Buts. Kw.
K. (Ser. 2) 5 1910 (249–251). [6005].
40635

——— and Manabe, K[aichiro].
Radioactivity of hot springs in Yuga-
wara, Izusan and Atami. Tokyo Su.

Buts. Kw. K. (Ser. 2) 5 1910 (206–249). [4275]. 40636

Issel, Arturo. Le misure di gravità e il presagio dei parossismi vulcanici. Riv. ligure sc. lett. ar. Genova 32 1910 (65–75). [0845]. 40637

Ives, Herbert E[ugene]. Note on Crova's method of heterochromatic photometry. Physic. Rev. Ithaca N.Y. 32 1911 (316–323 with text fig.). [3010]. 40638

————— Spectral luminosity curves obtained by the equality of brightness and flicker photometers. [Abstract.] Physic. Rev. Ithaca N.Y. 32 1911 (441–442). [4450 3010]. 40639

————— and Luckiesh, M. The effect of red and infra-red on the decay of phosphorescence in zinc sulphide. Astroph. J. Chicago Ill. 34 1911 (173–196 with fig.); [abstract] Physic. Rev. Ithaca N.Y. 32 1911 (240–241). [4230]. 40640

————— A form of neutral tint absorbing screen for photometric use. Physic. Rev. Ithaca N.Y. 32 1911 (522–529 with fig. table). [3010]. 40642

Ives, James E. An approximate theory of an elastic string vibrating in its fundamental mode, in a viscous medium. Phil. Mag. London (Ser. 6) 21 1911 (742–744). [9410]. 40643

————— Eine Näherungstheorie für die Antenne mit grossem Widerstande. (Uebers.) Physik. Zs. Leipzig 12 1911 (303–306). [6615]. 40644

————— and Mauchly, S. J. A new form of earth inductor. Phil. Mag. London (Ser. 6) 21 1911 (579–583). [6000]. 40645

Jachino, A. Telemetro e telemetrista. Riv. marìtt. Roma 4. trim. 1911 (219–245). [3090]. 40645A

Jacobitti, L. Apparecchio per la lettura in officina delle tensioni dei centri di distribuzione senza fili piloti. Elettricista Roma (Ser. 2) 10 1911 (209–211). [6010]. 40645B

Jacot, E. The effect of the electric discharge on water vapour. Cape Town Trans. Roy. Soc. S. Afric. 2 pt. 2 1911 (137–155 pls. ii–iii). [5685 6800]. 40646

[Jacoviello, Felice.] Produzione di correnti oscillatorie ad alta frequenza per mezzo dell' arco Jacoviello. Industria Milano 24 1910 (369–370). [6610]. 40646A

Jadanza, Nicodemo. Storia del cannochiale. Riv. astr. sci. affini Torino 4 1910 (1–17). [0010]. 40646B

————— Sopra alcuni sistemi composti di due lenti e sul livello di II. Wild costruito dalla Casa Zeiss in Jena. Torino Atti Acc. sc. 46 1911 (350–370). [3050]. 42734

Jaeckel, W. Mathematische Untersuchung über die scheinbare Hebung eines unter Wasser befindlichen Punktes. Unterrichtsbl. Math. Berlin 17 1911 (34–35). [3020]. 40647

Jaeger, F[rans] M[aurits]. De fotochemische omzettingen van ferritrichloorazetaat-oplossingen. [The photochemical transformations of ferritrichloro-acetate solutions.] Amsterdam Versl. Wis. Nat. Afd. K. Akad. Wet. 20 [1911] (295–308) (Dutch); Amsterdam Proc. Sci. K. Akad. Wet. 14 [1911] (342–356) (English). [4225]. 40648

————— Bijdrage tot de kennis der natuurlijke sulfo-antimonieten. I. [Contribution to the knowledge of the natural sulfo-antimonides. I.] Amsterdam Versl. Wis. Nat. Afd. K. Akad. Wet. 20 [1911] (497–510 with 1 pl.). [1810 1887]. 40649

————— en Klooster, H[endrik] S[joerd] van. Bijdrage tot de kennis der sulfo-antimonieten. II. [Contribution to the knowledge of the sulfo-antimonides. II.] Amsterdam Versl. Wis. Nat. Afd. K. Akad. Wet. 20 [1911] (510–516 with 1 pl.). [1810 1887]. 40650

————— en Kregten, J[acob] R[ein] N[icolaas] van. Over de vraag naar de mengbaarheid in vasten toestand tusschen aromatische nitro- en nitroso-verbindingen. III. [The question as to the miscibility in the solid condition between aromatic nitro- and nitroso-compounds. III.] Amsterdam Versl. Wis. Nat. Afd. K. Akad. Wet. 20 1912 (700–712 with 4 fig.) (Dutch); Amsterdam Proc. Sci. K. Akad. Wet. 14 1912 (729–740 with 4 fig.) (English). [1920]. 40651

————— en Menke, J. B. Studien over het tellurium. II. Over verbindingen van tellurium en jodium. [Studies on tellurium. II. On compounds of tellurium and iodine.] Amsterdam Versl. Wis. Nat. Afd. K. Akad. Wet. 21 1912 (695–700) (Dutch);

Amsterdam Proc. Sci. K. Akad. Wet. **14** 1912 (724–729) (English). [1920].
40652

Jaensch, A. *v.* Görges, H.

Jaffé, George. Über einen Fall von elektrolytischen Sättigungsstrom. Ann. Physik Leipzig (4. Folge) **36** 1911 (25–48). [6240 6250]. 40653

Janet, P., **Laporte** et **Jouaust**, R. Détermination de la force électromotrice en valeur absolue de l'élément Weston normal. Paris C. R. Acad. sci. **153** 1911 (718–719). [6210]. 40654

Janke, Georg. Ueber die Abhängigkeit der spezifischen Wärme des Wassers von der Temperatur. Diss. Rostock. Berlin (Druck v. O. Rahneberg) 1910 (28). 28 cm. [1620]. 40655

Jans, C. de. Sur une liaison entre la loi de Coulomb et la loi de Biot et Savart. J. phys. Paris (sér. 4) **9** 1910 (906–912). [6420]. 40656

Jaubert de Beaujeu *v.* Chaspoul.

Jeans, J. H. Molecule. Encycl. Brit. (ed. 11) **18** 1911. [0100]. 40657

Jégou, Paul. Réception d'un signal horaire hertzien de la Tour Eiffel. Paris C. R. Acad. sci. **151** 1910 (1042–1044). [6043 6615]. 40658

—————— Hertzsche Signale zur Zeitbestimmung und zur Messung von geographischen Längenunterschieden. Jahrb. drahtlos. Telegr. Leipzig **4** 1911 (628–635) ; II. Empfang der Zeit und Pendelsignale. (Übers.) *op. cit,* **5** 1911 (1–5). [6615 6043]. 40659

Jellinek, Karl. Ueber die Leitfähigkeit und Dissociation von Natriumhydrosulfit und hydroschwefliger Säure im Vergleich zu analogen Schwefelsauerstoffverbindungen. Ein Beitrag zur Dissociation ternärer Elektrolyte. Zs. physik. Chem. Leipzig **76** 1911 (257–354). [6240]. 40660

Jellinek, O. E. Zur Nomenklatur der radioaktiven Strahlungen. Radium Leipzig **1** 1911 (142–144). [4275]. 40661

Jensen, Chr. Einiges über die neutralen Punkte der Atmosphäre. Jahrb. Phot. Halle **25** 1911 (63–82). [3230]. 40662

—————— *v.* Busch, F.

Jentsch, Otto. Der deutsche Anteil an der Entwicklung der drahtlosen Telegraphie. Elektrot. Zs. Berlin **32** 1911 (25–27). [6615]. 40663

Jervis, T. Manuale pratico di elettrotecnica. [Trad.] Ed. 2. Torino (S. Lattes e C.) 1910 (519). 16 cm. [0030 4900]. 40664

Job, A. *v.* Bouasse, H.

Joffé, A. Ueber das magnetische Feld der Kathodenstrahlen. Ann. Physik Leipzig (4. Folge) **34** 1911 (1026–1032). [6845]. 40665

—————— Zur Theorie der Strahlungserscheinungen. Ann. Physik Leipzig (4. Folge) **36** 1911 (534–552). [4200]. 40666

—————— Zu den Abhandlungen von F. Ehrenhaft : „Ueber die Frage nach der atomistischen Konstitution der Elektrizität". Physik. Zs. Leipzig **12** 1911 (268). [4960]. 40667

Johannesson, P. Die physikalischen Uebungen am Sophiencalgymnasium zu Berlin. Zs. physik. Unterr. Berlin **24** 1911 (65–74). [0050]. 40668

Johnson, Arden Richard. On the dissolution of a metal in a binary solution, one component acid. Physic. Rev. Ithaca N.Y. **33** 1911 (27–42 with fig. table). [6240]. 40669

Johnston, John und **Adams**, L. H. Der Einfluss des Druckes auf die Schmelzpunkte einiger Metalle. (Uebers. von J. Koppel.) Zs. anorg. Chem. Hamburg **72** 1911 (11–30). [1810]. 40670

Jolibois, Pierre. Recherches sur le phosphore et les phosphures métalliques. J. Éc. polytech. Paris (sér. 2) **1911** (109–196 av. fig.). [1930]. 40671

—————— Sur les relations entre le phosphore blanc, le phosphore rouge et le phosphore pyromorphique. Paris C. R. Acad. sci. **151** 1910 (382–384). [1930]. 40672

Joly, John. Radiant matter. Dublin Proc. R. Soc. **13** 1911 (73–87). [4275]. 40673

—————— On a method of investigating the quantity of radium in rocks and minerals, etc. Phil. Mag. London (Ser. 6) **22** 1911 (134–150). [4275]. 40674

—————— and **Smyth**, L. B. On the amount of radium emanation in the soil and its escape into the atmosphere.

Dublin Proc. R. Soc. 13 1911 (148-161). [4275]. 40675

Joly, Maurice. Sur des transformateurs statiques de fréquence. Paris C. R. Acad. sci. 152 1911 (699-702). [6040]. 40676

—— Sur un tripleur statique de fréquence. Paris C. R. Acad. sci. 152 1911 (856-859). [6040]. 40677

Jonas, J. Mathematische Zeichen [für Phasenverschiebung]. Elektrot. Zs. Berlin 32 1911 (1144). [5900 0070]. 40678

Jones, Chapman. On the relationship between the size of the particle and the colour of the image. Phot. J. London 51 1911 (159-172). [4225]. 40679

Jones, H. C. et Strong, W. W. Spectres d'absorption des solutions. Possibilité d'une méthode pour déterminer la présence de composés intermédiaires dans les réactions chimiques. Journ. Chim. Phys. Genève 8 1910 (131-134). [3850 3860]. 40680

—— —— A study of the absorption spectra of solutions of certain salts of potassium, cobalt, nickel, copper, chromium, erbium, praseodymium, neodymium, and uranium as affected by chemical agents and by temperature. [With bibliography.] Washington (Carnegie Inst. Pub. No. 130) 1910 (ix + 159 with pl. text fig. tables). 26.2 cm. [3860]. 40681

—— v. Schmidt, M. R.

Jones, L. A. Effect on the cathode fall in gases produced by the evolution of gas from the cathode. Physic. Rev. Ithaca N.Y. 32 1911 (328-340 with tables text fig.). [6845]. 40682

Jonker, W[illem] P[ieter] A[ndries]. Ternaire stelsels waarvan een der komponenten een kolloid is. [Systèmes ternaires dont l'une des composantes est une substance colloidale.] Handl. Ned. Nat. Geneesk. Congres 13 1911 (209-213). [1887]. 40683

Jordan, F. W. The Thomson and Peltier effects. Nature London 86 1911 (380). [5710]. 40684

—— The direct measurement of the Peltier effect. Phil. Mag. London (Ser. 6) 21 1911 (454-464). [5710]. 40685

Jordan, H. Messung dielektrischer Verluste an faserigen Isolierstoffen. Nach einem Vortrag . . . Elektrot. Zs. Berlin 32 1911 (127-130 160-162). [5252]. 40686

Jordis, Eduard. Generalregister zu Band 1-10, Jg 1894-1904 der Zeitschrift für Elektrochemie und angewandte physikalische Chemie. Hrsg. von der Deutschen Bunsen-Gesellschaft für angewandte physikalische Chemie. Tl 1: Namenverzeichnis. Halle a. S. (W. Knapp) 1910 (113). 30 cm. 11,50 M. ; Tl 2: Sachverzeichnis. ibid. 1911 (115-315 + IV). 30 cm. 18,50 M. [0020]. 40687

Jorissen, W[illem] P[aulinus]. Quelques remarques sur la chaleur d'hydratation. Haarlem Arch. Néerl. Sci. Soc. Holl. (Sér. 3 A) 1 1911 (24-42). [1690]. 40688

—— et Woudstra, H[erman] W[ybe]. Sur l'action des rayons du radium sur les colloides. Haarlem Arch. Néerl. Sci. Soc. Holl. (Sér. III A) 1 1911 (43-50); Traduit de: Amsterdam Chem. Weekbl. 7 [1910] (941-948); Zs. Kolloide Dresden 8 1911 (8-11). [0340 4275]. 40689

Josse, A. Sur un calorimètre à lance prismatique teintée et sur un étalon calorimétrique. Sucr. belge Bruxelles 1906 (37-45). [1610]. 40690

Josse, E. Ueber die Verwendung von Wasserdampf als Kälteträger in Kältemaschinen. Zs. KälteInd. München 13 1911 (137-141). [2495]. 40691

—— Neue Versuche über Strömungsvorgänge und ihre Anwendung bei Dampfturbinen, Kondensationen und Kälteerzeugung. Jahrb. schiffbaut. Ges. Berlin 13 1912 (340-387). [2490 2495]. 40692

Jouaust, R. v. Janet, P.

Jouguet. Sur les points indifférents. Paris C. R. Acad. sci. 153 1911 (346-349). [1887]. 40693

—— Sur la vitesse et l'accélération des ondes de choc de seconde et de troisième espèce dans les fils. Paris C. R. Acad. sci. 153 1911 (1062-1064). [0840]. 40694

Joye, Paul. Influence de l'intensité maximum du courant sur le spectre de la décharge oscillante. Fribourg

Mém. Soc. Sc. Nat. Math. Phys. 1 1909 (43–198 av. 26 fig.). [6820 4206].
40695

Jüptner, Hans v. Heat energy and fuels, pyrometry, combustion analysis of fuels and manufacture of charcoal, coke and fuel gas. Translated by Oskar Nagel. New York (McGraw) 1908 (v + 305). [0900]. 40696

Jüttner, Ferencz. Das Maxwell'sche Gesetz der Geschwindigkeitsverteilung in der Relativtheorie. Ann. Physik Leipzig (4. Folge) 34 1911 (856–882). [0200 2415]. 40697

———— Die Dynamik eines bewegten Gases in der Relativtheorie. Ann. Physik Leipzig (4. Folge) 35 1911 (145–161). [0200]. 40698

———— Ueber die Ableitung der Nernstschen Formeln für Reaktionen in kondensierten Systemen. Zs. Elektroch. Halle 17 1911 (139–143). [2400 2415]. 40699

———— Über die allgemeinen Integrale der gewöhnlichen chemischen Kinetik. Zs. physik. Chem. Leipzig 77 1911 (735–743); [In : Festschrift zur Jahrhundertfeier der Univ. Breslau am 2. Aug. 1911.] Breslau (Trewendt & Granier) 1911 (31–40). [2472]. 40700

Julius, W[illem] H[endrik]. De lijnen H en K in het spectrum van de verschillende deelen der zonneschijf. [The lines H and K in the spectrum of the various parts of the solar disk.] Haarlem Arch. Néerl. Sci. Soc. Holl. (Sér. 3 A) 1 1912 (259–271); Traduit de : Amsterdam Versl. Wis. Nat. Afd. K. Akad. Wet. 19 1911 (1395–1406) (Dutch); Amsterdam Proc. Sci. K. Akad. Wet. 13 1911 (1263–1273) (English). [3850]. 40701

———— Absorption sélective et diffusion anomale de la lumière dans les masses étendues des gaz. Haarlem Arch. Néerl. Sci. Soc. Holl. (Sér. 3 A) 1 1912 (239–258); Traduit de : Amsterdam Versl. Wis. Nat. Afd. K. Akad. Wet. 19 1911 (1007–1022) (Dutch); Amsterdam Proc. Sci. K. Akad. Wet. 13 1911 (881–897) (English); Physik. Zs. Leipzig 12 1911 (329–338) (German). [3800 4200 3850 4960]. 40702

———— und Plaats, B. J. van der. Beobachtungen über anomale Dispersion des Lichtes in Gasen. Zs. wiss. Phot. Leipzig 10 1911 (62–67 mit 2 Taf.). [3850]. 40704

Jung, F. Zur Bewertung physikalischer Erkenntnistheorien. Ann. Natphilos. Leipzig 10 1911 (408–414). [0000]. 40705

Jurisch, E. r. Sieverts, A.

Just, C. r. Haber, F.

Kaemmerer, Paul. Ueber die Interferenzerscheinungen an Platten optisch aktiver, isotroper, durchsichtiger Kristalle [Natriumchlorat] im konvergenten polarisierten Licht. N. Jahrb. Min. Stuttgart 1911 II (20–29). [3830 4050 3610]. 40706

Kämpf, Carl. Die historische Entwicklung des photographischen Objektives. Centralztg Opt. Berlin 32 1911 (332–333 346–348). [3085]. 40707

Kaempf, F. Fluoreszenzabsorption und Lambertsches Absorptionsgesetz beim Fluoreszein. Physik. Zs. Leipzig 12 1911 (761–763). [4230 3810]. 40708

Kaestner, Georg. Robert Bunsen (zum 100 jährigen Geburtstag). Wiss. Rdsch. Leipzig 1911 (303–306). [0010]. 40709

Kahane, Max. Ueber Hochfrequenzströme und ihre Indikationen. Zs. physik. Ther. Leipzig 15 1911 (449–463 519–531 600–611). [5900]. 40710

Kahn, R[ichard] H. Elektrokardiogrammstudien. Arch. ges. Physiol. Bonn 140 1911 (627–649). [5900]. 40711

Kailan, Anton. Über das spezifische Gewicht des absoluten Äthylalkohols bei 25°. Berlin Ber. D. chem. Ges. 44 1911 (2381–2384). [0845]. 40712

———— Über das spezifische Gewicht und die Hygroskopizität des Glyzerins. Zs. anal. Chem. Wiesbaden 51 1912 (81–101). [1890 0845]. 40713

Kalähne, Alfred. Frequenz- und Dämpfungsberechnung gekoppelter Schwingungskreise nach der Cohenschen Methode. Jahrb. drahtlos. Telegr. Leipzig 4 1911 (357–381). [6450 6043]. 40714

Kalandyk, S. r. Goldmann, A.

Kalischer, [Salomon]. Bemerkung über die Wanderung der Ionen bei der Elektrolyse. Elektrot. Zs. Berlin 33 1912 (55). [6240]. 40715

Kamerlingh Onnes, H[eike]. Verdere proeven met vloeibaar helium. C. Over de verandering van den galvanischen weerstand van zuivere metalen bij zeer lage temperaturen enz. IV. De weerstand van zuiver kwik bij heliumtemperaturen. [Further experiments with liquid helium. C. On the change of electric resistance of pure metals at very low temperatures, etc. IV. The resistance of pure mercury at helium temperature.] Amsterdam Versl. Wis. Nat. Afd. K. Akad. Wet. 19 1911 (1479-1481) (Dutch); Amsterdam Proc. Sci. K. Akad. Wet. 13 1911 (1274-1276) (English); Leiden Comm. Physic. Lab. No. 120 C 1911 (3-5) (English). [5660]. 40716

———— Verdere proeven met vloeibaar helium. D. Over de verandering van den galvanischen weerstand van zuivere metalen bij zeer lage temperaturen enz. V. Het verdwijnen van den weerstand van kwik. [Further experiments with liquid helium. D. On the change of the electrical resistance of pure metals at very low temperatures, etc. V. The disappearance of the resistance of mercury.] Amsterdam Versl. Wis. Nat. Afd. K. Akad. Wet. 20 [1911] (81-83) (Dutch); Amsterdam Proc. Sci. K. Akad. Wet. 14 [1911] (113-115) (English); Leiden Comm. Physic. Lab. No. 122 C 1911 (13-15) (English). [5660]. 40717

———— Verdere proeven met vloeibaar helium. E. Een helium-cryostaat. Opmerkingen over de vorige mededeelingen. [Further experiments with liquid helium. E. A helium-cryostat. Remarks on the preceding communications.] Amsterdam Versl. Wis. Nat. Afd. K. Akad. Wet. 20 [1911] (162-168) (Dutch); Amsterdam Proc. Sci. K. Akad. Wet. 14 [1911] (204-210) (English); Leiden Comm. Physic. Lab. 1911 No. 123 (1-8) (English). [1012 4210 4250]. 40718

———— Verdere proeven met vloeibaar helium. F. Isothermen van eenatomige gassen enz. IX. Thermische eigenschappen van helium. [Further experiments with liquid helium. F. Isotherms of monatomic gases, etc. IX. Thermal properties of helium.] Amsterdam Versl. Wis. Nat. Afd. K. Akad. Wet. 20 [1911] (793-799 with 1 pl.) (Dutch); Amster-

dam Proc. Sci. K. Akad. Wet. 14 [1911] (678-684 with 1 pl.) (English); Leiden Comm. Physic. Lab. 124b 1912 (11-18 with 1 pl.) (English). [1880 1450]. 40719

Kamerlingh Onnes, H[eike]. Verdere proeven met vloeibaar helium. G. Over den galvanischen weerstand van zuivere metalen enz. VI. De sprong bij het verdwijnen van den weerstand van kwik. [Further experiments with liquid helium. G. On the electrical resistance of pure metals, etc. VI. On the sudden change in the rate at which the resistance of mercury disappears.] Amsterdam Versl. Wis. Nat. Afd. K. Akad. Wet. 20 [1911] (799-802 with 1 pl.) (Dutch); Amsterdam Proc. Sci. K. Akad. Wet. 14 1912 (818-821 with 1 pl.) (English); Leiden Comm. Physic. Lab. 124c 1912 (21-25 with 1 pl.) (English). [5660]. 40720

———— La liquéfaction de l'hélium. Avec des notes sur le laboratoire cryogène de Leyde et sur des expériences à faire aux températures extrêmement basses. (Extrait de: Rapports et communications au premier congrès international de froid, Octobre 1908, 2. 101-126). Leiden Comm. Physic. Lab. Supplement No. 21 to No. 121-132 [1911] (1-34 avec 4 pl.). [1870 1012]. 40721

———— Bericht über die im cryogenen Laboratorium zu Leyden ausgeführten Untersuchungen. [Reprinted from: Bericht über den 2ten internationalen Kältencongress, Wien, Oktober 1910, II, 1-14.] Leiden Comm. Physic. Lab. Supplement No. 21 to No. 121-132 [1911] (37-55). [2455 4230 5460 1012]. 40722

———— en Crommelin, C[laude] A[ugust]. Isothermen van eenatomige stoffen en hunne binaire mengsels. X. Het gedrag van argon ten opzichte van de wet der overeenstemmende toestanden. [Isotherms of monatomic substances and of their binary mixtures. X. The behaviour of argon with respect to the law of corresponding states.] Amsterdam Versl. Wis. Nat. Afd. K. Akad. Wet. 20 [1911] (68-72 with 2 pl.) (Dutch); Amsterdam Proc. Sci. K. Akad. Wet. 14 [1911] (158-163 with 2 pl.) (English); Leiden Comm. Physic. Lab. No. 121b 1911

L

(21–26 with 1 pl.) (English). [1450
1885]. 40723

Kamerlingh Onnes, H[eike] en Crommelin, C[lau]de [August]. Isothermen van eenatomige stoffen en hunne binaire mengsels. XI. Opmerkingen betreffende de kritische temperatuur van neon en het smeltpunt van zuurstof. [Isotherms of monatomic substances and of their binary mixtures. XI. Remarks upon the critical temperature of neon and upon the melting point of oxygen.] Amsterdam Versl. Wis. Nat. Afd. K. Akad. Wet. 20 [1911] (73–74) (Dutch); Amsterdam Proc. Sci. K. Akad. Wet. 14 [1911] (163–165) (English); Leiden Comm. Physic. Lab. No. 121c 1911 (29–31) (English). [1880 1810]. 40724

—————— en Perrier, A[lbert]. Onderzoekingen over magnetisme. III. Over paramagnetisme en diamagnetisme bij zeer lage temperaturen. [Researches on magnetism. III. On para- and diamagnetism at very low temperatures.] Amsterdam Versl. Wis. Nat. Afd. K. Akad. Wet. 20 [1911] (75–81) (Dutch); Amsterdam Proc. Sci. K. Akad. Wet. 14 [1911] (115–122) (English); Leiden Comm. Physic. Lab. No. 122a 1911 (3–10) (English). [5460]. 40725

—————— Onderzoekingen over magnetisme. IV. Over paramagnetisme bij zeer lage temperaturen. V. De aanvangssusceptibiliteit van nikkel bij zeer lage temperaturen. [Researches on magnetism. IV. On paramagnetism at very low temperatures. V. The initial susceptibility of nickel at very low temperatures.] Amsterdam Versl. Wis. Nat. Afd. K. Akad. Wet. 20 [1911] (803–807) 1912 (1138–1144) (Dutch); Amsterdam Proc. Sci. K. Akad. Wet. 14 [1911] (674–678) 1912 (1004–1007) (English); Leiden Comm. Physic. Lab. 124 1912 (3–8) 126a 1912 (3–6) (English). [5460]. 40726

—————— v. Becquerel, H.

[Kanevskij, B. I.] Каневскій, Б. И. Термическія пары. [Les piles thermiques.] St. Peterburg Žurn. russ. fiz.-chim. Obsc. Fiz. Otd. 41 1909 (115–130). [5610 5710 6255]. 40727

Kann, L. Apparat zur Bestimmung der konstanten elektrischen Schwingungskreise (wie der Frequenz, Dämpfung u.s.w.) mittels Nullmethoden. Jahrb. drahtlos. Telegr. Leipzig 4 1911 (296–301). [6043]. 40728

Kanolt, C[larence] W[hitney]. The determination of melting points at high temperatures. [Abstract.] Physic. Rev. Ithaca N.Y. 32 1911 (443–444). [1810]. 40729

Kapp, Gisbert. Elektrische Wechselströme. 4. Aufl. (Leiners technische Bibliothek. Bd 6.) Leipzig (O. Leiner) 1911 (IV + 118). 19 cm. 2,85 M. [6045 5705]. 40730

Kármán, Th. v. Ueber die Formänderung dünnwandiger Rohre, insbesondere federnder Ausgleichrohre. Berlin Zs. Ver. D. Ing. 55 1911 (1889–1895). [0835]. 40731

—————— Ueber den Mechanismus des Widerstandes, den ein bewegter Körper in einer Flüssigkeit erfährt. Göttingen Nachr. Ges. Wiss. math.-phys. Kl. 1911 (509–517). [4940]. 40732

—————— Ueber die Turbulenzreibung verschiedener Flüssigkeiten. (Bemerkung zu der Arbeit von Frau Margrete Bose und Herrn E. Bose.) Physik. Zs. Leipzig 12 1911 (283–284). [0325]. 40733

Karpenko, W. Die Entropietafel für Gase und ihre Verwendung zur Berechnung der Verbrennungsmaschinen. Gasmotorentechnik Berlin 11 1911 (1–3 37–41 55–58 mit 1 Taf.). [2490]. 40734

Karrer, J. Partiell beaufschlagte Dampfturbinen. Zs. Turbinenwesen München 8 1911 (513–516). [2490]. 40735

Kasper, Franz Joseph. Messungen am Silberspektrum. Zs. wiss. Phot. Leipzig 10 1911 (53–62); Diss. Bonn. [1205]. 40736

Kassel, R. v. Drucker, K.

Kato, Y[ogoro]. Studies on colloidal barium sulphate. Kyoto Mem. Coll. Sci. Eng. 2 1910 (187–215). [0340]. 40737

Katz, David. Die Erscheinungsweisen der Farben und ihre Beeinflussung durch die individuelle Erfahrung. Zs. Psychol. Leipzig Abt. 1 ErgBd 7 1911 (XVIII + 425). [4450]. 40738

Katz, J. R. Onderzoekingen over de analogie tusschen opzwellen en mengen. Opzwelbare kristallen en mengkristallen. [Experimental researches on the analogy between swelling (imbibition) and mixing.] Amsterdam Versl. Wis. Nat. Afd. K. Akad. Wet. 19 [1910] (649–666 with 1 pl. 781–787 with g pl.) (Dutch); Amsterdam Proc. Sci. K. Akad. Wet. 13 1911 (958–981 with 2 pl.) (English). [0340 2457]. 40739

Katz, W. Röntgenaufnahmen auf Bromsilberpapier. Med. Klinik Berlin 6 (1449). [4240]. 40740

Kaufmann, W[alter]. Ein einfacher Vorlesungsapparat. [Unsichtbarkeit durchsichtiger Objekte bei gleichförmiger Beleuchtung.] Physik. Zs. Leipzig 12 1911 (29). [0050]. 40741

———— und **Meier**, W. Magnetische Eigenschaften elektrolytischer Eisenschichten. Physik. Zs. Leipzig 12 1911 (513–522). [5440 5466]. 40742

Kavan, J. Umělé chlazení v lučebním prūmyslu. [Künstliche Kälteproduktion in der chemischen Industrie.] Listy Chem. Prag 1910 (436–440). [2495]. 40743

Kaye, G. W. C. Some notes on the tilted gold leaf electrometer, with suggestions as to the manipulation of gold leaf suspensions, suitable insulators for electrometer work, etc. London Proc. Physic. Soc. 23 1911 (209–218). [6005]. 40744

———— A silica standard of length. London Proc. R. Soc. (Ser. A) 85 1911 (430–447). [0807]. 40745

Kayser, H[einrich]. Zur Spektroskopie des Sauerstoffs. [Entgegnung auf die Arbeit von W. Steubing.] Ann. Physik Leipzig (4. Folge) 34 1911 (498–504). [4205]. 40746

———— Die Volumenänderung des Betons beim Erhärten. Armiert. Beton Berlin 4 1911 (396–397). [1400]. 40747

———— Die Geburt der Spektroskopie. [Robert Wilhelm Bunsen.] Zs. Elektroch. Halle 17 1911 (205–206). [0010 3030]. 40748

———— Normalen aus dem Bogenspektrum des Eisens im internationalen System. Zs. wiss. Phot. Leipzig 9 1911 (173–185). [3430 4205]. 40749

Kayser, H[einrich], **Fabry**, Ch. and **Ames**, J[oseph] S[weetman]. Additional secondary standards, international system, in the arc spectrum of iron. Astroph. J. Chicago Ill. 33 1911 (85 with table). [3430 4205]. 40750

———— v. Steubing, W.

Keesom, W[illem] H[endrik]. Spektrophotometrische Untersuchung der Opaleszenz eines einkomponentigen Stoffes in der Nähe des kritischen Zustandes. Ann. Physik Leipzig (4. Folge) 35 1911 (591–598). [3810 1880]. 40751

———— De verdampingswarmte van waterstof. [La chaleur de vaporisation de l'hydrogène.] Handl. Ned. Nat. Geneesk. Congr. 13 1911 (181–186). [1680]. 40752

Keil, Georg. Die Beziehung der sensibilisierenden Wirkung des Uranylsulfates zu seiner Fluorescenz. Diss. München (Druck v. Kastner & Callwey) 1911 (22). 22 cm. [4230 4225]. 40753

Keller, Gustav Adolf. Hirn, sein Leben und seine Werke. Beitr. Gesch. Technik Berlin 3 1911 (20–60). [0010]. 40754

Keller, Hans. Werdegang der modernen Physik. (Aus Natur und Geisteswelt. Bd 343.) Leipzig (B. G. Teubner) 1911 (IV + 113). 18 cm. 1,25 M. [0010 0030]. 40755

Kellermann. Über die Technologie beim Blechinstrumentenbau. D. InstrbauZtg Berlin 12 1911 (545–546 561–563). [9410]. 40756

Kelley, George Leslie v. Richards, T. W.

Kelvin, Lord. Mathematical and Physical Papers, vol. 5. Cambridge 1911 (618). [0030]. 40757

Kemna, G. Apparat zum Nachweis des Pascalschen Gesetzes der Druckfortpflanzung. Zs. physik. Unterr. Berlin 24 1911 (221–223). [0050]. 40758

Kemp, P. e **Stephens**, W. A. La scarica elettrica nell'aria provocata da differenze di potenziale alternanti. [Recensione. Trad.] Atti Ass. elettrotecn. Milano 15 1911 (45–46). [6820]. 40759

Kennelly, A[rthur] E[dwin]. Vectordiagrams of oscillating-current circuits. [With bibliography.] Boston Proc.

Amer. Acad. Arts Sci. 46 1911 (371–421 with fig.). [6460 6820]. 40760

Kent, William. A kinetic theory of gravitation. Science New York (N. Ser.) 33 1911 (619–620). [0700]. 40761

Kerbacher, Mario. Risultati degli ultimi studi sulle scariche elettriche oscillatorie. Elettricista Roma (Ser. 2) 10 1911 (17–18). [6820]. 40762

Kerbaker, Mario. L'avvenire dell'arco voltaico. Elettricista Roma (Ser. 2) 9 1910 (313–315). [6830]. 40763

Kerber, Arthur. Ein von P. Rudolph berechnetes Planar. Mechaniker Berlin 20 1912 (5–7 1819). [3085]. 40764

———— Ein Doppelanastigmat aus Pariser Gläsern. Mechaniker Berlin 19 1911 (37–39). [3085]. 40765

———— Abänderung des Doppelanastigmaten aus Pariser Gläsern. Mechaniker Berlin 19 1911 (110). [3085]. 40766

———— Ein Aplanat aus Jenaer Gläsern. Mechaniker Berlin 19 1911 (121–122 135–137). [3085]. 40767

———— Ein Dreimenisken-Objektiv. Mechaniker Berlin 19 1911 (169–170 185–186). [3085]. 40768

Kerillis, C. de. Observations faites au Labrador à l'occasion de l'éclipse totale de Soleil du 29–30 août 1905 par les Missions du croiseur Chasse-loup-Laubat, commandé par M. le capitaine de vaisseau C. de Kerillis. Ann. bur. longit. Paris 8 1911 (Q. 1 à Q. 22). [4205]. 40769

Kern, Felix. Erzeugung von geradsichtigem, polarisiertem Licht durch einfache Glasprismen. Centralztg Opt. Berlin 32 1911 (153–154). [4010]. 40770

Kernot, G. Sulla presenza di elementi radioattivi in alcune incrostazioni delle fumarole del Vesuvio. Napoli Rend. Soc. sc. (Ser. 3) 16 1910 (48–50). [4275]. 40771

———— e **Pomilio, U.** Ricerche sul comportamento crioscopico e viscosimetrico di alcune soluzioni di chinolina. Napoli Rend. Soc. sc. (Ser. 3) 17 1911 (359–372). [0325]. 40772

Kesseldorfer, W. I contatori a mercurio con speciale riguardo al tipo Isaria. [Sunto. Trad.] Atti Assoc. elettrotecn. Milano 15 1911 (946–949). [6010]. 40773

———— Theorie und Konstruktion der Quecksilber-Motorzähler mit besonderer Berücksichtigung des Fabrikates der Isaria-Zählerwerke A.-G., München. Elektrot. Zs. Berlin 32 1911 (684–690). [6070]. 40774

Kettner, Cornelis Hendrik. De oplosbaarheid van natriumkarbonaat. [La solubilité du carbonate de soude.] Amsterdam Chem. Weekbl. 8 1911 (391–393). [1887]. 40775

Kiebitz, Franz. Über die Geschichte der Erdantennen. Berlin Verh. D. physik. Ges. 14 1912 (10–17). [6615]. 40776

———— Neuere Versuche über gerichtete drahtlose Telegraphie mit Erdantennen. Berlin Verh. D. physik. Ges. 13 1911 (876–889). [6615]. 40777

———— Erwiderung auf den Aufsatz des Herrn Zehnder: Ueber gerichtete drahtlose Telegraphie mit Erdströmen. [Nebst] Antwort von L. Zehnder. Berlin Verh. D. physik. Ges. 13 1911 (1058–1059 1059–1060). [6615]. 40778

———— Über aperiodische Detektorkreise. Elektrot. Zs. Berlin 33 1912 (132–133). [6043 6615]. 40779

Kilchling, K. v. Koenigsberger, J.

Kimura, Masamichi and **Tamaki, Kajuro.** Oscilloscopic study of condenser discharge with the application to crystals-contact detector for electric oscillation. Kyoto Mem. Coll. Sci. Eng. 3 1911 (189–192 with pl.). [6820 6043]. 40780

———— and **Yamamoto, Kiyoshi.** Arc characteristics in gases and vapours. Kyoto Mem. Coll. Sci. Eng. 2 1910 (47–58). [6830]. 40781

———— On the unilateral electric conductivity of certain minerals in contact and of certain minerals and metals in contact. Kyoto Mem. Coll. Sci. Eng. 2 1910 (63–82). [6047]. 40782

———— Crystals and crystal-metal contact detectors for electric oscillations. Kyoto Mem. Coll. Sci. Eng. 2 1910 (83–106). [6043] 40783

———— and **Ichinohe, Ryujiro.** Preliminary note on the thermoelectric properties of some minerals. Kyoto Mem. Coll. Sci. Eng. 2 1910 (59–64). [5710].   40784

Kimura, M[asamichi] r. Ichinohe, R.

Kimura, Shunkichi. 1000-Funkenfrequenz. Jahrb. drahtlos. Telegr. Leipzig 5 1911 (222–235). [6615 6820]. 40785

King, Edward S[kinner]. Transformation of prismatic to normal spectra. Cambridge Mass. Ann. Obs. Harvard Coll. **59** [1910] (205–222 with fig. pl. tables). [3030].   40786

———— The effect of pressure upon electric furnace spectra. Astroph. J. Chicago Ill. **34** 1911 (37–56 with tables pl.); [abstract] Physic. Rev. Ithaca N.Y. **32** 1911 (440–441). [4206 4208].
                                                40787

———— The influence of a magnetic field upon the spark spectra of iron and titanium – summary of results. Astroph. J. Chicago Ill. **34** 1911 (225–250 with pl. tables). [4208].   40788

Kinoshita, M[asao] and **Ichinohe**, R[yujiro]. A glow phenomenon in vacuum bulbs. Kyoto Mem. Coll. Sci. Eng. 2 1910 (171–186). [6840]. 40789

———— On ionization due to an incandescent metallic filament in a vacuum tube. Kyoto Mem. Coll. Sci. Eng. 3 1911 (171–188). [6805 5685].
                                                40790

———— r. Ichinohe.

Kinoshita, S[uekichi]. **Nishikawa**, S[eiji] and **Ono**, S[uminosuke]. On the amount of the radioactive products present in the atmosphere. Tokyo Su. Buts. Kw. K. (Ser. 2) 6 1911 (92–111). [4275].   40791

Kinoshita, Toosaku. Über den Einfluss mehrerer aufeinanderfolgender wirksamer Reize auf den Ablauf der Reaktionsbewegungen bei Wirbellosen. Mitt. 2 u. 3 : Versuche an Cölenteraten. Arch. Ges. Physiol. Bonn **140** 1911 (167–208).   40792

Kinsloe, Ch. L. Effetto della forma delle correnti alternate sulla durata e sul consumo specifico dei vari tipi di lampade ad incandescenza. [Sunto.] Atti Ass. elettrotecn. Milano **15** 1911 (50–52). [6480].   40793

Kinzbrunner, C. Die Gleichstrommaschine. 2., verb. Aufl. (Sammlung Göschen. 257). Leipzig (G. J. Göschen) 1911 (154). 16 cm. 0,80 M. [6060].   40794

Kionka, H[einrich]. Die Radioaktivität der Mineralwässer. D. med. Wochenschr. Leipzig 37 1911 (769–774). [4275].   40795

———— Das Radium vom biologischen Standpunkt. Med. Klinik Berlin 7 1911 (685–690). [4275]. 40796

Kirkby, P. J. A theory of the chemical action of the electric discharge in electrolytic gas. London Proc. R. Soc. (Ser. A) **85** 1911 (151–174). [6800].
                                                40797

Kistner, A. Physikalische Irrtümer im Wandel der Zeit. Wiss. Rdsch. Leipzig **1911–12** 1911 (10–15). [0010].
                                                40798

Kjellin, F. A†. Die elektrolytische Dissociationstheorie unter Berücksichtigung der elektrischen Energie der Ionen. Zs. physik. Chem. Leipzig **77** 1911 (192–212). [6250].   40799

Kleeman, R. D. An investigation o. the determinations of the law of chemical attraction between atoms from physical data. Phil. Mag. London (Ser. 6) **21** 1911 (83–102). [0150].
                                                40800

———— Relations between the density, temperature and pressure of substances. Phil. Mag. London (Ser. 6) 21 1911 (325–341). [0100]. 40801

———— Molecular attraction and the properties of liquids. Phil. Mag. London (Ser. 6) **22** 1911 (566–586). [6020].   40802

Klein, G. Untersuchungen an Federmanometern. Zs. Dampfkessel Berlin **34** 1911 (285–288 297–300). [0835 0840].   40803

———— Die elastische Nachwirkung der Federmanometer. Zs. Dampfkessel Berlin **34** 1911 (405–408). [0835].   40804

Kleinpeter, H. Zur Systematik des Unterrichtsganges in der Elektrizitätslehre. Zs. physik. Unterr. Berlin **24** 1911 (129–137). [0050]. 40805

———— Projektion von Linienspektren. Zs. physik. Unterr. Berlin **25** 1912 (39–40). [0050].   40806

Klemenc, Alfons. Zur Messung der elektrischen Leitfähigkeit. ChemZtg Cöthen 35 1911 (1420). [6240]. 40807

Klemensiewicz, Z. Über die Entstehung positiver Ionen an erhitzten Metallen. Ann. Physik Leipzig (4. Folge) **36** 1911 (796–814). [6800 6805]. 40808

——— O powstawaniu dodatnich ionów na ogrzanych metalach. [Sur les ions positifs qui prennent naissance à la surface des métaux portés à des températures élevées.] Kraków Rozpr. Akad. **11 A** 1911 (159–177). [6805]. 40809

——— O powstawaniu dodatnich ionów na ogrzanych metalach. [Über die Bildung positiver Ionen an erhitzten Metallen.] Kraków Bull. Intern. Acad. **1911 A** (417–424). [6805]. 40810

Klimont, J. Ueber die Refraktionskonstanten bei vegetabilischen Oelen. Zs. angew. Chem. Leipzig **24** 1911 (254–256). [3020]. 40811

Klinckowstroem, Carl Graf v. Der Erfinder des Teleskops. Mitt. Gesch. Med. Hamburg **10** 1911 (249–257). [0010]. 40812

Kling, André. Influence des catalyseurs dans les déterminations de densités de vapeur. Paris C. R. Acad. sci. **152** 1911 (702–704). [0810]. 40813

Klingelfuss, Fr. Exakte Dosierung therapeutischer Voll- und Teildosen und praktische Eichung einer Röntgenröhre. Verh. D. Röntgenges. Hamburg **7** 1911 (120–129). [6080 4240]. 40814

——— Zeitschalter. Zwangläufige Steuerung eines Induktoriums zur vollständigen Ausschaltung der Schliessungsinduktion. Verh. D. Röntgenges. Hamburg **7** 1911 (148–149). [6040]. 40815

Klooster, H[endrik] S[joerd] van r. Jaeger, F. M.

Klughardt, August. Ueber einige Erscheinungen, die bei der Beugung des Lichtes durch Gitter auftreten. Diss. Jena. Leipzig (Druck v. Sturm & Koppe) 1911 (59). 22 cm. [3630]. 40816

Kneser, Adolf. Die Integralgleichungen und ihre Anwendungen in der mathematischen Physik. Vorlesungen . . . Braunschweig (F. Vieweg & S.) 1911 (VIII + 243). 23 cm. 6 M. [2010 9100 9110 9135]. 40817

Knipp, Ch. T. Ein leistungsfähiger und schnell wirkender Apparat zur

Destillation von Quecksilber. **Physik.** Zs. Leipzig **12** 1911 (270–271). [0090]. 40818

Knoblauch, Oskar und **Mollier**, Hilde. Die spezifische Wärme c_p des überhitzten Wasserdampfes für Drücke von 2 bis 3 kg qcm und Temperaturen von 350 bis 550° C. Berlin Zs. Ver. D. Ing. **55** 1911 (665–673); Mitt. ForschArb. Ingenieurw. Berlin H. **108-109** 1911 (79–106). [1640]. 40819

Knoblauch, W. Messapparate und Messmethoden für den praktischen Installateur . . . 2. Aufl. (Leiner's techn. Bibliothek. Bd 2.) Leipzig (O. Leiner) 1911 (VII + 263). 19 cm. Geb. 4,50 M. [6010]. 40821

Knoche, Walter. Bestimmungen des Emanationsgehaltes im Meerwasser und der induzierten Aktivität der Luft zwischen der chilenischen Küste und der Osterinsel. I. II. Physik. Zs. Leipzig **13** 1912 (112–115 152–157). [4275]. 40822

Knosp, Gaston. Notes sur la musique indo-chinoise. Riv. music. Torino **17** 1910 (415–432). [9400]. 40823

Knothe, A. Neue Entdeckungen betreffend die optischen Erscheinungen und die Strahlenwege am Prisma. Centralztg Opt. Berlin **32** 1911 (246–247 261–262 275–276). [3155]. 40824

Knowlton, A[nsel] A[lphonso]. Preparation and properties of the Heusler alloys. Physic. Rev. Ithaca N.Y. **32** 1911 (54–68 with fig. tables). [5466]. 40825

Knudsen, Martin. Luftarters termiske Molekulartryk i Rør. [The thermal molecular pressure of gases in tubes.] Kobenhavn Vid. Selsk. Overs. **1910** (437–450 with 1 pl.). [0200]. 40826

——— Die molekulare Wärmeleitung der Gase und der Akkomodationskoeffizient. Ann. Physik Leipzig (4. Folge) **34** 1911 (593–656). [2035 0200]. 40827

——— Erwiderung an Hrn. M. v. Smoluchowski [betr. Theorie des absoluten Manometers]. Ann. Physik Leipzig (4. Folge) **34** 1911 (823–826). [0835 0200]. 40828

——— Molekularströmung des Wasserstoffs durch Röhren und das Hitzdrahtmanometer. Ann. Physik Leipzig (4. Folge) **35** 1911 (389–396). [0325 0835 0200]. 40829

Knudsen, Martin. Zur Theorie der Wärmeleitung in verdünnten Gasen und der dabei auftretenden Druckkräfte. Erwiderung an Hrn. M. v. Smoluchowski. Ann. Physik Leipzig (4. Folge) 36 1911 (871–872). [2035]. 40830

—————— Luftarters Varmeledning og Accomodationskoefficient. [Conduction of heat through gases and the coefficient of accommodation.] Kobenhavn Vid. Selsk. Overs. 1911 (139–200 with pl.). [0200 2035]. 40831

—————— und **Weber,** Sophus. Luftwiderstand gegen die langsame Bewegung kleiner Kugeln. Ann. Physik Leipzig (4. Folge) 36 1911 (981–994). [6845]. 40832

Kobayashi, M[atsusuke]. Metallographische Untersuchung über die Legierungen des Tellurs mit Cadmium und Zinn. Kyoto Mem. Coll. Sci. Eng. 2 1910 (353–363 with pl.). [1840]. 40833

Koch, Hermann. Das Absorptionsspektrum des Anilins im Ultravioletten. Zs. wiss. Phot. Leipzig 9 1911 (401–414 mit 1 Taf.); Diss. Bonn. Leipzig (J. A. Barth) 1911 (19 mit 1 Taf.). 24 cm. [3860]. 40834

Koch, John. Über die Reflexion des Lichtes an Kalkspat in der Nähe von dessen metallischer Reflexionsbande bei ca. 6,6 μ. 1. Ark. Matem. Stockholm 7 No. 9 1911 (16 mit 8 Fig.). [3850 3860]. 40835

Koch, K. R. Ueber die äussere Reibung tropfbarer Flüssigkeiten. Ann. Physik Leipzig (4. Folge) 35 1911 (613–616). [0300 0325]. 40836

—————— Das Phonendoskop als Wünschelrute. Physik. Zs. Leipzig 12 1911 (112–113). [0090]. 40837

—————— Der Neubau des physikalischen Instituts der technischen Hochschule Stuttgart. Physik. Zs. Leipzig 12 1911 (818–831). [0000]. 40838

Koch, Peter Paul. Ueber die Messung der Intensitätsverteilung in Spektrallinien. 1. Mit Anwendungen auf Interferenzspektroskopie. Zum Teil gemeinsam mit Anton Ernst Weber. Ann. Physik Leipzig (4. Folge) 34 1911 (377–444 mit 1 Taf.). [4205 4210 3610]. 40839

—————— Zur Frage der Dissymmetrie der Zeemanschen Triplets. Bemerkung zu einer Veröffentlichung des Hrn. Voigt. Ann. Physik Leipzig (4. Folge) 35 1911 (1034–1036). [6660 4208]. 40840

Koch, Peter Paul. Zahl der Zentren von Lichtemission und Intensitätsverhältnisverschiedener Interferenzordnungen. Bemerkung zu einer Arbeit von Hrn. Stark. [Photographisches-photometrisches Messverfahren.] Physik. Zs. Leipzig 12 1911 (12–14). [4225 3630]. 40841

—————— Über ein einfaches Montierungsverfahren für Etalons nach Fabry und Perot. Zs. Instrumentenk. Berlin 31 1911 (378–380). [3610 3165]. 40842

—————— und **Friedrich,** Walter. Über den Nachweis anomaler Dispersion in leuchtendem Quecksilberdampf. Physik. Zs. Leipzig 12 1911 (1193–1197 mit 1 Taf.). [3850 4205]. 40843

—————— v. Stark, J., Tchougaeff, L.

Kock, F. Lichtbogengenerator für Laboratoriumszwecke. Physik. Zs. Leipzig 12 1911 (124–126). [6830]. 40844

—————— Apparat zur Aufnahme und Demonstration von Resonanzkurven. Physik. Zs. Leipzig 12 1911 (379–386). [0050 6800 6660]. 40845

—————— Aufnahme von Resonanzkurven unter Anwendung eines Kurvenzeichners. Diss. Berlin (Druck v. A. W. Schade) 1912 (33). 27 cm. [6015 6820 6043]. 40846

Köhler, A. Flüssigkeitskondensoren von grosser Apertur. Zs. Instrumentenk. Berlin 31 1911 (270–276). [3090 0050]. 40847

—————— Eine neue Nernstlampe für Mikroprojektion und Mikrophotographie. Zs. wiss. Mikrosk. Leipzig 27 1911 (477–488). [3082]. 40848

Köhler, Otto. Steigerung der spezifischen Leistung von Viertakt-Gasmaschinen mit Druckluftspülung. [Nebst Bemerkung von Wilh. Hellmann.] Berlin Zs. Ver. D. Ing. 55 1911 (1582–1584). [2490]. 40849

—————— Thermodynamische Untersuchung schnellaufender Dieselmotoren. [Nebst Bemerkung von M. Seiliger.] Berlin Zs. Ver. D. Ing. 56 1912 (241–243 243–244). [2490]. 40850

Köllner, [Hans]. Praktische Ergebnisse aus dem Gebiete der Augenheilkunde. Die diagnostische Bedeutung der erworbenen Farbensinnstörungen. Berliner klin. Wochenschr. **48** 1911 (846-849 897-900). 40851

Kölsch, O. Die langsam laufende, zwangläufige Frikart-Steuerung. Dinglers polyt. J. Berlin **326** 1911 (593-599 612-615). [2490]. 40852

König, Edmund. Die Materie. (Wege zur Philosophie. Nr. 2.) Göttingen (Vandenhoeck & Ruprecht) 1911 (IV + 108). 19 cm. 1.50 M. [0000]. 40853

König, W[alter]. Neuere Untersuchungen zur Theorie der Kundtschen Staubfiguren. Berlin Verh. D. physik. Ges. **13** 1911 (805-812) ; Physik. Zs. Leipzig **12** 1911 (991-994). [9130 9320]. 40854

————— Zwei Modelle zur Optik. [I. Fadenmodell zum Astigmatismus. II. Apparat zur Demonstration des Strahlenganges beim Regenbogen.] Zs. physik. Unterr. Berlin **24** 1911 (1-5). [0050 4430 3640]. 40855

Koenigsberger, Joh. Polarisation des Lichtes an Gittern mit sehr kleiner Gitterkonstante. (Analogon zu dem Gitterversuch von H. Hertz.) Physik. Zs. Leipzig **12** 1911 (637-639). [4010]. 40856

————— Ueber die Bestimmung der Zahl schwingender Teile in Dämpfen, Lösungen, leuchtenden Gasen. Physik. Zs. Leipzig **12** 1911 (1-5). [4960 6625 3850 3800]. 40857

————— Physikalische Messungen der chemischen Affinität durch Elektrizitätsleitung und Kanalstrahlen. Physik. Zs. Leipzig **12** 1911 (1084-1090); Berlin Verh. D. physik. Ges. **13** 1911 (931-944). [6800 5675 6345]. 40858

————— Ueber die Atomwärmen der Elemente. Zs. Elektroch. Halle **17** 1911 (289-293). [1660 1600]. 40859

————— Methoden zur Erkennung submikroskopischer Strukturen. Zs. wiss. Mikrosk. Leipzig **28** 1911 (34-41). [3082]. 40860

————— Zur Wärmeleitung von Graphit und Diamant. Berlin Verh. D. physik. Ges. **14** 1912 (9). [2020]. 40861

————— Über die Wirkung der Gravitation auf die Elektronen. Berlin Verh. D. physik. Ges. **14** 1912 (185-188). [6845]. 40862

Koenigsberger, Joh. und **Kilchling,** K. Zu P. Zeeman, Considerations concerning light radiation usw. [Einfluss des elektrischen Feldes auf die Lichtemission.] Ann. Physik Leipzig (4. Folge) **37** 1912 (345-346). [6635]. 40863

————— und **Küpferer,** K. Zur Absorption des Lichtes in festen und gasförmigen Körpern. Ann. Physik Leipzig (4. Folge) **37** 1912 (601-641). [3810 3860 3850 4230]. 40864

————— und **Kutschewski,** J. Notiz über gerade Dispersion von Kanalstrahlen. Berlin Verh. D. physik. Ges. **13** 1911 (151-153). [6840]. 40865

————— Über das Verhalten der Heliumkanalstrahlen verglichen mit dem der α-Strahlen und dem des Heliumatoms und über die Affinität der Atome zum Elektron. Heidelberg SitzBer. Ak. Wiss. math-natw. Kl. **1911** Abh. 8 (13). [6845]. 40866

————— Über den Durchgang von Kanalstrahlen durch Gase. Ann. Physik Leipzig (4. Folge) **37** 1912 (161-232). [6845]. 40867

————— Bildung und Geschwindigkeit negativer Ionen im Kanalstrahl. Berlin Verh. D. physik. Ges. **14** 1912 (1-8 168). [6845]. 40868

————— Über das Verhalten von Kanalstrahlen beim Durchgang durch Gase. [Referat.] Heidelberg SitzBer. Ak. Wiss. math.-natw. Kl. **1912** Abh. 1 (6). [6845 3875]. 40870

————— und **Müller,** W. J. Bemerkung zu einer Bestimmung des Molekulardurchmessers und über minimale optisch wirksame Schichtdicke. Physik. Zs. Leipzig **12** 1911 (606). [0150 3800]. 40871

Reichenheim, O[tto] und **Schilling,** K. Bemerkung zu der Abhandlung von F. Streintz und A. **Wellik.** Über den Widerstand zwischen Metall und Kristall an ebenen Grenzflächen. Physik. Zs. Leipzig **12** 1911 (1139-1142). [5640 5660]. 40872

————— und **Weiss,** J. Ueber die thermoelektrischen Effekte (Thermokräfte, Thomsonwärme) und die Wärmeleitung in einigen Elementen und

Verbindungen und über die experimentelle Prüfung der Elektronentheorie. Ann. Physik Leipzig (4. Folge) 35 1911 (1-46). [5710 2020 5675].
40873

Koenigsberger, Joh. v. Bahr, E.

Koenigsberger, Leo. Hermann von Helmholtz. Gekürzte Volksausgabe. Braunschweig (F. Vieweg & S.) 1911 (XII + 356 mit 2 Portr.). 23 cm. [0010].
40874

Körber, Friedrich. Zu Hrn. Lussanas Bemerkung: Ueber den Einfluss von Druck und Temperatur auf das elektrolytische Leitvermögen von Lösungen. Zs. physik. Chem. Leipzig 77 1911 (420-422). [6240].
40875

Korber, Heinrich. Widerstandsmaterial mit variablem Temperaturkoeffizienten. Zs. angew. Chem. Leipzig 24 1911 (1402-1405). [5060].
40876

Kohlrausch, Friedrich. Gesammelte Abhandlungen. Hrsg. von Wilhelm Hallwachs [u. a.]. Bd 2. Elektrolyte . . . Mit einem Lebensbild des Verf. von A. Heydweiller. Leipzig (J. A. Barth) 1911 (LXXII + 1305 mit 5 Taf.). 23 cm. 30 M. [0030 6200 6240 0010].
40877

Kohlrausch, K. W. F. u. Schweidler, E. v. Über die experimentelle Untersuchung der Schwankungen der radioaktiven Umwandlung. (Vorl. Mitt.) Physik. Zs. Leipzig 13 1912 (11-14). [4275 6845].
40878

Kohlschütter, V[olkmar]. Chemische Wirkungen von Kanalstrahlen. Zs. Elektroch. Halle 17 1911 (393-398). [6845].
40880

Kohnstamm, Ph[ilipp] en Ornstein, L[eonard] S[alomon]. Het warmtetheorema van Nernst en de chemische feiten. [Nernst's theorem of heat and chemical facts.] Amsterdam Versl. Wis. Nat. Afd. K. Akad. Wet. 20 1912 (822-839) (Dutch); Amsterdam Proc. Sci. K. Akad. Wet. 14 1912 (802-818) (English). [2415].
40881

———— en Reeders, J[ohan] C[hristiaan]. Over de condensatieverschijnselen bij mengsels van koolzuur en nitrobenzol in verband met dubbele retrograde condensatie. [On the phenomena of condensation for mixtures of carbonic acid and nitrobenzene in connection with double retrograde condensation.] Amsterdam Versl. Wis. Nat. Afd. K. Akad. Wet. 20 [1911] (359-367) (Dutch); Amsterdam Proc. Sci. K. Akad. Wet. 14 [1911] (270-278) (English). [2457].
40882

Kolb, R. Vergleich von Anhydrit, Cölestin, Baryt und Anglesit in bezug auf die Veränderung ihrer geometrischen und optischen Verhältnisse mit der Temperatur. Zs. Krystallogr. Leipzig 49 1911 (44-61). [3830].
40883

———— v. Rinne, F.

Kolbe, Bruno. Neue Versuche mit dem elektrodynamischen Pendel. Zs. physik. Unterr. Leipzig 24 1911 (276-278). [6420 0050].
40884

Kolhorster, Werner. Beiträge zur Kenntnis der radioaktiven Eigenschaften des Karlsbader Sprudels. Diss. Halle a. S. (Druck v. H. John) 1911 (55 mit Taf.). 22 cm. [4275].
40885

Kolowrat, L. Sur une tentative faite pour déceler la conductibilité électrique du radium D. Radium Paris 8 1911 (401-404 av. fig.). [4275].
40886

Komp, Rudolf. Die grüne Kohlenbande. λ = 5635. Zs. wiss. Phot. Leipzig 10 1911 (117-134); Diss. Bonn. Leipzig (J. A. Barth) 1911 (23). 24 cm. [4205].
40887

Konrad, Paul. Nouvel appareil de commande automatique des aiguilles de voie. Neuchâtel Bul. Soc. Sci. Nat. 37 1910 (147-157 av. 3 fig.). [0090].
40888

Koref, F. Messungen der spezifischen Wärme bei tiefen Temperaturen mit dem Kupferkalorimeter. Ann. Physik Leipzig (4. Folge) 36 1911 (49-73). [1620 1610 1680].
40889

Korn, A[rthur]. Weiterführung eines mechanischen Bildes der elektromagnetischen Erscheinungen. Berlin Verh. D. physik. Ges. 13 1911 (249-256). [4940].
40890

———— Ueber die jüngsten Fortschritte der Bildtelegraphie. Berlin Verh. D. physik. Ges. 13 1911 (257-265); Zs. Schwachstromtechn. München 5 1911 (117-120). [6480].
40891

———— L'état hélicoïdal de la matière électrique; hypothèses nouvelles pour expliquer mécaniquement les phénomènes électromagnétiques. Paris C. R. Acad. sci. 152 1911 (306-309). [6410].
40892

Korn, A[rthur]. Die Entwicklung der Bildtelegraphie. Fortschr. natw. Forschg Berlin **1** 1910 (177–194). [6480].
40893

———— und **Glatzel,** Bruno. Handbuch der Phototelegraphie und Telautographie. Leipzig (O. Nemnich) 1911 (XVI + 488). 24 cm. Geb. 28 M. [6480].
40894

[**Korolikov,** A[leksej] L[ivovič] et **Bartoševič,** A. M.] Королькóвъ, А[лексѣй Лвовичъ] и Бартошевичъ, А. М. Изслѣдованіе цирконовыхъ лампъ накаливанія. [Recherches sur les lampes à incandescence de zirconium.] St. Peterburg Žurn. russ. fiz.-chim. Obšč. Fiz. otd. **41** 1909 (258–261 rés. franç. 262). [5660 5720 1410 6080].
40895

Korteweg, D[iederik] J[ohannes] en **Schreinemakers,** F[rans] A[nton] H[ubert]. Algemeene beschouwingen over de raakkrommen van oppervlakken met kegels, met toepassing op verzadigings- en binodale lijnen in ternaire stelsels. [General considerations on the curves of contact of surfaces with cones, with application to the lines of saturation and binodal lines in ternary systems.] Amsterdam Versl. Wis. Nat. Afd. K. Akad. Wet. **20** [1911] (476–490 with fig.) (Dutch); Amsterdam Proc. Sci. K. Akad. Wet. **14** [1911] (510–524 with fig.) (English). [2457].
40896

Kossel, Walther. Über die sekundäre Kathodenstrahlung in Gasen in der Nähe des Optimums der Primärgeschwindigkeit. Ann. Physik Leipzig (4. Folge) **37** 1912 (393–424). [6845].
40897

Kotelow, K. J. v. Über die Ionisation der Atmosphäre in Jekaterinoslaw während des Durchganges des Halley-schen Kometen. Berlin Verh. D. physik. Ges. **13** 1911 (307–312). [5270].
40898

Kousleff, Christo. Conductibilité thermique et électrique des principales matières obturatrices. Schweiz. Vierteljahrschr. Zahnheilk Zürich **19** 1909 part. franç. (36–51). [2020 5220].
40899

Kovařik, Alois F. Bemerkung über den Wert der Zerfall-periode des Act. C. (Note on the half-period value of Act. C.) (Uebers.) Physik. Zs. Leipzig **12** 1911 (83). [4275].
40900

———— c. **Geiger,** H.

Kowalski, Joseph von. Untersuchungen über Phosphoreszenz organischer Verbindungen bei tiefen Temperaturen. Physik. Zs. Leipzig **12** 1911 (956–969). [4230 3860].
40901

———— et **Dzierzbicki,** J. de. Influence des groupements fonctionnels sur le spectre de phosphorescence progressive. Paris C. R. Acad. sci. **152** 1911 (83–85). [4230].
40902

Kraft, Kamil. O pewnej tożsamości w Analizie wektoryalnej czterowymiarowej i o jej zastosowaniu do Elektrodynamiki. [Eine Identität in der vierdimensionalen Vektoranalysis und deren Anwendung in der Elektrodynamik.] Kraków Bull. Intern. Acad. **1911** A (537–541). [4940 6410].
40903

———— O całkowaniu bezpośredniem typowych wyrażeń różniczkowych wektorów czasowo - przestrzennych. [Über die direkte Integration der typischen Differentialausdrücke von Raum-Zeit-Vektoren.] Kraków Bull. Intern. Acad. **1911** A (564–576). [4940 6410].
40904

———— O wyrażeniu całkowem wektorów elektromagnetycznych, wprowadzonych przez Minkowskiego do Elektrodynamiki poruszających się ciał materyalnych. [Zum Problem der Integraldarstellung der elektromagnetischen Vektoren in bewegten Körpern nach Minkowski's „Grundgleichungen".] Kraków Bull. Intern. Acad. **1911** A (596–619). [4940 6410].
40905

Kranz, Walther. Die ältesten Farbenlehren der Griechen. Hermes Berlin **47** 1912 (126–140). [0010].
40906

Kraus, Edward H. Eine neue Jolly'sche Federwage zur Bestimmung des spezifischen Gewichts. Centralbl. Min. Stuttgart **1911** (366–368). [0825].
40907

Krause, Robert L[oui]s. Ueber die Einwirkung von Hydrazin, Wasserstoffsuperoxyd und Hydroxylamin auf Zinkäthyl und Magnesiumhalogenalkyle, und über die Pseudoradioaktivität des Zinkperoxyds. Diss. Heidelberg (Druck v. Rössler & Herbert) 1910 (82). 22 cm. [4270].
40908

Krauss, [F.]. Polarisation. [Nachträge.] [In : Die Methoden der organischen Chemie. Hrsg. v. Th. Weyl.

Bd 2.] Leipzig (G. Thieme) 1911 (1372-1375). [4000]. 40909

Krawetz, T. Ueber einen möglichen Unterschied zwischen Emissions- und Absorptionsspektren. Physik. Zs. Leipzig **12** 1911 (510-511). [4205 4960]. 40910

Kregten, J[acob] R[ein] N[icolaas] van _v._ Jaeger, F. M.

Kretzschmar, F. E. Die Krankheiten des stationären elektrischen Blei-Akkumulators, ihre Entstehung, Feststellung . . . München u. Berlin (R. Oldenbourg) 1912 (VII + 162). 22 cm. Geb. 6 M. [5620]. 40911

Kreul, Wilhelm. Thermodynamische Untersuchung schnellaufender Dieselmotoren. [Nebst Bemerkung von M. **Seiliger.**] Berlin Zs. Ver. D. Ing. **55** 1911 (1493-1495). [2490]. 40912

Kreutz, St. Piezooptyczne własności salmiaku. [Piezooptisches Verhalten von Salmiak.] Kraków Bull. Intern. Acad. 1911 A (118-122). [3855]. 40913

Kreybig, Ludwig von. Pyknometer für Dichtebestimmungen. ChemZtg Cöthen **35** 1911 (1120). [0810]. 40914

Kreybig, Rezső. Prizmás kézi messzelátók. [Hand-Prismenfernrohre.] Termt. Közl. Budapest **43** 1910 (92-105). [3080]. 40915

Kristensen, K. S. Lyshinde paa Overflader, der træffes af en Bunsenflamme. [Colouring of surfaces when struck by a Bunsen flame.] Kobenhavn Fysisk Tids. **9** 1911 (139-141). [4270]. 40916

Kröner. Über einige Begleiterscheinungen beim Betrieb von Dampfturbinen. Turbine Berlin **7** 1911 (139-143). [2490]. 40918

Krüger, F[riedrich]. Ueber die Anwendung der Thermodynamik auf die Elektronentheorie der Thermoelektrizität. II. Physik. Zs. Leipzig **12** 1911 (360-368). [5710 5675]. 40919

——— Emil Boses Wirken. Physik. Zs. Leipzig **12** 1911 (1244-1247). [0010]. 40920

——— Ueber das Wesen der elektrolytischen Dissoziation und Lösungstension. Zs. Elektroch. Halle **17** 1911 (453-466). [6250]. 40921

Krüse, K. Schallfortpflanzung in einer Flüssigkeit. Zs. physik. Unterr. Berlin **24** 1911 (295). [9310 9200]. 40922

Krüss, Hugo. Stephan Lindeck. D. MechZtg Berlin **1911** (233-234). [0010]. 40923

——— Einfaches Kontrast-Photometer. J. Gasbeleucht. München **54** 1911 (121-122). [3010]. 40924

——— Spektrophotometer und Farbenmisch-Apparat. Zs. Instrumentenk. Berlin **32** 1912 (6-13). [3010 3155]. 40925

Kruss, Paul. Universalbogenlampe mit festem Lichtpunkt. D. MechZtg Berlin **1911** (241-242). [6080]. 40926

Krug, Karl. Das Kreisdiagramm der Induktionsmotoren. Berlin (J. Springer) 1911 [1912] (69). 24 cm. 2.80 M.; Diss. Darmstadt 1911. [6070]. 40927

Krulla, Rudolf. Die direkte Messung von Dampfdruckänderungen und der dampfdruckanalytische Nachweis von Verbindungen als Vorlesungsversuch. ChemZtg Cöthen **35** 1911 (471-472). [1920 0050]. 40928

——— Die quantitativen Verhältnisse bei der Teilung eines Körpers zwischen zwei Phasen: Adsorption. Zs. physik. Chem. Leipzig **76** 1911 (497-508). [1887 0300]. 40929

Krumhaar, Hermann. Optische Untersuchungen über Carboniumsalze und verwandte Verbindungen. Zur Kenntnis der gelben und roten Formen des p-Diamidoterephtalsäureesters und der Anile. Diss. Leipzig. Weida i. Th. (Druck v. Thomas & Hubert) 1911 (58). 23 cm. [3860]. 40930

Kruyt, H[ugo] R[udolf]. De betrekking tusschen de drie tripelpunten der zwavel. [Die Beziehung zwischen den drei Tripelpunkten des Schwefels.] Amsterdam Chem. Weekbl. **8** 1911 (643-648). [1887]. 40931

Kruyt, H. R. _v._ Ginneken: Olie.

Kučera, Bohumil. Experimentální studie o novém způsobu měření velmi vysokých potenciálů. [Experimentalstudie ueber eine neue Methode zur Messung sehr hoher Potentiale.] Prag Rozpr. České Ak. Frant. Jos. **1910** (24). [6010 5700]. 40932

Kühl, A. Über die Abhängigkeit der Sternhelligkeit von der Okularvergrösserung. Eine Bemerkung zur physiologischen Optik. Astr. Nachr. Kiel **190** 1912 (321-330 mit 1 Taf.). [4400 4430 3080 3010]. 40933

Kühn, A. Korrekturteilung für verschiedene Eintauchtiefen an Quecksilberthermometern. ChemZtg Cöthen **35** 1911 (373). [1210]. 40934

Kühn, Ludwig. Ueber Spannungsgefahren an geerdeten, eisernen Masten. Diss. Hannover. Erlangen (Druck v. Junge & S.) 1910 (103). 22 cm. [6000 5240]. 40935

Kuenen, J[ohan] P[ieter]. Distillatie van mengsels. [Destillation des mélanges.] Amsterdam Chem. Weekbl. **8** 1911 (349–370). [2457]. 40936

———— Enkele opmerkingen aangaande het beloop der binodale lijnen in de v-x figuur bij het driephasenevenwicht. [Some remarks on the direction of the binodal curves in the v-x diagram in a three phase equilibrium.] Amsterdam Versl. Wis. Nat. Afd. K. Akad. Wet. **20** [1911] (423–427) (Dutch); Amsterdam Proc. Sci. K. Akad. Wet. **14** [1911] (420–424) (English); Leiden Comm. Physic. Lab. Supplement No. 22 1911 (1–8) (English). [2457]. 40937

———— Onderzoekingen omtrent mengbaarheid van vloeistoffen. [Investigations concerning the miscibility of liquids.] Amsterdam Versl. Wis. Nat. Afd. K. Akad. Wet. **20** [1911] (725–730) (Dutch); Amsterdam Proc. Sci. K. Akad. Wet. **14** [1911] (644–649) (English); Leiden Comm. Physic. Lab. **125** 1912 (3–8) (English). [2457]. 40938

———— On the effect of passing a mixture of two vapours into a mixture of the liquids. Leiden Comm. Physic. Lab. Supplement No. 22 to No. 121–132 [1911] (11–16). [2457]. 40939

Küpferer, K. v. Koenigsberger, J.

Küster, F[r.] W. Logarithmische Rechentafeln für Chemiker, Pharmazeuten . . . 11., neu berechnete Aufl. Leipzig (Veit & Comp.) 1911 (106). 18 cm. Geb. 2,40 M. [0030]. 40940

———— Namen- und Sachregister zu den Bdn 25–50 der Zeitschrift für physikalische Chemie, Stöchiometrie und Verwandtschaftslehre. Hrsg. v. Wilh. Ostwald und J. H. van't Hoff. Lfg 10, 11. Leipzig (W. Engelmann) 1911 (Bd 2 : 545–920). 8vo. 5,60 M. 7,60 M. [0032]. 40941

Küster, Karl Heinrich. Bestimmung des Verhältnisses der spezifischen Wärmen bei constantem Druck und bei

$$\text{constantem Volumen } k = \frac{C_p}{C_v} \text{ von Sauer-}$$

stoff. Diss. Marburg (Druck v. R. Friedrich) 1911 (48). 22 cm. [1640]. 40942

Kullgren, Carl. Über die Einwirkung der atmosphärischen Feuchtigkeit auf den Feuchtigkeitsgehalt und die Verbrennungsgeschwindigkeit des Schwarzpulvers. Ark. Kemi Stockholm **4** No. 17 1911 (20). [0250]. 40943

Kulmann, K. Isolatori per alta tensione. [Sunto. Trad.] Atti Ass. elettrotec. Milano **15** 1911 (124–128). [5770]. 40944

Kummer, W. Die Magnetisierung des Eisens bei sehr kleinen Feldstärken [Hysteresis]. [Nebst Bemerkung von E. Gumlich, W. Rogowski.] Elektrot. Zs. Berlin **32** 1911 (380–381). [5450]. 40945

Kunz, Jakob. On the positive potential of metals in the photoelectric effect and the determination of the wave-length equivalent of Roentgen rays. Physic. Rev. Ithaca N.Y. **33** 1911 (208–214 with fig. tables). [4240 5210]. 40946

Kurlbaum, F[riedrich]. Messung der Sonnentemperatur. Berlin SitzBer. Ak. Wiss **1911** (541–554). 40947

Kutschewski, J. Notiz über Geschwindigkeitsänderung von Kanalstrahlen. Physik. Zs. Leipzig **12** 1911 (163–164). [6845]. 40948

———— v. Koenigsberger, J.

Kuźma, Bohumil v. Baborovský, J.

Kyll, Jacob. Intensitätsmessungen im positiven Bandenspektrum des Stickstoffs. Diss. Münster i. W. Borna-Leipzig (Druck v. R. Noske) 1911 (57 mit 2 Taf.). 23 cm. [4202 4205 4210 6840]. 40949

Laar, J[ohannes] J[acobus] van. Sur l'état solide. (Suite) Haarlem Arch. Néerl. Sci. Soc. Holl. (Sér. III A) **1** 1911 (51–89 272–294 avec 2 pl.); Traduit de : Amsterdam Versl. Wis. Nat. Afd. K. Akad. Wet. **19** [1910] (405–426 avec 1 pl. 675–688 avec 1 pl.) (Hollandais); Amsterdam Proc. Sci. K. Akad. Wet. **13** [1910] (454–475 avec 1 pl. 636–649 avec 1 pl.) (Anglais); VII. Conclusion.

149

Amsterdam Versl. Wis. Nat. Afd. K.
Akad. Wet. 20 [1911] (3–19) (Dutch);
Amsterdam Proc. Sci. K. Akad. Wet.
14 [1911] (48-100) (English). [2455].
40950

Laar, [Johannes] Jacobus van.
Over de veranderlijkheid der groot
heid *b* in de toestandsvergelijking
van Van der Waals, ook in verband
met de kritische grootheden. I. II.
III. IV. [On the variability of the
quantity *b* in Van der Waals' equation
of state, also in connection with the
critical quantities. I. II. III. IV.]
Amsterdam Versl. Wis. Nat. Afd. K.
Akad. Wet. 20 1911 (367-385 415-459
608-624); 1912 (777-789) (Dutch);
Amsterdam Proc. Sci. K. Akad. Wet.
14 1911 (278-297 428-442 563-579);
1912 (711-723) (English). [1880 2455].
40952

——— Ueber „einfache" und
„nicht-einfache" Systeme der thermodynamischen Chemie. Zs. physik. Chem.
Leipzig 76 1911 (67-74). [2472 2457].
40954

——— Over eenige bij het kritisch
punt geldende betrekkingen. [On
some relations holding for the critical
point.] Amsterdam Versl. Wis. Nat.
Afd. K. Akad. Wet. 20 1912 (923-933)
(Dutch); Amsterdam Proc. Sci. K.
Akad. Wet. 14 1912 (771-781) (English).
[2455 1889]. 40955

——— Over de waarde van
eenige differentiaal-quotienten in het
kritische punt, in verband met de co-
existeerende phasen in de nabijheid van
dat punt en met den vorm der toestandsvergelijking. [On the value of
some differential quotients in the
critical point, in connection with the
coexisting phases in the neighbourhood
of that point and with the form of the
equation of state.] Amsterdam Versl.
Wis. Nat. Afd. K. Akad. Wet. 20 1912
(1229-1245) (Dutch); Amsterdam Proc.
Sci. K. Akad. Wet. 14 1912 (1091-1105)
(English). [2455]. 40956

La Baume Pluvinel, A. de et **Baldet,** F.
Sur le spectre de la comète Kiess
(1911 b). Paris C. R. Acad. sci. 153
1911 (459-462). [4205]. 40958

Labozzetta, Rosario. Sul periodo
delle oscillazioni dei pendoli orizzontali
adoperati in sismometria. Riv. fis.
mat. sc. nat. Pavia 20 1909 (414-418).
[0845]. 40959

Laby, T. H. and **Burbidge,** P. The
nature of γ-rays. Nature London 87
1911 (144). [1275]. 40960

Lachmann, [Sally]. Die Radioaktivität der Heilquellen. Balneol.
Ztg Berlin 22 1911 wiss.-techn. Tl (1-3).
[4275]. 40961

Lacour, E. *v.* Violette, H.

Lacroix, A. Les minéraux radioactifs de Madagascar. Paris C. R. Acad.
sci. 152 1911 (559-564). [4275]. 40962

Ladenburg, Albert. Die chemische
Konstitution der Materie. Vortrag . . .
[*In*: A. Ladenburg. Naturwiss. Vorträge.] Leipzig Akad. Verlagsgesellschaft) 1911 (33-52). [0500]. 40963

——— Stereochemie. Vortrag
. . . [*In*: A. Ladenburg. Naturwiss.
Vorträge.] Leipzig (Akad. Verlagsgesellschaft) 1911 (71-87). [4040].
40964

——— Die Aggregatzustände und
ihr Zusammenhang. Vortrag . . . [*In*:
A. Ladenburg. Naturwiss. Vorträge.]
Leipzig (Akad. Verlagsgesellschaft) 1911
(89-124). [1800]. 40965

——— Die vier Elemente des
Aristoteles. Vortrag . . . [*In*: A.
Ladenburg. Naturwiss. Vorträge.]
Leipzig (Akad. Verlagsgesellschaft) 1911
(125-138). [0040]. 40966

——— Die Spektralanalyse und
ihre kosmischen Konsequenzen. Rede
. . . [*In*: A. Ladenburg. Naturwiss.
Vorträge.] Leipzig (Akad. Verlagsgesellschaft) 1911 (139-171). [4205
3030]. 40967

——— Das Radium und die
Radioaktivität. Vortrag . . . [*In*:
A. Ladenburg. Naturwiss. Vorträge.]
Leipzig (Akad. Verlagsgesellschaft) 1911
(209-227). [4275]. 40968

——— Theorie der Lösungen.
Vortrag . . . [*In*: A. Ladenburg.
Naturwiss. Vorträge.] Leipzig (Akad.
Verlagsgesellschaft) 1911 (313-326).
40969

——— Naturwissenschaftliche
Vorträge in gemeinverständlicher Dar-
stellung. 2., bedeutend verm. Aufl.
Leipzig (Akad. Verlagsgesellschaft) 1911
VII + 326 mit 1 Tab. . 24 cm. 5 M.
[0030]. 40970

Ladenburg, Rudolf. Ueber das Verhältnis von Emissions- und Absorptionsvermögen des leuchtenden Wasserstoffs. Physik. Zs. Leipzig **12** 1911 (5–9). [4210 4205 4960]. 40971

———— Astrophysikalische Bemerkungen im Anschluss an Versuche über Absorption und anomale Dispersion in leuchtendem Wasserstoff. Physik. Zs. Leipzig **12** 1911 (9–12). [3850 4205]. 40972

———— *v.* Born, M.

Ladoff, Isador. The titanium arc. J. Ind. Engin. Chem. Easton Pa. **1** 1909 (711–723 with ff. tables). [4202]. 40973

Lafay, A. Sur la mesure des pressions élevées déduite des variations de résistivité des inducteurs soumis à leur action. Ann. chim. phys. Paris (sér. 8) **19** 1910 (289–297 av. fig.). [0835 5660]. 40974

———— Sur un procédé d'observation des trajectoires suivies par les éléments d'un courant d'air gêné par des obstacles de formes variables. Paris C. R. Acad. sci. **152** 1911 (318–320). [0835]. 40975

———— Sur l'utilisation du procédé d'exploration à l'acétylène pour la mesure de la vitesse du vent et l'étude du champ aérodynamique. Paris C. R. Acad. sci. **152** 1911 (694–696). [0835]. 40976

Lagrange, E. L'électricité atmosphérique dans les régions antarctiques. Ciel et Terre Bruxelles **1906** (137–138). [5270]. 40977

———— L'électricité atmosphérique. Ciel et Terre Bruxelles **1903** (438–445). [5270]. 40978

———— L'histoire du thermomètre De Römer et le thermomètre Fahrenheit. Ciel et Terre Bruxelles **1910** (245–251). [0010]. 40979

Lagrula, J. Ph. et **Chrétien.** H. Sur la comète Kiess (1911 b). Son aspect photographique et son spectre. Paris C. R. Acad. sci. **153** 1911 (378–380). [4205]. 40980

———— Sur la comète Brooks (1911 c); son aspect photographique et son spectre. Paris C. R. Acad. sci. **153** 1911 (926–927). [4206]. 40981

Laguna, C. L'elettrochimica. Milano (Soc. ed. milanese) 1909 (57). 17 cm. [0030 4900]. 40982

———— Della pila e delle correnti elettriche. Milano (Soc. ed. milanese) 1909 (58). 17 cm. [0030 4900]. 40983

———— Le correnti variabili e loro applicazioni. Milano (Soc. ed. milanese) 1909 (61). 17 cm.; *ibid.* 1910 (59). 17 cm. [0030 4900]. 40984

———— Le correnti alternate e le loro applicazioni. Milano (Soc. ed. milanese) 1909 (63). 17 cm.; *ibid.* 1910 (61). [0030 4900]. 40985

Lahrs, Hinrich. Ueber den Einfluss der thermischen Behandlung auf die magnetischen Eisensiliciumlegierungen. Diss. Halle a. S. (Druck v. C. A. Kaemmerer & Co.) 1911 (49 mit Taf.). 22 cm. [5466]. 40986

Lama (De), Nicandro. Sul concetto di resistenza elettrica. Mortara (A. Pagliarini) 1910 (15). 20 cm. [5675]. 40987

Lampa, Anton. Wechselstromversuche. (Die Wissenschaft. H. 42.) Braunschweig (F. Vieweg & S.) 1911 (X + 176). 22 cm. 5 M. [6400 6460]. 40989

Lampe, Hans. Ueber die faradokutane Sensibilität. Diss. Leipzig. Borna-Leipzig (Druck v. R. Noske) 1911 (30). 22 cm. [5900]. 40990

Lamprecht, Hermann. Das Bandenspektrum des Bleies. Zs. wiss. Phot. Leipzig **10** 1911 (16–29 33–52 mit 2 Taf.); Diss. Bonn. Leipzig (J. A. Barth) 1911 (39 mit Taf.). 24 cm. [4205]. 40991

Land, W[illiam] J[esse] G[oad]. An electrical constant temperature apparatus. Bot. Gaz. Chicago **52** 1911 (391–399 with 4 ff.). [1014]. 40992

Landau, B. Ueber den Einfluss des Lösungsmittels auf das Drehungsvermögen optisch-aktiver Körper. Verh. Ges. D. Natf. Leipzig **82** (1910) II 1 1911 (34–35). [4040]. 40993

Landau, Marc. Action des rayons ultraviolets sur l'acide lactique. Paris C. R. Acad. sci. **152** 1911 (1308–1309). [4225]. 40994

Landis, Edward H. Some of the laws concerning voltaic cells. [With bibliography.] Philadelphia J. Frank lin Inst. 168 1909 (399-420 with ff. tables). [5610]. 40995

Landschütz, Hilda r. Martin.

Lang, Georg. Ueber den Einfluss des Mangans auf die Eigenschaften des Flusseisens. Metallurgie Halle S 1911 (15-21 49-53 mit Taf.). [5466 5660]. 40996

Lange, Max. Umformung der Seidelschen Bildfehlerausdrücke. Zs. Instrumentenk. Berlin 31 1911 (307-313). [3070]. 40997

—————— Entwickelung des ersten Gliedes der Aberration endlich geöffneter Lichtbüschel für den Achsenobjektpunkt einer lichtbrechenden Rotationsfläche, deren Querschnitt ein Kegelschnitt ist. Zs. Instrumentenk. Berlin 31 1911 (348-349). [3070]. 40998

Langennan, [Fritz]. Ergebnisse diasklereler Augendurchleuchtung mit starker Lichtquelle. Nachweis angeborenen spaltförmigen Mangels des retinalen Irispigmentes nach unten (rudimentärste Form des Iriscolobome). Graefes Arch. Ophthalm. Leipzig 79 1911 (137-144 mit 1 Taf.). [4470]. 40999

Langer, P[aul]. Über Gasturbinen. Stahl u. Eisen Düsseldorf, 31 1911 (1701-1706). [2490]. 41000

Langevin. Exposé expérimental des phénomènes fondamentaux de l'électrostatique au moyen de l'électromètre à quadrants. (C. R. par J. Villey.) J. phys. Paris (sér. 5) 1 1911 (460-466). [5200]. 41001

Langford, Grace. The selective reflection of ortho-, meta- and pyrophosphates in the infra-red spectrum. Physic. Rev. Ithaca N.Y. 33 1911 (137-151 with fig. table). [3855 3860]. 41002

Langford, T. H. r. Morris.

Lanis, E. r. Bakunin. M.

Laphores, Jean r. Scheuer, O.

Lapicque, M. et Lapicque, Mme. Durée utile des décharges de condensateurs, expériences sur l'escargot. Paris C. R. Acad. sci. 153 1911 (125-128). [6820]. 41003

Laporte r. Janet.

Larguier des Bancels, J. r. Bierry, H.

La Rosa, Michele. Sullo spettro della luce che accompagna il riscaldamento elettrico di un bastoncino di carbone. Nuovo Cimento Pisa (Ser. 5) 20 1910 (341-353); Ann. Physik Leipzig (4. Folge) 34 1911 (222-234 mit 1 Taf.). [4205 4202]. 41004

—————— Due regole semplici per l'interpolazione grafica fra due curve particolari di magnetizzazione. Nuovo Cimento Pisa (Ser. 6) 1 1911 (115-119). [5450]. 41005

—————— Distribuzione del flusso d'induzione concatenato col secondario di un rocchetto. Nuovo Cimento, Pisa (Ser. 6) 1 1911 (394). [6440]. 41006

—————— Sulla fusione del carbonio per mezzo dell'effetto Joule. Nuovo Cimento Pisa (Ser. 6) 2 1911 (418-424). [1810]. 41007

—————— Ueber das Schmelzen des Kohlenstoffs mittels des Jouleschen Effektes. Ann. Physik Leipzig (4. Folge) 34 1911 (95-105); 36 1911 (841-847). [1810 6830 5720]. 41008

—————— e Muglia, B. La potenza specifica e la struttura spettrale nell'arco di piccola intensità. Nuovo Cimento Pisa (Ser. 6) 1 1911 (283-286); Palermo Giorn. sc. nat. econ. 28 1911 (103-106). [4205 4210]. 41010

—————— e Pasta, G. La distribuzione del flusso d'induzione concatenato lungo il secondario; e la scelta delle dimensioni più convenienti per gli organi più importanti di un rocchetto d'induzione. Nuovo Cimento Pisa (Ser. 6) 1 1911 (81-114). [6040]. 41011

Larose, H. Sur le problème du câble limité dans les deux sens. Paris C. R. Acad. sci. 152 1911 (1051-1054). 41012

—————— Sur la propagation d'une discontinuité sur une ligne télégraphique avec perte uniforme. Paris C. R. Acad. sci. 152 1911 (1468-1471). [6480]. 41013

Larmor, Sir Joseph. Radiation. Encycl. Brit. (ed. 11) 22 1911. [4200]. 41014

Larsen, Absalon. Ein akustischer Wechselstromerzeuger mit regulierbarer Periodenzahl für schwache Ströme. Elektrot. Zs. Berlin 32 1911 (284-285). [6045]. 41015

Lasareff, P. Studien über das Weber-Fechner'sche Gesetz. Einfluss der Grösse des Gesichtsfeldes auf den Schwellenwert der Gesichtsempfindung. Arch. ges. Physiol. Bonn **142** 1911 (235–240). [4455]. 41017

—————— Über den Temperatursprung an der Grenze zwischen Metall und Gas. Ann. Physik Leipzig (4. Folge) **37** 1912 (233–246). [2000]. 41018

—————— Über das Ausbleichen von Farbstoffen im sichtbaren Spektrum. (Zweite Mitt.) Ann. Physik Leipzig (4. Folge) **37** 1912 (812–822). [4225 3810]. 41019

Laue, M[ax]. Zur Dynamik der Relativitätstheorie. Ann. Physik Leipzig (4. Folge) **35** 1901 (524–542). [4980 4940]. 41020

—————— Über einen Versuch zur Optik der bewegten Körper. München SitzBer. Ak. Wiss. math.-phys. Kl. **41** 1911 (405–412). [3420 6630 4960]. 41021

—————— Zur Diskussion über den starren Körper in der Relativitätstheorie. Physik. Zs. Leipzig **12** 1911 (85–87). [4960]. 41022

—————— Bemerkungen zum Hebelgesetz in der Relativitätstheorie. Physik. Zs. Leipzig **12** 1911 (1008–1010). [4980]. 41023

—————— Zwei Einwände gegen die Relativitätstheorie und ihre Widerlegung. Physik. Zs. Leipzig **13** 1912 (118–120). [0600]. 41024

—————— Ueber den Begriff der Energieströmung. [On the conception of the current of energy.] Amsterdam Versl. Wis. Nat. Afd. K. Akad. Wet. **20** 1912 (955–958) (German); Amsterdam Proc. Sci. K. Akad. Wet. **14** 1912 (825–828) (English). [6630]. 41025

—————— Das Relativitätsprinzip. (Die Wissenschaft. H. 38.) Braunschweig (F. Vieweg & S.) 1911 (X + 208). 22 cm. 6,50 M. [4940 6630 4980]. 41026

Laugier, H. v. Cardot, H.

Lauriol, P. Mesure des débits des injecteurs et mesure des densités des gaz au moyen des orifices-étalons. J. phys. Paris (sér. 5) **1** (466–468 av. fig.). [0810]. 41027

Lauriol, P. Procédé rapide pour la photométrie des becs à incandescence par le gaz. J. phys. Paris (sér. 5) **1** 1911 (469–473 av. fig.). [3010]. 41028

—————— Les essais de pouvoir calorifique du gaz d'éclairage à Paris. J. phys. Paris (sér. 5) **1** 1911 (726–737). [1610]. 41029

La Vespa, Paolo. Ricerche di radioattività e in specie delle acque termali di Termini Imerese (Sicilia). Giorn. sc. nat. econ. Palermo **28** 1911 (77–88). [4275]. 41030

Léauté, André. Recherches sur la décharge des condensateurs. J. Éc. polytech. Paris (sér. 2) **1910** (1–70 av. fig.). [6820]. 41031

—————— Sur les irrégularités du potentiel disruptif. Paris C. R. Acad. sci. **152** 1911 (1474–1476). [6820]. 41032

—————— Sur certaines difficultés que présente l'emploi des développements exponentiels. Paris C. R. Acad. sci. **153** 1911 (1064–1066). [5680 2010]. 41033

—————— Sur le développement d'une fonction en série d'exponentielles; application au transport de force à 100,000 volts de l'Exposition de Turin. Paris C. R. Acad. sci. **154** 1912 (28–31). [6020]. 41034

[Lebedev, P[etr] N[ikolajevič].] Лебедевъ, П[етръ] Н[иколаевичъ]. Еще разъ по поводу наблюденій проф. П. П. Мышкина. [A propos des expériences de M. le professeur N. P. Myšćin.] St. Peterburg Žurn. russ. fiz.-chim. Obšč. Fiz. otd. **41** 1909 (263–264) [4215]. 41035

—————— Die Grenzwerte der kürzesten akustischen Wellen. Ann. Physik Leipzig (4. Folge) **35** 1911 (171–174). [9200]. 41036

[Lebedinskij, V[ladimir] K[onstantinovič].] Лебединскій, В[ладимиръ] К[онстантиновичъ]. О нѣкоторыхъ случаяхъ раздѣленія радіаціи (статья вторая). [Nouveaux cas du partage des rayonnements [par l'action sur la décharge].] St. Peterburg Žurn. russ. fiz.-chim. Obšč. Fiz. otd. **41** 1909 (97–109). [6850]. 41037

—————— Измѣненіе искрового потенціала подъ дѣйствіемъ радіаціи. [La variation de potentiel de l'étincelle électrique sous l'influence des radiations.] St. Peterburg Žurn. russ. fiz.-chim. Obšč. Fiz. otd. 41 1909 (211-213). [6850]. 41038

Le Bel, J. A. A propos de l'inversion optique de Walden. Journ. Chim. Phys. Genève 9 1911 (323-324). [4050]. 41039

———— Essai de cosmologie rationelle. Journ. Chim. phys. Genève 9 1911 (559-577). [0000]. 41040

———— Sur l'échauffement singulier des fils minces de platine. Paris C. R. Acad. sci. 152 1911 (129-131). [1810-4210]. 41041

Lebeuf, A. et **Chofardet, P.** Observation de l'éclipse totale de Soleil du 29-30 août 1905 à Cistierna, province de Léon (Espagne). Rapport des membres de la Mission de l'Observatoire de Besançon. Ann. bur. longit. Paris 8 1911 (C. 1 à C. 22 av. pl.). [4205]. 41042

Leblanc, Maurizio. Lampada di quarzo a vapore di mercurio. Elettricità Milano 36 1911 (325-329). [6030]. 41043

———— r. Darmois, E.

Le Blanc, M[ax]. Über eine chemisch-passive unpolarisierbare Elektrode. Zs. Elektroch. Halle 17 1911 (677-679). [6230-5610]. 41044

———— Lehrbuch der Elektrochemie. 5. verm. Aufl. Leipzig (O. Leiner) 1911 (VIII + 331). 23 cm. 6 M. [6200-0030]. 41045

Le Bon, Gustave. Sur les variations de transparence du quartz pour la lumière ultraviolette et sur la dissociation de la matière. Paris C. R. Acad. sci. 153 1910 (49-51). [3850]. 41046

Le Cadet, G. Sur l'origine des manifestations électriques des orages, à l'occasion de l'observation des cyclones en mer de Chine. Paris C. R. Acad. sci. 153 1911 (985-986). [5270]. 41047

Le Chatelier, Henry. L'œuvre de Van 't Hoff. Rev. gén. sci. Paris 22 1911 (353-359). [0010]. 41048

———— Introduction à l'étude de la métallurgie. Le chauffage industriel. Paris (Dunod et Pinat) 1912 (528). 25 cm. [1010]. 41049

Lecher, Ernst. Einiges über das Elektron. Wien Schr. Ver. Verbr. Naturw. Kenntn. 51 1910-11 1911 (335-355). [4960]. 41050

Le Dantec, F. r. Bouasse, H.

Leduc, A. Compressibilité des gaz; volumes moléculaires et poids atomiques. Ann. chim. phys. Paris (sér. 8) 19 1910 (411-476). [1880]. 41051

———— Application des principes à un cas de magnetostriction. Paris C. R. Acad. sci. 152 1911 (853-855). [5462]. 41052

———— Sur le travail d'aimantation. Paris C. R. Acad. sci. 152 1911 (1243-1245). [5460]. 41053

———— Nouvelle méthode pour déterminer le rapport γ des chaleurs spécifiques C et c des vapeurs. Paris C. R. Acad. sci. 152 1911 (1752-1755). [1640]. 41054

———— Sur la détente des vapeurs et la variation du rapport γ de leurs chaleurs spécifiques avec la température et la pression. Paris C. R. Acad. sci. 153 1911 (51-54). [1640]. 41055

———— Pression interne dans les gaz; formules d'état et loi des attractions moléculaires. Paris C. R. Acad. sci. 153 1911 (179-182). [1880]. 41056

Leduc, H. Application du principe de Lenz aux phénomènes qui accompagnent la charge des condensateurs. Paris C. R. Acad. sci. 152 1911 (313-315). [2475-5220]. 41057

Leduc, Stephan. Der elektrische Widerstand des menschlichen Körpers. Arch. physik. Med. Leipzig 4 1909 (212-216). [5900]. 41058

Lee, Oliver J. Effects of variations of vapor-density on the calcium lines H, K, and g (λ 4227). Astroph. J. Chicago 34 1911 (397-403 with pl. fig. tables). [4206]. 41059

Leenhardt, Ch. Recherches expérimentales sur la vitesse de cristallisation des sels hydratés. Paris (Hermann) 1908 (145 av. fig.). 25 cm. 41060

———— et **Boutaric, A.** Cryoscopie dans l'hyposulfite de sodium cristallisé à 5 molécules d'eau. Paris C. R. Acad. sci. 154 1912 (113-115). [1920]. 41061

Lees, Charles H. On the effect of a narrow saw-cut in the edge of a conducting strip on the potential and stream lines in the strip and on the resistance of the strip. London Proc. Physic. Soc. **23** 1911 (361–366). [5680]. 41063

Leeuw, H. L. de. Über das System Acetaldehyd-Äthylalkohol. Zs. physik. Chem. Leipzig **77** 1911 (284–314). [1230]. 41063A

———— v. Smits, A.

Legonez, R. Motori a collettore. Atti Ass. elettrotecn. Milano **15** 1911 (899–901). [6070]. 41064

Legrand, Emmanuel. Essai de la résistance au choc du filament des lampes métalliques. Paris C. R. Acad. sci. **154** 1912 (274–275). [6080]. 41065

Le Heux, J. W. N. Lissajoussche Stimmgabelkurven in stereoskopischer Darstellung. Leipzig (J. A. Barth) 1911 (8 mit 18 Taf.). 18 cm. In Mappe 6 M. [9110]. 41066

Lehfeldt, R. A. Gravity in South Africa. Cape Town Trans. R. Soc. S. Afric. **2** pt. 2 1911 (63–126). [0700 0845]. 41067

Lehmann, Erich. Eine neue Photometerkonstruktion. (Nach gemeinsam mit A. Miethe angestellten Versuchen.) Berlin Verh. D. physik. Ges. **13** 1911 (335–337). [3010]. 41068

———— Erwiderung auf die Bemerkung des Herrn J. Hartmann zu dem Aufsatz über „Eine neue Photometerkonstruktion. (Nach gemeinsamen Versuchen mit A. Miethe.)" Berlin Verh. D. physik. Ges. **13** 1911 (503–504). [3010]. 41069

Lehmann, H. Lumineszenzanalyse mittels der UV-Filterlampe. Berlin Verh. D. physik. Ges. **13** 1911 (1101–1104); Physik. Zs. Leipzig **13** 1912 (35–36). [3165 4230 4205]. 41070

———— Das Fernspektroskop. Zs. Instrumentenk. Berlin **32** 1912 (1–6). [3165 0050]. 41071

———— Das UV-Filter und die UV-Filterlampe als Apparate zur Lumineszenzanalyse. Zs. Instrumentenk. Berlin **32** 1912 (43–54). [3165 4230 0090]. 41072

———— Die Kinematographie, ihre Grundlagen und ihre Anwendungen. (Aus Natur und Geisteswelt. Bd 358.) Leipzig (B. G. Teubner) 1911 (IV + 118 mit 2 Taf.). 18 cm. 1.25 M. [3090 0050 4490]. 41073

Lehmann, O[tto]. Ueber Molekularstruktur und Optik grosser flüssiger Kristalle. Ann. Physik Leipzig (4. Folge) **35** 1911 (193–219). [3830]. 41074

———— Die Umwandlung unserer Naturauffassung infolge der Entdeckung des Relativitätsprinzips. Aus d. Natur Leipzig **6** 1911 (705–711 751–761). [0040]. 41075

———— Konische Strukturstörungen bei flüssigen Pseudokristallen. Berlin Verh. D. physik. Ges. **13** 1911 (338–344). [3830]. 41076

———— Struktur und Optik grosser Kristalltropfen. Physik. Zs. Leipzig **12** 1911 (540–546 mit 2 Taf.). 41077

———— Kristallinische und amorphe Flüssigkeiten. Physik. Zs. Leipzig **12** 1911 (1032–1035); Berlin Verh. D. physik. Ges. **13** 1911 (945–951). [0400]. 41078

———— Geschichte des physikalischen Instituts der technischen Hochschule Karlsruhe. Festgabe . . . Karlsruhe i. B. (G. Braun) 1911 (99). 25 cm. 2.40 M. [0060]. 41079

———— Die neue Welt der flüssigen Kristalle und deren Bedeutung für Physik. Chemie. Technik und Biologie. Leipzig (Akadem. Verlagsges.) 1911 (VI + 388). 23 cm. 12 M. [0400]. 41080

Lehmann, Th. v. Benischke, G.

Leimbach, Gotthelf. Variiert p mit λ? Bemerkung zu der Arbeit des Herrn J. Stark über: „Das Schwärzungsgesetz der Normalbelichtung". Ann. Physik Leipzig (4. Folge) **36** 1911 (198–202). [4225 3010]. 41081

———— Drahtlose Telegraphie mit Erdinnern. Elektrot. Zs. Berlin **32** 1911 (237–238). [6615]. 41082

———— Die Strahlungseigenschaften der elektrischen Glühlampen. Elektrot. Zs. Berlin **32** 1911 (266–267). [6080 4202]. 41083

———— Unipolares Leitvermögen von Kontaktdetektoren und ihre Gleichrichterwirkung. Physik. Zs. Leipzig **12** 1911 (228 231). [6643]. 41084

———— Über eine neue Methode zur Verminderung der schädlichen

Wärmestrahlen im Projektionsapparat. [Beugung durch Drahtgitter.] Physik. Zs. Leipzig **12** 1911 (791–798). [3620 3630 0050 0090]. 41085

Leineweber, Norbert. Über die elektrische Leitfähigkeit von Salzdämpfen. Diss. Münster i. W. (Westfälische Vereinsdruckerei) 1911 (55). 22 cm. [5685]. 41086

Leiser, R. Über elektrische Doppelbrechung der Gase. Physik. Zs. Leipzig **12** 1911 (955–956); Berlin Verh. D. physik. Ges. **13** 1911 (903–905). [6640]. 41087

Leiss, C. Monochromator für das Praktikum. D. MechZtg Berlin **1911** (67–69). [3165]. 41088

——— Ultrarot-Spektrometer. Physik. Zs. Leipzig **12** 1911 (1252–1254). [3165 0090]. 41089

Lemale, Ch. Évolution de la chaleur dans les turbines. Technique moderne Paris **3** 1911 (68–70). [2490]. 41090

Lémeray, E. M. Sur la pression de radiation. J. phys. Paris (sér. 5) **1** 1911 (559–565). [4215]. 41091

——— Le principe de relativité et les forces qui s'exercent entre corps en mouvement. Paris C. R. Acad. sci. **152** 1911 (1465–1468). [4650]. 41092

Lemoult, P. Recherches sur les dérivés du styrolène; rectification de quelques erreurs expérimentales. Paris C. R. Acad. sci. **152** 1911 (1402–1404). [1695]. 41093

Lenard, P[hilipp]. Ueber die Absorption der Nordlichtstrahlen in der Erdatmosphäre. Heidelberg SitzBer. Ak. Wiss. math.-natw. Kl. **1911** Abh. 12 (9). [3875 6845]. 41094

——— Über die Elektrizitätsleitung und Lichtemission metallhaltiger Flammen. Heidelberg SitzBer. Ak. Wiss. math.-natw. Kl. **1911** Abh. 34 (22). [5685 4202 6895]. 41095

——— Über Äther und Materie. Vortrag . . . . 2. ausführlichere und mit Zusätzen versehene Aufl. Heidelberg (C. Winter) 1911 (51). 24 cm. 1 M. [0690 0500 4900]. 41096

——— und **Ramsauer**, C. Ueber die Wirkungen sehr kurzwelligen ultravioletten Lichtes auf Gase und über eine sehr reiche Quelle dieses Lichtes. Tl 4: Ueber die Nebelkernbildung durch Licht in der Erdatmosphäre und

in anderen Gasen, und über Ozonbildung. Heidelberg SitzBer. Ak. Wiss. math.-natw. Kl. **1911** Abh. 16 (27); Tl 5: Wirkung des stark absorbierbaren Ultraviolett und Zusammenfassung. *op. cit.* Abh. 24 (54). [6895 6880 1840]. 41097

Lenard, P[hilipp] und **Ramsauer**, C. De l'action de la lumière ultraviolette de très courte longueur d'onde sur les gaz et sur une source très puissante de ces rayons. Radium Paris **8** 1911 (115–119 av. fig.); [sunto. trad.] Riv. fis. mat. sc. nat. Pavia **23** 1911 (374–376). [6895 5685]. 41099

Lent, W. F. v. Mendenhall. C. E.

Lenz, Emil. Experimentelle Studien über die Kombination von Hochfrequenzströmen und Röntgenstrahlen. (A. d'Arsonvalströme. B. Diathermie.) Fortschr. Röntgenstr. Hamburg **17** 1911 (257–301). [5900]. 41100

Lenz, W. Ergänzung zu dem Bericht von J. Nicholson über den effektiven Widerstand einer Spule. Jahrb. drahtlos. Telegr. Leipzig **4** 1911 (481–489). [6460]. 41101

——— Ueber das elektromagnetische Wechselfeld der Spulen und deren Wechselstrom-Widerstand, Selbstinduktion und Kapazität. Diss. München. Leipzig (J. A. Barth) 1911 (85). 23 cm. [6440 6040]. 41102

Leonard, Alfred Godfrey Gordon. Ueber Anilidsäuren, Anile und Pyrazolone der Diphenylizindioxyweinsäure und deren Absorptionsspektren. Diss. Bonn (Druck v. H. Ludwig) 1910 (50). 22 cm. [3860]. 41103

Lepape, A. v. Moureu, C.

Leprince-Ringuet, F. Loi de la transmission de la chaleur entre un fluide en mouvement et une surface métallique. Paris C. R. Acad. sci. **152** 1911 (436–439; 588–590). [2030]. 41104

——— Propriétés géométriques du point représentant la Terre dans le diagramme des voltages d'un réseau polyphasé. Paris C. R. Acad. sci. **153** 1911 (1069–1071 av. fig.). [5705]. 41106

Le Roux, J. Sur l'incurvation et la flexion dans les déformations finies. Paris C. R. Acad. sci. **152** 1911 (1655–1657). [0840]. 41107

Lerp, K. Untersuchung der Fehlerquellen in den älteren Bestimmungen der spezifischen Ladung des Elektrons. [6845 4960]. 41107A

Leslie, Mll. May Sybil. Sur le poids moléculaire de l'émanation du thorium. Paris C. R. Acad. sci. 153 1911 (328 331). [4275]. 41108

———— Le thorium et ses produits de désagrégation. Radium Paris 8 1911 (356 363). [4275]. 41109

Levi, Augusto. Il calore specifico delle leghe metalliche. Venezia Atti Ist. ven. 68 parte 2 1909 (47 63 345 359). [1620]. 41110

Levi, Mario Giacomo v. Nasini, R.

Levites, S. Studien über organische Kolloide. Zs. Kolloide Dresden 8 1911 (4 8). [0340]. 41111

———— Studien über Adsorption. Zs. Kolloide Dresden 9 1911 (1 5). [0300]. 41112

Levitsky, M. Eine neue Form des geschlossenen Resonators zur Messung der Dämpfung kurzer elektrischer Wellen. Physik. Zs. Leipzig 12 1911 (386 391). [6043 6600]. 41113

Levy, Herbert. Über die Molekularwärme des Wasserdampfes. Nachtrag zu den Arbeiten von W. Nernst und H. Levy. Berlin Verh. D. physik. Ges. 13 1911 (926 928). [1640]. 41114

Lévy-Bruhl, L. v. Bouasse, H.

Lexin, L.. **Miethe,** A[dolf] und **Stenger,** E[rich]. Ueber die Sensibilisierung von photographischen Platten für das äusserste Rot und Infrarot. Arch. ges. Physiol. Bonn 142 1911 (403 404). [4225]. 41115

Lewis, W. C. McC. Note on the internal pressure of a liquid. Phil. Mag. London (Ser. 6) 22 1911 (193 197). [1430]. 41116

———— Latent heat of vaporization of liquids. Phil. Mag. London (Ser. 6) 22 1911 (268 276). [1680]. 41117

———— Beiträge zum Studium des flüssigen Zustands. I. Ein Ausdruck für die latente Verdampfungswärme. (Übers. von W. **Neumann.**) Zs. physik. Chem. Leipzig 78 1911 (24 38). [1680 0840]. 41118

Lewis, Warren K. The theory of fractional distillation. J. Ind. Engin. Chem. Easton Pa. 1 1909 (522 533 with ff.). [1840]. 41119

Lex, Franz. Hans Haselbach†. Carinthia II. Klagenfurt 101 1911 (1 7). [0040]. 41120

Ley, H[einrich]. Die Beziehungen zwischen Farbe und Konstitution bei organischen Verbindungen. Unter Berücksichtigung der Untersuchungsmethoden dargestellt. (Abhandlungen aus Physik und Chemie.) Leipzig (S. Hirzel) 1911 (VIII — 246 mit 2 Taf.). 24 cm. 7 M. [3860 3150]. 41121

Lichtenecker, K. Ueber die Poggendorfsche Kompensationsmethode. Zs. physik. Unterr. Berlin 24 1911 (91 93). [0050 5640]. 41122

Lichtenstein, Leon. Über den gegenwärtigen Stand und die nächsten Aufgaben der Hochspannungs-Kabeltechnik. Elektrot. Zs. Berlin 32 1911 (208 213). [6660]. 41123

Liebermann, Paul v. Verschmelzungsfrequenzen von Farbenpaaren. Zs. Psychol. Leipzig Abt. 2 45 1911 (117 128). [4450]. 41124

———— und **Marx,** Eugen. Über die Empfindlichkeit des normalen und des protanopischen Sehorgans für Unterschiede des Farbentons. Zs. Psychol. Leipzig Abt. 2 45 1911 (103 108). [4450]. 41125

Liebisch, Th[eodor]. Über den Schichtenbau und die elektrischen Eigenschaften des Zinnerzes. Berlin SitzBer. Ak. Wiss. 1911 (414 422). [4205 5710 6640]. 41126

Liebreich, Erik. Ueber die Veränderung der Brechungsexponenten mit der Temperatur im ultraroten Gebiete bei Steinsalz, Sylvin und Fluorit. Berlin Verh. D. physik. Ges. 13 1911 (1 18). [3822 3830]. 41127

———— Über die optischen Temperaturkoeffizienten für Steinsalz, Sylvin und Fluorit im Bereiche der tieferen Temperaturen. Berlin Verh. D. physik. Ges. 13 1911 (700 712). [3822 3830]. 41128

Liesegang, F. P. Esperimenti sull'assorbimento di raggi calorifici negli apparecchi di proiezione. Boll. Soc. fot. Firenze 22 1910 (321 322). [3855]. 41129

———— Rationelle Einstellung und Abblendung des photographischen Objektivs. Jahrb. Phot. Halle 25 1911 (45 50). [3085]. 41130

Lietzau, Willy. Beiträge zur Kenntnis der disruptiven Entladung. Fribourg Mém. Soc. Sc. Nat. Math. Phys. **1** 1904 (1 42 mit 10 Fig. u. 8 Taf.). [6820]. 41131

Litchitz. La photographie et la reproduction d'une courbe sonore. J. phys. Paris (sér. 5) **1** 1911 (565 575 av. fig.). [9310]. 41132

——— La reproduction sonore d'une courbe périodique. Paris C. R. Acad. sci. **152** 1911 (301 404 av. fig.). [9120]. 41133

——— Ecartement des particules dans les mouvements Browniens à l'aide des chocs sonores très rapides. Paris C. R. Acad. sci. **152** 1911 (761 762). [0240 9020]. 41134

——— v. Henri, V.

Lignana, Giuseppe. Trasformatori di misura. Torino (V. Bona) 1910 (51). 24 cm. [6040]. 41135

Lilienfeld, Julius E. Die Elektrizitätsleitung im extremen Vakuum. Leipzig Ber. Ges. Wiss. math.-phys. Kl. **63** 1911 (534 539). [6840]. 41136

——— Die Arbeitsleistung zur Abscheidung von N und O aus atmosphärischer Luft. Zs. komprim. Gase Weimar **13** 1911 (117 124). [0320 2415]. 41137

——— Das Laboratorium für tiefe Temperaturen (Luft- und Wasserstoffverflüssigung) des physikalischen Instituts der Universität Leipzig. Zs. komprim. Gase Weimar **13** 1911 (165 189 185 193). [0090 1870]. 41138

Limb, C. Compoundage des alternateurs au moyen des soupapes électrolytiques. Paris C. R. Acad. sci. **152** 1911 (252 255). [6230 6045]. 41139

Lind, J. C. Sur quelques effets chimiques des rayons du radium. Radium Paris **8** 1911 (289 292). [4275]. 41140

Linde, C. Die Abkühlung von Gasen beim Ausströmen durch eine Drosselstelle. Zs. Kältelnd. München **13** 1911 (132 137). [1150]. 41141

Linde, F. Über die Trennung von Gasgemischen mit Hilfe der Verflüssigung. Berlin Verh. Ver. Gewerbfl. **90** 1911 SitzBer. (9 29). [1870]. 41142

Lindeck, St. Ueber eine Beziehung zwischen dem Temperaturkoeffizienten und dem spezifischen Widerstand einiger Metalle, insbesondere von Kupfer. Berlin Verh. D. physik. Ges. **13** 1911 (65 71 281 282). [5660]. 41143

Lindemann, Charles L. Über die Temperaturabhängigkeit des thermischen Ausdehnungskoeffizienten. Physik. Zs. Leipzig **12** 1911 (1197 1199). [2000 2020]. 41145

——— und **Lindemann, F. A.** Die Abhängigkeit des Durchdringungsvermögens der Röntgenstrahlen von Druck und Gasinhalt. Physik. Zs. Leipzig **13** 1912 (404 406). [4240 6845]. 41146

Lindemann, Frederick. Ueber das Dulong-Petitsche Gesetz. Diss. Berlin (Druck v. G. Schade) 1911 (55). 22 cm. [1660 1600 1610]. 41147

Lindemann, F. A. Untersuchungen über die spezifische Wärme bei tiefen Temperaturen. IV. [Beziehungen zwischen der elektrischen Leitfähigkeit der Metalle und ihrem Energiegehalt.] Berlin SitzBer. Ak. Wiss. **1911** (316 321). [5675 1660]. 41148

——— Über die Berechnung der Eigenfrequenzen der Elektronen im selektiven Photoeffekt. Berlin Verh. D. physik. Ges. **13** 1911 (482 488). [6850 4960]. 41149

——— Über Beziehungen zwischen chemischer Affinität und Elektronenfrequenzen. Berlin Verh. D. physik. Ges. **13** 1911 (1107 1116). [0100 4200 6850]. 41150

——— v. Lindemann, C. L.; Nernst, D.

Lindemann, Max. Die Radioaktivität der Atmosphäre in Kiel, und ihre Abhängigkeit von meteorologischen Faktoren. Kiel Schr. natw. Ver. **15** 1911 (99 126). [4275 5270]. 41151

Lindemann, R. Untersuchungen über die Widerstandszunahme von Drahtlitzen bei schnellen elektrischen Schwingungen. Jahrb. drahtlos. Telegr. Leipzig **4** 1911 (561 604). [6460 6470]. 41152

Lindholm, F. Étude de la loi de Beer sur l'absorption dans le spectre infrarouge. Ark. Matem. Stockholm **7** No. 2 1911 (12 av. 4 pls. et 4 figs.). [3810 3855]. 41153

Lindstedt, Mlle v. Perot, A.

Link, Thomas. Das Deutsche Museum im Dienste des physikalischen Unterrichts. München (M. Kellerer) [1911] (44). 24 cm. 0,80 M. [0060 0050]. 41154

Linker, A. Bestimmung des Wirkungsgrades elektr. Maschinen nach der Hilfsmotormethode. Elektr. Betr. Leipzig **14** 1911 (1–3 33–36 44–48). [6070]. 41155

Lioret, H.. **Ducretet.** F. et **Roger,** E. Dispositif d'enregistrement à distance d'une transmission téléphonique sur cylindres ou disques phonographiques. Paris C. R. Acad. sci. **152** 1911 (1476–1478). [6485]. 41156

Lippmann, Alexander. Elektrische Doppelbrechung in Flüssigkeiten und ihre Beziehung zu chemischer Zusammensetzung und Konstitution. Zs. Elektroch. Halle **17** 1911 (15–20 mit 1 Tab.). [6640 3860]. 41157

Lippmann, G. Sur la réduction des tracés sismographiques. Ann. bur. longit. Paris **8** 1911 (1–4). [0825]. 41158

———— Action de forces extérieures sur la tension des vapeurs saturées et des gaz dissous dans un liquide. J. phys. Paris (sér. 5) **1** 1911 (261–264) ; Paris C. R. Acad. sci. **152** 1911 (239–241). [1840 0300 2465 0310]. 41159

———— Contacts électriques efficaces sans pression. Paris C. R. Acad. sci. **151** 1910 (1015–1016). [6020]. 41160

Liska, J. Die magnetische Prüfung von Eisenblech. [Nebst Erwiderung von J. Epstein.] Elektrot. Zs. Berlin **32** 1911 (601). [5435]. 41161

Livens, G. H. The initial accelerated motion of a perfectly conducting electrified sphere. Phil. Mag. London (Ser. 6) **21** 1911 (640–647). [6620 4980]. 41163

———— The initial accelerated motion of a rigidly charged dielectric sphere. Phil. Mag. London (Ser. 6) **22** 1911 (169–173). [4980]. 41164

———— Some further problems connected with the motion of charged spheres. Phil. Mag. London (Ser. 6) **22** 1911 (943–948). [6620]. 41165

Lloyd, M[orton] G[ithens]. Effect of wave form upon incandescent lamps. [Abstract.] Physic. Rev. Ithaca N.Y. **32** 1911 (256). [6080]. 41166

Lockemann, Georg. Zum hundertjährigen Jubiläum von Avogadros Hypothese. (Nach einem . . . Vortrage.) Arch. Gesch. Natw. Leipzig **3** 1911 (357 364). [0010]. 41167

———— Ueber die Adsorption von Arsen durch Eisenhydroxyd. Verh. Ges. D. Natf. Leipzig **82** (1910) II 1 1911 (25–28). [0300]. 41168

Lockyer, Norman. On the sequence of chemical forms in stellar spectra. London Proc. R. Soc. (Ser. A) **84** 1910 (426–432). [4205]. 41169

Lodge, Oliver. The mode of conduction in gases illustrated by the behaviour of electric vacuum valves. Phil. Mag. London (Ser. 6) **22** 1911 (1–7 657–658). [6805]. 41170

———— Der Weltäther. Übers. von Hilde **Barkhausen.** (Die Wissenschaft. H. 41.) Braunschweig (F. Vieweg & S.) 1911 (IX + 107 mit Taf.). 22 cm. 3 M. [0600 0500 0700]. 41171

Loeb, Leo. Influence of variation in specific heat of water on calorimetry of fuels. J. Ind. Engin. Chem. Easton Pa. **3** 1911 (175–177 with fig. table). [1600]. 41172

Löhlein, W[alter] und **Gebb,** H[einrich]. Erwiderung auf den Artikel des Herrn. F. Landolt. „Noch einmal die Sehprüfung". Arch. Augenheilk. Wiesbaden **68** 1911 (193–195). [4455]. 41173

Loessner, Fritz. Ueber Reaktionen der unterphosphorigen Säure und Wasserstoffverbindungen der Schwermetalle. Diss. Leipzig. Weida i. Th. (Druck v. Thomas & Hubert) 1911 (92). [5660]. 41174

Lowe, F. Reflexionsprisma mit scharfer Kante. Zs. Instrumentenk. Berlin **31** 1911 (245–247). [3090]. 41175

Loewenthal, S[iegfried]. Ueber Messmethoden und Einheiten in der biologischen Radiumforschung. Vortrag . . . Physik. Zs. Leipzig **12** 1911 (143–147). [4275]. 41176

Löwy, Heinrich. Dielektrizitätskonstante und Leitfähigkeit der Gesteine. Ann. Physik Leipzig (4. Folge)
36 1911 (125-133); Centralbl. Min.
Stuttgart 1911 (573-579). [5252-5660
6610]. 41177

———— Eine elektrodynamische
Methode zur Erforschung des Erdinnern. Beitr. Geophysik Leipzig 11
1911 Kl. Mitt. (1-8); Centralbl. Min.
Stuttgart 1911 (241-249). [6610].
41178

———— Die Fizeausche Methode
zur Erforschung des Erdinnern. Physik. Zs. Leipzig 12 1911 (1001-1004).
[6615]. 41179

Lohuizen, T[eunis] van. Reeksen in
de spectra van tin en antimoon.
[Series in the spectra of tin and antimony.] Amsterdam Versl. Wis.
Nat. Afd. K. Akad. Wet. 20 [1912]
(7-22 with 1 pl.) (Dutch); Amsterdam
Proc. Sci. K. Akad. Wet. 15 [1912]
(31-45 with 1 pl.) (English). [4205].
41180

———— Bijdrage tot de kennis van
lijnenspectra. [Contribution à l'étude
des spectres de lignes.] 's Gravenhage
(Drukkerij Transvaka) 1912 (102 av.
2 pl.). 26 cm. [4205]. 41181

Loif, Josef. Über induzierte Ströme
in einem ruhenden Netze linearer
Leiter und das Prinzip der kleinsten
Aktion. Berlin Verh. D. physik. Ges.
14 1912 (123-136). [6440-6400].
41182

Lombardi, Luigi. Standardizzazione
elettrica. Atti Ass. elettrotecn.
Milano 14 1910 (48-62). [5000]. 41183

———— Sulla magnetizzazione
del ferro entro a campi continui ed a
campi alternativi. Atti Ass. elettrotecn. Milano 15 1911 (247-294);
Nuovo Cimento Pisa (Ser. 6) 2 1911 (159-
212). [5430-5440]. 41184

———— Comportamento del ferro
in campi magnetici continui ed alternativi. Atti Soc. ital. prog. sci.
Roma 4 1911 (736-737). [5440].
41185

———— Relazione della commis-
sione per lo studio delle questioni
relative alle unità elettriche. Roma
(G. Bertero) 1910 (49). 26 cm. [4900].
41186

Lommel, E. von. Lehrbuch der
Experimentalphysik. 17.-19. neubearb.

Aufl. hrsg. von Walter König. Leipzig
(J. A. Barth) 1911 (X + 644 mit 1 Taf.).
22 cm. 6,60 M. [0030]. 41187

London, E[tim] S[emen]. Das
Radium in der Biologie und Medizin.
(Mit einem Literaturverzeichnis.) Leipzig (Akademische Verlagsges. M. b. H.)
1911 (VII + 199). 23 cm. 6 M.
[4275]. 41188

Lonkhuyzen, van. Eine neue Mess-
anordnung zur Prüfung von Eisen-
blechen nach den Verbandsnormalien.
Elektrot. J. Berlin 32 1911 (1131-1134).
[5435-6440]. 41189

Loose, Gustav. Die Luft-Fern-
regulierung der Röntgenröhren nach
Bauer. (Vorl. Mitt.). Münchener med.
Wochenschr. 58 1911 (2275-2276).
[6080]. 41190

Loperfido, Antonio. Il problema
geodetico e le misure della gravità.
Riv. Artig. Genio Roma 1. trim. 1911
(89-310). [0845]. 41191

Lorentz, H. A. Light (nature of).
Encycl. Brit. (ed. 11) 16 1911. [6600].
41192

———— Lotsy, J. P. et Bosscha,
J[ohannes]+. Haarlem. Arch. Néerl.
Sci. Soc. Holl. (Sér. A) 1 [1911] (1-
XVIII Programme pour l'année 1911).
[0010]. 41193

Lorenz, C. r. Rein. H.

Lorenz, Hans. Neue Theorie und
Berechnung der Kreiseräder. Wasser-
und Dampfturbinen... 2., neu bearb.
u. verm. Aufl. München u. Berlin (R.
Oldenbourg) 1911 (XII + 240). 24 cm.
Geb. 11 M. [2490]. 41194

Lori, Ferdinando. Un fotometro a
selenio. Padova Atti Mem. Acc. (N.
Ser.) 26 1910 (127-129). [3010]. 41195

———— Le dimensioni più opportune dei rocchetti di antoinduzione
senza ferro per ottenere fenomeni di
risonanza elettromagnetica. Venezia
Atti Ist. ven. 68 parte 2 1909 (17-22).
[6040]. 41196

———— Alcuni problemi relativi
ai circuiti con forze elettromotrici
alternate. Venezia Atti Ist. ven. 69
parte 2 1910 (731-735). [6440]. 41197

Loria, Gino. In memoria di Evangelista Torricelli. Riv. ligure se. lett. ar.
Genova 31 1909 (83-94). [0010]. 41198

Loria, L. r. Ganterio, G.

Loria, Stanislaw. Der magneto-optische Kerr-Effekt bei ferromagnetischen Verbindungen und Legierungen. [The magneto-optic Kerr-effect in ferromagnetic compounds and alloys.] Amsterdam Versl. Wis. Nat. Afd. K. Akad. Wet. **20** 1912 (1086 1099) (German); Amsterdam Proc. Sci. K. Akad. Wet. **14** 1912 (970–983) (English). [6650]. 41199

——— O metodach liczenia czastek w gazie. (Liczba Avogadry.) [Ueber die Methoden zur Bestimmung der Avogadro'schen Zahl.] Kosmos Lwów **36** 1911 (1–14). [0150]. 41200

Loschge, August. Neue Beiträge zur Dampfturbinentheorie. Zs. Turbinenwesen München **8** 1911 (193–199 212–217 241–245 279–283 297 301 309 316 321–330 339–346). [2490]. 41201

——— Allgemeine Beziehungen der Dampfturbinen. Zs. Turbinenwesen München **8** 1911 (545–547 568–570). [2490]. 41202

Losehand, O. Der Kreisel als Resonanzerreger. Zs. physik. Unterr. Berlin **24** 1911 (94–95). [0050]. 41203

Losio, Luigi. Lezioni ai conduttori di caldaie a vapore. Pavia (Succ. Marelli) 1909 (115). 22 cm. [0030 0900]. 41204

Lotsy, J. P. v. Lorentz, H. A.

Lottermoser, Alfred. Beiträge zur Elektrolytwirkung auf Hydrosole. Verh. Ges. D. Natf. Leipzig **81** (1909) 11 1 1910 (66–68). [0340]. 41205

——— Bericht über die Arbeiten auf dem Gebiete der Kolloidchemie im Jahre 1908. Zs. Elektroch. Halle **17** 1911 (295–330). [0340]. 41206

——— Adsorption in Hydrosolen. Zs. Elektroch. Halle **17** 1911 (806–809). [0340]. 41207

——— Anomale Adsorption. Zs. Kolloide Dresden **9** 1911 (135–136). [0340]. 41208

Love, Ernest Frederick John and **Smeal**, Glenny. The psychrometric formula. Melbourne Proc. R. Soc. Vict. N.S. **24** Pt. 11 1912 (201–220 pl. XLVIII.). [1890]. 41209

Lubowsky, Kurt. Drahtlose Telegraphie und Luftschiffahrt. Elektrot. Zs. Berlin **32** 1911 (1265 1266). [6615]. 41210

Lucchini, Virginio. Elettroliti nuovi ed usati d'elementi secondari al piombo. Ind. chim. Torino **11** 1911 (277–280). [5620]. 41211

Luck, Kurt von. Beiträge zur Kenntnis radioaktiver Bestandteile von natürlichen Wassern. Diss. Erlangen (Druck v. E. Th. Jacob) 1910 (36). 22 cm. [4275]. 41212

Luckiesh, M. v. Ives, H. E.

Ludeling, C. Observations d'électricité atmosphérique effectuées à bord de la "Belgica" en 1907 pendant la croisière arctique du duc d'Orléans. Ciel et Terre Bruxelles **1910** (395–417). [5270]. 41213

Ludewig, Paul. Über Unregelmässigkeiten beim Betriebe des Wehneltunterbrechers. Fortschr. Röntgenstr. Hamburg **17** 1911 (207–212 mit Taf.). [6040]. 41214

——— Der Freiballon als Empfangsstation für drahtlose Telegraphie. Physik. Zs. Leipzig **12** 1911 (604–606). [6615]. 41215

——— Ein Dämpfungsmesser für die Praxis der drahtlosen Telegraphie. Physik. Zs. Leipzig **12** 1911 (763–771). [6043 6615]. 41216

——— Luftschiffahrt und drahtlose Telegraphie. Luftschiffahrt Bielefeld **2** 1911 Nr. 5 (1–4) Nr. 6 (1–4). [6615]. 41217

Ludwig, K. [Umschlagtit.:] Reduktions-Tabelle für Heizwert und Volumen von Gasen. München u. Berlin (R. Oldenbourg) 1911 (8). 22 cm. 1.20 M. [0030]. 41218

Lüdtke, Heinrich. Beiträge zur Behandlung der elektromagnetischen Lichttheorie und der Lehre von den elektrischen Schwingungen. Nebst einem Anhang über die Geschwindigkeit der Elektrizität. Abh. Didakt. Natw. Berlin **2** 1911 (235–354). [6610 0050]. 41219

Lüppo-Cramer. Ueber die Natur des latenten Röntgenstrahlenbildes. Arch. physik. Med. Leipzig **4** 1909 (102–iii). [4225 4240]. 41220

——— Mikroskopische Beobachtungen über den Reifungsvorgang. Phot. Rdsch. Halle **25** 1911 (176–177 mit 1 Taf.). [4225]. 41221

Lüppo-Cramer. Photographie mit unsichtbaren Strahlen. Umschau Frankfurt a. M. 51 1911 (760–764). [1225].
41222

—————— Kolloidchemie und Photographie. VI. Zs. Kolloide Dresden 8 1911 (42–43 97–101 210 215); 9 1911 (22–25 73–76 116–118 240 241 mit 1 Taf.). [4225].
41223

—————— Das latente Bild. (Encyklopädie der Photographie. H. 78.) Halle a. S. (W. Knapp) 1911 [1912] (VII + 66). 22 cm. 3,60 M. [4225].
41224

Luers. Schnellbetrieb auf langen Unterseekabeln. Arch. Post Berlin 40 1912 (65–70). [6480].
41225

Lüschen, F. Messungen an unsymmetrischen Fernsprechdoppelleitungen. Berlin Verh. D. physik. Ges. 13 1911 (1034–1046). [6485].
41226

—————— Zweite internationale Zusammenkunft von Telegraphentechnikern . . . Elektrot. Zs. Berlin 32 1911 (387–390 409–413). [6485 6480].
41227

Lütke, Heinrich. Untersuchungen über das Gesetz von Wiedemann und Franz an Metalllegierungen. Diss. Breslau (Druck der Schles. Volkszeitung) 1911 (11 mit 4 Taf.). 28 cm. [5660].
41228

Lüttig, Otto. Das Zeeman-Phänomen im sichtbaren Spektrum von Mangan und Argon. Diss. Halle a. S. (Druck v. Hohmann) 1911 (48). 22 cm. [4208].
41229

Lumière, A. e Lumière, L. Fotografia dei colori e la tricromia. Prog. fotogr. Milano 17 1910 (5 7). [4225].
41230

—————— et Seyewetz, A. Différenciation par voie de développement chimique des images latentes obtenues au moyen des émulsions au chlorure et au bromure d'argent. Paris C. R. Acad. sci. 152 1911 (766 768). 41231

—————— —————— Sur le développement des images photographiques après fixage. Paris C. R. Acad. sci. 152 1911 (102–110). [4225]. 41232

Lumière, L. v. Lumière, A.

Lummer, Otto. Die Helligkeitsempfindlichkeitskurve des Auges und ihre Benutzung zur Temperaturbestimmung. Vortrag . . . Unterrichtsbl. Math. Berlin 17 1911 (2 12). [4455 1450 3010]. 41233

—————— und Reiche, Fritz. Die Abbildung nichtselbstleuchtender Objekte (Bildentstehung im Mikroskop). Arch. Math. Leipzig (3. Reihe) 17 1911 (301 333). [3082 3050 3650 3630]. 41234

Lundén, Harald. Influence de la température sur l'énergie interne et l'énergie libre des dissociations électrolytiques des acides et bases faibles. Stockholm Medd. Vet.-Ak. Nobelinst. 1 No. 12 1908 (16 av. 1 fig. dans le texte). [6250]. 41237

—————— Das Nobelinstitut für physikalische Chemie in Stockholm. Stockholm Medd. Vet.-Ak. Nobelinst. 1 No. 15 1909 (11 mit 7 Textfig.). [6060]. 41238

—————— La constante de dissociation de la tropine et sa variation avec la température. J. Chim. Phys. Genève 8 1910 (331–336). [2457]. 41239

Luneland, Harald. Ueber die Struktur einiger Spektrallinien und ihren Zeemaneffekt in schwachen Magnetfeldern. Ann. Physik Leipzig (4. Folge) 34 1911 (505–542). [4207 4208]. 41240

—————— Ueber das Verhalten des Trabanten – 0,121 A.-E. der Quecksilberlinie 5790 A.-E. im magnetischen Felde. Physik. Zs. Leipzig 12 1911 (511–512). [4208]. 41241

Lungo (Del), Carlo. Le forze capillari e l'evaporazione. Nuovo Cimento Pisa (Ser. 6) 2 1911 (425–430). [1840]. 41242

—————— Leggi e Principi di Fisica. Parte 1. Firenze (G. C. Sansoni) 1909 (448). 21 cm. [0030]. 41243

Lunkenheimer, Fritz. Über das Intensitätsverhältnis der Serienlinien des Wasserstoffs im Kanalstrahlenspektrum. Ann. Physik Leipzig (4. Folge) 36 1911 (134–152). [4205 6845]. 41244

—————— Entgegnung auf Starks Bemerkung zu meiner Abhandlung über das Intensitätsverhältnis der Serienlinien des Wasserstoffs im Kanalstrahlenspektrum. Ann. Physik Leipzig (4. Folge) 37 1912 (823–831). [6845 4205]. 41245

Lupi, D. Alcune ricerche e conclusioni sul fattore di potenza dei circuiti trifasi. Atti Ass. elettrotecn. Milano 14 1910 (3–30). [5720]. 41246

Lusby, S. G. The mobility of the positive flame ion. Cambridge Proc. Phil. Soc. 16 1911 (25–34). [5685]. 41247

Luterbacher, Jos. Die Radioaktivität der Gurnigel-Bad-Quellen. Bern Mitt. Natf. Ges. 1911 1912 (12–17 1 fig.). [4275]. 41248

Luther, R. v. Abegg. R.

Lummer, O[tto] und Reiche, F. Bemerkung zur Abhandlung von L. Mandelstam: Zur Abbeschen Theorie der mikroskopischen Bilderzeugung. Ann. Physik Leipzig (4. Folge) 37 1912 (839–844). [3650]. 41235

————— und Waetzmann, E[rich]. Einige Demonstrationsversuche. Physik. Zs. Leipzig 12 1911 (1135 1139). [0050]. 41236

————— v. Waetzmann.

Luziani, Luciano. Sulla viscosimetria e tensimetria clinica e sulle variazioni di viscosità e di tensione superficiale del sangue vivente sotto l'azione dei difenoli. Sperimentale Firenze 64 1910 (351–388). [0325]. 41249

Lyman, Theodore. The spectra of some gases in the Schumann region. Astroph. J. Chicago Ill. 33 1911 (98–107 with text fig. tables). [3440 4206]. 41250

Lyons, William J. A method of exact determination of the continuous change in absolute density of a substance, e.g. wax, in passing through its fusion stage. Dublin Proc. R. Soc. 13 1911 (63–72). [1410]. 41251

Maarse, J. v. Smits, A.

Macallum, E. N. v. McLennan, J. C.

Maccioni, Otto. Le onde elettromagnetiche e i fenomeni sismici. Riv. fis. mat. sc. nat. Pavia 22 1910 (360–365). [6600]. 41252

McDermott, F. Alex. Some observations on a photogenic micro-organism

Pseudomonas lucifera Molisch. Washington D. C. Proc. Biol. Soc. 24 1911 (179–183). [4200]. 41253

McDaniel, A. S. Chemistry of the silver voltameter. Science New York (N. Ser.) 34 1911 (159–160). [6010]. 41254

Macdonald, Hector Munro. The integration of the equations of propagation of electric waves. London Proc. Math. Soc. (Ser. 2) 10 1911 (91–95). [6620]. 41255

McGinnis, C. S. and Harkins, M. R. The transmission of sound through porous and non-porous materials. Physic. Rev. Ithaca N.Y. 33 1911 (128–136 with fig. table). [9320 9250]. 41256

Mach, Ernst v. Stallo, J. B.

McKeehan, L. W. Die Endgeschwindigkeit des Falles kleiner Kugeln in Luft bei vermindertem Druck. (The terminal velocity of fall of small spheres in air at reduced pressures.) [Übers.] Physik. Zs. Leipzig 12 1911 (707–721). [0325]. 41257

————— v. Zeleny, J.

McKendrick, J. G. Further experiments with the gramophone. Nature London 86 1911 (244–245). [9420]. 41258

Macků, B. Vliv předčasného vyhasnutí jiskry na měření útlumu. [Ueber den Einfluss des frühzeitigen Auslöschens des Funkens auf Dämpfungsmessungen.] Prag Věstn. České Spol. Náuk. 1911 No. 1 (27); Ann. Physik Leipzig (4. Folge) 34 1911 (941–970). [6820]. 41259

————— Zur Theorie der Goldschmidtschen Hochfrequenzmaschine. Jahrb. drahtlos. Telegr. Leipzig 5 1911 (5–14). [6045]. 41260

————— Zur Theorie der Dämpfung bei Hertzschen Wellen. Physik. Zs. Leipzig 12 1911 (224). [6615 9135]. 41261

————— O účinku magnetického pole na Voltův effekt. [Ueber die Einwirkung des magnetischen Feldes auf den Voltaschen Effekt.] Prag Rozpr. České Ak. Frant. Jos. 20 1911 No. 13 (6). [6455]. 41262

McLaren, S. B. Hamilton's equations and the partition of energy between matter and radiation. Phil. Mag. London (Ser. 6) **21** 1911 (15–26). [0500]. 41264

———— The emission and absorption of energy by electrons. Phil. Mag. London (Ser. 6) **22** 1911 (66–83). [4980]. 41265

Maclaurin, Richard C. Light. (Columbia University Lectures.) New York (Columbia University Press) 1909 (ix + 251 with portr. text fig. tables). 20.4 cm. [2990]. 41266

McLennan, J. C. and **Macallum**, E. L. The intensity of the earth's penetrating radiation at different altitudes and a secondary radiation excited by it. Phil. Mag. London (Ser. 6) **22** 1911 (639–646). [4275]. 41268

———— On the resolution of the spectral lines of mercury. [Abstract.] Physic. Rev. Ithaca N.Y. **32** 1911 (342–343 with text fig.). [4207]. 41269

Maennel, Kurt. Ueber die spezifischen Wärmen einiger Salzlösungen bei tiefen Temperaturen. Diss. Halle a. d. S. (Druck d. Buchdruckerei d. Waisenhauses) 1911 (75 mit Taf.). 23 cm. [1620]. 41270

Maercks, J. Kolbenmaschinen. [In: Lehrbuch des Maschinenbaues. Hrsg. von Karl Esselborn. Bd 1.] Leipzig (W. Engelmann) 1911 (147–339). [2490 6791]. 41271

Maey, E. Zwei Pendel für drei verschiedene Resonanzen. Zs. physik. Unterr. Berlin **24** 1911 (213–215). [0050]. 41272

Maffia, P. Über das Adsorptionsgleichgewicht im Grahamschen Eisenoxydhydrosol. Kolloidchem. Beih. Dresden **3** 1911 (85–122); Diss. Dresden (Th. Steinkopff) 1911 (39). 23 cm. [0340]. 41273

Magin, E. Optische Darstellung schwingender Vorgänge. Zs. physik. Unterr. Berlin **24** 1911 (197–201). [9030 0050]. 41274

Magini, R. Ricerche sulla tensione superficiale di alcuni liquidi. Nuovo Cimento Pisa (Ser. 6) **1** 1911 (462–483). [0300]. 41275

———— Sulle misure di tensione superficiale. Roma Rend. Acc. Lincei (Ser. 5) **20** 1. sem. 1911 (30–37). [0300]. 41276

Magini, C. Nuovo dispositivo per la separazione di scariche elettriche alternative. Atti Ass. elettrotecn. Milano **14** 1910 (489–494). [6047]. 41277

———— I raggi X alla portata di tutti. Milano (V. Strazza e C.) 1911 (36). 19 cm. [6845]. 41278

Magli, G. v. Piutti, A.

Magornow, N. und **Rotinjanz**, L. Eine einfache direkte Bestimmungsmethode der Verdampfungswärme von Flüssigkeiten mittels elektrischer Heizung. Zs. physik. Chem. Leipzig **77** 1911 (700–706). [1680 1610]. 41279

Mahillon. Nos stéthoscopes au point de vue acoustique. Presse méd. belge Bruxelles **1906** (13–15). [9220]. 41280

Mainka, C. Anordnung einer Flüssigkeitsdämpfung bei Erdbebenapparaten. Mechaniker Berlin **19** 1911 (205–207). [0090]. 41281

Majone, Pasquale. Metodo semplice per misurare il potere di assorbimento capillare nei materiali da costruzione. Ann. Igiene Roma **19** 1909 (123–137). [0300]. 41282

Majorana, Quirino. La telefonia a grande distanza. Riv. Leg. Stat. comp. Roma **1** 1908 (69–77). [6485]. 41283

———— Ricerche ed esperimenti di telefonia elettrica senza filo. [Sunto.] Riv. fis. mat. sc. nat. Pavia **19** 1909 (519–552). [6615]. 41284

———— Le radiazioni come mezzo di segnalazione a distanza. Riv. Comm. Roma **3** 1910 (1086–1092). [6615]. 41285

———— Posta, telegrafo, telefono. Cinquanta anni di storia italiana. Milano (Hoepli) 1911 (1–35). [0010 4900]. 41286

Makino, K[engo]. Effect of nonvoltage wave upon the performance of a transformer. Tokyo Denki Gakkwai Zasshi [J. Elect. Soc.] 1910 (313–370). [6047]. 41287

Makower, A. J. v. Eccles. W. H.; Galletti, R. C.

Makower, Walter and **Russ**, Sidney. Notes on scattering during radioactive recoil. Manchester Mem. Lit. Phil. Soc. 55 1911 (1–14). [4275].
41288

———— *c.* Fajans, K.

Malassez, J. Recherches sur les rayons cathodiques. Ann. chim. phys. Paris (sér. 8) 23 1911 (231–275 397–424 491–522). [6845].
41289

———— Sur l'émission des rayons cathodiques. Radium Paris 8 1911 (67–72 av. fig.). [6845].
41290

Malchair, A. Description et emploi du planimètre. Bul. mens. mus. enseign. indust. prof. prov. Hainaut Charleroi 1906 (281–290). [0800].
41291

Malclès, L. Sur l'effet dit "de pénétration" dans les diélectriques. Ann. chim. phys. Paris (sér. 8) 23 1911 (348–363). [5252].
41292

Maltitano, Giovanni. Ueber den mizellaren oder „kolloiden" Zustand. Untersuchungen über die Dispersionsvorgänge in den Hydro-Oxy-Chloro-Ferri-Systemen. (Übers. von Hans **Handovsky**.) Kolloidchem. Beih. Dresden 2 1910 (142–212). [0340].
41293

———— Cristalloïdes et colloïdes ou état moléculaire et état micellaire. Ann. chim. phys. Paris (sér. 8) 24 1911 (502–553) ; 25 1912 (159–253). [0340].
41294

———— Ciò che sono i colloidi. Atti Soc. ital. prog. sci. Roma 4 1911 (375–391). [0340].
41295

Malikov, M[ichail Feodoséjević] *v.* Alekséjev, A.

Mallik, D. N. Lines of force due to given static charges. Phil. Mag. London (Ser. 6) 22 1911 (177–190). [5220].
41296

Mallock, A. The damping of sound by frothy liquids. London Proc. R. Soc. (Ser. A) 84 1910 (391–395). [9240].
41297

Mallock, H. R. A. Pendulum clocks and their errors. London Proc. R. Soc. (Ser. A) 85 1911 (505–526). [0809 0825].
41298

Malloux, C. O. Determinazione della corrente costante che produce lo stesso riscaldamento di una corrente variabile. Atti Ass. elettrotecn. Milano 15 1911 (1021–1024). [5720].
41299

Malmström, R. Technische Anwendungen eines allgemeinen Satzes über erzwungene Schwingungen. Zs. Math. Leipzig 60 1912 (136–144). [9135].
41300

Malosse, Henri. Photométrie pratique pour le contrôle du pouvoir lumineux des becs servant à l'éclairage public ou privé. Paris C. R. Acad. sci. 152 1911 (1748–1749). [3010].
41301

———— Pouvoir rotatoire spécifique du camphre dissous dans l'acétone. Paris C. R. Acad. sci. 153 1911 (54–57). [4050].
41302

Mameli, Efisio. Conducibilità elettrica degli acidi clorcacetici in soluzione acquosa. Rend. Soc. chim. ital. Roma (Ser. 2) 2 1910 (324–325) ; Atti Soc. ital. prog. sci. Roma 4 1911 (760–761) ; Gazz. chim. ital. Roma 41 1. sem. 1911 (294–319). [6240].
41303

Manabe, K[aichiro] *v.* Isitani, D.

Mancini, J. *v.* Raffo, M.

Mandelstam, L. Zur Abbeschen Theorie der mikroskopischen Bildererzeugung. Ann. Physik Leipzig (4 Folge) 35 1911 (881–897). [3650 3082].
41305

———— Pendelmodell zur Demonstration der Schwingungsvorgänge in elektrischen gekoppelten Kondensatorkreisen. Jahrb. drahtlos. Telegr. Leipzig 4 1911 (515–521). [6450 0050].
41306

———— und **Papalexi**, N. Ueber eine Methode zur Messung von logarithmischen Dekrementen und Schwingungszahlen elektromagnetischer Schwingungssysteme. Jahrb. drahtlos. Telegr. Leipzig 4 1911 (605–618). [6610 6450].
41307

Manetti, C. La bussola giroscopica Anschütz-Kämpfe. Riv. maritt. Roma 1. trim. 1911 (461–471). [0090]
41308

Mangold, Gg. Die Regulierfähigkeit der Dampfturbine bei stossfreiem Eintritt. Zs. Turbinenwesen München 8 1911 (401–407 424–427) ; Diss. Danzig. München (Druck v. R. Oldenburg) 1911 (81). 23 cm. [2490].
41309

Mannessier, Anna *v.* Oddo, G.

Manson, E[dmund] S[ewall], jun. A kinetic theory of gravitation. Science New York (N. Ser.) 33 1911 (894–895). [0700].
41310

Marc, Robert. Vorlesungen über die chemische Gleichgewichtslehre und ihre Anwendung auf die Probleme der Mineralogie, Petrographie und Geologie. Jena (G. Fischer) 1911 (VI + 212). 24 cm. 5 M. [1887]. 41312

―――― und **Ritzel**, A. Ueber die Faktoren, die den Kristallhabitus bedingen. Zs. physik. Chem. Leipzig **76** 1911 (584–590). [0400 2465]. 41313

Marcelin, R. Mécanique des phénomènes irréversibles à partir des données thermodynamiques. J. Chim. Phys. Genève **9** 1911 (399–415). [2415]. 41314

March, H. W. Über die Ausbreitung der Wellen der drahtlosen Telegraphie auf der Erdkugel. Ann. Physik Leipzig (4. Folge) **37** 1912 (29–50) ; Diss. München. Leipzig (Druck v. B. G. Teubner) 1911 (70). 24 cm. [6615]. 41315

Marchand, H. Les autocommutateurs téléphoniques. Rev. gén. sci. Paris **22** 1911 (113–123). [6485]. 41316

―――― L'avenir des stations centrales d'électricité. Rev. gén. sci. Paris **22** 1911 (753–762). [6060 6070]. 41317

[**Marchesini**, Matilde.] Tubi luminescenti al neon. [Sunte.] Elettricista Roma (Ser. 2) **10** 1911 (20–21). [6080]. 41318

Marchi, G. Manuale pratico per l'operaio elettrotecnico. Ed. 3. Milano (Hoepli) 1909 (X + 519). 15 cm. [0030 4900]. 41319

Marchis, L. Production of low temperatures, and refrigeration. [Transl. from Rev. gén. sci. Paris **20** 5 1909.] Washington D.C. Smithsonian Inst. Rep. 1909 1910 (207–224). [1012]. 41320

Marcillac, P. Observations aérostatiques sur l'électricité atmosphérique. Conquête de l'air Bruxelles 1910. [5270]. 41321

Marckwald, W[illy]. Das Radium vom chemisch-physikalischen Standpunkt. Berlin Veröff. Hufeland Ges. Balneol. **32** 1911 (35–44). [4275]. 41322

―――― Einiges aus dem Gebiete der radioaktiven Erscheinungen. Radium Leipzig **1** 1911 (2–14). [4275]. 41323

―――― und **Russell**, Al. S. Ueber den Radiumgehalt einiger Uranerze. (Vorl. Mitt.) Berlin Ber. D. chem. Ges. **44** 1911 (771–775) ; Jahrb. Radioakt. Leipzig **8** (1911) 1912 (457–470). [4275]. 41324

Marcolongo, Roberto. Sull' equazione della propagazione del calore nei corpi cristallizzati. Napoli Rend. Soc. sc. (Ser. 3) **17** 1911 (164–172). [2010]. 41326

Marconi, Guglielmo. Telegrafia senza fili. [Trad.] Industria Milano **24** 1910 (162–165 179–182 201–203). [0030 6615 4900]. 41327

―――― I progressi della radiotelegrafia. Elettricità Milano **37** 1911 (18 19–24). [6615]. 41328

―――― La telegrafia senza fili, sistema Marconi. [Trad.] Elettricista Roma (Ser. 2) **10** 1911 (193–199) ; Politecn. Milano **59** 1911 (617–635). [6615]. 41329

―――― Nobel lecture [on wireless telegraphy]. Les prix Nobel en **1909** 1910 (24 with 25 textfigs.). [6943 6615]. 41330

Maréchal. Les colloïdes. Riv. fis. mat. sc. nat. Pavia **22** 1910 (472–475). [0340]. 41331

[**Marenco di Moriondo**, Enrico.] Densità e temperatura dell' acqua superficiale del mare determinate durante la campagna di circumnavigazione della R. Nave " Calabria " (4 febbraio 1905–3 febbraio 1907). Ann. idrogr. Genova **6** 1909 (263–272). [0810]. 41332

Mareš, Jar. Měření koncentrace iontu vodíka. [Konzentrationsmessung der Wasserstoffionen.] Listy Chem. Prag **1911** (290–292). [6210]. 41333

Marguerre, F. Beiträge zur Kenntnis der Wechselstrom-Kommutatormotoren. Elektr. Kraftbetriebe München **9** 1911 (541–545). [6070]. 41334

Marino, Luigi e **Porlezza**, C. Sulla luminosità del fosforo—esperienza da lezione. Roma Rend. Acc. Lincei (Ser. 5) **20** 1. sem. 1911 (442–446). [0050 2990]. 41335

Marmier, Louis. Action des rayons ultra-violets sur l'hyposulfite de sodium. Paris C. R. Acad. sci. **154** 1912 (32–33). [4225]. 41336

Marschall, Oswald c. Rabe, P.

Marsh, S. and **Nottage**, W. H. On the formation of dust striations by an electric spark. London Proc. Phys. Soc. 23 1911 (264–276). [6820]. 41337

Marsden, E. and **Barratt**, T. The probability distribution of the time intervals of α particles with application to the number of α particles emitted by uranium. London Proc. Physic. Soc. 23 1911 (367–373). [4275]. 41338

Martens, A. Ueber die technische Prüfung des Kautschuks und der Ballonstoffe im Königlichen Material-prüfungsamt zu Gross-Lichterfelde (West). Berlin SitzBer. Ak. Wiss. 1911 (346–366). [0090]. 41339

——— Handbuch der Materialienkunde für den Maschinenbau. Tl 2 : Die technisch wichtigen Eigenschatten der Metalle und Legierungen von E[mil] **Heyn**. Hälfte A. Die wissenschaftlichen Grundlagen für das Studium der Metalle und Legierungen. Metallographie. Berlin (J. Springer) 1912 (XXXII + 506 mit 19 Taf.). 28 cm. Geb. 42 M. [1200 5466]. 41340

Martin [q. b. **Landschütz**], Hilda v. Beobachtungen an metallischen Leitern von sehr hohem Widerstand und elektronentheoretische Folgerungen. Physik. Zs. Leipzig 12 1911 (41–48). [5660 6850 5675]. 41341

Martinelli, M. Le pile elettriche e loro applicazioni. Ed. 2. Milano (E. Bignami e C.) 1910 (447). 19 cm. [0030 4900]. 41342

Martini, Tito. Beniamino Franklin elettricista. Riv. fis. mat. sc. nat. Pavia 20 1909 (3–17). [0010]. 41343

——— Intorno a una memoria del Sig. K. Dörsing sulla velocità del suono nei liquidi. Venezia Atti Ist. ven. 68 parte 2 1909 (817–820). [9210]. 41344

Marvin, Charles F[rederick]. The pressure of saturated vapor from water and ice as measured by different authorities. [With bibliography.] Washington D.C. U. S. Dept. Agric. Mon. Weath. Rev. 37 1909 (3–9 with tables). [1840]. 41345

——— Methods and apparatus for the observation and study of evaporation. Washington D.C. U. S. Dept. Agric. Mon. Weath. Rev. 37

1909 (141 146 182–191 with fl.). [1840]. 41346

Marx, Erich. Sind meine Versuche über die Geschwindigkeit der Röntgenstrahlen durch Interferenz elektrischer Luftwellen erklärbar ? (Antwort an die Herren Franck und Pohl.) Ann. Physik Leipzig (4. Folge) 35 1911 (397–400). [4240]. 41347

——— Über die Messungen der Geschwindigkeit der Röntgenstrahlen. Jahrb. Radioakt. Leipzig 8 (1911) 1912 (535–548). [6845 4240]. 41348

Marx, Eugen und **Trendelenburg**, Wilhelm. Über die Genauigkeit der Einstellung des Auges beim Fixieren. Zs. Psychol. Leipzig Abt. 2 45 1911 (87–102 mit 1 Taf.). 41349

——— c. Liebermann, P. v.

Marx, H. Gravitation und Wärme. [Die Funktionen und mechanische Funktionen der Zustandsänderungen eines idealen Gases.] Turbine Berlin 7 1911 (213–215 231–233 267–279 330–334 357–360). [0200 1450]. 41350

Mascarelli, Luigi. Sul contegno delle aldeidi benzoica e paratoluica in presenza di iodio e sotto l'azione della luce. Atti Soc. ital. prog. sci. Roma 4 1911 (776–779). [4225]. 41351

——— e **Babini**, V. Solubilità allo stato solido fra composti aromatici ed i relativi esaidrogenati. Gazz. chim. ital. Roma 41 1. sem. 1911 (89–103). [1920]. 41352

——— e **Costantino**, A. Il cicloesano come solvente crioscopico. Gazz. chim. ital. Roma 40 1. sem. 1910 (31–42). [1920]. 41353

——— e **Musatty**, I. Il cicloesano come solvente crioscopico. Gazz. chim. ital. Roma 41 1. sem. 1911 (73–82 82–89). [1920]. 41354

——— ——— Sul comportamento crioscopico reciproco di sostanze differenti fra loro per i gruppi CO e CH₂. Gazz. chim. ital. Roma 41 1. sem. 1911 (103–110). [1920]. 41355

Mascart, Jean. Les applications récentes de la télégraphie sans fil aux bateaux de pêche. Rev. gén. sci. Paris 22 1911 (671–672). 41356

Masche, Walther. Physikalische Uebungen. Ein Leitfaden für die Hand des Schülers. Tl 1. (Beil. zum Jahresber. des k. Kaiser Wilhelms-Realgymnasiums in Berlin, Ostern 1910.) Berlin (Druck v. A. W. Hayns Erben) 1910 (47). 21 cm. [0050]. 41357

Mašek, Bohumil. Přehled pokroků fysiky za rok 1908. 5. Elektřina a magnetismus. [Uebersicht der physikalischen Fortschritte im J. 1908. 5. Elektrizität und Magnetismus.] Prag Věstn. České Ak. Frant. Jos. 1911 (53–88 105–119). [0030 4900]. 41358

Massink, A. v. Schreinemakers, F. A. H.

Massol, G. et Faucon, A. Sur la chaleur latente de fusion et la chaleur spécifique des acides gras. Paris C. R. Acad. sci. 154 1911 (268–270). [1670]. 41359

Mastrobuono, Luigi. Sulla viscosità dell' umor acqueo. Siena Atti Acc. Fisiocritici (Ser. 4) 20 1908 (459–494 con 1 tav.). [0325]. 41360

Mastrodomenico, Francesco. La gravitazione universale, ossia il mondo materiale e il gioco delle forze che ne animano la macchina. Napoli (Tip. De Rosa e Polidori) 1909 (36). 20 cm. [0700]. 41361

Mather, F. Sound vibrations produced by electric sparks. Elect. London 66 1911 (960). [9130]. 41362

Mathesius, Walther. Studie über die magnetischen Eigenschaften von Mangan- und Nickelstahl. Diss. Berlin. Düsseldorf (Druck v. A. Bagel) 1911 (30 mit Taf.). 28 cm. [5466]. 41363

Mathews, Joseph] Howard v. Richards. T. W.

Matignon, Camille. Sur la formation synthétique du protoxyde d'azote. Paris C. R. Acad. sci. 154 1912 (203–206). [2472]. 41364

Matsumoto, N]arazo] v. Takamine, T.

Matthies, W. Über eine neue Methode zur Bestimmung des Potentialgradienten bei der Glimm- und Bogenentladung in zylindrischen Glas- und Quarzröhren. Berlin Verh. D. physik. Ges. 13 1911 (552–568). [6840]. 41365

――― Findet im Quecksilber-Vakuumlichtbogen ein elektrischer Massentransport statt und tritt an der Hg-Anode ein von der Stromdichte und dem Anodenfalle abhängiger Reaktionsdruck auf ? Bemerkung zu der Arbeit des Hrn A. Perot : „Sur la luminescence de l'arc au mercure dans le vide". Ann. Physik Leipzig (4. Folge) 37 1912 (721–738). [6830]. 41366

Matthies, W. und Struck, H. Über den Potentialgradienten auf der ungeschichteten positiven Säule des Glimm-, bzw. Bogenstromes in N₂ und H bei hohen Strom- u. Gasdichten. Berlin Verh. D. physik. Ges. 14 1912 (83–103). [6840]. 41367

Mattausch, G. Die Verlegungs- oder Reductionsmethode von Frick zur Ermittelung der Stromverteilung in Leitungsnetzen. Zs. Elektrot. Potsdam 14 1911 (229–232 241–243 257–259 269–271 313–315). [5630]. 41368

Matuschek und Nenning. Über das Auftreten von chemisch wirksamen Strahlen bei chemischen Reaktionen. ChemZtg Cöthen 36 1912 (21). [4270]. 41369

Mau, W. v. Riesenfeld, E. H.

Mauchly, S. J. v. Ives, J. E.

Mauguin, Ch. Liquides biréfringents à structure hélicoïdale. Paris C. R. Acad. sci. 151 1910 (1141–1144). [1930]. 41370

――― Orientation des cristaux liquides par le champ magnétique. Paris C. R. Acad. sci. 152 1911 (1680–1684). [4030]. 41371

――― Über O. Lehmanns flüssige Kristalle. Physik. Zs. Leipzig 12 1911 (1011–1015). 41372

Maunder, E. W. L'origine solaire des perturbations du magnétisme terrestre. Ciel et Terre Bruxelles 1905 (51–56). [5490]. 41373

Maurain, Ch. Les états physiques de la matière. Paris (Alcan) 1910 (327). 19 cm. 3 fr. 50. [0500]. 41374

Mauro, Francesco. La trasmissione del calore negli isolanti per basse temperature. Politecn. Milano 58 1910 (691–696). [2020]. 41375

Mauthner, Erich von. Abhängigkeit des Gewichtes eines Körpers von seiner elektrischen Ladung. [Nebst Erwiderung.] Elektrot Zs. Berlin 32 1911 (552). [0810]. 41376

Maxted, Edward B[radford]. Ueber die Nitride von Eisen, Nickel und Kobalt. Ueber das Bleicoulometer. Diss. Berlin (Druck v. E. Ebering) 1911 (55). 23 cm. [6010]. 41377

Mayer, Emil. Verwendung von Zusatzpolen bei Einankerumformern. [Nebst Erwiderungen von Robert **Pohl** und J. **Jonas.**] Elektrot. Zs. Berlin 32 1911 (1096–1097). [6047]. 41378

Mayer, Karl. Die Farbenmischungslehre und ihre praktische Anwendung. Berlin (J. Springer) 1911 (V + 83 mit 6 Taf.). 24 cm. 4 M. [2990]. 41379

Mayer, Robert. Die Mechanik der Wärme. 2 Abhandlungen. Hrsg. von A. von **Oettingen**. (Ostwald's Klassiker der exakten Wissenschaften. Nr. 180.) Leipzig (W. Engelmann) 1911 (90 mit 1 Portr.). 19 cm. 1,60 M. [2405 0010]. 41380

————— Elektrotechnische Messkunde. Tl 1: Messinstrumente und Messmethoden. Für den Gebrauch an höheren technischen Lehranstalten . . . bearb. Leipzig u. Wien (F. Deuticke) 1912 (VII + 311). 24 cm. 7 M. [5600 6010 5435 6440 3010]. 41381

————— Über die Erhaltung der Kraft. Vier Abhandlungen, neu hrsg. . . . von Albert **Neuburger**. (Voigtländers Quellenbücher. Bd 12.) Leipzig (R. Voigtländer) [1912] (128). 18 cm. 0,90 M. [2405 0010]. 41382

Mazzotto, Domenico. Trasformazione delle leghe di piombo e stagno e di altre leghe binarie allo stato solido. Modena Mem. Acc. (Ser. 3) 9 1910 (81–86). [1695]. 41383

Mazzucchelli, Arrigo. Il teorema di Nernst. Rend. Soc. chim. ital. Roma (Ser. 2) 1 1909 (254–265 277–298). [2472]. 41384

————— Numeri di trasporto e complessità molecolare. Roma Rend. Acc. Lincei (Ser. 5) 20 2. sem. 1911 (124–129). [6240]. 41385

Meara [O]. W. A. I. I differenti sistemi di telegrafia multipla. Atti Ass. elettrotecn. Milano 15 1911 (1145–1151). [6130]. 41386

Mebes, [Albert]. Farbenphotographie mit Farbrasterplatten,

Theorie und Praxis der Autochrom-Thames-, Omnicolore-, Aurora-, Dioptichrom-Platte und der deutschen, Farbenfilms. Bunzlau i. Schl. (L. Fernbach) 1911 (VIII + 301 mit 2 Taf.). 22 cm. 4 M. 41387

Méchain und **Delambre**. Grundlagen des dezimalen metrischen Systems oder Messung des Meridianbogens . . . **Borda** und **Cassini**: Versuche über die Länge des Sekundenpendels in Paris . . . In Auswahl übers. und hrsg. von Walter **Block**. (Ostwald's Klassiker der exakten Wissenschaften. Nr. 181.) Leipzig (W. Engelmann) 1911 (200 mit 2 Taf.). 19 cm. Geb. 3,40 M. [0895]. 41388

Mees, C. E. Kenneth and **Piper**, C. Welborne. On the fogging powers of developers. Phot. J. London 51 1911 (226–241). [4225]. 41389

Meier, W. v. Kaufmann.

Meinecke, Wilhelm. Bildort bei einfacher Brechung. (Jahresber. der Bismarck-Realschule zu Stettin. Jg 2.) Stettin (Druck v. H. Saran) 1910 (1–9). 26 cm. [3020]. 41390

Meisenheimer. Optisch aktive Aminoxyde. Liebigs Ann. Chem. Leipzig 385 1911 (117–155) 41391

Meitner, Lise. Ueber einige neuere Ergebnisse auf dem Gebiete der Radioaktivität. Ergebn. wiss. Med. Leipzig 2 1911 (188–200). [4275]. 41392

————— Die radioaktiven Eigenschaften der Thoriumreihe. Natw. Rdsch. Braunschweig 26 1911 (353–356). [4275]. 41393

————— Über einige einfache Herstellungsmethoden radioaktiver Zerfallsprodukte. Physik. Zs. Leipzig 12 1911 (1094–1099). [4275]. 41394

————— v. Baeyer, O. v. ; Franck, J.

Melchissédec et **Frossard**. Sur la théorie mécanique de quelques tuyaux sonores. Paris C. R. Acad. sci. 153 1911 (176–179). [9130]. 41395

Mellecœur, R. Recherches expérimentales sur le thermo-calorimètre. Ann. chim. phys. Paris (sér. 8) 23 1911 (556–566). [1610]. 41396

Mendenhall, C[harles] E[llwood]. On the emissive power of wedge-shaped cavities and their use in temperature measurements. Astroph. J. Chicago Ill. **33** 1911 (91-97 with text fig.). [4210]. 41397

———— Notes on optical pyrometry. Physic. Rev. Ithaca N.Y. **33** 1911 (74-76 with fig. table). [3010]. 41398

———— and **Lent,** W. F. A method of measuring the susceptibility of weakly magnetic substances and a study of the susceptibility of alloys of bismuth with tellurium and thallium. Physic. Rev. Ithaca N.Y. **32** 1911 (406-417 with tables text fig.). [5440 5466]. 41399

———— *r.* Watts, O. P.

Meneghini, Domenico *r.* Bruni, G.

Menke, J. B. *r.* Jaeger, F. M.

Menneret, M. Mouvement oscillatoire et mouvement uniforme des liquides dans les tubes cylindriques. Frottement interne. J. phys. Paris (sér. 5) **1** 1911 (753-767 797-804). [0325]. 41400

Menzel. Physikalische Wandtafeln. Nr. 26. Wirkung der Brillen. 4. Aufl. Breslau (E. Morgenstern) [1912] (1 Ta..). 63 × 50 cm. 1 M. [0050]. 41401

Menzies, Alan W. C. Ueber einen bequemen Apparat zur Messung der Dampfdichten flüchtiger Stoffe. (Uebers. von Alexander Smith.) Zs. physik. Chem. Leipzig **76** 1911 (355-359). [0510]. 41402

———— *r.* Smith, A.

Mercanton, Paul L. Einige einfache Vorlesungsversuche. (Quelques expériences de cours simples.) [I. Wärmeleitung durch Gase. II. Edlunds Wärmeäquivalentmessung. III. Änderung der inneren Reibung mit der Temperatur.) (Übers.) Physik. Zs. Leipzig **13** 1912 (84-86). [0050]. 41403

Merczyng, H. O dyspersyi elektrycznej wody i alkoholu etylowego w okolicy fal bardzo krótkich. [Elektrische Dispersion von Wasser und Äthylalkohol für sehr kurze Wellen.] Kraków Bull. Intern. Acad. **1911 A** (123-133) ; Ann. Physik Leipzig (4. Folge) **34** 1911 (1015-1025). [3875]. 41405

(c-1388)

Merczyng. H. O zalamaniu promieni elektrycznych o małej długości fali w ciekłem powietrzu. [Über die Brechung elektrischer Strahlen von sehr kurzer Wellenlänge in flüssiger Luft.] Kraków Bull. Intern. Acad. **1911 A** (489-492) ; Ann. Physik Leipzig (4. Folge) **37** 1912 (157-169). [3875]. 41406

———— Zarys obecnych granic poznania natury w przestrzeni i czasie. [Les limites de notre connaissance de la Nature par rapport au temps et à l'espace.] Wszechświat Warszawa **30** 1911 (161-165 181-183). [0000]. 41407

———— O zasadzie względności w pojęciu fizycznem czasu i przestrzeni. [Le principe de relativité ; les notions fondamentales du temps et de l'espace.] Wszechświat Warszawa **30** 1911 (657-659 678-683 690-693). [0000]. 41408

Merritt, Ernest. The silicon detector used with short electric waves, and the theory of contact rectifiers. [Abstract.] Physic. Rev. Ithaca N.Y. **32** 1911 (630-631). [6043 6047]. 41410

———— *r.* Nichols, E. L.

Merservey, A. B. Investigation of the potentials required to produce discharges in gases at low pressures. Phil. Mag. London (Ser. 6) **21** 1911 (479-499). [6840]. 41411

Merton, Thomas Ralph. A method of calibrating fine capillary tubes. Phil. Mag London (Ser. 6) **21** 1911 (386-390). [0300]. 41412

Meslin, Georges. Étude sur la structure des raies spectrales à l'aide d'appareils à grande dispersion. Ann. chim. phys. Paris (sér. 8) **24** 1911 (87-134 av. fig.). [4207]. 41413

———— Sur la double réfraction circulaire du chlorate de sodium. Paris C. R. Acad. sci. **152** 1911 (1666-1668). [4040]. 41414

———— Sur les vitesses des circulaires inverses dans la polarisation rotatoire. Paris C. R. Acad. sci. **152** 1911 (1841-1843). [4040]. 41415

———— Sur l'emploi des prismes biréfringents pour obtenir des franges d'interférence. Paris C. R. Acad. sci. **153** 1911 (1145-1147). [3610 4060]. 41416

———— Sur le pouvoir dispersif des combinaisons de prismes. Application

N

aux spectroscopes. J. phys. Paris
(sér. 5) 1 1911 (88–104 av. fig.). [3165].
41417

Meslin, Georges. Application de la
télégraphie sans fil à la mesure des coefficients de self-induction. Paris C. R.
Acad. sci. 154 1912 (275–276). [6440
6615]. 41418

Méttler, G. Hohe Flammtemperaturen durch Gase, ihre chemische
und physikalische Erzeugung. Wasser
u. Gas Oldenburg 1 1911 (526–532).
[4202]. 41419

Mettler, Hans. Graphische Berech-
nungs-Methoden. Im Dienste der
Naturwissenschaft. I, II, III. Zürich-
Fehnau (Leemann u. Cie.) 1910–1912
(70 + 78 + 130 mit 43 + 71 + 92
Zeichnungen). 16 cm. [0030]. 41420

Metzner, P. Über „dunkle" Funken.
(Vorl. Mitt.) Berlin Verh. D. physik.
Ges. 13 1911 (612–616). [6820].
41421

Meunier, J. Sur les spectres de
combustion des hydrocarbures et de
différents métaux. Paris C. R. Acad.
sci. 152 1911 (1760–1763). [4205].
41422

―――――― Sur les conditions de la
production du spectre de Swan et sur
ce qu'on peut en conclure relativement
aux comètes qui possèdent ce spectre.
Paris C. R. Acad. sci. 153 1911 (863–
866). [4206]. 41423

Mewes, Rudolf. Vergleich der
eigenen Verfahren mit anderen Luft-
verflüssigungs- und Sauerstoff-Stick-
stoffgewinnungs-Verfahren. [Forts.
folgt.] Zs. Sauerstoffind. Leipzig 3
1911 (53–55 126–130 147–151). [1870].
41424

Meyer, Alfred R. Über die Änderung des elektrischen Widerstandes
reines Eisens mit der Temperatur in
dem Bereiche 0 bis 1000° C. Diss.
Greifswald ; [Auszug] Berlin Verh.
D. physik. Ges. 13 1911 (689–692).
[5660]. 41425

―――――― r. Girani, M. von.

Meyer, Bruno. Die Zerstreuung des
Lichts im Negativ. Phot. Ind. Berlin
1911 (350–351 387–389). [4225].
41426

Meyer, Edgar. Über Schweidlersche
Schwankungen. (Bemerkungen zu der
gleichnamigen Arbeit von N. Campbell.)
Mit einer Nachschrift von Norman

Campbell. Physik. Zs. Leipzig 13 1912
(73–83). (Übers.) [4275]. 41427

Meyer, Edgar. Über die Struktur der
γ-Strahlen. II. Ann. Physik Leipzig
(4. Folge) 37 1912 (700–720). [6845
4275]. 41428

Meyer, G. Über die Kapillaritätskonstanten von Amalgamen. Berlin
Verh. D. physik. Ges. 13 1911 (793–
795) ; Physik. Zs. Leipzig 1 1911
(975–976). [0300]. 41429

Meyer, Georg J. Nachträge zur
Theorie der Abschmelzsicherungen.
Elektr. Kraftbetriebe München 9 1911
(124–127). [5720 6600]. 41430

―――――― Die Verwendung verlustlos regelbarer Drehstrommotoren.
Elektr. Kraftbetriebe München 9 1911
(421–427 453–457 462–468). [6070].
41431

Meyer, Gustav M. Kurzschlüsse in
Wechselstromnetzen, ihre Rückwirkung
auf die Generatoren, insbesondere bei
Turbodynamos . . . Zs. Elektrot.
Potsdam 13 1910 (413–416 437–439
467). [6060 5720]. 41431A

Meyer, Gustav W. Maschinen und
Apparate der Starkstromtechnik, ihre
Wirkungsweise und Konstruktion. Ein
Lehrbuch für den Gebrauch an technischen Lehranstalten . . . Leipzig
u. Berlin (B. G. Teubner) 1912 (IV +
590). 25 cm. 15 M. [6000]. 41432

Meyer, Julius. Zur Kenntnis des
negativen Druckes in Flüssigkeiten.
Zs. Elektroch. Halle 17 1911 (743–
745) ; (Abhandlungen der D. Bunsen-
Gesellschaft . . . Nr. 6.) Halle
a. S. (W. Knapp) 1911 (53 mit Taf.).
25 cm. 2,10 M. [0842 1880 1430].
41433

Meyer, Kurt H. und **Wieland,**
Heinrich. Über das Absorptionsspektrum des Triphenylmethyls und
der Triphenylcarbinolsalze. Berlin
Ber. D. chem. Ges. 44 1911 (2557–
2559). [3860]. 41434

Meyer, O. E†. Zur Theorie des
Kymographions. Aus dem Nachlass
herausgegeben von Cl[emens] **Schaefer.**
Arch. ges. Physiol. Bonn 138 1911
(292–318). [0835]. 41435

Meyer, Richard. Spektrographische
Studien in der Phtaleingruppe. Natw.
Rdsch. Braunschweig 27 1912 (53–55
69–71). [3860]. 41436

Meyer, Ultilas. Über einen möglichen Unterschied zwischen Emissions- und Absorptionsspektren. Bemerkung zu der Arbeit des Herrn T. Krawetz. Physik. Zs. Leipzig **12** 1911 (869–870). [4205 4960]. 41437

Meyer-Lierheim v. Groedel. T.

Meyer-Wülfing, Heinrich. Die doppelt verkettete Streuung beim Zweiphasenmotor und beim Dreiphasenmotor mit Zweiphasenrotor. Diss. Jena. Coburg (Druck v. A. Rossteuscher) 1911 (57). 23 cm. [6070]. 41438

Mezzanotte, Carlo. Telegrafo stampante. [Sunto.] Mon. tecn. Milano **17** 1911 (519–520). [6480]. 41439

Michaelis, Leonor. Die Bestimmung der Wasserstoffionenkonzentration durch Gasketten. [In: Handbuch der biochem. Arbeitsmeth., hrsg. v. E. Abderhalden. Bd 5. Tl 1.] Berlin (Urban & Schwarzenberg) 1911 (500–524). [6250 6255]. 41441

Michaud, Félix. Sur les piles de gravitation. J. phys. Paris (sér. 5) **1** 1911 (123–127). [2475]. 41442

———— Sur les causes qui peuvent produire la variation, à température constante, de la tension de vapeur d'un liquide. Paris C. R. Acad. sci. **152** 1911 (849–851). [2465]. 41443

Michel, Franz. Verstellbares elektrisches Signalthermometer. ChemZtg Cöthen **35** 1911 (1111). [1250]. 41444

Michelson, A[lbert] A[braham]. Recent progress in spectroscopic methods. [Address of the president, American Association for the Advancement of Science, Washington meeting, December, 1911.] Science New York (N. Ser.) **34** 1911 (893–902). [4200]. 41445

———— Lichtwellen und ihre Anwendungen. Übers. und durch Zusätze erweitert von Max Iklé. [Mit einer Literaturübersicht seit 1889.] Leipzig (J. A. Barth) 1911 (IV + 236 mit 3 Taf.). 22 cm. 7.60 M. [3600 0805 4208 0032 0600 0807]. 41446

Mickle, Kenneth A. Flotation of minerals. Part II. Melbourne Proc., R. Soc. Vict. N.S. **23** pt. 2 1911 (555–585); **24** pt. 1I 1912 (301–339). [0250 0300]. 41447

Middlekauff, George W[iles]. A new form of direct-reading candlepower

(c-4388)

scale and recording device for precision photometers. Washington D.C. Dept. Comm. Lab. Bull. Bur. Stand. **7** 1911 (11–43 with fig.). [3010]. 41447A

Mie, Gustav. Antwort auf die Bemerkung des Hrn. G. Seibt zu der Arbeit des Hrn. K. Settnik. „Die Entstehung von sehr wenig gedämpften Wellen usw.". Ann. Physik (4. Folge) **36** 1911 (207–208). [6610]. 41448

———— Ionen und Elektronen. Fortschr. natw. Forschg Berlin **2** 1911 (163–192). [4960 6845 0100]. 41449

———— Grundlagen einer Theorie der Materie. 1. Mitt. Ann. Physik Leipzig (4. Folge) **37** 1912 (511–534). [0500 4940]. 41450

———— Moleküle, Atome, Weltäther. 3. Aufl. (Aus Natur und Geisteswelt. Bd 58.) Leipzig (B. G. Teubner) 1911 (VI + 174). 18 cm. 1.25 M. [0100 0600]. 41451

Miethe, A[dolf]. Farbenphotographie. Fortschr. natw. Forschg Berlin **1** 1910 (1–14). [4225]. 41452

———— Neuer Schwärzungsmesser für Negative. Jahrb. Phot. Halle **25** 1911 (256–260). [3010 4225]. 41453

———— Die chemische Wirkung des Lichtes. [In: Der Mensch u. die Erde. hrsg. v. H. Kraemer. Bd 7.] Berlin Leipzig Wien Stuttgart (Bong & Co.) [1911] (319–384). [4225]. 41454

———— und **Seegert,** B. Ueber Wellenlängenmessungen an einigen Platinmetallen im kurzwelligen ultravioletten Spektrum. Zs. wiss. Phot. Leipzig **10** 1911 (245–249). [3440 4205]. 41455

———— v. Lehmann, F.; Lewin, L.

Milch, Maurice. I motori monofasi a eccitazione in serie ed il probabile loro sviluppo. Industria Milano **25** 1911 (54–56). [6070]. 41456

Miller, J. M. v. Rosa, E. B.

Millikan, R[obert] A[ndrews]. The isolation of an ion, a precision measurement of its charge, and the correction of Stokes's law. Physic. Rev. Ithaca N.Y. **32** 1911 (349–397) with tables text fig.). [4960 0325 0150]. 41457

———— and **Fletcher,** Harvey. On the question of valency in gaseous

s 2

ionization. Phil. Mag. London (Ser. 6) 21 1911 (753-770); [abstract] Physic. Rev. Ithaca N.Y. 32 1911 (239). [6805]. 41458

Millikan, R[obert] A[ndrews] and Fletcher, Harvey. Ursachen der scheinbaren Unstimmigkeiten zwischen neueren Arbeiten über e. (Causes of apparent discrepancies in recent work on e.) (Uebers.) Physik. Zs. Leipzig 12 1911 (161-163). [4960 6845]. 41459

Millis, John. Brownian movements and molecular reality. Science New York (N. Ser.) 33 1911 (426-427). [0100]. 41460

Millochau, G. Contribution à l'étude des effets spectraux des décharges électriques dans les gaz et les vapeurs. Paris C. R. Acad. sci. 153 1911 (808-812). [4205]. 41461

Mills, J. E. The foundations of science. [Address of the President before the North Carolina section of the American Chemical Society, Raleigh, N.C., Jan. 9th, 1909.] Chapel Hill N.C. J. Elisha Mitchell Sci. Soc. 25 1909 (4-14). [0000]. 41462

Milon, H. Les nouveaux systèmes téléphoniques automatiques. Technique moderne Paris 3 1911 (9-12). [6485]. 41463

Miner, H[arlan] S[herman] and Whitaker, M. C. The rare earths—their production and application. J. ind. engin. chem. Easton Pa. 1 1909 (235-245 with if. table). [4202]. 41464

Minguin, J. Dissociation des tartrates, malates et camphorates d'amines, mise en évidence par le pouvoir rotatoire. Ann. chim. phys. Paris (sér. 8) 25 1912 (145-159). [4950 1930]. 41465

——— r. Guntz.

Mises, R. v. Über den Englerschen Flüssigkeitsmesser. Physik. Zs. Leipzig 12 1911 (812-814). [0325]. 41466

——— Dynamische Probleme der Maschinenlehre. [Encyklopädie d. mathem. Wissenschaften. Bd 4. Abt. 1. H.] Leipzig (B. G. Teubner) 1911 (153-355). [6060]. 41467

Mitchell, H. Note on the ratios which the amounts of substances in radio-active equilibrium bear to one another. Phil. Mag. London (Ser. 6) 21 1911 (40-42). [4275]. 41468

Miyazaka, Sanju. Hotoke no goko ni tsuite. [On the Heiligenschein.] Rigakukai [Science] Tokyo 7 1910 (736-737). [3220]. 41469

Miyazawa, T[orao] r. Fujiwara, S.

Mizuno, T[oshinojo]. On the application of the principle of relativity to electromagnetic problems. Kyoto Mem. Coll. Sci. Eng. 2 1910 (159-170). [4940]. 41470

Möller, H. G. Über die Widerstandszunahme unterteilter Leiter bei schnellen Schwingungen. Ann. Physik Leipzig (4. Folge) 36 1911 (738-778). [6460 6440]. 41471

Moller, Hans Jacob. Internationale Farbenbestimmungen. Zs. Farbenind. Berlin 10 1911 (127-132); Textil Berlin 4 1911 (Nr. 1096 1097). [2990]. 41472

Möller, K. und Möller, Th. Beziehungen zwischen Widerstand, Filterfläche, Filterdichte und Luftmenge. Zs. Sauerstoffind. Leipzig 3 1911 (89). [0320]. 41473

Möller, Th. r. Möller, K.

Mollier, Hilde r. Knoblauch, O.

Möllinger und Gewecke. Zum Diagramm des Spannungswandlers. Elektrot. Zs. Berlin 32 1911 (922). [6947 6040]. 41474

Mogendorff, E[duard] E[staell]. Som en verschiltrillingen in lijnenspectra. [Summational and differential vibrations in line spectra.] Amsterdam Versl. Wis. Nat. Afd. K. Akad. Wet. 20 [1911] (434-445) (Dutch); Amsterdam Proc. Sci. K. Akad. Wet. 14 [1911] (470-481) (English). [4205]. 41475

Mohr, Erich. Ueber Adsorption und Kondensation von Wasserdampf an blanken Glasflächen. Diss. Halle a. S. (Druck v. H. John) 1911 (49 mit Taf.). 22 cm. [0250 1840]. 41476

Moir, J. The absorption-spectrum of oxygen and a new law of spectra. Cape Town Trans. R. Soc. S. Afric. 2 pt. 2 1911 (157-159). [3430 3860]. 41477

Moir, Margaret B. On the influence of temperature upon the magnetic properties of a graded series of carbon steels. Edinburgh Proc. R. Soc. 31 1911 (505-516). [5460]. 41478

Mojoin, Pierre r. Dutoit, P.

Monasch, Berthold. Attuale sviluppo delle lampade ad incandescenza al tungsteno. Atti Ass. elettrotecn. Milano **15** 1911 (1036-1037). [6080].
41479

——— Die Entwicklung der Glühlampentechnik. Bayr. IndBl. München **97** 1911 (21-25 31-35). [6080].
41480

Monckton, C. C. F. Prevention of interference in wireless telegraph working. Elect. Engineering London **7** 1911 (193). [6615].
41481

Monier. L'atome primordial est soumis à la loi de l'attraction universelle comme la matière pondérable. [0500].
41482

Monod, G. v. Bonasse, H.

Montangerand, L. Observation de l'éclipse totale de Soleil du 30 août 1905 à Guelma (Algérie). Rapport. Ann. bur. longit. Paris **8** 1911 (P. 1 à P. 41 av. pl.). [4205].
41483

Montefinale, Tito. Goniometro panoramico a doppia visione. Riv. Artig. Genio Roma 2. trim. **1911** (274-282 con 1 tav.). [3090].
41484

Montessus de Ballore, de. Sur l'application de la suspension à la Cardan aux sismographes. Paris C. R. Acad. sci. 153 1911 (743-744). [0825].
41485

Monti, G. Vernici isolanti. Elettricità Milano **35** 1910 (395-396). [5252].
41486

——— Osservazioni critiche sui materiali isolanti adoperati in elettrotecnica. Elettricità Milano **36** 1911 (157-158). [5770].
41487

Monti, N. La radioattività delle acque minerali di S. Pellegrino. Idrol-Climatol. Ter. tis. Firenze **22** 1911 (57-61). [4275].
41488

Montpellier, T. A. L'accumulatore alcalino a ferro-nichel. Atti Ass. elettrotecn. Milano **15** 1911 (1177-1179). [5620].
41489

Motta, Giacinto. La calcolazione di massimo tornaconto delle linee per trasmissione elettrica di energia. Mon. tecn. Milano **16** 1910 (603-606 627-631). [5705].
41490

Montù, Carlo. La elettricità alla esposizione univ. internaz. di Bruxelles 1910. Atti Ass. elettrotecn. Milano **15** 1911 (159-194). [0020 4900].
41491

|**Moore.**| Luce Moore. Industria Milano **25** 1911 (23-25). [6080].
41492

Moore, B[arton] E[vans]. On the magnetic separation of the spectral lines of calcium and strontium. Astroph. J. Chicago Ill. **33** 1911 (385-394 with tables); (Uebers.) Physik. Zs. Leipzig 12 1911 (443-445). [4208].
41493

Moosbrugger, Willy. Spectrochemische und thermochemische Untersuchungen an ungesättigten organischen Verbindungen. Diss. Greifswald (Druck v. H. Adler) 1911 (75). 24 cm. [3860].
41494

Moravesik, Ernst Emil. Experimente über das psychogalvanische Reflexphänomen. J. Psychol. Leipzig **18** 1911 (186-199). [5900].
41495

More, Louis T. On the recent theories of electricity. Phil. Mag. London (Ser. 6) **21** 1911 (196-218). [4960].
41496

Moreau, Georges. Conductibilité électrique des fluorures et rayonnements corpusculaires. Ann. chim. phys. Paris (sér. 8) **24** 1911 (289-314). [6805 5685].
41497

——— Sur l'ionisation corpusculaire des vapeurs salines et la recombinaison des ions d'une flamme. Paris C. R. Acad. sci. 152 1911 (1664-1666). [6805].
41498

Morgan, J[ohn] Livingston R[utgers]. Das Gewicht eines fallenden Tropfens und die Gesetze von Tate. III. Ein Apparat zur raschen und genauen Bestimmung des Gewichts eines fallenden Flüssigkeitstropfens. (Übers. v. W. Neumann.) Zs. physik. Chem. Leipzig **77** 1911 (339-355); IV. Die Eichung eines Mundstücks und die Berechnung der Oberflächenspannung und des Molekulargewichts einer Flüssigkeit aus dem Gewicht ihrer fallenden Tropfen. op. cit. **78** 1911 (129-147). [0300 0690].
41499

——— Ein einfaches Bad für konstante Temperatur zum Gebrauch sowohl oberhalb als auch unterhalb Zimmertemperatur. (Übers. von W. Neumann.) Zs. physik. Chem. Leipzig **78** 1911 (123-128). [1014]. 41500

——— und **Daghlian,** G. K. Das Gewicht eines fallenden Tropfens und die Gesetze von Tate. VI. Die

Tropfengewichte von 20 weiteren nicht-associierten Flüssigkeiten und die für sie berechneten Molekulargewichte. (Übers. von W. **Neumann**.) Zs. physik. Chem. Leipzig **78** 1911 (169–184). [0300]. 41501

Morgan, J[ohn] Livingston R[utgers] und **Schwartz**, Frederick W. Das Gewicht eines fallenden Tropfens und die Tateschen Gesetze. VII. Die Tropfengewichte von einigen der niedern Ester und die daraus berechneten Oberflächenspannungen und Molekulargewichte. (Übers. von W. **Neumann**.) Zs. physik. Chem. Leipzig **78** 1911 (183–207). [0300]. 41502

————— und **Thomssen**, Edgar C. Das Gewicht eines fallenden Tropfens und die Gesetze von Tate. V. Die Tropfengewichte 15 nichtassociierter Flüssigkeiten, wie sie sich mit Hilfe der neuen Gestalt des Apparats ergeben, und die für sie berechneten Molekulargewichte. (Übers. von W. **Neumann**.) Zs. physik. Chem. Leipzig **78** 1911 (148–168). [0300]. 41503

Morini, Giuseppe. Dimostrazione dell' esistenza dell' unità fondamentale della materia. Firenze (E. Yanni) 1910 (9). 20 cm. [0500]. 41504

Morris, Charles. Gravitation. Philadelphia J. Franklin Inst. **167** 1909 (219–234). [0700]. 41505

Morris, J. T. and **Langford**, T. H. The method of constant rate of change of flux as a standard for determining magnetisation curves of iron. London Proc. Physic. Soc. **23** 1911 (277–300). [5440]. 41506

Morris, Wilson C. Attempts to explain gravitation. Pop. Sci. Mon. New York **79** 1911 (252–260 with fig.). [0700]. 41507

Morse, Harry W. Storage batteries. New York (Macmillan) 1912 (ii + 266). 19 cm. [5620]. 41508

————— and **Sargent**, Ledyard W. The internal resistance of the lead accumulator. [With bibliography.] Boston Proc. Amer. Acad. Arts Sci. **46** 1911 (587–612 with text fig. tables). [5620]. 41509

Morton, Réginald. Les rayons X. Monde **1911** juin (82–89). [4240]. 41510

Morton, W. B. On cusped waves of light and the theory of the rainbow. London Proc. Physic. Soc. **23** 1910 (58–65). [3040]. 41511

Moseley, B. A. and **Fajano**, K. Radio-active products of short life. Phil. Mag. London (Ser. 6) **22** 1911 (629–638). [4275]. 41513

Moser, Robert. Beitrag zur Bestimmung der Hauptabmessungen elektrischer Maschinen unter besonderer Berücksichtigung des Drehstrommotors. Elektr. Kraftbetriebe München **9** 1911 (161–166). [6070]. 41514

————— Einfacher graphischer Beweis des genauen Diagramms des Drehstrommotors. Elektrot. Zs. Berlin **32** 1911 (427–428). [6070]. 41515

————— Synchronmaschinen zur selbsttätigen Spannungs- oder Stromregelung. Elektrot. Zs. Berlin **32** 1911 (1127–1130 1156–1160). [6060]. 41516

Mosler, [Hugo]. Tickerempfang mit aperiodischem Kreis. Elektrot. Zs. Berlin **32** 1911 (1027–1028). [6043]. 41517

————— Radiotelegraphische Empfangsversuche im Freiballon. Elektrot. Zs. Berlin **32** 1911 (1204–1206). [6615]. 41518

————— v. **Rinkel**, R.

Moss, Herbert v. **Callendar**, H. L.

Moulin, M. Recherches sur l'ionisation produite par les rayons α. Ann. chim. phys. Paris (sér. 8) **21** 1911 (550–567 av. fig.). [4275]. 41519

————— Pompe à mercure à vide rapide. J. phys. Paris (sér. 5) **1** 1911 (60–65 av. fig.). [0835]. 41520

Moureu, Ch. et **Lepape**, A. Méthode spectrophotométrique de dosage du krypton. Paris C. R. Acad. sci. **152** 1910 (691–694). [4205]. 41521

————— Sur le rapport de l'argon à l'azote dans les mélanges gazeux naturels et sa signification. Paris C. R. Acad. sci. **152** 1911 (1533–1535). [4205]. 41522

————— Dosage spectrophotométrique du xénon. Constance des rapports xénon-argon et xénon-krypton dans les mélanges gazeux naturels. Paris C. R. Acad. sci. **153** 1911 (740–743). [4205]. 41523

————— Sur les rapports des gaz rares entre eux et avec l'azote dans

les grisous. Paris C. R. Acad. sci.
153 1911 (1043–1045). 41524

Mouton, H. v. Cotton, A.

Müller, W. v. Berndt, O ; Koenigsberger, J.

Muller, Ernst. Die Farbe der Silberpartikelchen in kolloidalen Ag-Lösungen, berechnet aus der Mieschen Theorie. Ann. Physik Leipzig (4. Folge) **35** 1911 (500–510). [0340 3810]. 41525

Müller, Frank. Zur Kenntnis der Absorption von Gasen durch Metalle. Diss. Leipzig. Weida i. Th. (Druck v. Thomas & Hubert) 1911 (75 mit Taf.). 23 cm. [0250 0320 5660]. 41526

Müller, Friedrich C. G. Ueber die Feldstärke innerhalb eines Kreisstromes. Zs. physik. Unterr. Berlin **24** 1911 (226–227). [6410]. 41527

——— Über die Pole gerader Drahtmagneten. Zs. physik. Unterr. Berlin **24** 1911 (346–348). [5410]. 41528

Müller, Johannes. Ueber induzierte elektrische Phänomene am menschlichen Körper und darauf beruhendes Tönen der Haut. [In : Festschrift, Wilhelm v. Leube gewidmet.] Leipzig (F. C. W. Vogel) 1910 (235–243). [5900]. 41529

Müller, Kurt. Die Geschichte der Dioptrica. Centralztg Opt. Berlin **32** 1911 (215–216). [3084 4430 0010]. 41530

Müller, Paul. Gegenstrom- und Kurzschlussbremsung bei Reihenschlusskommutatormotoren. Elektr. Kraftbetriebe München **9** 1911 (641–645 721–726) ; Diss. Berlin. München (Druck v. R. Oldenbourg) 1911 (18). 32 cm. [6070]. 41531

——— Die elektrische Leitfähigkeit der Metallegierungen im flüssigen Zustande. Diss. Aachen. Halle a. S. (W. Knapp) 1911 (57). 28 cm. [5660]. 41532

Müller, Willy. Ueber den elektrischen Widerstand von nichtbewehrtem Beton und seinen Einzelbestandteilen. Diss. Darmstadt. Berlin (W. Ernst & S.) 1911 (V + 71). 27 cm. [5660]. 41533

Müller-Uri, R. Neue Vorlesungsapparate. Physik. Zs. Leipzig **12** 1911 (1004–1005). [0050]. 41534

Muffone, Giovanni. Come dipinge il sole. Fotografia per i dilettanti. Ed. 7. Milano (Hoepli) 1910 (XX + 491). 15 cm. [0030 2990]. 41535

Muglia, B. v. La Rosa, M.

Muller, J. A. Sur les chaleurs de combustion et les poids spécifiques des méthylamines. Ann. chim. phys. Paris (sér. 8) **20** 1910 (116–131). [1695 0810]. 41536

[Murani, Oreste.] La ionizzazione dei gas. [Sunto.] Gaz Venezia **9** 1911 (1273–1274). [6895]. 41537

——— Radioattività delle sorgenti minerali dell'Aspio (Marche). Milano Rend. Ist. lomb. (Ser. 2) **44** 1911 (78–83). [4275]. 41538

——— Onde hertziane e telegrafo senza fili. Ed. 2. Milano (Hoepli) 1909 (XV + 397). 15 cm. [0030 4900 6615]. 41539

——— Trattato elementare di fisica. Ed. 4. vol. 1. Milano (Hoepli) 1909 (XXIII + 708). 24 cm. ; vol. 2. ibid. 1910 (XXIV + 871). 24 cm. [0030]. 41540

Muraoka, H[anichi]. Über die Unterschiedsschwellen der Tonhöhe. Kyoto Mem. Coll. Sci. Eng. **2** 1910 (263–276). [9430]. 41542

Murawski, Walter. Optische und thermische Untersuchungen an ungesättigten organischen Verbindungen. Diss. Greifswald (Druck v. H. Adler) 1911 (77). 24 cm. [3860]. 41543

Murdoch, W. H. F. A friction permeameter. Elect. London **67** 1911 (930). [5440]. 41544

Murphy, L. The nomenclature of primary and secondary sources of light. Elect. London **67** 1911 (511–512). [3010]. 41545

Murray, Donald. Printing telegraphy. London J. Inst. Electr. Engin. **47** 1911 (459–529). [6480]. 41546

Musatty, I. v. Mascarelli, L.

[Myškin, N[ikolaj] P[avlovič].] Мышкинъ, Н[иколай] П[авловичъ]. Пондеромоторныя силы свѣтового поля. [Les forces pondéromotrices dans le cham o de la lumière.] St. Peterburg Žurn. russ. fiz.-chim. Obšč. Fiz. Otd. **41** 1909 (161–190). [4215]. 41547

Myslakowski, Zygmunt. O. Waleryan Magni i kontrowersya w sprawie odkrycia próżni (1638-1648). [Le R. P. Valerien Magni; les différends relatifs à la découverte du vide.] Kraków Rozpr. Akad. 11 A 1911 (325-377 454-458). [0010]. 41548

Naccari, Giuseppe. Il terzo centenario dell'invenzione del cannocchiale. Riv. Astron. sci. affini Torino 3 1909 (258-263); Venezia Ateneo Veneto 32 2. sem. 1909 (93-107). [0010] 41549

Nachtikal, Frant. Přehled pokroků fysiky za rok 1908. 1. Mechanika. 2. Akustika. [Fortschritte in der Physik im Jahre 1908. 1. Mechanik. 2. Akustik.] Prag Věstn. České Ak. Frant. Jos. 1910 (183-203 245-259). [0030 8990]. 41550

Nádai, Arpád. Untersuchungen der Festigkeitslehre mit Hilfe des thermoelektrischen Temperaturmessverfahrens. Diss. Berlin (Druck v. E. Ebering) 1911 (55). 27 cm. 41552

Nadrowski, J. Beitrag zur Frage der Wirtschaftlichkeit der Gleichdruck-Gas- und Gas-Dampf-Turbinen. Turbine Berlin 8 1911 (5-8 31-33 61-66). [2490]. 41553

Nagaoka, H[antaro]. Note on a hypergeometrical series for the mutual inductance of two parallel coaxial circles. Tokyo Su. Buts. Kw. K. (Ser. 2) 6 1911 (10-14). [6440]. 41554

———— A table for facilitating the calculation of mutual inductance of two parallel coaxial circles. Tokyo Su. Buts. Kw. K. (Ser. 2) 6 1911 (47-51). [6440]. 41555

———— Attraction between two coaxial circular currents. Tokyo Su. Buts. Kw. K. (Ser. 2) 6 1911 (152-158). [6440]. 41556

Nakamura, S[eiji]. A camera for a complete panoramic view. Tokyo Su. Buts. Kw. K. (Ser. 2) 6 1911 (114-119). [3085]. 41557

Namias, R. Ottenimento d'imagini dei più svariati colori. Boll. Soc. fot. Firenze 22 1910 (12-15). [4225]. 41558

———— Fotografia dei colori e tricromia. Prog. fot. Milano 18 1911 (71-74). [4225]. 41559

Namias, R. Influenza dello spessore e rapidità delle lastre fotografiche sulla ricchezza del chiaro-scuro dell'imagine negativa. Prog. fot. Milano 18 1911 (257-259). [4225]. 41560

———— Uno strano fenomeno fotografico. Prog. fot. Milano 18 1911 (303-305). [4225]. 41561

———— La fotografia ordinaria e ortocromatica. Milano (Prog. fot.) 1909 (112 con 8 tav.). 19 cm. [4225]. 41562

Nasini, Raffaele. La teoria atomica e l'opera di Stanislas Cannizzaro. Atti Soc. ital. prog. sci. Roma 4 1911 (153-199). [0500]. 41563

———— e Levi, Mario Giacomo. Sopra la radioattività di materiali italiani. Gazz. chim. ital. Palermo 40 2. sem. 1910 (101-122). [4275]. 41564

———— e Ageno, F. Indagini chimicofisiche e analisi dell'acqua ferrico-arsenicale di Roncegno. Venezia Atti Ist. ven. 68 parte 2 1909 (935-970). [4275]. 41565

Nasmyth, George W[illiam]. Experiments in impact excitation. 1. The characteristics of short arcs between metal electrodes. Physic. Rev. Ithaca N.Y. 32 1911 (69-102 with text fig. table); 2. The intensity of the Lepel arc oscillations as a function of the arc current, capacity and inductance. t.c (103-114 with text fig. tables); 3. The frequency of the Lepel oscillations. t.c. (152-177 with fig. tables). [6043 6610]. 41566

Nassauer. Versuche über die Wirksamkeit des Schutzes durch Isolierschemel und die Kapazität des menschlichen Körpers. Elektr. Kraftbetriebe München 9 1911 (172-173). [5900]. 41567

Natanson, Wladyslaw. O teoryi statystycznej promieniowania. [On the statistical theory of radiation.] Kraków Bull. Intern. Acad. 1911 A (134-148); (Übers.) Physik. Zs. Leipzig 12 1911 (659-666). [2990 4210]. 41569

Neesen, F[riedrich]. Über das Ätherkalorimeter. Physik. Zs. Leipzig 12 1911 (1073-1074); Berlin Verh. D. physik. Ges. 13 1911 (1023-1026). [1610]. 41570

Negro, Carlo. Sulla radioattività della rugiada. Boll. bimens. Soc. meteor. ital. Torino (Ser. 3) **29** 1910 (14-16); Roma Atti Acc. Nuovi Lincei **63** 1910 (62-66). [4275]. 41571

———— Sulle cause di ionizzazione al di sopra degli oceani. Roma Atti Acc. Nuovi Lincei **63** 1910 (25-29). [4275 6805]. 41572

———— Contributo allo studio della dispersione elettrica atmosferica. Roma Atti Acc. Nuovi Lincei **63** 1910 (97-103). [6805]. 41573

———— Sulla elettricità e radioattività della precipitazione atmosferica. Roma Mem. Acc. Nuovi Lincei **28** 1910 (167-197); [sunto] Riv. fis. mat. sc. nat. Pavia **23** 1911 (249-250). [4275] 41574

Nehru, Shri Shridhara. Ueber die Strömung von Gasen durch Röhren und den Widerstand kleiner Kugeln und Cylinder in bewegten Gasen. Diss. Heidelberg. Bingen a. Rh. (Druck v. W. Polex) 1911 (IX + 70). 22 cm. [0325]. 41575

Neklepajew, N. Ueber die Absorption kurzer akustischer Wellen in der Luft. Ann. Physik Leipzig (4 Folge) **35** 1911 (175-181). [9250]. 41576

Nenning v. Matuschek.

Nernst. Introduction à quelques principes fondamentaux de la physique moderne. Rev. sci. Paris **48** 1910 (513-520). [0000 0100]. 41577

———— Ueber die Unverträglichkeit des von mir aufgestellten Wärmetheorems mit der Gleichung von Van der Waals bei sehr tiefen temperaturen. [On the inconsistency of my heat-theorem and Van der Waals' equation at very low temperatures.] Amsterdam Versl. Wis. Nat. Afd. K. Akad. Wet. **20** [1911] (64-67) (German); Amsterdam Proc. Sci. K. Akad. Wet. **14** [1911] (201-204) (English). [2415]. 41578

———— Der Energieinhalt fester Stoffe. Ann. Physik Leipzig (4. Folge) **36** 1911 (395-439). [1620 1610 1660 1600]. 41579

———— Über neuere Probleme der Wärmetheorie. Berlin SitzBer. Ak. Wiss. **1911** (65-90). [2400 0040 0100]. 41580

Nernst. Untersuchungen über die spezifische Wärme bei tiefen Temperaturen. III. Berlin SitzBer. Ak. Wiss. **1911** (306-315). [1620 1660 5660 5675]. 41581

———— Über ein allgemeines Gesetz, das Verhalten fester Stoffe bei sehr tiefen Temperaturen betreffend. Physik. Zs. Leipzig **12** 1911 (976-979); Berlin Verh. D. physik. Ges. **13** 1911 (921-925). [1600 2435 5675]. 41582

———— Sur quelques nouveaux problèmes de la théorie de la chaleur. Scientia Bologna **10** 1911 (278-306). [2400]. 41583

———— Zur Theorie der spezifischen Wärme und über die Anwendung der Lehre von den Energiequanten auf physikalisch-chemische Fragen überhaupt. Zs. Elektroch. Halle **17** 1911 (265-275). [1600 0200 4200 1660 2400]. 41584

———— Über einen Apparat zur Verflüssigung von Wasserstoff. Zs. Elektroch. Halle **17** 1911 (735-737). [1870]. 41585

———— Thermodynamik und spezifische Wärme. Berlin SitzBer. Ak. Wiss. **1912** (134-140). [2435 2415 2425 1660 5710]. 41586

———— und **Lindemann**, F. A. Untersuchungen über die spezifische Wärme bei tiefen Temperaturen. V. Berlin SitzBer. Ak. Wiss. **1911** (494-501). [1660 1600]. 41587

———— ———— Spezifische Wärme und Quantentheorie. Zs. Elektroch. Halle **17** 1911 (817-827). [1600 1660]. 41588

Nesper, Eugen. Frequenzmesser und Messung der Wellenlänge in der drahtlosen Telegraphie und Telephonie. Elektrot. Anz. Berlin **27** 1910 (1231-1232 1243-1245 1269-1270 1295-1296 1309-1310). [6043]. 41589

———— Die Entwickelung der Apparatur in der drahtlosen Telegraphie. [Forts.] Jahrb. drahtlos. Telegr. Leipzig **3** 1910 (376-391). [6043]. 41590

———— Vielton-Stationen für drahtlose Nachrichten-Übermittlung.— Postes à transmissions musicales multiples pour la télégraphie sans fil.—

Vielton stations for wireless transmission of communications. [Deutsch, franz. u. engl.] Helios Leipzig 17 1911 (Export-Zs. (993-996 1037-1041). [6043]. 41591

Nesper, Eugen. Ungesteuerte und gesteuerte Stossender für drahtlose Telephonie. Jahrb. drahtlos. Telegr. Leipzig 4 1911 (241-249). [6043]. 41592

——— Detektoren der drahtlosen Telegraphie und Telephonie. Jahrb. drahtlos. Telegr. Leipzig 4 1911 (312-326 423-438 534-551). [6043]. 41593

——— v. Rein, H.

Neubauer, Hans. Versuch einer Elementartheorie des Dreiphasenstromes und seines Generators. Oesterr. Zs. BergHüttwes. Wien 59 1911 (281-284 309-313 328-332 343-345 357-360). [6060]. 41594

Neumann, Franz. Gesammelte Werke. Bd 3. . . . Hrsg . . . . von C[arl] Neumann, W[oldemar] Voigt, A[lbert] Wangerin. Leipzig (B. G. Teubner) 1912 (XII + 500). 29 cm. 36 M. [0030 3800 6400]. 41595

Neuscheler, Karl. Untersuchung stehender Schallschwingungen mit Hilfe des Widerstandsthermometers. Diss. Tübingen. Leipzig (J. A. Barth) 1910 (41). 22 cm.; Ann. Physik Leipzig (4. Folge) 34 1911 (131-160). [9230 1230 1610 0090]. 41596

Nicastro, U. Nuovo sistema di dirigibilità delle onde elettromagnetiche utilizzate per la radiotelegrafia. Riv. maritt Roma 1910 1. trim. (404-407). [6615]. 41598

——— Alcune notizie sullo sviluppo della radiotelegrafia nella Marina degli Stati Uniti. Riv. maritt. Roma 1910 1. trim. (407-408). [6615]. 41599

Nicaud, O. Annales de l'Université de Grenoble. Tables alphabétique et analytique des vingt premières années (1889-1908). Paris (Gauthier-Villars) 1909 (42). 25 cm. [0030]. 41600

Nicolis, U. v. Bonacini, C.

Nichols, Edward L[eamington]. The effects of temperature on phosphorescence and fluorescence. Philadelphia Proc. Amer. Phil. Soc. 49 1910 (267-280 with text ff.). [4230]. 41601

Nichols, Edward L[eamington]. Some recent advances in fluorescence and phosphorescence. [Abstract.] Science New York (N. Ser.) 33 1911 (696-700 with ff.). [4230]. 41602

——— and Merritt, Ernest. Studies in luminescence. 5. On fluorescence and phosphorescence between + 20° and − 190°. Physic. Rev. Ithaca N.Y. 32 1911 (38-53 with text fig.). [4230]. 41603

Nicholson, J. W. A possible relation between uranium and actinium. Nature London 87 1911 (515). [4275]. 41604

——— On the bending of electric waves round a large sphere. Phil. Mag. London (Ser. 6) 21 1911 (62-68 281-295). [6610]. 41605

——— On the damping of the vibrations of a dielectric sphere, and the radiation from a vibrating electron. Phil. Mag. London (Ser. 6) 21 1911 (438-446). [4960]. 41606

——— On the number of electrons concerned in metallic conduction. Phil. Mag. London (Ser. 6) 22 1911 (245-266). [6625 5675]. 41607

——— Note on the optical properties of fused metals. Phil. Mag. London (Ser. 6) 22 1911 (266-268). [5680]. 41608

Niederstadt. Radiumfärbung anorganischer Körper. Elektroch. Zs. Berlin 18 1911 (131-133). [4275]. 41609

Nienhaus, Heinrich. Ueber das lichtelektrische Verhalten von Lösungen. Zs. wiss. Phot. Leipzig 10 1911 (250-263); Diss. Münster i. W. Leipzig (J. A. Barth) 1911 (19). 24 cm. [5660 6850]. 41610

Niethammer, Th. Methoden und neuere Ergebnisse der Schweremessungen. Fortschr. natw. Forschg Berlin 1 1910 (141-176). [0825]. 41611

——— Piccoli antitrasformatori per lampade ad incandescenza. [Sunto. Trad.] Atti Ass. elettrotecn. Milano 15 1911 (763-765). [6040]. 41612

——— Über das Pendeln von Synchronmaschinen. Elektr. Kraftbetriebe München 9 1911 (70-72). [6060]. 41613

——— Der Quecksilberdampf-Gleichrichter und seine Verwendung als Periodenwandler. Elektr. Kraftbetriebe München **9** 1911 (185–189). [6047]. 41614

Niethammer, Th. Das direktzeigende Wattmeter und seine Verwendung. Elektrot. Anz. Berlin **28** 1911 (299–300 327–329 365–367 377–379). [6040]. 41615

—————— Einfache Formel für die Überlastbarkeit des Asynchronmotors. [Nebst Erwiderung von **Auerbach.**] Elektrot. Zs. Berlin **32** 1911 (843). [6070]. 41616

—————— Über Wirbelstrombremsen. Elektr. Kraftbetriebe München **9** 1911 (601–605). [6070]. 41617

—————— Erwärmung elektrischer Maschinen. Elektr. Kraftbetriebe München **10** 1912 (130–134). [6000]. 41618

—————— und **Czepek,** R. Mechanische Kräfte zwischen Stromleitern. Elektr. Kraftbetriebe München **9** 1911 (6–11). [6420 6490]. 41619

—————— und **Siegel,** E. Doppelt verkettete Streuung von Drehstrommotoren. [Nebst Erwiderung von **W. Rogowski.**] Elektrot. Zs. Berlin **32** 1911 (252 481–482). 41620

Niewolak, Franciszek. Nauka fizyki w gimnazyum. [L'enseignement de la Physique au lycée.] Sprawozdanie XXXIII c. k. gimn. im. Rudolfa w Brodach za r. 1910–11 Brody (Nakl. gimnazyum) 1911 (1–44). 8vo. [0050]. 41621

Nikiforowsky, P. v. Zwaardemaker, H.

[**Nikolai,** E[vgenij] L[eopoldovič].] Николаи, Е. Л. О колебаніяхъ тонкостѣннаго цилиндра. [Sur les oscillations d'un cylindre à mur mince.] St. Peterburg Žurn. russ. fiz.-chim. Obšč. Fiz. Otd. **41** 1909 (214–227). [9110]. 41622

[**Nikolaev,** V[ladimir] V[asilevič].] Николаевъ, В[ладимиръ] В[асилевичъ]. О магнитострикціи. [Sur la magnétostriction.] St. Peterburg Žurn. russ. fiz.-chim. Obšč. Fiz. Otd. **41** 1909 (232–233). [5462]. 41623

—————— Особый случай электролиза. [Cas particulier de l'électrolyse.] St. Peterburg Žurn. russ. fiz.-chim. Obšč. Fiz. Otd. **41** 1909 (237). [6200]. 41624

—————— Диффузія пары вода-алкоголь подъ вліяніемъ тока. [Diffusion de la paire eau-alcohol sous l'influence du courant électrique.] St. Peterburg Žurn. russ. fiz.-chim. Obšč. Fiz. Otd. **41** 1909 (237–238). [6255]. 41625

[**Nikolaev,** V[ladimir] V[asilevič].] Николаевъ, В[ладимиръ] В[асилевичъ]. Опредѣленіе электрической проницаемости металловъ изъ опытовъ Хагена и Рубенса. [Bestimmung der Dielektrizitäts-konstante der Metalle aus den Versuchen von Hagen und Rubens.] St. Peterburg Žurn. russ. fiz.-chim. Obšč. Fiz. Otd. **41** 1909 (238–240). [6627]. 41626

—————— Электрострикція на границѣ двухъ электролитовъ и искровой разрядъ въ одномъ изъ нихъ. [Elektrostriktion an der Grenze zweier Elektrolyte und Funkenentladung in einem derselben.] St. Peterburg Žurn. russ. fiz.-chim. Obšč. Fiz. Otd. **41** 1909 (240–244). [5253 6820]. 41627

Nikolopulos, Andreas N. Ueber die Beziehungen zwischen den Absorptionsspektren und der Konstitution der Wernerschen Salze. Diss. Leipzig. Weida i. Th. (Druck v. Thomas & Hubert) 1911 (54 mit Taf.). 23 cm. [3860]. 41628

Nipher, Francis E[ugene]. New phenomena of electrical discharge. Science New York (N. Ser.) **33** 1911 (151–153). [6800]. 41629

—————— Theories of electrical discharge. Science New York (N. Ser.) **34** 1911 (282–283). [6800]. 41630

—————— Phenomena of forked lightning. Science New York (N. Ser.) **34** 1911 (442). [6800]. 41631

—————— The positive ion in electrical discharge through gases. Science New York (N. Ser.) **34** 1911 (917). [6805]. 41632

Nishikawa, S[eiji] v. Kinoshita, S.

Niven, Charles. On the measurement of specific inductive capacity. London Proc. R. Soc. (Ser. A) **85** 1911 (139–145). [5252]. 41633

Noack, K. Untersuchung der Ablenkung, die ein Magnet an einer Kompassnadel hervorruft, um die er in verschiedenen Stellungen im Kreise herumgeführt wird. Eine Aufgabe für physikalische Schülerübungen. Zs. physik. Unterr. Berlin **24** 1911 (6–11). [5435 0050]. 41634

Noack, K. Ein Apparat zur Demonstration der magnetischen Schirmwirkung. Zs. physik. Unterr. Berlin 24 1911 (31–32). [0050]. 41635

—————— Ein Apparat zum Nachweis des Boyleschen Gesetzes bei Schülerübungen. Zs. physik. Unterr. Berlin 25 1912 (17–21). [0050]. 41636

Nodon, Albert. Recherches sur le magnétisme terrestre. Bruxelles Bul. Soc. astron. 1910 (208–209). [5490]. 41637

—————— Recherches sur les variations de l'intensité du magnétisme terrestre. Ciel et Terre Bruxelles 1910 (445–449). [5490]. 41638

Noeggerath, J. E. Ueber die Stromabnahme. . . . Elektr. Kraftbetriebe München 9 1911 (81–87 101–107); Mit besonderer Berücksichtigung hoher Geschwindigkeiten. Diss. Hannover. München (Druck v. R. Oldenbourg) 1911 (19). 32 cm. [6060]. 41639

Nogier, Ch. r. Courmont, J.

Nonn, H. Kriegswissenschaften. [In: Angewandte Photographie in Wissenschaft u. Technik. Hrsg. v. K. W. Wolf-Czapek. Tl 3.] Berlin (Union) 1911 (33–47 mit 7 Taf.). [3085]. 41640

Norden, Konrad. Die Schattenbildung und ihre Berechnung. Elektrot. Zs. Berlin 32 1911 (607–609). [3010]. 41641

Nordmann, Charles. Diverses recherches relatives au magnétisme terrestre, à l'ionisation atmosphérique et au champ électrique de la Terre, exécutées notamment à l'occasion de l'éclipse totale de Soleil du 30 août 1905. Ann. bur. longit. Paris 8 1911 (D. 1 à D. 60.) [5270]. 41642

—————— Sur les diamètres effectifs des étoiles. Paris C. R. Acad. sci. 152 1911 (73–75). [1210]. 41643

Nordstrom, Gunnar. Zur Relativitäts-mechanik deformierbarer Körper. Physik. Zs. Leipzig 12 1911 (854–857). [4960 4980]. 41644

Norsa, Renzo. Alcune considerazioni sul fattore di potenza e sui sistemi polifasi non equilibrati. Atti Ass. elettrotecn. Milano 14 1910 (31–45). [5720]. 41645

Norzi, G. r. Porlezza, C.

Nottage, W. H. r. Marsh.

Novak, Franz. Gelbfilter für Autochromblitzlichtaufnahmen. Jahrb. Phot. Halle 25 1911 (190). [4225]. 41646

Novák, J. Zur Theorie der Turbokompressoren. Zs. Turbinenwesen München 8 1911 (385–388). [2490]. 41647

Novák, Vladimir. Přehled pokroků fysiky za rok 1908. 4. Nauka o vlnivém pohybu étheru. [Fortschritte in der Physik 1908. 4. Wellenbewegung des Äthers. Prag Věstn. České Ak. Frant. Jos. 1910 (359–398 413–449). [0030 2990]. 41648

Nowak, J. Maschine zum Berechnen elektrischer Leitungsnetze. Elektrot. Zs. Berlin 32 1911 (973–975 1006–1010). [5600 5630]. 41649

Nusselt, Wilhelm. Der Wärmeübergang im Kreuzstrom. Berlin Zs. Ver. D. Ing. 55 1911 (2021–2024). [2000]. 41650

Nuttall, J. M. v. Geiger, H.

Nutting, P[erley] G[ilman]. The visibility of radiation. A recalculation of König's data. Washington D.C. Dept. Comm. Lab. Bull. Bur. Stand. 7 1911 (235–238 with tables). [4450]. 41651

—————— A photometric attachment for spectroscopes. Washington D.C. Dept. Comm. Lab. Bull. Bur. Stand. 7 1911 (239–241 with fig.). [3010]. 41652

—————— and Tugman, Orin. The intensities of some hydrogen, argon, and helium lines in relation to current and pressure. Washington D.C. Dept. Comm. Lab. Bull. Bur. Stand. 7 1911 (49–70 with fig. tables). [4206]. 41653

Nylén, P. G. Torrelementat "R R," ett nytt svenskt fabrikat. [Das Trockenelement „R R", ein neues schwedisches Fabrikat.] Sv. Km. Tidskr. Stockholm 23 1911 (14–16). [5610]. 41654

Ōba, T[akashi] v. Takamine, T.

Occhialini, Augusto R. Ricerche sull'arco elettrico. [Sunto.] Riv. fis. mat. sc. nat. Pavia 20 1909 (440–441). [6830]. 41655

—————— Lo spettro di righe nell'arco. [Sunto.] Riv. fis. mat. sc. nat. Pavia 23 1911 (372–374). [4205]. 41660

—————— Sulla definizione di intensità di corrente elettrica. Elettricista Roma (Ser. 2) 10 1911 (182–184); Nuovo Cimento Pisa (Ser. 6) 1 1911 (65–73). [5600]. 41656

—————— Scintille a basso potenziale. Nuovo Cimento Pisa (Ser. 6) 2 1911 (223–228). [6830]. 41657

—————— Le condizioni di esistenza dell'arco fra carboni. Nuovo Cimento Pisa (Ser. 6) 2 1911 (329–336). [6830]. 41658

—————— Come si stabiliscono i fenomeni luminosi all'inizio dell'arco. Nuovo Cimento Pisa (Ser. 6) 2 1911 (431–436). [6830]. 41659

—————— I fenomeni luminosi all'inizio dell'arco. Roma Mem. Acc. Lincei (Ser. 5) 8 1911 (Mem. 17 654–662 con 1 tav.). [6830]. 41661

—————— v. Battelli, A.

O'Connor, E. Ueber das Spektrum des Poulsenschen Lichtbogens. (On the spectrum of the Poulsen arc.) (Uebers.) Physik. Zs. Leipzig 12 1911 (196–198). [4205 4202]. 41662

Oddo, Giuseppe e **Mannessier**, Anna. L'ossicloruro di fosforo come solvente in crioscopia. Gazz. chim. ital. Roma 41 2. sem. 1911 (212–223); Zs. anorg. Chem. Leipzig 73 1911 (259–269). [1920]. 41663

Oddone, Emilio. Sul coefficiente elastico di restituzione delle principali roccie costituenti la crosta terrestre. Roma Rend. Acc. Lincei (Ser. 5) 19 2. sem. 1910 (648–656). [0800]. 41665

—————— Sul coefficiente di attrito interno in misura assoluta delle lave fluide e solide e sull'isteresi terrestre. Atti soc. ital. prog. sci. Roma 4 1911 (745–746); Nuovo Cimento Pisa (Ser. 6) 1 1911 (VI–VII). [0325]. 41666

O'Donnell, P. S. v. Schiller, H.

Odén, Sven. Die Bedeutung des Dispersitätsgrades bei Untersuchung der allgemeinen Eigenschaften der Schwefelhydrosole. Zs. Kolloide Dresden 9 1911 (100–106). [0340]. 41667

Oettli, Max. Pergamentschlauch statt Schweinsblase für osmotische Versuche. Monatshefte natw. Unterr. Leipzig 4 1911 (79). [0090]. 41668

Ogorodnikoff, A. v. Tschugaeff, L.

Ohlsberg, Otto. Handbuch für Funkentelegraphisten. Lehr- und Übungsbuch auch für den Selbstunterricht. Amtlich eingeführtes Lehrbuch bei der staatl. Navigationsschule Hamburg. Mit einem einleitenden Vorwort von Bolte. Berlin (R. v. Decker) 1911 (XI + 224 mit Taf. u. 1 Karte). 22 cm. Geb. 6 M. [6615]. 41669

Oinuma, Soroku v. Inouye, N.

Okada, T[akematsu]. Contribution to the studies of psychrometer covering (2d. Note). Tokyo Kisho Sh. 29 1910 (210–213). [1890]. 41670

—————— and **Yoshida**, T[okuichi]. Pyrheliometric observations on the summit and at the base of Mt. Fuji. Tokyo Bull. Cent. Met. Obs. 3 1910 (1–8). [3810]. 41671

Olie, Jr., J[acob] en **Kruyt**, H[ugo] R[udolph]. Photoelectrische verschijnselen bij zwavel-antimonium (Antimoniet). [Photo-electric phenomena with antimony sulphide (Antimonite).] Amsterdam Versl. Wis. Nat. Afd. K. Akad. Wet. 20 1912 (692–695) (Dutch); Amsterdam Proc. Sci. K. Akad. Wet. 14 1912 (740–743) (English). [5660]. 41672

Olivari, F. Sugli equilibri di solubilità fra l'iodio e le sostanze organiche. Roma Rend. Acc. Lincei (Ser. 5) 20 1. sem. 1911 (470–474). [1887]. 41673

Ollive, F. Sur la force élastique des vapeurs saturantes. Paris C. R. Acad. sci. 154 1912 (188–190). [1840]. 41674

Ollivier, H. Aimantation hystérétique des électro-aimants droits. Ann. chim. phys. Paris (sér. 8) 25 1912 (276–285). [5450]. 41675

Olper, L. La trasformazione della frequenza. Elettricista Roma (Ser. 2) 10 1911 (225–226). [6460]. 41676

Olszewski, Karol. Skraplanie gazów. [La liquéfaction des gaz.] Chem. pols. Warszawa 11 1911 (385–392 414–420 442–447). [1870]. 41677

—————— Skroplenie wodoru przy całkowitem uchyleniu strat zimna.

[La liquéfaction de l'hydrogène ; procédé permettant d'éviter les pertes de froid.] Chem. pols. Warszawa **11** 1911 (457–469). [1870]. 41678

Olszewski, Karol. Verflüssigung des Wasserstoffes bei vollkommener Vermeidung von Kälteverlusten. Vorl. Mitt. Zs. komprim. Gase Weimar **14** 1911 (1–3). [1870]. 41679

Oltay, Károly. Nehézséggyorsulásmérések Budapesten. [Messung der Schwerkraftbeschleunigung in Budapest.] Math. Termt. Ért. Budapest **29** 1911 (229–245). [0700 0825].
41680

O'Meara, W. A. J. Submarine cables for long-distance telephones. London J. Inst. Electr. Engin. **46** 1911 (309–427). [6485]. 41682

Omori, F[usakichi]. On the velocity of sound waves of the noon gun of Tokyo observed on Mt. Tsukuba. Kisho Sh. Tokyo **29** 1910 (41–48). [9210]. 41683

Ono, S[uminosuke] v. Kinoshita, S.

Oosterhuis, E[kko]. Eene methode ter bepaling van het Peltier effekt. [Une méthode pour la détermination de l'effet Peltier.] Handl. Ned. Nat. Geneesk. Congr. **13** 1911 (172). [5710]. 41683A

———— Over het Peltier-effect en de thermoketen ijzer-kwikzilver. [Sur le phénomène de Peltier et sur la pile thermo-électrique fer-mercure.] Groningen (M. de Waal) 1911 (55 + 4 pl.). 23 cm. [5710]. 41684B

Oosting, H. J. Ein Experiment über den Luftdruck. Zs. physik. Unterr. Berlin **24** 1911 (353–354). [0050]. 41685C

———— Proeven met een verbeterd instrument voor gedwongen trillingen van draden en staven. [Expériences avec un instrument amélioré pour la démonstration des vibrations forcées de fils et de verges.] Handl. Ned. Nat. Geneesk. Congres **13** 1911 (162–164). [9135]. 41686D

Orlandini, O. Sul decorso dei raggi e formazione delle imagini dopo refrazione attraverso un mezzo diottrico centralmente opaco. Clin. ocul. Roma **13** 1911 (683–692) con 1 tav.). [3050]. 41691

Orlich, E. Stephan August Lindeck Zs. Instrumentenk. Berlin **31** 1911 (329–331 mit Portr.). [0010]. 41692

———— Die Theorie der Wechselströme. (Mathematischphysikalische Schriften für Ingenieure und Studierende. Hrsg. von E. Jahnke. 12.) Leipzig u. Berlin (B. G. Teubner) 1912 [1911] (IV + 94). 21 cm. 2,40 M. [6460 5705]. 41693

[**Orlov**, Nik[olaj Alekséevič].] Орловъ, Ник[олай Алексѣевичъ]. Къ методикѣ сравненія электродвижущихъ силъ. [Deux nouvelles méthodes potentiométriques.] St. Peterburg Žurn. russ. fiz.-chim. Obšč. Fiz. Otd. **41** 1909 (86–90). [5695]. 41694

Ornstein, L[eonard] S[alomon]. Eenige opmerkingen over de grondslagen der warmteleer. [Some remarks on the mechanical foundation of thermodynamics.] Amsterdam Versl. Wis. Nat. Afd. K. Akad. Wet. **19** [1910] (809–824) 1911 (947–954) (Dutch); Amsterdam Proc. Sci. K. Akad. Wet. **13** 1911 (804–817 858–865) (English); Haarlem Arch. Néerl. Sci. Soc. Holl. (Sér. III A) **1** 1911 (159–183) (French). [0200 2400].
41695

———— Entropie en waarschijnlijkheid. [Entropy and probability.] Amsterdam Versl. Wis. Nat. Afd. K. Akad. Wet. **20** [1911] (243–258) ; Handl. Ned. Nat. Geneesk. Cong. **13** 1911 (118–144) (Dutch) ; Amsterdam Proc. Sci. K. Akad. Wet. **14** 1912 (840–853) (English). [0200 2415].
41696

———— Opmerking over het verband der methode van Gibbs met die van den viriaal en van de gemiddelde weglengte bij de afleiding van de toestandsvergelijking. [Remarks on the relation of the method of Gibbs for the determination of the equation of state with that of the virial and the mean free path.] Amsterdam Versl. Wis. Nat. Afd. K. Akad. Wet. **20** [1911] (790–793) (Dutch); Amsterdam Proc. Sci. K. Akad. Wet. **14** 1912 (853–856) (English). [0200]. 41697

———— Over den vasten toestand. 1. Éénatomige stoffen. [On the solid state. 1. Monatomic substances.] Amsterdam Versl. Wis. Nat. Afd. K. Akad. Wet. **20** 1912 (1117–1125) (Dutch) ; Amsterdam Proc. Sci.

K. Akad. Wet. **14** 1912 (983–991)
(English). [0400].   41699

Ornstein, L[eonard] S[alomon] *v.*
Kohnstamm, Ph.

Ortvay, Rudolf. Über die Dielektrizitätskonstante einiger Flüssigkeiten
bei hohem Druck. Ann. Physik Leipzig
(4. Folge) **36** 1911 (1–24). [5252].
                                     41700

Osann. Bericht über die im Auftrage des Vereins unternommenen
wissenschaftlichen Arbeiten. Ergebnisse von Versuchen behufs Feststellung des Wärmeleitungsvermögens
feuerfester Steine in Winderheizern.
Ber. Ver. D. Fabr. feuerfester Produkte Berlin **29** 1909 (14–45). [2020].
                                    41700A

Ossanna. Über die Dimensionierung der einphasigen Kommutatormotoren mit besonderer Berücksichtigung der schweren Zugförderung. Vortrag . . . Elektrot. Zs. Berlin **32**
1911 (581–584 614–618). [6070].
                                     41701

Osten, Hermann. Das Phasophon,
ein neues Instrument für die Betriebskontrolle in Drehstromwerken. Elektr.
Kraftbetriebe München **9** 1911 (610–
612). [5770].   41702

Ostertag, P. Theorie und Konstruktion der Kolben- und Turbo-Kompressoren. Berlin (J. Springer) 1911
(VI + 232). 28 cm. Geb. 11 M.
[2495].   41703

Ostwald, W. L'énergie. Traduit
par E. Philippi. Paris (Alcan) 1910
(X + 238). 19 cm. [0000 0010
2430].   41704

——— Energi. Bemynd.
öfvers. av Anna Sundquist. [Energie.
Übers.] (Vetenskap och bildning. 3.)
Stockholm (Bonnier) 1910 (172). 22
cm. 2.75 kr. [2400 0030].   41705

——— Esquisse d'une philo-
sophie des sciences, traduit par Dorole.
[Bibliothèque de philosophie contem-
poraine.] Paris (Alcan) 1911 (IV + 184).
18 cm. 2 fr. 50. [0000].   41706

Ostwald, Wilh[elm]. Lehrbuch der
allgemeinen Chemie. (In 2 Bdn.)
Bd 2. 1 Tl. Chemische Energie.
2. umgearb. Aufl. 3. Abdr. Leipzig
(W. Engelmann) 1911 (XV + 1104).
24 cm. 34 M. [0030].   41705A

Ostwald, Wilhelm. Abbe unser
Führer. Ann. Naturphilos. Leipzig **11**
1911 (1–16). [0010].   41707

——— Grosse Männer. Studien
zur Biologie des Genies. Bd 1. 3. u.
4. Aufl. Leipzig (Akad. Verlagsgesellschaft) 1910–1911 (XII + 424). 14 M.
[0010].   41708

Ostwald, Wo[lfgang]. Grundriss
der Kolloidchemie. 2. völlig umgearb.
und wesentl. verm. Aufl. 1. Hälfte.
Dresden (Th. Steinkopff) 1911 (VI +
329 mit 1 Portr. u. Taf.). 23 cm.
9 M. [0340].   41705B

——— Zur Theorie der kritischen
Trübungen. Ann. Physik Leipzig
(4. Folge) **36** 1911 (848–854). [1580
0340].   41709

——— Ueber Farbe und Dis-
persitätsgrad kolloider Lösungen. Kolloidchem. Beih. Dresden **2** 1911 (409–
487). [0340 3860].   41710

——— *v.* Bottazzi, F.

Oswald, Marcel. Sur une relation
simple entre le coefficient de dilatation
des liquides et la température. Paris
C. R. Acad. sci. **154** 1912 (61–63).
[1885].   41711

Ottinger und **Weiss**, J. Eine Bestimmung der Fallbeschleunigung am
frei fallenden Körper. Zs. physik.
Unterr. Berlin **24** 1911 (148–151).
[0050 0820].   41712

Owen, D. Corpi magnetici composti
di elementi non magnetici. [Sunto.
Trad.] Atti Ass. elettrotecn. Milano
15 1911 (537–538). [5410].   41713

Owen, E. A. On the scattering of
Röntgen radiation. Cambridge Proc.
Phil. Soc. **16** 1911 (161–166). [4240].
                                     41714

——— The change of resistance
of nickel and iron wires placed longitudinally in strong magnetic fields.
Phil. Mag. London (Ser. 6) **21** 1911
(122–130). [5460].   41715

Owen, Gwilym. Note on the production of nuclei in air by intense
cooling. Phil. Mag. London (Ser. 6)
22 1911 (563–566). [1940].   41716

——— and **Pealing**, Harold.
On condensation nuclei produced by
the action of light on iodine vapour.
Phil. Mag. London (Ser. 6) **21** 1911
(465–479). [5685].   41717

Owen, Morris. Magnetochemische Untersuchungen. Die thermomagnetischen Eigenschaften der Elemente. II. Ann. Physik Leipzig (4. Folge) 37 1912 (657–699) ; Amsterdam Versl. Wis. Nat. Afd. K. Akad. Wet. 20 [1911] (673–681) (English) ; Amsterdam Proc. Sci. K. Akad. Wet. 14 [1911] (637–644) (English). [5460 5466 5470 5446]. 41718

Oxley, A. E. On the magnetic susceptibilities of certain compounds. Cambridge Proc. Phil. Soc. 16 1911 (102–111). [5467]. 41719

Pacini, D. La radiation pénétrante sur la mer. Radium Paris 8 1911 (307–312) ; [sunto] Riv. fis. mat. sc. nat. Pavia 24 1911 (274–275). [4275]. 41720

Pacinotti, Antonio. Descrizione di una macchinetta elettromagnetica. Ri-prodotto dal Nuovo Cimento Giugno 1864. Atti Assoc. elettrotecn. Milano 15 1911 (635–641). [0010]. 41721

Padoa, Maurizio. Relazioni fra fototropia e costituzione chimica. Atti Soc. ital. prog. sci. Roma 4 1911 (780–781). [4225]. 41723

————— Esperienze sulla foto-tropia di alcuni fenilidrazoni. Gazz. chim. ital. Roma 41 1. sem. 1911 (203–210). [3850]. 41724

————— Tentativo di sintesi asimmetrica con la luce polarizzata circolarmente. Gazz. chim. ital. Roma 41 1. sem. 1911 (469–472). [4005]. 41725

————— e Bovini, F. Relazioni fra la costituzione e la fototropia. Roma Rend. Acc. Lincei (Ser. 5) 20 2. sem. 1911 (712–717). [4225]. 41726

————— e Graziani, F. Ricerca di nuove sostanze fototrope. Gazz. chim. ital. Roma 41 1. sem. 1911 (210–215 215-220). [3850]. 41727

————— Relazioni tra la costituzione e la fototropia. Gazz. chim. ital. Roma 41 1. sem. 1911 (385–391). [3850]. 41728

Padova, E. Il fotometro di Zöllner-Wolfer applicato allo studio del fotometro registratore Müller. Venezia Atti Ist. ven. 70 parte 2 1911 (675–691) ; [sunto] Riv. Astron. sci. affini Torino 5 1911 (216–219). [3010]. 41729

Paillat, J., Ducretet, F. et Roger, E. Nouveau procédé de désélectrisation des matières textiles au moyen des courants électriques de haute fréquence. Paris C. R. Acad. sci. 152 1911 (583–585). [6470] 41730

Painlevé, P. r. Bonasse, H.

Palagi, Ferdinando. Nozioni elementari di chimica inorganica e organica precedute dalle nozioni preliminari di fisica. Ed. 5. Torino (E. Loescher) 1909 (VIII + 231). 23 cm. [0100]. 41731

Palladino, Pietro. Di alcune inesatte descrizioni sperimentali dei fenomeni capillari. Riv. fis. mat. sc. nat. Pavia 22 1910 (223–236). [0300]. 41735

Palma (Di), Francesco. Nuovo generatore di corrente elettrica primaria. Elettricista Roma (Ser. 2) 10 1911 (19–20). [5610]. 41736

Palmer, Frederic, jun. Volume ionization produced by light of extremely short wave-length. Physic. Rev. Ithaca N.Y. 32 1911 (1–22 with text fig.). [6805] 41737

Pampanini, G. r. Amadori, M.

Panebianco, Giuseppe. Sulla suscettibilità magnetica dei metalli ferromagnetici in campi deboli. Napoli Rend. Soc. sc. (Ser. 3) 16 1910 (216–221). [5440]. 41738

Panomareff, R. D. Ein neuer Apparat zum Nachweis der Spannkraft verschiedener Dämpfe. Zs. physik. Unterr. Berlin 24 1911 (290–292). [1840 0050]. 41739

Panther, H. Das Zielfernrohr. Schuss u. Waffe Neudamm 4 1911 (229–233 246–249 267–270 288–291). [3080]. 41740

Paoli, Alessandro. La scuola di Galileo nella storia della filosofia. Ann. univ. tosc. Pisa 29 1910 (Mem. 3 1–102). [0010]. 41741

Papalexi, N. r. Mandelstam, L.

Papenfus, Franz. Die Brauchbarkeit der Koinzidenzmethode zur Messung von Wellenlängen. Zs. wiss. Phot. Leipzig 9 1911 (332–346 349–360) ; Diss. Münster i. W. Leipzig (J. A. Barth) 1911 (32). 24 cm. [3430 3160]. 41742

Pardo, Ruggero. L'alterazione di grandezza e l'alterazione di forma delle imagini quali fattori della diminuzione di V (visus) determinata dalla prospettiva. Clin. ocul. Roma 13 1911 (565-573). [4430]. 41746

Parenty, H. Sur un compteur de vapeur. Paris C. R. Acad. sci. 154 1912 (25-28 av. fig.). [0835]. 41747

—————— Sur la régulation progressive des pressions à l'entrée d'une conduite de distribution d'eau, de gaz ou de vapeur. Paris C. R. Acad. sci. 154 1912 (186-188). [0835]. 41748

—————— Sur un régulateur thermique de précision. Paris C. R. Acad. sci. 154 1912 (326). [1044]. 41749

Parmentier, Jacques. Vérification de la loi de Stefan-Boltzmann au moyen d'un tour Memker. Ann. chim. phys. Paris (sér. 8) 22 1911 (417-428 av. fig.). [4210]. 41750

Parr, W. Alfred. Osservazioni spettroscopiche solari con mezzi semplici. Riv. Astron. sci. affini Torino 3 1909 (337-339). [4205]. 41751

Parsons, Charles A. Further experiments with the gramophone. Nature London 86 1911 (416). [9420]. 41752

—————— and **Cook, S. S.** Experiments on the compression of liquids at high pressure. London Proc. R. Soc. (Ser. A) 85 1911 (332-348). [0810]. 41753

Parsons, C. S. v. Elliott, J. W.

Partzsch, A. Zur Theorie des lichtelektrischen Stromes in Gasen. Berlin Verh. D. physik. Ges. 14 1912 (69-73). [6850]. 41754

Pascal, Blaise. Œuvres. Édition L. Braunschweig et P. Boutroux. Tomes I, II, III (collection " Les grands écrivains de la France "). Paris (Hachette) 1908. Tome I (LXI + 406); Tome II (571); Tome III (600). 23 cm. 41755

Pascal, P. Recherches magnéto-chimiques. Ann. chim. phys. Paris (sér. 8) 19 1910 (5-70 av. fig.); 25 1912 (289-377 av. fig.). [5466 5467 5481]. 41756

—————— Sur un mode de contrôle optique des analyses magnéto-chimiques. Paris C. R. Acad. sci. 152 1911 (1852-1855). [5489]. 41757

—————— Recherches magnéto-chimiques sur la structure atomique des halogènes. Paris C. R. Acad. sci. 152 1911 (862-865). [5489 5466]. 41759

(e-4388)

Paschen, F[riedrich]. Über die Seriensysteme in den Spektren von Zink, Cadmium und Quecksilber. II. Ann. Physik Leipzig (4. Folge) 35 1911 (860-880). [4207 4208 4205]. 41760

—————— Über die Dispersion des Quarzes im Ultrarot. Ann. Physik Leipzig (4. Folge) 35 1911 (1005-1008). [3830 3034]. 41761

—————— Kritisches zur genauen Wellenlängenmessung ultraroter Spektrallinien. Ann. Physik Leipzig (4. Folge) 36 1911 (191-197). [3435 3160]. 41762

—————— Erweiterung der Seriengesetze der Linienspektra auf Grund genauer Wellenlängenmessungen im Ultrarot. Jahrb. Radioakt. Leipzig 8 1911 (174-186). [4205 3435]. 41763

—————— Intensitätsverteilung im Kanalstrahl-Dopplerstreif. Ann. Physik Leipzig (4. Folge) 37 1912 (599-600). [6845]. 41764

—————— und **Wolff, K.** Die Bestimmung des mechanischen Wärmeäquivalentes in Vorlesung und Praktikum. Physik. Zs. Leipzig 12 1911 (113-115). [2410 C050]. 41765

Pasqualini, Luigi. Un metodo per la verifica degli specchi per proiettori. Riv. maritt. Roma 1910 2. trim. (323-325). [3020]. 41766

Pasquier, Ern. Équilibre statique, dynamique. Union ing. Louvain 1910 (104-114). [5200]. 41767

Passavant. Definitionen für die internationale elektrotechnische Kommission. Elektrot. Zs. Berlin 32 1911 (323-324). [0070]. 41768

Pasta, G. v. La Rosa, M.

Paternò, Emanuele. Le soluzioni colloidali. Gazz. chim. ital. 40 2. sem. 1910 (537-548); [ristampa] Rend. Soc. chim. ital. Roma (Ser. 2) 2 1910 (301-313). [0340]. 41769

—————— e **Chieffi, Generoso.** Sintesi in chimica organica per mezzo della luce. Nota 5. Gazz. chim. ital. Palermo 40 2. sem. 1910 (321-331). [4225]. 41770

—————— e **Forli Forti, G.** Sintesi in chimica organica per mezzo della luce. Nota 6. Gazz. chim. ital. Palermo 40 2. sem. 1910 (332-341). [4225]. 41771

o

Pauli, Richard. Über die Beurteilung der Zeitordnung von optischen Reizen im Anschluss an eine von E. Mach beobachtete Farbenerscheinung. Arch. ges. Psychol. Leipzig 21 1911 (132–218). [4450]. 41772

Pauli, W. E. Über Phosphoreszenz. Physik. Zs. Leipzig 13 1912 (39–46). [4230]. 41773

———— Über ultraviolette und ultrarote Phosphoreszenz. Ann. Physik Leipzig (4. Folge) 34 1911 (739–779 mit 1 Taf.); [Auszug] Heidelberg SitzBer. Ak. Wiss. math.-natw. Kl. 1911 Abh. 1 (24). [4230]. 41774

Pawlow, P. Ueber die Anwendung der thermodynamischen Theorie der dispersen Systeme auf Hydrometeore. Zs. Kolloide Dresden 8 1911 (18–24). [1800 2435 0340 5270]. 41775

———— Zur Frage über den Niederschlagsformkoeffizienten von P. P. von Weimarn. [Nebst Bemerkungen von P. P. von Weimarn.] Zs. Kolloide Dresden 8 1911 (138–141 141–143). [2457]. 41776

———— Zur Thermodynamik der kondensierten dispersen Systeme. Zs. physik. Chem. Leipzig 76 1911 (450–468). [2455 2465 1887 0340]. 41777

Pealing, Harold v. Owen.

Pécheux, H. Proprietà elettriche dei filamenti delle lampade elettriche ad incandescenza. [Sunto. Trad.] Atti Ass. elettrotecn. Milano 15 1911 (620–624). [6080]. 41778

———— Résistivité et thermo-électricité du tantale. Paris C. R. Acad. sci. 153 1911 (1140–1141). [5710 5660]. 41779

———— Les lampes électriques. Paris (Gauthier-Villars et Masson) 1910 (186 av. fig.). 19 cm. [6080]. 41780

Pecsi, Gustavo. Crisi degli assiomi della fisica moderna. [Trad.] Roma (Desclée e C.) 1910 (106). 19 cm. [2495]. 41781

Peddie, W. The problem of partition of energy, especially in radiation. Phil. Mag. London (Ser. 6) 22 1911 (663–668). [4210]. 41782

Pedersen, P. O. La ricerca della segretezza nella comunicazioni radio-telegrafiche. Atti Ass. elettrotecn. Milano 15 1911 (1141–1145). [6610]. 41783

———— Resonanz in gekoppelten Schwingungskreisen. Jahrb. drahtlos. Telegr. Leipzig 4 1911 (449–459). [6450]. 41784

———— Wirbelstromverluste in und effektiver Widerstand von geraden, runden Metallzylindern. Formelsammlung und Tabellen. Jahrb. drahtlos. Telegr. Leipzig 4 1911 (501–515). [6440]. 41785

———— Drahtlose Schnelltelegraphie. Jahrb. drahtlos. Telegr. Leipzig 4 1911 (524–531). [6615]. 41786

Peek, W. Le leggi del fenomeno della corona e la rigidità dielettrica dell'aria. [Sunto. Trad.] Atti Ass. elettrotecn. Milano 15 1911 (945–946). [6460]. 41787

Peineke, W. Die Konstruktionen elektrischer Maschinen. (Elektrotechnik in Einzel-Darstellungen. Hrsg. von G. Benischke. H. 16.) Braunschweig (F. Vieweg & S.) 1912 (VII + 113). 22 cm. 3,60 M. [6600]. 41788

Peirce, B[enjamin] Osgood. The effects of sudden changes in the inductances of electric circuits as illustrative of the absence of magnetic lag and of the Von Waltenhofen phenomenon in finely divided cores. Certain mechanical analogies of the electrical problems. Boston Proc. Amer. Acad. Arts Sci. 46 1911 (539–585 with text fig. pl.). [6400 5440]. 41789

Pélabon, H. Sur la résistivité des séléniures d'antimoine. Paris C. R. Acad. sci. 152 1911 (1302–1305). [5660]. 41790

———— Sur la métallographie des systèmes sélénium-antimoine. Paris C. R. Acad. sci. 153 1911 (343–346 349–360). [1920]. 41791

Pellat, Solange. Notice sur les travaux de Henri Pellat. Paris (Basset et Cie) 1911 (44 av. portr.). 22 cm. [0010]. 41793

Peller, W. Neuerungen an galvanischen Elementen. Elektroch. Zs. Berlin 17 1911 (340–142); 18 1911 (7–9 31–36). [5610]. 41794

Pellerano, L. L'autocromia e le applicazioni artistiche. Boll. Soc. tot. Firenze 22 1910 (6-12). [3850]. 41795

——— L'ultima parola sulle lastre autocrome. Boll. Soc. fot. Firenze 22 1910 (97-102). [3850]. 41796

Peri, Guido. Le moderne lampade ad arco metallico in serie su corrente continua costante con apparecchi raddrizzatori a mercurio. Industria Milano 25 1911 (486-490 503-509 520-521). [6080]. 41797

Perlewitz, K. Neues Verfahren zur Isolation von Spulen für Hochspannungsmaschinen. Elektrot. Zs. Berlin 32 1911 (1028-1029). [6000]. 41798

Perlia, R[ichard]. Ein vereinfachtes Stereoskopometer. Klin. Monatsbl. Augenheilk. Stuttgart (49) N.F. 12 1911 (192-194). [4470]. 41799

Perot, A. Sur la luminescence de l'arc au mercure dans le vide. J. phys. Paris (sér. 5) 1 1911 (609-626). [6840]. 41800

——— Sur la spectroscopie solaire. Paris C. R. Acad. sci. 152 1911 (36-38). [3420 4205 6805]. 41802

——— Les principes de Doppler-Fizeau et de W. Michelson et les raies d'absorption. J. phys. Paris (sér. 5) 2 1912 (171-176 av. fig.). [3420 3850]. 41803

——— Sur la longueur d'onde de la raie solaire D₁. Paris C. R. Acad. sci. 154 1912 (326-329). [3430]. 41804

——— et Lindstedt, Mlle. Sur la longueur d'onde de la raie solaire b. Paris C. R. Acad. sci. 152 1911 (1367-1370 av. fig.). [3430]. 41805

Perotti, Pierluigi. Telefonografia. Riv. Comun. Roma 4 1911 (96-103); Elettricista Roma (Ser. 2) 10 1911 (104-105); Elettricità Milano 36 1911 (380-382 394-396). [6485]. 41806

Perrier, Albert. Les variations thermiques de l'hystérèse tournante et l'hystérèse alternative. J. phys. Paris (sér. 4) 9 1910 (785-819 865-887 av. fig.). [5450]. 41807

——— r. Kamerlingh Onnes, H.

Perrin, Jean. Mouvement brownien et molécules. Journ. Chim. Phys. Genève 8 1910 (57-91). [0400]. 41808

——— Movimento browniano e grandezze molecolari. [Sunto.] Riv. (c-4388)

lis. mat. sc. nat. Pavia 21 1910 (295-296). [0150]. 41809

Perrin, Jean. Les grandeurs moléculaires (nouvelles mesures). Paris C. R. Acad. sci. 152 1911 (1380-1382). [0150]. 41810

——— et Bjerrum, N. L'agitation moléculaire dans les fluides visqueux. Paris C. R. Acad. sci. 152 1911 (1569-1571). [0200]. 41811

Perrot, F. Louis. Sur quelques constantes physicochimiques des gaz liquéfiés. Genève C. R. Soc. Phys. Hist. Nat. 28 1912 (40-41). [1870]. 41812

——— r. Baume, G.

Pescio, Amedeo. Antonio Pacinotti e il cinquantenario della dinamo. Agric. ital. Pisa (Ser. 4) 7 1911 (204-208). [0010]. 41813

Pesenti, M. Il telegrafista. Milano (Soc. ed. milanese) 1909 (119). 16 cm. [0030 4900]. 41814

Peters, Gustav. Zur Kenntnis hydroaromatischer Substanzen mit konjugierten Doppelbindungen. Diss. Greifswald (Druck v. H. Adler) 1910 (71). 24 cm. [3860]. 41815

Petersen, W. Hochspannungstechnik. Stuttgart (F. Enke) 1911 (VIII + 358). 25 cm. 11 M. [6000]. 41816

Peterson, Joseph. Combination tones and other related auditory phenomena. [With bibliography.] Psych. Rev. Monogr. Suppl. Baltimore Md. 9 No. 3 1908 (i-xiii 1-136). [9400]. 41817

Petíra, Stanislav. Přehled pokroku fysiky za rok 1908. 3. Nauka o teple. [Fortschritte in der Physik 1908. 3. Wärmelehre.] Prag Věstn. České Ak. Frant. Jos. 1910 (333-359). [0030 0090]. 41818

Petrie, J. M. r. Chapman, H. G.

Petrowsky, A. Einige Bemerkungen über Strahlungsdekrement, wirksame Kapazität und Selbstinduktion einer Antenne. Ann. Physik Leipzig (4. Folge) 35 1911 (189-190). [6615]. 41819

Peukert, W[ilhelm]. Das Spiegelgalvanometer nach Deprez-d'Arsonval als Ersatz des Elektrometers. Elektrot. Zs. Berlin 32 1911 (362-363). [6010]. 41820

Pioro, Jan. Ueber den Zusammen hang zwischen Sensibilisierung und Fluoreszenz. Diss. München (Bayerische Druckerei & Verlagsanstalt) 1911 (18). 22 cm. [4230 4225]. 41847

[**Piotrovskij,** M[ichail Julianovič].] Пиотровскій, М[ихаилъ Юліано вичъ]. Развитіе теоріи индукціонной катушки. [Die Entwickelung der Theorie des Funkeninduktors.] Vopr. fiziki St. Peterburg 3 1909 (206 228). [0010]. 41848

Piper, C. Welborne r. Mees, C. E. K.

Piper, H[ans]. Ueber die Aktionsströme der Krebsscherenmuskeln. Med. Klinik Berlin 7 1911 (435). [5900]. 41849

Pirani, M. v. Ueber optische Temperaturmessungen. Berlin Verh. D. physik. Ges. 13 1911 (19-25). [3810]. 41850

———— Notiz über das Absorptionsvermögen der Auermasse. Berlin Verh. D. physik. Ges. 13 1911 (26). [3810]. 41851

———— Notiz über eine Darstellungsweise für den Temperaturkoeffizienten des elektrischen Widerstandes. Berlin Verh. D. physik. Ges. 13 1911 (929-930). [5660]. 41852

———— Über die Photometrierung verschiedenfarbiger Lichtquellen. Zs. wiss. Phot. Leipzig 9 1911 (270-272). [3010 3860]. 41853

———— und **Meyer,** Alfred R. Über den Schmelzpunkt und den Temperaturkoeffizienten des spezifischen Widerstandes des Tantals. Zs. Elektroch. Halle 17 1911 (908-910). [5660]. 41854

———— Über die Eichung von Pyrometerlampen vermittels zweier Temperaturfixpunkte. Zs. wiss. Phot. Leipzig 10 1911 (135-137). [3010]. 41855

Pirret, Ruth and **Soddy,** Frederick. The ratio between uranium and radium in minerals. Phil. Mag. London (Ser. 6) 21 1911 (652-658). [4275]. 41856

Pirro (Di), Giovanni. Problem tecnico-scientifici della telegrafia e telefonia. Riv. Leg. stat. com. Roma 1 1908 (497-508). [6480]. 41857

———— Sulla telefonia a grande distanza. Atti Ass. stat. comp. elettrotecn. Milano 15 1911 (1119-1126). [6485]. 41858

Piutti, Arnaldo. Ricerche sull' elio. L'elio nell' aria di Napoli e nel Vesuvio. Gazz. chim. ital. 40 1. sem. 1910 (435-476). [4202]. 41859

———— Ricerche sull'elio. Minerali radioattivi contenenti elio. Gazz. chim. ital. 40 1. sem. 1910 (476-488). [4275]. 41860

———— L'Elio nei minerali recenti. Napoli Rend. Soc. sc. (Ser. 3) 16 1910 (30-32 con tab.). [4275]. 41861

———— Ricerche sull'elio. Sull'assorbimento dell' elio nei sali e nei minerali. Nota IV. Napoli Rend. Soc. sc. (Ser. 3) 16 1910 (253-255). [0250]. 41862

———— Ricerche sull' elio. Atti Soc. ital. prog. sci. Roma 4 1911 (277-315 con 4 tav.). [4202]. 41863

———— Sur la présence de l'hélium dans les autunites et sur la période de la vie de l'ionium. Radium Paris 8 1911 (204-205 av. fig.). [4275]. 41864

———— La ricerca dell' elio nell'atmosfera. Atti VII. Cong. geogr. ital. Palermo (Vezzi) 1911 (177-211 con 3 tabelle). 25 cm. [4202]. 41865

———— e **Magli,** G. Sul potere assorbente per l'aria di alcune varietà di carboni vegetali. Gazz. chim. ital. 40 1. sem. 1910 (569-577). [0250]. 41866

———— Sulla radioattività dei prodotti della recente eruzione dell'Etna. Napoli Rend. Soc. sc. (Ser. 3). 16 1910 (159-163); Gazz. chim. ital. Roma 41 1. sem. 1911 (717-722). [4275]. 41867

Pizzighelli, Giuseppe. Gli strumenti ottici usati in fotografia. Boll. soc. fot. Firenze 22 1910 (47-48). [3085]. 41868

———— Il sensitometro a scalinata. Boll. Soc. fot. 22 1910 (156-159). [3850]. 41869

———— La fotografia a grandi distanze colla Téléphot-Camera. Boll Soc. fot. Firenze 22 1910 (258-260) [3085]. 41870

———— Sopra alcuni fenomeni anormali nel campo della fotografia. [Trad.] Boll. Soc. fot. Firenze 22 1910 (286-291). [4450]. 41871

———— La fotografia con raggi invisibili di R.W.Wood. [Trad. Sunto.]

Boll. Soc. fot. Firenze 22 1910 (322–323). [4225]. 41872

Pizzighelli, Giuseppe. Obbiettivi, condensatori e sorgenti di luce per ingrandimento. [Trad.] Firenze Boll. Soc. fot. 22 1911 (41–46). [3085]. 41873

———— Il nuovo filtro di R. A. Houston e J. Logie per i raggi calorifici. [Trad.] Firenze Boll. Soc. fot. 22 1911 (49–51). [3855]. 41874

———— La fototelegrafia o la trasmissione elettrica di imagini a grandi distanze. Firenze Boll. Soc. fot. 22 1911 (286–293). [6480]. 41875

Pizzuti, Michele. Protezione delle condutture aeree dalle sovraelevazioni di tensione. Atti Ass. elettrotecn. Milano 14 1910 (713–724). [6450]. 41876

———— Sulla protezione degli impianti elettrici da sovratensioni. Atti Ass. elettrotecn. Milano 15 1911 (1016–1017). [6440]. 41877

———— e Ferrari, Carlo. Accorciatore di onde. Protezione delle condutture elettriche. Atti Ass. elettrotecn. Milano 14 1910 (495–499). [6450]. 41878

Plaats, B. J. van der. Eenige waarnemingen betreffende anomale dispersie van het licht in absorbeerende gassen. [Quelques observations sur la dispersion anomale des gaz absorbants.] Handl. Ned. Nat. Gneesk Congres 13 1911 (178–181). [3850]. 41879

———— v. Julius, W. H.

Planck, Max. Energie et température. J. phys. Paris (sér. 5) 1 1911 (345–359). [0200–2425]. 41880

———— Zur Hypothese der Quantenemission. Berlin SitzBer. Ak. Wiss. 1911 (723–731). [4200]. 41881

———— Eine neue Strahlungshypothese. Berlin Verb. D. physik. Ges. 13 1911 (138–148). [4200–4960]. 41882

———— Energie und Temperatur. Vortrag . . . Physik. Zs. Leipzig 12 1911 (681–687). [2400–2435–2425]. 41883

———— Über die Begründung des Gesetzes der schwarzen Strahlung. Ann. Physik Leipzig (4. Folge) 37 1912 (642–656); Berlin Verb. D. physik. Ges. 14 1912 (113–118). [4210–4200]. 41884

Planck, Max. Über neuere thermodynamische Theorien. (Nernstsches Wärmetheorem und Quanten-Hypothese.) (Vortrag . . .) Berlin Ber. D. chem. Ges. 45 1912 (5–23); Physik. Zs. Leipzig 13 1912 (165–175); Leipzig (Akadem. Verlagsges.) 1912 (34). [2400–2115–4200]. 41885

———— Vorlesungen über Thermodynamik. 3., erweit. Aufl. Leipzig (Veit & Comp.) 1911 (VIII + 288). 23 cm. Geb. 7.50 M. [2400–0030]. 41886

Planer, V. Eine neue Methode für Fehlermessungen an Drehstromkabeln mit unterbrochener Ader und gleichzeitigem Erdschluss. Elektrot. Anz. Berlin 28 1911 (894–895). [5770]. 41887

Plank, Rudolph. Das Verhalten des Querkontraktionskoeffizienten des Eisens bis zu sehr grossen Dehnungen. Berlin Zs. Ver. D. Ing. 55 1911 (1479–1483). [0840]. 41888

Platania, Gaetano. Effetti magnetici del fulmine sulle lave di Stromboli. Acireale Atti Acc. Zelanti (Ser. 3) 5 (Classe Scienze) (1905–06) 1909 (163–167). [6800]. 41889

Platania, Giovanni. Radioattività di materiali etnei. Catania Bull. Acc. Gioenia (Ser. 2) 15 1911 (25–28). [4275]. 41890

Pleier, Franz. Zum Kapitel: Tageslichtmessung. Zs. Schulgesundhtspfl. Hamburg 1911 (197–200). [3010]. 41891

Plesch, J[ohann]. Zur biologischen Wirkung der Radiumemanation. D. med. Wochenschr. Leipzig 37 1911 (488–490). [4275]. 41892

Plotnikow, Joh. Photochemische Studien. II. Ueber die Klassifikation der Lichtreaktionen. Zs. physik. Chem. Leipzig 77 1911 (472–481 mit 2 Taf.); III. Über räumlich fortschreitende Lichtreaktionen op. cit. 78 1911 (293–298). [4225–0050]. 41893

———— Photochemische Versuchstechnik. Leipzig (Akadem. Verlagsges.) 1912 (XV + 371 mit 3 Taf.). 24 cm. Geb. 11 M. [4225]. 41894

Pochettino, Alfredo. Sui fenomeni di luminescenza catodica nei minerali. Nuovo Cimento Pisa (Ser. 6) 1 1911 (21–64). [4230]. 41895

Pochettino, Alfredo. Sulla sensibilità alla luce dei preparati di selenio. Nuovo Cimento Pisa (Ser. 6) 1 1911 (147–210); Riv. fis. mat. sc. nat. Pavia 24 1911 (173–179). [5660]. 41896

—————— Su alcuni nuovi metodi di preparare soluzioni di selenio colloidale. Roma Rend. Acc. Lincei (Ser. 5) 20 1. sem. 1911 (428–433). [0340]. 41898

Pochhammer, L. Die Zustandsgleichung in angenäherter Rechnung. Ann. Physik Leipzig (4. Folge) 37 1912 (103–130). [1890 1880]. 41899

Poensgen, Richard. Die Bestimmung der Wärmeleitfähigkeit plattenförmiger Materialien. Bayr. Ind. Bl. München 97 1911 (471–472). [2020]. 41900

Pöschl, Viktor. Einführung in die Kolloidchemie. Ein Abriss der Kolloidchemie für Lehrer . . . 3. verb. Aufl. Dresden (Th. Steinkopff) 1911 (80). 23 cm. 2 M. [0340]. 41901

Pogány, Béla. Ueber einige Beobachtungen über die Polarisation des von Metallgittern gebeugten Lichtes. (Vorl. Mitt.) Physik. Zs. Leipzig 12 1911 (279–283). [3630 3840]. 41902

—————— Untersuchungen über die Polarisationsverhältnisse des von Metallgittern gebeugten Lichtes. Ann. Physik Leipzig (4. Folge) 37 1912 (257–288 mit 2 Taf.). [3630 3820 4905 3840]. 41903

Pohl, R[obert]. Über eine Beziehung zwischen dem selektiven Photoeffekt und der Phosphoreszenz. Berlin Verh. D. physik. Ges. 13 1911 (961–966). [4230]. 41904

—————— Zusatzpole für Umformer. Elektrot. Zs. Berlin 32 1911 (847–849). [6947]. 41905

—————— Bericht über die Methoden zur Bestimmung des elektrischen Elementarquantums. Jahrb. Radioakt. Leipzig 8 1911 (406–439). [6845]. 41906

—————— und **Pringsheim,** P. Bemerkung über die lichtelektrischen Effekte an kolloidalen Alkalimetallen. Berlin Verh. D. physik. Ges. 13 1911 (219–223). [6850]. 41907

—————— Über den selektiven Photoeffekt ausserhalb der Alkaligruppe. Berlin Verh. D. physik. Ges. 13 1911 (474–481). [6850]. 41908

Pohl, R[obert] und **Pringsheim,** P. Über den selektiven Photoeffekt des Lithiums und Natriums. Berlin Verh. D. physik. Ges. 14 1912 (46–59). [6850]. 41909

—————— The normal and selective photo-electric effect. Phil. Mag. London (Ser. 6) 21 1911 (155–161). [6850]. 41910

—————— v. Franck, F.

Pohlhausen, A. Die Dampfturbinen. Bd 2 des Werkes: Die Dampfmaschinen. Lehr- und Handbuch für Studierende . . . Lfg 1–5. Mittweida (Polyt. Buchhandlung) [1911] (1–120 mit Taf.). 28 cm. Die Lfg 0,60 M.; Lfg 6,7. ibid. (121–168 mit Taf.). 28 cm. Die Lfg 0,60 M. [2490]. 41911

Poincaré, Henri. Über einige Gleichungen in der Theorie der Hertzschen Wellen. Math.-natw. Bl. Berlin 8 1911 (49–53). [6690]. 41912

—————— Sur la théorie des quanta. Paris C. R. Acad. sci. 153 1911 (1103–1108). [4200]. 41913

—————— Savants et écrivains. Paris (Flammarion) 1910 (XIV + 279). 19 cm. [0040]. 41914

—————— Leçons sur les hypothèses cosmogoniques, professées à la Sorbonne (cours de la Faculté des sciences de Paris) rédigées par Henri Vergne. Paris (Hermann) 1911 (XXV + 294). 8vo. [2415 2040 4215 0200]. 41915

Poirot, J[ean]. Die Phonetik. [In: Handbuch d. vergl. Methodik, hrsg. v. R. Tigerstedt. Bd 3, Abt. 6.] Leipzig (S. Hirzel) 1911 (276). [9510]. 41916

[**Pokrovskij,** S[ergej] Ivanovič.] Покровскій, С[ергѣй] Ивановичъ. О возможности опредѣленія температуры чернаго тѣла изъ спектрофотометрическихъ измѣреній по закону, аналогичному закону смѣщенія Вина и объ изслѣдованіи такимъ образомъ функцій хроматической чувствительности глаза. [Sur la possibilité de la détermination de la température du corps noir d'après les mesures spectrophotométriques en se servant de la loi analogue de celle de Wien et sur la méthode de trouver la fonction de sensibilité chromatique de l'œil.] St. Peterburg Žurn. russ. fiz.-chim. Obšč. Fiz. otd. 41 1909 (73–80 rés. fr. 80). [4210 4450]. 41917

[**Pokrovskij**, S[ergej Ivanovič].]
Покровскій, С[ергѣй Ивановичъ].
Über das Spektrohelioskop (astronomischer Monochromator.) Astr. Nachr.
Kiel 189 1911 (369-372). [3465].
41918

———— Ein einfaches Projektionsverfahren der Erscheinungen der chromatischen Polarisation des Lichtes in
konvergenten Strahlen. D. MechZtg
Berlin 1911 (124). [0050]. 41919

———— Ueber die Anwendung des
polarisierten Lichtes in der Interferometrie. Physik. Zs. Leipzig 12 1911
(459). [3610 4000]. 41920

———— Ueber das Dopplersche
Prinzip. Physik. Zs. Leipzig 12 1911
(459-460 1115-1118). [3420 4207
6640]. 41921

———— Ueber das spektrophoto-
metrische Verschiebungsgesetz. (Vorl.
Mitt.) Physik. Zs. Leipzig 12 1911
(549-551). [3010 4450]. 41922

———— Anwendung des Prinzips
virtueller Verschiebungen auf die in
eine Strahlung versenkten Systeme.
Physik. Zs. Leipzig 12 1911 (1118-
1125). [4200 3400]. 41923

———— Notiz über die Halbschatteninterferometrie. Physik. Zs. Leipzig
12 1911 (1142-1143). [3610 4000].
41924

———— Ponderomotorische Wirkungen zirkularpolarisierter Strahlen.
Physik. Zs. Leipzig 13 1912 (158-161).
[4005 3405]. 41925

Pokrowsky v. Pokrovski.

Polara, Giovanni. Sulla conducibilità elettrica della saliva mista del-
l'uomo. Catania Atti Acc. Gioenia (Ser.
5) 3 1910 (Mem. 6 1-5 con 1 tav.).
[5660]. 41926

Pole, Joseph. Zur Photometrie
geradlinig ausgedehnter Lichtquellen.
Elektrot. Zs. Berlin 32 1911 (440-443).
[3010]. 41927

———— Photometrische Untersuchungen an Quecksilberdampflampen.
Elektrot. Zs. Berlin 33 1912 (153-156).
[4202 6080]. 41928

Pollitzer, F. Bestimmung spezifischer Wärmen bei tiefen Temperaturen
und ihre Verwertung zur Berechnung
elektromotorischer Kräfte. Zs. Elektroch. Halle 17 1911 (5-14). [1620
5610 1670]. 41929

Pollitzer, F. Zur Thermodynamik des
Clarkelements. Zs. physik. Chem.
Leipzig 78 1911 (371-383). [5610
2475]. 41930

Polotsky, A. v. Herzog, R.

Poma, Gualtiero. Colore e idratazione. Gazz. chim. ital. Roma 40
1. sem. 1910 (176-193). [3860]. 41931

Pomey. Ondes cylindriques périodiques dans un conducteur. J. phys.
Paris (sér. 5) 2 1912 (203-205). [6460].
41932

Pomilio, U. v. Kernot, G.

Ponti, G. G. Metodi razionali per
la misura commerciale dell'energia
elettrica. Atti Ass. elettrotecn.
Milano 15 1911 (1181-1184). [6010].
41933

Ponzini, Alfredo. Apparecchio ad
induzione per convertire industrialmente in calore l'energia elettrica anche
ad alto potenziale. [Sunto.] Industria
Milano 24 1910 (66-68). [6090]. 41934

———— Apparecchio ad induzione
per transformare industrialmente in
calore l'energia elettrica. Atti Ass.
elettrotecn. Milano 14 1910 (217-225).
[5720]. 41935

Poole, Horace H. On the rate of
evolution of heat by pitchblende.
Phil. Mag. London (Ser. 6) 21 1911
(58-62). [4275]. 41936

Popoff, Kyrille. Sur une cause qui
peut influer sur l'estimation de la
grandeur des étoiles. Paris C. R. Acad.
sci. 153 1911 (1210-1211). [4225
3010]. 41937

Poppelreuter, Walther. Beiträge zur
Raumpsychologie. Mathematische
Theorie des Wahrnehmungsraumes.
Quantitativer Vergleich der binoku-
laren und monokularen empirischen
Raumwahrnehmung. Zs. Psychol.
Leipzig Abt. 1 58 1911 (200-262).
[4440]. 41938

Poppendieck, Robert. Ueber Vario-
meter für die Horizontalintensität mit
vier Ablenkungsmagneten. Diss. Gies-

sen. Darmstadt (Druck v. L. C. Wittich) 1911 (63). 22 cm. [5435].
41939

Porlezza, C. Contributo alla conoscenza del secondo spettro dell'idrogeno. Roma Rend. Acc. Lincei (Ser. 5) **20** 1. sem. 1911 (819-828); 2. sem. (176-183). [4205].
41940

———— Contributo alla conoscenza dello spettro a bande del tetrafluoruro di silicio. Roma Rend. Acc. Lincei (Ser. 5) **20** 2. sem. 1911 (486-490). [4205].
41941

———— Lo spettro a righe dell'azoto in tubo di Geissler. Roma Rend. Acc. Lincei (Ser. 5) **20** 2. sem. 1911 (584-587 642-645). [4205].
41942

———— e **Norzi,** G. Nuovi studi sui gas dei soffioni boraciferi di Larderello. Roma Rend. Acc. Lincei (Ser. 5) **20** 2. sem. 1911 (338-342). [4275].
41943

———— ———— Concentrazione dell'emanazione radioattiva dei gas dei soffioni boraciferi mediante il carbone a bassa temperatura. Roma Rend. Acc. Lincei (Ser. 5) **20** 1. sem. 1911 (932-934). [4275].
41945

———— ———— Sul tufo radioattivo di Fiuggi—Gas occlusi—Contenuto in radio ed uranio. Roma Rend. Acc. Lincei (Ser. 5) **20** 1. sem. 1911 (935-939). [4275].
41946

———— r. Marino, L.

Porter, H. L. r. Bragg.

Poske, F. Die Hypothese in Wissenschaft und Unterricht. Zs. physik. Unterr. Berlin **25** 1912 (1-7). [0000 0050].
41947

Pote, F. W. r. Earhart, R. F.

Poulsen, Valdemar. La telefonia senza fili. Atti Ass. elettrotecn. Milano **15** 1911 (1132-1137). [6615].
41948

———— La radiotelefonia. Elettricità Milano **37** 1911 (264-265 276-278). [6615].
41949

———— Ueber drahtlose Telephonie. Nach einem . . . Vortrag. Elektrot. Anz. Berlin **28** 1911 (1120-1121 1124). [6615].
41950

Poynting, J. H. On small longitudinal material waves accompanying lightwaves. London Proc. R. Soc. (ser. A) **85** 1911 (474-476). [3405 3420].
41951

———— Sound. Encycl. Brit. (ed. 11) **25** 1911. [8990].
41952

Pozdena, Rudolf F. Eine halbautomatische Etalonbrücke zur Untersuchung von Massstäben. Mechaniker Berlin **20** 1912 (1-5 16-18). [0807].
41953

Pradel. Zum Schoop'schen Metallisierungsverfahren. Elektroch. Zs. Berlin **18** 1911 (23-24). [0090]. 41954

Prescott, J. On the rigidity of the earth. Phil. Mag. London (Ser. 6) **22** 1911 (481-505). [0840]. 41955

Preston, Thomas. The theory of light. 4th Ed. Edited by William Edward Thrift. London (Macmillan) 1912 (xxiii + 618). 22 cm. 15s. [0030]. 41956

Prieth, Gabriel. Ueber die Veränderung der Kapillaritätskonstante des Wassers durch gelöste Gase. Programm des Staats-Gymnasiums in Salzburg 1910-11. Salzburg **1911** (3-21). [0250 0300]. 41957

Pringsheim, P. r. Franck, J.. Pohl, R.

Pritschow. Die Dioptrieeinteilung an optischen Instrumenten. Centralztg Opt. Berlin **32** 1911 (61-64). [4430 3080]. 41958

Pritzsche, K. Die Verwendung der Lumière'schen Farbenplatten in der Mikrophotographie. Natw. Wochenschr. Jena **26** 1911 (353-356 mit 1 Taf.). [4225]. 41959

Profilo, S. C. Su l'azione degli idrati di sodio e di potassio nelle soluzioni di glucosio rispetto all'azione ottica. Napoli Rend. Soc. sc. (er. 3) **17** 1911 (174-181). [4040]. 41960

Proszyński, C. de. Application du gyroscope et de l'air comprimé à la prise des vues cinématographiques. Paris C. R. Acad. sci. **151** 1910 (1342-1344). [4225]. 41961

———— La prise des vues cinématographiques à la main (cinématographe détective). J. phys. Paris (sér. 5) **1** 1911 (129-131). [4225].
41964

Protz, Ludwig. Abhängigkeit der kubischen Kompressibilität von der Temperatur für Kalium und Natrium. Diss. Marburg. Frankfurt a. M. (Druck v. W. Gätje) 1909 (63 mit Taf.). 21 cm. [0840 1620]. 41962

Provenzal, Giulio. La trasmutazione degli elementi. Nuova Antologia Roma (Ser. 5) 149 1910 (299-305). [0500]. 41963

Przibram, Karl. Die Untersuchungen über die Kondensation von Dämpfen an Kernen (Bericht). Jahrb. Radioakt. Leipzig 8 1911 (285-308). [6805 1840]. 41965

———— Ladungsbestimmungen an Nebelteilchen. Physik. Zs. Leipzig 12 1911 (62-63 260-261); 13 1912 (106-108). [6805 0150 4690 5685]. 41966

Puccianti, Luigi. Recensione di "H. Kayser. Handbuch der Spectroscopie, vol. 5." Nuovo Cimento Pisa (Ser. 6) 1 1911 (78-80). [0030]. 41968

———— Necrologia di Luigi Magri. Nuovo Cimento Pisa (Ser. 6) 2 1911 (407-417). [0010]. 41969

Pugliese, Alberto. Necrologia di Giuseppe Gerosa. Nuovo Cimento Pisa (Ser. 6) 1 1911 (7-20 con ritratto). [0010]. 41970

Pugliese, Augusto. La nuova lampada a fiamma a lunga accensione di T. L. Carbone. Atti Ass. elettrotecn. Milano 15 1911 (151-158). [6830]. 41971

Puiseux. Rapport sur l'observation de l'éclipse totale de Soleil du 30 août 1905 à Cistierna (Espagne). Ann. bur. longit. Paris 8 1911 (B. 1 à B. 23 av. pl.). [4205]. 41972

Pulfrich, Carl. Stereoskopisches Sehen und Messen. Mit einem Literaturverzeichnis seit 1900. Jena (G. Fischer) 1911 (40). 29 cm. 1 M. [4440 3090]. 41973

Punga, Franklin. Versuche über das kritische GD von Drehstromgeneratoren. Elektrot. Zs. Berlin 32 1911 (385-387). [6060]. 41974

Puppini, Umberto. La filtrazione per mezzi non omogenei. Mon. tecn. Milano 17 1911 (512-515). [0300]. 41975

Purcell, Béla Baron. Másolható szines fotografiai fölvételek. [Kopierbare farbige photographische Aufnahmen.] Termt. Közl. Budapest 43 1911 (272-275). [4225]. 41976

Purvis, J. E. Note on the Zeeman effect for chromium. Astroph. J. Chicago Ill. 34 1911 (312-313 with table). [4208]. 41977

Putscher, Henry. Zur Charakteristik des elektrischen Lichtbogens in Alkalidämpfen. Diss. Göttingen (Druck v. Dieterich) 1911 (62). 22 cm. [6830]. 41978

Puxeddu, E. Azione chimica della luce sulla vanillina e i snoi eteri. Roma Rend. Acc. Lincei (Ser. 5) 20 2. sem. 1911 (717-723). [4225]. 41979

Quartaroli, A. Sull' energia degli elementi e sulla quantità che resta nelle combinazioni. Saggio di una teoria energetica dell' isomeria. Gazz. chim. ital. 40 1. sem. 1910 (325-379). [2472]. 41980

Quartulli, Giovanni. Nuovo metodo per lo studio della conducibilità termica dei metalli. Cefalù (Tip. S. Gussio) 1910 (11). 28 cm. [2029]. 41981

Quentin, H. Drachenphotographie. Phot. Ind. Berlin 1911 (1322-1324). [3085]. 41982

Quervain, A. de. Ueber die Bestimmung der Einstellungsträgheit von Thermometern. Met. Zs. Braunschweig 28 1911 (88-90). [1200]. 41983

———— Die instrumentelle Einrichtung der schweizerischen Erdbebenwarte in Degenried bei Zürich. Aarau Verh. Schweiz. Natf. Ges. 94 1912 212-213). [0060]. 41984

Quidor, A. De la vision binoculaire. Ann. chim. phys. Paris (sér. 8) 19 1910 (233-289 av. fig.). [4440]. 41985

Quincke, Georg. Die Elektrochemie in Heidelberg vor 55 Jahren. [Robert Wilhelm Bunsen.] Zs. Elektroch. Halle 17 1911 (207). [0010]. 41986

Quix, F[rançois] H[ubert]. Het verschijnsel van Hensen en de accommodatie van het oor. [Le phénomène de Hensen et l'accommodation des oreilles.] Ned. Tijdschr. Geneesk. Amsterdam 54 2 1910 (981-985). [9520]. 41987

Rabe, Paul und **Marschall**, Oswald. Fluorescenzerscheinungen bei Chinaalkaloiden. (13. Mitt. : Zur Kenntnis der Chinaalkaloide.) Liebigs Ann. Chem. Leipzig **382** 1911 (360–364). [4230]. 41988

Radt, M. Die Eisenverluste in elliptischen Drehfeldern. Karlsruhe, Arb. elektrot. Inst. 2 (1910–1911) 1911 (249–296). [6060 6440 5450]. 41989

—— —— Le perdite magnetiche nei campi rotanti ellittici. [Sunto. Trad.] Atti Ass. elettrotecn. Milano **15** 1911 (461–463). [5450]. 41990

Ratto, G. Ancora sulla densità di alcune lave dell' Etna del Vesuvio e di alcuni mattoni. Catania Ball. Acc. Gioenia (Ser. 2) **18** 1911 (4–10). [0810]. 41991

—————— und **Mancini**, J. Beitrag zur Kenntnis des Kolloiden Schwefels. 3. Mitt. (Übers. von Felix **Fraenckel**.) Zs. Kolloide Dresden **9** 1911 (58–61). [0349]. 41992

Ragonot, E. Costruzione ed impiego degli interruttori automatici. Atti Ass. elettrotecn. Milano **15** 1911 (913–920). [6920]. 41993

Raimondi, E. Procedimento analitico per determinare la capacità di alcuni tipi di condensatori. Riv. Artig. Genio Roma 1. trim. 1910 (99–103). [5620]. 41994

Raisch, R. Über das Anoden und Kathodengefälle und das Minimumpotential in Chlor. Ann. Physik Leipzig (4. Folge) **36** 1911 (907–928); Diss. Freiburg i. Br. Emmendingen (Druck d. Druck- u. Verlags-Ges.) 1911 (34). 22 cm. [6840]. 41995

Rajs, A. Die Kaskadenschaltung von dreiphasigen Induktions-motoren und Kommutatormotoren. Karlsruhe Arb. elektrot. Inst. 2 (1910–1911) 1911 (297–350); Diss. Karlsruhe. Berlin (J. Springer) 1911 (III + 55). 23 cm. [6070]. 41996

Ra'kowski, Adam. Zur Kenntnis der Adsorption, II. Über die chemische Hysteresis. Zs. Kolloide Dresden **10** 1912 (22–31). [0349 1920]. 41997

Raman, C. V. Photographs of vibration curves. Phil. Mag. London (Ser. 6) **21** 1911 (615–618 with pl.). [9310]. 41998

—————— The photometric measurement of the obliquity factor of diffraction. Phil. Mag. London (Ser. 6) **21** 1911 (618–626 with pl.). [3620]. 41999

Raman, C. V. Remarks on a paper by J. S. Stokes on "Some curious phenomena observed in connection with Melde's experiment." Physic. Rev. Ithaca N.Y. **32** 1911 (307–308). [9105]. 42000

—————— The small motion at the nodes of a vibrating string. Physic. Rev. Ithaca N.Y. **32** 1911 (309–315 with text fig.). [9110]. 42001

Ramsauer, C. Über die Wirkungen sehr kurzwelligen, ultravioletten Lichtes auf Gase. Physik. Zs. Leipzig **12** 1911 (997–998); Berlin Verh. d. physik. Ges. **13** 1911 (899–902). [6800]. 42002

—————— und **Hausser**, W. Ueber die aktinodielektrische Wirkung bei den Erdalkaliphosphoren; nach Versuchen von Rob. **Oeder**. Ann. Physik Leipzig (4. Folge) **34** 1911 (445–454). [6850 4230]. 42003

—————— v. Lénard, P.

Ramsay, Sir William. Les mesures de quantités infinitésimales de matières. J. phys. Paris (sér. 5) **1** 1911 (429–442 av. fig.). [0810]. 42004

—————— Action du niton (émanation du radium) sur les sels de thorium. Paris C. R. Acad. sci. **153** 1911 (373–374). [4275]. 42005

—————— v. Gray, R. W.

Ramsey, R[olla] R[oy]. Polarization of cadmium cells. Indianapolis Ind. Proc. Acad. Sci. **1909** 1910 (229–231 with table). [5610]. 42006

Ramstedt, Eva. Sur la solubilité de l'émanation du radium dans les liquides organiques. Radium Paris **8** 1911 (253–256). [4275]. 42007

Randall, H[arrison] M[cAllister]. Some infra-red spectra. Astroph. J. Chicago Ill. **34** 1911 (1–20 with text fig. tables). [4205 3435 4207]. 42008

—————— Residual rays of selenite. Astroph. J. Chicago Ill. **34** 1911 (308–311 with fig.). [3840]. 42009

Randhagen, Richard. Gleichstrommessungen der Praxis . . . Instrumente . . . . Berlin (H. Meusser). 1911 (VIII + 183). 22 cm. Geb. 6 M. [6010]. 42010

Rane, Albert v. Bierry, H.

Rankine, A. O. On the relation between viscosity and atomic weight for the inert of gases; with its applica-

tion to the case of radium emanation.
Phil. Mag. London (Ser. 6) **21** 1911
(45–53). [0325]. 42011

Raoult, F. r. Hanriot, H.

Raphael, F. Charles. Isolationsmessungen und Felderbestimmungen
an elektrischen Starkstromleitungen.
Autoris. deutsche Bearb. von Richard
Apt. 2., verb. Aufl. Berlin (J. Springer)
1911 (VII + 192). 21 cm. Geb. 6 M.
[5770]. 42012

Raps, A. Über automatische Telephonie. Elektrot. Zs. Berlin **32** 1911
(433–436 466–469 493–495). [6485].
42013

Rasch, G. Umwandlung von Dreiin Zweiphasenstrom. Elektrot. Zs.
Berlin **32** 1911 (681–684 712–715).
[6047]. 42014

———— Über die Anwendung des
Görgesschen Diagrammes auf Teillochwicklungen. Elektrot. Zs. Berlin **33**
1912 (7–11 36–39). [6045]. 42015

Raus, František. Změna galvanického odporu rtuti v magnetickém poli.
[Galvanische Widerstandsänderung des
Quecksilbers in Magnetfelde.] Prag
Rozpr. České Ak. Frant. Jos. 19 **1910**
No. 57 (12 mit 3 Taf.). [5660 6455].
42016

———— Experimentální příspěvek
k methodice měření Hallova efektu;
jeho asymetrie. methoda Koláčkova s
modifikací Kučerovou. [Experimentalbeitrag zur Methodik der Messung des
Halleffekts; seine Assymmetrie.
Methode von Koláček mit der Modifikation von Kučera.] Prag Rozpr.
České Ak. Frant. Jos. 20 **1911** No. 29
(16). [6455]. 42017

Raveau, C. Calcul de la différence
de marche introduite par une lame
mince isotrope. J. phys. Paris (sér. 5)
1 1911 (127–128 av. fig.). [3610].
42018

Ravelli, Agostino. L'energia del
moto ondoso del mare e la sua utilizzazione a scopo industriale. Venezia
Ateneo Veneto 33 1. sem. 1910 (149–
176). [0855]. 42019

Rayet, G. et Courty, F. Rapport sur
les observations faites à Burgos (Espagne) à l'occasion de l'éclipse totale
de Soleil du 29 30 août 19 5. Ann.
bur. longit Paris 8 1911 (II. 1 à II. 21).
[4205]. 42020

Rayleigh. On the sensibility of the
eye to variations of wave-length in the
yellow region of the spectrum. London
Proc. R. Soc. (Ser. A) **84** 1911 (464–
468). [4450]. 42021

———— Breath figures. Nature
London 86 1911 (416–417). [1800].
42022

———— Note on Bessel's functions
as applied to the vibrations of a circular
membrane. Phil. Mag. London (Ser. 6)
21 1911 (53–58). [9120]. 42023

———— Aberration in a dispersive
medium. Phil. Mag. London (Ser. 6)
22 1911 (130–133). [3420 0420].
42024

———— On the calculation of
Chladni's figures for a square plate.
Phil. Mag. London (Ser. 6) **22** 1711
(225–229). [9120]. 42025

———— Problems in the conduction of heat. Phil. Mag. London (Ser.
6) 22 1911 (381–395). [2010 2000].
42026

———— On the general problem
of photographic reproduction with
suggestions for enhancing gradation
originally invisible. Phil. Mag. London
(Ser. 6) 22 1911 (734–739). [3085].
42027

———— On the propagation of
waves through a stratified medium,
with special reference to the question
of reflexion. London Proc. R. Soc.
(Ser. A) 86 1912 (207–226). [3820].
42028

———— On departures from
Fresnel's laws of reflexion. Phil. Mag.
London (Ser. 6) 23 1912 (431–438).
[3820]. 42029

Rayner, E. H. On an optical lever
of high power suitable for the determinations of small thicknesses and
displacements. London Proc. Physic.
Soc. 23 1911 (198–200). [3090]. 42030

Raymond, G. Résultats de mesures
photoélectriques faites à Antibes pendant l'année 1911. Paris C. R. Acad.
sci. 154 1912 (45–48). [6850]. 42031

Rebenstorff, H. Einfachste Ausführung von Versuchen mit Kohlensäure. Zs. physik. Unterr. Berlin **24**
1911 (230–231). [0050]. 42032

———— Schülerversuch über den
thermischen Ausdehnungskoeffizienten
von Gasen. Zs. physik. Unterr. Berlin
25 1912 (34–36). [0050]. 42033

Rebenstorff, H. Physikalisches Experimentierbuch. II. (Schluss-) Tl. Anleitung zum selbständigen Experimentieren . . . (Bastian Schmids naturwissenschaftliche Schülerbibliothek. 2.) Leipzig u. Berlin (B. G. Teubner) 1912 (VI + 178). 20 cm. Geb. 3 M. [0050]. 42034

Reboro, Gino. Ricerche sperimentali sugli isolatori di vetro e di porcellana. Atti Ass. elettrotecn. Milano **14** 1910 (665–712); Mon. tecn. Milano **16** 1910 (350–352); Elettricità Milano **36** 1911 (108–110 142–144 158–159 173–176 189–192). [5770]. 42035

———— La temperatura delle macchine elettriche rilevata col termometro a mercurio. Atti Ass. elettrotecn. Milano **15** 1911 (487–499); [sunto] Mon. tecn. Milano **17** 1911 (359). [6400 6440]. 42036

———— Il rotore delle macchine a corrente continua. Elettricità Milano **37** 1911 (11–16 24–28). [6060]. 42037

———— Raffreddamento ed isolamento dei trasformatori. Elettricità Milano **37** 1911 (55–59 72–75). [5620]. 42038

Reboul, G. Impressions photographiques sur cuivre. Paris C. R. Acad. sci. **153** 1911 (1215–1216). [4225]. 42039

———— Conductibilité accompagnant des réactions chimiques. Paris C. R. Acad. sci. **152** 1911 (1660–1662). [6805 5685]. 42040

———— Conductibilité électrique et réactions chimiques. Radium Paris **8** 1911 (376–381 av. fig.). [6805 5685]. 42041

———— et **Grégoire de Bollemont,** E. Sur l'émission des charges positives par les métaux chauffés. Radium Paris **8** 1911 (406–411 av. fig.). [6845]. 42042

———— ———— Transport de particules métalliques sous l'action de la chaleur. Paris C. R. Acad. sci. **153** 1911 (628–630); **152** 1911 (758–760). [2040]. 42043

Recoura, A. et **Colin,** G. Action des rayons émis par la lampe à quartz à vapeurs de mercure sur la colorabilité des bacilles acido-résistants. Paris C. R. Acad. sci. **153** 1911 (1253–1256). [4225]. 42045

[**Reden** v.] Реденъ. Ртутный воздушный насосъ п вакууметръ.

[Переводъ.] [Quecksilberluftpumpe und Vacuummeter.] [Übers.] Vopr. fiziki St. Peterburg **3** 1909 (188–191). [6090]. 42046

Reelers, J[ohan] C[hristiaan] v. Kohnstamm, Ph.

Regener, Erich. Ueber Ladungsbestimmungen an Nebelteilchen. (Zur Frage nach der Grösse des elektrischen Elementarquantums.) Physik. Zs. Leipzig **12** 1911 (135–141). [6805 4960]. 42047

———— Ueber die Zerfallskonstante des Poloniums. Berlin Verh. D. physik. Ges. **13** 1911 (1027–1033). [4275]. 42048

———— Über den Einfluss der Kondensatorform auf den Verlauf der α-Strahlen-Sättigungsstromkurven. Berlin Verh. D. physik. Ges. **12** 1911 (1065–1073). [6845]. 42049

———— Die Strahlen der radioaktiven Substanzen I. II. Radium Leipzig **1** 1911 (39–45 71–78 97–104). [4275 6845]. 42050

———— Über die Radioaktivität. Intern. Monatschr. Wiss. Berlin **6** 1912 (511–526 639–650). [4275]. 42051

Rehfisch, Eugen. Einführung in die Lehre vom Elektrokardiogramm. Berliner Klinik H. **269** 1910 (1–25). [5900]. 42052

Reich, M[ax]. Über den dämpfenden Einfluss der Erde auf Antennenschwingungen. Jahrb. drahtlos. Telegr. Leipzig **5** 1911 (176–188); **5** 1912 (253–261). [6615]. 42053

Reichard, C. Ueber geologische Zeitbestimmung und das Radium als Zeitmesser für das Alter der Erde. Pharm. Zentralhalle, Dresden **52** 1911 (95–100). [4275]. 42054

Reiche, Fritz. Die Berechnung einer einfachen Brechungserscheinung mittels des Huygensschen Prinzips. Ann. Physik Leipzig (4. Folge) **34** 1911 (177–181). [6620]. 42055

———— Die Beugung des Lichtes an einem ebenen, rechteckigen Keil von unendlicher Leitfähigkeit. Ann. Physik Leipzig (4. Folge) **37** 1912 (131–156). [3620 6627]. 42056

———— v. Lummer, O.; Schaefer, C.

Reichenheim, Otto *r*. Gehrcke, E.

Reichert, C[arl]. [Apparate zur Dunkelfeldbeleuchtung.] Wien Verh. Zool.Bot. Ges. 61 1911 ((60)–(69)). [3482]. 42057

Reichert, Karl. Das Fluoreszenzmikroskop. Physik. Zs. Leipzig 12 1911 (1010–1011). [3082]. 42058

Reichinstein, D. Die Belastungsfähigkeit der galvanischen Elemente. I. Zs. Elektroch. Halle 17 1911 (85–90). [5610]. 42059

———— Die chemische Polarisation der umkehrbaren elektrolytischen Elektrode. Zs. Elektroch. Halle 17 1911 (699–719). [5610 6230]. 42060

Reiffer, Alberto. A proposito di un dispositivo di carica per batterie di accumulatori. Elettricista Roma (Ser. 2) 10 1911 (239–240). [5620]. 42061

Reiger, R. Ueber die Ausbreitung scherender Deformationen in Gasen. Ann. Physik Leipzig (4. Folge) 34 1911 (258–276). [0325]. 42062

———— Über die unselbständige Strömung bei der Ionisation durch die leuchtende Entladung. (Vorl. Mitt.) Berlin Verh. D. physik. Ges. 13 1911 (283–306). [6849]. 42063

Reimerdes, Ernst *r*. Domke, J.

Rein, H. Der radiotelegraphische Gleichstrom-Tonsender. [Nebst Erwiderung von E. Nesper und C. Lorenz.] Physik. Zs. Leipzig 12 1911 (70–71); Diss. Darmstadt. Langensalza (Druck v. H. Beyer & S.) 1912 (63). 23 cm. [6615 6843]. 42064

Reinders, W[illem]. Over de constitutie der photohaloïden. [Sur la constitution des photo-haloïdes.] Amsterdam Chem. Weekbl. 8 1911 (316–321); [Die Konstitution der Photohaloïden. III.] *op. cit.* 9 1912 (242–247). [4225]. 42065

Reinganum, Max. Streuung und photographische Wirkung der *α*-Strahlen. Berlin Verh. D. physik. Ges. 13 1911 (848–849); Physik Zs. Leipzig 12 1911 (1076–1077); Heidelberg SitzBer. Ak. Wiss. math.-natw. Kl. 1911 Abh. 10 (22); 1. II. Physik. Zs. Leipzig 12 1911 (575–580 666–671). Über die Änderung der inneren Reibung der Gase der Argongruppe mit der Temperatur. Zur Abhandlung von A. O. Rankine. Physik. Zs. Leipzig

12 1911 (779–780). [4275 5675 5685 0325]. 42066

Reinkober, Otto. Ueber Absorption und Reflexion ultraroter Strahlen durch Quarz, Turmalin und Diamant. Ann. Physik Leipzig (4. Folge) 34 1911 (343–372). [3810 3855]. 42070

Reinstein, E. Untersuchung der Schwingungen gleichförmig gespannter elliptisch begrenzter Membranen. Ann. Physik Leipzig (4. Folge) 35 1911 (109–144 mit 2 Taf.). [9120]. 42071

———— Untersuchungen über die Transversalschwingungen der gleichförmig gespannten elliptisch oder kreisförmig begrenzten Vollmembran und Kreismembran sowie von Vollkreis- und Kreisringmembran mit nach speziellen Gesetzen variierter ungleichförmiger Spannung. Diss. Göttingen. Leipzig (J. A. Barth) 1911 (134 mit 10 Taf.). 23 cm. [9120 9100]. 42072

Reis, Alfred. Ueber ammoniakund stickoxydhaltige Flammen. Zs. physik. Chem. Leipzig 76 1911 (560–568). [4202 4205]. 42073

Reiss, Emil. Die elektrische Entartungsreaktion. Klinische und experimentelle Studien über ihre Theorie. Berlin (J. Springer) 1911 (VII + 119). 22 cm. 4.80 M. [5900]. 42074

Reithoffer, Max. Neuerungen in der drahtlosen Telegraphie. Wien Schr. Ver. Verbr. Natw. Kenntn. 50 1909–10 [1910] (181–196). [6615]. 42075

———— Ein elektrisches Zentraluhrensystem für Wien. Wien Schr. Ver. Verbr. Naturw. Kenntn. 51 1910–11 [1911] (439–456). [0809]. 42076

Reko, Victor A. Tonempfindliche Kunststoffe. [Sprechmaschinen.] Kunststoffe München 1 1911 (5–7 22–25) [9420]. 42077

———— Klanggefässe. Phon. Zs. Leipzig 12 1911 (127–129). [9410]. 42078

———— Die Geschichte von der doppelt wirkenden Schalldose. Phon. Zs. Berlin 12 1911 (383–386 401–402). [9420]. 42079

———— Neue Dokumente zur Geschichte der Sprechmaschinen. Phon. Zs. Berlin 12 1911 (415–417). [9420]. 42080

———— Akustische Phänomene. Phon. Zs. Berlin 12 1911 (893–894 919 921). [9200]. 42081

Remele, A. Neue Beobachtungen über dunkle Strahlungen [des Borstickstoffs.] Berlin Verh. D. physik. Ges. **13** 1911 (771–777); Physik. Zs. Leipzig **12** 1911 (969–972). [4270]. 42082

Renan, Henri. Résultats de la discussion des observations faites par MM. Lancelin et Tsatsopoulos pour déterminer par la télégraphie sans fil la différence de longitude entre Paris et Bizerte. Paris C. R. Acad. sci. **153** 1911 (1211–1214). [6615]. 42083

Renaux, J. Observations de l'éclipse de Soleil du 30 août 1905. Rapport de la Mission d'Alger. Ann. bur. longit. Paris **8** 1911 (C. 1 à C. 37 av. pl.). [4205]. 42084

Rengade, E. Sur la forme théorique des courbes de refroidissement dans les mélanges binaires. J. Chim. Phys. Genève **8** 1910 (42–56). [2457]. 42085

——— v. Damour, E.

Reppert, Rudolf. Über die Ursache der Schwerkraft. München (G. Müller) 1911 (29). 25 cm. 1 M. [0700]. 42086

Réthy, Moritz. Über die Anstrengungslinien der Metalle. Math.-natw. Ber. Ungarn Leipzig **27** (1909) 1911 (22–44). [9059]. 42087

Reuss, Fritz v. Stobbe, H.

Revello, E. I motori a scoppio " Mietz-Weiss." Riv. ing. san. Torino **6** 1910 (197–201). [2490]. 42088

Revessi, Giuseppe. Le correnti tramviarie di ritorno. Roma Ann. Soc. ing. **26** 1911 (341–347). [6200]. 42089

Révész, Géza. Ueber eine neue Methode der heterochromen Photometrie. (Bestimmung der Helligkeitswerte der Farben durch Kontrast: Kontrastmethode.) Ber. Kongr. exp. Psych. Leipzig **4** 1911 (217–219). [3010 4450]. 42090

Rey, J. v. Blondel, A.

Rezelman, J. The reactance of asynchronous motors. Elect. London **66** 1911 (857–861). [6070]. 42091

——— The reactance of asynchronous motors with squirrel-cage rotors. Elect. London **67** 1911 (291–293). [6070]. 42092

——— The determination of synchronous and asynchronous reactance. Elect. London **67** 1911 (961–963 1000–1003). [6045]. 42093

Ribot, C. v. Bouasse, H.

Riccò, A. Anomalie de la pesanteur et du champ magnétique terrestre en Calabre et en Sicile, mises en rapport avec la constitution du sol. Ciel et Terre Bruxelles 1908 (157 205–212). [5490]. 42094

——— Risultati delle osservazioni pireliometriche eseguite a varie altezze sull' Etna. Catania Bull. Acc. Gioenia (Ser. 2) **8** 1909 (18–20). [3260]. 42095

——— Risultati recenti degli studi solari. [Sunto.] Riv. fis. mat. sc. nat. Pavia **24** 1911 (438–455). [3060]. 42096

Richards, Theodore William] and **Kelley,** George Leslie. The transition temperatures of sodium chromate as convenient fixed points in thermometry. Boston Proc. Amer. Acad. Arts Sci. **47** 1911 (169–188). [1260]. 42097

——— and **Mathews,** J[oseph] Howard. A method for determining heat of evaporation as applied to water. Boston Proc. Amer. Acad. Arts Sci. **46** 1911 (509–538 with fig.). [1680]. 42098

Richardson, O[wen] W[illiams]. The theory of dispersion and the residual rays. [Abstract.] Physic. Rev. Ithaca N. Y. **32** 1911 (619–620). [3820]. 42099

——— and **Cooke,** H. L. The heat liberated during the absorption of electrons by different metals. Phil. Mag. London (Ser. 6) **21** 1911 (404–410). [6805]. 42100

Richarz, F[ranz]. Anwendung der Elektronentheorie auf den Magnetismus. Marburg SitzBer. Ges. Natw. **1910** 1911 (67–71). [5480]. 42101

——— Friedrich Kohlrausch, † 17. Januar. Marburg SitzBer. Ges. Natw. **1910** 1911 (13–16). [0010]. 42102

——— Ueber den Magnetismus von Legierungen. Physik. Zs. Leipzig **12** 1911 (151–158). [5466]. 42103

Richter, M. M. Über Fluorescenz in der p-Benzochinon-Reihe. Berlin Ber. D. chem. Ges. **44** 1911 (3469–3473). [4220]. 42104

Richter, Rudolf. Zur Funkenunterdrückung bei Wechselstrom-Kommu-

tatormotoren. Elektr. Zs. Berlin 32
1911 (1258–1262 1291–1295). [6070].
42105

Ridolfi, Carlo. Sulla collazione delle
lauree in Fisica. Replica al Memoriale
della R. Università di Pisa. Firenze
(A. Meozzi) 1910 (13). 27 cm. [0050].
42106

Riebesell, P. Das Weltbild der
modernen Physik. [Relativitätsprinzip :
alte und neue Mechanik ; die neue
Optik u. Elektrodynamik.] Monatshefte natw. Unterr. Leipzig 4 1911
(536–543). [4940]. 42107

Riecke, E. Le concezioni moderne
sulla natura dello stato metallico.
[Sunto.] Riv. fis. mat. sc. nat. Pavia 20
1909 (441–442). [0500]. 42108

————— Zur Theorie des Interferenzversuches von Michelson. Göttingen Nachr. Ges. Wiss. math.-phys.
Kl. 1911 (271–277). [3420 3610].
42109

————— Zur Erniedrigung des
Schmelzpunktes durch einseitigen Zug
oder Druck. Centralbl. Min. Sutttgart
1912 (97–104). [1810]. 42110

————— Lehrbuch der Physik zu
eigenem Studium und zum Gebrauche
bei Vorlesungen. Bd 1. Mechanik.
Molekularerscheinungen und Akustik.
Optik. 5., verb. u. verm. Aufl. Leipzig
(Veit & Co.) 1912 (XVI + 600). 24 cm.
12 M. [0030]. 42111

Riegger, Hans. Über gekoppelte
Kondensatorkreise bei sehr kurzer
Funkenstrecke. Jahrb. drahtlos.
Telegr. Leipzig 5 1911 (35–59) ; Diss.
Strassburg. Leipzig (J. A. Barth) 1911
(36). 23 cm. [6820]. 42112

Rieke, Reinhold. Die Schmelzpunkte
der Segerkegel 022 bis 15. Keram.
Rdsch. Berlin 19 1911 (549–552 561–
564) ; TonindZtg Berlin 35 1911 (1751–
1757). [1240]. 42113

Riemann, Hugo. Tonhöhenbewusstsein und Intervallurteil. Zs. intern.
Musikges. Leipzig 13 1912 (269–272).
[9150]. 42113A

Riemann, Ludwig. Das Wesen des
Klavierklanges und seine Beziehungen
zum Anschlag. Eine akustisch-
ästhetische Untersuchung . . . Leipzig
(Breitkopf & Härtel) 1911 (VIII +
279). 24 cm. 6 M. [9410]. 42114

Ries, Chr. Der Spannungseffekt am
Selen und Antimonit. Ann. Physik
Leipzig (4. Folge) 36 1911 (1055–1065).
[5660]. 42115

————— Die Ursache der Lichtempfindlichkeit des Selens. I. Physik.
Zs. Leipzig 12 1911 (480–490 522–533) ;
Umschau Frankfurt a. M. 15 1911
(897–898). [5660 6850]. 42116

Riesenfeld, E. H. Stille elektrische
Entladungen in Gasen bei Atmosphärendruck. Zs. Electroch. Halle 17 1911
(725–731). [6820]. 42117

————— und Mau, W. Stille
elektrische Entladungen in Gasen bei
Atmosphärendruck. I. Heidelberg
SitzBer. Ak. Wiss. math.-natw. Kl.
1911 Abh. 19 (17). [6820]. 42118

Riéty, L. Force électromotrice
produite par l'écoulement d'une solution de sulfate de cuivre dans un tube
capillaire. Paris C. R. Acad. sci. 152
1911 (1375–1377). [5240] 4235].
42119

Righi, A. Nouvelles recherches sur
le potentiel de décharge dans le champ
magnétique. Radium Paris 8 1911 (135–
139 196–204 373–375 av. fig.). [6840].
42121

————— De l'influence du champ
magnétique sur l'intensité du courant
dans l'air raréfié. Radium Paris 8
1911 (415–416 av. fig.). [6840]. 42122

Righi, Aldo. Lampada ad arco
trifase a quattro carboni. Atti Ass.
elettrotecn. Milano 14 1910 (253–258) ;
Politecn. Milano 58 1910 (539–542).
[6830 6080]. 42123

Righi, Augusto. Sulla traiettoria
percorsa da un elettrone attorno ad
un ione nel campo magnetico. Bologna
Mem. Acc. sc. (Ser. 6) 7 1910 (3–31).
[4960]. 42124

————— Ricerche sperimentali sui
raggi magnetici. Bologna Mem. Acc.
sc. (Ser. 6) 6 1909 (89–107 con 1 tav.) ;
[trad. sunto] Riv. fis. mat. sc. nat.
Pavia 22 1910 (63–71). [4960 6845].
42125

————— Comete ed elettroni. Bologna Mem. Acc. Sc. (Ser. 6) 7 1910
(Supplemento 10–31) ; Riv. fis. mat.
sc. nat. Pavia 24 1911 (264–269) ;
[Attualità scientifiche. 13.] Bologna
(N. Zanichelli) 1910 (63). 28 cm.;
Leipzig (Akademische Verlagsgesellschaft) 1911 (64). 22 cm. 2,40 M.
[4960 4215]. 42126

Righi, Augusto. Sulla ionizzazione dell'aria entro un tubo di scarica posto nel campo magnetico. Bologna Rend. Acc. sc. (N. Ser.) **14** 1910 (49–58). [6805]. 42127

—————— Sul potenziale necessario a provocare la scarica in un gas posto nel campo magnetico. Bologna Rend. Acc. sc. (N. Ser.) **14** 1910 (151–177). [6850]. 42128

—————— Nuove ricerche sul potenziale di scarica nel campo magnetico. Nuovo Cimento Pisa (Ser. 6) **2** 1911 (5–38); (Übers.) Physik. Zs. Leipzig **12** 1911 (424–439). [6840 6845 6455]. 42130

—————— Sur l'action ionisante probable du champ magnétique. Paris C. R. Acad. sci. **152** 1911 (250–252). [5685]. 42131

—————— Due nuove esperienze sui raggi magnetici. Roma Rend. Acc. Lincei (Ser. 5) **20** 2. sem. 1911 (163–167); (Übers.) Physik. Zs. Leipzig **12** 1911 (835–837). [4960 6845]. 42135

—————— Dell' influenza del campo magnetico sull' intensità di corrente nell' aria rarefatta. Roma Rend. Acc. Lincei (Ser. 5) **20** 2. sem. 1911 (167–170); (Übers.) Physik. Zs. Leipzig **12** 1911 (833–835). [5685 6845]. 42136

—————— Über die Funkenentladung in einem verdünnten Gase und ihre Umwandlung in ein Bündel magnetischer Strahlen. (Sulla scarica a scintilla in un gas rarefatto e sulla sua trasformazione in un fascio di raggi magnetici. Vortrag . . . (Übers.) Physik. Zs. Leipzig **13** 1912 (65–73). [6840]. 42137

—————— La materia radiante ed i raggi magnetici. Bologna (N. Zanichelli) 1909 (VI + 308 con 11 tav.). 23 cm.; Ed. 2. 1910 (VI + 344 con 10 tav.). 22 cm. [0030 4900 6840 2990]. 42138

Righini, Carlo. Metodo per calcolare i reostati d'avviamento dei motori a corrente continua. Industria Milano **24** 1910 (359–361). [6070]. 42141

Rihl, Wilhelm. Über die Schallintensität des tönenden Lichtbogens. Ann. Physik Leipzig (4. Folge) **36** 1911 (647–680). [6830]. 42142

Rimbach, E[berhard] und **Volk,** H. Polarimetrische Aviditätsbestimmun-

(c–1388)

gen an schwachen Basen in nichtwässeriger Lösung. Zs. physik. Chem. Leipzig **77** 1911 (385–410). [4050]. 42143

Rinkel, R. Radiotelegraphische Empfangsversuche im Freiballon. [Nebst] Erwiderung von **Mosler.** Elektrot. Zs. Berlin **33** 1912 (24). [6615]. 42144

Rinne, F[ritz] und **Kolb,** R. Optisches zur Modifikationsänderung von α- in β-Quarz sowie von α- in β-Leucit. N. Jahrb. Min. Stuttgart **1910** II [1911] (138–158). [3822 3830]. 42145

Risco, Martínéz. Die Asymmetrie der Zeeman-schen Tripletts. (Übers.) Physik. Zs. Leipzig **13** 1912 (137–142 mit 1 Taf.). [4208]. 42146

Ritter, F. Eine Einrichtung zum Messen von Knallstärken. Zs. Schiesswesen München **6** 1911 (341–344). [9320]. 42147

Ritzel, A. r. Mare, R.

Rivett, A. C. D. Neutral salt action as exhibited in the freezing points of mixtures in aqueous solution. Stockholm Medd. Vet.-Ak. Nobelinst. **2** No. 9 1911 (32 with 5 figs.). [1920]. 42148

Rixon, J. W. Ein einfacher Regulierwiderstand für das Laboratorium. Zs. Elektroch. Halle **17** 1911 (374). [6020]. 42149

Rizzo, G. L'Esposizione internazionale di Bruxelles. Elettricista Roma (Ser. 2) **9** 1910 (297–303 331–335). [6000]. 42150

Robertson, D. Rotor hysteresis in polyphase induction motors. Elect. London **68** 1911 (12–14). [6070]. 42151

Robin, Félix. Sur la hauteur du son dans les alliages et ses variations en fonction de la température. Paris C. R. Acad. sci. **153** 1911 (665–668). [9110]. 42152

Robinson, James. Electric dust figures. Phil. Mag. London (Ser. 6) **21** 1911 (268–270); Physik. Zs. Leipzig **12** 1911 (439–440 mit 1 Taf.). [6820 5200 9320]. 42153

—————— Bericht über die Versammlung der British Association for the Advancement of Science zu Portsmouth, 30. Aug. bis 6. Sept. 1911. (Übers.) Physik. Zs. Leipzig **12** 1911 (1179–1191). [0020]. 42155

r

Roe, E. D. *junr.* and **Graham, W. P.**
Suggestions for a new theory of
comets. [Elektronentheorie.] Astr.
Nachr. Kiel **187** 1911 (17–22). [4960].
42156

Roeder, Hans. Ist die magnetische
Nachwirkung auf Selbstinduktion im
Magnetisierungskreise zurückzuführen ?
Diss. Halle a. S. (Druck v. H. John)
1911 (50 mit Taf.). 22 cm. [6440
5430]. 42157

Röhrs, Fritz. Molekularrefraktion,
Molekularvolumen und Dissoziation
in nichtwässerigen Lösungsmitteln. Ann.
Physik Leipzig (4. Folge) **37** 1912 (289–
329). [3020 3860]. 42158

Ronnholm, Albin. Om strömtätheten
och värmentveeklingen på katoden i
förtunnade gaser vid elektriska urladd-
ningar. [Über die Stromdichte und
Wärmeentwicklung an der Kathode in
verdünnten Gasen bei elektrischen
Entladungen.] Akad. afh. Uppsala
1911 (84). [6840]. 42159

Roger, E. v. Lioret, H., Paillat, J.

Rogowski, W. Über die Gegen- und
Querwindungen eines Drehstromgenerators. Elektrot. Zs. Berlin **32** 1911
(290–292). [6060]. 42160

———— *v.* Epstein, T., Gumlich.
E., Kummer, W., Niethammer, F.,
Sumec.

Rohland, [Paul]. Schopenhauer als
Chemiker und Physiker. Arch. Gesch.
Natw. Leipzig **3** 1911 (263–268).
[0010]. 42161

Rohmann, Hermann. Messung von
Kapazitätsänderungen mit schnellen
Schwingungen, angewandt auf die
Vergleichung der Dielektrizitätskon-
stanten von Gasen. Ann. Physik
Leipzig (4. Folge) **34** 1911 (979–1002).
[5740 5252]. 42162

———— Über Stosserregung bei
zahlreichen Partialentladungen. Physik. Zs. Leipzig **12** 1911 (649–652).
[6820]. 42163

———— Ein Modell zum Rela-
tivitätsprinzip. Physik. Zs. Leipzig **12**
1911 (1227–1230). [0050]. 42164

Rohr, M. von. Professor Allvar
Gullstrand als Optiker. Tekn. Tidskr.
Stockholm **40** 1910 Veckouppl. (9–13
mit Portr.). [0010]. 42165

———— Das Biotar, ein Projektionssystem mit besonders grosser

Öffnung und ebenem Felde. Zs. Instrumentenk. Berlin **31** 1911 (265–270).
[3090 0050]. 42166

Rohr, M. von. Über die Würdigung
des Augendrehpunktes und seine Berücksichtigung in der konstruktiven Optik.
Zs. Instrumentenk. Berlin **31** 1911
(380–386). [3060 4420 4400]. 42167

———— Über Verbesserungen an
den optischen Systemen der Cystoskope. Zs. Urol. Berlin **5** 1911 (881–
919). [3060]. 42168

———— Die optischen Instrumente. 2., verm. und verb. Aufl. (Aus
Natur und Geisteswelt. Bd **88.**)
Leipzig (B. G. Teubner) 1911 (VI +
140). 18 cm. 1,25 M. [3000]. 42169

Roiti, Antonio. Conferenza internazionale per le unità e i campioni
elettrici, tenuta a Londra nell' ottobre
1908. Roma (G. Bertero) 1909 (26).
26 cm. [5000]. 42170

Rolla, Luigi. Su la diffusione degli
elettroliti nei colloidi. Roma Rend.
Acc. Lincei (Ser. 5) **20** 2. sem. 1911
(47–51). [0320]. 42172

———— Su la dissociazione dei
sali idrati. Roma Rend. Acc. Lincei
(Ser. 5) **20** 1. sem. 1911 (112–119).
[6250]. 42173

Romberg, Gisbert *Freiherr* von.
Praktische Winke für die Ausführung
von Hygroskopizitätsbestimmungen
nach Rodewald-Mitscherlich. Landw.
Versuchsstat. Berlin **75** 1911 (483–484).
[1890]. 42174

Ronceray, P. Recherches sur
l'écoulement dans les tubes capillaires.
Ann. chim. phys. Paris (sér. 8) **22** 1910
(107–125). [0300]. 42175

Roop, W. P. Eine neue Methode für
Untersuchungen über die magnetische
Permeabilität der Gase. Physik. Zs.
Leipzig **12** 1911 (48–56). [5440 5435].
42176

———— Die magnetischen Eigenschaften der Flammen. Physik. Zs.
Leipzig **12** 1911 (56). [5440]. 42177

Roozeboom, H. W. Bakhuis. Die
heterogenen Gleichgewichte vom Standpunkte der Phasenlehre. H. 3. Die
ternären Gleichgewichte. Tl. 1.
Systeme mit nur einer Flüssigkeit ohne
Mischkristalle und ohne Dampf von
F. A. H. **Schreinemakers.** (Deutsch
von J. J. B. **Deuss.**) Braunschweig

(F. Vieweg & S.) 1911 (XII + 315). 23 cm. 10 M. [1887]. 42178

Rosa, E. B. La candela internazionale. Atti Ass. elettrotecn. Milano 15 1911 (1034-1036). [3010]. 42179

———— and Crittenden, E. C. The pentane lamp as a primary light standard. [Abstract.] Physic. Rev. Ithaca N.Y. 32 1911 (241-242). [3010]. 42180

———— Dorsey, N. E. and Miller, J. M. The Bureau of Standards' current balances. [Abstract.] Physic. Rev. Ithaca N.Y. 32 1911 (599-601). [6010 5610]. 42181

Roschansky, D. Über den Einfluss des Funkens auf die oszillatorische Kondensatorentladung. Ann. Physik Leipzig (4. Folge) 36 1911 (281-307 mit 2 Taf.). [6820]. 42182

Rosenberg, E. Hunting of direct current interpole motors. Elect. London 67 1911 (670-673). [6070]. 42183

———— Elektrische Starkstromtechnik. Eine leichtfassl. Darstellung. 3. verm. Aufl. Leipzig (O. Leiner) 1911 (VIII + 293). 21 cm. 6,50 M. [6000]. 42184

Rosenberg, Karl. Experimentierbuch für den Unterricht in der Naturlehre. In zwei Bänden. Zweite . . . Aufl. Zweiter Band. Wien (Hölder) 1910 (X + 550). 25 cm. [0050]. 42185

Rosenhain, Walter and Archbutt. Sydney L. The constitution of the alloys of aluminium and zinc. London Phil. Trans. R. Soc. 211 1911 (315-343). [1810]. 42186

Rosenstiehl, A. Cohésion et pression osmotique. J. phys. Paris (sér. 5) 1 1911 (52-60). [0310]. 42187

———— Eau polymérisée et eau de cristallisation. J. phys. Paris (sér. 5) 1 1911 (288-294). [1430]. 42188

———— L'harmonie des couleurs réalisée par l'emploi des camaïeux complémentaires. Paris C. R. Acad. sci. 153 1911 (715-718). [4450]. 42189

———— Données historiques relatives à la force osmotique. Rectification de noms d'auteurs. Paris C. R. Acad. sci. 152 1911 (1305-1308). [0310 0010]. 42190

Rosický, Vojtěch. O vztahu mezi hustotou a svetelným lomem. [Ueber die Beziehung zwischen der Dichtigkeit und Lichtbrechung.] Prag Rozpr. České Ak. Frant. Jos. 1911 (8). [3822]. 42191

———— Die Brille als optisches Instrument. [In: Graefe-Saemisch Handbuch der gesamten Augenheilkunde. 2. neu bearb. Aufl. Anhang.] Leipzig (W. Engelmann) 1911 (IX + 169 mit 1 Taf.). 22 cm. 4 M. [4430]. 42192

Ross, Alexandre. Sur les propriétés singulières de certains alliages ternaires de cuivre. J. phys. Paris (sér. 5) 1 1911 (117-123). [5460]. 42193

———— and Gray, Robert C. On the magnetism of the copper-manganese-tin alloys under varying thermal treatment. Edinburgh Proc. R. Soc. 31 1910-1911 (85-99). [5460]. 42194

Rossander, C. A. Stato attuale e futuro sviluppo del riscaldamento elettrico. Atti Ass. elettrotecn. Milano 15 1911 (1027-1032); Elettricista Roma (Ser. 2) 10 1911 (311-314). [6090]. 42195

Rosselet, A. Les rayons ultra-violets. Rev. Suisse Méd. 1910 (369-372). [3040]. 42196

Rossem, A[driaan] van r. Böeseken, J.

Rossi, Andrea Guilio. Un metodo didattico per ricavare le due leggi fondamentali della propagazione ondulatoria. Nuovo Cimento Pisa (Ser. 6) 1 1911 (287-306). [0050]. 42197

———— Esperienze sul piano inclinato. Nuovo Cimento Pisa (Ser. 6) 1 1911 (335-347). [0800]. 42198

———— Il convertor. [Sunto.] Riv. maritt. Roma 1910 1. trim. (607-610). [6043]. 42199

Rossi, Gaetano. Variazione di resistenza del mercurio e delle amalgame di bismuto nel campo magnetico. Nuovo Cimento Pisa (Ser. 6) 2 1911 (337-348). [5660]. 42200

Rossi (De), Guglielmo. Lampade a filamento metallico e trasformatori. Atti Ass. elettrotecn. Milano 15 1911 (473-480). [6080]. 42201

Rossi, Guido. Contributo allo studio dell' influenza della temperatura sulle osservazioni polarimetriche. Roma (Tip. Un. ed.) 1909 (6). 24 cm. [4040]. 42202

(c-1388)

p 2

Rossi, Paolo. La doppia rifrazione accidentale nel caucciù studiata in rapporto al comportamento elastico. Napoli Rend. Soc. sc. (Ser. 3) **16** 1911 (125–134). [3835]. 42203

———— La doppia rifrazione accidentale e le azioni elastiche susseguenti nel caucciù. Napoli Rend. Soc. sc. (Ser. 3) **16** 1910 (142–151). [3835]. 42204

———— La doppia rifrazione accidentale delle gelatine studiata in rapporto al loro comportamento elastico. Napoli Rend. Soc. sc. (Ser. 3) **16** 1910 (181–192). [3835]. 42205

———— La doppia rifrazione accidentale del celluloide e del vetro studiata in rapporto al loro comportamento elastico. Napoli Rend. Soc. sc. (Ser. 3) **16** 1910 (206–215). [3835]. 42206

———— Osservazioni su taluni fenomeni di rilassamento. Napoli Rend. Soc. sc. (Ser. 3) **17** 1911 (207–212); Nuovo Cimento Pisa (Ser. 6) **2** 1911 (151–158). [0325]. 42207

———— Doppia rifrazione accidentale di talune sostanze studiate in rapporto al loro comportamento elastico. Atti Soc. ital. prog. sci. Roma **4** 1911 (743–745); Nuovo Cimento Pisa (Ser. 6) **1** 1911 (III–IV). [3835]. 42208

Rossi, R. The effect of pressure on the arc spectrum of vanadium. Astroph. J. Chicago Ill. **34** 1911 (21–25 with tables pl.). [4206 4208]. 42209

———— On the pressure displacement of spectral lines. Phil. Mag. London (Ser. 6) **21** 1911 (499–504); [trad.] Riv. fis. mat. sc. nat. Pavia **24** 1911 (455–456). [4206]. 42210

Rossi, V. Sopra uno speciale " Relais " telefonico. Elettricista Roma (Ser. 2) **10** 1911 (81–83). [6485]. 42211

Rossiter, A. L. r. Hambly, H. R.

Rotarski, Tadeusz. Cząsteczkowo-mechaniczna teorya cieczy różnokierunkowych, czyli t.zw. kryształów ciekłych. [Théorie moléculaire et cinétique des liquides acotropes ou des milieux nommés " cristaux liquides."] Chem. pols. Warszawa **11** 1911 (289–293 332–347). [0400]. 42212

Roth, W[alter] A. und **Eisenlohr,** F. Refraktometrisches Hilfsbuch. Mit Logarithmen. Leipzig (Veit & Comp.) 1911 (VIII + 146 27). 23 cm. Geb. 6 M. [3020 3800 0810]. 42213

Rothé, A. Sur la réception des radiotélégrammes météorologiques avec antennes réduites. Paris C. R. Acad. sci. **154** 1912 (193–196). [6615]. 42214

Rother, Franz. Der Elektrizitätsübergang bei sehr kleinen Kontaktabständen. Physik. Zs. Leipzig **12** 1911 (671–674). [6820 6810]. 42215

Rotinjanz, L. r. Magornow, N.

Rottgardt, Karl. Der Kathodenfall in Argon (Luft, Stickstoff, Wasserstoff) und das periodische System der Elementen. Ann. Physik Leipzig (4. Folge) **33** 1910 (1161–1194). [6840]. 42215A

———— Über Entstehung und Vermeidung von Lichtbögen bei Verwendung von Resonanztransformatoren. Physik. Zs. Leipzig **12** 1911 (652–657). [6820]. 42216

———— Über den Einfluss von Elektrodenmaterial und Medium der Funkenstrecke auf die Bildung von Lichtbögen bei Verwendung von Resonanztransformatoren. Physik. Zs. Leipzig **12** 1911 (1160–1162). [6820]. 42217

Roy, Louis. De la viscosité dans le mouvement des membranes flexibles. Paris C. R. Acad. sci. **153** 1911 (1132–1134). [9120]. 42218

———— De la viscosité dans le mouvement des fils flexibles. Paris C. R. Acad. sci. **152** 1911 (1228–1231). [9110]. 42219

———— Les équations générales des membranes flexibles. Paris C. R. Acad. sci. **154** 1912 (109–112). [9120]. 42220

———— Recherche sur les propriétés thermodynamiques des corps solides. Thèse. Paris (Gauthier-Villars) 1910 (69). 27 cm. [2460]. 42221

Royal-Dawson, W. G. The flow of thin liquid films. Nature London **86** 1911 (110). [0325]. 42222

Royds, T. The reflective power of lamp- and platinum-black. Phil. Mag. London (Ser. 6) **21** 1911 (166). [3855]. 42223

Rozzi, Norberto. Studi sul nucleo terrestre. Teramo (Tip. del Corriere) 1910 (62). 24 cm. [0700]. 42224

Rubens, H[einrich]. Über langwellige Reststrahlen des Kalkspats. Berlin Verh. D. physik. Ges. 13 1911 (102–110). [3855]. 42225

————— Bemerkung zu der Arbeit von H. Rubens und R. W. Wood. „Einfache Methode zur Isolierung sehr langwelliger Wärmestrahlung". Berlin Verh. D. physik. Ges. 13 1911 (179–180). [3855]. 42226

————— Ueber die Energieverteilung der von der Quarzquecksilberlampe ausgesandten langwelligen Strahlung. Berlin SitzBer. Ak. Wiss. 1911 (666–677). [4205]. 42227

————— und Baeyer, O. von. Ueber eine äusserst langwellige Strahlung des Quecksilberdampfs. Berlin SitzBer. Ak. Wiss. 1911 (339–345). [4202 3855 3435]. 42228

————— On extremely long waves emitted by the quartz mercury lamp. Phil. Mag. London (Ser. 6) 21 1911 (689–695); Radium Paris 153 1911 (139–142 av. fig.). [3855]. 42229

————— und Wartenberg, H. v. Absorption langwelliger Wärmestrahlen in einigen Gasen. Berlin Verh. D. physik. Ges. 13 1911 (796–804); Physik. Zs. Leipzig 12 1911 (1080–1084). [3855 4202]. 42230

————— und Wood, R. W. Einfache Anordnung zur Isolierung sehr langwelliger Wärmestrahlung. Berlin Verh. D. physik. Ges. 13 1911 (88–100). [3855]. 42231

————— Focal isolation of long heat-waves. Phil. Mag. London (Ser. 6) 21 1911 (249–261). [3435]. 42232

————— Isolement de rayons calorifiques de grande longueur d'onde à l'aide de lentilles de quartz. Radium Paris 8 1911 (44–51 av. fig.). [3855]. 42233

————— v. du Bois, H.

Rubien, Erich. Brechungsexponent für Natriumlicht und Dissoziationsgrad wässeriger Salzlösungen. Diss. Rostock (o. V.) 1911 (34). 23 cm. [3860 3020]. 42234

Rubner, Max. Die Kalorimetrie. [In: Handbuch d. physiologischen Methodik, hrsg. v. R. Tigerstedt. Bd 1, Abt. 3.] Leipzig (S. Hirzel) 1911 (150–228). [1610]. 42235

Rudel. Zur Bestimmung der Einstellungsträgheit von Thermometern. Met. Zs. Braunschweig 28 1911 (90–93). [1200]. 42236

Rudeloff, M. Die Bestimmung der Wärmeausdehnung von Zementbeton und anderen Baustoffen. Armiert. Beton Berlin 4 1911 (172–183 207–214). [1410]. 42237

Rudge, W. A. A constant temperature, porous plug experiment. Cambridge Proc. Phil. Soc. 16 1911 (48–54). [1450]. 42238

————— Observations on the surface tension of liquid sulphur. Cambridge Proc. Phil. Soc. 16 1911 (55–163). [0300]. 42239

————— Notes on the electrification of the air near the Zambesi falls. Phil. Mag. London (Ser. 6) 21 1911 (611–615). [5270]. 42240

Rudolfi, E. Uebersicht über die neueren Ansichten über die Radioaktivität. Natw. Wochenschr. Jena 26 1911 (321–327). [4275]. 42241

Rudolph, H. Messeinrichtung für Gleich- und Wechselstrom mit grossem Messbereich und Schutz gegen Überlastung des empfindlichen Galvanometers. Elektrot. Zs. Berlin 32 1911 (1055–1056). [0050 6010]. 42242

————— Messeinrichtung für Gleich- und Wechselströme. Zs. physik. Unterr. Berlin 24 1911 (341–344). [0050 6010]. 42244

————— Die Stellung der Physik und Naturphilosophie zur Weltätherfrage. Zs. Balneol. Berlin 3 1911 (528–530 567–572 602–607). [0600]. 42243

Rudolph, Wilhelm. Erzeugung kurzer elektrischer Wellen mit Gleichstrom und ihre Verwendung zur Bestimmung von Dielektrizitätskonstanten und Absorptionen. Diss. Leipzig Weida i. Th. (Druck v. Thomas & Hubert) 1911 (117). 23 cm. [6610 5252 3875 6830]. 42245

Rüdenberg, Reinhold. Über die Stabilität, Kompensierung und Selbsterregung von Drehstrom-Serienmaschinen. Elektrot. Zs. Berlin 32 1911 (233–237 264–266). [6070]. 42246

————— Selbsterregende Drehstromgeneratoren für veränderliche Frequenz. Elektrot. Zs. Berlin 32 1911 (391–395 413–416). [6060]. 42247

Rüdenberg, Reinhold. Der Drehstrom-Kollektorgenerator im Leerlauf. Elektrot. Zs. Berlin 32 1911 (489–493). [6045]. 42248

Rümelin, G. Doppelter Schlüssel für Quadrantenelektrometer. Physik. Zs. Leipzig 12 1911 (460–461). [6905]. 42249

Ruff, O[tto]. Ueber das sogenannte Sulfammonium und den Nachweis neuer Verbindungen auf spektrometrischem Wege. Verh. Ges. D. Natf. Leipzig 82 (1910) II 1 1911 (24–25). [3860]. 42250

——— Ueber die Lichtdurchlässigkeit von Gemischen mehrerer lichtabsorbierender Stoffe. (Nachweis von Molekülarten auf spektrometrischem Wege.) [Nebst einem Anhang von Leopold Hecht.] Zs. physik. Chem. Leipzig 76 1911 (21–57). [3860 3810]. 42251

——— und Hecht, Leopold. Ueber das Sulfammonium und seine Beziehungen zum Schwefelstickstoff. Zs. anorg. Chem. Hamburg 70 1911 (49–69). [3860]. 42252

Ruhmer, Ernst. Researches on multiplex telephony. Elect. London 66 1911 (995). [6485]. 42253

——— Prove di telefonia multipla. Elettricità Milano 36 1911 (341–345). [6485]. 42254

——— Versuche mit MultiplexTelephonie. Mechaniker Berlin 19 1911 (157–158 171–173). [6485]. 42255

——— Ein bedeutsamer Fortschritt im Fernsehproblem. (Der Rosingsche Fernseher.) Umschau Frankfurt a. M. 15 1911 (508–510). [6480]. 42256

Ruhstrat, E. Rheogött-Widerstand. Elektroch. Zs. Berlin 18 1911 (61–62). [6010]. 42257

Rumi, S. A. Antonio Pacinotti. L'uomo e l'inventore. Boll. tecn. ligure Genova 9 1911 (1–19). [0010]. 42258

——— Illuminanti e illuminazione. Elettricista Roma (Ser. 2) 10 1911 (145–154). [4200]. 42259

Rumpf, [Theodor]. Ueber physikalische und physiologische Erscheinungen der oszillierenden Ströme. Arch. ges. Physiol. Bonn 137 1910 (329–338). [5900]. 42260

Runge, C[arl]. Ueber die Radioaktivität der Luft auf dem offenen Meere. Göttingen Nachr. Ges. Wiss. math.-phys. Kl. 1911 (99–109). [4275]. 42261

Runge, J. v. Sommerfeld, A.

Ruppersberg, Emma A. v. Blake, F. C.

Rusch, E. Die Goldschmidtsche Hochfrequenzmaschine. Jahrb. drahtlos. Telegr. Leipzig 4 1911 (348–357). [6470]. 42262

Rusch, F. Der Repulsionsmotor. Elektrot. Zs. Berlin 32 1911 (157–160 190–192). [6070]. 42263

——— Plattenförmige Leiter in zylinderischem Wechselfeld. Jahrb. drahtlos. Telegr. Leipzig 4 1911 (459–480). [6440 5680]. 42264

——— Die Berechnung der Magnetisierungskurve bei Mehrlochwicklungen. Elektrot. Zs. Berlin 32 1911 (311–314). [6060 6030]. 42265

Russ, Sidney v. Makower, W.

Russell, Alexander. The electric stress at which ionisation begins in air. London Proc. Physic. Soc. 23 1911 (86–97). [6805]. 42266

——— The capacity coefficients of spherical electrodes. London Proc. Physic. Soc. 23 1911 (352–360). [5220]. 42267

——— Messungen von spezifischen Wärmen bei tiefen Temperaturen. Physik. Zs. Leipzig 13 1912 (59–64). [1660 1620]. 42268

——— and Soddy, Frederick. The γ-rays of thorium and actinium. Phil. Mag. London (Ser. 6) 21 1911 (130–154). [4275]. 42269

——— v. Marckwald, W.

Russenberger, J. H. Sur l'extension des lois de la capillarité. Paris C. R. Acad. sci. 153 1911 (57–60). [0300]. 42270

Russner, Johannes. Die Strahlungseigenschaften elektrischer Glühlampen. Elektrot. Zs. Berlin 32 1911 (1026–1027). [6080 4202]. 42271

Rutherford, Ernest. Radio-activity of thorium. London J. Röntgen Soc. 7 1911 (23–30). [4275]. 42272

——— The transformation of radium. London J. Soc. Chem. Indust. 30 1911 (659–662). [4275]. 42273

Rutherford, Ernest. The scattering of α and β particles by matter and the structure of the atom. Phil. Mag. London (Ser. 6) 21 1911 (669-688). [4275]. 42271

——— Radiumnormalmasse und deren Verwendung bei radioaktiven Messungen. Deutsch von B. **Finkelstein**. Leipzig (Akadem. Verlagsges.) 1911 (45). 22 cm. 1,50 M. [4275]. 42275

——— and **Geiger**, H. Transformation and nomenclature of the radio-active emanations. Phil. Mag. London (Ser. 6) 22 1911 (621-629). [4275]. 42276

——— v. Boltwood, B. B.

Ryan, Harris J. Luft und Öl als Hochspannungsisolatoren. Glimmen von Freileitungen. (Vortrag . . .) Elektrot. Zs. Berlin 32 1911 (1104-1108). [6810 6805 5250 6820]. 42277

Rybár, István. A lanthán és a kobalt spektrálvonalainak Zeeman effektusáról. [Über die Zeeman-Effekte der Spektrallinien des Lanthans und Kobalts.] Math. Phys. L. Budapest 20 1911 (128-156 198-248). [4208]. 42278

——— Über die Zerlegung der Spektrallinien von Lanthan und Kobalt im magnetischen Felde. Physik. Zs. Leipzig 12 1911 (889-900). [4208]. 42279

Rybczyński, W. O ruchu postępowym kuli ciekłej w ośrodku lepkim. [Sur le mouvement progressif d'une sphère liquide à travers un milieu visqueux.] Kraków Rozpr. Akad. 11 A 1911 (5-7); Kraków Bull. Intern. Acad. 1911 A (40-46). [0325]. 42280

Sabatier, Paul. Sur un procédé pour faire réagir deux corps dans l'arc électrique. Paris C. R. Acad. sci. 151 1910 (1328). [6830]. 42282

Sachs, Stanislaus. Messungen an den Elektrizitätsträgern und Nebelkernen, welche durch ultraviolettes Licht in Gasen erzeugt werden. Ann. Physik Leipzig (4. Folge) 34 1911 (469-497). [6805 0150]. 42283

——— Ueber die Wirkung des ultravioletten Lichtes auf Gase und über die dabei erzeugten Nebelkerne. Diss. Heidelberg (Druck v. C. Pfeffer) 1910 (49). 22 cm. [6805 0150]. 42284

Sackur, O[tto]. Zur kinetischen Begründung des Nernstschen Wärmetheorems. [Entropie und Wahrscheinlichkeit.] Ann. Physik Leipzig (4. Folge) 34 1911 (455-468); Breslau Jahresber. Ges. vaterl. Cultur. 88 (1910) 1911 natw. Sect. (93-104). [0200 2400 2415]. 42285

——— Die Anwendung der kinetischen Theorie der Gase auf chemische Probleme. Ann. Physik Leipzig (4. Folge) 36 1911 (958-980). [0200]. 42286

——— Physikalische Chemie. Jahrb. Chem. Braunschweig 20 (1910) 1911 (1-61). [0020]. 42287

——— Geschmolzene Salze als Lösungsmittel. I. Kryoskopische Untersuchungen. II. Löslichkeitsbestimmungen. Zs. physik. Chem. Leipzig 78 1912 (550-563 564-572). [1920]. 42288

Sadler, Charles A. The transformation of the energy of homogeneous Röntgen radiation into energy of corpuscular radiation. Phil. Mag. London (Ser. 6) 22 1911 (447-458). [4240]. 42289

——— and **Steven**, A. J. An apparent softening of Röntgen rays in transmission through matter. Phil. Mag. London (Ser. 6) 21 1911 (659-668). [4240]. 42290

Saegmüller, George M. Ueber Phosphoreszenz von Gläsern. Diss. Jena (Druck v. G. Neuenhahn) 1911 (23 mit Taf.). 23 cm. [4230]. 42291

Sagnac, Georges. Les systèmes optiques en mouvement et la translation de la Terre. Paris C. R. Acad. sci. 152 1911 (310-313). [3420]. 42292

——— La translation de la Terre et les phénomènes optiques dans un système purement terrestre. Paris C. R. Acad. sci. 152 1911 (1835-1838). [3420]. 42293

——— Strioscopie et striographie interférentielles analogues à la méthode optique des stries de Foucault et de Topler. Paris C. R. Acad. sci. 153 1911 (90-93). [3610]. 42294

——— Quelques paradoxes au sujet des actions optiques du premier ordre de la translation de la Terre. Paris C. R. Acad. sci. 153 1911 (243-245). [3420]. 42295

Sagnac, Georges. Limite supérieure d'un effet tourbillonnaire optique dû à un entraînement de l'éther lumineux au voisinage de la Terre. Radium Paris 8 1911 (1 8 av. fig.). [3420]. 42296

———— Strioscope et striographe interférentiels. Forme interférentielle de la méthode optique des stries. Radium Paris 8 1911 (241–253). [3610]. 42297

Salet, P. Observation de l'éclipse totale de Soleil du 30 août 1905 faite à Robertville (Algérie). Ann. bur. longit. Paris 8 1911 (E. 1 à E. 22 av. pl.). [4205]. 42298

———— Sur la diffusion de la lumière du Soleil par les météorites. Bul. astr. Paris 29 1912 (25–29). [3800]. 42299

———— Sur quelques applications de l'étude de la polarisation en astronomie. Radium Paris 8 1911 (156–158). [3230]. 42300

Salles, Ed. La diffusion des ions gazeux. Radium Paris 8 1911 (59–62). [6805 5685]. 42301

Salmon, E. A. Sur un procédé pour faire réagir deux corps dans l'arc électrique. Paris C. R. Acad. sci. 151 1910 (1057–1058). [6830]. 42302

Salomonson, Wertheim. On the induction coil. London J. Röntgen Soc. 7 1911 (31–47). [6040]. 42303

Saltini, G. Telefono a batteria centrale a 40 volt. Elettricità Milano 37 1911 (52–55). [6485]. 42304

Salvadori, Riccardo. Sulla posizione delle centrali telefoniche. Roma Ann. Soc. ing. 25 1910 (70–72). [6485]. 42305

———— Le difficoltà della telefonia. Boll. tecn. ligure Genova 9 1911 (10–12). [6485]. 42306

Salzer, Michael. Optische Schülerübungen. Zs. physik. Unterr. Berlin 24 1911 (142–148). [0050]. 42307

Sande Bakhuyzen, H[endricus] G[erardus] van de. De toestand van de natuurwetenschappen in den tijd van Spinoza. [Der Zustand der Naturwissenschaften zur Zeit Spinoza's.] 's Gravenhage (Belinfante) 1911 (20). 21 cm. [0010]. 42308

Sander, Wilhelm. Über die Löslichkeit der Kohlensäure in Wasser und einigen andern Lösungsmitteln unter höhern Drucken. Zs. physik. Chem. Leipzig 78 1912 (513–549). [0250]. 42309

Sanderson, James Cox. Der wahrscheinliche Einfluss des Bodens auf die örtliche atmosphärische Radioaktivität. (The probable influence of the soil on local atmospheric radioactivity.) (Übers.) Physik. Zs. Leipzig 13 1912 (142–151). [4275]. 42310

Sanford, Fernando. On positive atomic charges. Pyhsic. Rev. Ithaca N.Y. 32 1911 (512–517 with fig. tables). [4960 6200]. 42311

———— Atomic charges and cohesion. Physic. Rev. Ithaca N.Y. 32 1911 (518–521 with tables). [4960 0150]. 42312

———— Dr. Brush's theory of gravitation. Science New York (N. Ser.) 33 1911 (933). [0700]. 42313

Sang, Alfred. The underlying facts of science. Pop. Sci. Mon. New York 78 1911 (564–583). [0500]. 42314

Sangster, Robert B. Consequences of Fresnel's reflection of light theory, with formulæ for determining the angle of incidence in order to reflect 1 ten the incident light. Phil. Mag. London (Ser. 6) 22 1911 (305–322). [3820]. 42315

Santoponte, Giovanni. Annuario della fotografia e delle sue applicazioni. Roma 1909 (XV + 192 con 15 tav.). 17 cm. [4225]. 42316

Š[apošnikov] A[leksandr] Aleksandrovič. Ш[апошниковъ], А[лександръ] Александровичъ]. Аккумуляторная батарея высокаго напряжения. [Ueber eine Hochspannungsakkumulatorenbatterie.] Vopr. fiziki St. Peterburg 3 1909 (107–109). [5620]. 42317

Sarasin, Ed. et **Tommasina,** Th[omas]. Constatation de quelques faits nouveaux en radioactivité induite. Genève C. R. Soc. Phys. Hist. Nat. 28 1911 (7–11 3 figg.). [4275]. 42318

———— Action de faibles élévations de température sur la radioactivité induite. Paris C. R. Acad. sci. 152 1911 (434–436 av. fig.). [4275]. 42319

———— ———— Etude de l'action de la chaleur sur l'air ionisé par la radioactivité induite. Constatation d'une différence de nature entre le produit de la désactivation lente et celui de la désactivation rapide. Genéve C. R. Soc. Phys. Hist. Nat. 28 1912 (30 34) 2 figg.). [4275].   42320

Sargent, Ledyard W. r. Morse, H. W.

Sartori, Giuseppe. Macchine a corrente alternata a collettore. Mon. teen. Milano 17 1911 (31 34 114 118 135-139 155-160). [6060].   42321

Sassi, L. I primi passi in fotografia. Ed. 2. Milano (Hoepli) 1909 (X 205 con 13 tav.). 15 cm. [2990].   42322

Satterly, J. The radium-content of salts of potassium. Cambridge Proc. Phil. Soc. 16 1911 (67-70). [4275].
42323

Scal, C. r. Urbain, G.

Scala, Alberto r. Traube Mengarini, M.

Scarpa, Oscar. La ionizzazione dell'aria nelle vicinanze di alcune sorgenti termali dell'isola d'Ischia. Elettricista Roma (Ser. 2) 9 1910 (113-114); Napoli Atti 1st. incoragg. sc. nat. 62 1911 (37-42). [4275 6805].   42324

————— Analisi della radioattività di alcune acque termali dell'isola d'Ischia. Gazz. chim. ital. Palermo 40 2. sem. 1910 (285-325). [4275].   42325

————— Sulla misura della viscosità dei liquidi e dei lubrificanti. Un nuovo viscosimetro a efflusso. Napoli Atti 1st. incoragg. sc. nat. (Ser. 6) 61 1910 (207-245); Gazz. chim. ital. Palermo 40 2. sem. 1910 (261-285). [0325 0090].   42326

————— Sugli ultramicroscopi a riflessione totale. Napoli Atti 1st. incoragg. sc. nat. (Ser. 6) 61 1910 (323-331). [3090].   42327

————— Sulla legge della diluizione. Nuovo Cimento Pisa (Ser. 5) 20 1910 (445-454); Rend. Soc. chim. ital. Roma (Ser. 2) 2 1910 (211-215). [6250 1930].   42328

————— Un nuovo apparecchio per la misura dei numeri di trasporto. Rend. Soc. chim. ital. (Ser. 2) 2 1910 (215-17). [6240].   42329

————— Su un singolare risultato di alcune esperienze di diffusione. Rend. Soc. chim. ital. Roma (Ser. 2) 2 1910 (290-293). [0320].   42330

————— Su alcune esperienze di diffusione. Atti Soc. ital. prog. sci.

Roma 4 1911 (769-770) ; Nota 2 e 3. Gazz. chim. ital. Roma 41 I. sem. 1911 (113-121 122 126) ; Nuovo Cimento Pisa (Ser. 6) 1 1911 (320-329 330-334). [0320 6255].   42331

Scarpa, Oscar. Analisi della radioattività delle acque termali Fornello e Fontana di Porto d'Ischia e Manzi di Casamicciola. Napoli Atti 1st. incoragg. sc. nat. (Ser. 6) 62 1911 (1-36). [4275].   42332

————— Sull'esistenza dell'emanazione di torio nelle acque termali di Porto d'Ischia. Napoli Atti 1st. incoragg. sc. nat. 62 1911 (197-200). [4275].   42334

————— Su un problema e su alcune esperienze di diffusione. Nuovo Cimento Pisa (Ser. 6) 1 1911 (431-436). [0320].   42335

————— Sul calcolo dei numeri di trasporto reali. Nuovo Cimento Pisa (Ser. 6) 2 1911 (141-150). [6240].   42336

Schade, H[einrich]. J[acobus] H[enricus] van 't Hoff†. Münchener med. Wochenschr. 58 1911 (803-804). [0010].   42337

Schäfer. Nachweis von Induktionsströmen. Zs. physik. Unterr. Berlin 24 1911 (231-232). [0050].   42338

Schäfer, Béla B. Ein neuer Quecksilberdampf-Gleichrichter für grosse Leistungen. Elektrot. Zs. Berlin 32 1911 (2-5). [6047].   42339

Schaefer, Clemens. Über die Beugung elektromagnetischer Wellen an isolierenden zylindrischen Hindernissen. (Vortrag.) Physik. Zs. Leipzig 10 1909 (261-272). [3875 6640].   42340

————— Erwiderung an O[tto] Frank. Arch. ges. Physiol. Bonn 145 1911 (410-422). [9100 0835].   42341

————— und **Reiche**, Fritz. Zur Theorie des Beugungsgitters. Ann. Physik Leipzig (4. Folge) 35 1911 (817-850). [3630 6627].   42342

Schaefer, Ernst. Untersuchungen über Dichte, Reibung und Kapillarität kristallinischer Flüssigkeiten. Diss. Halle a. S. (Druck v. C. A. Kaemmerer & Co.) 1911 (41 mit Tab.). 22 cm. [0325 0300].   42343

Schaefer, Karl L. Über eine neue Methode der Schwingungszahlenbestimmung. Verh. D. otol. Ges. Jena 20 1911 (309–313). [9320]. 42344

——— r. Szivessy.

Schäffer, W. Hintereinanderschaltung von Bogenlampen und Glühlampen. Elektrot. Zs. Berlin 32 1911 (425–427 450–452). [6080]. 42345

Schaffers, V. La loi de Coulomb. Rev. quest. scient. Bruxelles 11 1907 (449–493). [5200]. 42346

Schalamberidse, Michael. Ueber Chromoisomerie von Nitro-Anilinen und Nitro-Acetanilinen sowie Nitro-Phenoläther. Ueber den Zustand des dampfförmigen, flüssigen und gelösten Acetons auf Grund von optischen und thermischen Messungen sowie von Verteilungsversuchen. Diss. Leipzig (Druck v. Bomboes & Schneider) 1911 (59). 23 cm. [3860]. 42347

Schall, C. Über Demonstration photochemischer Wirkungen im ultravioletten Licht mittels sensibler Schichten und Messungen an denselben. Zs. wiss. Phot. Leipzig 10 1911 (89–116). [4225]. 42348

Schatte. Über eine neue Methode der Kinematographie mit elektrischen Funken. Zs. Schiesswesen München 7 1912 (65–67 mit taf.). [0090]. 42349

Schaum, Karl. Über die sogenannten „dunkeln" Funken. Berlin Verh. D. physik Ges. 13 1911 (676–679). [4225]. 42350

——— Photographische Probleme. Jahrb. Phot. Halle 25 1911 (174–178). [4225]. 42351

——— Leistungen und Aufgaben der wissenschaftlichen Photographie. Natw. Rdsch. Braunschweig 26 1911 (29–33 41–44). [4225]. 42352

——— Über die Verwendung von Kinoobjektiven für Spektrographen. Zs. Wiss. Phot. Leipzig 9 1911 (414–416). [3165]. 42353

——— Vorlesungsversuche. [1. Ablenkbares Lichtbündel. 2. Absorptionsgefäss mit stark sich ändernder Schichtdicke.] Zs. wiss. Phot. Leipzig 10 1911 (29–30). [0050]. 42354

——— und **Wustenfeld,** Heinrich. Über selektive Absorption und Emission. Zs. wiss. Phot. Leipzig 10 1911
(213–237 mit 2 Taf.). [3850] 4210 4206 4205]. 42355

Scheel, Karl. Präzisionswage für 10 kg Belastung nach Thiesen. Zs. Instrumentenk. Berlin 31 1911 (237–245). [0810]. 42356

——— Die Wärmeausdehnung des Quarzglases. Zs. Instrumentenk. Berlin 32 1912 (14–18). [1410]. 42357

——— Grundlagen der praktischen Metronomie. (Die Wissenschaft H. 36.) Braunschweig (F. Vieweg & S.) 1911 (XII + 168). 22 cm. 5.50 M. [0800 1410]. 42358

——— und **Heuse,** Wilhelm. Die spezifische Wärme C, der Luft bei Zimmertemperatur und tiefen Temperaturen. Physik. Zs. Leipzig 12 1911 (1074–1076); Berlin Verh. D. physik. Ges. 13 1911 (870–873); Ann. Physik Leipzig (4. Folge) 37 1912 (79–95). [1640]. 42359

——— ——— Über die Wärmeausdehnung des Quecksilbers. Bemerkungen zu einer Arbeit von Callendar u. Moss. Berlin Verh. D. physik. Ges. 14 1912 (139–144). [1430]. 42360

Scheffer, F[rans] E[ppo] C[ornelis]. Over het systeem zwavelwaterstofwater. [On the system hydrogen sulphide-water.] Amsterdam Versl. Wis. Nat. Afd. K. Akad. Wet. 20 [1911] (104–109) (Dutch); Amsterdam Proc. Sci. K. Akad. Wet. 14 [1911] (195–201) (English). [1887]. 42361

——— Heterogene Gleichgewichte bei dissoeiierenden Verbindungen. Tl 3. Zs. physik. Chem. Leipzig 76 1911 (161–173). [1887]. 42362

——— Over gasevenwichten. [On gas equilibria.] Amsterdam Versl. Wis. Nat. Afd. K. Akad. Wet. 20 1912 (761–776) (Dutch); Amsterdam Proc. Sci. K. Akad. Wet. 14 1912 (743–758) (English). [2472]. 42363

——— en **Treub,** J. P. Dampspanningsbepalingen van het stikstoftetroxyd. [Determinations of vapour tensions of nitrogen tetroxide.] Amsterdam Versl. Wis. Nat. Afd. K. Akad. Wet. 20 [1911] (529–542) (Dutch); Amsterdam Proc. Sci. K. Akad. Wet. 14 [1911] (536–549) (English). [1840 1930]. 42364

Scheffer, W[ilhelm]. Ueber Licht-höfe. Jahrb. Phot. Halle 25 1911 (242-256). [4225]. 42365

Scheiber, Johannes. Über die Homologie von Anthranil und Methylanthranil. Berlin Ber. D. chem. Ges. 44 1911 (2409-2418). [3860]. 42366

Schell, Curt. Photographisch-photometrische Absorptionsmessungen an Jodsilber im ultravioletten Spektrum. Ann. Physik Leipzig (4. Folge) 35 1911 (695-727 mit 1 Taf.). [3810 4225 3010]. 42367

Schenkel, M. Über elektrische Bremsung mit Wechselstrom-Kommutatormotoren. Elektr. Kraftbetriebe München 10 1912 (119-120). [6070]. 42368

Scherbius, A. Nuovo sistema per regolare la velocità dei motori a corrente trifase e confronto cogli altri sistemi sinora in uso. [Trad.] Industria Milano 24 1910 (211-215 229-233). [6015]. 42369

Scheuer, Otto und **Saphores,** Jean. Bericht über die Jahresausstellung der französischen physikalischen Gesellschaft. [Apparate.] Physik. Zs. Leipzig 12 1911 (639-647). [0090]. 42370

Schicht, Franz. Zur Robervalschen Wage. Zs. physik. Unterr. Berlin 25 1912 (33-34). [0810]. 42371

———— Der Fritter im Hertzspiegel. Zs. physik. Unterr. Berlin 25 1912 (40). [6610]. 42372

Schidlof, A. Zur Aufklärung der universellen elektrodynamischen Bedeutung der Planckschen Strahlungskonstanten h. Ann. Physik Leipzig (4. Folge) 35 1911 (90-100). [4210 4960]. 42373

———— Sur quelques problèmes récents de la théorie du rayonnement. Genève C. R. Soc. Phys. Hist. Nat. 28 1912 (17-20 28-30). [4270]. 42374

Schiffner, C., **Weidig,** M. und **Friedrich,** R. Radioaktive Wässer in Sachsen. Tl 3. Freiberg i. S. (Craz & Gerlach) 1911 (145-216 mit 2 Taf.). 25 cm. 3 M. [4275]. 42375

Schiller, Heliodor und O'Donnell, P. S. Induzierte Radioaktivität durch Röntgenstrahlen. Fortschr. Röntgenstr. Hamburg 16 1911 (283-284). [4240 4275]. 42376

Schiller, Ludwig. Die Änderung der Dielektrizitätskonstante des Kautschuks bei Zug senkrecht zu den Kraftlinien. Ann. Physik Leipzig (4. Folge) 35 1911 (931-982); Diss. Leipzig. Weida i. Th. (Druck v. Thomas & Hubert) 1911 (84 mit Taf.). 23 cm. [5252 0840 5250]. 42377

Schilling, K. r. Koenigsberger, J.

Schilling, Martin. Catalog mathematischer Modelle für den höheren mathematischen Unterricht. 7. Aufl. Leipzig (M. Schilling) 1911 (XIV + 172). 23 cm. 1,20 M. [0050]. 42378

Schillo, Joh. Messung hoher Umlaufzahlen mittels des Stroboskops. Elektrot. Zs. Berlin 33 1912 (159-160). [0820]. 42379

Schimmack, Rudolf. Über die Verschmelzung verschiedener Zweige des mathematischen Unterrichts. Habvortr. Zs. math. Unterr. Leipzig 42 1911 (569-581). [0050]. 42380

Schincaglia, Ignazio. I raggi X. Bergamo (Istituto Artigrafiche) 1910 (152 e 27 tav.). 26 cm. [0030 4900]. 42381

Schindler, A. Eine einfache Methode zur Bestimmung des Dampfverbrauches von Dampfturbinen. Zs. Turbinenwesen München 8 1911 (356-360 369-372). [2490]. 42382

Schlee, G. Methoden und Apparate zur Widerstandsmessung. Mechaniker Berlin 19 1911 (145-147 160-162 173-175 186-188 195-197 210-212). [6010 5640]. 42383

Schleicher, G. Über die Schnellformation von Bleiakkumulatoren mit Lösungen von Schwefelsäure und Chlorat bezw. Perchlorat. Zs. Elektroch. Halle 17 1911 (554-569). [5620]. 42384

Schliephacke, Gerhard. Ueber die Mutarotation der Maltose. Diss. Hannover (Druck v. Göhmann) 1909 (38 mit 2 Taf.). 22 cm. [4050]. 42385

Schmidt, Ad. Zur Frage der Zerlegung des erdmagnetischen Feldes. Met. Zs. Braunschweig 28 1911 (49-53). [5490]. 42386

Schmidt, Erich. Optische Eigenschaften von Flussspath, Schwefel, Phosphor u. Selen. Diss. Rostock. Berlin (H. Hadorff) 1911 (40). 22 cm. [3810 3020 3830]. 42387

212

Schmidt, Friedrich. Ueber die
Veränderung der Oberflächenspannung
durch Metallzusatz. Diss. Freiburg
i. Br. (Druck d. Caritas-Druckerei) 1911
(VII + 40 mit Taf.). 22 cm. [0300].
42388

Schmidt, C. C. Ueber die Elektrizitätsleitung von Salzdämpfen. Ann.
Physik Leipzig (4. Folge) 35 1911 (401–
443). [5685]. 42389

———— Über Adsorption von
Lösungen. 2. Abh. Zs. physik. Chem.
Leipzig 77 1911 (641–660). [0250].
42390

Schmidt, Hans. Leitvermögen des
Oberflächenwassers der Nordsee. Jahrb.
drahtlos. Telegr. Leipzig 4 1911 (636–
638). [6240]. 42391

Schmidt, Harry. Zwei einfache
Versuche zur Demonstration der Impedanz einer Drahtspule. Monatschr.
natw. Unterr. Stuttgart 1910–11 1911
(231–232). [0050]. 42392

———— Röntgen- und lichtelektrische Versuche. Natur u. Unterr.
Stuttgart 3 1912 (61–62). [0050].
42393

———— Anleitung zur Anfertigung
einer einfachen Stark- oder Schwachstromschalttafel. Natur u. Unterr.
Stuttgart 3 1912 (65–67). [6020].
42394

———— v. Cermak, P.

Schmidt, M. R. and Jones, Harry C.
Conductivity and viscosity in mixed
solvents containing glycerol. [Eleventh
communication.] Amer. Chem. J.
Baltimore 42 1909 (37–95 with fig.
tables). [0325]. 42395

Schmidt, W. Die spezifische und
Erstarrungswärme des geschmolzenen
Roheisens. Aachen Mitt. eisenhüttenmänn. Inst. 4 1911 (91–94). [1620].
42396

———— Vom Äther, von der
Atomauflösung und ihrer Beziehung
zur Ionisierung. Karlsruhe (C. F.
Müller) 1911 (27). 23 cm. 0,80 M.
[0100]. 42397

Schmiedel, Karl. Reibung von
Elektrizitäts-Zählern mit rotierendem
Anker und Einfluss der Reibung auf die
Fehlerkurve. [Schluss.] Berlin Verh.
Ver. Gewerbfl. 90 1911 (111–129).
[6010]. 42398

Schmutzer, J[osef]. Over de orien-
teering van kristaldoorsneden met
behulp van de traces van twee vlakken
en de optische uitdooving. [On the
orientation of crystal sections with the
help of the traces of two planes and the
optic extinction.] Amsterdam Versl.
Wis. Nat. Afd. K. Akad. Wet. 20
[1911] (35–38 with 2 pl.) (Dutch);
Amsterdam Proc. Sci. K. Akad. Wet.
14 [1911] (128–132 with 2 pl.) (English).
[4030]. 42399

———— Over de optische uitdooving als hulpmiddel bij de bepaling
van een kristal in een preparaat.
[Ueber die optische Auslöschung als
Hilfsmittel bei der Bestimmung der
Lage eines Krystalles in einem Dünn-
schliffe.] Handl. Ned. Nat. Geneesk.
Congres 13 1911 (406–411). [4030].
42400

Schneckenberg, Erich. Schlupfzähler für Induktionsmotoren. Elektrot. Zs. Berlin 32 1911 (1162–1163).
[6070]. 42401

———— Ueber die scheinbaren
Kontaktpotentialdifferenzen zwischen
einem Metall und elektrolytischen Lösungen. Elektroch. Zs. Berlin 18 1912
(307–308). [5210 6210]. 42402

Schneiders, Fr. v. Spalekhaver, R.

Schneider, Hans. Die Energie der
aus glühendem CaO entweichenden
Elektronen. Ann. Physik Leipzig (4.
Folge) 37 1912 (569–593); Diss.
Berlin (Druck v. J. Jagert) 1911 (42).
24 cm. [6845 6800 4210]. 42404

Schnerr, Al. v. Estreicher, T.

Schofield, J. The anti-kathodes of
X-ray tubes. Nature London 87 1911
(215). [6800]. 42405

Scholl, H. Theorie der elektro-
statischen Messinstrumente. Helios
Leipzig 17 1911 Fach-Zs. (285–291
303–306). [6005]. 42406

Schorr, Carl. Untersuchungen über
physikalische Zustandsänderungen der
Kolloide. 12. Mitt. Ueber Eigenschaften der Eiweissionen. Biochem.
Zs. Berlin 37 1911 (424–451). [0340].
42407

Schoop, M. U. Weiteres über das
Schoop'sche Metallisierungsverfahren.
Elektroch. Zs. Berlin 17 1911 (355–
356). [0090]. 42408

Schouten, J. A. Über die Gegen und Querwindungen eines Drehstromgenerators. [Nebst Erwiderung von W. **Rogowski.**] Elektrot. Zs. Berlin **32** 1911 (935–936). [6060]. 42409

Schramm. Neuerungen am Ferndrucker von Siemens & Halske. Arch. Post Berlin **39** 1911 (465–471). [6480]. 42410

Schreber, K. Explosionsmotoren mit Einführung verdampfender Flüssigkeiten. Dinglers polyt. J. Berlin **326** 1911 (8–12 26–28). [2490]. 42411

———— Die Grundlagen der Masssysteme. Elektrot. Zs. Berlin **32** 1911 (1125–1126). [0800]. 42412

———— Les moteurs à explosion à injection de liquides volatils. Rev. gén. sci. Paris **22** 1911 (404–411). [2490]. 42413

Schreinemakers, F[rans] A[nton] H[ubert]. Evenwichten in het stelsel: water - natriumsulfaat - natriumchlorid-kopersulfaat-koperchlorid. [Equilibria in the system: water-sodium sulphate-sodium chloride-copper sulphate-cupric chloride.] Amsterdam Versl. Wis. Nat. Afd. K. Akad. Wet. **19** 1911 (1222–1235) (Dutch); Amsterdam Proc. Sci. K. Akad. Wet. **13** 1911 (1163–1177) (English). [1887]. 42414

———— en **Deuss, J[oseph] J[ohan] B[althasar].** Over het stelsel: water-alcohol-manganosulfaat. [On the system: water-alcohol-manganous sulphate.] Amsterdam Versl. Wis. Nat. Afd. K. Akad. Wet. **20** 1912 (933–936) (Dutch); Amsterdam Proc. Sci. K. Akad. Wet. **14** 1912 (924–927) (English). [1887]. 42415

———— en **Figee, Th.** Het stelsel: water-calcium chloride-calciumhydroxyde bij 25°. [Das System: Wasser-Kalziumchlorid-Kalziumhydroxyd bei 25.] Amsterdam Chem. Weekbl. **8** 1911 (683–688). [1887]. 42416

———— en **Massink, A.** Over enkele verbindingen van nitraten en sulfaten. [Some compounds of nitrates and sulphates.] Amsterdam Versl. Wis. Nat. Afd. K. Akad. Wet. **20** 1912 (1084–1086) (Dutch); Amsterdam Proc. Sci. K. Akad. Wet. **14** 1912 (1042–1044) (English). [1887]. 42417

———— c. Korteweg, D. J.

Schroder, Wilhelm. Quantitative Messungen des Absorptionsvermögens des Natrium-Dampfes. Diss. Kiel. Bremen (Druck v. C. Schünemann) 1909 (28). 24 cm. [3810 4210 4206]. 42419

Schrutka, Lothar v. c. Pichelmayer,K.

Schück, A. Die Vorgänger des Kompasses. Centralztg Opt. Berlin **32** 1911 (103–105 121 122 138–140 156–158 171–172 185–186). [5435]. 42420

———— Der Kompass. [Entwicklung desselben.] Hamburg (Selbstverl. d. Verf.) 1911 (18 mit 46 Taf.). 36 cm. 21 M. [5435]. 42421

Schück, B. c. Caro, N.

Schüle, W. Die Eigenschaften des Wasserdampfes nach den neuesten Versuchen. Berlin Zs. Ver. D. Ing. **55** 1911 (1506–1512 1561–1567 mit 2 Taf.). [1840 1880 1680]. 42422

Schüler, L. Die Praxis des Parallelbetriebes. Elektrot. Zs. Berlin **32** 1911 (1199–1202). [6060]. 42423

Schuen, W. Thermostat für hohe Temperaturen. Elektroch. Zs. Berlin **17** 1911 (301–303). [1014]. 42425

———— c. Bölling, E.

Schunemann, Julius. Untersuchungen über den elektrischen Zustand der Luft in Höhlen und Kellern. Diss. Göttingen. Braunschweig (Druck v. F. Vieweg & S.) 1910 (36). 22 cm. [5270 4275]. 42424

Schulemann, Otto. Das Funkenspektrum des Indiums. Zs. wiss. Phot. Leipzig **10** 1911 (263–280). [4205]. 42426

Schuller, A. Wie entsteht das „Weiss" auf der Autochromplatte? Zs. wiss. Phot. Leipzig **10** 1912 (368–374). [4225]. 42427

Schultze, H. Die Untersuchung von Spannungstransformatoren mittels des Quadrantelektrometers. Zs. Instrumentenk. Berlin **31** 1911 (332–346). [6040 6005]. 42428

Schulz, Ernst. Lasthebemagnete. Helios Leipzig **17** 1911 Fach-Zs. (309–313). [6030]. 42429

———— Die elektrischen Maschinen ... Berlin (H. Meusser) [1911] (111 + 221). 19 cm. Geb. 3.75 M. [6060]. 42430

Schulz, Hans. Ueber eine neue Interferenzerscheinung im parallelen Licht. Physik. Zs. Leipzig 12 1911 (306–310). [3610]. 42431

———— Über Interferenzpunkte an einem System rechtwinkliger Prismen. Physik. Zs. Leipzig 12 1911 (1211–1213). [3610]. 42432

———— Polarisationsprismen aus Glas. Zs. Instrumentenk. Berlin 31 1911 (180–183). [4000]. 42433

Schulz, Karl. Ueber die mittlere spezifische Wärme einiger Silikate im kristallisierten und im amorphen Zustande zwischen 20° und 100°. Centralbl. Min. Stuttgart 1911 (632–640). [1620]. 42434

Schulze, Alfred. Die spezifische Wärme binärer Gemische I. Berlin Verh. D. physik. Ges. 14 1912 (189–210). [1925 1620]. 42435

———— Untersuchungen über die Dielektrizitätskonstante und das langwellige Refraktionsvermögen binärer Gemische. Zs. Elektroch. Halle 18 1912 (77–93). [5252 5250 3800]. 42436

Schulze, Erich Edgar. Ueber funkentelegraphische Küsten- und Binnenlandstationen. Ein Begleitwort zu den drei Funkentelegraphenkarten. Petermanns geogr. Mitt. Gotha 57 1911 (I 49–51 mit 3 Karten). [6615]. 42437

———— und **Trier**, G. Über das spezifische Drehungsvermögen des Glutamins, nebst Bemerkungen über glutaminsaures Ammonium. Berlin Ber. D. chem. Ges. 45 1912 (257–262). [4050]. 42438

Schulze, F[ranz] A[rthur]. Zur Theorie der Kombinationstöne. Ann. Physik Leipzig (4. Folge) 34 1911 (817–822). [9140]. 42439

———— Die Wärmeleitfähigkeit einiger Reihen von Edelmetallegierungen. Berlin Verh. D. physik. Ges. 13 1911 (856–864); Physik. Zs. Leipzig 12 1911 (1028–1031). [2020 5660]. 42440

———— Bestimmung der oberen Hörgrenze mit der Zahnradsirene. Marburg SitzBer. Ges. Natw. 10 1911 (73–76). [9430]. 42441

———— Ermüdung des Ohres. Marburg SitzBer. Ges. Natw. 1910 1911 (76–77). 42442

Schulze, Fritz. Ueber Metallzerstäubung durch ultra-violettes Licht. Diss. Berlin (Druck v. Ebering) 1911 (35), 23 cm. [6825]. 42443

Schulze, Günther. Der Einfluss der Elektrolyte auf die Maximalspannung der elektrolytischen Ventilwirkung. Ann. Physik Leipzig (4. Folge) 34 1911 (657–710). [6200 6220 6047]. 42444

———— Die Maximalspannung der elektrolytischen Ventilwirkung in geschmolzenen Salzen. Zs. Elektroch. Halle 17 1911 (509–514). [6220]. 42445

———— Die Bildung schlechtleitender Schichten bei der Elektrolyse des Glases. Ann. Physik Leipzig (4. Folge) 37 1912 (435–471). [5660 6200]. 42446

———— Ueber die Kapazitäten der elektrolytischen Ventilwirkung in geschmolzenen Salzen und in absoluter Schwefelsäure. Zs. Elektroch. Halle 18 1912 (22–29). [6200 6220]. 42447

Schulze, Paul. Allgemeine Theorie unsymmetrischer Ablenkungen bei Systemen mit einem Freiheitsgrad und deren Zusammenhang mit der allgemeinen Theorie unsymmetrischer Schwingungen gleicher Systeme, nebst Anwendungen auf besondere Fälle. Zs. Math. Leipzig 59 1911 (298–311). [5435 6010]. 42448

Schwartz, Alfred. Über die Beeinflussung der Leitungsfähigkeit des polarisierten Nerven durch die den strom zuführenden Ionen. Einfluss der Kationen Ca, Na, K, auf die anodische Strecke. Arch. ges. Physiol. Bonn 138 1911 (487–524). 42449

———— Technische und wissenschaftliche Messinstrumente auf der Weltausstellung Brüssel 1910. Elektrot. Zs. Berlin 32 1911 (103–108 131–135 162–164). [6010]. 42450

———— Elektrische Temperaturmessung und Fernablesung unter besonderer Berücksichtigung der thermoelektrischen Verfahrens. Berlin Zs. Ver. D. Ing. 56 1912 (223–229 259–264). [1230 1250]. 42451

Schwartz, Frederick W. v. Morgan, J[ohn] Livingston R.

Schwarz, Emil. Osmotische Versuche. TonindZtg Berlin 35 1911 (828–830). [0310]. 42452

Schwarzhaupt, P. Sonnenlicht, Gebirge und Wellentelegraphie. Elektrot. Zs. Berlin 32 1911 (1313–1314). [6615]. 42453

Schweidler, E. v. r. Kohlrausch.

Schwenckenbecher, P. Der Quecksilberdampf-Lichtbogen und seine Anwendungsgebiete. — Le circuit à vapeur de mercure et ses applications. — The mercury vapour arc and its uses. [Deutsch, franz., engl.] Helios Leipzig 17 1911 Export Zs. (1313 1317 1363 1368 1405 1410 1453 1457 1495 1500). [6080]. 42454

Schwenn, Richard. Elektrische Temperatur - Messapparate. Helios Leipzig 17 1911 Fach-Zs. (437 439 449–454 485–490 497 503 532 535). [1230]. 42455

Schwers, F. La densité et l'indice de réfraction des solutions. Nouvelles contributions à l'étude des solutions. J. Chim. Phys. Genève 8 1910 (630–697); 9 1911 (15–99 4 pl.). [3020 0845]. 42456

————— Densité, polarisation rotatoire magnétique et indice de réfraction des mélanges binaires. Nouvelles contributions à l'étude des solutions. J. Chim. Phys. Genève 9 1911 (325–351). [3822 3860 4040]. 42457

————— Nouvelles contributions à l'étude des solutions. III. Relation entre la densité et la polarisation rotatoire magnétique des mélanges binaires. Rec. Trav. chim. Leiden 30 1911 (101–107). [4040]. 42458

————— Nouvelles contributions à l'étude des solutions. IV. Densité, rotation magnétique et réfraction chez les mélanges binaires dissociés. Rec. Trav. chim. Leiden 30 1911 (108–115). [4040 3822]. 42459

————— Sur la densité du sucre liquide et de ses solutions aqueuses. Rec. Trav. chim. Leiden 30 1911 (225–237). [1920]. 42460

————— La densità e la rifrazione nel sistema furfurolo ÷ acqua. Roma Rend. Acc. Lincei (Ser. 5) 20 2. sem. 1911 (398–405). [3860]. 42461

————— Risposta a una critica del Sig. A. Mazzucchelli "a proposito di uno studio recente su l'indice di rifrazione dei miscugli binari". Roma Rend. Acc. Lincei (Ser. 5) 20 2. sem. 1911 (510–518). [3860]. 42462

Schwietring, Fr. Über den Polarisationswinkel der durchsichtigen inaktiven Kristalle. Berlin SitzBer. Ak. Wiss. 1911 (423–435). [3820]. 42463

Schwoerer, Emile. Nouvelles recherches sur la détente adiabatique des gaz et sur l'équivalent mécanique de la chaleur. [Avec] Rapport sur le mémoire de M. E. Schwoerer. Par Roger Hartmann. Mülhausen Bull. Soc. Ind. 81 1911 (230–255 256–263). [1450 2410]. 42464

————— Le principe de l'équivalence. Paris (Gauthier-Villars) 1912 (47). [2405]. 42465

Scotti, C. Ein Hitzdraht- und ein Resonanz-Instrument für die Projektion. Zs. physik. Unterr. Berlin 24 1911 (29). [0050]. 42466

Searle, G. F. C. On resistances with current and potential terminals. Elect. London 66 1911 (999–1002 1029–1033); 67 (12–14). [5630]. 42467

————— Aldis, A. C. W. and Dobson, G. M. B. On a revolving table method of determining the curvature of spherical surfaces. Phil. Mag. London (Ser. 6) 21 1911 (218–224). [3090]. 42468

Šebor, Jan. Chemické a fysikální vlastnosti skel. [Chemische und physikalische Eigenschaften der Glassorten.] Listy Chem. Prag 1910 (58–64). [2990]. 42469

————— r. Horák, V.

Seddig, Max. Ein absolutes Bolometer und neue Vorlesungsapparate. Berlin Verh. D. physik. Ges. 13 1911 (53–64). [1230 0050]. 42470

————— Messung der Temperatur-Abhängigkeit der Brown-Zsigmondyschen Bewegung. Zs. anorg. Chem. Leipzig 73 1912 (360–384). [0200]. 42471

————— Ingenieurwesen und Industrie. [In: Angewandte Photographie in Wissenschaft u. Technik. Hrsg. v. K. W. Wolf-Czapek. Tl. 3.] Berlin (Union) 1911 (49–76 mit 13 Taf.). [3085]. 42472

Seegert, B. r. Miethe, A.

Seeliger, H[ugo]. Über den Einfluss des Lichtdrucks auf die Bewegung planetarischer Körper. Astr. Nachr. Kiel 187 1911 (417–422). [3405]. 42473

Seeliger, R. Über die Bremsung eines Elektrons in einem verdünnten Gase. Berlin Verh. D. physik. Ges. **13** 1911 (1094-1100). [6845 4960].
42474

—————— Über Gasionisation durch Kanalstrahlen. (Vorl. Mitt.) Physik. Zs. Leipzig **12** 1911 (839-842). [6805 6845].
42475

Seemann, J[ohn] und Victoroff, C. Elektrokardiogramm-studien am veratrinvergifteten Froschherzen. I. Zs. Biol. München **56** 1911 (91-138 mit 1 Taf.). [5900].
42476

Seibert, H. Über einen elektrischen Widerstandsofen mit Heizwiderstand aus unedlen Metallen. ChemZtg Cöthen **35** 1911 (443). [6090].
42477

Seibt, G. Bemerkung zu der Arbeit des Hrn. Karl Settnik: „Die Entstehung von sehr wenig gedämpften Wellen mit rein metallischer Leitungsbahn bei Nebenschaltung von Antennen an die Funkenstrecke eines Oszillators". Ann. Physik Leipzig (4. Folge) **35** 1911 (191-192). [6615 6820].
42478

—————— Ein Instrumentarium zur Untersuchung und Demonstration von Mineralien auf Empfindlichkeit gegen elektrische Schwingungen. Centralbl. Min. Stuttgart **1911** (588-592 614-622). [6043 6610].
42479

—————— Der radiotelegraphische Gleichstrom-Tonsender. Physik. Zs. Leipzig **12** 1911 (184-185). [6615].
42480

—————— Ein Präzisionsdrehplatten-kondensator und eine Methode zum Vergleichen von Kapazitäten. Zs. Schwachstromtechn. München **5** 1911 (649-655). [5740].
42481

Seidl, Sándor. Petzval József. Újabb adatok egy magyar tudós tudományos munkásságából. [Josef Petzval. Neuere Daten zur wissenschaftlichen Tätigkeit eines ungarischen Gelehrten.] Termt. Közl. Budapest **43** 1911 (141-145). [0010].
42482

Seiterheld, Hermann. Ueber Dampfspannungen verdünnter wässeriger Lösungen von Nichtelektrolyten, absolut gemessen. Diss. Tübingen. Leipzig (J. A. Barth) 1911 (22). 23 cm. [1920].
42483

Seiliger, M. Thermodynamische Untersuchung schnelllaufender Dieselmotoren. Berlin Zs. Ver. D. Ing. **55** 1911 (587-592 625-628). [2490].
42484

Selényi, Paul. Ueber Lichtzerstreuung im Raume Wienerscher Interferenzen und neue, diesen reziproke Interferenzerscheinungen. Ann. Physik Leipzig (4. Folge) **35** 1911 (444-460). [3610].
42485

—————— Adalékok az üvegrácson elhajlitott fény polárosságának elméletéhez. [Beiträge zur Theorie der Polarisation des von Glasgittern gebeugten Lichtes.] Math. Termt. Ért. Budapest **29** 1911 (45-75): (Deutsch) Math.-natw. Ber. Ungarn Leipzig **27** (1909) 1911 (45-75). [3820 3620 3610 6625 4000 4010].
42486

—————— A Wiener-féle és a reciprok interferencziajelenségekről. [Über die Wiener'schen und reciproken Interferenzerscheinungen.] Math. Termt. Ért. Budapest **29** 1911 (601-640). [3610].
42488

Seliger, Paul. Die stereoskopische Messmethode in der Praxis. Tl 1. Berlin (J. Springer) 1911 (XI + 227). 24 cm. 7 M.
42489

Sella, Alfonso. Introduzioni teoriche ad alcuni esercizi pratici di fisica. Firenze (Succ. Le Monnier) 1909 (VIII — 133). 24 cm. [0030].
42490

Sendtner, Albert. Die Bestimmung der Dampffeuchtigkeit mit dem Drosselkalorimeter und die Anwendung desselben zur Prüfung von Wasserabscheidern. Berlin Zs. Ver. D. Ing. **55** 1911 (1421-1427): Mitt. ForschArb. Ingenieurw. Berlin H. **98-99** 1911 (47-84). [1890 1840].
42491

Senouque, A. Sur des expériences de télégraphie sans fil en aéroplane. Paris C. R. Acad. sci. **152** 1910 (186-187). [6615].
42493

[Šerkov, S[ergej] V[ladimirovič].] Серков, С[ергѣй] В[ладимирович]. Электропроводность растворов электролитовъ въ водѣ, въ метиловомъ и этиловомъ алкоголяхъ, въ ацетонѣ и въ бинарныхъ смѣсяхъ этихъ растворителей. [Leitfähigkeit einiger Salze in Wasser, Methyl- und Aethylalkohol, in Aceton und in binären Gemischen dieser Flüssigkeiten.] St. Peterburg Žurn. russ. fiz.-chim. Obšč. Fiz. otd. **41** 1909 (1-43 deutsch. Res. 44-45). [4240 6250].
42494

Settnik, Karl. Die Entstehung von sehr wenig gedämpften Wellen mit rein metallischer Leitungsbahn bei Neben-

schaltung von Antennen an die Funkenstrecke eines Oszillators. Diss. Greifswald. Leipzig (J. A. Barth) 1910 (30). 23 cm.; Ann. Physik Leipzig (4. Folge) 34 1911 (565–589). [6615–6820].
42495

Sève, Pierre. Sur la mesure des champs magnétiques en valeur absolue. Paris C. R. Acad. sci. 152 1911 (1478–1480). [5440].
42496

Seyewetz, A. r. Lumière, A.

Shambaugh, Geo. E. Die Frage der Tonempfindung. Uebers. v. J. Holinger. Arch. ges. Physiol. Bonn 138 1911 (155–158). [9520].
42497

Sharp, C. H. Il contatore elettrico, avuto riguardo alla natura del carico ed ai vari regimi di questo. Atti Ass. elettrotecn. Milano 15 1911 (969–971). [6010].
42498

———— I contatori elettrici considerati nei differenti regimi di carico. Elettricità Milano 37 1911 (312–315 330–333 343–346 360–362). [6010].
42499

Shaw, A. Norman. Increased accuracy in the use of bifilar suspensions. Phil. Mag. London (Ser. 6) 22 1911 (433–447). [0840].
42500

———— r. Bronson.

Shaw, P. E. The measurement of end-standards of length. London Proc. R. Soc. (Ser. A) 84 1911 (589–595). [0807].
42501

Sheard, Charles r. Blake, F. C.

Shedd, John C. The genesis of the law of gravity. Pop. Sci. Mon. New York 78 1911 (313–340 with illus. portr.). [0700].
42502

Shepherd, E. Sanger. The cause of reversal and its remedy, with some notes on the photographic process. Phot. J. London 51 1911 (249–257). [4225].
42503

Shibata, Yuji r. Hantzsch, A.

Shoemaker, M. P. r. Wolff, F. A.

Sichling, Konrad. Ueber die Natur der Photochloride des Silbers und deren Lichtpotentiale. Bemerkungen zu dieser Arbeit von Emil Baur. Zs. physik. Chem. Leipzig 77 1911 (1–65). [6850].
42504

Sieg, L[ee] P[aul]. On the function of rest in restoring a platinum-iridium wire to its annealed condition. [Abstract.] Physic. Rev. Ithaca N.Y. 32 1911 (212–213). [0849].
42505

Siegbahn, Manne. Untersuchungen von elektrischen Schwingungen dritter Art in einem Lichtbogen. Lund Univ. Arsskr. N.F. 4 No. 5 | Fysiogr. Sällsk. Handl. N.F. 19; 5] 1909 (16 mit 2 Taf.). [6830].
42506

———— Magnetische Feldmessung. Lund Univ. Arsskr. N.F. 7 Afd. 2 No. 2 | Fysiogr. Sällsk. Handl. N.F. 22 No. 2] 1911 (64 mit Textfigg.); Diss. [5435 5440].
42507

Siegel, E. r. Niethammer, F.

Sieglerschmidt, H. Elastizitätsmodul und Wärmeausdehnung der Metalle. Ann. Physik Leipzig (4. Folge) 35 1911 (775–782). [1410 0840].
42508

Sieveking, H[erm]. Die Radioaktivität der Mineral- und Thermalquellen. (Vortrag.) J. Gasbeleucht. München 54 1911 (1183–1186). [4275].
42509

Sieverts, Adolf. Die Löslichkeit von Wasserstoff in Kupfer, Eisen und Nickel. Zs. physik. Chem. Leipzig 77 1911 (591–613). [0250].
42510

———— und Jurisch, E. Platin, Rhodium und Wasserstoff. Berlin Ber. D. chem. Ges. 45 1912 (221–229). [0250].
42511

Signorini, A. Sulle vibrazioni luminose di un mezzo cristallino uniassico dovute alla presenza di un unico centro luminoso. Roma Rend. Acc. Lincei (Ser. 5) 20 1 sem. 1911 (555–562). [3830].
42512

Silber, Paolo r. Ciamician, G.

Silberberg, P. Die Ableitung des Ossannakreises. Elektrot. Zs. Berlin 32 1911 (323). [6070 6045].
42513

Silberstein, Ludovico. Sulla massa mutua di due elettroni. Nuovo Cimento Pisa (Ser. 6) 1 1911 (IV–VI). [4960].
42514

———— Ueber die gegenseitige Masse kugelförmiger Elektronen. Physik. Zs. Leipzig 12 1911 (87–91). [4960].
42515

———— Fale elektromagnetyczne. Ciąg dalszy. [Les ondes électromagnétiques. Suite.] Przegl. techn. Warszawa 49 1911 (117–119). [6600].
42516

Silberstein, Ludovico. Fale nieciągłości w ośrodku przewodzącym. [Ueber Unstetigkeitswellen in einem Halbleiter.] Warszawa Spraw. Tow. Nauk. **4** 1911 (256–262). [6627]. 42517

—————— Kwaternionowa postać teoryi względności. [Quaternionenform der Relativitätstheorie.] Warszawa Spraw. Tow. Nauk. **4** 1911 (506–547). [0000 2990 4900]. 42518

Silva, G. r. Alessio, A.

Silvey, Oscar William. An investigation of a point discharge in a magnetic field. Indianapolis Ind. Proc. Acad. Sci. **1909** 1910 (233–242 with ff.). [6810]. 42519

—————— An investigation of a point discharge in magnetic and electrostatic fields. Indianapolis Ind. Proc. Acad. Sci. **1910** 1911 (247–268 with ff. tables). [6810]. 42520

Simon, H. Physik und Technik der Thermopenetration. Zs. med. Elektrol. Leipzig **13** 1911 (97–131 mit 1 Taf.). [5900]. 42521

—————— Der elektrische Lichtbogen. Experimentalvortrag ... Leipzig (S. Hirzel) 1911 (III — 52 mit 1 Taf.). 24 cm. 2 M. [6830]. 42522

Simonin. Éclipse totale de Soleil du 30 août 1905. Mission de l'Observatoire de Nice. Rapport. Ann. bur. longit. Paris **8** 1911 (O. 1 à O. 43 av. pl.). [4205]. 42523

Simons, Arthur. Crampi bei amyotrophischer Lateralsklerose. Mit einem Anhang : Untersuchung der Aktionsströme der Muskeln während des Crampus, von Paul Hoffmann. Zs. ges. Neurol. Berlin Orig. **5** 1911 (23–28). [5900]. 42524

Simons, Konrad. Elektrotechnik. Taschenbuch Math. Leipzig **2** 1911 (447–489). [6400 6000]. 42525

Simpson, G. C. and **Wright**, C. S. Atmospheric electricity over the ocean. London Proc. R. Soc. (Ser. A.) **85** 1911 (175–199). [5270]. 42526

Sirk, H. Die Beziehungen zwischen dem Gesetz von Avogadro und der kinetischen Gastheorie. Wien Viertelj.-Ber. Ver. Förd. PhysChem. Unterr. **16** 1911 (120–130). [0200 1450]. 42527

—————— r. Doelter, C.

Sitter de W. On the bearing of the principle of relativity on gravitational astronomy. London Mon. Not. R. Astron. Soc. **71** 1911 (388–415). [4940]. 42528

Sizes, Gabriel. Sur la résonance multiple des cloches. Paris C. R. Acad. sci. **154** 1912 (340–342). [9120]. 42529

Skinner, Clarence] A[urelius] und **Tuckerman** jr., L. B. Halbschatteninterferometer. (Half shade interferometers.) (Übers.) Physik. Zs. Leipzig **12** 1911 (620–626). [3610 4000]. 42530

Skrabal, Anton. Chemische und strahlende Energie. Wien Schr. Ver. Verbr. Naturw. Kenntn. **51** 1910–11 1911 (225–256). [3260]. 42531

Skworzow, J. Aggregation und Kristallistation des Wassers in Zusammenhang mit der Frage von dem physikalischen Zustand der Körper. Zs. Kolloide Dresden **9** 1911 (107–112). [0100 0400]. 42532

Slaby, A[dolf]. Otto von Guericke. D. Mus. Vortr. München H. **3** 1906 (13 mit Portr. u. Taf.). [0010]. 42533

Smallwood, Julian C. The exception to Hooke's law. Physic. Rev. Ithaca N.Y. **33** 1911 (317–321 with fig.). [0840]. 42534

Smeal, Glenny r. Love. E. F. J.

Smedts, Arthur. Recherches sur la polarisation produite par le passage du courant électrique dans la flamme. Bruxelles Bul. Acad. roy. **1905** (333–359). [6805]. 42535

[**Smirnov**, D[mitrij] A[leksandrovič].] Смирновъ, Д[митрій] А[лександровичъ]. О нѣкоторыхъ явленіяхъ, наблюденныхъ при раскручиваніи проволока изъ фосфорной бронзы. [Sur quelques phénomènes observés pendant la détorsion des fils de phosphore-bronze.] St. Peterburg. Žurn. russ. fiz-chim. Obsc. Fiz. otd. **41** 1909 (244–245). [0840]. 42536

—————— Объ очкахъ для видѣнія подъ водой. [Lunettes pour voir dans l'eau.] St. Peterburg Žurn. russ. fiz.-chim. Obsc. Fiz. otd. **41** 1909 (232). [3090]. 42537

Smith, Alexander und **Menzies**, Alan W. C. Dampfdruckuntersuchungen. VII. Der Dampfdruck von getrock-

netem Kalomel. Zs. physik. Chem.
Leipzig **76** 1911 (713–720). [1900].
42538

Smith, Alpheus W[ilson]. The Hall
effect and some allied effects in alloys.
Physic. Rev. Ithaca N.Y. **32** 1911
(178–200 with text fig.). [6455 5669
5710].
42539

————— The transverse thermomagnetic effect in nickel and cobalt.
Physic. Rev. Ithaca N.Y. **33** 1911
(295–306 with fig. tables). [2020
6455].
42540

Smith, Arthur Whitmore. Heat of
evaporation of water at 100° C. [Ab-
stract.] Physic. Rev. Ithaca N.Y. **32**
1911 (628–629). [1680].
42541

————— Heat of evaporation of
water. Physic. Rev. Ithaca N.Y. **33**
1911 (173–183 with fig. tables). [1680].
42542

Smith, C. A. Vibrating wires and
the measurement of distance. Electr.
Rev. London **69** 1911 (124–126).
[0807].
42543

Smith, C. F. Irregularities in the
rotating field of the polyphase induction motor. London J. Inst. Electr.
Engin. **46** 1911 (132–170). [0070].
42544

Smith, F. E. v. Glazebrook, R. T.

Smith, S. P. The non-salient pole
turbo-alternator. London J. Inst.
Electr. Engin. **47** 1911 (562–606).
[6045].
42545

Smits, A[ndreas]. Over terugloopende damplijnen. I. [On retrogressive vapour-lines. I.] Amsterdam
Versl. Wis. Nat. Afd. K. Akad. Wet. **20**
[1911] (136–141) (Dutch); Amsterdam
Proc. Sci. K. Akad. Wet. **14** [1911]
(177–182) (English). [2457].
42546

————— Over terugloopende smeltlijnen. II. [On retrogressive melting
point lines. II.] Amsterdam Versl.
Wis. Nat. Afd. K. Akad. Wet. **20**
[1911] (57–64) (Dutch); Amsterdam
Proc. Sci. K. Akad. Wet. **14** [1911]
(170–177) (English). [2457]. 42547

————— De toepassing van de
nieuwe theorie der allotropie op het
stelsel zwavel. [The application of the
new theory of allotropy to the system
sulphur.] Amsterdam Versl. Wis. Nat.
Afd. K. Akad. Wet. **20** [1911] (232–
238) (Dutch); Amsterdam Proc. Sci.
(c 4388)

K. Akad. Wet. **14** [1911] (263–270)
(English). [1887].
42548

Smits, A[ndreas]. Het systeem ijzer-
koolstof. [The system iron-carbon.] Amsterdam Versl. Wis. Nat. Afd. K. Akad.
Wet. **20** [1911] (542–548) (Dutch);
Amsterdam Proc. Sci. K. Akad. Wet.
14 [1911] (530–536) (English). [1887].
42549

————— Eine neue Theorie der
Erscheinung Allotropie. Zs. physik.
Chem. Leipzig **76** 1911 (421–444).
[1887 1940].
42550

————— „Das Gesetz der Um-
wandlungsstufen" in het licht van de
theorie der allotropie. [„Das Gesetz
der Umwandlungsstufen" in the light
of the theory of allotropy.] Amsterdam
Versl. Wis. Nat. Afd. K. Akad. Wet.
20 1912 (749–761) (Dutch); Amsterdam
Proc. Sci. K. Akad. Wet. **14** 1912 (788–
801) (English). [1930]. 42551

————— en **Leeuw**, H[erman]
L[ouis] de. Over het stelsel zwavel.
[On the system sulphur.] Amsterdam
Versl. Wis. Nat. Afd. K. Akad. Wet.
20 [1911] (400–407) (Dutch); Amsterdam Proc. Sci. K. Akad. Wet. **14**
[1911] (461–468) (English). [1887].
42552

————— en **Maarse**, J. Over het
stelsel water-phenol. [On the system
water-phenol.] Amsterdam Versl. Wis.
Nat. Afd. K. Akad. Wet. **20** [1911]
(100–104) (Dutch); Amsterdam Proc.
Sci. K. Akad. Wet. **14** [1911] (192–195)
(English). [1887]. 42553

————— en **Treub**, J. P. Over
terugloopende smeltlijnen. III. [On
retrogressive melting point lines. III.]
Amsterdam Versl. Wis. Nat. Afd. K.
Akad. Wet. **20** [1911] (148–151) (Dutch);
Amsterdam Proc. Sci. K. Akad. Wet.
14 [1911] (189–191) (English). [2457].
42554

————— ————— Over den loop der
P-T-lijnen voor standvastige samenstel-
ling in het stelsel aether-anthrachinon.
[On the course of the P-T-lines for
constant concentration in the system
ether - anthraquinone.] Amsterdam
Versl. Wis. Nat. Afd. K. Akad. Wet.
20 [1911] (142–148) (Dutch); Amsterdam Proc. Sci. K. Akad. Wet. **14**
[1911] (183–188) (English). [1887
2457].
42555

Smoluchowski, M. v. Bemerkung zur Theorie des absoluten Manometers von Knudsen. Ann. Physik Leipzig (4. Folge) 34 1911 (182–184). [0200 1450 0835]. 42556

———— Über Wärmeleitung pulverförmiger Körper und ein hierauf gegründetes neues Wärme-Isolierungsverfahren. Vortrag . . . Kältelnd. Hamburg 8 1911 (59–62). [2020]. 42557

———— Uwagi teoretyczne o przewodnictwie cieplnem w gazach rozrzedzonych oraz o występujących w nich ciśnieniach. [Zur Theorie der Wärmeleitung in verdünnten Gasen und der dabei auftretenden Druckkräfte.] Kraków Bull. Intern. Acad. 1911 A (432–453); Ann. Physik Leipzig (4. Folge) 35 1911 (983–1004). [2035]. 42559

———— Przyczynek do teoryi opalescencyi w gazach w stanie krytycznym. [Beitrag zur Theorie der Opaleszenz von Gasen im kritischen Zustande.) Kraków Bull. Intern. Acad. 1911 A (493–502). [0200 1880]. 42560

———— Dalsze studya nad przewodnictwem cieplnem ciał sproszkowanych. [Études sur la conductibilité calorifique des corps pulvérisés. (Suite).] Kraków Bull. Intern. Acad. 1911 A (548–557). [0200 2035]. 42561

———— O oddziaływaniu wzajemnem kul poruszających się w ośrodku lepkim. [Sur l'action réciproque qui s'exerce entre plusieurs sphères qui se meuvent à travers un milieu visqueux.] Kraków Rozpr. Akad. 11 A 1911 (1–3); Kraków Bull. Intern. Acad. 1911 A (28–39). [0325]. 42562

———— Some remarks on conduction of heat through rarefied gases. Phil. Mag. London (Ser. 6) 21 1911 (11–14). [3035]. 42563

———— Ewolucya teoryi atomistycznej. [L'évolution de la théorie atomique.] Wiad. mat. Warszawa 15 1911 (201–216); Kraków (Nakl. Akad. Um.) (Spółka Wyd. Pol.) 1911 (24). 8vo. hal. 50. [0100]. 42564

Smyth, L. B. v. Joly, J.

Soddy, Frederick and Berry, Arthur John. Conduction of heat through rarefied gases. London Proc. R. Soc. (Ser. A.) 84 1911 (576–585). [2035]. 42565

———— v. Pirret, R., Russell, A. S.

Soennecken, Alfred. Der Wärmeübergang von Rohrwänden an strömendes Wasser. Mitt. ForschArb. Ingenieurw. Berlin H. 108–109 1911 (33–78). [2000]. 42566

[Sokolov, F[edor] F[edorovič.] Соколовъ, О[едоръ] О[еторовичъ]. Дисперсія въ космическомъ пространствѣ. [Lichtdispersion im Weltraum.] Vopr. fiziki St. Peterburg 3 1909 (176–186 195–206). [0600 3460]. 42567

Solari, Luigi. Circa la priorità nell'invenzione della telegrafia senza fili. Riv. maritt. Roma 1910 4. trim. (75–76). [0010]. 42568

———— Le invenzioni di Marconi e di Pacinotti. Elettricista Roma (Ser. 2) 10 1911 (205–206). [0010 4900]. 42569

Soleri, E. Sostegni per cavi ad alta tensione. Elettricista Roma (Ser. 2) 10 1911 (97–102). [5770]. 42570

Somerville, A. A. Temperature coefficients of electrical resistance. 3. Physic. Rev. Ithaca N.Y. 33 1911 (77–80 with fig.). [5660]. 42571

Somigliana, Carlo. Sull' elasticità della terra. Atti Soc. ital. prog. sci. Roma 4 1911 (115–129). [0840]. 42572

Somma, Raffaele. Il cannocchiale geometrico in relazione all'ottica fisiologica. Napoli (F. Perrella) 1909 (214 con 9 tav.). 25 cm. [3080]. 42573

Sommerfeld, A[rnold]. Das Plancksche Wirkungsquantum und seine allgemeine Bedeutung für die Molekularphysik. Berlin Verh. D. physik. Ges. 13 1911 (1074–1093); Physik. Zs. Leipzig 12 1911 (1057–1069). [4200 4960 0100]. 42574

———— Ueber die Struktur der γ-Strahlen. München SitzBer. Ak. Wiss. math.-phys. Kl. 41 1911 (1–60). [6845 4275]. 42575

———— Ausbreitung der Wellen in der drahtlosen Telegraphie. Einfluss der Bodenbeschaffenheit auf gerichtete und ungerichtete Wellenzüge. Physik. Zs. Leipzig 12 1911 (158). [6615]. 42576

———— und Runge, J. Anwendung der Vektorrechnung auf die Grundlagen der geometrischen Optik. Ann. Physik Leipzig (4. Folge) 35 1911 (277-298). [3000]. 42578

Soret, A. Audiphone magnétique bilatéral. Paris C. R. Acad. sci. 153 1911 (1214-1215). [6485]. 42579

Sorkau, Walter. Experimentelle Untersuchungen über die innere Reibung einiger organischer Flüssigkeiten im turbulenten Strömungszustande. Physik. Zs. Leipzig 12 1911 (582 595). [0325]. 42580

Sosman, Robert B. r. Day, A. L.

Southall, James P[owell] C[ocke]. Abolition of two of the spherical errors of a thin lens-system. Astroph. J. Chicago Ill. 33 1911 (330 337 with table). [3070]. 42581

Spalckhaver, R. und **Schneiders,** Fr. Die Dampfkessel nebst ihren Zubehörteilen und Hilfseinrichtungen. Ein Hand- und Lehrbuch zum praktischen Gebrauch für Ingenieure . . . Berlin (J. Springer) 1911 (VIII — 419). 32 cm. Geb. 24 M. [2490]. 42582

Sparrow, C. M. r. Anderson, J. A.

Spath, Friedrich. Absolutes und relatives elektrisches Potential. Zs. physik. Unterr. Berlin 24 1911 (97 98). [5240]. 42583

Spencer, James Frederick. Ueber eine Elektrode dritter Art zur Messung der Potentiale des Thalliumions. (Uebers. von W. Neumann.) Zs. physik. Chem. Leipzig 76 1911 (360-366). [5610]. 42584

Speranski, Alexander. Über den Dampfdruck und über die integrale Lösungswärme der gesättigten Lösungen. Zs. physik. Chem. Leipzig 78 1911 (86-109). [1925 1920 1690]. 42585

Squier, George O[wen] and **Crehore,** Albert C. Note on oscillatory interference bands and some practical applications. Washington D.C. Dept. Comm. Lab. Bull. Bur. Stand. 7 1911 (131-142 with fig. pl.). [3600 5740 5720 6000]. 42587

Stach, Ernst. Messgeräte für Druck und Geschwindigkeit von Gasen und Dämpfen. Stahl u. Eisen Düsseldorf 31 1911 (1752-1758 1880-1886). [0835]. 42589

Stadthagen, H. Die Sicherung richtigen Längenmasses unter besonderer Berücksichtigung der Endmassnormale. Berlin Zs. Ver. D. Ing. 55 1911 (1525 1529). [0807]. 42590

Staffieri, Emanuele. Manuale di telegrafia e telefonia. Matera (B. Conti) 1910 (56). 21 cm. [0030 4900]. 42591

Stahl, Willy. Untersuchungen über die Spektren des Argons. Zs. wiss. Phot. Leipzig 9 1911 (302 312). [4205]. 42592

Staiger, Fritz. Optische Veränderungen von Azo- und Nitrokörpern durch Lösungsmittel und Aggregatzustand. [Mit einem Anhang: Ueber Absorptionsspektren von Diazokörpern.] Diss. Leipzig. Weida i. Th. (Druck v. Thomas & Hubert) 1910 (39). 23 cm. [3860]. 42593

Stallo, J. B. Die Begriffe und Theorien der modernen Physik. Nach der 3. Aufl. . . . übers. u. hrsg. von Hans **Kleinpeter.** Mit einem Vorwort von Ernst **Mach.** 2. Aufl. Leipzig (J. A. Barth) 1911 (XXIV + 328). 20 cm. 7 M. [0000]. 42594

[**St. Peterburg.** Comité spécial de la Section de Physique de la Société Physico-Chimique russe.] С. Петербургъ. Коммисія при физическомъ отдѣлѣ Русскаго физико-Химическаго Общества. Участіе А.С. Попова въ возникновеніи безпроволочной телеграфіи. [La part de A. S. Popov dans l'histoire de la radio-télégraphie.] St. Peterburg Žurn. russ. fiz.-chim. Obšč. Fiz. otd. 41 1909 (63-72 avec des lettres de E. Branley et de O. Lodge). [0010]. 42595

[**St. Peterburg.** Die Section der Physik der Russischen Physiko-Chemischen Gesellschaft.] С. Петербургъ. Физическое отдѣленіе Русскаго физико-Химическаго Общества. Годовой отчетъ за 1908 г. [Jahresbericht für das Jahr 1908.] St. Peterburg Žurn. russ. fiz.-chim. Obšč. Fiz. otd. 41 1909 (I-XXVI). [0020]. 42596

——— Протоколы засѣданій Отдѣленія отъ 268-го до 277-го. (Procès verbaux des séances 268-277.) St. Peterburg Žurn. russ. fiz.-chim. Obšč. Fiz. otd. 41 1909 (110-114 228 246 319-328 399 410). [0020]. 42597

Staněk, Vl. Ueber das Entwässern der Hydrogele mit Äther. Hoppe-Seylers Zs. physiol. Chem. Strassburg 72 1911 (93 96). [0340]. 42598

Staniewski, M. Cieplo wlaseiwe pewnych pierwiastków stalych w temperaturach niskich. [La chaleur spécifique de quelques éléments solides aux températures basses.] Wszechświat Warszawa 30 1911 (497–499). [1620]. 42599

Stanton, T. E. The mechanical viscosity of fluids. London Proc. R. Soc. (Ser A) 85 1911 (366–376). [0325]. 42600

Stapfer, Marcel. Sur la rotation de la Terre, d'après MM. F. Klein et A. Sommerfeld. Ann. obs. Bordeaux 14 1911 (1–74 av. fig.). 42601

Stark, J[ohannes]. Ueber das Schwärzungsgesetz der Normalbelichtung und über photographische Spektralphotometrie. Ann. Physik Leipzig (4. Folge) 35 1911 (461–485). [4225 3010]. 42602

———— Zahl der Zentren von Lichtemission und Intensitätsverhältnis verschiedener Interferenzordnungen. III. Weitere Beobachtungen. Ann. Physik Leipzig (4. Folge) 35 1911 (486–499). [3060 4200 3610]. 42603

———— Bemerkung zu der Mitteilung des Hrn. Baerwald: „Untersuchung der Einwirkung des Magnetfeldes auf den Dopplereffekt der Kanalstrahlen". Ann. Physik Leipzig (4. Folge) 35 1911 (755–760). [6845]. 42604

———— Erwiderung auf die Bemerkungen des Hrn. Leimbach zu meiner Untersuchung über das Schwärzungsgesetz der Normalbelichtung. Ann. Physik Leipzig (4. Folge) 36 1911 (855–858). [4225 3010]. 42605

———— Antwort auf die Bemerkung des Hrn. Baerwald betreffend die Einwirkung des Magnetfeldes auf den Doppler-Effekt der Kanalstrahlen. Ann. Physik Leipzig (4. Folge) 36 1911 (859–860). [6845 4208]. 42606

———— Bemerkung zu einer Abhandlung des Hrn. Lankenheimer über das Intensitätsverhältnis der Serienlinien des Wasserstoffs im Kanalstrahlenspektrum. Ann. Physik Leipzig (4. Folge) 36 1911 (861–865). [6845 4106 4205]. 42607

———— Bemerkungen zur Diskussion über die Intensitätsverteilung im Dopplereffekt von Kanalstrahlen. Berlin Verh. D. physik. Ges. 13 1911 (193–202). [6845]. 42608

Stark, J[ohannes]. Bemerkung zu den Beobachtungen der Herren Gehrcke und Reichenheim über den Dopplereffekt von Wasserstoffkanalstrahlen. Berlin Verh. D. physik. Ges. 13 1911 (353–356). [6845]. 42609

———— Zur Frage nach dem Träger und dem Sitz der Emission von Serienlinien. Berlin Verh. D. physik. Ges. 13 1911 (405–416); Jahrb. Radioakt. Leipzig 8 1911 (231–240). [4205]. 42610

———— Bemerkungen über das photographische Schwärzungsgesetz. Herrn P. P. Koch zur Antwort. Nebst einer Erwiderung von Peter Paul **Koch**: Zahl der Zentren von Lichtemission . . . Physik. Zs. Leipzig 12 1911 (104–107 268–269 310). [4225]. 42611

———— Zur Diskussion über die Struktur der γ-Strahlen. Bemerkung zu einer Mitteilung von E. Meyer. Physik. Zs. Leipzig 13 1912 (161–162). [6845 4275]. 42612

———— Über einen Zusammenhang zwischen chemischer Energie und optischer Frequenz. Bemerkung zu einer Mitteilung von F. Haber. Berlin Verh. D. physik. Ges. 14 1912 (119–122). 42613

———— Prinzipien der Atomdynamik. Tl 2. Die elementare Strahlung. Leipzig (S. Hirzel) 1911 (XV + 286). 22 cm. 7,80 M. [4200 4205 6800 6845 6620]. 42614

Stacke, Willy. Die Radioaktivität einiger Brunnen der Umgegend von Halle. Diss. Halle a. S. (Druck v. C. A. Kaemmerer & Co.) 1911 (54 mit Tab. u. Taf.). 22 cm. 42615

Starling, S. G. Demonstration of Peltier and Thomson effects. Nature London 85 1911 (512). [5710]. 42616

Statesca, C. Solutions de sels magnétiques hétérogènes dans un champ magnétique hétérogène. Paris C. R. Acad. sci. 153 1911 (547–549). [5467]. 42617

Staub, Th. Physikunterricht bei den Blinden. Verh. Schweiz. Natf. Ges. Aarau 94 1912 (223–225). 42618

Stauffer, K. Die Verunreinigungen der Akkumulatorensäure. Elektr. Betr. Berlin 14 1911 (17–19 29–30). [5629]. 42619

Staus, Anton. Der Indikator und seine Hilfseinrichtungen. Berlin (J. Springer) 1911 (VII + 188). 24 cm. Geb. 6 M. [0820]. 42620

Stead, G. On the anode and cathode spectra of various gases and vapours. London Proc. R. Soc. (Ser. A) 85 1911 (393–401). [4205]. 42621

Stefanini, Annibale. La distribuzione del flusso d'induzione concatenato col secondario di un rocchetto. Nuovo Cimento Pisa (Ser. 6) 1 1911 (236). [6449]. 42622

————— e **Tonietti,** P. Un fonometro per la voce afona. Torino Giorn. Acc. med. (Ser. 4) 17 1911 (155–163). [9500]. 42624

Steffens, Paul. Witterungswechsel und Rheumatismus. Zugleich ein Beitrag zur Erklärung der Wirkung radioaktiver Bäder. Anhang: Beschreibung einer einfachen Einrichtung zur Bestrahlung mit Hochspannungs-Gleichstrom („Anionen - Behandlung"). Vortrag. Leipzig (O. Nemnich) 1910 (16). 23 cm. 0,60 M. [4275]. 42625

Stell, Edmund. Untersuchungen über Solenoide und über ihre praktische Verwendbarkeit für Strassenbahnbremsen. Diss. Berlin (Druck v. A. W. Schade) 1911 (41). 27 cm. [6030]. 42626

Stein, A. Die lineare Ausdehnung der festen Elemente als Funktion der absoluten Schmelztemperatur. Zs. anorg. Chem. Leipzig 73 1911 (270–273). [1410 1400 1810]. 42627

Steinberg, Karl. Über den Halleffekt bei jodhaltigem Kupferjodür. Ann. Physik Leipzig (4. Folge) 35 1911 (1009–1033). [6455 5660]. 42628

————— Ueber den Halleffekt und die Widerstandsänderung im Magnetfelde bei jodhaltigem Kupferjodür. Diss. Jena. Leipzig (J. A. Barth) 1911 (35). 23 cm. [6455 5660]. 42629

Steiner, Desider. Die Hysteresisverluste der ferromagnetisierbaren Manganaluminiumbronzen in Abhängigkeit von der Frequenz des Wechselfeldes. Ann. Physik Leipzig (4. Folge) 35 1911 (727–574 mit 2 Taf.); Diss. Darmstadt. Leipzig (J. A. Barth) 1911 (49 mit 5 Taf.). 23 cm. [5466 5450]. 42630

Steiner, Szilárd. Szines fotografiak. [Farbige Photographien.] Termt.

Közl. Budapest 43 1911 (395–401). [4225]. 42631

Steinhaus, W. Über die Angaben von Hitzdrahtinstrumenten bei schnellen Schwingungen. Physik. Zs. Leipzig 12 1911 (657–659). [5705]. 42632

Steinmetz, Charles P. La natura dei " Transients " in elettrotecnica. Atti Ass. elettrotecn. Milano 15 1911 (1000–1003). [6449]. 42633

Stelzner, Otto. Mathematik und Naturwissenschaften an den neuhumanistischen Schulen unter Einwirkung von Gesner, Ernesti, Heyne und Wolf. Ein Beitrag zur Geschichte des mathematisch-naturwissenschaftlichen Unterrichts. Diss. Leipzig Halle a. S. (Druck v. H. John) 1911 (VI + 90). 22 cm. [0050 0010]. 42634

Stenger, Erich. Ueber das Nachreifen panchromatischer Platten. Jahrb. Phot. Halle 25 1911 (50–54). [4225]. 42635

————— Die Gradation von Bromsilbergelatineschichten im Ultraviolett. Physik. Zs. Leipzig 12 1911 (580–582). [4225]. 42636

————— und **Heller,** H. Ueber den Intensitätsunterschied des Schleiers auf belichteten und nicht belichteten Trockenplatten. Atel. Phot. Halle 18 1911 (45–48 61–63). [4225]. 42637

Stéphan, E. Rapport sur l'observation de l'éclipse totale de Soleil du 30 août 1905, à Guelma (Algérie), adressé à M. le Président du Bureau des Longitudes. Ann. bur. longit. Paris 8 1911 (L. 1 à L. 17 av. pl.). [4205]. 42638

Stephens, W. A. v. Kemp, P.

Stephenson, Andrew. On absorption and dispersion. Phil. Mag. London (Ser. 6) 22 1911 (303–305). [3800]. 42639

Štěrba, Jan. O radioaktivitě sedlin pramenů teplickošanovských. [Ueber die Radioaktivität der Quellensedimente von Teplitz-Schönau.] Prag Rozpr. České Ak. Frant. Jos. 1910 (10); Jahrb. Radioakt. Leipzig 8 1911 (23–34). [4275]. 42640

Stern, Seigfried. Ein Beitrag zur Geschichte der elektrischen Strahlungserscheinungen. Arch. Gesch. Natw. Leipzig 3 1911 (236–237). [6840 0010]. 42642

Stern, Oscar. Determinazione dei campi magnetici di un motore monofase a repulsione sistema Déri. [Sunto. Trad.] Atti Ass. elettrotecn. Milano 15 1911 (229–231). [5440].　42643

―――― Untersuchung der Statorfelder eines Einphasenmotors. Karlsruhe Arb. elektrot. Inst. 2 (1910–1911) 1911 (227–248). [6070].　42644

Sterry, John. Reversal and re-reversal. Phot. J. London 51 1911 (320–322). [4225].　42645

―――― Light and development. Phot. J. London 51 1911 (328–330). [4255].　42646

Steubing, W[alter]. Zweite Antwort an Hrn. Kayser. [Betr. Sauerstoffspektrum]. Ann. Physik Leipzig (4. Folge) 36 1911 (1077–1080). [4205].　42647

―――― Versuche zu der Arbeit von Herrn Wood: Eine neue strahlende Emission seitens des Funkens. Physik. Zs. Leipzig 12 1911 (626–630 mit 2 Taf.). [4270 4292 4205 6820].　42648

―――― Stark, [Johannes]. Zur Spektroskopie des Sauerstoffs. Nebst einer Erwiderung von H[einrich] Kayser. Ann. Physik Leipzig (4. Folge) 34 1911 (1003–1014); 35 (698–612). [4205].　42649

Steuer, Karl. Untersuchung von Dampfdiagrammen auf Grund der Dynamik der Dampfströmung in der Kolbendampfmaschine. Diss. Danzig. Leipzig (Druck v. O. Leiner) 1911 (44). 22 cm. [2490].　42650

Steven, A. I. s. Sadler, C. A.

Stevens. La vitesse du son. Rev. sci. ind. 1906 (58). [9210].　42651

Stewart, A[lfred] W[alter] und Wright Robert. Studien über Absorptionsspektren. IV. Einfluss des Lösungsmittels und der Verdünnung auf die Gültigkeit des Beer'schen Gesetzes. Berlin Ber. D. chem. Ges. 44 1911 (2819–2826 mit 1 Taf.). [3860 3810].　42652

Stewart, G[eorge] W[alter]. The acoustic shadow of a rigid sphere. [Abstract.] Physic. Rev. Ithaca N.Y. 32 1911 (248–249). [9050].　42653

Stewart, O[scar] M[ilton]. The second postulate of relativity and the electromagnetic emission theory of light.

Physic. Rev. Ithaca N.Y. 32 1911 (418–428). [6620 3400].　42654

Stifler, W. W. The magnetization of cobalt as a function of the temperature and the determination of its intrinsic magnetic field. Physic. Rev. Ithaca N.Y. 33 1911 (268–294 with fig. tables). [5440 4960 5460].　42655

―――― Tests on certain electrical insulators at high temperatures. Physic. Rev. Ithaca N.Y. 32 1911 (429–432 with text fig.). [5770].　42656

―――― The saturation value of the specific intensity of magnetization of cobalt at various temperatures. [Abstract.] Physic. Rev. Ithaca N.Y. 32 1911 (625–626). [5440].　42657

Stille, C. Telegraphen- und Fernsprechtechnik. Braunschweig (F. Vieweg & S.) 1911 (XVI + 350 mit 1 Taf.). 24 cm. 12 M. [6480 6485 6960].　42658

Stilling, J[akob]. Ueber den Mechanismus der Akkommodation. Zs. Augenheilk. Berlin 25 1911 (15–27 141–153 mit 1 Taf.). [4420].　42659

Stobbe, Hans und Ebert, Erich. Die Lichtabsorption einiger korrespondierender Äthan-, Äthylen- und Acetylen-Derivate. Berlin Ber. D. chem. Ges. 44 1911 (1289–1294). [3860].　42660

―――― Fluorescenz und Radiolumineszenz einiger Kohlenwasserstoffe mit Äthan-, Äthylen- und Acetylen-Resten. Berlin Ber. D. chem. Ges. 44 1911 (1294–1297). [4230].　42661

―――― und Reuss, Fritz. Die Lichtrefraktion der Allo- und Isozimtsäuren. Berlin Ber. D. chem. Ges. 44 1911 (2735–2739). [3810].　42662

Stock, Alfred. Ein Projektionsapparat für die Chemievorlesung. Zs. Elektroch. Halle 17 1911 (995–1002). [0050].　42663

Stock, J. O ruchu kuli w ośrodku lepkim wzdłuz ściany płaskiej. (Über die Bewegung einer Kugel in einem zähen Medium längs einer ebenen Wand.) Kraków Bull. Intern. Acad. 1911 A (18–27). [0325].　42664

Stöckl, K. Vakuum-Röhren-Licht. Bayr. Ind.Bl. München 97 1911 (301–304). [6080].　42665

Stohr, Adolf. Monokulare Plastik. Vortrag . . . (Wiss. Beilage z. 23. Jahresber. (1910) d. Philos. Ges. zu Wien.) Leipzig (J. A. Barth) 1911 (21–39). [4400 4440]. 42666

Stoermer. Neue Methoden zur Erzeugung hoher Temperaturen. Ber. Ver. D. Fabr. Feuerfester Produkte Berlin 31 1911 (80–83). [1010]. 42667

Störmer, Carl. Sur la structure de la couronne du Soleil. Paris C. R. Acad. sci. 152 1911 (425–428 av. fig.). [6845]. 42668

——— La structure de la couronne du Soleil dans la théorie d'Arrhenius. Paris C. R. Acad. sci. 152 1911 (571–574). [6845]. 42669

Stoll, Otto. Ueber die specifische Wärme C, von elektrolytischem Sauerstoff und die theoretische Berechnung des mechanischen Wärmeäquivalentes. Diss. Marburg (Druck v. R. Friedrich) 1911 (V + 40 mit 1 Taf.). 22 cm. [1640 2410]. 42670

Stoltzenberg, H[ugo]. Optische Aktivität und kristallinisch-flüssiger Zustand. Diss. Halle-Wittenberg. Gräfenhainichen (Druck v. C. Schulze & Co.) 1911 (74). 23 cm. [4940]. 42671

Stolze, F. Handbuch des Vergrösserns auf Papieren und Platten. 3., neubearb. Aufl. Hrsg. von A. Streissler. (Encyklopädie der Photographie. H. 17.) Halle a. S. (W. Knapp) 1911 [1912] (VII + 206). 22 cm. 6 M. [4225]. 42672

Stone, John Stone. Maximum current in the secondary of a transformer. Physic. Rev. Ithaca N.Y. 32 1911 (398–405 with text fig.). [6040]. 42673

——— Schwingungszahlen und Dämpfungskoeffizienten gekoppelter Oszillatoren. Elektrot. Zs. Berlin 33 1912 (111–114). [6450 6470 6610 6820]. 42674

Strahl. Untersuchung und Berechnung der Blasrohre und Schornsteine von Lokomotiven. Organ Eisenbahnw. Wiesbaden (N. F.) 48 1911 (321–328 341–348 359–366 379–387 399–406 419–423). [2490]. 42675

Strauss, Carl. Schulversuch zum Nachweis des Gay-Lussac'schen Gesetzes. Zs. physik. Unterr. Berlin 25 1912 (36–37). [6650]. 42676

Strecker, Hans. Aus der Praxis der Kolloidchemie. Ein neues Druckverfahren: Stagmatypie. [Nebst Entgegnung von Wa. Ostwald.] Zs. Elektroch. Halle 18 1912 (18–22 mit Taf. 127). [4225]. 42677

[Strecker, Karl]. A E F. Ausschuss für Einheiten und Formelgrössen. Berlin Verh. D. physik. Ges. 13 1911 (519–526). [0070 0805]. 42678

——— Einheiten und Formelgrössen. Elektrot. Zs. Berlin 32 1911 (721–723). [5000 0070 0805]. 42679

Strehl, Karl. Ueber die Leistungsgrenzen und Empfindungsstärke unseres Sehorgans bei Abbildung von Fixsternen und Planeten mit und ohne Fernrohr. Astr. Nachr. Kiel 188 1911 (385–388). [4400]. 42680

Streintz, F. und Wellik, A. Über den Widerstand zwischen Metall und Kristall an ebenen Grenzflächen. Physik. Zs. Leipzig 12 1911 (845–854). [5640 5660]. 42681

Streit, Hermann. Einige akustische Untersuchungen mit Hilfe des Endophonoskops. Münchener med. Wochenschr. 58 1911 (792–793). [9430]. 42682

Strong, W. W. Experiments on the radioactivity of erbium, potassium and rubidium compounds. Amer. Chem. J. Baltimore 42 1909 (147–150). [4275]. 42683

——— Report. Recent progress in our knowledge of the radioactive elements. Amer. Chem. J. Baltimore 42 1909 (541–558 with tables). [4275]. 42684

——— Glossary of atmospheric electricity terms. Terr. Mag. Baltimore Md. 15 1910 (145–158 with table). [1600]. 42685

——— Spectroscopic evidences of molecular clustering. [Abstract.] Physic. Rev. Ithaca N.Y. 32 1911 (621–624). [3860]. 42686

——— v. Jones, H. C.

Struck, H. v. Matthies, W.

Strutt, R. J. The afterglow of electric discharge. London Proc. Physic. Soc. 23 1910 (66–73). [6840]. 42687

——— On flames of low temperature supported by ozone. London Proc. Physic. Soc. 23 1911 (147–151). [4202]. 42688

Strutt, R. J. A chemically active modification of nitrogen, produced by the electric discharge. London Proc. R. Soc. (Ser. A) **85** 1911 (219–229). [6840]. 42689

—— The flame arising from the nitrogen-burning arc. London Proc. R. Soc. (Ser. A.) **85** 1911 (533–536). [6830]. 42690

—— The afterglow of electric discharge in nitrogen. Nature London **85** 1911 (439–440). [6840 4205]. 42691

—— v. Fowler.

Struycken, H. J. L. Beobachtungen über die physiologische obere Hörgrenze für Luft- und Knochenleitung. Beitr. Anat. Ohr. Berlin **5** 1911 (1–6). [9430]. 42692

Stubbs, C. M. Conductivity of aqueous solutions of carbon-dioxide prepared under pressure at various temperatures; with special reference to the formation of a hydrate at low temperatures. Wellington Trans. N.-Zeal. Inst. **43** 1911 (11 25). [6240]. 42693

Stuhlmann, Otto, jun. The difference in the photoelectric effect caused by incident and emergent light. [Abstract.] Physic. Rev. Ithaca N.Y. **32** 1911 (621). [5260]. 42694

Stumpf, C[arl]. Differenztöne und Konsonanz. 2. Artikel. Beitr. Akustik Leipzig H. **6** 1911 (151–165); Zs. Psychol. Leipzig Abt. 1 **59** 1911 (161–175). [9450]. 42695

—— Konsonanz und Konkordanz. Nebst Bemerkungen über Wohlklang und Wohlgefälligkeit musikalischer Zusammenklänge. Zs. Psychol. Leipzig Abt. 1 **58** 1911 (321–355). [9450]. 42696

—— Die Anfänge der Musik. Leipzig (J. A. Barth) 1911 (209). 20 cm. 6,60 M. [9400]. 42697

Stumpf, F. Optische Beobachtungen an einer flüssig-kristallinischen aktiven Substanz. Ann. Physik Leipzig (4. Folge) **37** 1912 (351–379 mit 1 Taf.). [3830 4050]. 42698

Stumpf, J[ohann]. Die Wärmeausnutzung der heutigen Kolbendampfmaschine. [Nebst Erwiderung von K. Heilmann.] Berlin Zs. Ver. D. Ing. **55** 1911 (1699 1708). [2490]. 42699

—— Die Gleichstrom-Dampfmaschine. München u. Berlin (R.

Oldenbourg) 1911 (VII + 184 mit 7 Taf.). 28 cm. 10 M. [2490]. 42700

Subkis, Solomon. Der Einfluss der Koppelung bei langsamen ungedämpften Schwingungen. Diss. Braunschweig. Leipzig (J. A. Barth) 1910 (31). 23 cm. [6820]. 42701

Suchý, Julius. O změně elektrického odporu ocelových a železných drátů při mechanickém napjeti. [Ueber die Aenderung des elektrischen Widerstandes der Stahl- und Eisendrähte bei mechanischer Spannung.] Prag Rozpr. České Ak. Frant. Jos. **1910** (13). [5660]. 42702

—— Wärmestrahlung und Wärmeleitung. Ann. Physik Leipzig (4. Folge) **36** 1911 (341–382). [4200 2000]. 42703

Süchting, Fritz. Über einen neuen elektrischen Zeigertelegraphen (Kommandoapparat). Elektrot. Zs. Berlin **32** 1911 (516–519 543–546). [6480]. 42704

Süring, R. Messungen der neutralen Punkte der atmosphärischen Polarisation. Berlin Veröff. met. Inst. No. **240** 1911 (X–XXVIII). 42705

—— Ballonphotographie. [In: Angewandte Photographie in Wissenschaft u. Technik. Hrsg. v. K. W. Wolf-Czapek. Tl 3.] Berlin (Union) 1911 (25–31 mit 2 Taf.). [3085]. 42706

Sumec. Gegen- und Querwindungen. [Nebst] Erwiderung von W. **Rogowski**.] Elektrot. Zs. Berlin **32** 1911 (1194–1195); **33** 1912 (51). [6060]. 42707

Sumec, J. Spannungsabfall von Drehstromgeneratoren. Elektrot. Zs. Berlin **32** 1911 (77–80). [6060]. 42708

Sutherland, William. On weak electrolytes and towards a dynamical theory of solutions. Phil. Mag. London (Ser. 6) **22** 1911 (17–66). [1430]. 42709

Svedberg, The. Diffusionsgeschwindigkeit und Teilchengrösse disperser Systeme. Ark Kemi Stockholm **3** No. 22 1909 (1–8); **4** No. 12 1911 (7 mit 1 Fig.). [0320]. 42710

—— Über die Bildung disperser Systeme durch Bestrahlung von Metallen mit ultraviolettem Licht und Röntgenstrahlen. Zs. Kolloide Dresden **6** 1910 (129–136). [0340 6825]. 42712

—— Prüfung der Gültigkeit der van der Waalsschen Zustandsgleichung für kolloide Lösungen. Zs. Kolloide Dresden 9 1911 (219–224). [0310 0310 1800 1920]. 42713

Svedberg, The. und Andreen-Svedberg, Andrea. Diffusionsgeschwindigkeit und relative Grösse gelöster Moleküle. Zs. physik. Chem. Leipzig 76 1911 (145–155). [0320 0150 3860]. 42714

——— und Estrup, Knud. Ueber die Bestimmung der Häufigkeitsverteilung der Teilchengrössen in einem dispersen System. Zs. Kolloide Dresden 9 1911 (259 261). [0340 0150]. 42715

——— und Inouye, Katsuji. Über die Eigenbewegung der Teilchen in kolloiden Lösungen. 3. Ark. Kemi Stockholm 4 No. 19 1911 (20 mit 9 Fig.). [0300 0340]. 42716

——— Zur Kenntnis der Struktur ultramikroskopischer Teilchen. Zs. Kolloide Dresden 9 1911 (49–53). [0550 0340]. 42717

——— Ultramikroskopische Beobachtung einer Temperaturkoagulation. Zs. Kolloide Dresden 9 1911 (153–154). 42718

——— Eine neue Methode zur Prüfung der Gültigkeit des Boyle-Gay-Lussacschen Gesetzes für kolloide Lösungen. (2. Mitt.) Zs. physik. Chem. Leipzig 77 1911 (145–191). [0340 0842 0150]. 42719

Swann, W. F. G. The problem of the uniform rotation of a circular cylinder in its connexion with the principle of relativity. Phil. Mag. London (Ser. 6) 21 1911 (342–348). [0810 0820]. 42720

——— The longitudinal and transverse mass of an electron. Phil. Mag. London (Ser. 6) 21 1911 (733–735). [6620 4960]. 42721

——— The magnetic field produced by a charged condenser moving through space. Phil. Mag. London (Ser. 6) 22 1911 (150–168). [6435]. 42722

Swinburne, James. Separation of oxygen by cold. London Trans. Faraday Soc. 6 1911 (212–224). [1870]. 42723

Swinne, Richard. Über einige zwischen den radioaktiven Elementen bestehende Beziehungen. Physik. Zs. Leipzig 13 1912 (14–21). [4275 6845]. 42724

——— Bemerkung zu Niels Bjerrum: Ueber die spezifische Wärme der Gase. [Nebst] Antwort von Niels Bjerrum. Zs. Elektroch. Halle 17 1911 (994 995). [1640]. 42725

Szabó v. Bigyon, Andreas. Zur Fehlerregelung der Klupperung. Wien ZentrBl. Forstw. 37 1911 (441–447). [0807]. 42588

Szanto, Hugo. Messung des Brechungsexponenten des Wassers mit einfachen Mitteln. Natur u. Unterricht Stuttgart 3 1912 (71–72). [0050]. 42726

Szillard, B. Über einen Apparat zur Messung der Radioaktivität. ChemZtg Cöthen 35 1911 (539 540). [4275]. 42727

——— Frau Pierre Curie und ihr Werk. ChemZtg Cöthen 35 1911 (1361–1362). [0010]. 42728

——— Elektromos hullámok kiáramlása fémekből. [Ausströmung elektrischer Wellen aus Metallen.] Math. Termt. Ért. Budapest 29 1911 (76–90). [5210 5660 6043]. 42729

——— Készülék a Röntgensugaraknak abszolut egységekben való mérésére, főképen therapiai czélokra. [Apparat zur Messung der Röntgenstrahlen in absoluten Einheiten, besonders für therapeutische Zwecke.] Math. Termt. Ért. Budapest 29 1911 (246–257). [0090 4240]. 42730

Szivessy, G. Über den Voltaeffekt bei Kristallen. Ann. Physik Leipzig (4. Folge) 36 1911 (183–186). [6210 5210]. 42731

——— und Schäfer, K. Ueber die Erhöhung des elektrischen Leitvermögens bei flüssigen Dielektrika durch Bestrahlung mit ultraviolettem Lichte. Ann. Physik Leipzig (4. Folge) 35 1911 (511–523). [5660 6850]. 42732

Szyszkowski, Bohdan. Politropiczne cieplo właściwe oraz jego zastosowania. [Sur la chaleur spécifique polytrope et ses applications.] Wektor Warszawa 1 1911 (268–276). [2400]. 42733

Takamine, T[oshio]. Ōba, T[akashi] and Matsumoto, N[arazo]. Experimental determination of induced magnetism in an elliptic toroid in different magnetic fields. Tokyo Su. Buts. Kw. K. (Ser. 2) 5 1910 (303–308). [5440]. 42735

Take, E. Alterungs- und Umwandlungs-Studien an Heuslerschen ferromagnetisierbaren Aluminium-Man-

ganbronzen, insbesondere an Schmiedeproben. (Göttingen Abh. Ges. Wiss.
math.-phys. Kl. 8 1911 No. 2 (IV +
127); Natw. Rdsch. Braunschweig 26
1911 (505-508 521-524). [5466].
42736

Talsch, Ernst. Untersuchungen über
gekoppelte elektrische Schwingungskreise. (Mitteilungen der physikalischen Versuchs-Station Halle-Cröllwitz.)
(No. 28.) Diss. Halle a. S. (Druck v.
C. A. Kaemmerer & Co.) 1912 (46 mit
Taf.). 29 cm. [6450 6470 6610
6940 6043]. 42737

Tamaki, K[ajuro]. Electric field due
to Hertzian doublet oscillators. Kyoto
Mem. Coll. Sci. Eng. 2 1910 (121-131).
[6610]. 42738

—————— Electric and magnetic
force due to a moving electric charge.
Kyoto Mem. Coll. Sci. Eng. 2 1910
(151-158). [4940]. 42739

—————— Note on general equations
for an electromagnetic field in a moving
medium. Kyoto Mem. Coll. Sci. Eng.
3 1911 (103-111). [4940 6400 6410].
42740

—————— On fundamental equations
for an electromagnetic field in a moving
medium. Kyoto Mem. Coll. Sci. Eng.
3 1911 (113-119). [4940 6400 6410].
42741

—————— Energy radiated by a
damped Hertzian oscillator. Kyoto
Mem. Coll. Sci. Eng. 3 1911 (121-127).
[6490 6610]. 42742

—————— Mean flow of energy from
three Hertzian doublet oscillators.
Kyoto Mem. Coll. Sci. Eng. 3 1911
(129-136). [6490]. 42743

—————— Motion of an electron in
the neighbourhood of a negatively
charged sphere. Kyoto Mem. Coll. Sci.
Eng. 3 1911 (137-140). [4960]. 42744

—————— v. Kimura, M.

Tamarkine, J. Sur le problème des
vibrations transversales d'une verge
élastique homogène. Paris C. R. Acad.
sci. 154 1912 (267-271). [9110]. 42745

Tammann, G[ustav]. Zur Thermodynamik der Gleichgewichte in Einstoffsystemen. 1. Ann. Physik Leipzig
(4. Folge) 36 1911 (1027-1054); Zs.
Elektroch. Halle 17 1911 (745-749).
[2400 1810 1930 1887]. 42746

—————— Zur Molekulargewichtsbestimmung krystallisierter Stoffe. Ber-

lin Ber. D. chem. Ges. 44 1911 (3618-
3628). [1810 0300]. 42747

Tammann, G[ustav]. Zur Thermodynamik der Gleichgewichte in Einstoffsystemen. 1. Die Gleichgewichte
isotroper und anisotroper Phasen. II.
Der Polymorphismus. Göttingen
Nachr. Ges. Wiss. math.-phys. Kl. 1911
(236-260 325-360). [2400 1810 1930].
42748

—————— Ueber Zustandsgleichungen im Gebiete kleiner Volumen.
Göttingen Nachr. Ges. Wiss. math.-
phys. Kl. 1911 (527-562). [1800 1885
2445]. 42749

Tangl, Karl. Experimentaluntersuchungen über die Oberflächenspannung an der Trennungsfläche fest-
flüssig. Ann. Physik Leipzig (4. Folge)
34 1911 (311-342). [0300 0320].
42750

Tannery, J. v. Bouasse, H.

Tardivo, Cesare. La trasmissione
telegrafica delle fotografie per mezzo
del telestereografo Belin. Roma Ann.
Soc. ing. 25 1910 (510-516). [6000].
42751

Taylor, J. E. Wireless telegraphy in
relation to interference and perturbation. London J. Inst. Electr. Engin.
47 1911 (119-166). [6615]. 42752

Taylor, T. S. On the ionization of
different gases by the Alpha particles
from polonium and the relative amounts
of energy required to produce an ion.
Phil. Mag. London (Ser. 6) 21 1911
(571-579); [abstract] Physic. Rev.
Ithaca N.Y. 32 1911 (236). [4275
6805]. 42753

Tchougaeff v. Tschugaeff.

Teichmüller, [Joachim]. Schnelle
Ermittelung der mittleren hemisphäri-
schen und mittleren sphärischen Licht-
stärke mittels Rechenschiebers. J.
Gasbeleucht. München 55 1912 (190-
194). [3010]. 42755

Tejessey, M. Utilizzazione del
vapore di scappamento. [Trad.] Industria Milano 24 1910 (68-70 117-119
131-134). [2490]. 42756

[Terešin, S[ergěj] Jakovlevič].]
Терешинъ, С[ергѣй] Яковлевичъ].
Соотношеніе между плотностью и сте-
пени диссоціаціи водныхъ рас-
творовъ. [La relation entre la densité
et le degré de dissociation des dissolutions aqueuses.] St. Peterburg

Zorn, russ. fiz.-chim. Obšč. Fiz. otd. **41** 1909 (155–160). [0100]. 42757

Ter Gazarian, G. Sur une relation générale entre les propriétés physiques des corps ; application aux densités. Paris C. R. Acad. sci. **153** 1911 (871–874) ; Application à la viscosité, la capillarité, l'énergie superficielle, la chaleur, la vaporisation, le diamètre rectiligne. *l.c.* (1071–1074). [1885 0325–0300 1680–1850]. 42758

Terlanday, Emil. A kettőstörés utánzása üveglemezekkel. [Nachbildung der Doppelbrechung mittels Glasplatten.] Math. Phys. L. Budapest **20** 1911 (302–330). [3820–3830]. 42759

Texett, Frank B. Telefonia a grande distanza in America. Atti Ass. elettrotecn. Milano **15** 1911 (1126–1132). [6485]. 42760

Thibaut, R. Die spezifische Wärme verschiedener Gase und Dämpfe. Ann. Physik Leipzig (4. Folge) **35** 1911 (347–377). [1640]. 42761

Thieme, Bruno. Notiz zur elektrischen Abscheidung von Kohlenstoff aus Flammen. Zs. Elektroch. Halle **18** 1912 (131). [5685]. 42762

———— Abscheidungen aus Flammen durch Elektrizität. Zs. physik. Chem. Leipzig **78** 1912 (490–499). [5685]. 42763

———— Der Selbstinduktionsversuch von Lodge in einer neuen Anordnung. Zs. physik. Unterr. Leipzig **24** 1911 (279–283). [6440–0050]. 42764

Thierry (De, J. H. L'imitatore per corrente alternata e continua. Elettricità Milano **36** 1911 (196–198). [6020]. 42765

Thirion, J. Pascal ; l'horreur du vide et la pression atmosphérique. Rev. quest. sci. Bruxelles **13** 1908 (149–248). [0010]. 42766

Thomalen, A. Die Ableitung des Ossannaschen Kreises. Elektrot. Zs. Berlin **32** 1911 (131). [6070–6045]. 42767

———— Das Stromdiagramm des Drehstrom-Serienmotors. Elektrot. Zs. Berlin **32** 1911 (1108–1109). [6070]. 42768

———— Berücksichtigung der Streuung im Diagramm des Drehstrom-Serienmotors. Elektrot. Zs. Berlin **32** 1911 (1319–1321). [6070]. 42769

Thomas, P. *v.* Bouasse, H.

Thomas, Viktor. Die Stimmgabel. Eine Skizze zu ihrem Zweihundertjahrsjubiläum. D. Instrban-Ztg Berlin **13** 1911 (42–43). [9410]. 42770

Thompson, Silvanus P. Sul ciclo di isteresi e le figure di Lissajous e sulla energia dissipata in un ciclo di isteresi. [Sunto, Trad.] Atti Ass. elettrotecn. Milano **15** 1911 (452–454). [5450]. 42771

———— Motori-generatori, convertitori e raddrizzatori. (Congresso delle Applicazioni elettriche, Torino, 1911.) Elettricista Roma (Ser. 2) **10** 1911 (293–297) ; [sunto] Atti Ass. elettrotecn. Milano **15** 1911 (889–892). [6047]. 42772

———— Nouvelle méthode d'analyse harmonique par la sommation algébrique d'ordonnées indéterminées. Paris C. R. Acad. sci. **153** 1911 (88–90). [0805]. 42773

———— *v.* Huygens.

Thomsen, Ernst. Über die innere Reibung von Gasgemischen. Ann. Physik Leipzig (4. Folge) **36** 1911 (815–833) ; Diss. Kiel (Druck v. H. Fiencke) 1911 (35). 23 cm. [0325]. 42774

Thomson, Arthur. On a variation in the intensity of the penetrating radiation at the earth's surface observed during the passage of Halley's comet. [Abstract.] Physic. Rev. Ithaca N.Y. **32** 1911 (343–347). [4275]. 42775

[**Thomson,** [Sir] Joseph] J(ohn).] Томсонъ, Дж. Дж. Взаимоотношеніе между матеріей и эфиромъ по новѣйшимъ изслѣдованіямъ въ области электрическа ; переводъ съ англійскаго. [Über die Beziehungen der Materie und des Aethers nach neuen Untersuchungen im Gebiet der Elektrizität ; übers. aus dem englischen.] Vopr. fiziki St. Peterburg **3** 1909 (81–97). [0100]. 42777

———— Energia raggiante e materia. [Sunto, Trad.] Atti Ass. elettrotecn. Milano **15** 1911 (364–368). [3400]. 42776

———— A new method of investigating the positive rays. Cambridge Proc. Phil. Soc. **16** 1911 (120). [4250 6485]. 42778

———— Rays of positive electricity. Phil. Mag. London (Ser. 6) **21** 1911

(225 249); (Uebers.) Jahrb. Radioakt.
Leipzig 8 1911 (197 226 mit 1 Taf.).
[6845 4250].   42779

Thomson, [Sir] J[oseph] J[ohn].
Eine neue Methode der chemischen
Analyse. [Spektrum der positiven
Strahlen.] Jahrb. Radioakt. Leipzig 8
1911 (226 230). [4205 6840]. 42789

———————— Magneto-optics. Encycl.
Brit. (ed. 11) 17 1911. [6635]. 42782

Thomssen, Edgar G. r. Morgan,
J. L. R.

Thorkelsson, Thorkell. Drei Formen
der Zustandsgleichung und die innere
Verdampfungswärme. Physik. Zs.
Leipzig 12 1911 (633 637).   [1880
1689].   42783

Thorner, W[alther]. Die stereoskopische Photographie des Augenhintergrundes. Verh. Ges. D. Natf.
Leipzig 81 (1909) II 2 1910 (224–226).
[4470].   42784

Thornton, W. M. On thunderbolts.
Phil. Mag. London (Ser. 6) 21 1911
(630–634). [5270].   42785

Thovert, J. Photométrie et utilisation des sources colorées. Paris C. R.
Acad. sci. 151 1910 (1347–1349).
[3040].   42786

———————— Photométrie des sources
colorées. J. phys. Paris (sér. 2) 2 1912
(34–49). [3940].   42787

Thrift, William Edward r. Preston.

Thürmel, Erich. Das Lummer-
Pringsheimsche Spektral-Flickerphotometer als optisches Pyrometer. Breslau
Jahresber. Ges. vaterl. Cultur 88 (1910)
1911 natw. Sect. (12–47); Diss. Breslau
(Druck v. Grass, Barth & Comp.) 1910
(43). 21 cm. [3040 4202].   42788

Thurn. H. Demonstrationsapparat
für drahtlose Telephonie mittels elektrischer Wellen. Techn. Monatshefte
Stuttgart 1911 (48–52). [6615 0050
6043].   42789

Tian. Sur la nature de la décomposition de l'eau oxygénée produite par
la lumière. Paris C. R. Acad. sci. 151
1910 (1040–1042). [4225].   42790

———————— Sur les radiations qui
décomposent l'eau et sur le spectre
ultraviolet extrême de l'arc au mercure.
Paris C. R. Acad. sci. 152 1911 (1483
1486). [4225 4205].   42791

Tiede, Erich r. Fischer, F.

Tiersot, Louis. Vérification du vide
dans les lampes à incandescence. Eau
éclairage chauffage 1910 (265–267).
[6980].   42792

Tietze, Curt. Untersuchungen über
die Brauchbarkeit des Thermoelementes
zu energetischen Messungen. (Mittei-
lungen der physikalischen Versuchs-
Station Halle-Cröllwitz.) (No. 27.)
Diss. Halle a. S. (Druck v. C. A.
Kaemmerer & Co.) 1911 (34 mit Tab. u.
Taf.). 29 cm. [6043 5705 5700].
                                42793

Tikhoff, G. A. L'enregistrement
photographique et la reproduction de la
scintillation des étoiles. Paris C. R.
Acad. sci. 154 1912 (329–331). [3165].
                                42794

[Timiriazev, A[rkadij] Klimentovič].]
Тимирязев, Аркадій Клименто-
вичъ]. Электромагнитная теорія
тепловаго излученія. [Elektromag-
netische Theorie der Wärmestrahlung.]
Vopr. fiziki St. Peterburg 3 1909 (157–
176). [6620 4980 0040].   42795

Timmermans, J. Recherches sur le
point de congélation des liquides
organiques. Bruxelles Bul. Soc. chim.
1911 (300–327). [1920].   42796

———————— Recherches sur la densité
des liquides en dessous de zéro.
Bruxelles Bul. Soc. chim. 1907 (395–
402). [1430 0810].   42797

———————— Nouvelles recherches sur
la densité des liquides sous 0°. Bruxelles Bul. Soc. chim. 1908 (427–439).
[0810 1430].   42798

Timofejew, G. Piezochemische
Studien. VIII. Der Einfluss des
Druckes auf die Affinität. II. Zs.
physik. Chem. Leipzig 78 1911 (299–
320). [5610 6200 2475].   42799

Timoschenko, Steph. Erzwungene
Schwingungen prismatischer Stäbe. Zs.
Math. Leipzig 59 1911 (163–203).
[9135 9110].   42800

Tissot, C. Contribution à l'étude
des contacts des détecteurs solides.
J. phys. Paris (sér. 4) 9 1910 (807–901
av. fig.). [6043].   42801

———————— Die geographische Längen-
bestimmung mittels drahtloser Telegraphie. (La détermination des
longitudes par télégraphie sans fil.)
(Uebers.) Jahrb. drahtlos. Telegr.
Leipzig 4 1911 (618–627). [6615].
                                42802

Tissot, C. Sur la détermination exacte des périodes des oscillations électriques. Paris C. R. Acad. sci. **152** 1911 (684–685). [6610]. 42803

Titow, W. S. Beitrag über die Radium-emanationsgehaltsbestimmung durch Ionisationsströme. Physik. Zs. Leipzig **12** 1911 (476–480). [4275]. 42804

Tiwald, Wilh. Einige interessante Versuche über Wärmeleitung und Wärmestrahlung. Natur u. Unterr. Stuttgart **3** 1911 (31–35). [0050]. 42805

Tobey, W. Rigidità dielettrica del-l'olio. [Sunto. Trad.] Atti Ass. elettro-tecn. Milano **15** 1911 (135–136). [5252]. 42806

Todd, G. W. The mobility of the positive ion in gases at low pressures. Cambridge Proc. Phil. Soc. **16** 1911 (21–25); Radium Paris **8** 1911 (113–115). [6805–5685]. 42807

Tolman, Richard C. Non-Newtonian mechanics.—The direction of force and acceleration. Phil. Mag. London (Ser. 6) **22** 1911 (458–463). [0820]. 42808

Tommasina, Th[omas]. Sur une modification donnant une plus grande liberté d'allure et plus de sûreté aux aéroplanes. Genève C. R. Soc. Phys. Hist. Nat. **28** 1912 (43–46 av. fig.). [0090]. 42809

———— Sur un appareil d'aviation non renversable et effectuant automatiquement le vol plané en cas d'arrêt du moteur. Genève C. R. Soc. Phys. Hist. Nat. **28** 1912 (48–52 av. 3 fig.). [0090]. 42810

———— La nature de l'électricité et la dynamique de l'électron. Genève C. R. Soc. Phys. Hist. Nat. **28** 1912 (69–72). [4900–4980]. 42811

———— c. Sarasin.

Tonietti, P. c. Stefanini, A.

Tosi, A. c. Bellini, E.

Toula, Franz. Festschrift zur Feier des fünfzigjährigen Bestandes des Ver-eines zur Verbreitung naturwissen-schaftlicher Kenntnisse in Wien. Wien 1910 (1–267) Selbstverlag. 19 cm. [0020]. 42813

Townsend, John S. The charges on ions in gases, and some effects that influence the motion of negative ions. London Proc. R. Soc. (Ser. A) **85** 1911 (25–29); Phil. Mag. London (Ser. 6) **22** 1911 (204–211). [5685–6805]. 42814

———— The mode of conduction in gases. Phil. Mag. London (Ser. 6) **22** 1911 (656–658). [5685–6805]. 42815

Trabacchi, Giulio Cesare. Misure di velocità di otturatori fotografici. Roma Rend. Acc. Lincei (Ser. 5) **20** 2. sem. 1911 (701–705). [3085]. 42816

Trabert, Wilhelm. Lehrbuch der kosmischen Physik. Leipzig u. Berlin (B. G. Teubner) 1911 (X + 662 mit 1 Taf.). 24 cm. 20 M. [3200]. 42817

Traube, I[sidor]. Étude théorique sur la tension d'attraction et la pression osmotique. J. Chim. Phys. Genève **8** 1910 (515–537). [0300–0310]. 42818

———— Die Theorie des Haft-drucks (Oberflächendrucks). V. Arch. ges. Physiol. Bonn **140** 1911 (109–134). [0300]. 42819

Traube Mengarini, Margherita e **Scala**, Alberto. Azione dell' acqua distillata e dell' acqua distillata con-tenente elettroliti sul piombo metallico. Roma Mem. Acc. Lincei (Ser. 5) **8** 1911 Mem. 14 (576–598 con 2 tav.). [0340]. 42820

———— —— La solubilità dei metalli nell' acqua distillata. Atti Soc. ital. progr. sci. Roma **4** 1911 (201–215). [1920]. 42821

Trautz, Max. Der Temperatur-koeffizient chemischer Reaktionsge-schwindigkeiten. V. Reaktionsweg und status nascendi. Der obere Grenzwert der chemischen Reaktionsgeschwindig-keit und die Temperaturen, bei denen er erreicht wird. Zs. physik. Chem. Leipzig **76** 1911 (129–144). [2472]. 42822

Travers, Morris W., **Gwyer**, A. G. C. and **Usher**, F. L. Researches on the attainment of very low temperatures. Part. 2. Further notes on the self intensive process for liquefying gases. Washington D.C. Smithsonian Inst. Misc. Collect. **49** (Pub. 1652) 1906 (1–14 with ff. tables). [1012]. 42823

Trendelenburg, W[ilhelm]. Willibald A. Nagel. Nachruf. Klin. Monatsbl. Augenheilk. Stuttgart (49) N.F. 11 1911 (387–390 mit Portr.). [0040].
42824

——— r. Marx. E.

Treub, J. P. r. Scheffer, F. E. C.; Smits, A.

Triepel, Hermann. Modell der Schwingungsebenen des Lichtes im Polarisationsapparat. Zs. wiss. Mikrosk. Leipzig 28 1911 (42–45). [4000].
42825

Trier, G. r. Schulze. E.

Tripold. Die Radioaktivität der Thermen von Warmbad Villach und die Bedeutung der Piszinen für die Wirksamkeit radioaktiver Bäder. Zs. Balneol. Berlin 4 1911 (33–37). [4275].
42826

Trivelli, A[drian] P[eter] H[ermann]. Over de konstitutie der fotohaloiden. II. III. [Ueber die Konstitution der Photohaloiden. II. III.] Amsterdam Chem. Weekbl. 9 1912 (1–11 248–257). [4225].
42827

——— Het expositieverschil bij physische en chemische werking. [Der Expositionsunterschied bei physikalischer und chemischer Entwicklung.] Amsterdam Chem. Weekbl. 9 1912 (32–36). [4225].
42828

——— Neuere Theorien der photochemischen Vorgänge in der Bromsilbergelatine-Platte. Jahrb. Radioakt. Leipzig 8 1911 (334–383 mit 2 Taf.).
42829

——— Ostwalds Gesetz der Umwandlungsstufen und die photochemische Zersetzung der Silberhaloide. Zs. wiss. Phot. Leipzig 9 1911 (185–187). [4225].
42830

——— Ueber die Natur der Schaumschen Substanz B. Zs. wiss. Phot. Leipzig 9 1911 (187–193). [4225].
42831

Trotter, A. P. The nomenclature of primary and secondary sources of light. Elect. London 67 1911 (204–205 552). [3040].
42832

Trouton, F. T. A demonstration of the phase difference between the primary and secondary currents of a transformer by means of simple apparatus. London Proc. Physic. Soc. 23 1911 (98–102). [6450].
42833

Trowbridge, Augustus. The ether drift. Philadelphia Proc. Amer. Phil. Soc. 49 1910 (52–56). [0600].
42834

——— Concerning the echelette grating. Astroph. J. Chicago Ill. 34 1911 (317–319). [3160 3630]. 42835

——— and Crandall, T. B. Groove-form and energy distribution of diffraction gratings. Phil. Mag. London (Ser. 6) 22 1911 (534–547). [3630].
42836

Trowbridge, C[harles] C[hristopher]. Measurements of the rate of decay of gas phosphorescence. Physic. Rev. Ithaca N.Y. 32 1911 (129–151 with text fig. tables). [4230]. 42837

——— The origin of luminous meteor trains. Pop. Sci. Mon. New York 79 1911 (191–203 with ff.). [6805]. 42838

True, Heinrich. Über die Erdströme in der Nähe einer Sendeantenne für drahtlose Telegraphie. Jahrb. drahtlos. Telegr. Leipzig 5 1911 (125–175). [6615]. 42839

Tschernobaéff, D. et Wologdine, L. Sur les chaleurs de formation de quelques silicates. Paris C. R. Acad. sci. 154 1912 (206–208). [1695]. 42840

Tschugaeff, L. Über einen neuen Typus der anomalen Rotationsdispersion. Ein Beitrag zur Kenntnis der optischen Superposition. (Vorl. Mitt.) Berlin Ber. D. chem. Ges. 44 1911 (2023–2030). [4040]. 42841

——— Ueber Rotationsdispersion. III. Farblose Verbindungen. Zs. physik. Chem. Leipzig 76 1911 (469–483). [4050]. 42842

——— et Koch, P. Sur une anomalie de la réfraction moléculaire dans la série des glyoximes substitutées. Paris C. R. Acad. sci. 153 1911 (259–262). [3860]. 42754

——— et Ogorodnikoff, A. Sur la dispersion anormale des corps colorés et actifs. Ann. chim. phys. Paris (sér. 8) 22 1911 (137–144). [4050]. 42843

Tswett, M. Eine Hypothese über den Mechanismus der photosynthetischen Energieübertragung. Zs. physik. Chem. Leipzig 76 1911 (413–419). [4225]. 42844

Tuckermann, jun. L. B. v. Skinner, Clarence A.

Tagman, Orin v. Nutting. P. G.

Turner, H. H. Characteristics of the observational sciences. Nature London 87 1911 (289–296). [6040]. 42845

Turnwald, Carl. Exper.mentelle Untersuchungen über den Zusammenhang zwischen Potentialdifferenz und Stromstärke in einem metallischen Leiter. Diss. Zürich 1909 (48 mit 2 Fig.). 23 cm. [5240 5700]. 42846

Turpain, A. Curieux effets d'un coup de foudre sur une antenne réceptrice d'ondes électriques. J. phys. Paris (sér. 5) 1 1911 (372–381 av. fig.). [5270]. 42847

—————— Microampèremètre enregistreur. J. Phys. Paris (sér. 5) 1 1911 (1003–1004); Radium Paris 8 1911 (388–389 av. fig.). [6910 6010]. 42848

—————— Appareils enregistreurs et préviseurs des orages. J. phys. Paris (sér. 5) 1 1911 (1005–1015 av. fig.); Radium Paris 8 1911 (419–423 av. fig.). [6043 5270]. 42849

—————— Étude et enregistrement des orages. Leur prévision. Radium Paris 8 1911 (419–423 av. fig.). [6043 5270]. 42850

—————— La protection de nos hôtels des postes contre l'orage. Rev. gén. sci. Paris 22 1911 (747–748). [5270 6615]. 42851

—————— Inscription graphique des signaux de l'heure émis par la Tour Eiffel. Possibilité d'enregistrement des télégrammes sans fil. J. phys. Paris (sér. 5) 2 1912 (105–112). [6615 0809]. 42852

Tyndall, A. M. On the discharge from an electrified point. Phil. Mag. London (Ser. 6) 21 1911 (585–603 with pl.). [6810]. 42853

Tyrer, D. The law of molecular attraction. Phil. Mag. London (Ser. 6) 23 1912 (101–113). [2400]. 42854

Ubbelohde, Leo. Elektrische Laboratoriumsöfen mit Wicklung aus unedlem Metall. ChemZtg Cöthen 35 1911 (1493–1494); Zs. Elektroch. Halle 17 1911 (1002–1003). [6090]. 42855

Ubisch, Gertrud von. Schwingungszahl und Dämpfung im leuchtenden (c-4388)

und nichtleuchtenden Na-Dampfe. Diss. Strassburg. Leipzig (J. A. Barth) 1911 (36). 23 cm.; [Auszug] Ann. Physik Leipzig (4. Folge) 35 1911 (790–816).] [6660 6620 6650 4200]. 42856

Ugrimoff, Bor's von. Die unipolare Gleichstrommaschine. Karlsruhe Arb. elektrot. Inst. 2 (1910–1911) 1911 (132–226). [6060]. 42857

Ujj, Gyula. Leneserend-zerek töpontjainak és föfelületeinek kisérleti meghatározásáról. [Über die experimentelle Bestimmung der Hauptpunkte und Hauptflächen der Linsensysteme.] Math. Phys. L. Budapest 20 1911 (357–379). [3060]. 42858

Uljanin, W. v. Die Zehndersche Röhre als Indikator für elektrische Schwingungen. Ann. Physik Leipzig (4. Folge) 36 1911 (119–124). [6660]. 42859

Uller, Karl. Elektrische Leitfähigkeiten von Meer und Land. Jahrb. drahtlos. Telegr. Leipzig 4 1911 (638–640). [6240 5660]. 42860

Ulrich, Reinhold. Bestimmung von Dampfdichten nach der Bunsenschen Ausströmungsmethode. Diss. Marburg (Druck v. R. Friedrich) 1910 (54 mit 2 Taf.). 22 cm. [0810 1850]. 42861

Ulmer, Fritz. Das erste Telephon — ein Sprachrohrtelegraph aus dem Jahre 1796. Arch. Gesch. Natw. Leipzig 3 1911 (256–262). [0010]. 42862

Unruh, Franz. Beiträge zur Methodik luftelektrischer Messungen. Diss. Kiel. Berlin (Druck v. J. Sittenfeld) 1911 (88). 23 cm. [6805 5270 5685]. 42863

Urasow, G. G. Bestimmte Verbindungen mit veränderlicher Zusammensetzung der festen Phase. Leitfähigkeit und Härte der Magnesium-Cadmiumlegierungen. [Übers. von J. **Pinsker**.] Zs. anorg. Chem. Leipzig 73 1911 (31–47 mit 1 Taf.). [5660]. 42864

Urbain, G. Sur un nouvel élément qui accompagne le lutécium et le scandium dans les terres de la gadolinite; le celtium. Paris C. R. Acad. sci. 152 1911 (141–143). [4205]. 42865

—————— Sur une balance-laboratoire à compensation électromagnétique destinée à l'étude des systèmes qui dégagent des gaz avec une vitesse sensible. Paris C. R. Acad. sci. 154 1912 (347–349). [0810]. 42866

Urbain, G. et **Scal,** G. Sur les systèmes monovariants qui admettent une phase gazeuse. Paris C. R. Acad. sci. 152 1911 (769–772). [2472]. 42867

—————— et **Feige,** A. Sur un nouveau type de lampe à arc à cathode de mercure et à lumi re blanche. Paris C. R. Acad. sci. 152 1911 (255–286). [6810]. 42868

Usher, Francis L. Die chemische Einzelwirkung und die chemische Gesamtwirkung der α- und der β-Strahlen. (Übers.) Jahrb. Radioakt. Leipzig 8 1911 (323–334). [4275]. 42869

—————— r. Travers, M. W.

Vacca, Giovanni r. Garbasso, A.

Vaillant, P. Application de l'évaporation à la mesure des coefficients de diffusion. J. phys. Paris (sér. 5) 1 1911 (877–896 av. fig.). [0320 1840]. 42870

—————— Nouvelle méthode permettant de constater par la radiographie si un enfant déclaré né mort a vécu ou n'a réellement pas vécu. Paris C. R. Acad. sci. 152 1911 (220–223). [4240]. 42871

—————— Sur les variations de la conductibilité d'un corps phosphorescent sous l'action de la lumière. Paris C. R. Acad. sci. 155 1911 (1141–1144). [5660 4230]. 42872

Valenta, E. Fortschritte auf dem Gebiete der Photochemie und Photographie im Jahre 1910. ChemZtg Cöthen 35 1911 (941–943 962–963). [4225]. 42873

—————— r. Eder, J. M.

Valentin, Ernst. Messungen der Funkenkonstanten in Luft. Chlor, Brom- und Joddämpfen bei verschiedenen Drucken. Diss. Rostock. Berlin (Druck v. L. Simion Nf.) 1910 (42). 22 cm. [6820]. 42874

Valentiner, S. Willy Wien. ChemZtg Cöthen 35 1911 (1363). [0010]. 42875

—————— Waserstoffabsorption durch Palladium bei niedrigen Drucken und tiefen Temperaturen. Berlin Verh. D. physik. Ges. 13 1911 (1003–1022). [0250]. 42876

Valla, Elena. Sugli spettri di assorbimento di sali inorganici complessi. Roma Rend. Acc. Lincei (Ser. 5) 20 2. sem. 1911 (406–411). [3860]. 42877

Vallauri, Giancarlo. Alcune misure sopra un condensatore a celluloide. Atti Ass. elettrotecn. Milano 14 1910 (227–235). [5252]. 42878

—————— Tentativi di transformazione statica della frequenza di correnti alternate. Atti Ass. elettrotecn. Milano 14 1910 (655–664). [6460]. 42879

—————— Isteresi del ferro nei cicli asimmetrici di magnetizzazione alternativa. Atti Ass. elettrotecn. Milano 15 1911 (79–92). [5450]. 42880

—————— Perdite per magnetizzazione alternativa e rotante nelle macchine elettriche. Atti Ass. elettrotecn. Milano 15 1911 (781–815). [5460]. 42882

—————— Raddoppiatore statico di frequenza. Atti Ass. elettrotecn. Milano 15 1911 (391–404); Elettricità Milano 37 1911 (28–30). [6040]. 42883

Vallot, J. Sur la protection contre la foudre des observatoires de grande altitude. Paris C. R. Acad. sci. 153 1911 (986–988). [5270]. 42884

Van der Mensbrugghe, G. Sur les quatre propriétés providentielles de l'eau. Rev. quest. sci. Bruxelles 1911 (90–108). [1800]. 42885

Van der Noot, L. L'acoustique des salles R. de l'Institut des hautes études et de l'École de Musique et de déclamation d'Ixelles. (15–18). [9255]. 42886

—————— Recherches expérimentales sur la tension superficielle au contact de deux liquides. Bruxelles Bul. Acad. roy. 1911 (493–502). [0300]. 42887

Vanino, L[udwig] und **Zumbusch,** E. Über die Bologneser Leuchtsteine. (3. Mitt.) J. prakt. Chem. Leipzig (N. F.) 84 1911 (305–317). [4220 4230]. 42888

Vanzetti, B. Lino. Idrolisi di sali in soluzione. Milano Rend. Ist. lomb. (Ser. 2) 42 1909 (870–876). [6250]. 42890

—————— Su alcune esperienze di diffusione. Nuovo Cimento Pisa (Ser. 5) 20 1910 (442–444). [0320]. 42891

—————— Nuove esperienze di diffusione di elettroliti in soluzione

235

acquosa. Rend. Soc. chim. ital. Roma
(Ser. 2) 2 1910 (376 379); Atti Soc.
ital. prog. sci. Roma 4 1911 (769).
[0320]. 42892

Varicak, V[ladimir]. Zum Ehrenfestschen Paradoxon. Physik. Zs.
Leipzig 12 1911 (169 170). [4960].
42894

Vassura, Giuseppe. Evangelista
Torricelli. Malnate (Tip. A. de Mohr.)
1909 (14), 23 cm. [1010]. 42895

Vater, R. Der gegenwärtige Stand
der Entwicklung der Wärmekraftmaschinen in Deutschland. Himmel u.
Erde Leipzig 23 1911 (337 348 406
422). [2490]. 42896

Vampel, Wilhelm. Untersuchungen
über die Dielektrizitätskonstante flüssiger Kristalle. Diss. Halle a. S. (Druck
v. C. A. Kaemmerer & Co.) 1911 (34
mit Taf.). 22 cm. [5252]. 42897

Veen, A[braham] L[ouis] W[illem]
E[duard] van der. Physisch- en
kristallographisch onderzoek naar de
symmetrie van diamant. [Recherches
physico-chimiques et cristallographi-
ques sur la symétrie du diamant.]
Leiden (A. W. Sijthoff's Uitg. Mij.)
1911 (1-58 avec 2 pl. et 3 stéréo-
photogr.). 27 cm. [5260]. 42898

———— Piëzo- e Pyro-electrisch
onderzoek van diamant. [Recherches
piëzo- et pyroélectriques sur le diamant.]
Handl. Ned. Nat. Genee-k. Congr. 13
1911 (164-168). [5260]. 42899

Veillon, [Henri] und **Forel,** F. A.
Prof. Dr. Eduard Hagenbach-Bischoff.
Verh. Schweiz. Natf. Ges. Aarau 94
2 1912 (1-17 m. Portr.). [0020]. 42900

Veit, Th. r. Wedekind, E[dgar].

Venske, O. Vergleichende erd-
magnetische Messungen in Potsdam
und Wilhelmshaven. Berlin Veröff.
met. Inst. No. 229 1911 (142 149).
[5435]. 42901

Verain, L. Sur la constante diélectrique de l'anhydride carbonique au
voisinage du point critique. Paris C. R.
Acad. sci. 154 1912 (345-347). [5252].
42902

Verhoeckx, P[aulus] M[arinus].
Proeve eener theorie van het roteerend
magnetisch veld. [Essai d'une théorie
du champ magnétique tournant.] 's
Gravenhage (Giunta d'Albani) 1912
(210). 24 cm. [6070]. 42903

(c-4388)

Veroi, Gomberto. Elementi di
elettrotecnica. Vol. 2. Torino (Un.
Tip. Ed.) 1909 (XII + 712). 25 cm.
[0030 4900]. 42904

Verschaffelt, J. E. Sur l'existence
d'un maximum de déviation dans la
réfraction de la lumière à travers un
prisme cristallin. Bruxelles Bul. Acad.
roy. 1910 (125 132). [3020]. 42905

Very, Frank W. On the need of
adjustment of the data of terrestrial
meteorology and of solar radiation, and
on the best value of the solar constant.
Astroph. J. Chicago 34 1911 (371-387
with ff.). [3240]. 42906

Veselý, Vítězslav. O viskosité skla.
[Ueber die Viskosität des Glases.]
Listy Chem. Prag 1911 (246 254).
[0325]. 42907

Vèses, M. Sur la définition de
l'essence de térébenthine commercialement pure. Bordeaux Proc.-verb. soc.
sci. phys. nat. 1909-1910 (22 27 71-80).
[4950]. 42908

Victoroff, C. r. Seemann, J.

Vieweger, H. Aufgaben und Lösungen
aus der Gleich- und Wechselstromtechnik. Ein Übungsbuch für den Unterricht an technischen Hoch- und
Fachschulen . . . 3., verb. Aufl. Berlin
(J. Springer) 1911 (VII + 282 mit 2
Taf.). 23 cm. 7 M. [0030 4900
0050]. 42909

Vigneron, H. Répartition des raies
spectrales dans les spectres d'émission.
J. phys. Paris (sér. 5) 1 1911 (294-301
381-388). [4205]. 42910

Vignolo-Lutati, F. Pel centenario
della legge di Amedeo Avogadro. Ind.
chim. Torino 11 1911 (2 5). [0010].
42911

Vigouroux, E. Sur le système nickel-
argent. Bordeaux Proc.-verb. soc. sci.
phys. nat. 1909-1910 (44-45). [6210].
42912

Villard, P. et **Abraham,** H. Mesures
de potentiels explosifs entre 20,000
volts et 300,000 volts. Paris C. R.
Acad. sci. 153 1911 (1200-1204). [6005].
42913

———— Sur une grande machine
électrostatique. Paris C. R. Acad. sci.
152 1911 (1813-1814). [6025]. 42914

———— r. Abraham.

R 2

Villey, Jean. Sur les couples électriques dans les électromètres. Paris C. R. Acad. sci. **153** 1911 (367–369). [6005]. 42915

Vincent, J. H. Electrical experiments with mercury contained in tubes. Phil. Mag. London (Ser. 6) **22** 1911 (506–533). [6840]. 42916

Violette, H., **Lacour**, E. et **Florian**, Ch. Lunette de pointage pour pièces marines de petit calibre. Paris C. R. Acad. sci. **151** 1910 (1119–1122 av. fig.). [3080]. 42917

Viscidi, P. Le proprietà magnetiche del ferro e leghe relative in campi intensi. Elettricista Roma (Ser. 2) **10** 1911 (86–88). [5466]. 42918

———— Generatore di corrente alternata ad alta frequenza. Elettricista Roma (Ser. 2) **10** 1911 (331–332). [6040]. 42919

Vlès, Fred. Propriétés optiques des muscles. Thèse. Paris (Hermann) 1912 (XVIII + 372). 23 cm. [3850 4010 4050]. 42920

Voege, W. Elektrostatische Messinstrumente. Helios Leipzig **17** 1911 Fach-Zs. (321–325 333–336). [6005]. 42921

———— Ueber Licht- und Wärmestrahlung der künstlichen Lichtquellen. J. Gasbeleucht. München **54** 1911 (295–299). [4202]. 42922

Volker, Carl August. Die Lackierkunst der alten Meister. Musikinstrumentenztg Berlin **21** 1911 (413–414). [9410]. 42923

Vogel, Emil. Ueber die Temperaturänderung von Luft und Sauerstoff beim Strömen durch eine Drosselstelle bei 10° C und Drücken bis zu 150 Atmosphären. Mitt. ForschArb. Ingenieurw. Berlin H. **108 109** 1911 (1–31); Zs. komprim. Gase Weimar **14** 1911 (3–10 25–31). [1450]. 42924

———— Taschenbuch der Photographie. Ein Leitfaden für Anfänger und Fortgeschrittene. Bearb. von Paul Hanneke. 26.–28. Aufl. 92.–100. Taus. Berlin (G. Schmidt) 1911 (VIII + 335 mit 24 Taf.). 17 cm. Geb. 2.50 M. [3085]. 42925

Vogel, Walther. Die Einführung des Kompasses in die nordwesteuropäische Nautik. Hansische GeschBl. Leipzig 1911 (1–32). [0010]. 42926

Vogl, Seb. r. Björnbo, A. A.

Vogler, A. Die elektrischen Wellen, deren Erzeugung und Anwendung zur drahtlosen oder Funkentelegraphie, Regelung der Uhren und Fernzeiger, . . . 2., verm. u. verb. Aufl. (Jedermann Elektrotechniker. Bd 14.) Leipzig (M. Schäfer) 1912 (64). 20 cm. 1 M. [0050 6610]. 42927

Voigdt, Paul. Beitrag zum Gültigkeitsbereich der Fresnelschen Reflexionsformeln. Diss. Münster i. W. Berlin (Druck v. G. Schade) 1911 (40). 23 cm. [3820]. 42928

Voigt, Kurt. Absorption und Konstitution von Nitroverbindungen. Diss. Leipzig (Druck v. A. Hoffmann) 1911 (57 mit Taf.). 23 cm. [3860]. 42929

———— r. Hantzsch, A.

Voigt, W[oldemar]. Über die Schwingungen im zweiten Medium bei totaler Reflexion. Ann. Physik Leipzig (4. Folge) **34** 1911 (797–860). [3824 6620]. 42930

———— Zur Frage der Dissymmetrie der Zeemanschen Triplets. Ann. Physik Leipzig (4. Folge) **35** 1911 (101–108). [6660 4208]. 42931

———— Zwei Antworten. [Betr. Intensitätsverteilung in Spektrallinien u. Totalreflexion.] Ann. Physik Leipzig (4. Folge) **36** 1911 (866–870). [4205 3824]. 42932

———— Zur Theorie der komplizierten Zeemaneffekte. Ann. Physik Leipzig (4. Folge) **36** 1911 (873–906). [4208]. 42933

———— Beiträge zu Lord Rayleigh's Theorie der Gitterbeugung. Göttingen Nachr. Ges. Wiss. math.-phys. Kl. **1911** (41–57). [3630 3800 3840]. 42934

———— Allgemeines über Emission und Absorption in Zusammenhang mit der Frage der Intensitätsmessungen beim Zeeman-Effekt. Nach Beobachtungen von C. Försterling. Mit einem Zusatz von H[endrik] A[ntoon] **Lorentz**. Göttingen Nachr. Ges. Wiss. math.-phys. Kl. **1911** (71–97). [4210 6660]. 42935

Volk, H. r. Rimbach, E.

Volkmann, P. Franz Neumann als Experimentator. Verh. Ges. D. Natf. Leipzig **82** (1910) II 1 1911 (7–8). [0010]. 42936

Volkmann, Wilhelm. Die beste
Gestalt für die Spulen eines Nadelgalvanometers. Berlin Verh. D.
physik. Ges. 13 1911 (172-178). [6010].
42937

———— Über Galvanometerspulen
und ihre beste Gestalt. Mechaniker
Berlin 19 1911 (133-135 147-149 159-
160). [6010]. 42938

———— Die Leistungsgrenze der
Spiegelablesung. Physik. Zs. Leipzig
12 1911 (30-32). [0090]. 42939

———— Eine einfache schütter-
freie Aufhängung. Physik. Zs. Leipzig
12 1911 (75). [0090]. 42940

———— Die zweckmässige Grösse
des Galvanometerspiegels. Physik. Zs.
Leipzig 12 1911 (76-77). [0090 6010].
42941

———— Ueber Spiegelablesungen
mit mehrfacher Spiegelung. Physik.
Zs. Leipzig 12 1911 (183-184). [0090].
42942

———— Ueber Versuche, die
Spiegelablesung zu verfeinern. Physik.
Zs. Leipzig 12 1911 (223-224). [0050].
42943

———— Neue Klemmenformen.
Physik. Zs. Leipzig 12 1911 (734).
[0090]. 42944

———— Kleine Verbesserungen an
Schieberwiderständen. Physik. Zs.
Leipzig 12 1911 (733). [6010]. 42945

———— Zwei Ablesemikroskope.
Physik. Zs. Leipzig 12 1911 (734-735).
[0090 3082]. 42946

———— Ein Lichtzeiger für objektive Spiegelablesung. Zs. physik.
Unterr. Berlin 24 1911 (17-19). [0050].
42947

———— Ein lehrreicher Pendelversuch. Zs. physik. Unterr. Berlin
24 1911 (157-158). [0050]. 42948

———— Ueber den Fresnelschen
Interferenzspiegel und eine zuver-
lässige Form desselben. Zs. physik.
Unterr. Berlin 24 1911 (218-220).
[3610 0090]. 42949

Vondráček, R. Elektrická pec v
železářství. [Elektrischer Ofen in der
Eisenindustrie.] Listy Chem. Prag
1911 (25-28 64-66). [0090]. 42950

Vorländer, D[aniel] und **Huth**, M. E.
Ueber den Charakter der Doppelbrechung flüssiger Kristalle. Zs.
physik. Chem. Leipzig 75 1911 (641-
650). [3830]. 42951

Vosmaer, A. Fysico-analyse.
[Analyse physique.] Amsterdam
Chem. Weekbl. 8 1911 (907-911).
[0090]. 42952

Voss, R. von. Die Berechnung von
Elektromagnet- und Widerstandsrollen.
Taschenbuch f. Präzisionsmechaniker
Nikolassee 12 1912 [1911] Beih. 1
(1-32). [6030]. 42953

———— Der Elektromagnet in
Theorie und Praxis mit besonderer
Berücksichtigung der Schwachstromtechnik. Taschenbuch f. Präzisionsmechaniker Nikolassee 11 1911 (1-74).
[6030]. 42954

Voženílek, Jindřich c. Baborovský, J.

Waals, J. D. van der. Nobel-
Vortrag [über das Wesen der Gase und
der Flüssigkeiten]. Les prix Nobel en
1910 1911 (14). [0200]. 42955

———— Opmerkingen over de
waarde der kritische grootheden. [On
the value of the critical quantities.]
Amsterdam Versl. Wis. Nat. Afd. K.
Akad. Wet. 19 1911 (1310-1330)
(Dutch); Amsterdam Proc. Sci. K.
Akad. Wet. 13 1911 (1211-1231)
(English); Haarlem Arch. Néerl. Sci.
Soc. Holl. (Ser. III A) 1 1911 (136-
150) (French). [1880 1885 2455].
42956

———— Opmerkingen over de
grootte der volumina van de co-exi-
steerende phasen van een enkele stof.
[Some remarks on the value of the
volumes of the coexisting phases of a
simple substance.] Amsterdam Versl.
Wis. Nat. Afd. K. Akad. Wet. 19 1911
(1458-1467) (Dutch); Amsterdam
Proc. Sci. K. Akad. Wet. 13 1911
(1253-1262) (English). [1880 1885].
42957

———— Bijdrage tot de kennis der
binaire mengsels. XVI, XVII, XVIII,
XIX. [Contribution to the theory of
binary mixtures. XVI, XVII, XVIII,
XIX.] Amsterdam Versl. Wis. Nat.
Afd. K. Akad. Wet. 20 1911 (597-603
654-673); 1912 (937-955 1215-1229)
(Dutch); Amsterdam Proc. Sci. K.
Akad. Wet. 14 1911 (594-509 655-673);
1912 (875-892 1049-1063) (English).
[2457]. 42958

———— Association apparente ou
aggrégation moléculaire. Haarlem
Arch. Néerl. Sci. Soc. Holl. (Ser. III A)
1 1911 (90-135); Traduit de: Amsterdam Versl. Wis. Nat. Afd. K. Akad.

Wet. **19** [1910] (78 105 549–561)
(Hollandais); Amsterdam Proc. Sci.
K. Akad. Wet. **13** [1910] (107–134 494–
503) (Anglais). [2455 0200]. 42959

Waals, J. D. van der. Remarques
sur la grandeur des volumes des phases
coexistantes d'une substance simple.
Haarlem Arch. Néerl. Sci. Soc. Holl.
(Sér. 3 A) **1** 1912 (292–303); [Traduit
de: Amsterdam Versl. Wis. Nat. Afd.
K. Akad. Wet. **19** 1911 (1458–1467)
(Dutch); Amsterdam Proc. Sci. K.
Akad. Wet. **13** [1911] (1253–1262) (Eng-
lish).] [1880 1885 2455]. 42960

———— Die Zustandsgleichung.
Rede . . . Leipzig (Akademische Verlagsges.) 1911 (24). 22 cm. 1,20 M.
[1800 1450 0200]. 42961

**Waals, Jr., J[ohannes] D[iderik] van
der.** Energie en massa. [Energy and
mass.] Amsterdam Versl. Wis. Nat.
Afd. K. Akad. Wet. **20** [1911] (342–
389); **20** 1912 (962–965) (Dutch);
Amsterdam Proc. Sci. K. Akad. Wet.
14 [1911] (239–255); **14** 1912 (822–824)
(English). [4960 0810 4215 6630].
42962

———— Zur Deutung von Gibbs'
„Canonical Ensembles". Ann. Physik
Leipzig (4. Folge) **35** 1911 (185–188).
[2400]. 42963

———— Ueber die Erklärung der
Naturgesetze auf statistischmechani-
scher Grundlage. Physik. Zs. Leipzig
12 1911 (547–549). [0000]. 42964

———— Über die Frage nach den
fundamentalsten Naturgesetzen. Physik. Zs. Leipzig **12** 1911 (600–603).
[0040 0000]. 42965

———— Over het begrip energie-
strooming. [On the conception of
the current of energy.] Amsterdam
Versl. Wis. Nat. Afd. K. Akad. Wet.
20 1912 (958–962) (Dutch); Amsterdam
Proc. Sci. K. Akad. Wet. **14** 1912
(828–831) (English). [6630]. 42966

Wachsmuth, B. Ungenaue Massbezeichnungen in der Technik. Verkehrstechn. Woche Berlin **6** 1912
(369–370). [0800 0070]. 42968

Waetzmann, E. Ueber mögliche
Erweiterungen der Helmholtzschen
Theorie der Kombinationstöne. Ann.
Physik Leipzig (4. Folge) **35** 1911
(378–380). [9140]. 42969

———— Über ein neues akustisches
Interferenzrohr (mit Demonstration).

Breslau Jahresber Ges. vaterl. Cultur
88 (1910) 1911 natw. Sect. (7–9).
[9030 9230]. 42970

Waetzmann, E. Ueber den Zusammenklang zweier einfacher Töne. [I. Zur
Analyse der Resultierenden. II.
Schwebungen. III. Kombinationstöne.] Physik. Zs. Leipzig **12** 1911
(231–238). [9340 9230 9140]. 42971

———— Demonstration von Wasserwellen. Physik. Zs. Leipzig **12** 1911
(866–867). [9030]. 42972

———— Ueber die „Ausdehnung"
der Tonempfindungen. Folia Neuro-
biologica Haarlem **6** 1912 (24–26).
[9520]. 42973

———— Die Resonanztheorie des
Hörens. Als Beitrag zur Lehre von
den Tonempfindungen. Braunschweig
(F. Vieweg & S.) 1912 (XII + 163).
23 cm. 5 M. [9520 9140 8990].
42973A

———— und **Lummer, O[tto].**
Neue Interferenzkurven gleicher Neigung. Ann. Physik Leipzig (4. Folge)
36 1911 (383–394). [3610]. 42974

Waetzoldt. Vorschläge zur Far-
benterminologie. [In: Offizieller
Bericht über die Verhandlungen des
IX. internationalen kunsthistorischen
Kongresses.] Leipzig (E. A. Seemann)
1911 (100–108). 27 cm. [0070]. 42975

Wagener, A. Feindruckmesser mit
Schreibvorrichtung zur Untersuchung
von Druck u. Geschwindigkeitsverteilung in nahezu beständigen Luftströ-
men.] Motorwagen Berlin **14** 1911
(864–868 mit 1 Taf.). [0835]. 42976

———— Beiträge zur Frage der
Verwendung von Zweitaktmaschinen
für Luftfahrzeuge. [Forts.] Zs. Flugtechnik München **2** 1911 (93–98 109–
111 125–128). [2490]. 42977

Waggoner, C[hauncey] W[illiam].
The elastic properties of a series of
iron-carbon alloys. [Abstract.] Physic. Rev. Ithaca N.Y. **32** 1911 (624–
625). [0840]. 42978

Wagner, Franz Ludwig. Das ultraviolette Funkenspektrum der Luft.
Zs. wiss. Phot. Leipzig **10** 1911 (69–89);
Diss. Bonn. Leipzig (J. A. Barth) 1911
(27). 24 cm. [4205]. 42979

Wagner, Karl Willy. Ueber Kabelprobleme und ähnliche Randwertaufgaben, die auf Reihenentwicklungen nach nicht orthogonalen Eigenfunktionen führen. Arch. Math. Leipzig (3. Reihe) 18 1911 (230–241). [6450 6490]. 42980

————— Über die Verbesserung des Telephons. Elektrot. Zs. Berlin 32 1911 (80–83 110–112). [6485]. 42981

————— Die Fortpflanzung von Strömen in Kabeln mit unvollkommenem Dielektrikum. Elektrot. Zs. Berlin 32 1911 (258–262). [6460]. 42982

————— Elektromagnetische Ausgleichsvorgänge in Freileitungen und Kabeln. (Eine experimentelle Untersuchung.) Elektrot. Zs. Berlin 32 1911 (899–903 928–931 947–951). [6450 6460 6480 6610]. 42983

————— Zur Messung dielektrischer Verluste mit der Wechselstrombrücke. Elektrot. Zs. Berlin 32 1911 (1001–1002). [5740]. 42984

Wagner, P. Dampfdurchgangsquerschnitte von Regelventilen. Berlin Zs. Ver. D. Ing. 55 1911 (1379–1384). [2490]. 42985

Waidner, C[harles] W[illiam]. The temperature work of the Bureau of Standards. J. Ind. Engin. Chem. Easton Pa. 2 1910 (49–63 with ff. tables). [1200]. 42986

————— and **Burgess,** G[eorge] K[imball]. On the constancy of the sulphur boiling point. Washington D.C. Dept. Comm. Lab. Bull. Bur. Stand. 7 1911 (127–130). [1840 1260]. 42987

————— ————— Note on the temperature scale between 100° and 500° C. [With bibliography.] Washington D.C. Dept. Comm. Lab. Bull. Bur. Stand. 7 1911 (1–9 with pl. tables). [2425 1840 1840]. 42988

Wainoff, Julius. Ueber die elektrische Leitfähigkeit von Salzen und Salzgemischen. Diss. Königsberg i. Pr. (Druck d. Vereinsdruckerei) [1910] (55). 22 cm. [6240]. 42989

————— v. Benrath, A.

Wallen, P. Sur l'inversion optique des composés organiques. ("Inversion de Walden"). J. Chim. Phys. Genève 9 1911 (160–197). [4050]. 42990

————— Zur Geschichte der kolloiden Kieselsäure. Zs. Kolloide Dresden 9 1911 (145–146). [0340]. 42991

————— Über den Zusammenhang zwischen dem Grenzwert der molekularen Leitfähigkeit und der innern Reibung. Zs. physik. Chem. Leipzig 78 1911 (257–283). [6240 0325]. 42992

Walker, G. W. An electrostatic voltmeter for photographic recording of atmospheric potential. London Proc. R. Soc. (Ser. A) 84 1911 (585–588). [6010]. 42993

Walker, Henry. The variation of Young's modulus under an electric current. Part III. Edinburgh Proc. R. Soc. 31 1910–11 (186–192). [0840]. 42994

Wall, E. J. Die Farbe photographischer Bilder. Jahrb. Phot. Halle 25 1911 (38–41). [4225]. 42995

Wallot, J. Über den Einfluss von Hüllen und Schirmen auf elektromagnetische Drahtwellen. Ann. Physik Leipzig (4. Folge) 36 1911 (684–737). [6610 5252]. 42996

————— Elektrische Drahtwellen. Berlin Verh. D. physik. Ges. 13 1911 (813–820); Physik. Zs. Leipzig 12 1911 (994–997). [6610 5252]. 42997

Walter, B. Über das Bauersche Qualimeter. Fortschr. Röntgenstr. Hamburg 17 1911 (212–225). [6080 4240]. 42998

————— Absorptionsspektra phosphoreszierender Stoffe. Physik. Zs. Leipzig 13 1912 (6–11 mit 1 Taf.). [3850 4230]. 42999

Walter, L. H. Accuracy of the Bellini-Tosi wireless compass for navigational purposes. Elect. London 67 1911 (749–751). [6615]. 43000

Wamsler, Friedrich. Die Wärmeabgabe geheizter Körper an Luft. Berlin Zs. Ver. D. Ing. 55 1911 (599–605 628–633); Mitt. ForschArb. Ingenieurw. Berlin H. 98 99 1911 (1–45). [2040 4210]. 43001

Wartenberg, H. v. Zur Kenntnis der kristallinen Flüssigkeiten. Physik. Zs. Leipzig **12** 1911 (837 839). [0400 6640 6655]. 43002

―――― v. Rubens, H.

Washburn, Ed. W. Système simple de chimie thermodynamique basée sur une modification de la méthode de Carnot. J. Chim. Phys. Genève **8** 1910 (358 414). [2415]. 43003

―――― Loi fondamentale pour une théorie générale des solutions. J. Chim. Phys. Genève **8** 1910 (538 568). [0200 1920]. 43004

Wassmuth, Anton. Die Bewegungsgleichungen des Elektrons und das Prinzip der kleinsten Aktion. Berlin Verh. D. physik. Ges. **14** 1912 (76). [4960]. 43005

Watson, F[loyd] R[owe]. Echoes in an auditorium. [Abstract.] Physic. Rev. Ithaca N.Y. **32** 1911 (231-232). [9220 9255]. 43006

―――― Musical echoes. Science New York (N. Ser.) **34** 1911 (454-455). [9220]. 43007

Watson, Herbert Edmeston. On regularities in the spectrum of neon. Astroph. J. Chicago Ill. **33** 1911 (399-405 with tables). [4205]. 43008

Watson, W. Isopiestic expansibility of water at high pressures and temperatures. Edinburgh Proc. R. Soc. **31** 1911 (456-477). [1430]. 43009

―――― Das Volumen des Wassers bei hohen Drucken und Temperaturen. Leipzig Ber. Ges. Wiss. math.-phys. Kl. **63** 1911 (264 268). [0810 0845 1430]. 43010

Watts, O. P. und **Mendenhall**, C. E. On the fusion of carbon. Physic. Rev. Ithaca N.Y. **33** 1911 (65-69 with fig.); [Übers.] Ann. Physik Leipzig (4. Folge) **35** 1911 (783 789). [1810]. 43012

Weber, Albert. Gleichstromwickungen, l. Strelitz i. M. (M. Hittenkofer) [1912] (23). 27 cm. 1 M. [6060]. 43013

Weber, Anton. Die Lorentzkontraktion bei einem idealen Gas. Berlin Berh. D. physik. Ges. **13** 1911 (695-699). 43014

―――― Geschwindigkeitsänderung eines bewegten Hohlraums infolge von Kompression. Zs. Math. Leipzig **59** 1911 (311-312). [2435 4200]. 43015

Weber, Anton. Die Transformation von Energie und Bewegungsgrösse. Zs. Math. Leipzig **59** 1911 (313-314). [2435 4200]. 43016

Weber, Anton Ernst v. Koch, P. P.

Weber, L[eonhard]. Das Relativ-Photometer. Kiel Schr. natw. Ver. **15** 1911 (158 162). [3010]. 43017

Weber, Rudolf H. Ueber Kontinuität zwischen Brechung und Reflexion. Rostock SitzBer. natf. Ges. N.F. **2** 1910 [1911] (53-58). [3820]. 43018

―――― Die Magnetisierbarkeit der Oxyd- und Oxydulsalze der Eisengruppe. Ann. Physik Leipzig (4. Folge) **36** 1911 (624-646). [5467]. 43019

―――― Reversible und umkehrbare Prozesse. Gelieferte und geleistete Arbeit. Rostock SitzBer. natf. Ges. N.F. **2** 1910 [1911] (361-369). [2415]. 43020

―――― Ueber die Bedeutung des absoluten Nullpunktes der Temperatur. Rostock SitzBer. natf. Ges. (N.F.) **3** 1911 Abh. (383-390). [2425 1260]. 43021

Weber, Sophus v. Knudsen, M.

Webster, A. G. Sur un nouveau problème mixte de l'équation des télégraphistes. Paris C. R. Acad. sci. **153** 1911 (590-503). [6480]. 43022

Wedekind, E[dgar]. Magnetochemie. Beziehungen zwischen magnetischen Eigenschaften und chemischer Natur. Berlin (Gebr. Borntraeger) 1911 (VIII + 114). 22 cm. [5467 5466]. 43023

―――― und **Horst**, C. Über die Magnetisierbarkeit und die Magnetonenzahlen der Oxyde und Sulfide des Vanadiums. Berlin Ber. D. chem. Ges. **45** 1912 (262-270). [5467]. 43024

―――― und **Veit**, Th. Über einige weitere ferromagnetische Verbindungen des Mangans. Berlin Ber. D. chem. Ges. **44** 1911 (2663-2670). [5466]. 43025

Wegener, Alfred. Untersuchungen über die Natur der obersten Atmosphärenschichten. II. Physik. Zs. Leipzig **12** 1911 (214-222). [4205]. 43026

Wegner von Dallwitz. Wärmelehre in Theorie und Anwendung. Bd 1: Wärmetheorie und ihre Beziehungen zur Technik und Physik. Berlin (C. J. E. Volckmann Nachf.) 1912 (XVIII + 331 mit 2 Taf.). 25 cm. 10 M. [2400 0900 0030]. 43027

Wezscheider, Rud. Zur Verdampfung des Salmiaks. Zs. physik. Chem. Leipzig 76 1911 (126). [1840 1900]. 43028

Wehnelt, A[rthur]. Über die Zuverlässigkeit von Sondenmessungen im dunkeln Kathodenraume. Berlin Verh. D. physik. Ges. 13 1911 (505 510). [6840]. 43029

————— Die Ionenbewegung in der Glimmlichtentladung. (Vorl. Mitt.) Erlangen SitzBer. physik. Soc. 42 (1910) 1911 (89 96). [6840]. 43030

————— Ueber eine neue Methode zur Erzeugung von Kathoden-, Röntgenstrahlen und anderen Lichterscheinungen in Geisslerschen Röhren. Natur Leipzig 3 1911 (74–78). [6840]. 43031

Weichsel, H. Die Berechnung der Magnetisierungskurve bei Mehrlochwicklungen. Elektrot. Zs. Berlin 32 1911 (812). [6060 6030]. 43032

Weicker, W. Lo studio sperimentale del comportamento elettrico degli isolatori delle linee aeree ad alta tensione. [Sunto. Trad.] Atti Ass. elettrotecn. Milano 15 1911 (128 131). [5770]. 43033

————— Protezione delle sovratensioni per gli isolatori nelle condutture aeree e specialmente negli isolatori a sospensione. Atti Ass. elettrotecn. Milano 15 1911 (1013). [6440]. 43034

————— Zur Kenntnis der Funkenspannung bei technischem Wechselstrom. Berlin Zs. Ver. D. Ing. 55 1911 (554 559); Elektrot. Zs. Berlin 32 1911 (436–440 460 464); Mitt. Forsch-Arb. Ingenieurw. Berlin H. 100 1911 (1–48). [6820]. 43035

————— Korona-Bildung und Korona-Verluste an Hochspannungsleitungen. Helios Leipzig 17 1911 Fach. Zs. (559 561 571–574). [6810]. 43036

————— Zur Beurteilung von Hochspannungs-Freileitungs-Isolatoren, nebst einem Beitrag zur Kenntnis von Funkenspannungen. Diss. Dresden. Berlin (Druck v. A. W. Schade) 1910 (99 mit 2 Taf.). 27 cm. [6000 6820]. 43037

Weidig, Max. Metallurgische und technologische Studien auf dem Gebiete der Legierungs-Industrie, insbesondere über das Ausglühen von Metallen und Legierungen. Berlin Verh. Ver. Gewerbfl. 90 1911 (445 514 525–587). [5660]. 43038

————— Radioaktive Quellen von ganz einzigartig hoher Aktivität bei Brambach im sächsischen Vogtlande. Zs. öff. Chem. Plauen 17 1911 (221 224). [4275]. 43039

————— Radioaktive Gase oder Emanationen, ihre Natur und ihre praktische Bedeutung. Zs. öff. Chem. Plauen 18 1912 (61–72). [4275]. 43040

————— r. Schiffner.

Weidig, P. r. Görges, H.

Weigert, Fritz. Eine einfache Methode zur Konstruktion von Schwärzungskurven photographischer Platten. Jahrb. Phot. Halle 25 1911 (57–58). [4225]. 43041

————— Die chemischen Wirkungen des Lichts. Samml. chem. Vortr. Stuttgart 17 1911 (183–296). [4225]. 43042

————— Zur Einteilung der photochemischen Reaktionen. Zs. wiss. Phot. Leipzig 10 1911 (1–15). [4225]. 43043

————— r. Goldberg, E.

Weigle, G. F. Natürliche und künstliche Obertöne, einfache Töne. Mixturen. Zs. InstrBau Leipzig 31 1911 (1307–1309). [9450]. 43044

Weiler, W. Das kritische CD' von Drehstromgeneratoren. Elektrot. Zs. Berlin 32 1911 (677). [6045]. 43045

————— Ursprung des Erdmagnetismus und der Luftelektrizität. Uns. Welt Godesberg 3 1911 (555–562). [5490 5270]. 43046

————— Die galvanischen Induktionsapparate. Leichtfassliche Anleitung zur Anfertigung . . . Unter Mitwirkung von E. Zobel. 2., vielfach verb. und stark verm. Aufl. Leipzig (M. Schäfer) [1911] (XVI + 180 mit 1 Taf.). 20 cm. 4 M. [0050 4900]. 43047

[**Weimarn,** P[etr] P[etrovič] von.]
Беймарнъ, П[етръ] П[етровичъ]
фонъ]. Ультрамикроскопическія
изслѣдованія жидкихъ кристалловъ.
[Ultramikroskopische Untersuchungen
kristallinischer Flüssigkeiten.] St.
Peterburg Žurn. russ. fiz.-chim. Obšč.
Fiz. otd. **41** 1909 (90–96). [0400].
43048

—————— Uebersättigung und Unterkühlung als grundlegende Ursachen
des dispersen Zustandes der Materie.
Kolloidchem. Beih. Dresden **1** 1910
(331–374). [0340]. 43049

—————— Die Theorie der Herstellung und der Stabilität kolloider
Lösungen, I. Kolloidchem. Beih.
Dresden **1** 1910 (396–422). [0340].
43050

—————— Der kolloide Zustand
und seine Bedeutung für die verschiedenen Zweige der Naturwissenschaft.
Kolloidchem. Beih. Dresden **1** 1911
(399–408). [0340]. 43051

—————— Theorie der Uebergangserscheinungen zwischen kolloiden und
wahren Lösungen. Zs. Kolloide Dresden **8** 1911 (24–33). [0100 0340].
43052

—————— Zur Frage der Untersuchungsmethoden kapillarchemischer
Probleme. Zs. Kolloide Dresden **8** 1911
(133–138). [0300 1810]. 43053

—————— Beiträge zur Kenntnis der
Natur der dispersen Systeme. Zs.
physik. Chem. Leipzig **76** 1911 (212–
230). [0340]. 43054

—————— Grundzüge der Dispersoidchemie. Dresden (Th. Steinkopff) 1911
(VIII + 127 mit Taf.). 23 cm. 4 M.
[0340 0400]. 43055

Wiener, Hugo. Ueber die Umkehr
des Zuckungsgesetzes bei der Entartungsreaktion. Bemerkungen zu dem
Buche Reiss: „Die elektrische Entartungsreaktion". D. Arch. klin. Med.
Leipzig **103** 1911 (188–194). [5900].
43056

Weinhold, Adf. F. Physikalische
Demonstrationen. Anleitung zum
Experimentieren im Unterricht an
höheren Schulen u. techn. Lehranstalten. 5. verb. u. verm. Aufl. (In 3
Lfgn.) Lfg 1. 2. Leipzig (J. A. Barth)
1911 (VI + IV + 704 mit 5 Taf.).
25 cm. 11 M. [0050]. 43057

Weinstein, B[ernhard]. Die Grundgesetze der Natur und die modernen
Naturlehren. (Wissen und Können.
19.) Leipzig (J. A. Barth) 1911 (VIII
+ 279). 23 cm. Geb. 6 M. [0000].
43058

Weiss, E. Ladungsbestimmungen
an Silberteilchen. (Vorl. Mitt.) Physik. Zs. Leipzig **12** 1911 (630–633).
[5220 6845 0150]. 43059

Weiss, J. Einiges aus der Theorie
der Thermoelektrizität. Zs. physik.
Unterr. Berlin **24** 1911 (238–248).
[5710]. 43060

—————— Thermoelektrische Versuche. Zs. physik. Unterr. Berlin **24**
1911 (344–346). [5710 0050]. 43061

—————— Experimentelle Beiträge
zur Elektronentheorie aus dem Gebiet
der Thermoelektrizität. Diss. Freiburg i. Br. Emmendingen (Druck d.
Druck- u. Verlags-Ges.) 1910 (71).
22 cm. [5710 2020 5675]. 43062

—————— v. Koenigsberger, J.

Weiss, Otto. Temperaturmessungen
auf Schiffen der Kriegs- und Handels-
marine. Jahrb. schiffbaut. Ges. Berlin
12 1911 (222–244). [1250]. 43063

Weiss, Pierre. Über die rationalen
Verhältnisse der magnetischen Momente
der Moleküle und das Magneton. Berlin Verh. D. physik. Ges. **13** 1911 (718–
755); Physik. Zs. Leipzig **12** 1911
(935–952); J. phys. Paris (sér. 5) **1** 1911
(900–912 965–988 av. fig.); Radium
Paris **8** 1911 (301–307 av. fig.); Zürich
Vierteljahrschr. Natf. Ges. **56** 1911
(213–228 mit 3 Fig.); [sunto. trad.]
Riv. fis. mat. sc. nat. Pavia **24** 1911
(272–274). [5480 5490]. 43064

—————— Sur une propriété nouvelle
de la molécule magnétique. Paris
C. R. Acad. sci. **152** 1911 (79–81).
[5480]. 43066

—————— Sur la rationalité des
rapports des moments magnétiques des
atomes et un nouveau constituant
universel de la matière. Paris C. R.
Acad. sci. **152** 1911 (187–189). [5480].
43067

—————— Sur la grandeur du
magnéton déduite des coefficients
d'aimantation des sels de fer. Paris
C. R. Acad. sci. **152** 1911 (367–369).
[5450]. 43068

Weiss. Pierre. Une idée de Walther Ritz sur les spectres de bandes. Paris C. R. Acad. sci. **152** 1911 (585 588). [4205]. 43069

———— Sur le magnéton dans les corps solides paramagnétiques. Paris C. R. Acad. sci. **152** 1911 (688 691). [5480]. 43070

———— Spectres de bandes. D'après quelques notes manuscrites de Ritz et une conversation. Radium Paris **8** 1911 (177–180). [4207]. 43071

———— et **Bloch,** O. Sur l'aimantation du nickel, du cobalt et des alliages de nickel et de cobalt. Paris C. R. Acad. sci. **153** 1911 (941 943). [5466]. 43072

———— et **Foex,** G. Étude de l'aimantation des corps ferromagnétiques en dessus du point de Curie. J. phys. Paris (sér. 5) **1** 1911 (274 288 744 753 805 814 av. fig.). [5460]. 43073

Weisz, Eduard. Ungeregelte Verhältnisse bei Bestimmung und Bewertung der Radiumemanation. Berlin Veröff. HufelandGes. Balneol. **31** 1910 (121–128). [4275]. 43074

Weitzel, Karl. Ueber die Temperaturkoeffizienten der Leitfähigkeit einiger Elektrolyten in nichtwässrigen Lösungsmitteln. Diss. Bonn (Druck v. H. Ludwig) 1911 (58). 22 cm. [6240]. 43075

Wellik, A. v. Streintz, F.

Wellisch, E. M. Ueber die Vorgänge beim Transport des aktiven Niederschlages. (Uebers.) Berlin Verh. D. physik. Ges. **13** 1911 (159-171). [6845]. 43076

Wellmer, W. Ein Jahr physikalischer Schülerübungen. Monatschr. natw. Unterr. Stuttgart **1910-11** 1911 (222–230). [0050]. 43077

Wendler, A. Die Methode der Autokollimation im Schülerpraktikum. (Ein Beitrag zur Anwendung des Ohmannschen Feld-Winkelmessers.) Zs. physik. Unterr. Berlin **24** 1911 (95–97). [0090 0050 3020]. 43079

———— Mikrometerwage für magnetische Messungen. Zs. physik. Unterr. Berlin **24** 1911 (272 276). [5435]. 43080

Wendt, G. Untersuchungen an Quecksilberlinien. Struktur. Ver-

änderung der Linien und des Spektrums bei Verdünnung des Metalldampfes. Zeemaneffekt in schwachen und starken Feldern. Ann. Physik Leipzig (4. Folge) **37** 1912 (535 560) ; Diss. Tübingen. Leipzig (J. A. Barth) 1911 (32). 23 cm. [4207 4208 4206]. 43081

Wengner, M. Theoretische und experimentelle Untersuchungen an der synchronen Einphasenmaschine. [Nebst Erwiderung von J. **Rezelmann.**] Elektrot. Zs. Berlin **32** 1911 (552). [6060]. 43082

Wenner, F. The stretching of a conductor by its own current. Elect. London **66** 1911 (960 961). [6420]. 43083

———— Method for eliminating the effect of all connecting resistances in the Thomson bridge. [Abstract.] Physic. Rev. Ithaca N.Y. **32** 1911 (614 616 with fig.). [6010]. 43084

Werner, Otto. Zur Physik Leonardo da Vincis. Diss. Erlangen (Druck v. Junge & S.) 1910 (179). 22 cm. ; Berlin (Intern. Verlagsanst. f. Kunst u. Literatur) [1911] (VII + 184). 23 cm. 2 M. [0010]. 43085

Werner, W. Odkrycie Galvani'ego i Volty. [Les découvertes de Galvani et d. Volta.] Wektor Warszawa **1** 1911 (66 99). [0010]. 43086

———— Über den Einfluss einer permanenten Dehnung auf die elektrische und thermische Leitfähigkeit der Metalle. Diss. Freiburg (Schweiz) 1909 (82). 22 cm. [5675]. 43087

Werner-Bleines. Tönende Telefunken. D. TechnZtg Berlin **28** 1911 (643 647 658 663 707–711 741–746). [6615]. 43088

———— Neue Apparate zur drahtlosen Telephonie nach Dr. Erich Huth. Mechaniker Berlin **19** 1911 (81 91). [6043]. 43089

Wertenstein. Sur un rayonnement ionisant extrêmement absorbable émis par le radium C. Paris C. R. Acad. sci. **152** 1911 (1657–1660). [4275]. 43090

Werth, F. La galvanoplastica. Ed. 2. Milano (Hoepli) 1910 (XIV + 333). 16 cm. [6030 4900]. 43091

Wertheimer, Alfred. Ueber Strom- und Spannungsverlauf (Charakteristik) an Röntgenröhren. Zs. Röntgenkunde

Leipzig 13 1911 (292–306); Leipzig (S. Hirzel) 1911 (III + 42 mit 2 Taf.). 25 cm. 2 M. [6840 6080 4240].
43092

Wertheimer, E. Zur Theorie des Wasserdampfes. Dinglers polyt. J. Berlin 326 1911 (676–680); Physik. Zs. Leipzig 12 1911 (91–94). [1800 1880 1840 2455].
43093

—————— Die Plancksche Konstante h und der Ausdruck h v. Physik. Zs. Leipzig 12 1911 (408–412). [4200 4960].
43094

Wertheim-Salomonson, J. K. A. Die Aktions-Ströme der willkürlichen und reflektorischen Kontraktionen der menschlichen Muskeln. Arch. physik. Med. Leipzig 4 1909 (203–204). [5900].
43095

—————— Die günstigste Unterbrechungsfrequenz bei dem Induktorbetrieb. Arch. physik. Med. Leipzig 6 1911 (58 61). [6040].
43096

—————— High sound vibrations produced by electric sparks. Elect. London 66 1911 (959–960). [9130].
43097

—————— Milliampèremeter und Röntgenlicht. Fortschr. Röntgenstr. Hamburg 16 1911 (291–296). [4240 6845].
43098

—————— v. Salomonson.

Wesendonk, K[arl] v. Zur Theorie der Klangfarbe. Berlin Verh. D. physik. Ges. 13 1911 (278–280). [9450].
43099

Westphal, Wilh. H. Zur Dynamik eines idealen Gases vom Standpunkt des Relativitätsprinzips und der kinetischen Gastheorie. Berlin Verh. D. physik. Ges. 13 1911 (590–600). [0200].
43100

—————— Zur Dynamik der bewegten Hohlraumstrahlung. Berlin Verh. D. physik. Ges. 13 1911 (607–611). [4200].
43101

—————— Zur Arbeit: Zur Dynamik eines idealen Gases vom Standpunkte der kinetischen Gastheorie und des Relativitätsprinzips. Berlin Verh. D. physik. Ges. 13 1911 (974 977). [0200].
43102

—————— v. Franck, J.

Weszelszky, Gyula. A rádioaktivitásról, tekintettel a rádiummal való gyógyitásra. [Über die Radioaktivität, mit Rücksicht auf die Radiotherapie.]

Termt. Közl. Budapest 43 1911 (441–457). [4275].
43103

Wetterer, Josef. Zwei neue Instrumente zur qualitativen und quantitativen Messung der X-Strahlen. Das Villard'sche Radiosklerometer und das Quantitometer. Arch. physik. Med. Leipzig 4 1909 (205–212). [4240].
43104

Wetthauer, August. Ueber die Breite und den Ort der Interferenzstreifen bei keilförmigen Blättchen. Diss. Marburg (Druck v. C. Schaaf) 1911 (56 mit Taf.). 22 cm. [3610].
43105

Weve, H. v. Zeeman, W. P. C.

Weyl, H[ermann]. Ueber die Abhängigkeit der Eigenschwingungen einer Membran von deren Begrenzung. J. Math. Berlin 141 1912 (1–11). [9120].
43106

—————— Das asymptotische Verteilungsgesetz der Eigenwerte linearer partieller Differentialgleichungen (mit einer Anwendung auf die Theorie der Hohlraumstrahlung). Math. Ann. Leipzig 71 1912 (441–479). [4205 4210 6620 9120].
43107

Wheeler, Lynde P. An experimental investigation on the reflexion of light at certain metal-liquid surfaces. Phil. Mag. London (Ser. 6) 22 1911 (229–245). [3810].
43108

Wherry, Edgar T[heodore] v. Boyer, C.

Whetham, W. C. D. Lo stato attuale della fisica. [Trad. con note.] Palermo (R. Sandron) 1909 (XXIV + 341 con 6 ritr. e 7 tav.). 22 cm. [0030 0100].
43109

Whiddington, R. The production of characteristic Röntgen radiations. Cambridge Proc. Phil. Soc. 16 1911 (150–154); London Proc. R. Soc. (Ser. A) 85 1911 (323–332); Radium Paris 8 1911 (286–288 av. fig.). [4240]. 43110

—————— The production and properties of soft Röntgen radiation. London Proc. R. Soc. (Ser. A) 85 1911 (99–118). [4240].
43111

Whipple, R. S. Some recent improvements in pyrometers. Elect. London 68 1911 (132–134). [1255].
43112

Whitaker, M. C. v. Miner, H. S.

White, Walter P[orter]. A method
for increasing calorimetric accuracy.
[Abstract.] Physic. Rev. Ithaca N.Y.
32 1911 (601–602). [1610].   43113

——————— The detection of small
heat effects at high temperatures.
[Abstract.] Physic. Rev. Ithaca N.Y.
32 1911 (604–606). [1600].   43114

——————— Schmelzpunktsbestim-
mungen. (Uebers. von J. **Koppel.**)
Zs. anorg. Chem. Hamburg 69 1911
(305–330). [1810].   43115

——————— Schmelzpunktsmethoden
bei hohen Temperaturen. (Uebers.
von J. **Koppel.**) Zs. anorg. Chem.
Hamburg 69 1911 (331–352). [1810].
                                      43116
Whittaker, E. T. On the dynamical
nature of the molecular systems which
emit spectra of the banded type.
London Proc. R. Soc. (Ser. A) 85 1911
(262–270). [4207].   43117

Wiebe, H. F. Die Brauchbarkeitsgrenze der hochgradigen Thermometer. D. MechZtg Berlin 1912 (21–23
33–40). [1250 1210].   43119

——————— Über die verschiedenen
Konstruktionen der ärztlichen Maxi-
mum-Thermometer. D. MechZtg
Berlin 1911 (77–79 89–90 189–191).
[1250].   43120

——————— und **Hebe,** P. Über die
Unzuverlässigkeit ungeprüfter Fieber-
thermometer. D. MechZtg Berlin
1911 (65–67). [1250].   43121

Wiechert, E. Relativitätsprinzip
und Äther. I. II. Physik. Zs. Leipzig
12 1911 (689–707 737–758). [0600
4940].   43122

Wiedemann, Eilhard. Zur Optik
von Kamâl al Dîn. Arch. Gesch.
Natw. Leipzig 3 1911 (161–177).
[0010].   43123

——————— Zu den optischen Kennt-
nissen von Qutb al Dîn al Schirâzi.
Arch. Gesch. Natw. Leipzig 3 1911
(187–193). [0010].   43124

——————— Beiträge zur Geschichte
der Naturwissenschaften. XIX. Über
die Brechung des Lichtes in Kugeln
nach Ibn al Haitam und Kamâl al Dîn
al Fârisi. Erlangen SitzBer. physik.
Soc. 42 (1910) 1911 (15–58). [3020
0010 3640].   43125

——————— v. Heiberg, J. L.

Wiegner, Georg. Ueber Emulsionskolloide (Emulsoide) nebst Bemerkungen zur Methodik der ultramikroskopischen Teilchenbestimmung. Kolloidchem. Beih. Dresden 2 1911 (213–242).
[0340 0450].   43126

——————— Die Adsorption der
Zucker in wässeriger Lösung. Nach
Versuchen mit Frerik **Burmeister.** Zs.
Kolloide Dresden 8 1911 (126–133).
[0300].   43127

——————— Beiträge zur ultramikroskopischen Untersuchung einiger Kolloidkoagulationen durch Elektrolyte.
Zs. Kolloide Dresden 8 1911 (227–232).
[0340].   43128

Wieland, Heinrich v. Meyer, K. H.

Wieleitner, H. Ueber das virtuelle
Bild eines unter Wasser befindlichen
Punktes. Unterrichtsbl. Math. Berlin
17 1911 (132–133). [3020].   43129

Wien, W[ilhelm]. Bestimmung der
mittleren freien Weglänge der Kanalstrahlen. Berlin SitzBer. Ak. Wiss.
1911 (773–786). [6845].   43130

——————— Über die Gesetze der
Wärmestrahlung. Nobel-Vortrag . . .
Leipzig (J. A. Barth) 1912 (21). 24 cm.
1 M. [4200].   43131

Wiesent, H. Eine Quecksilber-
Reibungselektrisiermaschine. Zs. physik. Unterr. Berlin 24 1911 (225–226).
[5210].   43132

Wiesner, Siegbert. Ein Wirkungsprinzip der Natur. Ann. Natphilos.
Leipzig 10 1911 (392–396). [0000].
                                      43133
Wigand, Albert. Die umkehrbare
Lichtreaktion des Schwefels. Zs.
physik. Chem. Leipzig 77 1911 (423–
471). [3810].   43134

Wild, J. Die Ursache der zusätzlichen
Eisenverluste in umlaufenden glatten
Ringankern. Beitrag zur Frage der
drehenden Hysterese. Diss. Stuttgart.
Berlin (Druck v. A. W. Schade) 1911
(58). 26 cm. [5450].   43135

Wild, L. W. Magnetic testing of
transformer iron. London J. Inst.Electr.
Engin. 46 1911 (217–232); [sunto. trad.]
Atti Ass. elettrotecn. Milano 15 1911
(460–461). [5450 5440].   43136

Wildermuth, Filipp. Experimentelle
Untersuchungen über den spezifischen
Leitungswiderstand und über die spezi-

lische Wärme der Gewebe des menschlichen Körpers als Grundlage für die Beurteilung des Weges von wärmeerregenden Hochfrequenzströmen. Mitt. Grenzgeb. Med. Chir. Jena **22** 1911 (511–527). [5900]. 43137

Wilke. Der Einfluss des magnetischen Feldes auf die Emission des Lichtes. Natw. Wochenschr. Jena **26** 1911 (737–742). [6660]. 43138

Wilke, E. und Ätzler, E. Versuche, die Reizwellen im Nerven durch Interferenz sichtbar zu machen. Arch. ges. Physiol. Bonn **142** 1911 (372–376). [5900]. 43139

Willcox, F. W. Effect of alternating current on drawn tungsten wire. Elect. London **67** 1911 (827). [6180]. 43140

Williams, E. H. A comparison of the influence of planes of transverse section on the magnetic properties of iron and of nickel bars. [Abstract.] Physic. Rev. Ithaca N.Y. **32** 1911 (231). [5400]. 43141

———— Spark discharge at very small distances. Physic. Rev. Ithaca N.Y. **32** 1911 (585–590 with fig. tables). [6820 6850]. 43142

———— Increase of magnetic induction in nickel bars due to transverse joints. Physic. Rev. Ithaca N.Y. **33** 1911 (60–64 with fig. tables). [5430]. 43143

Williams, S[amuel] R[obinson]. Experimental indications of the nature of magnetization. [Abstract.] Physic. Rev. Ithaca N.Y. **32** 1911 (249–250). [5430]. 43144

———— A study of the Joule and Wiedemann magnetostrictive effects in steel tubes. Physic. Rev. Ithaca N.Y. **32** 1911 (281–296 with tables text fig.). [5462]. 43145

Willows, R. S. and Picton, T. Notes on the behaviour of incandescent lime kathodes. London Proc. Physic. Soc. **23** 1911 (257–263). [6840]. 43146

Willstatter, Richard. Untersuchungen über Chlorophyll. XVIII. Absorptionsspektra der Komponenten und ersten Derivate des Chlorophylls; von Richard **Willstatter.** Arthur **Stoll** und Max **Utzinger.** — Über die Reduktion des Chlorophylls. I.; von Richard **Willstatter** und Yasuhiko **Asahina.** Liebigs Ann. Chem. Leipzig **385** 1911

(156 188 188 225 mit Taf.). [3860 3850]. 43147

Wilsar, Heinrich. Über den Ursprung der Träger der bewegten und der ruhenden Intensität der Kanalstrahlen. (Vorl. Mitt.) Physik. Zs. Leipzig **12** 1911 (1091–1094). 43148

Wilson, C. T. R. On a method of making visible the paths of ionising particles through a gas. London Proc. R. Soc. (Ser. A) **85** 1911 (285–288). [4960 6805]. 43149

Wilson, Ernest. High-tension electrostatic wattmeters. London Proc. Physic. Soc. **23** 1911 (246–252). [6010]. 43150

———— and **Budd, L. C.** Previous magnetic history as affected by temperature. London Proc. Physic. Soc. **23** 1911 (253–256). [5460]. 43151

———— and **Wilson, W. H.** Demonstration of a new method for producing high-tension discharges. London Proc. Physic. Soc. **23** 1910 (35–38). [6040]. 43152

Wilson, H. A. The velocity of the ions of alkali salt vapours. Phil. Mag. London (Ser. 6) **21** 1911 (711–718). [5685]. 43153

———— The number of electrons in the atom. Phil. Mag. London (Ser. 6) **21** 1911 (718–722). [0500]. 43154

Wilson, W. The variation of ionisation with velocity for the β-particles. London Proc. R. Soc. (Ser. A) **85** 1911 (240–248). [4275]. 43155

———— The effect of temperature on the absorption coefficient of iron for γ-rays. Phil. Mag. London (Ser. 6) **21** 1911 (532–534). [4275]. 43156

———— The discharge of positive electricity from hot bodies. Phil. Mag. London (Ser. 6) **21** 1911 (634–640). [6810]. 43157

Wilson, W. H. v. Wilson, E.

Wimmer, Franz Paul. Praxis der Makro- und Mikro-Projektion für die Lehrzwecke in Schule und Haus . . . Leipzig (O. Nemnich) 1911 (XIX + 360 mit 8 Taf.). 23 cm. Geb. 6 M. [0050 3085]. 43158

Winderlich, R. Das Problem der Materie. II. Monatshefte natw. Unterr. Leipzig **4** 1911 (21–32). [0500]. 43159

Winterberg, H[einrich]. Das Elektrokardiogramm, seine theoretische und praktische Bedeutung. Med. Klinik Berlin **7** 1911 (761–766 804 807). [5900]. 43160

Winterstein, Hans. Linsen mit veränderlicher Krümmung [zur Demonstration physiologisch - optischer und physikalischer Erscheinungen]. Zs. biol. Techn. Leipzig **2** 1911 (206 208). [4490 3090 6050]. 43161

Winther, Chr. Über einen elektrischen Lichtakkumulator. Zs. Elektroch. Halle **18** 1912 (138 143). [5620 6850 6200]. 43162

————— Über die optische Sensibilisierung. Zs. wiss. Phot. Leipzig **9** 1911 (205 228). [4225]. 43163

————— Zur Theorie der Farbenempfindlichkeit. Zs. wiss. Phot. Leipzig **9** 1911 (229 237); **10** 1911 (209 211). [4225]. 43164

Wirtz, Karl r. Berndt, O.

Witkowski, A. O elektrycznem „napięciu". [Sur l'intensité du champ électrique.] Wektor Warszawa **1** 1911 (37–41). [5200]. 43165

————— O wartości hipotez naukowych. Odezyt wygłoszony na otwarcie roku szkolnego w Uniwersytecie Jagiellońskim w 1910 r. [Sur la valeur des hypothèses scientifiques. Discours prononcé à l'ouverture de l'année scolaire à l'Université de Cracovie en 1910.] Kraków 1911 (s.) (16 str.). 1 kor. [0000]. 43166

Witte, Hans. Ueber den behaupteten inversen Kräftezusammenhang zwischen Elektro- und Hydrodynamik. Physik. Zs. Leipzig **12** 1911 (347–360). [4940]. 43167

Wittmann, Ferencz. Csillapodás nélküli és csillapított rezgésjelenségek kísérleti vizsgálata. [Experimentaluntersuchungen ungedämpfter und gedämpfter Oszillationsphänomene.] Math. Termt. Ért. Budapest **29** 1911 (931–957). [5705 6015 6460 9020 9110]. 43168

Wodetzky, József. A fény szineszóródása a világtérben. [Dispersion des Lichtes im Weltraum.] Pótf. Termt. Közl. Budapest **43** 1911 (1 16). [3030 3210 3400 3410]. 43169

Wogan, M. v. r. Gehreke, E.

Woitaschewsky, A. Die Abhängigkeit der integralen Lösungswärme von der Temperatur. Zs. physik. Chem. Leipzig **78** 1911 (110–122). [1925 1920 1690]. 43170

Wolf, Rudolf. Experimentelle Bestätigung des Vektorendiagramms für den Motor nach Winter-Eichberg-Latour. Diss. Dresden. Leipzig (Druck von B. G. Teubner) 1910 (64). 25 cm. [6070]. 43171

Wolf, W. Beiträge zur Entwicklung der Gleichstrommaschine, deren Erregung vom Anker aus mittels einer Hilfsspannung oder eines Hilfsfeldes selbsttätig geregelt wird. Berlin Verh. Ver. Gewerbfl. **90** 1911 (407–430). [6960]. 43172

————— Neuere Anordnungen zur Aufhebung von Wellenspannungen und Lagerströmen. Helios Leipzig **17** 1911 Fach-Zs. (263 264). [6960]. 43173

————— Nuovi alternatori con autoregolazione. [Trad.] Industria Milano **25** 1911 (283 284 292 293 425 426). [6045]. 43174

Wolf-Czapek, K. W. Die Kinematographie. Wesen, Entstehung und Ziele des leb. Bildes. 2. erweit. Aufl. Berlin (Union) 1911 (136). 23 cm. 3 M. [3090]. 43175

Wolff, F. A. e **Dellinger,** J. H. The electrical conductivity of commercial copper. Washington D.C. Dept. Comm. Lab. Bull. Bur. Stand. **7** 1911 (103–126 with fig. pl. tables) ; [sunto. trad.] Atti Ass. elettrotecn. Milano **15** 1911 (373 374). [5660]. 43176

————— **Shoemaker,** M. P. and **Briggs,** C. A. The construction of primary mercurial resistance standards. [Abstract.] Physic. Rev. Ithaca N.Y. **32** 1911 (692–694 with table). [5650]. 43178

Wolff, Hans Th. Bemerkungen zu der Frage nach den Kräften, welche die Ladung eines Elektrons zusammenhalten. Ann. Physik Leipzig (4. Folge) **36** 1911 (1066–1070). [4960]. 43179

————— Behandlung des Vorganges, dass eine ebene elektromagnetische Welle, die auf die ebene Oberfläche eines Körpers, insbesondere eines Leiters, auftrifft, von diesem reflektiert wird, auf Grund der Maxwellschen Gleichungen unter ausführlichem

Eingehen auf die Art der stattfinden-
den Energiefortpflanzung. Diss. Rostock. Borna-Leipzig (Druck v. R.
Noske) 1910 (V + 55). 22 cm. [6600
6627 3875]. 43180

Wolff, Hermann. Über Volumeffekte bei Lösungsvorgängen. Ann.
Physik Leipzig (4. Folge) 36 1911 (177–
182). [2457 1925]. 43181

Wolff, K. r. Paschen, F.

Wolfke, Mieczyslaw. Ueber die
Abbildung eines Gitters bei künstlicher
Begrenzung. Diss. Breslau (Druck v.
H. Fleischmann) 1910 (52 mit 2 Taf.).
21 cm. ; Ann. Physik Leipzig (4. Folge)
34 1911 (277–310). [3630]. 43182

————— Über die Abbildung eines
Gitters bei asymmetrischer Abblendung.
Ann. Physik Leipzig (4. Folge) 37 1912
(96–102). [3630]. 43183

————— Über die Abbildung eines
durchlässigen Gitters. Ann. Physik
Leipzig (4. Folge) 37 1912 (797–811).
[3630 3650]. 43184

Wolletz. Hahnrohr für den Torricellischen Versuch und für Untersuchungen von Dämpfen. Zs. physik. Unterr.
Berlin 25 1912 (31). [8050]. 43185

Wollmann, Mme E. r. Duclaux, J.

Wologdine, L. r. Tschernobaeff, D.

Wolter, Peter. Über die ultravioletten Banden des Kohlenoxydspektrums. Zs. wiss. Phot. Leipzig 9
1911 (361–387). [4205]. 43186

Wommelsdorf, Fortschritte im Bau
von Influenzmaschinen. Elektrot. Zs.
Berlin 32 1911 (1247). [5210]. 43187

Wood, R. W. Nickeled glass reflectors for celestial photography. Astroph. J. Chicago 34 1911 (404–409
with pl.). [3060]. 43188

————— The destruction of the
fluorescence of iodine and bromine
vapour by other gases. Phil. Mag.
London (Ser. 6) 21 1911 (309–313);
Berlin Verh. D. physik. Ges. 13 1911
(72–77). [4230]. 43189

————— The resonance spectra
of iodine. Phil. Mag. London (Ser. 6)
21 1911 (261–265). [4205]. 43190

————— The resonance spectra of
iodine vapour and their destruction by
gases of the helium group. Phil. Mag.
London (Ser. 6) 22 1911 (469–481);

Physik. Zs. Leipzig 12 1911 (1204–1211
mit 1 Taf.). [4205]. 43193

Wood, R. W. Bemerkungen zu der A.
Heurungschen Arbeit : Untersuchungen über die magneto-optischen Effekte
bei Chlor und Jod. Ann. Physik Leipzig
(4. Folge) 37 1912 (594–596). [6650].
43194

————— Kritische Bemerkung zu
der Arbeit des Herrn Steubing über die
strahlende Emission seitens des Funkens. [Criticism of Herr Steubing's
work on the radiant emission from the
spark.] (Übers.) Physik. Zs. Leipzig
13 1912 (32–34 mit 1 Taf.). [6820 4205
4270]. 43195

————— Physical Optics. (ed. 2)
New York 1911. [2990]. 43196

————— und **Franck, J.** Transformation of a resonance spectrum into
a band-spectrum by presence of helium.
Phil. Mag. London (Ser. 6) 21 1911 (265–
268); Berlin Verh. D. physik. Ges. 13
1911 (84–87); Physik. Zs. Leipzig 12
1911 (81–83). [4230 4205 4206].
43197

————— and **Galt, R. H.** The
cathode-ray fluorescence of sodium
vapor. Astroph. J. Chicago Ill. 33
1911 (72–89 with tables text ff. pl.).
[4230]. 43200

————— r. Franck, Rubens.

Worel, Karl. Fortschritte in der
Farbenphotographie im vorigen Jahre.
Jahrb. Phot. Halle 25 1911 (3–5).
[4225]. 43201

Worral, P. W. Fenomeni di com-
mutazione ed oscillazioni magnetiche
nelle dinamo a corrente continua.
[Recens. Trad.] Atti Ass. elettrotecn.
Milano 15 1911 (48–50). [6440]. 43202

Worthing, A. G. The ratio of the
two heat capacities of carbon dioxide
as a function of the pressure and the
temperature. [Abstract.] Physic.
Rev. Ithaca N.Y. 32 1911 (243–245
with tables). [1640]. 43203

————— The free-expansion and
Joule-Kelvin effects in air and in
carbon-dioxide. [Abstract.] Physic.
Rev. Ithaca N.Y. 32 1911 (245–246
with tables). [1450]. 43204

————— Some thermodynamic
properties of air and of carbon dioxide.
Physic. Rev. Ithaca N.Y. 33 1911 (217–
267 with fig. tables). [1450 2435].
43205

————— r. Guthe, K. E.

Woudstra, H[erman] W[ijbe]. De werking van electrolyten op kolloïde oplossingen. II. [L'action d'électrolytes sur les solutions colloïdales. II.] Amsterdam Chem. Weekbl. **8** 1911 (21–41). [0340]. 43206

—————— Dispersitätsgrad und innere Reibung. Zs. Kolloide Dresden **8** 1911 (73–80). [0340 0325]. 43207

—————— v. Jorissen, W. P.

Woy, R. Bad Reinerz in Schlesien und seine neuen Heilquellen. Zs. öff. Chem. Plauen **17** 1911 (181 192). [4275]. 43208

Wright, Charles E. The temperature rise in pulleys and flywheels under frictional load, and a description of an electro-magnetic brake. Mining and Engineering Melbourne **3** No. 28 1911 (181–183 figs. 1–7). [2410 6050]. 43209

Wright, C. S. v. Simpson.

Wright, Fred. Eugène. Über den Durchgang des Lichtes durch inaktive durchsichtige Krystallplatten mit besonderer Berücksichtigung der Erscheinungen im konvergenten polarisierten Lichte. Min. Petr. Mitt. Wien **30** N.F. 1911 (171–232). [3820 3830 4000 4030]. 43210

Wright, J. R. Photo-electric effects in aluminum as a function of the wave-length of the incident light. [Abstract.] Physic. Rev. Ithaca N.Y. **32** 1911 (243). [6200 6850 5210]. 43211

—————— The positive potential of aluminium as a function of the wave length of the incident light. Physic. Rev. Ithaca N.Y. **33** 1911 (43 52 with fig. tables); (Uebers.) Physik. Zs. Leipzig **12** 1911 (338–343). [5210 6850 6200]. 43212

Wright, Robert v. Stewart, A. W.

Wroczyński, A. Résumé des travaux concernant les courbes de point de fusion des mélanges binaires dont un composant au moins est un corps organique. J. Chim. Phys. Genève **8** 1910 (569–594). [0032 1920]. 43213

Wülfing, E[rnst] A[nton]. Ueber die Konstanten der Konometer. Heidelberg SitzBer. Ak. Wiss. math.-natw. Kl. **1911** Abh. 3 (12). [3082]. 43214

—————— Ueber die Lichtbrechung des Kanadabalsams. Heidelberg Sitz- (6–1388)

Wülfing, E[rnst] A[nton]. Ber. Ak. Wiss. math.-natw. Kl. **1911** Abh. 20 (26). [3020 3822 3830]. 43215

Wülfing, E[rnst] A[nton]. Über Projektion mikroskopischer Objekte insbesondere im polarisierten Licht. Heidelberg SitzBer. Ak. Wiss. math.-natw. Kl. **1911** Abh. 36 (40 mit 1 Taf.). [0050 0390]. 43216

Würschmidt, J. Über Zweigströme in Entladungsröhren. (Vorl. Mitt.) Berlin Verh. D. physik. Ges. **13** 1911 (359 378). [6840]. 43217

—————— Ueber das Spektrum des elektrischen Lichtbogens. Jahrb. Phot. Halle **25** 1911 (16–18). [4202]. 43218

—————— Ueber die Brennkugel. Monats-hefte natw. Unterr. Leipzig **4** 1911 (98–113). [3060 3020 0010]. 43219

Wüst, F[riedrich]. Ueber die Schwindung der Metalle und Legierungen. Aachen Mitt. eisenhüttenmänn. Inst. **4** 1911 (20–43 mit Taf.). [1410 1810]. 43220

Wustenfeld, Heinrich v. Schaum, K.

Wüstney, Paul. Ein neues Zeiger-Quadrantenelektrometer für niedere Spannungen. Physik. Zs. Leipzig **12** 1911 (1251–1252). [6005]. 43221

Wuite, J. P. P-T-Durchschnitte. Zs. physik. Chem. Leipzig **78** 1911 (71–85). [1887]. 43222

[**Wulf,** G. V.] Вульфъ, Г. В. О такъ называемыхъ жидкихъ кристаллахъ и кристаллическихъ жидкостяхъ. [Sur les cristaux liquides et sur les liquides cristallins.] St. Peterburg Zurn. russ. fiz.-chim. Obšč. Fiz. otd. **41** 1909 (191–210). [0700]. 43223

Wulf, Theod. Ueber die Radioaktivität als allgemeine Eigenschaft der Körper. Physik. Zs. Leipzig **12** 1911 (497–500). [4275 0500]. 43224

Wunder, L. Ueber die Bildung stehender Wellen in den Wandungen explodierender Gefässe. Zs. physik. Unterr. Berlin **24** 1911 (215–217). [9200]. 43225

—————— Ueber Thermoelemente. Zs. physik. Unterr. Berlin **24** 1911 (224–225). [5710]. 43226

Wuppermann, Georg. Ueber Verdampfungsgeschwindigkeit. Diss. Leipzig. Borna-Leipzig (Druck v. R.

Noske) 1910 (37). 23 cm. [1840]. 0320]. 43227

Wurm, Erich. Eine neue Messbrücke zur Untersuchung von Blitzableiteranlagen. Elektrot. Zs. Berlin 32 1911 (593–595). [6010 5640]. 43228

Yamamoto, K[iyoshi] r. Kimura, M.

Yensen, Trygve D. Starkstromkondensator für Hochspannungszwecke. Elektrot. Zs. Berlin 33 1912 (81–83). [6000]. 43229

Yoshida, T[okuichi] r. Okada, T.

Yvon. Sur la cataphotographie. Paris C. R. Acad. sci. 152 1911 (1298). [4225]. 43230

Žáček, Augustin. Příspěvek k theorii Einthovenova strunového Galvanometru. [Beitrag zur Theorie des Einthovenschen Saitengalvanometers.] Prag Rozpr. České Ak. Frant. Jos. 20 1911 No. 34 (14). [6010]. 43231

Zacharias. Die Erzeugung elektrischer Kraft auf elektrochemischem Wege . . . Ann. Gew. Berlin 69 1911 (46–53). [5610]. 43232

Zahn, Hermann. Über scheinbaren Halleffekt bei hochfrequenten Wechselströmen und ein hierauf beruhendes empfindliches Nullinstrument. Ann. Physik Leipzig (4 Folge) 36 1911 (553–574). [6455 5705]. 43233

————— Über ein empfindliches Drehspulgalvanometer von kleinem Widerstande. Zs. Instrumentenk. Berlin 31 1911 (145–148). [6010]. 43234

————— Über magnetischen Skineffekt von Metallscheiben in hochfrequenten Wechselfeldern. Ann. Physik Leipzig (4. Folge) 37 1912 (330–350). [6440 6400 5400]. 43235

Zakrzewski, Konstanty. O własnościach optycznych metali, część II. (Über die optischen Eigenschaften der Metalle 2. Mitt.) Kraków Bull. Intern. Acad. 1911 A (314–329). [5675]. 43236

————— O użyciu interferometru półcieniowego w celach fotometrycznych. (Das Halbschatteninterferometer als Photometer.) Kraków Bull. Intern. Acad. 1911 A (515–547). [3010 3600]. 43237

Zammarchi, Angelo. Il cinquantenario di un'invenzione. L'anello di

Pacinotti. Riv. fis. mat. sc. nat. Pavia 24 1911 (515–554). [0010]. 43238

Zangger, H[einr]. Eine neue einfache Methode zur Bestimmung der Avogadroschen Zahl N. Zs. Kolloide Dresden 9 1911 (216–218). [0150]. 43239

————— Die Bestimmungen der Avogadroschen Zahl N. ; die untere Teilungsgrenze der Materie (deren Bedeutung für die Biologie und Medizin). Zürich Vierteljahrschr. Natf. Ges. 56 1911 (167–182). [0100 0500]. 43240

Zanietowski, J[osef]. Ueber den Beschluss des Elektrologenkongresses zu Barcelona und über das Verhältnis desselben zu den bisherigen Resultaten meiner Kondensatorversuche. Zs. med. Elektrol. Leipzig 13 1911 (65–69). [5900]. 43241

————— Praktische Winke zur Berechnung der modernen Erregungskoeffizienten. (Anhang zum vorhergehenden Artikel.) Zs. med. Elektrol. Leipzig 13 1912 (145–154). [5900]. 43242

Zanotti Bianco, Ottavio. Determinazioni della gravità sull'Oceano indiano e sul Pacifico istituite dal prof. dott. O. Hecker. Riv. geogr. ital. Firenze 16 1909 (234–237). [0845]. 43243

————— La gravità alla superficie del mare e l'ipotesi di Pratt. Riv. geogr. ital. Firenze 17 1910 (1–46). [0700]. 43244

————— Inerzia ed energia. Riv. Astron. sci. affini Torino 5 1911 (2–11). [2405]. 43245

————— La figura della terra e le misure di gravità. Riv. Astron. sci. affini Torino 5 1911 (548–565). [0700]. 43246

Zàvada, Bohuslav. Anordnung zur Beseitigung der störenden Wirkungen der Trägheit von Selenzellen für telephotographische Zwecke. Elektrot. Zs. Berlin 32 1911 (1111–1112). [6480 5660]. 43247

————— Eine neue Form von Elektrodynamometer. Zs. Elektrot. Potsdam 14 1911 (407–408). [6010]. 43248

Záviška, Frant. Přehled pokroků fysiky za rok 1908. 5. Elektřina a magnetismus. [Uebersicht der physikalischen Fortschritte im J. 1908. 5. Elektrizität und Magnetismus.]

Prag Věstn. České Ak. Frant. Jos.
1911 (155–195 232–235). [0030 4900].
43249

Zavadzki, J. v. Haber, F.

Zeeman, P. L'origine des couleurs
du spectre. [Sunto.] Riv. fis. mat. sc.
nat. Pavia **19** 1909 (160–162). [4200].
43250

——— Beschouwingen over
lichtstraling onder den gelijktijdigen
invloed van electrische en magnetische
krachten en eenige naar aanleiding
daarvan genomen proeven. [Con-
siderations concerning light radiation
under the simultaneous influence of
electric and magnetic forces and some
experiments thereby suggested.] Amsterdam Versl. Wis. Nat. Afd. K. Akad.
Wet. **19** 1911 (957–967) (Dutch);
Amsterdam Proc. Sci. K. Akad. Wet.
14 [1911] (2–11) (English). [6660].
43251

——— Le cas général de la
décomposition magnétique des raies
spectrales et son application en astrophysique. J. phys. Paris (sér. 5) **1**
1911 (442 469); [Übers.] Physik. Zs.
Leipzig **13** 1912 (86–95). [6660 4208].
43252

——— Over het isoleerend
vermogen van vloeibare lucht voor
hooge spanning en over het electro-
optisch Kerr-effect in vloeistoffen.
[Note on the insulating power of liquid
air for high potentials and on the Kerr
electro effect of liquid air.] Amsterdam Versl. Wis. Nat. Afd. K. Akad.
Wet. **20** [1911] (731–736) (Dutch);
Amsterdam Proc. Sci. K. Akad. Wet.
[1911] (650–655) (English). [6640
5770 3835]. 43253

——— en **Hoogeboom**, C. M.
Electrische dubbele breking en nevels.
[Electric double refraction in some
artificial clouds and vapours.] Amsterdam Versl. Wis. Nat. Afd. K. Akad.
Wet. **20** [1911] (570–574) 1912 (921–
923) (Dutch); Amsterdam Proc. Sci. K.
Akad. Wet. **14** [1911] (558–562) 1912
(786–788) (English). [6640 3835].
43255

Zeeman, W. P. C. Linsenmessungen
und Emmetropisation. Graefes Arch.
Ophthalm. Leipzig **78** 1911 (93–128
mit 4 Taf.). [4410]. 43256

——— und **Weve**, H. Ein
Spektralapparat zur Untersuchung des
Farbensinnes. Klin. Monatsbl. Augen-
(c–4288)

heilk. Stuttgart (**49**) N. F. **11** 1911
(490–501). [4470 4450]. 43257

Zehnder, Ludwig. Über gerichtete
drahtlose Telegraphie mit Erdströmen.
Berlin Verh. D. physik. Ges. **13** 1911
(874–875). [6615]. 43258

——— Ueber die Beseitigung der
Antennen bei der drahtlosen Telegraphie. Elektrot. Anz. Berlin **28** 1911
(1315). [6615]. 43259

——— Beruht die drahtlose Telegraphie auf der Ausstrahlung Hertzscher Wellen in der Erde? [Nebst]
Erwiderung von F. Kiebitz. Elektrot.
Zs. Berlin **32** 1911 (1101–1102 1195
1219). [6615]. 43260

Zeleny, Anthony. The causes of
zero displacement and deflection hysteresis in moving-coil galvanometers.
Physic. Rev. Ithaca N.Y. **32** 1911
(297–306 with tables text fig.). [6010].
43261

Zeleny, John. A lecture electroscope
for radioactivity and other ionization
experiments. Physic. Rev. Ithaca
N.Y. **32** 1911 (581–584 with fig.); [ab-
stract] l.c. (255–256). [6005]. 43262

——— On the presence in point
discharge of ions of opposite sign.
Physic. Rev. Ithaca N.Y. **33** 1911 (70–
73 with fig. table). [6800]. 43263

——— and **McKeehan**, L. W. A
microscope plate micrometer. Physic.
Rev. Ithaca N.Y. **32** 1911 (530–532
with fig.). [3082]. 43264

Zemplén, Győző. A hanghullámok
hőhatásának kisérleti kimutatása. [Ex-
perimenteller Nachweis des Wärmeeffektes der Schallwellen.] Termt.
Közl. Budapest **43** 1911 (322–323).
[9320]. 43265

——— A képtelegrafia haladá-
sáról. [Über die Fortschritte der
Bildtelegraphie.] Termt. Közl. Budapest **43** 1911 (425–428). [6480]. 43266

——— Törvényszerűségek az
elemek atomsúlyában és a radio-
aktivitás. [Gesetzmässigkeiten im Atom-
gewichte der Elemente und die Radioaktivität.] Termt. Közl. Budapest **43**
1911 (572–573). [4275]. 43267

——— A napsugarak felhaszná-
lása elektromos áram keltésére. [Die
Anwendung der Sonnenstrahlen zur
Erregung des elektrischen Stroms.]
Termt. Közl. Budapest **43** 1911 (819–
820). [5210]. 43268

s 2

Zemplén, Győző. A relativitás elvéről.
[Über das Relativitätsprinzip.] Math.
Phys. L. Budapest 20 1911 (331–347).
[0000 4940 4240]. 43269

—————— Vizsgálatok a gázok
belső surlódásáról. [Untersuchungen
über die innere Reibung der Gase.]
Math. Termt. Ért. Budapest 29 1911
(645–718). [0325]. 43270

Zenghelis, C. Nachweis, dass der
Siedepunkt des Wassers mit dem
Drucke sinkt. Zs. physik. Unterr.
Berlin 24 1911 (224). [0050]. 43271

Zenneck, J[onathan]. Energiemessung an Hochbogenspannungslichtbögen. Physik. Zs. Leipzig 12 1911
(343–346 mit 1 Taf.). [6830]. 43272

—————— Über einen lichtstarken
Spektrographen. Physik. Zs. Leipzig
12 1911 (1199–1201 mit 1 Taf.). [3165].
43273

Zerkowitz, Guido. Beitrag zur
Berechnung der Kompressoren auf
thermodynamischer Grundlage. Zs.
Turbinenwesen München 8 1911 (529–
532 548–552 564–568). [2495]. 43274

Zevi, Guido. Impiego di batterie di
accumulatori per regolare le reti a
corrente alternata. Elettricista Roma
(Ser. 2) 9 1910 (335–341). [6020].
43275

Ziegenberg, R. Neue Wechselstrom-
Präzisions - Messmethoden. Helios
Leipzig 17 1911 Fach-Zs. (150–154
177–181). [5705]. 43276

—————— Der Elektrolytzähler. Zs.
Beleuchtungsw. Berlin 17 1911 (86–89
101–103). [6010]. 43277

Zimmer, Otto. Ueber die innere
Reibung von Aethylen und Koh-
lenoxyd und ihre Aenderung bei tiefen
Temperaturen. Diss. Halle a. S.
(Druck v. H. John) 1911 (32 mit Taf.).
22 cm. [0325]. 43278

Zimmermann, Carl. Die Vibrationen
des Schädels beim Singen. Beitrag
zur Lehre von den objektiven Resonanzerscheinungen. Stimme Berlin 5
1911 (193–198). [9420 9140]. 43279

Zipp, Hermann. Indicatori di alte
tensioni. [Trad.] Industria Milano
24 1910 (325–327). [6010]. 43280

—————— Ein Beitrag zur Theorie
der Oberflächenentladungen. Elektr.
Kraftbetriebe München 9 1911 (361–
365). [5220 6810]. 43281

Zipp, Hermann. Experimentelle
Ermittlung des Hysteresedrehmo-
mentes. Elektrot. Zs. Berlin 32 1911
(652–654). [6045]. 43282

—————— Neue dynamometrische
Methoden zur Messung von L, C und ω.
Elektrot. Zs. Berlin 33 1912 (182–185).
[6440]. 43283

—————— Unter welchen Um-
ständen ist die Berührung einer elektrischen Anlage gefährlich ? Zs. Elektrot. Potsdam 14 1911 (215–217 249–
252). [6000 5900]. 43284

—————— Handbuch der elektrischen
Hochspannungstechnik. Mit besonderer Berücksichtigung der Energieübertragung. Lehrbuch für Ingenieure
und Studierende. Leipzig (O. Leiner)
1911 (VIII + 436 mit 4 Taf.). 25 cm.
13.50 M. [6000 6460]. 43285

Zöllich, H. v. Grober, M. K.

Zomparelli, Ennio. L'apoteosi del-
l'elettricità. Elettricista Roma (Ser. 2)
10 1911 (1–3). [0040 4900]. 43286

—————— La nuova lampada al
neon. Elettricista Roma (Ser. 2) 10
1911 (84). [6080]. 43287

—————— Il fenomeno della "corona"
nelle linee aeree ad alta tensione.
Elettricista Roma (Ser. 2) 10 1911
(88–89). [6460]. 43288

—————— Le proprietà elettriche
del selenio e loro pratiche applicazioni. Elettricista Roma (Ser. 2) 10
1911 (102–104). [5660]. 43289

—————— Forni elettrici. Elettricista
Roma (Ser. 2) 10 1911 (129–131).
[6090]. 43290

—————— Nuovo tipo di forno
elettrico. Elettricista Roma (Ser. 2)
10 1911 (180–182). [6090]. 43291

—————— Nuove invenzioni di
Tesla. Elettricista Roma (Ser. 2) 10
1911 (233–235). [6470]. 43292

—————— Sulla telefonia auto-
matica. Elettricista Roma (Ser. 2) 10
1911 (261–273). [6485]. 43293

—————— Termometria a distanza.
Elettricista Roma (Ser. 2) 10 1911
(302–303). [1230]. 43294

Zorn, Walter F. Ueber die Abhängigkeit der Dämpfung in Kondensatorkreisen mit Funkenstrecke von

der Gestalt und dem Material der Elektroden sowie von dem Dielektrikum in der Funkenstrecke. Jahrb. drahtlos. Telegr. Leipzig **4** 1911 (260–280 382 399). [6820]. 43295

Zoth, O[skar]. Weitere Versuche mit dem Fallphonometer. Arch. ges. Physiol. Bonn **137** 1911 (545–570). [9430]. 43296

Zschokke, W. Ueber Miniaturkameras. Jahrb. Phot. Halle **25** 1911 (34–38). [3085]. 43297

Zumbusch, Emilie. Ueber Luminophore. Mit einem Anhang: Ueber Wismut. Diss. München. Schongau (Druck v. C. F. Bornschein) 1911 (94). 23 cm. [4230]. 43298

Zumbusch, E. v. Vanino, L.

Zwaardemaker, H[endrik]. De afvloeiing van acustische energie uit het hoofd volgens proefnemingen van Dr. P. Nikiforowsky. [The effusion of acoustic energy from the head according to experiments of Dr. P. Nikiforowsky.] Amsterdam Versl. Wis. Nat. Afd. K. Akad. Wet. **20** [1911] (686–691) (Dutch); Amsterdam Proc. Sci. K. Akad. Wet. **14** [1911] (758–763) (Dutch). [9510]. 43299

———— The camera silenta of the physiological Laboratory at Utrecht. Utrecht Onderz. Physiol. Lab. (Ser. 5) **11** 1910 (151–158). [9240]. 43300

———— De acustiek der openbare gebouwen. [Die Akustik der öffentlichen Gebäude.] Utrecht Onderz. Physiol. Lab. (Ser. 5) **12** 1911 (59–77). [9255]. 43301

SUBJECT CATALOGUE.

The five-figure numbers following the name of the author refer to the position of the corresponding entry in the Author Catalogue where the full reference is to be found. In the case of societies and institutions which do not appear in the Author Catalogue the full reference is given under the earliest registration number.

References to previous volumes are given thus : v. C 10 = See THE VOLUME FOR PHYSICS IN THE TENTH ANNUAL ISSUE.

0000 PHILOSOPHY.

Beckenhaupt. 39142. Verhältnis der chemischen Elemente zu den Massen und Bewegungen der Himmelskörper und die ursprüngliche Art der Energie. 39143 : Existenz des Aethers und die mechanische Theorie. Wie weit sind Relativität und Vierdimensionalität begründet ?

Białobrzeski. 39239. Le principe du relativisme et ses applications. (Polish.)

Bouasse *et alii.* 39347. De la méthode dans les sciences, 2. éd.

Caraccio. 39510. Moto e materia o metamorfosi eterne universali.

Dochmann. 39774. Ostwalds Energetik.

Duhem. 39829. Wandlungen der Mechanik und der mechanischen Naturerklärung.

Einstein. 39896. Relativitätstheorie.

Frank. 40066. Gibt es eine absolute Bewegung ?

Froelich. 40088. Energie und Entropie.

Heffter. 40463. Vierdimensionale Welt Minkowskis.

Henk. 40477. Zur Methode und Philosophie Poincarés.

Isenkrahe. 40626. Energie, Entropie, Weltanfang, Weltende.

Jung. 40705. Bewertung physikalischer Erkenntnistheorien.

Konig. 40853. Die Materie.

Le Bel. 41040. Cosmologie rationelle.

Merczyng. 41405. Les limites de notre connaissance de la Nature par rapport au temps et à l'espace. 41408 : Le principe de relativité. (Polish.)

Mills. 41462. Foundations of science.

Nernst. 41577. Principes fondamentaux de la physique moderne.

Ostwald. 41704. L'énergie. [Trad.] 41706 : Esquisse d'une philosophie des sciences. [Trad.]

Picard. 41830. De la science.

Poske. 41947. Die Hypothese in Wissenschaft und Unterricht.

Silberstein. 42518. Quaternionenform der Relativitätstheorie. (Polish.)

Stallo. 42594. Begriffe und Theorien der modernen Physik.

Waals, *jr.* 42964. Erklärung der Naturgesetze auf statistisch-mechanischer Grundlage. 42965 : Frage nach den fundamentalsten Naturgesetzen.

Weinstein. 43058. Grundgesetze der Natur und moderne Naturlehren.

Wiesner. 43133. Ein Wirkungsprinzip der Natur.

Witkowski. 43166. Valeur des hypothèses scientifiques. (Polish.)

Zemplén. 43269. Relativitäts-prinzip. (Ungar.)

0010 HISTORY, BIOGRAPHY.

Les progrès de la physique et de la Chimie en Belgique pendant la période décennale 1899–1908. Chimiste au laboratoire et à l'usine, **1910** (129–132 145–147).

Sur l'invention de la boussole. Rev. univ. intern. illustrée Bruxelles **1910** (61–62).

ABBE r. Ostwald. 41707.

Albertotti. 38915. L'opera oftalmologica del prof. Reymond.

ARRHENIUS, Svante August r. Hamburger, H. J.

AVOGADRO, Amedeo r. Vignolo-lutati, F. 42911.

Baslini. 39103. Occhiali con astuccio del secolo XVII.

BECQUEREL, M. r. Becquerel, H. 39152.

BELLI, Giuseppe r. Pinauda. 41841.

BERLINER, Emil r. Grunwald, M. 40335.

Bjornbo † und **Vogl.** 39276. Alkindi, Tideus und Pseudo-Euklid. Drei optische Werke. Mit einem Gedächtniswort auf A. A. Björnbo.

BOSSCHA, J[ohannes] r. Lorentz. 41193.

MERCADIER r. Broca. 39399.

BUNSEN, R. r. Bosch, F. 39335 ; Kaestner, G. 40709 ; Kayser, H. 40748 ; Quincke, G. 41986.

Caiori. 39463. Storia della fisica elementare.

Cohen. 39594–5. Hundert Jahre in der Welt der Moleküle (1811–1911). (Holl.)

CURIE, Pierre r. Szilard. 42728.

DANIELSSON, Ernst. 19 – 1 1866 –15–8 1907. Stockholm Vet. - Ak. Årsbok 1910 (319–338 with portr. and text figs.).

De Heen. 39720. La succession des étapes de l'évolution des sciences physiques et les théories hybrides modernes. 39722 : Coup d'œil rétrospectif sur la science de l'électricité.

Dvořak. 39842. Entdeckung der Fallgesetze und das verkehrte Pendel.

D.velshauvers-Dery. 39843. L'évolution des forces.

Euler. 39951A. Dioptrica.

FRANKLIN, Benjamino r. Martini. 41343.

Favaro. 39976, 39977, 39978. Serie di scampoli Galileiani.

Galli. 40122. Come si svolse il primo concetto del termoscopio ad aria. 40123 : Come il termoscopio ad aria fu trasformato in termometro a liquido.

Garbasso e **Vacca.** 40138. Vecchia esperienza di Bennet e Volta.

GEROSA, Giuseppe r Pugliese. 41970.

GOETHE r. Geitel. 40168.

Graham. 40271. Abhandlungen über Dialyse (Kolloide).

KERNBAUM, Miroslas r. Grotowski, M. 40316.

GUERICKE, Otto von r. Slaby. 42533.

GULLSTRAND r. Rohr. 42165.

HAGENBACH - BISCHOFF, Eduard r. Veillon. 42900.

Hamburger. 40405. 25 Jahre „Osmotischer Druck" in den medizinischen Wissenschaften. Hugo de Vries, van 't Hoff, Svante Arrhenius.

HASELBACH r. Lex, F. H. 41120.

Heiberg und **Wiedemann.** 40465. Eine arabische Schrift über die Parabel und parabolische Hohlspiegel.

HELMHOLTZ, H. von r. Koenigsberger, L. 40874.

HIRN, G. A. r. Keller. 40754.

Jadanza. 40646b ; **Naccari.** 41549. Storia del cannocchiale.

HOFF, J[acobus] H[endrikus] van 't r. Hamburger, H. J. 40405 ; Le Chatelier. 41048 ; Schade. 42337.

Jeans. 40657. Molecule.

Keller. 40755. Werdegang der modernen Physik.

Kistner. 40798. Physikalische Irrtümer im Wandel der Zeit.

Klinckowstroem, Graf v. 40812. Der Erfinder des Teleskops.

KOHLRAUSCH, Friedrich r. Baborovský. 39033, Richarz. 42102.

Kohlrausch. 40877. Gesammelte Abhandlungen.

Kranz. 40906. Die ältesten Farbenlehren der Griechen.

Lagrange. 40979. L'histoire du thermomètre de Römer et le thermomètre Fahrenheit.

LINDECK, Stephan r. Krüss. 40923. Orlich. 41692.

Lockemann. 41167. Avogadros Hypothese.

BOSSCHA † r. Lorentz. 41193.

MAGRI, Luigi r. Pucciauti. 41969.

Majorana. 41286. Posta, telegrafo, telefono.

Mayer. 41382. Erhaltung der Kraft. 41380 : Mechanik der Wärme.

Muller. 41530. Geschichte der Dioptrien.

Mysłakowski. 41548. Valérien Magni et les différends relatifs à la découverte du vide. (Polish.)

NAGEL, W. A. r. Trendelenburg. 42824.

NEUMANN, Franz r. Volkmann, P. 42936.

OHM r. Bermbach. 39198.

Ostwald. 41704. L'énergie. [Trad.] 41708 : Grosse Männer.

Pacinotti. 41721. Descrizione di una macchinetta elettromagnetica.

PACINOTTI, Antonio. Onoranze ad Antonio Pacinotti. Atti Ass. elettrotecn. Milano 15 1911 (837–845).

————— r. Boccara. 39216 ; Pescio. 41813 ; Rumi. 42258.

Palazi. 41731. Nozioni elementari di chimica inorganica precedente dalle nozioni preliminari di fisica.

Paoli. 41741. La scuola di Galileo.

Pascal. 41755. Œuvres. Edition L. Braunschweig et P. Boutroux. Tomes I, II, III.

PELLAT, H. r. Pellat, S. 41793.

PETZVAL, Josef r. Seidl. 42482.

Picard. 41839. De la science.

Piotrovskij. 41848. Entwickelung der Theorie des Funkeninduktors. (Russ.)

Poincaré. 41914. Savants et écrivains.

Rohland. 42161. Schopenhauer als Physiker.

Rosenstiehl. 42190. Données historiques relatives à la force osmotique. Rectification de noms d'auteurs.

St. Peterburg. Comité special de la Section de Physique de la Société Physico-Chimique russe. 42595. Popov et l'histoire de la radiotélégraphie. (Russe avec des lettres fr. et angl.)

Spinoza r. Sande Bakhuyzen. 42308.

SCHRADER, G. J. F. r. Clemens, H. 39581.

SCHUSTER, Aimé r. Choppé. 39553.

SEMMOLA, Eugenio r. Chistoni. 39551 ; Pinto. 41843.

Smoluchowski. 42564. L'évolution de la Théorie Atomique. (Polish.)

Solari. 42568. Priorità nell'invenzione della telegrafia senza fili. 42569 : Le invenzioni di Marconi e di Pacinotti.

Stelzner. 42634. Mathematik und Naturwissenschaften an den neuhumanistischen Schulen. Diss.

Stern. 42642. Geschichte der elektrischen Strahlungserscheinungen.

Thirion. 42766. Pascal ; l'horreur du vide et la pression atmosphérique.

THOMPSON, S. P. r. Huygens. 40595.

TORRICELLI, Evangelista r. Giudice 40201 ; Thoria 41198 ; Vassura 42895.

Ulmer. 42862. Das erste Telephon : ein Sprachrohrtelegraph 1796.

Vogel. 42926. Einführung des Kompasses in die nordwesteuropäische Nautik.

VRIES, Hugo de r. Hamburger, H. J.

WATT, James r. Biedenkapp. 39244.

Werner. 43085. Zur Physik Leonardo da Vincis.

Werner. 43086. Découvertes de Galvani et de Volta. (Polish.)

Wiedemann. 43123-4. Optik von Kamâl al Din und Qutb al Din al Schîrâzî. 43125 : Brechung des Lichtes in Kugeln nach Ibn al Haitam und Kamâl al Din al Fârisî.

WIEN, Willy r. Valentiner. 42875.

WIND, Cornelius Harm †. (Dutch.) Amsterdam Versl. Wis. Nat. Afd. K. Akad. Wet. 20 [1911] 172-174).

WIRKEN, E. B. r. Krüger. 40920.

Würschmidt. 43219. Brennkugel.

ZAMBIASI, Giulio v. Gianfranceschi. 40181.

Zammarchi. 43238.

0020 PERIODICALS, REPORTS OF INSTITUTIONS, SOCIETIES, CONGRESSES, Etc.

Eis- und Kälte-Industrie. Monatsschrift für Natureis-Industrie . . . Hrsg. von Rich. **Stetefeld.** Bd. 13. Wittenberg (A. Ziemsen), 1911. 32 cm. Der Jg zu 12 Heften. 12 M. [Erschien früher in Berlin.] [0020].

Elektromotor. Süddeutsche Monatsschrift für Elektrizitäts-Verwendung und Verbreitung in Haus und Gemeinde, . . . Hrsg. **Greeff.** Jg 1. Berlin (U. Meyer) 1911. 26 cm. Der Jg zu 12 Nrn. 3,00 M. [0020 6000].

Jahrbuch der Elektrochemie v. C **6** p. 296. Berichte über 1906. Unter Mitwirkung der Herren P. Askenasy [u. a.] hrsg. von Heinrich **Danneel** und Julius **Meyer.** Jg 13. 1. Hälfte. (Bogen 1–31). 1911 (IV+497). Berichte über 1907. Unter Mitwirkung der Herren K. Elbs [u. a.] hrsg. von Julius **Meyer.** Jg 14. 1. Hälfte. (Bogen 1–31). Halle a. S. (W. Knapp) 1911 (III + 489). 23 cm. [6200].

Report of the National Academy of Sciences for the year 1907. Washington, 1908 (49); id. for 1908. 1909 (111); id. for 1909. 1910 (43); id. for 1909. 1910 (43); id. for 1910. 1911 (48). 24 cm.

Jordis. 40687. Generalregister zu Bd 1–10, Jg 1894–1904 der Zeitschrift für Elektrochemie.

Knudsen. 40826. Thermical molecular pressure of gases in tubes. (Danish.)

Montu. 41491. La elettricità alla esposizione univ. internaz. di Bruxelles 1910.

Robinson. 42155. Bericht über die Versammlung der British Association zu Portsmouth 1911.

Sackur. 42287. Physikalische Chemie.

St. Peterburg, Section de Physique de la Société Physico-Chimique Russe. II. Procès verbaux des séances. 42597. 42596 : 5. Jahresbericht für 1908. (Russ.)

Schriften der physikalisch-ökonomischen Gesellschaft zu Königsberg in Pr. 42418. Generalregister zu den Jahrgängen 26–50. 1885–1909.

Toula. 42813.

0030 GENERAL TREATISES, TEXT-BOOKS, DICTIONARIES, COLLECTED WORKS, TABLES.

Angewandte Photographie in Wissenschaft v. C **10** p. 243. Hrsg. von **Wolf-Czapek.** Tl 2 : Die Photographie im Dienste der organischen Naturwissenschaften. Tl 3 : Die Photographie im Dienste der Technik. Berlin (Union) 1911 (IV + 119 mit 41 Taf. ; IV + 95 mit 42 Taf.). 25 cm. Je 5 M. [3085 4225].

„Hütte" des Ingenieurs Taschenbuch. Hrsg. vom Akademischen Verein Hütte. 21. Aufl. Bd 1. 2. Berlin (W. Ernst & S.) 1911 (XVI + 1138 ; VII + 1043). 19 cm. Geb. 13 M. [0030].

Tables annuelles de constantes et données numériques de chimie, de physique et de technologie, publiées sous le patronage de l'Association internationale des Académies. Vol I, année 1910 Paris (Gauthier-Villars) 1912 (XXXIX + 727). 28 cm.

Tables électro-magnétiques et appareils magnétiques de tension. Industrie Bruxelles **1907** (169–170).

Baborovský. 39035. Fortschritte in der physikalischen Chemie 1907 u. 1908. Radioaktivität. (Čechisch).

Barreca. 39089. Correnti alternate. 39090 : Telegrafia e telefonia senza fili.

Berliner. 39197. **Donle.** 39786. **Lommel.** 41187. Lehrbücher der Experimentalphysik.

Borino. 39329 ; **Cantani.** 39485 ; **Pesenti.** 41814. Telegrafia.

Bracchi. 39375. Corso preparatorio per gli aspiranti telegrafisti.

Cataldi. 39514. La meccanica. Generatori di vapore, macchine termiche.

Ebert. 39852 ; **Grimsehl.** 40304 ; **Riecke.** 42111. Lehrbücher der Physik.

Ferrero. 39983. La locomotiva.

Clay. 39580. Practical light.

Föppl. 40021. Maxwellsche Theorie der Elektrizität.

Foveau de Cournelles. 40043. Progrès électriques en 1911.

Novák. 41648. Fortschritte in der Lehre über die Wellenbewegung des Aethers 1908. (Čechisch.)

Preston. 41956. Theory of light. 1912.

Puccianti. 41968. Recensione di " H. Kayser, Handbuch der Spectroscopie, Vol. 5."

Schincaglia. 42381. I raggi X.

0032   BIBLIOGRAPHIES.

Catalogus van boeken in Noord-Nederland verschenen van den vroegsten tijd tot op heden. I. Inleiding. Tijdschriften van gemengden inhoud, enz. Bibliographie. IX. Wis- en Natuurkunde. [Katalog von in den Nördlichen Niederlanden erschienenen Büchern von der frühesten Zeit bis auf heute. I. Einleitung. Zeitschriften gemischten Inhaltes u.s.w. Bibliographie. IX. Mathematik und Naturwissenschaften.] 's Gravenhage (Martinus Nijhoff) 1911 I (76 + Personenregister) IX (96 + Personenregister). 26 cm. [0010].

Fortschritte der Elektrotechnik v. C 10 p. 244. Hrsg. von K. **Strecker.** Jg 24. Das Jahr 1910. H. 2. 3. 4. Berlin 1911 (VIII + 317–1744 + IV). 24 cm. 10 M. 10,40 M. 15 M. [6000 4900].

International Catalogue of Scientific Literature. C Physics. Ninth annual issue 1911 (VIII + 424) ; Tenth annual issue 1912 (VIII + 397). London (Harrison). 22 cm.

Literatur der Elektrotechnik 1900–1910. Verzeichnis der Erscheinungen auf dem Gebiete der Elektrotechnik in den letzten 10 Jahren. Leipzig (Schulze & Co.) [1911] (28). 16 cm. 1 M.

Notice sur les travaux scientifiques de Mme P. Curie. Paris (Gauthier Villars) 1910 (56). 27 cm.

Schriften der physikalisch-ökonomischen Gesellschaft zu Königsberg in Pr. 42418. Generalregister zu den Jahrg. 26–50. 1885–1909.

Becquerel. 39152. Liste des ouvrages et memoires publiés de 1875 à 1908.

Küster. 40941. Namen- und Sachregister zu den Bdn 25–50 der Zeitschrift für physikalische Chemie.

Michelson. 41446. Lichtwellen und ihre Anwendungen. [Übers.]

Wroczyński. 43213. Courbes de point de fusion des mélanges binaires.

0040   ADDRESSES, LECTURES, Etc.

GENERAL.

Chwolson. 39559. Fortschritte in der Physik 1908. (Russ.)

Ciamician. 39560. La coopération des sciences.

Corbino. 39637. I fondamenti sperimentali delle nuove teorie fisiche.

Foley. 40027. Recent developments in physical science.

Ladenburg. 40966. Die vier Elemente des Aristoteles.

Lehmann. 41075. Umwandlung unserer Naturauffassung infolge der Entdeckung des Relativitätsprinzips.

Timiriazev. 42795. Elektromagnetische Theorie der Wärmestrahlung. (Russ.)

Turner. 42845. Characteristics of the observational sciences.

Waals, Van der. 42965. Fundamentalste Naturgesetze.

HEAT.

Nernst. 41580. Neuere Probleme der Wärmetheorie.

LIGHT.

Houllevigue. 40567. Revue annuelle d'optique.

ELECTRICITY.

Zomparelli. 43286. L'apoteosi dell' elettricità.

0050   PEDAGOGY. LECTURE APPARATUS AND EXPERIMENTS.

Le programme de physique à l'école moyenne. Par E. M. Gymnastique scolaire **1910** (72–74). [0050].

Amerio. 38951. Un'esperienza da lezione sulla ricomposizione della luce.

Askenasy. 39002. Ersatz für Diapositive für Projektionszwecke.

Bahrdt. 39051. Apparat zur Untersuchung der Gesetze des freien Falls.

Behrendsen und **Gotting.** 39163. Demonstrationsapparat zur Erläuterung des Ohm'schen Gesetzes.

Bernini. 39201. Magnetoskope für Unterrichtszwecke.

Brenken. 39393. Elektrostatischer Dynen- und Voltmesser. Apparat zum Nachweis des Coulombschen Gesetzes.

Bush. 39455. Value and limitations of quantitative work in physics and chemistry.

Cady. 39461. Isolierte Doppelklemmen.

Classen. 39570. Kleine Universalbogenlampe mit festem Lichtpunkt.

Corbino. 39638. Nozioni di fisica per le scuole secondarie.

Czudnochowski. 39677. Physikalische Projektions-Demonstrationen.

Dörge. 39777. Schulversuche aus der Akustik. 39778 : Siedepunktserhöhung bei erhöhtem Druck.

Eberlein. 39859. Elektrische Messungen und Rechnungen.

Ehrhardt. 39878. Versuch aus dem Gebiete der magnetischen Kraftlinien. 39879 : Hydromechanischer Apparat zur Erläuterung einiger beim galvanischen Element auftretenden Erscheinungen.

Fischer. 40004. Elektro-optische Aufnahme von physikalischen Vorgängen mit dem Oszillographen.

Glatzel. 40210. Maschine zur Demonstration von Wechselstromvorgängen. 40213 : Demonstrationsversuch über die Energieaufnahme in Wechselstromkreisen.

Glinzer. 40225. Ein neuer Luftverflüssigungsapparat.

Goldstein. 40254. Untersuchung der Emissionsspektra fester aromatischer Substanzen mit dem Ultraviolettfilter. 40256 : Farbige Projektion ungefärbter Spektrogramme.

Grix. 43008. Geschweisstes Spezial-Kompensationsmetall in besonderer Anordnung zur Hervorbringung relativ grosser Bewegungen bei Temperaturänderungen.

Grunfeld. 40327. Schülerübung zur Bestimmung des spezifischen Gewichts der Luft.

Hartmann. 40433. Herstellung von Schulapparaten.

Herweg. 40498. Knallgasvoltameter für den Unterricht.

Hoffmann. 40543. Demonstrationsapparat für Wechselstromversuche.

Holle. 40549. Apparat zur Demonstration des Boyle - Mariotteschen Gesetzes.

Johannesson. 40668. Physikalische Uebungen.

Kaufmann. 40741. Unsichtbarkeit durchsichtiger Objekte bei gleichförmiger Beleuchtung.

Kemna. 40758. Apparat zum Nachweis des Pascalschen Gesetzes der Druckfortpflanzung.

Kleinpeter. 40805. Unterrichtsgang in der Elektrizitätslehre. 40806 : Projektion von Linienspektren.

Kock. 40845. Apparat zur Aufnahme von Resonanzkurven.

Köhler. 40847. Flüssigkeitskondensoren von grosser Apertur.

König. 40855. Fadenmodell zum Astigmatismus. Apparat zur Demonstration des Strahlenganges beim Regenbogen.

Kolbe. 40884. Neue Versuche mit dem elektrodynamischen Pendel.

Krulla. 40928. Die direkte Messung von Dampfdruckänderungen und der dampfdruckanalytische Nachweis von Verbindungen.

Lehmann. 41071. Fernspektroskop. 41073 : Kinematographie.

Leimbach. 41085. Methode zur Verminderung der schädlichen Wärmestrahlen im Projektionsapparat.

Lichtenecker. 41122. Poggendorfsche Kompensationsmethode.

Link. 41154. Das Deutsche Museum im Dienste des physikalischen Unterrichts.

Losehand. 41203. Der Kreisel als Resonanzerreger.

Lüdtke. 41219. Elektromagnetische Lichttheorie und Lehre von den elektrischen Schwingungen. Geschwindigkeit der Elektrizität.

Lummer u. **Waetzmann.** 41236.

Maey. 41272. Zwei Pendel für drei verschiedene Resonanzen.

Magin. 41274. Optische Darstellung schwingender Vorgänge.

Mandelstam. 41306. Pendelmodell zur Demonstration der Schwingungsvorgänge in elektrischen gekoppelten Kondensatorkreisen.

Marino e **Porlezza.** 41335. Luminosità del fosforo.

Masche. 41357. Physikalische Uebungen.

Menzel. 41401. Wandtafeln. Wirkung der Brillen.

Mercanton. 41403. I. Wärmeleitung durch Gase. II. Edlunds Wärmeäquivalentmessung. III. Änderung der inneren Reibung mit der Temperatur.

Müller-Uri. 41534.

Niewolak. 41621. L'enseignement de la physique au lycée. (Polish.)

Noack. 41634. Untersuchung der Ablenkung, die ein Magnet an einer Kompassnadel hervorruft. 41635 : Apparat zur Demonstration der magnetischen Schirmwirkung. 41636 : Apparat zum Nachweis des Boyleschen Gesetzes.

Oosting. 41685c. Ein Experiment über den Luftdruck.

Ottinger und **Weiss.** 41712. Bestimmung der Fallbeschleunigung am frei fallenden Körper.

Panomareff. 41739. Apparat zum Nachweis der Spannkraft verschiedener Dämpfe.

Paschen und **Wolff.** 41765. Bestimmung des mechanischen Wärmeäquivalentes.

Plotnikow. 41893. Räumlich fortschreitende Lichtreaktionen.

Pokrowsky. 41919. Projektionsverfahren der Erscheinungen der chromatischen Polarisation des Lichtes in konvergenten Strahlen.

Poske. 41947. Die Hypothese in Wissenschaft und Unterricht.

Rebenstorff. 42032. Versuche mit Kohlensäure. 42033. Thermischer Ausdehnungskoeffizient von Gasen. 42034 : Anleitung zum selbständigen Experimentieren.

Ridolfi. 42106. Collazione delle lauree in fisica.

Rohmann. 42164. Ein Modell zum Relativitätsprinzip.

Rohr. 42166. Das Biotar, ein Projektionssystem mit besonders grosser Öffnung und ebenem Felde.

Rosenberg. 42185. Experimentierbuch für den Unterricht in der Naturlehre.

Rudolph. 42242, 4. Messeinrichtung für Gleich- und Wechselstrom.

Salzer. 42307. Optische Schülerübungen.

Schäfer. 42338. Nachweis von Induktionsströmen.

Schaum. 42354.

Schilling. 42378. Catalog mathematischer Modelle für den höheren mathematischen Unterricht. 7. Aufl.

Schimmack. 42380. Verschmelzung verschiedener Zweige des mathematischen Unterrichts.

Schmidt. 42392. Versuche zur Demonstration der Impedanz einer Drahtspule. 24393 : Röntgen- und lichtelektrische Versuche.

Scotti. 42466. Ein Hitzdraht- und ein Resonanz-Instrument für die Projektion.

Seddig. 42470. Absolutes Bolometer.

Staub. 42618. Physikunterricht bei den Blinden.

Stelzner. 42634. Mathematik und Naturwissenschaften an den neuhumanistischen Schulen.

Stock. 42663. Projektionsapparat für die Chemievorlesung.

Strauss. 42676. Nachweis des Gay-Lussacschen Gesetzes.

Szanto. 42726. Messung des Brechungsexponenten des Wassers.

Thieme. 42764. Selbstinduktionsversuch von Lodge.

Thurn. 42789. Demonstrationsapparat für drahtlose Telephonie mittels elektrischer Wellen.

Tiwald. 42805. Versuche über Wärmeleitung und Wärmestrahlung.

Vieweger. 42909. Gleich- und Wechselstromtechnik.

Vogler. 42927. Elektrische Wellen : Erzeugung und Anwendung.

Volkmann. 42943. Versuche, die Spiegelablesung zu verfeinern. 42947 : Ein Lichtzeiger für objektive Spiegelablesung. 42948 : Ein lehrreicher Pendelversuch.

Weiler. 43047. Die galvanischen Induktionsapparate.

Weinhold. 43057. Physikalische Demonstrationen.

Weiss. 43061. Thermoelektrische Versuche.

Wellmer. 43077. Physikalische Schülerübungen.

Wendler. 43079. Methode der Autokollimation.

Wimmer. 43158. Makro- und Mikro-Projektion für Lehrzwecke.

Winterstein. 43161. Linsen mit veränderlicher Krümmung.

Wolletz. 43185. Hahnrohr für den Torricellischen Versuch und für Untersuchungen von Dämpfen.

Wülfing. 43216. Projektion mikroskopischer Objekte insbesondere im polarisierten Licht.

Zenghelis. 43271. Nachweis, dass der Siedepunkt des Wassers mit dem Drucke sinkt.

0060 INSTITUTIONS, MUSEUMS, COLLECTIONS.

Visite du prince Albert de Belgique à l'Institut Montéfiore et à l'Hôtel de l'Association. Liége Bul. Ass. ing. électr. 1905 (514-518).

Börnstein. 39305. Physikalisches Institut der landwirtschaftlichen Hochschule in Berlin.

Bose. 39338. Physikalisches Institut der Universität La Plata.

Carhart. 39495. Bureau of standards.

Hantschel. 40418. Geschichte des physikalischen Kabinetts am Linzer Staatsgymnasium und seiner Kustoden vom Jahre 1754 bis zur Gegenwart.

Koch. 40838. Neubau des physikalischen Instituts der technischen Hochschule Stuttgart.

Lehmann. 41079. Geschichte des physikalischen Instituts der technischen Hochschule Karlsruhe.

Link. 41154. Das Deutsche Museum im Dienste des physikalischen Unterrichts.

Lundén. 41238. Das Nobelinstitut für physikalische Chemie in Stockholm.

Quervain, de. 41984. Die instrumentelle Einrichtung der schweizerischen Erdbebenwarte.

0070 NOMENCLATURE.

Emde et alii. 39914. „Feld" und „Fluss".

Jonas. 40678. Mathematische Zeichen [für Phasenverschiebung].

Passavant. 41768. Definitionen für die internationale elektrotechnische Kommission.

[**Strecker.**] 42678-9. A. E. F. Ausschuss für Einheiten und Formelgrössen.

Wachsmuth. 42968. Ungenaue Massbezeichnungen in der Technik.

Waetzoldt. 42975. Vorschläge zur Farbenterminologie.

0090 METHODS OF RESEARCH, INSTRUMENTS AND APPARATUS.

Calorimetro registratore pel saggio dei gas combustibili. [Sunto. Trad.] Riv. ing. san. Torino 5 1909 (91-92).

Andrade. 38960. Neue Methode, die Flammengeschwindigkeit zu bestimmen.

Andrews. 38966. Apparatus for illustrating Boyle's law.

Arons. 38990 ; **Haken.** 40397. Chromoskop.

Becker. 39148. Photographisches.

Beutell. 39233-4. Automatische Quecksilberluftpumpe.

Biffi. 39252. La mostra dell'elettricità all'esposizione internazionale di Torino 1911.

Bock. 39299. Neue Apparate der Cambridge Scientific Instrument Co.

Borchardt. 39323. Das Arousssche Chromoskop.

Broemser. 39401. Zur Theorie der registrierenden Apparate.

Brunn. 39434. Petroleum bei Kondensatorplatten.

Büeler de Florin. 39446. Zum Erschmelzen von Quarz.

Carpini. 39503. Barometro a peso.

du Bois. 39807. Geradsichtiger lichtstarker Monochromator.

Fleiss. 40010. Reibung beim Schreiben in Russ.

Frank. 40062. Kymographien, Schreibhebel, Registrierspiegel, Prinzipien der Registrierung.

Füchtbauer. 40094. Methode zur Untersuchung von Absorptionslinien mit dem Stufengitter.

Gehlhoff. 40151. Methode zur Reindarstellung von Edelgasen, Wasserstoff und Stickstoff.

Geiger. 40165. Steigerung der Empfindlichkeit bei der Gauss-Poggendorfschen Spiegelmethode.

Grix. 40308. Geschweisstes Spezial-Kompensationsmetall in besonderer Anordnung zur Hervorbringung relativ grosser Bewegungen bei Temperaturänderungen.

Hoffmann. 40544. Die durch verschiedene Messungsanordnungen in einem homogenen elektrischen Felde hervorgerufenen Störungen (Deformationen) der Niveauflächen.

Holzknecht. 40552. Ein neues Dosimeter für Röntgen-Strahlen.

Knipp. 40818. Apparat zur Destillation von Quecksilber.

Koch. 40837. Das Phonendoskop als Wünschelrute.

Konrad. 40888. Appareil de commande automatique des aiguilles de voie.

Lehmann. 41072. UV-Filter und Filterlampe zur Lumineszenanalyse.

Leimbach. 41085. Methode zur Verminderung der schädlichen Wärmestrahlen im Projektionsapparat.

Leiss. 41089. Ultrarot-Spektrometer.

Lilienfeld. 41138. Laboratorium für tiefe Temperaturen.

Mainka. 41281. Anordnung einer Flüssigkeitsdämpfung bei Erdbebenapparaten.

Manetti. 41308. La bussola giroscopica Anschütz-Kämpfe.

Martens. 41339. Prüfung des Kautschuks und der Ballonstoffe.

Morgan. 41499. Das Gewicht eines fallenden Tropfens und die Gesetze von Tate. III. Ein Apparat zur raschen und genauen Bestimmung des Gewichts eines fallenden Flüssigkeitstropfens. IV. Die Eichung eines Mundstücks und die Berechnung der Oberflächenspannung und des Molekulargewichts einer Flüssigkeit aus dem Gewicht ihrer fallenden Tropfen.

Neuscheler. 41596, 41597. Untersuchung stehender Schallschwingungen mit Hilfe des Widerstandsthermometers [Versilberung von Quarzfäden].

Oettli. 41668. Pergamentschlauch statt Schweinsblase für osmotische Versuche.

Petíra. 41818. Fortschritte in der Wärmelehre 1908. (Čechisch.)

Pigeon. 41839. Un stéréoscope à coulisses.

Reden. 42046. Quecksilberluftpumpe und Vacuummeter. (Russ.)

Rossi. 42197. Un metodo didattico per ricavare le due leggi fondamentali della propagazione ondulatoria.

Scarpa. 42326. Misura della viscosità dei liquidi e dei lubrificanti. Un nuovo viscosimetro ad efflusso.

Schatte. 42349. Kinematographie mit elektrischen Funken.

Scheuer und **Saphores.** 42370. Jahresausstellung der französischen physikalischen Gesellschaft.

Schoop. 42408. Das Schoop'sche Metallisierungsverfahren.

Szilárd. 42730. Apparat zur Messung der Röntgenstrahlen in absoluten Einheiten. (Ungar.)

Tommasina. 42809. Modification donnant une plus grande liberté d'allure et plus de sûreté aux aéroplanes. 42810: Appareil d'aviation non renversable etc.

Volkmann. 42939, 42. Spiegelablesung. 42940: Einfache schütter-

freie Aufhängung. 42941 : Zweckmässige Grösse des Galvanometerspiegels. 42944 : Neue Klemmenformen. 42946 : Zwei Ablesemikroskope.
42949 : Fresnelscher Interferenzspiegel.

Vosmaer. 42952. Analyse physique
[des alliages]. (Hollandais.)

Wendler. 43079. Autokollimation im
Schülerpraktikum.

GENERAL MOLECULAR PHYSICS.

0100 GENERAL.

Amann. 38943. Ultramikroskopische Beobachtungen.

Barus. 39098. Sedimentation.

Broglie (De). 39402. Sospensione
nei gas.

Cohen. 39594. Welt der Moleküle
(1811-1911). (Holländisch.)

Corbino. 39637. I fondamenti
sperimentali delle nuove teorie fisiche.

Darling. 39691. Formation of
spheres of liquids.

Debye. 39700. Atomistische
Struktur der Energie.

Duhem. 39829. Wandlungen der
Mechanik und der mechanischen Naturerklärung.

Ebert. 39852. Lehrbuch.

Einstein. 39893. Thermische Molekularbewegung in festen Körpern.

Gray and Ramsay. 40285. Density
of niton ("radium emanation") and
the disintegration theory.

Grüneisen. 40326. Theorie einatomiger fester Körper.

Haber. 40377. Der feste Körper
sowie Zusammenhang ultravioletter und
ultraroter Eigenwellenlängen im Absorptionsspektrum fester Stoffe und
seine Benutzung zur Verknüpfung der
Bildungswärme mit der Quantentheorie.
40378 : Elektronenemission bei chemischen Reaktionen.

———— und Just. 40379. Über
die Aussendung von Elektronenstrahlen
bei chemischen Reaktionen.

Kleeman. 40801. Relations between
the density, temperature, and pressure
of substances.

(c-1388)

Lehmann. 41078. Kristallinische
und amorphe Flüssigkeiten.

Lindemann. 41150. Beziehungen
zwischen chemischer Affinität und
Elektronenfrequenzen.

Mie. 41149. Ionen und Elektronen.
41151 : Moleküle, Atome, Weltäther.

Millis. 41460. Brownian movements
and molecular reality.

Nernst. 41577. Principes fondamentaux de la physique moderne.
41580 : Neuere Probleme der Wärmetheorie.

Perrin. 41808. Mouvement brownien
et molécules.

Sachs. 42284. Wirkung des ultravioletten Lichtes auf Gase und die dabei
erzeugten Nebelkerne.

Schmidt. 42397. Äther, Atomauflösung und ihre Beziehung zur Ionisierung.

Skworzow. 42532. Aggregation und
Kristallisation des Wassers in Zusammenhang mit der Frage von dem
physikalischen Zustand der Körper.

Sommerfeld. 42574. Das Plancksche Wirkungsquantum und seine
allgemeine Bedeutung für die Molekularphysik.

Stark. 42613. Zusammenhang
zwischen chemischer Energie und
optischer Frequenz.

Terešin. 42757. La relation entre
la densité et le degré de dissociation pour
des dissolutions aqueuses. (Russ.)

Thomson. 42777. Beziehungen der
Materie und des Aethers. (Russ.)

Weimarn. 43052. Theorie der Uebergangserscheinungen zwischen kolloiden und wahren Lösungen.

Whetham. 43109. Lo stato attuale
della fisica.

Zangger. 43240. Bestimmungen der
Avogadroschen Zahl N ; die untere
Teilungsgrenze der Materie.

0150 ESTIMATES AND CALCU-LATIONS OF MOLECULAR MAGNITUDES.

Acquino (D'). 38998A. Dimensioni
molecolari.

T

0200 THE MOLECULAR THEORY OF GASES AND LIQUIDS (GENERAL MATHEMATICAL THEORIES).

0250   ABSORPTION AND ADSORPTION OF GASES.

Piutti. 41862. Assorbimento dell'elio nei sali e nei minerali.

————— e Mogli. 41866. Potere assorbente per l'aria di alcune varietà di carboni vegetali.

Prieth. 41957. Veränderung der Kapillarkonstante des Wassers durch gelöste Gase.

Sander. 42309. Löslichkeit der Kohlensäure in Wasser und einigen andern Lösungsmitteln unter höhern Drucken.

Schmidt. 42390. Adsorption von Lösungen.

Sieverts. 42510. Löslichkeit von Wasserstoff in Kupfer, Eisen und Nickel.

————— und Jurisch. 42511. Platin, Rhodium und Wasserstoff.

Valentiner. 42876. Waserstoffabsorption durch Palladium bei niedrigen Drucken und tiefen Temperaturen.

0300 CAPILLARITY.

Bénard. 39174. Les tourbillons cellulaires.

Bohr. 39310. Determination of the tension of a recently formed water-surface.

Darling. 39692. Formation of stable columns of liquids.

Domke und Reimerdes. 39781. Bestimmung der Dichte von Flüssigkeiten.

Gautier. 40145. Porosité des bougies filtrantes.

Herzog. 40502. Negative Adsorption.

Koch. 40836. Äussere Reibung tropfbarer Flüssigkeiten

Krulla. 40929. Quantitativen Verhältnisse bei der Teilung eines Körpers zwischen zwei Phasen: Adsorption.

Lockemann. 41168. Adsorption von Arsen durch Eisenhydroxyd.

Levites. 41112. Adsorption

Magini. 41275-6. Tensione superficiale di alcuni liquidi.

Majone. 41282. Metodo per misurare il potere di assorbimento capillare nei materiali da costruzione.

Merton. 41112. Method of calibrating fine capillary tubes.

Meyer. 41129. Kapillaritätskonstanten von Amalgamen.

Mickle. 41447. Flotation of minerals.

Morgan. 41499. Das Gewicht eines fallenden Tropfens und die Gesetze von Tate. II. Ein Apparat zur raschen und genauen Bestimmung des Gewichts eines fallenden Flüssigkeitstropfens. IV. Die Eichung eines Mundstücks und die Berechnung der Oberflächenspannung und des Molekulargewichts einer Flüssigkeit aus dem Gewicht ihrer fallenden Tropfen. ————— et alii. 41501-3: Das Gewicht eines fallenden Tropfens und die Gesetze von Tate.

Palladino. 41735. Fenomeni capillari.

Prieth. 41957. Veränderung der Kapillaritätskonstante des Wassers durch gelöste Gase.

Puppini. 41975. La filtrazione per mezzi non omogenei.

Ronceray. 42175. L'écoulement dans les tubes capillaires.

Rudge. 42239. Surface tension of liquid sulphur.

Russenberger. 42270. L'extension des lois de la capillarité.

Schaefer. 42343. Untersuchungen über Dichte, Reibung und Kapillarität kristallinischer Flüssigkeiten.

Schmidt. 42388. Veränderung der Oberflächenspannung durch Metallzusatz.

Svedberg und Inouye. 42716. Eigenbewegung der Teilchen in kolloiden Lösungen.

Tammann. 42747. Molekulargewichtsbestimmung krystallisierter Stoffe.

Tangl. 42750. Oberflächenspannung an der Trennungsfläche fest-flüssig.

Ter Gazarian. 42758. Une relation générale entre les propriétés physiques des corps: application à la viscosité, la capillarité, l'énergie superficielle, la chaleur, la vaporisation, le diamétre rectiligne.

Traube. 42818. Tension d'attraction et pression osmotique.

Traube. 42819. Theorie des Haftdrucks (Oberflächendrucks).

Van der Noot. 42887. Tension superficielle au contact de deux liquides.

Weimarn. 43053. Untersuchungs-methoden kapillarchemischer Probleme.

Wiegner. 43127. Adsorption der Zucker in wässeriger Lösung.

0310 OSMOSIS, OSMOTIC PRESSURE. LIQUIDS AND SOLIDS. EFFUSION. TRANSPIRATION.

Antropoff. 38975. Die Dynamik osmotischer Zellen.

Bary. 39102. Phénomènes osmotiques dans les milieux non conducteurs.

Biltz. 39260. Dialyse und Osmose von Farbstofflösungen.

Fouard. 40038-9. Méthode de préparation des membranes semi-perméables et son application à la mesure du poids moléculaire au moyen de la pression osmotique. 40041 : Mécanisme de l'osmose.

Girard. 40195. L'osmose. 40196 : Rôle prépondérant de deux facteurs électrostatiques dans l'osmose des solutions d'électrolytes. Mouvements osmotiques normaux.

———— et Henri. 40197. Nouvelles hypothèses sur l'état moléculaire des corps en solution.

Lippmann. 41159. Action de forces extérieures sur la tension des vapeurs saturées et des gaz dissous dans un liquide.

Rosenstiehl. 42187. Cohésion et pression osmotique. 42190 : Données historiques relatives à la force osmotique.

Schwarz. 42452. Osmotische Versuche.

Svedberg. 42713. Prüfung der Gültigkeit der van der Waals'schen Zustandsgleichung für kolloide Lösungen.

Traube. Tension d'attraction et pression osmotique.

0320 DIFFUSION OF GASES, LIQUIDS, AND SOLIDS. EFFUSION. TRANSPIRATION.

Austerweil. 39016. Passage de l'hydrogène à travers le tissu caoutchouté des aérostats.

Barus. 39099. Gang der Luft durch eine Wasserwand.

Becker. 39115. Diffusion leuchtender Metalldämpfe in Flammen ; Lichtemissionszentren dieser Dämpfe.

Boselli. 39339. Vitesses de réactions dans les systèmes gaz-liquides.

Bruni e Meneghini. 39433. Formazione di soluzioni solide per diffusione allo stato solido.

Carlson. 39498. Diffusion of oxygen and carbon dioxide in water.

Gaede. 40103. Die äussere Reibung der Gase.

Garbasso. 40134 ; Grassi. 40278-9 ; Scarpa. 42330-1, 5 ; Vanzetti. 42891.

Griffiths. 40302. Movement of a coloured index along a capillary tube and its application to the measurement of the circulation of water in a closed circuit.

Harrison. 40428. Diffusion in Systemen von geschmolzenen Salzen.

Herzog. 40501. Lösungen der Farbstoffe.

Lilienfeld. 41137. Arbeitsleistung zur Abscheidung von N_2 und O_2 aus atmosphärischer Luft.

Möller und Möller. 41473. Beziehungen zwischen Widerstand, Filterfläche, Filterdichte und Luftmenge.

Müller. 41526. Absorption von Gasen durch Metalle.

Rolla. 42172. Diffusione degli elettroliti nei colloidi.

Svedberg. 42710. Diffusionsgeschwindigkeit und Teilchengrösse disperser Systeme.

Tangl. 42759. Oberflächenspannung an der Trennungsfläche fest-flüssig.

Vaillant. 42870. Application de l'évaporation à la mesure des coefficients de diffusion.

Vanzetti. 42892. Diffusione di elettroliti in soluzione acquosa.

Wuppermann. 43227. Verdampfungsgeschwindigkeit. [Diffusion.] Diss.

0325 VISCOSITY OF FLUIDS (INTERNAL FRICTION).

Arnold. 38989. Limitations imposed by slip and inertia terms upon Stokes's law for the motion of spheres through liquids.

Bancelin. 39064. La viscosité des émulsions. 39065 ; Viskosität von Suspensionen und die Bestimmung der Avogadroschen Zahl.

Bénard. 39174. Sur les tourbillons cellulaires.

Bingham. 39264. Viscosity and fluidity.

Borelli. 39328. Résistance au mouvement dans un fluide de petits corps non sphériques.

Bose und **Bose.** 39337. Turbulenzreibung verschiedener Flüssigkeiten.

Boussinesq. 39363. Aperçu théorique sur les oscillations d'une colonne de liquide dans un tube en V.

Clerici. 39582. Viscosità dei liquidi per la separazione meccanica dei minerali.

Doelter. 39770.

Doelter und **Sirk.** 39776. Bestimmung des Absolutwertes der Viskosität bei Silikatschmelzen.

Drucker und **Kassel.** 39802. Fluidität von binären Gemischen.

Einstein. 39892. Viskosität von Suspensionen.

Filippi. 39997. Rapporti tra i tramutamenti della viscosità e della tensione superficiale del sangue vivente sotto l'influenza dei vari farmaci.

Fisher. 40006. Kinetic pressuredrop correction in the transpiration method for gas-viscosity. 40007 ; Flow of a gas in a capillary tube when Boyle's law is not obeyed.

Freedericksz. 40074. Frottement intérieur des solides aux basses températures.

Fric. 40083. Modifications subies par les nitrocelluloses et les poudres qui en dérivent sous l'influence de la chaleur.

Gaede. 40103. Die äussere Reibung der Gase.

Gans. 40127. Wie fallen Stäbe und Scheiben in einer reibenden Flüssigkeit ?

Hadamard. 40385. Une question relative aux liquides visqueux.

Hatschek. 40413. Die Viskosität der Dispersoide.

Herzog. 40503. Viskosität kolloider Lösungen.

Hilditsch und **Dunstan.** 40519. Beizelung der Viskosität zu anderen physikalischen Eigenschaften. I. Äthen- und Äthinverbindungen.

Kármán. 40733. Turbulenzreibung verschiedener Flüssigkeiten.

Kernot e **Pomilio.** 40772. Comportamento crioscopico e viscosimetrico di alcune soluzioni di chinolina.

Knudsen. 40829. Molekularströmung des Wasserstoffs durch Röhren und das Hitzdrahtmanometer.

Koch. 40836. Äussere Reibung tropfbarer Flüssigkeiten.

Luziani. 41249. **Grassi.** 40277. Viscosimetria e tensimetria del sangue.

Mc Keehan. 41257. Terminal velocity of fall of small spheres in air at reduced pressures.

Mastrobuono. 41360. **Cavazzani.** 39519. Viscosità dell' umor acqueo.

Menneret. 41400. Mouvement oscillatoire et mouvement uniforme des liquides dans les tubes cylindriques. Frottement interne.

Millikan. 41457. Isolation of an ion, a precision measurement of its charge, and the correction of Stokes's law.

Mises. 41466. Englerscher Flüssigkeitsmesser.

Nehru. 41575. Strömung von Gasen durch Röhren und Widerstand kleiner Kugeln und Cylinder in bewegten Gasen.

Oddone. 41666. Coefficiente d'attrito interno in misura assoluta delle lave solide e fluide ; isteresi terrestre.

Pick. 41835. Innere Reibung kristallinisch-flüssiger Gemische von p-Azoxyanisol und p-Azoxyphenetol.

Rankine. 42011. Relation between viscosity and atomic weight for the inert gases ; with its application to the case of radium emanation.

Reiger. 42062. Ausbreitung scherender Deformationen in Gasen.

Reinganum. 42069. Änderung der inneren Reibung der Gase der Argongruppe mit der Temperatur.

Rossi. 42207. Fenomeni di rilassamento.

Royal-Dawson. 42222. The flow of thin liquid films.

Rybczyński. 42280-1. Mouvement progressif d'une sphère liquide à travers un milieu visqueux. [Polish.]

Scarpa. 42326. Misura della viscosità dei liquidi e dei lubrificanti.

Schaefer. 42343. Untersuchungen über Reibung und Kapillarität kristallinischer Flüssigkeiten.

Schmidt and Jones. 42395. Conductivity and viscosity in mixed solvents containing glycerol.

Smoluchowski. 42558, 62. Wechselwirkung von Kugeln, die sich in einer zähen Flüssigkeit bewegen.

Sorkau. 42580. Innere Reibung einiger organischer Flüssigkeiten im turbulenten Strömungszustande.

Stanton. 42600. The mechanical viscosity of fluids.

Stapfer. 42601. Rotation de la Terre d'après F. Klein et A. Sommerfeld.

Stock. 42664. Bewegung einer Kugel in einem zähen Medium längs einer ebenen Wand.

Ter Gazarian. 42758. Une relation générale entre les propriétés physiques des corps : application à la viscosité.

Thomsen. 42774. Innere Reibung von Gasgemischen.

Veselý. 42907. Viskosität des Glases. (Čechisch.)

Walden. 42992. Zusammenhang zwischen dem Grenzwert der molekularen Leitfähigkeit und der innern Reibung.

Woudstra. 43207. Dispersitätsgrad und innere Reibung.

Zemplén. 43270. Innere Reibung der Gase. (Ungarisch.)

Zimmer. 43278. Innere Reibung von Aethylen und Kohlenoxyd und ihre Aenderung bei tiefen Temperaturen.

0340 COLLOIDAL SUBSTANCES.

Amann. 38943. Bachmann. 39040. Ultramikroskopische Beobachtungen.

Antony. 38972. I colloidi inorganici.

—— e Bianchi. 38974.

Bancelin. 39065. Viskosität von Suspensionen.

Bary. 39101. Mode de dissolution des matières colloïdales.

Baur. 39130. Kolloide und molekulardisperse Lösungen.

Biltz. 39260. Osmotischer Druck der Kolloide.

Binaghi. 39261.

Bottazzi. 39342. Definition der kolloiden Systeme und Systematik der Kolloide.

Chiari. 39549. Glutinquellung in Säuren und Laugen.

Dexheimer. 39755. Darstellung anorganischer Kolloide in kolloidalen organischen Medien.

Duclaux et Wollmann. 39821. Pression osmotique des colloïdes.

Ellis. 39903. Elektrische Ladung der Ölemulsionen.

Fichter. 39996. Kapillarelektrische Fällung positiver Kolloide.

Frank. 40055. Schmelzwärme von Kolloiden. 40056 : Kontraktionen und Ausdehnungskoeffizienten kolloidaler Lösungen.

Freimann. 40075. Kolloide.

Graham. 40271. Abhandlungen über Dialyse (Kolloide).

Guareschi. 40340. Pseudosolutionen oder Scheinlösungen.

Handovsky. 40410. Kolloidchemie der Eiweisskörper.

Harrison. 40429. Farbe und Dispersitätsgrad kolloider Lösungen.

Hatschek. 40443. Viskosität der Dispersoide. 40444 : Bildung von Schichten in heterogenen Systemen.

Herzog. 40501. Lösungen der Farbstoffe. 40503 : Viskosität kolloider Lösungen.

Jorissen und Woudstra. 40689. Wirkung von Radiumstrahlen auf Kolloide.

Kato. 40737. Colloidal barium sulphate.

Katz. 40739. Analogy between swelling (imbibition) and mixing. (English.) (Dutch.)

Levites. 41111. Organische Kolloide.

Lorenz r. C 10 No. 37114. Pyrosole : Kolloidales Phänomen in der glühend flüssigen Materie.

Lottermoser. 41205. Elektrolytwirkung auf Hydrosole. 41206 : Arbeiten über Kolloidchemie 1908. 41207 : Adsorption in Hydrosolen. 41208 : Anomale Adsorption.

Maffia. 41273. Adsorptionsgleichgewicht im Grahamschen Eisenoxydhydrosol.

Malfitano. 41293. Dispersionsvorgänge in den Hydro-oxy-chloro-Ferri-Systemen. 41294 : Cristalloïdes et colloïdes ou état moléculaire et état micellaire. 41295 : Ciò che sono i colloidi.

Maréchal. 41331. Colloïdes.

Müller. 41525. Farbe der Silberpartikelchen in kolloidalen Ag-Lösungen berechnet aus der Mieschen Theorie.

Odén. 41667. Bedeutung des Dispersitätsgrades bei Untersuchung der allgemeinen Eigenschaften der Schwefelhydrosole.

Ostwald. 41705в. Grundriss der Kolloidchemie. 41709 : Theorie der kritischen Trübungen. 41710 : Farbe und Dispersitätsgrad kolloider Lösungen.

Paterno. 41769. Soluzioni colloidali.

Pawlow. 41775. Anwendung der thermodynamischen Theorie der dispersen Systeme auf Hydrometeore. 41777 : Zur Thermodynamik der kondensierten dispersen Systeme.

Pihlblad. 41840. Lichtabsorption in Silberhydrosolen.

Pochettino. 41898. Metodi di preparare soluzioni di selenio colloidale.

Poschl. 41901. Kolloidchemie.

Raffo und **Mancini.** 41992. Kolloider Schwefel. 3. Mitt.

Rakowski. 41997. Adsorption. II. Die chemische Hysteresis.

Schorr. 42407. Eigenschaften der Eiweissionen.

Stanêk. 42598. Entwässern der Hydrogele mit Äther.

Svedberg. 42712. Bildung disperser systeme durch Bestrahlung von metallen mit ultraviolettem Licht und Röntgenstrahlen. 42713 : Prüfung der Gültigkeit der van der Waalschen Zustandsgleichung für kolloide Lösungen.

Svedberg und **Estrup.** 42715. Bestimmung der Häufigkeitsverteilung der Teilchengrössen in einem dispersen System.

—— und **Inouye.** 42716. Eigenbewegung der Teilchen in kolloiden Lösungen. 3. 42717 : Struktur ultramikroskopischer Teilchen. 42718 : Ultramikroskopische Beobachtung einer Temperaturkoagulation. 42719 : Methode zur Prüfung der Gültigkeit des Boyle-Gay-Lussacschen Gesetzes für kolloide Lösungen.

Traube Mengarini e **Scala.** 42820. Azione dell'acqua distillata e dell'acqua distillata contenente elettroliti sul piombo metallico.

Walden. 42991. Kolloide Kieselsäure.

Weimarn. 43049. Uebersättigung und Unterkühlung als grundlegende Ursachen des dispersen Zustandes der Materie. 43050 : Theorie der Herstellung und der Stabilität kolloider Lösungen. 43051 : Der kolloide Zustand. 43052 : Theorie der Uebergangserscheinungen zwischen kolloiden und wahren Lösungen. 43054 : Natur der dispersen Systeme. 43055 : Grundzüge der Dispersoidchemie.

Wiegner. 43126. Emulsionskolloide (Emulsoide). 43128 : Zur ultramikroskopischen Untersuchung einiger Kolloidkoagulationen durch Elektrolyte.

Woudstra. 43206. L'action d'électrolytes sur des solutions colloïdales. II. (Hollandais.) 43207 : Dispersitätsgrad und innere Reibung.

0400 MOLECULAR THEORIES OF CRYSTALS AND OTHER SOLIDS.

Brillouin. 39394. Éléments cristallins et orientations moléculaires.

Einstein. 39889, 91. Beziehung zwischen dem elastischen Verhalten und der spezifischen Wärme bei festen Körpern mit einatomigem Molekül.

Grüneisen. 40325. Beziehungen zwischen Atomwärme, Ausdehnungskoeffizient und Kompressibilität fester Elemente.

Lehmann. 41077. Struktur und Optik grosser Kristalltropfen. 41078 : Kristallinische und amorphe Flüssigkeiten. 41080 : Flüssige Kristalle.

Marc und **Ritzel.** 41313. Faktoren, die den Kristallhabitus bedingen.

Ornstein. 41699. The solid state. I. Monatomic substances. (English, Dutch.)

Rotarski. 42212. Théorie moléculaire et cinétique des liquides aéolotropes ou des milieux nommés "cristaux liquides." (Polish.)

Skworzow. 42532. Aggregation und Kristallisation des Wassers in Zusammenhang mit der Frage von dem physikalischen Zustand der Körper.

Wartenberg. 43002. Kristalline Flüssigkeiten.

Weimarn, von. 43048. Ultramikroskopische Untersuchungen krystallinischer Flüssigkeiten. (Russ.). 43055 : Dispersoidchemie.

Wulf. 43223. Cristaux liquides et liquides cristallins. (Russ.)

ULTIMATE PHYSICAL THEORIES.

0500 THEORIES OF THE CONSTITUTION OF MATTER.

Alasia. 38909. Una nuova ipotesi cosmogonica.

Antony. 38973. La costituzione degli atomi.

Arrhénius. 38991. L'énergie libre.

Barreca. 39087. Legge di degradazione universale e una possibile disponibilità indefinita di energia degradabile.

Becquerel. 39153, S. La constitution de la matière.

Belot. 39171. Cosmogonie tourbillonnaire. L'origine dualiste des mondes.

Biltz. 39259. Das System der Elemente auf Grund der periodischen Abhängigkeit von Schwingungszahl und Gewicht der Atome.

Boissoudy (de). 39313. Constitution de l'atome.

Corbino. 39621. La massa dell'energia. 39637 : I fondamenti sperimentali delle nuove teorie fisiche.

Duclaux. 39820. Constitution de l'eau.

Dunoyer. 39833. Rayonnement matériel d'origine purement thermique.

Fletcher. 40018. Vérification de la théorie du mouvement brownien et détermination de la valeur de N pour l'ionisation des gaz.

Giovanetti. 40193. La natura elettrica della materia.

Gray and **Ramsay.** 40285. Density of niton (radium emanation) and the disintegration theory.

Hanriot. 40412. Nature de l'adhésivité.

Ladenburg. 40963. Chemische Konstitution der Materie.

Lenard. 41096. Äther und Materie.

Lodge. 41171. Weltäther.

McLaren. 41264. Hamilton's equations and the partition of energy between matter and radiation.

Maurain. 41374. Les états physiques de la matière.

Mie. 41450. Theorie der Materie.

Monier. 41482. L'atome primordial est soumis à la loi de l'attraction universelle.

Morini. 41504. Esistenza dell'unità fondamentale della materia.

Nasini. 41563. La teoria atomica e l'opera di Stanislao Cannizzaro.

Provenzal. 41963. La trasmutazione degli elementi.

Riecke. 42108. Natura dello stato metallico.

Sang. 42314.

Wilson. 43154. Number of electrons in the atom.

Winderlich. 43159. Materie.

Wulf. 43224. Radioaktivität als allgemeine Eigenschaft der Körper.

Zangger. 43240. Bestimmungen der Avogadroschen Zahl N ; die untere Teilungsgrenze der Materie.

0600 THEORIES OF THE ETHER.

Beckenhaupt. 39143. Existenz des Aethers und die mechanische Theorie.

Brisset. 39397. La matière et les forces de la nature.

Campbell. 39475 ; **Helm.** 40474 : **Lane.** 41024 ; **Wiechert.** 43122. Relativitätsprinzip und Äther.

Corbino. 39630. Massa dell'energia.

Hack. 40381. Aetherhypothese.

Lenard. 41096. Äther und Materie.

Lodge. 41171 ; Mie. 41451. Weltäther.

Michelson. 41446. Lichtwellen.

Rudolph. 42243. Stellung der Physik zur Weltätherfrage.

Sokolov. 42567. Lichtdispersion im Weltraum. (Russ.)

Trowbridge. 42834. The ether drift.

0700 DYNAMICAL THEORIES OF GRAVITATION.

Abraham. 38892-4. Teoria della gravitazione.

Arrhenius. 38995. Il divenire dei mondi. [Trad.]

Baraldi. 39066. Genesi del moto universale e formazione della materia.

Bottlinger. 39345. Zur Theorie der Lotschwankungen.

Brush. 39435 ; Kent. 40761 ; Manson. 21310 ; Sanford. 42313. A kinetic theory of gravitation.

Combebiac. 39613. Actions à distance.

Crudeli. 39667. Teoria dei fluidi rotanti.

Ely. 39912. Newton's law and the cause of gravitation.

Froelich. 40087. Newton.

Gerber. 40171. Gravitation und Elektrizität.

Hack. 40382. Schwerkraft.

Häussler. 40389. Wegweiser für die Gravitationsforschung.

Lehfeldt. 41067. Gravity in South Africa.

Lodge. 41171. Weltäther.

Mastrodomenico. 41361. La gravitazione universale, ossia il mondo materiale e il gioco delle forze che ne animano la macchina.

Morris. 41505. Gravitation.

Morris. 41507. Attempts to explain gravitation.

Oltay. 41680. Messung der Schwerkraftbeschleunigung in Budapest. (Ungar.)

Reppert. 42086. Ursache der Schwerkraft.

Rozzi. 42224. Nucleo terrestre.

Shedd. 42502. Genesis of the law of gravity.

Zanotti Bianco. 43244. La gravità alla superficie del mare e l'ipotesi di Pratt. 43246 ; La figura della terra e le misure di gravità.

MEASUREMENT OF MECHANICAL QUANTITIES. ELASTICITY.

0800 GENERAL.

Broca. 39398. La constitution d'axes de rotation assez stables pour permettre la mesure des angles géodésiques par la méthode de la répétition.

Duhem. 39827. Origines de la statique.

Fleiss. 40010. Reibung beim Schreiben in Russ.

Geiger. 40165. Steigerung der Empfindlichkeit bei der Gauss-Poggendorffschen Spiegelmethode.

Hass, de. 40376. Measurement of volume and pressure : volumenometer.

Malchair. 41291. Le planimètre.

Oddone. 41665. Coefficiente elastico di restituzione delle principali roccie.

Rossi. 42198. Piano inclinato.

Scheel. 42358. Metronomie.

Schreber. 42412. Masssysteme.

Wachsmuth. 42968. Ungenaue Massbezeichnungen.

0805 THEORY OF MEASUREMENT (COMBINATION OF OBSERVATIONS). HARMONIC ANALYSIS. UNITS AND DIMENSIONS.

Broniewski. 39411. Réduction du nombre d'unités fondamentales. (Polish.)

Budde. 39440. Kilogramm-Kraft und Kilogramm-Masse, ein Vorschlag zur Einigung.

Méchain und Delambre. 41388. Grundlagen des dezimalen metrischen Systems oder Messung des Meridianbogens.

Michelson. 41446. Lichtwellen und ihre Anwendungen. [Übers.]

Strecker. 42678-9. Ausschluss für Einheiten und Formelgrössen.

Thompson. 42773. Nouvelle méthode d'analyse harmonique par la sommation algébrique d'ordonnées indéterminées.

0807 MEASUREMENT OF LENGTH (MECHANICAL AND OPTICAL).

Andrade. 38959. Le mouvement ; mesures de l'étendue et mesures du temps.

Bourgeois. 39358. Erreur instrumentale des appareils de mesure de base.

Carpentier. 39502. Sphéromètre.

Crain. 39656. Maschinenbau nach dem Austauschverfahren.

Delambre. 39726. Grandeur et figure de la Terre.

Dokulil. 39779. Neue Ablesevorrichtungen für Teilkreise.

Gordon. 40262. Vernier arc.

Guillet. 40359. Machine à plan de référence électrique, propre à répéter une même translation donnée.

Kaye. 40745. A silica standard of length.

Michelson. 41446. Lichtwellen und ihre Anwendungen.

Pozdena. 41953. Eine halbautomatische Etalonbrücke zur Untersuchung von Massstäben.

Shaw. 42501. Measurement of end-standards of length.

Smith. 42543. Vibrating wires and the measurement of distance.

Stabó v. Bágyon. 42588. Zur Fehlerregelung der Klappierung.

Stadthagen. 42590. Sicherung richtigen Längenmasses unter Berücksichtigung der Endmassnormale.

0809 MEASUREMENT OF TIME (MECHANICAL AND ELECTRICAL).

Bureau des Longitudes. L'éclipse de Soleil du 17 avril 1912. Paris 1912 (16 av. 1 carte). 23 cm.

Andrade. 38958. Nouvel organe régulateur des chronomètres. 38959 :

Le mouvement ; mesures de l'étendue et mesures du temps.

Baillaud. 39052. Précision de la connaissance de l'heure à l'Observatoire de Paris.

Carlier. 39496.

Claude, Ferrié et Driencourt. 39571. L'emploi de la télégraphie sans fil pour la détermination des longitudes.

Féry. 39989. Nouveau chronomètre électrique.

Mallock. 41298. Pendulum clocks and their errors.

Reithoffer. 42076. Ein elektrisches Zentraluhrensystem für Wien.

Turpain. 42852. Inscription graphique des signaux de l'heure émis par la Tour Eiffel.

0810 MEASUREMENT OF MASS AND DENSITY. BALANCE.

Andreae. 38962. Methode des Schwebens zur Dichtebestimmung homogener fester Körper.

Batschinski. 39109 ; Hartmann. 40438. Empfindlichkeit der Wage.

Blackman. 39277. Weighing the earth.

Domke und Reimerdes. 39781. Handbuch der Aräometrie. Bestimmung der Dichte von Flüssigkeiten.

Gaehr. 40105. Relation between density and concentration of aqueous solutions.

Gray and Ramsay. 40285. Die Dichte des Nitons (,, Radiumemanation '') und die Zerfalltheorie.

Gülich. 40344. Bestimmung des spezifischen Gewichts und Molekulargewichts von Gasen.

Heyn und Bauer. 40516. Spannungen in kaltgereckten Metallen.

Kling. 40813. Influence des catalyseurs dans les déterminations de densités de vapeur.

Kreybig. 40914. Pyknometer für Dichtebestimmungen.

Lauriol. 41027. Mesure des débits des injecteurs et mesure des densités des gaz au moyen des orifices-étalons.

Marenco di Moriondo. 41332. Densità e temperatura dell'acqua superficiale del mare.

Mauthner. 41376. Abhängigkeit des Gewichtes eines Körpers von seiner elektrischen Ladung.

Menzies. 41402. Apparat zur Messung der Dampfdichten flüchtiger Stoffe.

Müller. 41536. Poids spécifiques des méthylamines.

Raffo. 41991. Densità di alcune lave.

Ramsay. 42004. Mesures de quantités infinitésimales de matières.

Roth und Eisenlohr. 42213. Refraktometrisches Hilfsbuch.

Scheel. 42356. Präzisionswage nach Thiesen.

Schicht. 42371. Robervalsche Wage.

Swann. 42720. Problem of the uniform rotation of a circular cylinder in its connexion with the principle of relativity.

Timmermans. 42797-8. Densité des liquides en dessous de zéro.

Ullrich. 42861. Bestimmung von Dampfdichten nach der Bunsenschen Ausströmungsmethode.

Urbain. 42866. Une balance-laboratoire à compensation électromagnétique destinée à l'étude des systèmes qui dégagent des gaz avec une vitesse sensible.

Waals, Jr., van der. 42962. Energy and mass. (English, Dutch.)

Watson. 43010. Das Volumen des Wassers bei hohen Drucken und Temperaturen.

0820 MEASUREMENT OF VELOCITY. ACCELERATION, ENERGY OF VISIBLE MOTION.

Bahrdt. 39051. Apparat zur Untersuchung des freien Falls.

Carlier. 39496. Appareils de mesures des vitesses et des accélérations.

Caro und Schück. 39501. Veränderung von Wasserstoff in Gasballons.

Esclangon. 39941. Système de synchronisation fixe ou différentielle. 39942 : Un régulateur rotatif à vitesse fixe ou variable.

Ottinger und Weiss. 41712. Bestimmung der Fallbeschleunigung am frei fallenden Körper.

Schillo. 42379. Messung hoher Umlaufzahlen mittels des Stroboskops.

Staus. 42620. Der Indikator und seine Hilfseinrichtungen.

Swann. 42720. Problem of the uniform rotation of a circular cylinder in its connexion with the principle of relativity.

Tolman. 42808. Non-newtonian mechanics : The direction of force and acceleration.

0825 MEASUREMENT OF FORCE. PENDULUM, SPRING BALANCE, TORSION BALANCE.

Agnew. 38904. Device for measuring the torque of electrical instruments.

Hecker. 40462. Gravity determinations at sea.

Kraus. 40907. Neue Jolly'sche Federwage zur Bestimmung des spezifischen Gewichts.

Lippmann. 41158. Réduction des tracés sismographiques.

Mallock. 41298. Pendulum clocks and their errors.

Montessus de Ballore, de. 41485. L'application de la suspension à la Cardan aux sismographes.

Niethammer. 41611. Schweremessungen.

Oltay. 41680. Messung der Schwerkraftbeschleunigung in Budapest. (Ungar.)

0835 MEASUREMENT OF FLUID PRESSURE AND FLUID VELOCITY.

Bayeux. 39132. Appareil de précision pour l'emploi de l'oxygène gazeux.

Christen. 39554. Arbeitsberechnung am Quecksilbermanometer.

Frank. 40057-8.60 ; **Hürthle.** 40584 ; **Schaefer.** 42341. Manometer. 40061 : Theorie des Lufttonographen. 40063 : Hämodynamik.

Gaede. 40103. Die äussere Reibung der Gase.

Holland. 40548. Quarzmanometer.

Kármán. 40731 : Formänderung dünnwandiger Rohre.

Klein. 40803-4. Federmanometer.

Knudsen. 40828; **Smoluchowski.** 42556. Theorie des absoluten Manometers. 40829: Hitzdrahtmanometer.

Lafay. 40974. La mesure des pressions élevées déduite des variations de résistivité des inducteurs soumis à leur action. 40975: Un procédé d'observation des trajectoires suivies par les éléments d'un courant d'air géné par des obstacles de formes variables. 40976: L'utilisation du procédé d'exploration à l'acétylène pour la mesure de la vitesse du vent et l'étude du champ aérodynamique.

Meyer. 41435. Kymographion.

Moulin. 41520. Pompe à mercure à vide rapide.

Parenty. 41747. Compteur de vapeur 41748: Régulation progressive des pressions à l'entrée d'une conduite de distribution d'eau, de gaz ou de vapeur.

Ravelli. 42019. L'energia del moto ondoso del mare.

Stach. 42589. Messgeräte für Druck und Geschwindigkeit von Gasen und Dämpfen.

Wagener. 42976. Feindruckmesser mit Schreibvorrichtung [zur Untersuchung von Druck u. Geschwindigkeitsverteilung in nahezu beständigen Luftströmen].

0840 ELASTIC DEFORMATION OF SOLIDS. COMPRESSIBILITY AND RIGIDITY. ELONGATION, TORSION, FLEXURE. YOUNG'S MODULUS.

Alfthan-Klotz. 38925. La compressibilité des récipients en verre de quartz et les constantes élastiques du quartz fondu. Thèse.

Almansi. 38933. Concetto di deformazione derivata applicato allo studio delle deformazioni dei solidi cilindrici.

Bemmelen, van. 39172. Plasticité des terres argileuses. [Trad.]

Boudouard. 39349. Essais des métaux pour l'amortissement des mouvements vibratoires.

Brillouin. 39395. Méthode interférentielle pour la détermination des modules de torsion des cristaux.

Cassebaum. 39511. Das Verhalten von weichem Flussstahl jenseits der Proportionalitätsgrenze.

Cheneveau et **Heim.** 39547. L'extensibilité du caoutchouc vulcanisé.

Coker. 39599. Photo-elasticity.

Daniele. 39684. Problema dell'equilibrio elastico nello spazio esterno ad un ellissoide per dati spostamenti in superficie.

Drucker und **Kassel.** 39802. Fluidität von binären Gemischen.

Einstein. 39889, 91. Beziehung zwischen dem elastischen Verhalten und der spezifischen Wärme bei festen Körpern mit einatomigem Molekül.

Ferri. 39984. Lo spostamento dell'asse di rotazione terrestre nella massa della terra in rapporto colle variazioni di latitudine e con i grandi terremoti mondiali.

Freedericksz. 40074. Frottement intérieur des solides aux basses températures.

Friedrich. 40085. Kubische Kompressibilität vom Kadmium.

Grablovitz. 40268. Velocità della propagazione sismica.

Grüneisen. 40325. Beziehungen zwischen Atomwärme, Ausdehnungskoeffizient und Kompressibilität fester Elemente. 40326: Zur theorie einatomiger fester Körper.

Guthe and **Harris.** 40369. Elastic properties of bismuth wires.

Hartmann. 40437. Mécanisme de la déformation permanente dans les métaux soumis à l'extension.

Heyn und **Bauer.** 40517. Spannungen in Kesselblechen.

Jouguet. 40694. Vitesse et l'accélération des ondes de choc de seconde et de troisième espèce dans les fils.

Klein. 40803. Federmanometer.

Le Roux. 41107. L'incurvation et la flexion dans les déformations finies.

Lewis, McC. 41118. Ausdruck für die latente Verdampfungswärme.

Nádai. 41552. Untersuchungen der Festigkeitslehre mit Hilfe des thermoelektrischen Temperaturmessverfahrens.

Parsons and **Cook.** 41753. Compression of liquids at high pressure.

Plank. 41888. Verhalten des Querkontraktionskoeffizienten des Eisens bis zu sehr grossen Dehnungen.

Watson. 43010. Das Volumen des Wassers bei hohen Drucken und Temperaturen.

Zanotti Bianco. 43243. Determinazioni della gravità sull' Oceano indiano e sul Pacifico.

HEAT.

0900 GENERAL.

Campetti. 39476. Misure e nuovi apparecchi relativi ai fenomeni termici.

Cataldi. 39514.

Cei. 39523.

Ebert. 39852. Lehrbuch.

Ferrero. 39983.

Garuffa. 40142.

Geigel. 40160. Die Wärme.

Humphreys. 40590. Laws of radiation and absorption.

Jüptner. 40696. Heat energy and fuels.

Lasio. 41204.

Wegner von Dallwitz. 43027. Wärmetheorie.

SOURCES OF HEAT AND COLD.

1010 METHODS OF PRODUCING HIGH TEMPERATURES.

Damour, Carnot, Rengade. 39680. Les sources de l'énergie calorifique.

Le Chatelier. 41049. Chauffage industriel.

Stoermer. 42667. Erzeugung hoher Temperaturen.

1012 METHODS OF PRODUCING LOW TEMPERATURES.

Handy. 40411. A convenient method of refrigeration (−75° C.)

Kamerlingh Onnes. 40718. A hélium-cryostat. 40721-2 : La liquéfaction de l'hélium. Laboratoire cryogène de Leyde ; expériences à faire aux températures extrêmement basses.

Marchis. 41320. Production of low temperatures, and refrigeration.

Travers, Gwyer and Usher. 42823. Self intensive process for liquefying gases.

1014 METHODS OF PRODUCING CONSTANT TEMPERATURES. THERMOSTATS.

Andrejev. 38965. Eine Anwendung des Thermostaten. (Russ.)

Esclangon. 39943 ; Parenty. 41749. Un régulateur thermique de précision.

Haas. 40376. Description of a thermostat.

Land. 40992. An electrical constant temperature apparatus.

Morgan. 41500. Bad für konstante Temperatur sowohl oberhalb als auch unterhalb Zimmertemperatur.

Schuen. 42425. Thermostat für hohe Temperaturen.

THERMOMETRY.

1200 GENERAL.

Le thermomètre. Rev. univ. intern. illustrée Bruxelles 1907 (98).

Bornstein. 39307.

Day and Sosman. 39699. High temperature gas thermometry.

Martens. 41340.

Rudel. 42236 ; Quervain. 41983. Einstellungsträgheit von Thermometern.

Waidner. 42986. Temperature work of Bureau of Standards.

1210 EXPANSION AND PRESSURE THERMOMETRY.

Darling. 39690. Pirometri industriali.

Kuhn. 40934. Korrekturteilung für verschiedene Eintauchtiefen an Quecksilberthermometern.

Häussler. 40390. Ein Thermometer aus dem Jahre 1636.

Wiebe. 43119. Brauchbarkeitsgrenze der hochgradigen Thermometer.

1230 ELECTRICAL THERMOMETRY.

Thermomètre électrique à distance. Eau éclairage chauffage Bruxelles 1908 (261-263).

Callendar. 39465. A thermoelectric balance for the absolute measurement of radiation.

Kamerlingh Onnes. 40719. Thermal properties of helium. (Dutch.)

——— and **Crommelin.** 40723. Isotherms of monatomic substances and of their binary mixtures. X. The behaviour of argon with respect to the law of corresponding states. (English.)

Linde. 41141. Abkühlung von Gasen beim Ausströmen durch eine Drosselstelle.

Marx. 41350. Gravitation und Wärme. [Die Funktionen und mechanischen Funktionen der Zustandsänderungen eines idealen Gases.]

Rudge. 42238. A constant temperature, porous plug experiment.

Schwoerer. 42464. Nouvelles recherches sur la détente adiabatique des gaz et sur l'équivalent mécanique de la chaleur.

Sirk. 42527. Beziehungen zwischen dem Gesetz von Avogadro und der kinetischen Gastheorie.

Smoluchowski. 42556. Theorie des absoluten Manometers von Knudsen.

Vogel. 42924. Temperaturveränderung von Luft und Sauerstoff beim Strömen durch eine Drosselstelle bei 10° C. und Drücken bis zu 150 Atmosphären.

Worthing. 43204. Free expansion and Joule-Kelvin effects in air and in carbon-dioxide. 43205 : Some thermodynamic properties of air and of carbon dioxide.

CALORIMETRY AND SPECIFIC HEAT.

1600 GENERAL UNITS OF HEAT.

Della calorimetria. Gaz Venezia **9** 1911 (1212–13).

Albaret. 38910. Nouvelle formule d'émission de le chaleur.

Bjerrum. 39275. Spezifische Wärme der Gase.

Einstein. 39889. Beziehung zwischen dem elastischen Verhalten und der spezifischen Wärme bei festen Körpern mit einatomigem Molekül. 39893 : Thermische Molekularbewegung in festen Körpern.

Emerson. 39916. Bomb calorimeter.

Eucken. 39948. Temperaturverlauf der spezifischen Wärme.

Grüneisen. 40324. Verhältnis der thermischen Ausdehnung zur spezifischen Wärme fester Elemente. 40326 : Theorie einatomiger fester Körper.

Koenigsberger. 40859. Atomwärmen der Elemente.

Lindemann. 41147. Das Dulong-Petitsche Gesetz. Diss.

Loeb. 41172. Influence of variation in specific heat of water on calorimetry of fuels.

Nernst. 41579. Der Energieinhalt fester Stoffe. 41582 : Verhalten fester Stoffe bei sehr tiefen Temperaturen. 41584, 41586 : Theorie der spezifischen Wärme.

——— und **Lindemann.** 41587. Spezifische Wärme bei tiefen Temperaturen. 41588 : Spezifische Wärme und Quantentheorie.

Sommerfeld. 42574. Das Plancksche Wirkungsquantum.

White. 43114. Detection of small heat effects at high temperatures.

1610 CALORIMETRIC METHODS.

Le calorimètre Junkers. Rev. techn. pet. indust. 1905 (99–101).

Börnstein. 39307 ; **Rübner.** 42235. Wärmemessung.

Eucken. 39947. Molekularwärme des Wasserstoffs bei tiefen Temperaturen.

Glikin. 40224. Kalorimetrie organischer Verbindungen.

Hayes. 40458. Errors in cooling curves.

Inchley. 40619. Calorific value of solid and liquid fuels.

Josse. 40690. Un calorimètre à lame prismatique teintée et un étalon calorimétrique.

Koref. 40889. Messungen der spezifischen Wärme bei tiefen Temperaturen mit dem Kupferkalorimeter.

Lauriol. 41029. Essais de pouvoir calorifique du gaz d'éclairage.

Lindemann. 41147. Diss.

Magornow und **Rotinjanz.** 41279. Bestimmung der Verdampfungswärme von Flüssigkeiten mittels elektrischer Heizung.

Mellecœur. 41396. Recherches sur le thermo-calorimètre.

Neesen. 41570. Ätherkalorimeter.

Nernst. 41579. Der Energieinhalt fester Stoffe.

Neuscheler. 41596, 41597. Untersuchung stehender Schallschwingungen mit Hilfe des Widerstandsthermometers. [Bestimmung der Verhältnisse der spezifischen Wärmen bei Gasen.]

White. 43113. Method for increasing calorimetric accuracy.

1620 SPECIFIC HEATS OF SOLIDS AND LIQUIDS.

Barschall. 39091 ; **Koref.** 40889 ; **Maennel.** 41270 ; **Nernst.** 41581 ; **Pollitzer.** 41929 ; **Russell.** 42268 ; **Staniewski.** 42599. Spezifische Wärmen bei tiefen Temperaturen.

Beuss. 39232. Spezifische Wärme von binären Flüssigkeitsgemischen.

Cotty. 39653. Chaleur spécifique de l'eau.

Deuss. 39748. Spezifische Wärme des Rubidiums und Cadmiums.

Einstein. 39889. Beziehung zwischen dem elastischen Verhalten und der spezifischen Wärme bei festen Körpern mit einatomigem Molekül.

Faasch. 39964. Spezifische Wärme von wässerigen Salzlösungen.

Gnesotte e **Fabrij.** 40350. Acetato sodico idrato.

Greenwood. 40291. Specific heats at high temperatures and the latent heats of fusion of metals.

Grüneisen. 40324. Verhältnis der thermischen Ausdehnung zur spezifischen Wärme fester Elemente.

Levi. 41110. Il calore specifico delle leghe metalliche.

Nernst. 41579. Energieinhalt fester Stoffe.

Protz. 41962. Abhängigkeit der kubischen Kompressibilität von der Temperatur für Kalium und Natrium.

Schmidt. 42396. Spezifische und Erstarrungswärme des geschmolzenen Roheisens.

Schulz. 42431. Mittlere spezifische Wärme einiger Silikate im kristallisierten und im amorphen Zustande zwischen 20° und 100°.

Schulze. 42435. Spezifische Wärme binärer Gemische.

1640 SPECIFIC HEATS OF GASES AND VAPOURS.

Bjerrum. 39275 ; **Drucker.** 39801 ; **Swinne.** 42725. Spezifische Wärme der Gase.

Eucken. 39947. Molekularwärme des Wasserstoffs bei tiefen Temperaturen.

Evetrs. 39959.

Knoblauch und **Mollier.** Die spezifische Wärme c_p des überhitzten Wasserdampfes für Drücke von 2 bis 3 kg qcm und Temperaturen von 350 bis 550° C.

Küster. 40942 ; **Stoll.** 42676. Spezifische Wärme von Sauerstoff.

Leduc. 41054. Nouvelle méthode pour déterminer le rapport γ des chaleurs spécifiques C et c des vapeurs. 41055 ; La détente des vapeurs et la variation du rapport γ de leurs chaleurs spécifiques avec la température et la pression.

Levy. 41114. Molekularwärme des Wasserdampfes.

Scheel und **Heuse.** 42359. Spezifische Wärme der Luft bei Zimmertemperatur und bei tiefen Temperaturen.

Thibaut. 42761. Spezifische Wärme verschiedener Gase und Dämpfe.

Worthing. 43203. Ratio of the two heat capacities of carbon dioxide as a function of the pressure and the temperature.

1660 CHEMICAL CONSTITUTION AND SPECIFIC HEAT (DULONG AND PETIT LAW, ETC.).

Eucken. 39947. Molekularwärme des Wasserstoffs bei tiefen Temperaturen.

Grüneisen. 40325. Beziehungen zwischen Atomwärme, Ausdehnungskoefficient und Kompressibilität fester Elemente.

Koenigsberger. 40859. Atomwärmen der Elemente.

Lindemann. 41147. Das Dulong-Petitsche Gesetz. Diss. 41148. Spezifische Wärme bei tiefen Temperaturen. IV. [Beziehungen zwischen der elektrischen Leitfähigkeit der Metalle und ihrem Energiegehalt.]

Nernst. 41579. Energieinhalt fester Stoffe. 41581, 41587. Spezifische Wärme bei tiefen Temperaturen. 41584, 41588. Spezifische Wärme und Quantentheorie.

Russell. 42268. Messungen von spezifischen Wärmen bei tiefen Temperaturen.

1670 HEATS OF FUSION.

Baud. 39115. Chaleur moléculaire de fusion.

Deuss. 39748. Schmelzwärme des Rubidiums.

Frank. 40055. Schmelzwärme von Kolloiden.

Massol et Faucon. 41359. Chaleur latente de fusion et chaleur spécifique des acides gras.

Pollitzer. 41929. Tiefe Temperaturen.

1680 HEATS OF VAPORISATION.

Sul calore totale del vapor d'acqua saturo. [Trad. Sunto.] Roma Ann. Soc. ing. **25** 1910 (17-18).

Barschall. 39092. Verdampfungswärme des Sauerstoffes.

Brandt. 39383. Innere latente Verdampfungswärme.

Cederberg. 39520. Beziehung zwischen Verdampfungswärme. Dampfdruck und Temperatur.

Estreicher und **Schnerr.** 39945. Verdampfungswärme einiger verflüssigter Gase.

Greenwood. 40292. Dampfdruckkurve und Verdampfungswärme einiger schwerflüchtiger Metalle.

Keesom. 40752. Chaleur de vaporisation de l'hydrogène.

Koref. 40889. Messungen der spezifischen Wärme bei tiefen Temperaturen mit dem Kupferkalorimeter.

Lewis. 41117. Latent heat of vaporization of liquids. 41118: Ein Ausdruck für die latente Verdampfungswärme.

Magornow und **Rotinjanz.** 41279. Bestimmungsmethode der Verdampfungswärme von Flüssigkeiten mittels elektrischer Heizung.

Richards and **Mathews.** 42098. Determination of heat of evaporation of water.

Schüle. 42422. Die Eigenschaften des Wasserdampfes.

Smith. 42541, 42542. Heat of evaporation of water.

Ter Gazarian. 42758. Une relation générale entre les propriétés physiques des corps.

Thorkelsson. 42783. Zustandsgleichung und die innere Verdampfungswärme.

1690 HEATS OF DISSOLUTION.

Colson. 39607. La particule dissoute.

Jorissen. 40688. Chaleur d'hydratation.

Speranski. 42585. Dampfdruck und integrale Lösungswärme der gesättigten Lösungswärme der gesättigten Lösungen.

Woitaschewsky. 43170. Abhängigkeit der integralen Lösungswärme von der Temperatur.

1695 HEATS OF TRANSFORMATION.

La determinazione sperimentale e la registrazione continua del potere calorifico dei gas. (Calorimetro Junkers.) [Sunto.] Roma Ann. Soc. ing. **25** 1910 (263-265).

Forcrand. 40030. Sels haloïdes et oxydes des métaux alcalins et alcalino-terreux.

Lemoult. 41093. Dérivés du styrolène.

Mazzotte. 41383. Trasformazione delle leghe binarie allo stato solido.

Muller. 41536. Chaleurs de combustion et poids spécifiques des méthylamines.

Tschernobaeff et Wologdine. 42840. Chaleurs de formation de quelques silicates.

PHENOMENA OF CHANGE OF STATE.

1800 GENERAL.

Amadori e Pampanini. 38936. Capacità degli alogenuri potassici di dare soluzioni solide, in rapporto colla temperatura.

Barus. 39097. A continuous record of atmospheric nucleation.

Block. 39288. Volumenänderung beim Schmelzen von Kristallen und die Wärmeausdehnung.

Dieterici. 39765; Pochhammer. 41899; Svedberg. 42713; Tammann. 42749; van der Waals. 42961. Theorie der Zustandsgleichung.

Grüneisen. 40326. Zur Theorie einatomiger fester Körper.

Hybl. 40596. Neue Tabellen für Ammoniakdampf.

Ladenburg. 40965. Aggregatzustände und ihr Zusammenhang.

Pawlow. 41775. Anwendung der thermodynamischen Theorie der dispersen Systeme auf Hydrometeore.

Rayleigh. 42022. Breath figures.

Van der Mensbrugghe. 42885. Les quatre propriétés providentielles de l'eau.

Wertheimer. 43093. Thermodynamik des Wasserdampfes.

1810 FUSION AND SOLIDIFICATION (GENERAL).

Beck. 39140. Bestimmung der Erweichungspunkte von Silikatgläsern.

Bénard. 39175. Formation des cirques lunaires.

Biltz. 39258. Schmelzpunkt und Atomschwingungszahl des Germaniums.

Day and Sosman. 39699. High temperature gas thermometry.

Doelter. 39775. Gleichgewichte in Silikatschmelzen.

Forsythe. 40037. Melting-points of tantalum and tungsten.

Fujiwara. 40096. Ice-formation.

Grüneisen. 40326. Zur Theorie einatomiger fester Körper.

Hackspill. 40384. Densité, coefficient de dilatation et variation de volume à la fusion des métaux alcalins.

Hanriot. 40412. L'adhésivité.

Hess. 40506. Plastizität des Eises.

Jaeger. 40649. 40650. Sulfoantimonites.

Johnston und Adams. 40670. Einfluss des Druckes auf die Schmelzpunkte einiger Metalle.

Kamerlingh Onnes and Crommelin. 40724. Critical temperature of neon. Melting point of oxygen. (English, Dutch.)

Kanolt. 40729. Determination of melting points at high temperatures.

Kobayashi. 40833. Legierungen des Tellurs mit Cadmium und Zinn.

La Rosa. 41007. 41008. Fusione del carbonio per mezzo dell'effetto Joule.

Le Bel. 41041. L'échauffement singulier des fils minces de platine.

Leenhardt. 41060. Vitesse de cristallisation des sels hydratés.

Riecke. 42110. Erniedrigung des Schmelzpunktes durch einseitigen Zug oder Druck.

Rosenhain and Archbutt. 42186. Constitution of the alloys of aluminium and zinc.

Stein. 42627. Lineare Ausdehnung der festen Elemente als Funktion der absoluten Schmelztemperatur.

Tammann. 42746, 42748. Thermodynamik der Gleichgewichte in Einstoffsystemen. 42747: Molekulargewichtsbestimmung krystallisierter Stoffe.

Waidner and Burgess. 42988. Temperature scale between 100° and 500° C.

Watts and Mendenhall. 43011. 43012. Fusion of carbon.

Weimarn. 43053. Untersuchungsmethoden kapillarchemischer Probleme.

White. 43115, 43116. Schmelz-
punktsbestimmungen. [Uebers.]

Wüst. 43220. Schwindung der
Metalle und Legierungen.

1840 SATURATED VAPOURS. PRESSURE. BOILING POINTS. EVAPORATION.

Becker. 39147. Kondensation von
Dämpfen.

Berkeley and **Appleby.** 39195.
Boiling - point of water. 39196 :
Boiling-point of some saturated solu-
tions.

Bieber. 39243. Kondensation von
Wasserdampf in Gegenwart von Ozon,
Stickstoffoxyden und Wasserstoffsuper-
oxyd. Kerne des blauen Nebels.

Bradley, Browne und **Hale.** 39377.
Wirkung von mechanischer Erschütterung auf Kohlensäure in der Nähe der
kritischen Temperatur.

Cederberg. 39520. Beziehung
zwischen Verdampfungswärme, Dampfdruck und Temperatur. 39521 : Zur
Dampfdruckfunktion.

Chapman. 39532. Equilibrium
temperatures in fog chambers.

Deckert. 39707. Temperaturmessung mittelst eines Widerstandsthermometers.

Greenwood. 40292. Dampfdruckkurve und Verdampfungswärme einiger
schwerflüchtiger Metalle.

Guthe and **Worthing.** 40370.
Formula for the vapor tension of water
between 0° and 200° C.

Hansen. 40414. Temperaturabnahmen hochmolekularer Dämpfe bei
kleinen Drucken. 40415 : Siedepunkt.

Hort. 40560. Dampfspannungs-
kurven von Nitrobenzol und Erdöldestillat.

Hýbl. 40596. Neue Tabellen für
Ammoniakdampf.

Lenard und **Ramsauer.** 41097.
Nebelkernbildung durch Licht.

Lewis. 41119. The theory of
fractional distillation.

Lippmann. 41159. Action des
forces extérieures sur la tension des
vapeurs saturées.

Lungo (Del). 41242. Le forze
capillari e l'evaporazione.

Marvin. 41345. Pressure of saturated vapor from water and ice. 41346 :
Methods for study of evaporation.

Mohr. 41476. Adsorption und
Kondensation von Wasserdampf an
blanken Glasflächen. Diss.

Ollive. 41674. Force élastique des
vapeurs saturantes.

Panomareff. 41739. Apparat zum
Nachweis der Spannkraft verschiedener
Dämpfe.

Przibram. 41965. Kondensation
von Dämpfen an Kernen.

Scheffer and **Treub.** 42364. Determinations of vapour tensions of nitrogen
tetroxide. (English, Dutch.)

Schüle. 42422. Eigenschaften des
Wasserdampfes.

Sendtner. 42491. Bestimmung der
Dampffeuchtigkeit mit dem Drosselkalorimeter.

Vaillant. 42870. Application de
l'évaporation à la mesure des coefficients de diffusion.

Waidner and **Burgess.** 42987. Constancy of the sulphur boiling point.
42988 : The temperature scale between
100° and 500° C.

Wegscheider. 43028. Zur Verdampfung des Salmiaks.

Wertheimer. 43093. Zur Theorie
des Wasserdampfes.

Wuppermann. 43227. Verdampfungsgeschwindigkeit. Diss.

1850 VAPOUR DENSITIES.

Ullrich. 42861. Bestimmung von
Dampfdichten nach der Bunsenschen
Ausströmungsmethode. Diss.

Ter Gazarian. 42758. Une relation
générale entre les propriétés physiques
des corps.

1860 EBULLITION.

Cegielskij. 39522. Sieden von
Elektrolyten bei Stromdurchgang.

1870 LIQUEFACTION OF GASES AND GASEOUS MIXTURES.

Claude. 39575. Fabrication industrielle de l'azote pur.

Glinzer. 40225. Ein neuer Luftver-flüssigungsapparat.

Kamerlingh Onnes. 40721. La liquéfaction de l'hélium.

Lilienfeld. 41138. Luft- und Wasserstoffverflüssigung.

Linde. 41142. Trennung von Gasgemischen mit Hilfe der Ver-flüssigung.

Mewes. 41424. Luftverflüssigungs-und Sauerstoff - Stickstoffgewinnungs-Verfahren.

Nernst. 41585. Apparat zur Verflüssigung von Wasserstoff.

Olszewski. 41677. La liquéfaction des gaz. 41678, 41679 : La liquéfaction de l'hydrogène ; procédé permettant d'éviter les pertes de froid. (Polish.)

Perrot. 41812. Constantes physico-chimiques des gaz liquéfiés.

Swinburne. 42723. Separation of oxygen by cold.

1880 CONTINUITY OF STATE. CRITICAL STATE, CRITICAL POINT, Etc. CHARACTERIS-TIC EQUATIONS.

Amagat. 38942. Pression intérieure des fluides et détermination du zéro absolu.

Batschinski. 39107. Equation of continuity of the liquid and gaseous states of matter. 39108 : Ermittlung des Grades der molekularen Association von Flüssigkeiten.

Bradley *et alii*. 39377. Wirkung von mechanischer Erschütterung auf Koh-lensäure in der Nähe der kritischen Temperatur.

Cardoso. 39493. Densités des phases coexistantes (densités ortho-bares) et le diamètre de l'anhydride sulfureux au voisinage du point critique.

Crismer. 39660. Détermination exacte de la densité des alcools absolus à l'aide de leur température critique de dissolution.

Kamerlingh Onnes. 40719. Thermal properties of helium. (Dutch.)

————— and **Crommelin.** 40724. Critical temperature of neon.

Keesom. 40751. Spektrophoto-metrische Untersuchung der Opaleszenz eines einkomponentigen Stoffes in der Nähe des kritischen Zustandes.

Laar, van. 40953. Variability of the quantity b in Van der Waals' equation of state, also in connection with the critical quantities. 40955 : Relations holding for the critical point. (Dutch.)

Leduc. 41051. Compressibilité des gaz ; volumes moléculaires et poids atomiques. 41056 : Pression interne dans les gaz ; formules d'état et loi des attractions moléculaires.

Meyer. 41433. Negativer Druck in Flüssigkeiten.

Ostwald. 41709. Zur Theorie der kritischen Trübungen.

Pochhammer. 41899. Zustands-gleichung in angenäherter Rechnung.

Schüle. 42422. Eigenschaften des Wasserdampfes.

Smoluchowski. 42560. Opaleszenz von Gasen im kritischen Zustande.

Thorkelsson. 42783.

Waals, van der. 42956. Value of the critical quantities. 42957, 42960 : Volumes of the coexisting phases of a simple substance.

Wertheimer. 43093. Wasserdampf.

1885 CORRESPONDING STATES.

Einstein. 39888. Gesetz von Eötvös [für Flüssigkeiten].

Kamerlingh Onnes and **Crommelin.** 40723. Behaviour of argon with respect to the law of corresponding states.

Oswald. 41711. Relation simple entre le coefficient de dilatation des liquides et la température.

Tammann. 42749. Zustandsglei-chungen im Gebiete kleiner Volumen.

Ter Gazarian. 42758. Relation générale entre les propriétés physiques des corps.

Waals, van der. 42956. Value of the critical quantities. 42957, 42960 : Grandeur des volumes des phases co-existantes d'une substance simple.

**1887 EQUILIBRIUM IN COEX-
ISTENT PHASES. PHASE
RULE. (GENERAL.)**

Boulouch. 39353, 39354. La loi
des phases.

Campetti e **Delgrosso.** 39479. Equilibrio di coppie di liquidi parzialmente
miscibili. Equilibrio tra le fasi liquide.

Dam, van et **Donk.** 39679. Equili-
bres dans le système : iodure d'argent,
iodure de potassium et eau. (Hollandais.)

Faucon. 39975. Mélanges d'eau et
d'acides gras.

Gay. 40146. Mélanges d'acide
acétique avec les liquides normaux.

Horiba. 40558. Equilibrium in the
system : water, ethyl alcohol and ethyl
ether.

Jaeger. 40649, 40650. Sulfoantimonites. (Dutch.)

Jonker. 40683. Systèmes ternaires,
dont l'une des composantes est une
substance colloïdale. (Hollandais.)

Jouguet. 40693. Points indifférents.

Kettner. 40775. Solubilité du
carbonate de soude. (Hollandais.)

Krulla. 40929. Quantitative
Verhältnisse bei der Teilung eines
Körpers zwischen zwei Phasen : Ad-
sorption.

Kruyt. 40931. Beziehung zwischen
den drei Tripelpunkten des Schwefels.
(Holl.)

Laar, van. 40951, 40957. The solid
state.

Marc. 41312. Die chemische
Gleichgewichtslehre.

Olivari. 41673. Equilibri di solubilità fra l'iodio e le sostanze organiche.

Pawlow. 41777. Thermodynamik der
kondensierten dispersen Systeme.

Roozeboom. 42178. Systeme mit
nur einer Flüssigkeit ohne Mischkristalle und ohne Dampf.

Scheffer. 42361. System hydrogen
sulphide-water. 42362 : Heterogene
Gleichgewichte bei dissociierenden Verbindungen.

Schreinemakers. 42414. Equilibria
in the system : water-sodium sulphate-
sodium chloride-copper-sulphate-cupric
chloride. (English, Dutch.)

———— and **Deuss.** 42415.
System water-alcohol-manganous sulphate.

———— und **Figee.** 42416. Das
System : Wasser-Kalziumchlorid-Kalziumhydroxyd bei 25°. (Holl.)

———— and **Massink.** 42417.
Compounds of nitrates and sulphates.
(English.)

Smits. 42548. Application of the
new theory of allotropy to the system
sulphur. 42549 : System iron-carbon.
42550 : Eine neue Theorie der Allotropie. ———— and **Leeuw.** 42552.
System sulphur. ———— and **Maarse**
42553 : System water-phenol. ————
and **Treub.** 42555 : Course of the
P-T-lines for constant concentration in
the system ether-anthraquinone.

Tammann. 42746. Thermodynamik
der Gleichgewichte im Einstoffsystem.

Wuite. 43222. P-T-Durchschnitte.

**1890 HYGROSCOPY AND
HYGROMETRY.**

Kailan. 40713. Spezifisches Gewicht und Hygroskopizitat des Glyzerins.

Love and **Smeal.** 41209. The
psychrometric formula.

Okada. 41670. Psychrometer
covering.

Romberg. 42174. Hygroskopizitätsbestimmungen.

Sendtner. 42491. Bestimmung der
Dampffeuchtigkeit mit dem Drosselkalorimeter.

**1900 VAPORIZATION OF SOLIDS.
SUBLIMATION.**

Smith und **Menzies.** 42538. Dampfdruck von getrocknetem Kalomel.

Wegscheider. 43028. Salmiak.

**1920 SOLUTIONS AND LIQUID
MIXTURES : MELTING-POINT,
BOILING-POINT, VAPOUR-
PRESSURE, Etc.**

Baume et alii. 39125, 39126. Courbes de fusibilité des mélanges gazeux.

Wroczyński. 43213. Courbes de points de fusion des mélanges binaires dont un composant au moins est un corps organique.

1925 SOLUTIONS : OTHER THERMAL PROPERTIES (LATENT HEAT). (See 1690.)

Colson. 39607. La particule dissoute. 39610 : La dissolécule et la formule de Van't Hoff.

Speranski. 42585 : **Woitaschewsky.** 43170. Integrale Lösungswärme der gesättigten Lösungen.

1930 DISSOCIATION. ALLO- TROPIC TRANSFORMATIONS.

Chauvenet. 39545. Dissociation de ThCl⁴ 18NH³.

Enklaar. 39919. Dissoziations-Konstante K_2 der Schwefelsäure und der Oxalsäure. (Holländisch.)

Forcrand. 40032. Hydrates des fluorures de rubidium et de cæsium.

Grenet. 40299. Trempe des bronzes.

Guillet. 40360. Le revenu des produits écrouis.

Jolibois. 40671. Phosphore et phosphures métalliques. 40672 : Relations entre le phosphore blanc, le phosphore rouge et le phosphore pyromorphique.

Scarpa. 42328. Legge della diluizione.

Scheffer and **Treub.** 42364. Determinations of vapour tensions of nitrogen tetroxide.

Smits. 42551. „Gesetz der Umwandlungsstufen" and theory of allotropy.

Tammann. 42746. Thermodynamik der Gleichgewichte in Einstoffsystemen. 42748 : Gleichgewichte isotroper und anistroper Phasen. Polymorphismus.

1940 RETARDATION PHENO- MENA (SUPERFUSION, SUPER- HEATING, SUPERSATURA- TION).

Berthoud. 39220. L'impossibilité de surchauffer un solide.

Owen. 41716. Production of nuclei in air by intense cooling.

Smits. 42550. Allotropie.

2000 GENERAL.

Baroni. 39084. Studi sugli scambi di calore.

Bryant. 39436. Curious thermal phenomenon.

Campetti. 39477. Leghe.

Gabelli. 40102. Sistema di rottura di lamine vitree per squilibrio termico.

Binder. 39262. 39263 : **Hinlein.** 40525. Erwärmung der elektrischen Maschinen.

Lasareff. 41018. Temperatursprung an der Grenze zwischen Metall und Gas.

Nusselt. 41650. Wärmeübergang im Kreuzstrom.

Rayleigh. 42026. Conduction of heat.

Soennecken. 42566. Wärmeübergang von Rohrwänden an strömendes Wasser.

Suchý. 42703. Wärmestrahlung und Wärmeleitung.

2010 MATHEMATICAL ANALYSIS AND APPLICATIONS (FOURIER).

Fujiwara and **Miyazawa.** 40098. Flow of heat in snow.

Kneser. 40817. Die Integralgleichungen.

Léauté. 41033. Difficultés que présente l'emploi des développements exponentiels.

Marcolongo. 41326. Equazione della propagazione del calore nei corpi cristallizzati.

Rayleigh. 42026. Conduction of heat.

2020 CONDUCTANCE OF SOLIDS.

Bacon. 39041. Conduttività per il calore di alcuni coibenti.

Carbonelli. 39489. Coibenti industriali specialmente per uso di bordo.

Darling. 39689. Heat-insulating materials : the relation between surface temperature and efficiency.

Eucken. 39946. Temperaturabhängigkeit der Wärmeleitfähigkeit fester Nichtmetalle. 39946A : Wärmeleitfähigkeit einiger Kristalle bei tiefen Temperaturen.

———— und **Gehlhoff.** 39950. Elektrisches, thermisches Leitvermögen und Wiedemann-Franzsche Zahl der Antimon-Cadmiumlegierungen zwischen 0° und 190° C.

Gröber. 40312. Wärmeleitfähigkeit von Isolier- und Baustoffen.

Grünzweig. 40328. Korkstein-Blätterholzkohle.

Grünzweig. 40329. Der Kork als Wärmeisolator.

Icole. 40607. Détermination à différentes températures de la conductibilité calorifique du graphite et du sulfure cuivreux.

Koenigsberger. 40861. Wärmeleitung von Graphit und Diamant.

———— und **Weiss.** 40873. Thermoelektrische Effekte (Thermokräfte, Thomsonwärme) und Wärmeleitung in einigen Elementen und Verbindungen.

Kousleff. 40899. Conductibilité thermique et électrique des principales matières obturatrices.

Mauro. 41375. Trasmissione del calore negli isolanti per basse temperature.

Osann. 41700A. Wärmeleitungsvermögen feuerfester Steine in Winderhitzern.

Poensgen. 41900. Bestimmung der Wärmeleitfähigkeit plattenförmiger Materialien.

Quartulli. 41981. Nuovo metodo per lo studio della conducibilità termica dei metalli.

Schulze. 42440. Wärmeleitfähigkeit einiger Reihen von Edelmetallegierungen.

Smith. 42540. Transverse thermomagnetic effect in nickel and cobalt.

Smoluchowski. 42557. Wärmeleitung pulverförmiger Körper.

Weiss. 43062. Elektronentheorie.

2030 LIQUIDS, CONDUCTANCE OF.

Goldschmidt. 40245. Wärmeleitfähigkeit von Flüssigkeiten.

Leprince-Ringuet. 41104. Loi de la transmission de la chaleur entre un fluide en mouvement et une surface métallique.

2035 CONDUCTANCE OF GASES.

Eucken. 39949. Temperaturabhängigkeit der Wärmeleitfähigkeit einiger Gase.

Heindlhofer. 40470. Bestimmung der Wärmeleitungsfähigkeit der Gase.

Knudsen. 40827. Molekulare Wärmeleitung der Gase und Akkomodationskoeffizient. 40831 : Conduction of heat through gases and the coefficient of accommodation. (Danish.) 40830 : **Smoluchowski.** 42559 : Zur Theorie der Wärmeleitung in verdünnten Gasen und der dabei auftretenden Druckkräfte.

Smoluchowski. 42561. Conductibilité calorifique des corps pulvérisés. 42563 : Conduction of heat through rarefied gases.

Soddy and **Berry.** 42565. Conduction of heat through rarefied gases.

2040 CONVECTION. LAWS OF COOLING. (See 4210.)

Amerio. 38952.

Boudry. 39351. Méthode d'utilisation à distance des eaux minérales thermales.

Binder. 39262. Äussere Wärmeleitung und Erwärmung elektrischer Maschinen.

Boussinesq. 39365. Vibrations spontanées d'une barre à bouts fixes et imperméables à la chaleur qui se met en équilibre thermique avec une atmosphère à température constante. 39366 : Vibrations spontanées d'une barre libre se refroidissant par contact à ses extrémités et par rayonnement ou convection à sa surface latérale.

Bryant. 39436. Thermal phenomenon.

David. 39696. Radiation in explosions of coal-gas and air.

Poincaré. 41915. Les hypothèses cosmogoniques.

Reboul et **Grégoire de Bollemont.** 42043. Transport de particules métalliques sous l'action de la chaleur.

Wamsler. 43001. Die Wärmeabgabe geheizter Körper an Luft.

THERMODYNAMICS.

2400   GENERAL.

Energia e materia. [Sunto. Trad.] Roma Ann. Soc. ing. 26 1911 (279-282).

Berthoud. 39221. Théorie cinétique des gaz et thermodynamique.

Callendar. 39466. Caloric theory of heat and Carnot's principle.

Duhem. 39828. Traité d'énergétique ou de thermodynamique générale. 39829: Wandlungen der Mechanik und der mechanischen Naturerklärung.

Ehrenfest. 39873. Das Prinzip von Le Chatelier-Braun und die Reziprozitätssätze der Thermodynamik.

———— und **Ehrenfest.** 39874. Begriffliche Grundlagen der statistischen Auffassung in der Mechanik.

Einstein. 39890. Mechanische Grundlagen der Thermodynamik.

Fleming. 40013. Thermodynamics.

Gambèra. 40125. Conseguenze dedotte dalla ipotesi moderna sulla entità del calorico e della temperatura.

Hargreaves. 40425. A kinematical theorem in radiation.

Hasenöhrl. 40442. Grundlagen der mechanischen Theorie der Wärme.

Hirshfeld. 40532. Engineering thermodynamics.

Jüttner. 40699. Ableitung der Nernstschen Formeln für Reaktionen in kondensierten Systemen.

Nernst. 41580, 3. Neuere Probleme der Wärmetheorie. 41584: Theorie der spezifischen Wärme und Anwendung der Lehre von den Energiequanten auf physikalischchemische Fragen.

Ornstein. 41695. Mechanical foundation of thermodynamics. [Thermodynamical definition of temperature.]

Ostwald. 41704. L'énergie. [Trad.] 41705: Energie. (Schwedisch.)

Planck. 41883. Energie und Temperatur. 41885: Über neuere thermodynamische Theorien. (Nernstsches Wärmetheorem und Quanten-Hypothese.) 41886: Thermodynamik.

Roy 42221. Propriétés thermodynamiques des corps solides.

Sackur. 42285. Kinetische Begründung des Nernstschen Wärmetheorems. [Entropie und Wahrscheinlichkeit.]

Szyszkowski. 42733. Chaleur spécifique polytrope et ses applications. (Polish.)

Tammann. 42746, 8. Thermodynamik der Gleichgewichte in Einstoffsystemen.

Tyrer. 42854. The law of molecular attraction.

Waals, jr., van der. 42963. Zur Deutung von Gibbs' „Canonical Ensembles".

Wegner von Dallwitz. 43027. Wärmetheorie.

2405   THE FIRST LAW. CONSERVATION OF ENERGY. DIFFERENT FORMS OF ENERGY.

Garbasso. 40136. Fisica d'oggi.

Mayer. 41380. Mechanik d. Wärme. 41382: Erhaltung der Kraft.

Pécsi. 41781. Fisica moderna.

Schwœrer. 42465. Le principe de l'équivalence.

Zanotti Bianco. 43245. Inerzia ed energia.

2410   MECHANICAL EQUIVALENT OF HEAT.

Everts. 39959; **Paschen u. Wolff.** 41766: **Stoll.** 42690. Bestimmung des mechanischen Wärmeäquivalentes.

※**Schwoerer.** 42464. La détente adiabatique des gaz et l'équivalent mécanique de la chaleur.

Wright. 43209. The temperature rise in pulleys and flywheels under frictional load.

2415 THE SECOND LAW. CAR-
NOT CYCLES. ENTROPY
AND AVAILABLE ENERGY.
IRREVERSIBLE PHENOMENA.
FREE ENERGY AND THER-
MODYNAMIC POTENTIALS.

Barreca. 39087. Una maggiore
precisazione della legge di degradazione
universale ed una possibile disponibilità
indefinita di energia degradabile.

Bloch. 39286. Théorèmes généraux
de mécanique et de thermodynamique.

Burstall. 39452. The energy
diagram for gas.

Décombe. 39708, 11, 12. Nature
de la chaleur non compensée. 39709 :
L'interprétation mécanique du principe
de Carnot-Clausius. 39710 ; La définition de l'entropie et de la température.
Les systèmes monocycliques. 39713 :
La chaleur de Siemens.

De Keyser. 39725. L'exposé des
principes élémentaires de la thermodynamique par la notion de l'entropie.

Jüttner. 40697. Das Maxwellsche
Gesetz der Geschwindigkeitsverteilung
in der Relativtheorie. 40699 : Ableitung der Nernstschen Formeln für
Reaktionen in kondensierten Systemen.

Kohnstamm and **Ornstein.** 40881.
Nernst's theorem of heat and chemical
facts.

Lilienfeld. 41137. Arbeitsleistung
zur Abscheidung von N und O aus
atmosphärischer Luft.

Marcelin. 41314. Mécanique des
phénomènes irréversibles à partir des
données thermodynamiques.

Nernst. 41578. Inconsistency of
my heat-theorem and Van der Waals'
equation at very low temperatures.
41586 : Thermodynamik und spezitische Wärme.

Ornstein. 41696, 8. Entropy and
probability.

Planck. 41885. Nernstsches
Wärmetheorem und Quanten-Hypothese.

Poincaré. 41915. Les hypothèses
cosmogoniques.

Sackur. 42285. Zur kinetischen
Begründung des Nernstschen Wärmetheorems. [Entropie und Wahrscheinlichkeit.]

Washburn. 43003. Système simple
de chimie thermodynamique.

Weber. 43020. Reversible und
umkehrbare Prozesse. Gelieferte und
geleistete Arbeit.

2425 ABSOLUTE TEMPERATURE
AND ITS DETERMINATION.

Amagat. 38942. Pression intérieure
des fluides et détermination du zéro
absolu.

Day and **Sosman.** 39699. High
temperature gas thermometry.

Nernst. 41586. Thermodynamik
und spezitische Wärme.

Planck. 41880, 41883. Énergie et
température.

Waidner and **Burgess.** 42988.
The temperature scale between 100°
and 500° C.

Weber. 43021. Bedeutung des
absoluten Nullpunktes.

2435 SPECIAL THERMODYNAMIC
RELATIONS.

Ehrenfest. 39873. Das Prinzip von
Le Chatelier-Braun und die Reziprozitätssätze der Thermodynamik.

Gay. 40147. La notion de tension
d'expansibilité. 40148 : La tension
d'expansibilité d'un fluide normal.

Nernst. 41582. Ein allgemeines
Gesetz, das Verhalten fester Stoffe bei
sehr tiefen Temperaturen betreffend.
41586 : Thermodynamik und spezifische Wärme.

Pawlow. 41775. Anwendung der
thermodynamischen Theorie der dispersen Systeme auf Hydrometeore.

Planck. 41883. Energie und
Temperatur.

Weber. 43015. Geschwindigkeitsänderung eines bewegten Hohlraums
infolge von Kompression. 43016 :
Die Transformation von Energie und
Bewegungsgrösse.

Worthing. 43205. Thermodynamic
properties of air and of carbon dioxide.

2445 THERMODYNAMIC
SURFACES, MODELS, Etc.

Block. 39288. Volumenänderung
beim Schmelzen von Kristallen und

die Wärmeausdehnung der Kristalle
und ihrer Schmelzen.

Tammann. 42749. Zustandsgleichungen bei kleiner Volumen.

2455 THERMODYNAMICS OF SINGLE SUBSTANCES.

Berthoud. 39221. Théorie cinétique des gaz et thermodynamique.

Eucken. 39947. Molekularwärme des Wasserstoffs bei tiefen Temperaturen.

Kamerlingh Onnes. 40722. Die im cryogenen Laboratorium zu Leyden ausgeführten Untersuchungen.

Laar. 40950-1, 7. L'état solide. 40952-3 : Variability of the quantity *b* in Van der Waals' equation of state : the critical quantities. 40955 : Relations holding for the critical point. 40956 : Value of some differential quotients in the critical point, in connection with the coexisting phases in the neighbourhood of that point and with the form of the equation of state. (English, Dutch.)

Pawlow. 41777. Thermodynamik der kondensierten dispersen Systeme.

Waals, van der. 42956. Value of the critical quantities. (Engl., Dutch, French.) 42959 : Association apparente ou aggrégation moléculaire. (Holl., Anglais.) 42960 : Grandeur des volumes des phases coexistantes d'une substance simple.

Wertheimer. 43093. Thermodynamik des Wasserdampfes.

2457 THERMODYNAMICS OF SOLUTIONS AND MIXTURES.

Arrhenius. 38992. Energieverhältnisse der Dampfbildung und der elektrolytischen Dissoziation.

Batschinski. 39108. Ermittlung des Grades der molekularen Association von Flüssigkeiten.

Baud. 39116. Une loi générale de la dissolution.

Carlson. 39497. Vitesse de solution dans le système gaz-fluide.

Colson. 39611. Théorie des dissolutions (peroxyde d'azote).

Dubrisay. 39815. Les équilibres chimiques en solution.

Einstein. 39888. Gesetz von Eötvös [für Flüssigkeiten].

Katz. 40739. Analogy between swelling (imbibition) and mixing. (Engl. and Dutch.)

Kohnstamm and Reeders. 40882. Phenomena of condensation for mixtures of carbonic acid and nitrobenzene in connection with double retrograde condensation. (Engl. and Dutch.)

Korteweg and Schreinemakers. 40896. Curves of contact of surfaces with cones, with application to the lines of saturation and binodal lines in ternary systems. (English, Dutch.)

Kuenen. 40936. Destillation des mélanges. (Hollandais.) 40937 : Direction of the binodal curves in the v-x diagram in a three phase equilibrium. 40938 : Miscibility of liquids. (Engl. and Dutch). 40939 : Effect of passing a mixture of two vapours into a mixture of the liquids.

Laar. 40954. „Einfache" und „nicht-einfache" Systeme der thermodynamischen Chemie.

Lundén. 41239. La constante de dissociation de la tropine.

Pawlow. 41776. Niederschlagsformkoeffizient von Weimarn.

Rengade. 42085. Courbes de refroidissement dans les mélanges binaires.

Smits. 42546. Retrogressive vapour lines. 42547 : Retrogressive melting point lines. (Engl. and Dutch.)

———— **and Treub.** 42554. Retrogressive melting point lines. 42555 : Course of the P-T-lines for constant concentration in the system ether - anthraquinone. (Engl. and Dutch.)

Waals, van der. 42958. Concentration of the gas phase between that of two coexisting liquid phases. (Engl. and Dutch.)

Wolff. 43181. Volumeffekte bei Lösungsvorgängen.

2465 THERMODYNAMICS OF SYSTEMS WITH EXTERNAL AND CAPILLARY FORCES.

Lippmann. 41159. Action de forces extérieures sur la tension des vapeurs saturées et des gaz dissous dans un liquide.

Marc und **Ritzel.** 41313. Faktoren, die den Kristallhabitus bedingen.

Michaud. 41143. Causes qui peuvent produire la variation à température constante de la tension de vapeur d'un liquide.

Pawlow. 41777. Kondensierte disperse Systeme.

2472 THERMODYNAMICS OF CHEMICAL PROCESSES.

Arrhenius. 38992. Energieverhältnisse der elektrolytischen Dissoziation.

Jüttner. 40700. Allgemeine Integrale der gewöhnlichen chemischen Kinetik.

Laar. 40954. „Einfache" und „nicht-einfache" Systeme der thermodynamischen Chemie.

Matignon. 41364. Formation synthétique du protoxyde d'azote.

Mazzucchelli. 41384. Teorema di Nernst.

Quartaroli. 41980. Energia degli elementi e quantità che resta nelle combinazioni.

Scheffer. 42363. Gas equilibria.

Trautz. 42822. Temperaturkoeffizient chemischer Reaktionsgeschwindigkeiten.

Urbain et **Scal.** 42867. Systèmes monovariants qui admettent une phase gazeuse.

2475 THERMODYNAMICS OF ELECTRO-CHEMICAL PROCESSES.

Arrhenius. 38992. Energieverhältnisse der Dampfbildung und der elektrolytischen Dissoziation.

Leduc. 41057. Application du principe de Lenz aux phénomènes qui accompagnent la charge des condensateurs.

Michaud. 41442. Les piles de gravitation.

Pollitzer. 41930. Thermodynamik des Clarkelements.

Timofejew. 42799. Einfluss des Druckes auf die Affinität.

Henning. 40478. Temperaturmessung mit Hilfe der Clapeyron-Clausiusschen Gleichung.

2490 THEORY OF HEAT ENGINES.

Le motrici tandem a valvole tipo Tosi. Politecn. Milano 58 1910 (577–582).

Macchine a corrente continua di vapore ed a movimento alternativo. [Sunto.] Riv. maritt. Roma 1910 2. trim. (430–432).

Motori Diesel tipo Polar. Riv. maritt. Roma 1910 3. trim. (467–472).

Sui motori tipo Diesel ad olio pesante. Riv. maritt. Roma 1910 2. trim. (195–206 con 3 tav.).

Allara. 38927. Trasformazione grafica del diagramma dinamico di una motrice a vapore nel diagramma entropico.

Barth. 39094. Dampfmaschinen.

Benasso. 39176. Le turbine a vapore marine.

Bignami. 39253. Macchine marine a vapore soprariscaldato con distribuzione a valvole. 39254 : Le macchine Stumpf.

Burstall. 39252. Energy diagram for gas.

Caprotti. 39488. Scappamento ed ammissione nei motori a due tempi.

Carvallo. 39598. Théorie des moteurs à gaz et à pétrole.

Christlein. 39557. Allgemeines Verhalten der Geschwindigkeitskoeffizienten von Leitvorrichtungen des praktischen Dampfturbinenbaues bei verschiedenen Betriebsbedingungen.

Cicali. 39562–3. Motrici termiche.

Emanaud. 39913. Fonctionnement interne des générateurs de vapeur.

Fehrmann. 39981. Maschinen-Betriebsführung in den Gärungsgewerben.

Gentsch. 40170. Verbrennungsturbinen.

Hanszel. 40417. Dreifach-Expansions-Dampfmaschine.

Heilmann. 40467 ; **Steuer.** 42650 ; **Stumpf.** 42699. Kolbendampfmaschine.

Hellenschmidt. 40473. Gemischbildungen der Gasmaschinen.

Heym. 40515. Strahlungen bei Gasexplosionen [Gasmaschinen].

Holzwarth. 40554 : **Langer.** 41000 ; **Loschge.** 41201-2 ; **Mangold.** 41309 ; Gasturbinen.

Hort. 40560. Untersuchung von Flüssigkeiten die als vermittelnde Körper im oberen Prozess einer Mehrstoffdampfmaschine Verwendung finden können.

Illies. 40616. Die ersten Dampfmaschinen.

Josse. 40692. Strömungsvorgänge und ihre Anwendung bei Dampfturbinen.

Karpenko. 40734. Entropietafel für Gase zur Berechnung der Verbrennungsmaschinen.

Karrer. 40735. Partiell beaufschlagte Dampfturbinen.

Köhler. 40849. Steigerung der spezifischen Leistung von Viertakt-Gasmaschinen mit Druckluftspülung. 40850 ; **Kreul.** 40912 ; **Seiliger.** 42484 : Thermodynamische Untersuchung schnellaufender Dieselmotoren.

Kölsch. 40852. Die langsam laufende, zwangläufige Frikart-Steuerung.

Kröner. 40918. Begleiterscheinungen beim Betrieb von Dampfturbinen.

Lemale. 41090. Évolution de la chaleur dans les turbines.

Lorenz. 41194. Neue Theorie und Berechnung der Kreiselräder. Wasserund Dampfturbinen.

Maercks. 41271. Kolbenmaschinen.

Nadrowski. 41553. Gleichdruck-Gas- und Gas-Dampf-Turbinen.

Novák. 41647. Theorie der Turbokompressoren.

Poblhausen. 41911 ; **Besig.** 39224. Die Dampfturbinen.

Revello. 42088. I motori a scoppio " Mietz-Weiss."

Schindler. 42382. Bestimmung des Dampfverbrauches von Dampfturbinen.

Schreber. 42411, 42413. Explosionsmotoren mit Einführung verdampfender Flüssigkeiten.

Spalckhaver und **Schneiders.** 42582. Die Dampfkessel.

Strahl. 42675. Untersuchung der Blasrohre und Schornsteine von Lokomotiven.

Stumpf. 42700. Die Gleichstrom-Dampfmaschine.

Tejessey. 42756. Utilizzazione del vapore di scappamento.

Vater. 42896. Entwicklung der Wärmekraftmaschinen.

Wagener. 42977. Verwendung von Zweitaktmaschinen für Luftfahrzeuge.

Wagner. 42985. Dampfdurchgangsquerschnitte von Regelventilen.

2495 REFRIGERATORS.

Hirsch. 40530. Verbesserung des Arbeitsvorganges der Kompressionskühlmaschinenanlagen.

Horst. 40559. Verbesserte CO_2-Expansions-Kältemaschine.

Josse. 40691. Verwendung von Wasserdampf als Kälteträger in Kältemaschinen. 40692 : Strömungsvorgänge und ihre Anwendung bei Kälteerzeugung.

Kavan. 40743. Künstliche Kälteproduktion in der chemischen Industrie. (Czechisch.)

Ostertag. 41703. Theorie und Konstruktion der Kolben- und Turbo-Kompressoren.

Zerkowitz. 43274. Berechnung der Kompressoren auf thermodynamischer Grundlage.

LIGHT AND INVISIBLE RADIATION.

2990 GENERAL.

Albertotti. 38915.

Amerio. 38951. Esperienza sulla ricomposizione della luce.

Baslini. 39103. Occhiali con astuccio del secolo XVII.

Battelli, Occhialini e **Chella.** 39113-4. La radioattività.

Białobrzeski. 39239. Le principe du relativisme et ses applications. [Polish.]

Bourcart. 39357. Appareil rotatif pour observer les nuances données par un mélange de couleurs.

Clay. 39580. Practical light.

Dosne. 39789. Complémentaire d'une couleur donnée, sa détermination par le calcul.

Henry et Diselez. 40485. Lumière et couleurs.

Maclaurin. 41266. Light.

Marino e **Porlezza.** 41335. Luminosità del fosforo.

Mayer. 41379. Farbenmischung.

Muffone. 41535. Come dipinge il sole.

Möller. 41472. Internationale Farbenbestimmungen.

Natanson. 41569. The statistical theory of radiation.

Nováz. 41648. Fortschritte in der Lehre über die Wellenbewegung des Aethers 1908 (Cechisch.)

Righi. 42138. La materia radiante ed i raggi magnetici.

Sassi. 42322. Fotografia.

Šebor. 42469. Physikalische Eigenschaften der Glassorten. (Cechisch.)

Silberstein. 42518. Quaternionenform der Relativitätstheorie. [Polish.]

Wood. 43196. Physical optics.

GEOMETRICAL OPTICS.

3000   GENERAL.

Ames. 38953. Theory of optics.

Björnbo und **Vogl.** 39276. Alkindi, Tideus und Pseudo-Euklid. Drei optische Werke.

Castelnuovo. 39513. Il principio di relatività e i fenomeni ottici.

Euler. 39951A. Dioptrica.

Gleichen. 40222. Die Optik in der Photographie. 40223: Theorie der modernen optischen Instrumente.

Haken. 40398. Entwicklung des Baues der optischen Instrumente.

Haubold. 40445. Der perfekte Optiker.

Hinrichs. 40526. Einführung in die geometrische Optik.

Riccò. 42096. Risultati recenti degli studi solari.

(e-1388)

Rohr. 42167. Der Augendrehpunkt und seine Berücksichtigung in der konstruktiven Optik. 42169 : Optische Instrumente.

3010   PHOTOMETRY. UNITS OF LIGHT. BRIGHTNESS. OPTICAL PYROMETRY. (See also 1255.)

Fotometro universale. [Sunto.] Gaz Venezia **8** 1910 (929).

Il nuovo fotometro Trotter. Riv. ing. san. Torino **6** 1910 (105).

I misuratori campione della luce e il loro impiego nella fotometria del gas. Gaz Venezia **8** 1910 (992).

L'illuminazione moderna. Giorn. Genio civ. Roma **48** 1910 (29-33).

Unità di misura luminosa internazionale. Gaz Venezia **8** 1910 (769).

Allen. 38928. New method of measuring the luminosity of the spectrum.

Bertolini. I proiettori elettrici per la difesa delle coste.

Bornstein. 39306. Beleuchtung und Lichtmessung.

Butterfield, Haldane and **Trotter.** 39457. Corrections for the effects of atmospheric conditions of photometric flame standards.

Contarino. 39615. Effetto della deformazione che subisce la sezione di un fascio di luce parallela traversante l'atmosfera terrestre sulle misure fotometriche che si fanno su di esso.

Eitner. 39899. Die in Deutschland gebräuchlichen photometrischen Methoden.

Féry. 39988. Spectrophotomètre à absorption.

Franz. 40067. Methoden der Lichtprüfung in Schulen.

Gage. 40106. A heterochromatic photometer. 40108 : Radiant efficiency of arc lamps.

Geiger. 40166. Schwärzung und Photometrie photographischer Platten.

Goldberg. 40240. Herstellung neutral-grauer Keile und verlaufender Filter für Photometrie.

Gross. 40314. Lambertsches Kosinusgesetz. Diss.

Jadanza. 42734. Alcuni sistemi composti di due lenti. Livello di H. Wild.

Lummer und **Reiche.** 41234. Abbildung nichtselbstleuchtender Objekte (Bildentstehung im Mikroskop).

Orlandini. 41691. Decorso dei raggi e formazione delle imagini dopo rifrazione attraverso un mezzo diottrico centralmente opaco.

3060 MIRRORS AND LENSES.

Coblentz. 39590. Preservation of silver mirrors.

Heiberg und **Wiedemann.** 40465. Eine arabische Schrift über parabolische Hohlspiegel.

Hulbert and **Bacon.** 40587. A liquid concave mirror.

Rohr. 42168. Verbesserungen an den optischen Systemen der Cystoskope.

Ujj. 42858. Experimentelle Bestimmung der Hauptpunkte und Hauptflächen der Linsensysteme. (Ungar.)

Wood. 43188. Nickeled glass reflectors for celestial photography.

Würschmidt. 43219. Brennkugel.

3070 ABERRATIONS, SPHERICAL AND CHROMATIC. DISTORTION, Etc. ACHROMATISM.

Blein. 39281. Aberrations dans le miroir parabolique.

Boulouch. 39355. Images stigmatiques des points d'un petit volume situé autour de l'axe d'un système centré. 39356 : La relation des sinus de Abbe est une condition de stigmatisme. Condition de l'aplanétisme vrai.

Carvallo. 39507. Goniomètre.

Harting. 40430. Theorie des sekundären Spektrums.

Hinrichs. 40527. Theorie der natürlichen Blende optischer Instrumente.

Lange. 40997. Umformung der Seidelschen Bildfehlerausdrücke. 40998: Entwickelung des ersten Gliedes der Aberration endlich geöffneter Lichtbüschel für den Achsenobjektpunkt einer lichtbrechenden Rotationsfläche, deren Querschnitt ein Kegelschnitt ist.

Southall. 42581. Abolition of two of the spherical errors of a thin lenssystem.

3080 TELESCOPES, FIELD GLASSES.

Abetti. 38886. Modo di illuminare il campo oppure il reticolo di un refrattore.

Borletti. 39331. Metodi per determinare l'ingrandimento di un cannocchiale astronomico.

Ferrara. 39982. Sistema di cannocchiale a due obbiettivi.

Hnatek. 40534. 38 cm-Objektiv.

Hofe. 40539. Fernoptik.

Kreybig. 40915. Hand-Prismenfernrohre. (Ungarisch.)

Kühl. 40933. Abhängigkeit der Sternhelligkeit von der Okularvergrösserung.

Panther. 41740. Zielfernrohr.

Pritschow. 41958. Dioptriceinteilung an optischen Instrumenten.

Somma. 42573. Il cannocchiale geometrico.

Violette et alii. 42917. Lunette de pointage pour pièces marines de petit calibre.

3082 MICROSCOPES.

Ignatowsky. 40614. Zur Geschichte des Kardioidkondensors.

Köhler. 40848. Neue Nernstlampe.

Koenigsberger. 40860. Erkennung submikroskopischer Strukturen.

Lummer und **Reiche.** 41234. Abbildung nichtselbstleuchtender Objekte (Bildentstehung im Mikroskop).

Mandelstam. 41305. Theorie der mikroskopischen Bilderzeugung.

Reichert. 42057. [Apparate zur Dunkelfeldbeleuchtung.]. 42058 : Das Fluoreszenzmikroskop.

Volkmann. 42946. Ablesemikroskope.

Wulfing. 43214. Konstanten der Konometer.

Zeleny and **McKeehan.** 43264. A microscope plate micrometer.

3084 EYE-PIECES.

Müller. 41539. Die Geschichte der Dioptrien.

3085 PHOTOGRAPHIC LENSES AND SYSTEMS.

Angewandte Photographie von K. W. **Wolf-Czapek** r. 0030.

Un progresso nella fotografia stereoscopica. Apparecchio a grandissimo angolo. Prog. fotogr. Milano 17 1910 (179-183).

Albert. 38912. Astigmatismo e costruzioni ottiche anastigmatiche. 38913 : Il diaframma e la limitazione dei raggi negli obbiettivi fotografici.

Aue. 39008. Bestimmung der allgemeinen Konstanten eines photographischen Objektives.

Bordoni. 39327. Impiego dei comuni obbiettivi fotografici per riproduzioni alla luce artificiale.

Eichberg. 39880. Apparecchio per la fotografia metrica.

Frey. 40081. Die Prüfung photographischer Objektive.

Gleichen. 40217. Helligkeit photographischer Objektive. 40218, 21 : Helligkeit, Tiefe und richtiger Betrachtungsabstand bei photographischen Aufnahmen. 40219 : Richtiger Betrachtungsabstand und perspektivische Übertreibung. 40220 : Scheinbare perspektivische Anomalie. 40222 : Optik in der Photographie.

Goldberg. 40239. Preparazione di prismi o di schermi di tono grigio neutro per usi fotometrici.

Heimstädt. 40468. Spiegelreflexkamera für mikrophotographische Zwecke. 40469 : Satzanastigmate aus drei miteinander verkitteten Linsen.

Holl. 40547. Verschlussgeschwindigkeit und Lichtverlust.

Hoyer. 40579. Tiefenschärfe bei konstantem Abbildungsmassstab.

Kämpf. 40707. Historische Entwicklung des photographischen Objektives.

Kerber. 40764. Ein von P. Rudolph berechnetes Planar. 40765 : Ein Doppelanastigmat aus Pariser Gläsern. 40766 : Abänderung des Doppelanastigmaten aus Pariser Gläsern. 40767 :

Ein Aplanat aus Jenaer Gläsern. 40768 : Ein Dreimenisken-Objektiv.

Liesegang. 41130. Rationelle Einstellung und Abblendung des photographischen Objektivs.

Nakamura. 41557. Camera for a complete panoramic view.

Pfenninger. 41823. Historisches über die Farbenkamera.

Piergrossi. 41838. Modo di regolare i contrasti in fotomicrografia.

Pizzighelli. 41868. Strumenti ottici usati in fotografia. 41870 : La fotografia a grandi distanze colla Téléphot-Camera. 41873 : Obbiettivi, condensatori e sorgenti di luce per ingrandimento.

Quentin. 41982. Drachenphotographie.

Rayleigh. 42027. Problem of photographic reproduction, with suggestions for enhancing gradation originally invisible.

Eder. 39863 ; **Becker.** 39148 ; **Nonn.** 41640 ; **Seddig.** 42472. Photographie.

Süring. 42706. Ballonphotographie.

Trabacchi. 42816. Misure di velocità di otturatori fotografici.

Vogel. 42925. Taschenbuch der Photographie.

Wimmer. 43158. Praxis der Makro- und Mikro-Projektion.

Zschokke. 43297. Miniaturkameras.

3090 OPTICAL APPARATUS NOT SCHEDULED ELSEWHERE. STEREOSCOPE.

Eijkman. 39886A. Anwendungen der Stereoskopie. 39887 : Symphanometrie in der Parallaxaufnahme.

Elias. 39901. Theorie lichtstarker Monochromatoren.

Hofe. 40539. Fernoptik.

Jachino. 40645A. Telemetro.

Köhler. 40847. Flüssigkeitskondensoren von grosser Apertur.

Lehmann. 41073 : **Wolf-Czapek.** 43175. Kinematographie.

Löwe. 41175. Reflexionsprisma mit scharfer Kante.

Montefinale. 41484. Goniometro panoramico a doppia visione.

Pigeon. 41839. Un stéréoscope à coulisses.

Pulfrich. 41973 : **Seliger.** 42489. Stereoskopisches Sehen und Messen.

Rayner. 42030. An optical lever of high power suitable for the determinations of small thicknesses and displacements.

Rohr. 42166. Das Biotar.

Scarpa. 42327. Ultramicroscopi a riflessione totale.

Searle. Aldis and **Dobson.** 42468. A revolving table method of determining the curvature of spherical surfaces.

Smirnov. 42537. Lunettes pour voir dans l'eau. (Russ.)

Winterstein. 43161. Linsen mit veränderlicher Krümmung.

Wülfing. 43216. Projektion mikroskopischer Objekte im polarisierten Licht.

APPARATUS FOR SPECTRUM ANALYSIS.

3150　GENERAL.

Fabinyi. 39965. Die Spektralanalyse und ihre Anwendung. (Ungarisch.)

Ley. 41121.

3155　PRISMS.

Fery. 39987. A prism with curved faces, for spectrograph or spectroscope.

Knothe. 40824. Optische Erscheinungen und Strahlenwege am Prisma.

Krüss. 40925. Spektrophotometer und Farbenmisch-Apparat.

3160　GRATINGS.

Anderson and **Sparrow.** 38957. Effect of the groove form on the distribution of light by a grating.

Biske. 39271. Krümmung der Spektrallinien beim Plangitter.

Eagle. 39845. On the curvature of the spectrum lines in a concave grating. 39846 : Neue Konkavgitter-Anordnung.

Goos. 40261. Dispersion und Ausmessung von Konkavgitterspektrogrammen.

Papenfus. 41742. Die Brauchbarkeit der Koinzidenzmethode zur Messung von Wellenlängen.

Paschen. 41762. Wellenlängenmessung ultraroter Spektrallinien.

Trowbridge. 42835. Echelette grating.

3165　SPECIAL SPECTROSCOPIC APPARATUS.

du Bois. 39807. Geradsichtiger lichtstarker Monochromator.

———— und **Elias.** 39811. Hochdispergierender lichtstarker Monochromator und Spektralapparat.

Elias. 39901. Theorie lichtstarker Monochromatoren.

Füchtbauer. 40094. Methode zur Untersuchung von Absorptionslinien mit dem Stufengitter.

Gehlhoff. 40150. Methode zur Erzeugung von Metallspektren in der Glimmentladung.

Gehrcke. 40153 : **Humphreys.** 40591. Anwendung der Zylinderlinse in Spektralapparaten.

Goldberg. 40240. Herstellung neutral-grauer Keile und verlaufender Filter.

Goldstein. 40255. Zur Orientierung an Spektrogrammen.

Goos. 40260. Toepferscher Messapparat für Spetrogramme.

Koch. 40842. Montierungsverfahren für Etalons nach Fabry und Perot.

Lehmann. 41070, 41072. Das UV-Filter und die UV-Filterlampe als Apparate zur Lumineszenzanalyse. 41071 : Fernspektroskop.

Leiss. 41088. Monochromator. 41089 : Ultrarot-Spektrometer.

Meslin. 41417. Pouvoir dispersif des combinaisons de prismes. Application aux spectroscopes.

Pokrowsky. 41918. Spektrohelioskop.

Tikhoff. 42794. L'enregistrement photographique et la reproduction de la scintillation des étoiles.

3420 ABERRATION AND MOVING MEDIA.

Belopolsky. 39169. Durée de rotation de la planète Vénus sur elle-même.

Budde. 39441. Das Dopplersche Prinzip für bewegte Spiegel und ein Versuch von Klinkerfues. 39442 : Zur Theorie des Michelsonschen Versuches.

Cotton. 39643, 59647. Doppler's principle : radial velocities on the sun.

Deslandres. 39738. Mouvements des couches atmosphériques solaires par le déplacement des raies spectrales. 39739, 39740 : Explication des protubérances solaires par des champs magnétiques très faibles. 39741 : Ionisation des gaz solaires. Relations entre le rayonnement et la rotation des corps célestes. 39742. 39744 : Mouvements des protubérances solaires.

————— et d'Azambuja. 39743. Vitesse de rotation des filaments noirs dans la couche supérieure de l'atmosphère solaire.

Dufour. 39825. Rotation spontanée dans un champ magnétique de l'arc à mercure.

Giuganino. 40202. Action de la translation terrestre sur les phénomènes lumineux.

Grünbaum. 40323 ; **Riecke.** 42109. Michelsonscher Interferenzversuch.

Laue. 41021. Zur Optik der bewegten Körper.

Perot. 41802. Spectroscopie solaire. 41803 : Les principes de Doppler-Fizeau et de W. Michelson et les raies d'absorption.

Pokrowsky. 41921. Das Dopplersche Prinzip.

Poynting. 41951. On small longitudinal material waves accompanying light waves.

Rayleigh. 42024. Aberration in a dispersive medium.

Sagnac. 42292, 42293, 42295. Systèmes optiques en mouvement et la translation de la Terre. 42296 : Limite supérieure d'un effet tourbillonnaire optique du à un entraînement de l'éther lumineux au voisinage de la Terre.

3430 MEASUREMENT OF WAVE-LENGTH OF RAYS IN THE LUMINOUS SPECTRUM.

Eversheim. 39958. Messungen im Eisenspektrum.

Exner und Haschek. 39961. Wellenlängentabellen.

Goos. 40261. Ausmessung von Konkavgitterspektrogrammen.

Kayser, Fabry and **Ames.** 40750, 40749. Additional secondary standards, international system, in the arc spectrum of iron.

Moir. 41477. Absorption-spectrum of oxygen and a new law of spectra.

Papenfus. 41742. Brauchbarkeit der Koinzidenzmethode zur Messung von Wellenlängen.

Perot. 41804. Longueur d'onde de la raie solaire D_1.

————— et **Lindstedt.** 41805. Longueur d'onde de la raie solaire b_2.

3435 MEASUREMENT OF WAVE-LENGTH OF INFRA-RED RAYS.

Exner und Haschek. 39961.

Paschen. 41762, 41763.

Randall. 42008. Infra-red spectra.

Rubens und Baeyer. 42228, 42229. Eine äusserst langwellige Strahlung des Quecksilberdampfs.

————— and **Wood.** 42232. Focal isolation of long heat-waves.

3440 MEASUREMENT OF WAVE-LENGTH OF ULTRA-VIOLET RAYS.

Exner und Haschek. 39961.

Lyman. 41250. Spectra of some gases in the Schumann region.

Miethe und Seegert. 41455. Wellenlängenmessungen an einigen Platinmetallen.

INTERFERENCE AND DIFFRACTION.

3600 GENERAL.

Michelson. 41446. Lichtwellen.

Pfund. 41827.

Squier and **Crehore.** 42587. Oscillatory interference bands.

Stark. 42603. Zahl der Zentren von Lichtemission und Intensitätsverhältnis verschiedener Interferenzordnungen. III.

Zakrzewski. 43237. Das Halbschatteninterferometer als Photometer.

3610 INTERFERENCE. INTERFERENTIAL REFRACTOMETERS. COLOURS OF THIN SHEETS.

Arons. 38999. Chromoskop.

Barus. 39096. Elliptic interference in connection with reflecting grating. 39100 : Elliptic interferences in relation to interferometry.

Cotton. 39645. La sensibilité des mesures interférentielles et les moyens de l'accroitre ; appareils interférentiels à pénombre.

Grünbaum. 40323. Zur Darstellung des Michelsonschen Interferenzversuches.

Kaemmerer. 40706. Interferenzerscheinungen an Platten optisch aktiver, isotroper, durchsichtiger Kristalle [Natriumchlorat] im konvergenten polarisierten Licht.

Koch. 40839. Messung der Intensitätsverteilung in Spektrallinien mit Anwendungen auf Interferenzspektroskopie. 40842 : Einfaches Montierungsverfahren für Etalons nach Fabry und Perot.

Meslin. 41416. L'emploi des prismes biréfringents pour obten'r des franges d'interférence.

Pokrowsky. 41920. Anwendung des polarisierten Lichtes in der Interferometrie. 41924 : Halbschatteninterferometrie.

Raveau. 42018. Calcul de la différence de marche introduite par une lame mince isotrope.

Riecke. 42109 : **Budde.** 39442. Theorie des Interferenzversuches von Michelson.

Sagnac. 42294, 42297. Strioscopie et striographie interférentielles.

Schulz. 42431. Interferenzerscheinung im parallelen Licht. 42432 : Interferenzpunkte an einem System rechtwinkliger Prismen.

Selényi. 42486. Theorie der Polarisation des von Glasgittern gebeugten Lichtes. 42488 : Wiener'sche und reciproke Interferenzerscheinungen. (Ungarisch.)

Skinner und **Tuckerman.** 42530. Halbschatteninterferometer.

Stark. 42602. Schwärzungsgesetz der Normalbelichtung und photographische Spektralphotometrie. 42603 : Zahl der Zentren von Lichtemission und Intensitätsverhältnis verschiedener Interferenzordnungen. III.

Volkmann. 42949. Fresnelscher Interferenzspiegel.

Waetzmann und **Lummer.** 42974. Interferenzkurven gleicher Neigung.

Wetthauer. 43105. Breite und Ort der Interferenzstreifen bei keilförmigen Blättchen.

3620 DIFFRACTION

Leimbach. 41085. Neue Methode zur Verminderung der schädlichen Wärmestrahlen im Projektionsapparat.

Raman. 41999. Photometric measurements of the obliquity factor ot diffraction.

Reiche. 42056. Beugung des Lichtes an einem ebenen, rechteckigen Keil von unendlicher Leitfähigkeit.

Selényi. 42486. Theorie der Polarisation des von Glasgittern gebeugten Lichtes.

Trowbridge and **Crandall.** 42836. Groove-form and energy distribution of diffraction gratings.

3630 SPECTRA FORMED BY DIFFRACTION AND BY GRATINGS.

Biske. 39271. Krümmung der Spektrallinien beim Plangitter.

Eagle. 39845. Curvature of the spectrum lines in a concave grating.

Klughardt. 40816. Erscheinungen, die bei der Beugung des Lichtes durch Gitter auftreten.

Koch. 40841. Zahl der Zentren von Lichtemission und Intensitätsverhältnis verschiedener Interferenzordnungen.

Leimbach. 41085.

Lummer und **Reiche.** 41234. Abbildung nichtselbstleuchtender Objekte (Bildentstehung im Mikroskop).

Pogány. 41902. 41903. Polarisation des von Metallgittern gebeugten Lichtes.

Schaefer und **Reiche.** 42342. Theorie des Beugungsgitters.

Trowbridge. 42835. Echelette grating.

Voigt. 42934. Rayleigh's Theorie der Gitterbeugung.

Woltke. 43182. Abbildung eines Gitters bei künstlicher Begrenzung. 43183: Abbildung eines Gitters bei asymmetrischer Abblendung. 43184: Abbildung eines durchlässigen Gitters.

3640 DIFFRACTION BY SMALL PARTICLES. THEORY OF RAINBOW, OPTICAL RESONANCE, Etc.

Busch und **Jensen.** 39453. Atmosphärische Polarisation.

König. 40855. Apparat zur Demonstration des Strahlenganges beim Regenbogen.

3650 DEFINITION OF OPTICAL INSTRUMENTS. GENERAL THEORY.

Lummer und **Reiche.** 41234. Abbildung nichtselbstleuchtender Objekte (Bildentstehung im Mikroskop).

Mandelstam. 41305; **Lummer.** 41235. Abbesche Theorie der mikroskopischen Bilderzeugung.

Woltke. 43184. Abbildung eines durchlässigen Gitters.

REFLEXION, REFRACTION, AND ABSORPTION OF RADIATION.

(*See also* 3320, 3030.)

3800 GENERAL.

Bahr und **Koenigsberger.** 39049. Farbe anorganischer Salze und Berechnung der schwingenden Teile.

Bôhle. 39309. Effects of uniformity and contrast on light.

Fleissner. 40011. Trübe Medien.

Havelock. 40453. Optical dispersion: its dependence upon physical conditions.

Hertz. 40496. Absorption ultraroter Strahlung durch Gase.

Humphreys. 40590. Certain laws of radiation and absorption.

Julius. 40702. Selektive Absorption und anomale Zerstreuung (Diffusion) des Lichtes in ausgedehnten Gasmassen. Theorie des Sonnenspektrums.

Koenigsberger. 40857. Bestimmung der Zahl schwingender Teile in Dämpfen, Lösungen, leuchtenden Gasen.

———— und **Müller.** 40871. Bestimmung des Molekulardurchmessers: minimale optische wirksame Schichtdicke.

Neumann. 41595. Werke.

Roth und **Eisenlohr.** 42213. Refraktometrisches Hilfsbuch.

Salet. 42299. Diffusion de la lumière du Soleil par les météorites.

Stephenson. 42639. Absorption and dispersion.

Voigt. 42934. Rayleigh's Theorie der Gitterbeugung.

3810 REFLECTING AND ABSORBING POWERS OF MATERIALS. IRREGULAR REFLEXION.

Bell. 39164. Opacity of certain glasses for the ultra violet.

Eberhard. 39849. Verwendung des Spurgeschen Röhrenphotometers für photometrische Messungen.

Hantzsch. 40419. Colorimetrisches Verdünnungsgesetz.

Hecht. 40461. Spektrometrische Untersuchung eines Gemisches mehrerer lichtabsorbierender Stoffe.

Houstoun. 40572. Absolute Lichtmessung.

Frëedericksz. 40072. Dispersion und Absorption in Chrom und Mangan.

Kaempf. 40708. Fluoreszenzabsorption und Lambertsches Absorptionsgesetz beim Fluoreszein.

Keesom. 40751. Spektrophotometrische Untersuchung der Opaleszenz eines einkomponentigen Stoffes in der Nähe des kritischen Zustandes.

Koenigsberger und **Küpferer.** 40861. Absorption des Lichtes in festen und gasförmigen Körpern.

Lasareff. 41019. Ausbleichen von Farbstoffen im sichtbaren Spektrum.

Lindholm. 41153. Loi de Beer sur l'absorption dans le spectre infrarouge.

Müller. 41525. Farbe der Silberpartikelchen in kolloidalen Ag-Lösungen, berechnet aus der Mieschen Theorie.

Okada and **Yoshida.** 41671. Pyrheliometric observations on the summit and at the base of Mt. Fuji.

Pihlblad. 41840. Lichtabsorption in Silberhydrosolen.

Pirani. 41850. Optische temperaturmessungen. 41851 : Absorptionsvermögen der Auermasse.

Reinkober. 42070. Absorption und Reflexion ultraroter Strahlen durch Quarz, Turmalin und Diamant.

Ruff. 42251. Lichtdurchlässigkeit von Gemischen mehrerer lichtabsorbierender Stoffe.

Schell. 42367. Photographisch-photometrische Absorptionsmessungen an Jodsilber im ultravioletten Spektrum.

Schmidt. 42387. Optische Eigenschaften von Flussspath, Schwefel, Phosphor u. Selen. Diss.

Schröder. 42419. Quantitative Messungen des Absorptionsvermögens des Natrium-Dampfes.

Selényi. 42485. Lichtzerstreuung im Raume Wienerscher Interferenzen.

Stewart und **Wright.** 42652. Einfluss des Lösungsmittels und der Verdünnung auf die Gültigkeit des Beerschen Gesetzes.

Stobbe und **Reuss.** 42662. Lichtrefraktion der Allo- und Isozimtsäuren.

Wheeler. 43108. Reflexion of light at certain metal-liquid surfaces.

Wigand. 43134. Die umkehrbare Lichtreaktion des Schwefels.

3820 DYNAMICAL THEORY OF REFLEXION AND REFRACTION IN TRANSPARENT MEDIA. POLARIZATION BY REFLEXION.

Forsterling. 40024. Formeln zur Berechnung der optischen Konstanten einer Metallschicht von beliebiger Dicke aus den Polarisationszuständen des reflektierten und des durchgegangenen Lichts.

Galli und **Forsterling.** 40124. Optisches Verhalten dünnster Metallschichten.

Pogány. 41903. Polarisationsverhältnisse des von Metallgittern gebeugten Lichtes.

Rayleigh. 42028. Propagation of waves through a stratified medium : reflexion. 42029 : Departures from Fresnel's laws of reflexion.

Richardson. 42099. Theory of dispersion and the residual rays.

Sangster. 42315. Consequences of Fresnel's reflection of light theory, with formulæ for determining the angles of incidence in order to reflect 1 nth the incident light.

Schwietring. 42463. Polarisationswinkel der durchsichtigen inaktiven Kristalle.

Selényi. 42486, 42487. Theorie der Polarisation des von Glasgittern gebeugten Lichtes.

Terlanday. 42759. Nachbildung der Doppelbrechung mittels Glasplatten. (Ungar.)

Voigdt. 42928. Gültigkeitsbereich der Fresnelschen Reflexions-formeln.

Weber. 43018. Kontinuität zwischen Brechung und Reflexion.

Wright. 43210. Durchgang des Lichtes durch inaktive durchsichtige Krystallplatten : Erscheinungen im konvergent polarisierten Lichte.

3822 REFRACTION : INFLUENCE OF TEMPERATURE, DENSITY AND CHANGE OF STATE.

Ambronn. 38944, 38945. Anomale Doppelbrechung beim Zelluloid. 38946 : Dispersion der Doppelbrechung in zweiphasigen Systemen.

Brauns. 39388. Aenderung des optischen Achsenwinkels in Gips bei höherer Temperatur.

Coker. 39599. Photo-elasticity.

Eykman. 39963. Recherches réfractométriques. (Hollandais.)

Gaubert. 40143. Indices de réfraction des cristaux liquides mixtes.

Gutton. 40371. Vitesse de la lumière dans les milieux réfringents.

Liebreich. 41127, 41128. Veränderung der Brechungsexponenten mit der Temperatur im ultraroten Gebiete bei Steinsalz, Sylvin und Fluorit.

Rinne und Kolb. 42145. Optisches zur Modifikationsänderung von α- in β-Quarz sowie von α- in β-Leucit.

Rosický. 42191. Beziehungen zwischen Dichtigkeit und Lichtbrechung. (Čechisch.)

Schwers. 42457, 42459. Densité, rotation magnétique et réfraction chez les mélanges binaires dissociés.

Wülfing. 43215. Lichtbrechung des Kanadabalsams.

3824 TOTAL REFLEXION.

Eichenwald. 39882. Bewegung der Energie bei Totalreflexion. (Russ.)

Voigt. 42930. Schwingungen im zweiten Medium bei totaler Reflexion. 42932 : Totalreflexion.

3830 REFRACTION IN CRYSTALLINE MEDIA.

Ambronn. 38945. Anomale Doppelbrechung beim Zelluloid.

Baumhauer. 39127. Krystallographisch-optische Untersuchungen.

Boussinesq. 39367. Construction simple (en recourant seulement aux deux ellipsoïdes inverse et direct) de la vibration du rayon lumineux et de la vitesse de ce rayon, pour chacun des deux systèmes d'ondes planes de direction donnée propagés dans un cristal transparent.

Brauns. 39388. Aenderung des optischen Achsenwinkels in Gips bei höherer Temperatur.

Kaemmerer. 40706. Interferenzerscheinungen an Platten optisch aktiver, isotroper, durchsichtiger Kristalle [Na-

triumchlorat] im konvergenten polarisierten Licht.

Kolb. 40883. Vergleich von Anhydrit, Cölestin, Baryt und Anglesit in bezug auf die Veränderung ihrer geometrischen und optischen Verhältnisse mit der Temperatur.

Lehmann. 41074. Molekularstruktur und Optik grosser flüssiger Kristalle. 41076 : Konische Strukturstörungen bei flüssigen Pseudokristallen. 41077 : Struktur und Optik grosser Kristalltropfen.

Liebreich. 41127, 41128. Optische Temperaturkoeffizienten für Steinsalz, Sylvin und Fluorit im Bereiche der tieferen Temperaturen.

Mauguin. 41372. O. Lehmanns flüssige Kristalle.

Paschen. 41761. Dispersion des Quarzes im Ultrarot.

Rinne und Kolb. 42145. Optisches zur Modifikationsänderung von α- in β-Quarz sowie von α- in β-Leucit.

Schmidt. 42387. Optische Eigenschaften von Flussspath, Schwefel, Phosphor u. Selen.

Signorini. 42512. Vibrazioni luminose di un mezzo cristallino uniassico dovute alla presenza di un unico centro luminoso.

Stumpf. 42698. Optische Beobachtungen an einer flüssig-kristallinischen aktiven Substanz.

Terlanday. 42759 Nachbildung der Doppelbrechung mittels Glasplatten. (Ungar.)

Vorländer und **Huth.** 42951. Charakter der Doppelbrechung flüssiger Kristalle.

Wright. 43210. Durchgang des Lichtes durch inaktive durchsichtige Krystallplatten : Erscheinungen im konvergent polarisierten Lichte.

Wülfing. 43215. Lichtbrechung des Kanadabalsams.

3835 REFRACTION IN STRAINED MEDIA.

Ambronn. 38946. Dispersion der Doppelbrechung in zweiphasigen Systemen.

Kreutz. 40913. Piezooptisches Verhalten von Salmiak.

Rossi. 42203, 42204, 42205, 42206, 42208; Cantone. 39486. La doppia rifrazione accidentale di talune sostanze studiata in rapporto al loro comportamento elastico.

Zeeman. 43253. Insulating power of liquid air for high potentials. Kerr electro effect in liquid air.

———— and Hoogenboom. 43255. Electric double refraction in some artificial clouds and vapours.

3840 METALLIC REFLEXION.

Coblentz. 39590. Reflecting power of various metals.

Forsterling. 40024. Formeln zur Berechnung der optischen Konstanten einer Metallschicht von beliebiger Dicke aus den Polarisations-zuständen des reflektierten und des durchgegangenen Lichts.

Freedericksz. 40072. Dispersion und Absorption in Chrom und Mangan für das sichtbare und ultraviolette Spektrum. 40073: Beziehungen zwischen den optischen Konstanten und dem Eigenpotential der Metalle.

Galli und Forsterling. 40124. Optisches Verhalten dünnster Metallschichten.

Pogány. 41902-41903. Polarisation des von Metallgittern gebeugten Lichtes.

Randall. 42009. Residual rays of selenite.

Voigt. 42934. Rayleigh's Theorie der Gitterbeugung.

3850 SELECTIVE REFLECTION AND ABSORPTION, INCLUDING OBJECTIVE COLOUR. DICHROISM. ANOMALOUS DISPERSION.

Ambronn. 38944, 38945. Anomale Doppelbrechung beim Zelluloid.

Arrhenius. 38994. Conditions physiques de la planète Mars.

Auwers. 39025. Spektrochemie der Enole und Enol-Derivate.

Auwers. 39026: Spektrochemisches Verhalten und Konstitution des Acetessigesters. 39027: Spektrochemie ungesättigter Verbindungen. 39028: I. Refraktion und Dispersion von organischen Substanzen mit mehreren isolierten Doppelbindungen; von Auwers und Morsbrugger. II. Spektrochemische Unterscheidung hydroaromatischer Verbindungen mit cicloeyclischer und mit semicyclischer Doppelbindung; von Auwers und Ellinger. III. Konstitution des Camphens; von Auwers.

Bahr. 39048. Veränderung von Absorptionslinien durch fremde Gase.

Boussinesq. 39364, 39368. Calcul de l'absorption dans les cristaux translucides.

Brahat. 39427. Dichroïsme rotatoire du diphényl-c-bornyldithiouréthane.

Clark. 39569. Selective reflection of salts of chromium acids.

Cotton. 39646. Dichroïsme circulaire et polarisation rotatoire.

Cremer. 39658. Das absorptionsspektrum des Toluols im Ultravioletten.

du Bois. 39809. Der verallgemeinerte Zeemaneffekt in selektiv absorbierenden Körpern.

———— und Elias. 39810. Einfluss von Temperatur und Magnetisierung bei selektiven Absorptions- und Fluoreszenzspektren.

Elias. 39900. Anomale magnetische Drehungsdispersion und selektive Absorption.

Evans and Antonoff. 39954. The absorption spectrum of selenium vapor, and the effect of temperature upon it.

Füchtbauer. 40094. Über eine Methode zur Untersuchung von Absorptionslinien mit dem Stufengitter und über die Veränderung von Absorptions-linien durch fremde Gase.

Goldschmidt. 40253. Lichtkreis und Lichtknoten an Kristallkugeln. [Almandin; Beryll; Rosenquarz.]

Hertz. 40496. Absorption ultraroter Strahlung durch Gase.

Houstoun. 40569. Aqueous solutions of nickel salts in the visible spectrum and the infra red.

———— and Anderson. 40573. Aqueous solutions of cobalt and nickel salts in the ultra-violet.

———— and Brown. 40574. Aqueous solutions of cobalt salts in the visible spectrum.

Dispersion der Doppelbrechung in zweiphasigen Systemen.

Auwers *et alii.* 39025-9 ; Eisenlohr. 39897 ; **Ellinger.** 39962. Spektro chemische Untersuchungen.

Bahr und **Koenigsberger.** 39049. Farbe anorganischer Salze und Berechnung der schwingenden Teile.

Bell. 39164. Opacity of certain glasses for the ultra violet.

Berget. 39192. Détermination précise de la salinité des eaux de mer par la mesure de l'indice de réfraction.

Bonacini. 39318. Tricromia.

Coblentz. 39586. Water of crystallization.

Cremer. 39658. Absorptionsspektrum des Toluols im Ultravioletten.

Dickson. 39758. Ultraviolette Fluoreszenz des Benzols.

Duval. 39841. Réfraction moléculaire de composés azoïques.

Ebert. 39851 ; **Murawski.** 41543 ; **Moosbrugger.** 41494. Optische Untersuchungen ungesättigter organischer Verbindungen.

Enklaar. 39918. Réfraction moléculaire et structure des hydrocarbures à plusieurs groupes éthénoïdes. (Hollandais.)

Evans and **Antonoff.** 39954. Absorption spectrum of selenium vapor and effect of temperature upon it.

Féry. 39988. Spectrophotomètre à absorption.

Fredenhagen. 40070. Beeinflussung der Absorption des Natriumdampfes durch neutrale Gase.

Fry. 40091-2. Dynamische Formeln und das Ultraviolettabsorptionsspektrum des Benzols und des Naphtalins.

Galissot. 40117. L'absorption sélective de l'atmosphère.

Gruschke. 40337. 40338. Brechung und Dispersion des Lichtes in einigen Gasen.

Hantzsch. 40419. Das colorimetrische Verdünnungsgesetz.

———— und **Shibata.** 40420. Farbenwechsel der Kobaltsalze.

———— und **Voigt.** 40421. Konjugierte aci-Nitrokörper.

Harrison. 40429. Farbe und Dispersitätsgrad kolloider Lösungen.

Hecht. 40461. Spektrometrische Untersuchung eines Gemisches mehrerer lichtabsorbierender Stoffe.

Houstoun. 40568. Aqueous solutions of cobalt salts in the infra-red. 40569 : Aqueous solutions of nickel salts in the visible spectrum and the infra-red.

———— and **Anderson.** 40573. Aqueous solutions of cobalt and nickel salts in the ultra violet.

———— and **Brown.** 40574. Aqueous solutions of cobalt salts in the visible spectrum.

Hübl. 40583. Ist eine farblose Dunkelkammerbeleuchtung möglich ?

Jones and **Strong.** 40680. Spectres d'absorption des solutions. Possibilité d'une méthode pour déterminer la présence de composés intermédiaires dans les réactions chimiques. 40681 : Absorption spectra of solutions of certain salts as affected by chemical agents and by temperature.

Koch. 40834. Absorptionsspektrum des Anilins im Ultravioletten. 40835 : Reflexion des Lichtes an Kalkspat in der Nähe von dessen metallischer Reflexionsbande bei ca. 6, 6, μ 1.

Koenigsberger und **Küpferer.** 40864. Absorption des Lichtes in festen und gasförmigen Körpern.

Kowalski. 40901. Phosphoreszenz organischer Verbindungen bei tiefen Temperaturen.

Krumhaar. 40930. Optische Untersuchungen über Carboniumsalze.

Langford. 41002. Selective reflection of ortho-, meta- and pyrophosphates in the infra-red spectrum.

Leonard. 41103 ; **Meyer** u. **Wieland.** 41434 ; **Meyer.** 41436 ; **Stobbe** u. **Ebert.** 42660 ; **Voigt.** 42929. Absorptionsspektren einiger organischer Verbindungen.

Ley. 41121. Beziehungen zwischen Farbe und Konstitution bei organischen Verbindungen.

Lippmann. 41157. Elektrische Doppelbrechung in Flüssigkeiten und ihre Beziehung zu chemischer Konstitution.

Mcir. 41477. Absorption-spectrum of oxygen and a new law of spectra.

Nikolopulos. 41628. Beziehungen zwischen den Absorptionsspektren und der Konstitution der Wernerschen Salze.

Ostwald. 41710. Farbe und Dispersitätsgrad kolloider Lösungen.

Peters. 41815. Hydroaromatische Substanzen mit konjugierten Doppelbindungen.

Pirani. 41853. Photometrierung verschiedenfarbiger Lichtquellen.

Poma. 41931. Colore e idratazione.

Röhrs. 42158. Molekularrefraktion, Molekularvolumen und Dissoziation in nichtwässerigen Lösungsmitteln.

Rubien. 42234. Brechungsexponent für Natriumlicht und Dissoziationsgrad wässeriger Salzlösungen.

Ruff. 42250-2. Nachweis neuer Verbindungen auf spektrometrischem Wege.

Schalamberidse. 42347. Chromoisomerie von Nitro-Anilinen und Nitro-Acetaniljnen sowie Nitro-Phenoläther. Zustand des dampfförmigen, flüssigen und gelösten Acetons auf Grund von optischen Messungen.

Scheiber. 42366. Homologie von Anthranil und Methylanthranil.

Schulze. 42436. Langwelliges Refraktionsvermögen binärer Gemische.

Schwers. 42457. Densité, polarisation rotatoire magnétique et indice de réfraction des mélanges binaires. 42461 : Densità e rifrazione nel sistema furfurolo acqua. 42462 : Indice di rifrazione dei miscugli binari.

Staiger. 42593. Optische Veränderungen von Azo- und Nitrokörpern durch Lösungsmittel und Aggregatzustand. [Absorptionsspektren von Diazokörpern.]

Stewart und **Wright.** 42652. Absorptionsspektren : Einfluss des Lösungsmittels und der Verdünnung auf die Gültigkeit des Beerschen Gesetzes.

Strong. 42686. Spectroscopic evidences of molecular clustering.

Svedberg und **Andreen - Svedberg.** 42714. Diffusionsgeschwindigkeit und relative Grösse gelöster Molekule.

Tchougaeff et **Koch.** 42754. Anomalie de la réfraction moléculaire dans la série des glyoximes substitutées.

Valla. 42877. Spettri di assorbimento di sali inorganici complessi.

Willstätter. 43147. Chlorophyll.

3070 ABERRATIONS. SPHERICAL AND CHROMATIC. DISTORTION, Etc. ACHROMATISM.

Foix. 40026. Construction de rayons marginaux dans les systèmes centrés aplanétiques.

3875 REFLEXION, REFRACTION AND ABSORPTION OF ELECTRIC RADIATION.

Andrejev. 38964. Dispersion gedämpfter Wellen. (Russ.)

Arndt. 38982. Methoden zur Bestimmung von Dielektrizitätskonstanten und Verfahren zur Erzeugung schwach gedämpfter Schwingungen.

Bahr. 39048. Veränderung von Absorptionslinien durch fremde Gase.

Barkla. 39077, 39078. The spectra of the fluorescent Röntgen radiations.

Baxmann. 39131. Absorption und Geschwindigkeitsverlust der β-Strahlen des Radiums.

Becker. 39146. Absorption der Kathodenstrahlen.

Koenigsberger und **Kutschewski.** 40870. Verhalten von Kanalstrahlen beim Durchgang durch Gase.

Lenard. 41094. Absorption der Nordlichtstrahlen in der Erdatmosphäre.

Merczyng. 41404-5. Elektrische Dispersion von Wasser und Äthylalkohol für sehr kurze Wellen. 41406, 9 : Brechung elektrischer Strahlen von sehr kurzer Wellenlänge in flüssiger Luft.

Rudolph. 42245. Erzeugung kurzer elektrischer Wellen mit Gleichstrom und ihre Verwendung zur Bestimmung von Dielektrizitätskonstanten und Absorptionen.

Schaefer. 42340. Beugung elektromagnetischer Wellen an isolierenden zylindrischen Hindernissen.

Wolff. 43180. Behandlung des Vorganges, dass eine ebene elektromagnetische Welle, die auf die ebene Oberfläche eines Körpers, insbesondere eines Leiters, auftrifft, von diesem reflektiert wird, auf Grund der Maxwellschen Gleichungen.

POLARISATION.

4000 GENERAL INSTRUMENTS AND METHODS.

Arons. 38990; **Haken.** 40397. Chromoskop.

du Bois und **Rubens.** 39812, 39814. Polarization of undiffracted long-waved heat rays by wire gratings.

Fischer. 40000. Mikropolarisation.

Friedel et **Grandjean.** 40084. Structure des liquides à coniques focales.

Gaubert. 40143. Indices de réfraction des cristaux liquides mixtes.

Krauss. 40909. Polarisation.

Meslin. 41416. L'emploi des prismes biréfringents pour obtenir des franges d'interférence.

Pokrowsky. 41920. Anwendung des polarisierten Lichtes in der Interferometrie. 41924; **Skinner** u. **Tuckerman.** 42530; Halbschatteninterferometrie.

Schulz. 42433. Polarisationsprismen aus Glas.

Selényi. 42487. Theorie der Polarisation des von Glasgittern gebeugten Lichtes.

Triepel. 42825. Modell der Schwingungsebenen des Lichtes im Polarisationsapparat.

Wright. 43210. Durchgang des Lichtes durch inaktive durchsichtige Krystallplatten; Erscheinungen im konvergent polarisierten Lichte.

4005 ELLIPTIC AND CIRCULAR POLARIZATION. GENERAL.

Padoa. 41725. Tentativo di sintesi asimmetrica con la luce polarizzata circolarmente.

Pogány. 41903. Polarisationsverhältnisse des von Metallgittern gebeugten Lichtes.

Pokrowsky. 41925. Ponderomotorische Wirkungen zirkularpolarisierter Strahlen.

(c-4388)

4010 PRODUCTION OF POLARIZED RADIATION.

du Bois und **Rubens.** 39812, 39814. Polarisation ungebeugter langwelliger Wärmestrahlen durch Drahtgitter.

Kern. 40770. Erzeugung von geradsichtigem, polarisiertem Licht durch einfache Glasprismen.

Koenigsberger. 40856. Polarisation des Lichtes an Gittern mit sehr kleiner Gitterkonstante.

Selényi. 42487. Polarisation des von Glasgittern gebeugten Lichtes. (Ungar.)

Vlès. 42920. Propriétés optiques des muscles.

4020 MEASUREMENT OF POLARIZED RADIATION.

du Bois und **Rubens.** 39812–4.

4030 RINGS AND BRUSHES OF CRYSTALS.

Mauguin. 41370. Liquides biréfringents à structure hélicoïdale. 41371; Orientation des cristaux liquides par le champ magnétique.

Schmutzer. 42399. Orientation of crystal sections with the help of the traces of two planes and the optic extinction. [Lines of optical extinction on crystal sections.] (English, Dutch.)

Wright. 43210. Durchgang des Lichtes durch inaktive durchsichtige Krystallplatten. Erscheinungen im konvergent polarisierten Lichte.

4040 ROTATORY POLARIZATION AND DISPERSION, STRUCTURAL AND MAGNETIC. GENERAL. (*See also* 6650, 6655.)

Brahat. 39427. Dichroïsme rotatoire du diphényl-ε-bornyldithiouréthane.

Cotton. 39646. Dichroïsme circulaire et polarisation rotatoire.

du Bois. 39809. L'effet Zeeman généralisé dans les absorbants sélectifs.

Elias. 39900. Anomale magnetische Drehungsdispersion und selektive Absorption.

Ewell. 39960. Rotationspolarisation durch Torsion.

Y

Hilditch. 40518. Wirkung molekularer Symmetrie auf die optische Aktivität und das relative Rotationsvermögen von aromatischen Stellungsisomeren.

Ladenburg. 40964. Stereochemie.

Landau. 40993. Einfluss des Lösungsmittels auf das Drehungsvermögen optisch-aktiver Körper.

Meslin. 41414. Double réfraction circulaire du chlorate de sodium. 41415 : Vitesses des circulaires inverses dans la polarisation rotatoire.

Profilo. 41960. L'azione degli idrati di sodio e di potassio nelle soluzioni di glucosio rispetto all'azione ottica.

Rossi. 42202. Influenza della temperatura sulle osservazioni polarimetriche.

Schwers. 42457-9. Relation entre la densité, l'indice de réfraction et la polarisation rotatoire magnétique des mélanges binaires.

Stoltzenberg. 42671. Optische Aktivität und kristallinisch-flüssiger Zustand.

4050 ROTATORY POWERS OF SUBSTANCES.

Darmois. 39693. Polarisation rotatoire naturelle et polarisation rotatoire magnétique.

Elias. 39900. Anomale magnetische Drehungsdispersion und selektive Absorption.

Fischer et alii. 40001. Optisch-aktive Dialkyl-essigsäuren.

Grossmann und **Bloch.** 40315. Rotationsdispersion und Mutarotation der Zuckerarten in Wasser, Pyridin und Ameisensäure.

Hilditch. 40518. Relatives Rotationsvermögen von aromatischen Stellungsisomeren.

Kaemmerer. 40706.

Malosse. 41302. Pouvoir rotatoire spécifique du camphre dissous dans l'acétone.

Meisenheimer. 41391. Optisch aktive Aminoxyde.

Minguin. 41465. Dissociation des tartrates, malates et camphorates

d'amines, mise en évidence par le pouvoir rotatoire.

Rimbach und **Volk.** 42143. Polarimetrische Aviditätsbestimmungen an schwachen Basen in nichtwässeriger Lösung.

Schliephacke. 42385. Mutarotation der Maltose. Diss.

Schulze und **Trier.** 42438. Spezifisches Drehungsvermögen des Glutamins.

Stumpf. 42698. Optische Beobachtungen an einer flüssig-kristallinischen aktiven Substanz.

Tschugaeff. 42842. Rotationsdispersion farbloser Verbindungen.

———— et **Ogorodnikoff.** 42843. La dispersion anormale des corps colorés et actifs.

Vèzes. 42908. La définition de l'essence de térébenthine commercialement pure.

Vlès. 42920. Propriétés optiques des muscles.

Walden. 42990 ; **Le Bel.** 41039. L'inversion optique des composés organiques.

THE EMISSION AND ANALYSIS OF RADIATION, PHOSPHORESCENCE, RADIOACTIVITY, SPECTRA, Etc.

4200 GENERAL.

Abbot. 38881. Silver disk pyrheliometer. 38882 : The sun.

———— and **Aldrich.** 38883. The pyrheliometric scale.

Blake. 39280. Is energy atomic in structure ?

Buisson et **Fabry.** 39450. La lumière ultraviolette.

Coblentz. 39589. Farbe des von Feuerfliegen und Leuchtkäfern ausgesandten Lichtes.

Ehrenfest. 39871. Welche Züge der Lichtquantenhypothese spielen in der Theorie der Wärmestrahlung eine wesentliche Rolle ?

Einstein. 39893. Thermische Molekularbewegung in festen Körpern. 39895 : Thermodynamische Begründung des photochemischen Äquivalentgesetzes.

4202 SOURCES : LAMPS, ARCS, VACUUM TUBES.

Gehlhoff. 40149. Glimmentladung und Emission der Alkalimetalldämpfe. 40150 ; Erzeugung von Metallspektren in der Glimmentladung.

Grebe. 40287. Strahlung der Quecksilberbogenlampe.

Kyll. 40949. Intensitätsmessungen im positiven Bandenspektrum des Stickstoffs.

Ladoff. 40973. The titanium arc.

La Rosa. 41009. Spektrum des die elektrische Erhitzung eines Kohlenstäbchens begleitenden Lichtes.

Leimbach. 41083. Strahlungseigenschaften der elektrischen Glühlampen.

Lenard. 41095. Elektrizitätsleitung und Lichtemission metallhaltiger Flammen.

Méttler. 41419. Hohe Flammtemperaturen durch Gase, ihre chemische und physikalische Erzeugung.

Miner and **Whitaker.** 41464. Rare earths.

O'Connor. 41662. Spektrum des Poulsenschen Lichtbogens.

Piutti. 41859, 63-5. Elio.

Pole. 41928. Photometrische Untersuchungen an Quecksilberdampflampen.

Reis. 42073. Ammoniak- und stickoxydhaltige Flammen.

Rubens und **Baeyer.** 42228. Eine äusserst langwellige Strahlung des Quecksilberdampfs.

——— und **Wartenberg. v.** 42230. Absorption langwelliger Wärmestrahlen in einigen Gasen.

Russner. 42271. Strahlungseigenschaften elektrischer Glühlampen.

Steubing. 42648. Neue strahlende Emission seitens des Funkens.

Strutt. 42688. Flames at low temperature supported by ozone.

Thürmel. 42788. Das Lummer-Pringsheimsche Spektral-Flickerphotometer als optisches Pyrometer [Nernstlampe].

Voege. 42922. Licht- und Wärmestrahlung der künstlichen Lichtquellen.

Würschmidt. 43218. Spektrum des elektrischen Lichtbogens.

4205 SPECTRA, DISTRIBUTION OF SPECTRAL LINES.

Bureau des Longitudes. L'éclipse de Soleil du 17 avril 1912. Paris 1912 (16 av. 1 carte). 23 cm.

André. 38961 : **Bigourdan.** 39255 ; **Bourget.** 39361 : **Leboeuf** et **Chofardet.** 41042 ; **Montangerand.** 41483 ; **Puiseux.** 41972 ; **Rayet** et **Courty.** 42020 ; **Renaux.** 42084 ; **Salet.** 42298 ; **Stephan.** 42638 ; **Kerillis.** 40769 ; **Simonin.** 42523. Observations faites à l'occasion de l'éclipse totale de Soleil du 30 août 1905.

Aretz. 38978. Langwelliger Teil des Kupferfunken- und Kupferbogenspektrums.

Barkla. 39077. Spectra of the fluorescent Röntgen radiations.

Barnes. 39081. The spectra of aluminium, copper and magnesium in the arc under reduced pressure.

Bevan. 39236. Absorption spectra of lithium and cæsium. 39237 : Dispersion in vapours of the alkali metals.

Bosler. 39341, 39341A. Spectre de la comète de Brooks [1911 c].

Buchwald. 39438. Untersuchungen von Flammenspektren mit dem Vakuumbolometer.

Busch und **Jensen.** 39453. Atmosphärische Polarisation.

Crew. 39659. Handbuch der Spectroscopie, Band V. Von H. Kayser.

Croze. 39665. Le second spectre de l'hydrogène dans l'extrême rouge. 39666 : Spectre du pôle négatif de l'oxygène.

Dickson. 39758. Ultraviolette Fluoreszenz des Benzols.

Dunz. 39834. Die Serien.

Eversheim. 39958. Weitere Messungen über Wellenlängennormale im Eisenspektrum.

Exner und **Haschek.** 39961. Die Spektren der Elemente bei normalem Druck.

Fabry et **Buisson, H.** 39966. Etudes de quelques propriétés spectroscopiques et électriques de l'arc entre métaux. 39967 ; **Henri.** 40479 : Le rayonnement des lampes à vapeur de mercure.

Fowler and **Strutt.** 40045. Spectroscopic investigations in connection with the active modification of nitrogen. I. Spectrum of the afterglow.

Froboese. 40086. Argon. Diss.

Gehrcke und **Reichenheim.** 40154. Dopplerspektrum der Wasserstoffkanalstrahlen.

Goldstein. 40254. Untersuchung der Emissionsspektra fester aromatischer Substanzen mit dem Ultraviolettfilter. 40258 : Emissionsspektra aromatischer Verbindungen in ultraviolettem Licht, in Kathodenstrahlen, Radiumstrahlen und Kanalstrahlen.

Harnack. 40427. Vergleichende Untersuchungen über Spektren in der Sauerstoff-Wasserstoff- und in der Chlor-Wasserstoff-Knallgasflamme.

Hemsalech. 40476. Le spectre de l'air donné par la décharge initiale de l'étincelle de self-induction.

Horton. 40562. Vacuum tube spectra of mercury. 40563 : Origin of spectra.

Hughes. 40586. Ultra-violet light from the mercury arc.

Idrac. 40608-9. Le spectre de la nouvelle étoile du Lézard.

Kasper. 40736. Messungen am Silber-spektrum.

Kayser. 40746 : **Steubing.** 42647 ; **Steubing** u. **Stark.** 42649. Spektroskopie des Sauerstoffs. 40749 : Normalen aus dem Bogenspektrum des Eisens im internationalen System. 40750 : Additional secondary standards, international system, in the arc spectrum of iron.

Koch. 40839. Messung der Intensitätsverteilung in Spektrallinien.

——— und **Friedrich.** 40843. Nachweis anomaler Dispersion in leuchtendem Quecksilberdampf.

Komp. 40887. Die grüne Kohlenbande. λ 5635.

Kowalski. 40901. Phosphoreszenz organischer Verbindungen bei tiefen Temperaturen.

Krawetz. 40910 ; **Meyer.** 41437. Unterschied zwischen Emissions- und Absorptionsspektren.

Kyll. 40949. Intensitätsmessungen im positiven Bandenspektrum des Stickstoffs.

Ladenburg. 40967. Spektralanalyse und ihre kosmischen Konsequenzen.

Ladenburg. 40971 Verhältnis von Emissions- und Absorptionsvermögen des leuchtenden Wasserstoffs. 40972 : Astrophysikalische Bemerkungen im Anschluss an Versuche über Absorption und anomale Dispersion in leuchtendem Wasserstoff.

La Baume Pluvinel et **Baldet.** 40958 ; **Lagrula** et **Chrétien.** 40980. Le spectre de la comète Kiess (1911 b).

Lamprecht. 40991. Das Bandenspektrum des Bleies.

La Rosa. 41004. Spettro della luce che accompagna il riscaldamento elettrico di un bastoncino di carbone.

——— e **Muglia.** 41010. La potenza specifica e la struttura spettrale nell' arco di piccola intensità.

Lehmann. 41070. Lumineszenzanalyse mittels der UV-Filterlampe.

Liebisch. 41126. Schichtenbau und elektrische Eigenschaften des Zinnerzes.

Lockyer. 41169. Sequence of chemical forms in stellar spectra.

Lohuizen, van. 41180. Series in the spectra of tin and antimony. 41181 : Spectres de lignes. (Hollandais.)

Lunkenheimer. 41244-5 ; **Stark.** 42607. Intensitätsverhältnis der Serienlinien des Wasserstoffs im Kanalstrahlenspektrum.

Meunier. 41422. Spectres de combustion des hydrocarbures et de différents métaux.

Miethe und **Seegert.** 41455. Wellenlängenmessungen an einigen Platinmetallen im kurzwelligen ultravioletten Spektrum.

Millchau. 41461. Effets spectraux des décharges électriques dans les gaz et les vapeurs.

Mogendorff. 41475. Summational and differential vibrations in line spectra.

Moureu et **Lepape.** 41521. Méthode spectrophotométrique de dosage du krypton. 41522 : Rapport de l'argon à l'azote dans les mélanges gazeux naturels et sa signification. 41523 : Dosage spectrophotométrique du xénon. Constance des rapports xénon-argon et xénon-krypton dans les mélanges gazeux naturels. 41524 : Rapports des gaz rares entre eux et avec l'azote dans les grisous.

Occhialini. 41660. Lo spettro di righe nell' arco.

O'Connor. 41662. Spektrum des Poulsenschen Lichtbogens.

Parr. 41751. Osservazioni spettroscopiche solari con mezzi semplici.

Paschen. 41760. Seriensysteme in den Spektren von Zink, Cadmium und Quecksilber. 41763 : Erweiterung der Seriengesetze der Linienspektra auf Grund genauer Wellenlängenmessungen im Ultrarot.

Perot. 41802. La spectroscopie solaire.

Porlezza. 41940, 4. Secondo spettro dell'idrogeno. 41941 : Spettro a bande del tetrafluoruro di silicio. 41942 : Spettro a righe dell'azoto in tubo di Geissler.

Randall. 42008. Infra-red spectra.

Reis. 42073. Ammoniak- und stickoxydhaltige Flammen.

Rubens. 42227. Energieverteilung der von der Quarzquecksilberlampe ausgesandten langwelligen Strahlung.

Schaum und **Wüstenfeld.** 42355. Selektive Absorption und Emission.

Schulemann. 42426. Das Funkenspektrum des Indiums.

Stahl. 42592. Spektren des Argons.

Stark. 42610. Träger und Sitz der Emission von Serienlinien. 42614 : Atomdynamik. Die elementare Strahlung.

Stead. 42621. Anode and cathode spectra of various gases and vapours.

Steubing und **Wood.** 43195. Eine neue strahlende Emission seitens des Funkens.

Strutt. 42691. The afterglow of electric discharge in nitrogen.

Thomson. 42780. Eine neue Methode der chemischen Analyse. [Spektrum der positiven Strahlen.]

Tian. 42791. Les radiations qui décomposent l'eau et le spectre ultraviolet extrême de l'arc au mercure.

Urbain. 42865. Un nouvel élément qui accompagne le lutécium et le scandium dans les terres de la gadolinite ; le cellium.

Vigneron. 42910. Répartition des raies spectrales dans les spectres d'émission.

Voigt. 42932. Intensitätsverteilung in Spektrallinien.

Wagner. 42979. Ultraviolettes Funkenspektrum der Luft. Diss.

Watson. 43008. Regularities in the spectrum of neon.

Wegener. 43026. Natur der obersten Atmosphärenschichten.

Weiss. 43069. Idée de Ritz sur les spectres de bandes.

Wertheim-Salomonson. 43098. Milliampèremeter und Röntgenlicht.

Weyl. 43107. Das asymptotische Verteilungsgesetz der Eigenwerte linearer partieller Differentialgleichungen (Anwendung auf die Theorie der Hohlraumstrahlung).

Wolter. 43186. Ultraviolette Banden des Kohlenoxydspektrums.

Wood. 43090, 2. Resonance spectra of iodine and their destruction by gases of the helium group.

——— und **Franck.** 43197-8. Ueberführung des Resonanzspektrums der Jodfluoreszenz in ein Bandenspektrum durch Zumischung von Helium.

4206 INFLUENCE OF PRESSURE, TEMPERATURE, Etc., ON SPECTRA.

Bahr. 39948. Veränderung von Absorptionslinien durch fremde Gase.

Barnes. 39081. Spectra of aluminium, copper and magnesium in the arc under reduced pressure.

Duffield. 39823. Effect of pressure upon arc spectra. Silver, λ 4000 to λ 4600. Gold.

Gale and **Adams.** 40112. Spectrum of the spark under pressure. 40113 : Pressure shift of the arc and spark lines of titanium.

Gehlhoff. 40149. Glimmentladung und Emission der Alkalimetalldämpfe.

Henri. 40480. Influence de diverses conditions physiques sur le rayonnement ultraviolet des lampes à vapeur de mercure en quartz.

Huber. 40581. Einfluss der Selbstinduktion auf die Spektren von Legierungen.

Joye. 40695. Influence de l'intensité maximum du courant sur le spectre de la décharge oscillante.

King. 40787. Effect of pressure upon electric furnace spectra.

Lagrula et **Ohrétien.** 40981. Spectre de la comète Brooks.

Lee. 41059. Effects of variations of vapor-density on the calcium lines H, K, and g (λ 4227).

Lyman. 41250. Spectra of some gases in the Schumann region.

Meunier. 41423. Conditions de la production du spectre de Swan et ce qu'on peut en conclure relativement aux comètes qui possèdent ce spectre.

Nutting and **Tugman.** 41653. Intensities of some hydrogen, argon, and helium lines in relation to current and pressure.

Rossi. 42209. Effect of pressure on the arc spectrum of vanadium. 42210 : Pressure displacement of spectral lines.

Schaum und **Wüstenfeld.** 42355. Selektive Absorption und Emission.

Schröder. 42419. Natrium-Dampf. [Umkehr der Na-Linie inbezug auf die Temperatur.]

Wendt. 43081. Veränderung der Quecksilberlinien bei Verdünnung des Metalldampfes.

Wood und **Franck.** 43197 43198. Ueberführung des Resonanzspektrums der Jodfluoreszenz in ein Bandenspektrum durch Zumischung von Helium.

4207 STRUCTURE OF SPECTRAL LINES.

Biske. 39271. Krümmung der Spektrallinien beim Plangitter.

Brotherus. 39416 Photometrische Untersuchung der Struktur einiger Spektrallinien.

Franck und **Pringsheim.** 40050. Das elektrische und optische Verhalten der Chlorflamme.

Lunelund. 41240. Struktur einiger Spektrallinien und ihr Zeemaneffekt in schwachen Magnetfeldern.

McLennan and **Macallum.** 41269. Resolution of the spectral lines of mercury.

Meslin. 41413. Structure des raies spectrales.

Paschen. 41760. Seriensysteme in den Spektren von Zink, Cadmium und Quecksilber.

Pokrowsky. 41921. Dopplersches Prinzip.

Randall. 42008. Infra-red spectra.

Stark. 42607. Lunkenheimers Abhandlung über das Intensitätsverhältnis der Serienlinien des Wasserstoffs im Kanalstrahlenspektrum.

4208 INFLUENCE OF MAGNETIC FIELD ON SPECTRA.

Babcock. 39032. Grouping of triplet separations produced by a magnetic field. 39030-1 : The Zeeman effect for vanadium and for chromium.

Baerwald. 39043. Untersuchung der Einwirkung des Magnetfeldes auf den Dopplereffekt des Kanalstrahlen.

Cotton. 39648, 39649. La théorie de Ritz du phénomène de Zeeman. 39650 : Mesures sur le phénomène de Zeeman. Changements magnétiques des raies d'émission des corps gazeux.

du Bois. 39312, 39809. Der verallgemeinerte Zeemaneffekt in selektiv absorbierenden Körpern.

——— und **Elias.** 39810. Der Einfluss von Temperatur und Magnetisierung bei selektiven Absorptions- und Fluoreszenzspektren.

Dufour. 39824, 6 ; **Guadet.** 41339. Phénomène de Zeeman.

Graftdijk. 40270. Le phénomène de Zeeman dans les spectres du nickel, du cobalt et du fer de λ = 4400 jusqu'à λ = 6500. (Hollandais.)

King. 40787. Effect of pressure upon electric furnace spectra. 40788 : Influence of a magnetic field upon the spark spectra of iron and titanium.

Lüttig. 41229. Zeeman-Phänomen im sichtbaren Spektrum von Mangan und Argon.

Lunelund. 41240. Struktur einiger Spektrallinien und ihr Zeemaneffekt in schwachen Magnetfeldern. 41241 : Verhalten des Trabanten — 0,121 Å.-E. der Quecksilberlinie 5790 Å.-E. im magnetischen Felde.

Michelson. 41446. Lichtwellen und ihre Anwendungen. [Übers.]

Moore. 41493. Magnetic separation of the spectral lines of calcium and strontium.

Paschen. 41760. Seriensysteme in den Spektren von Zink, Cadmium und Quecksilber.

Purvis. 41977. Zeeman effect for chromium.

Rossi. 42209. Effect of pressure on the arc spectrum of vanadium.

Rybár. 42278. Zeeman-Effekte der Spektrallinien des Lanthans und Kobalts. (Ungar.) 42279 : Zerlegung der Spektrallinien von Lanthan und Kobalt im magnetischen Felde.

Stark. 42606 ; **Baerwald.** 39043A. Einwirkung des Magnetfeldes auf den Doppler-Effekt der Kanalstrahlen.

Voigt. 42933. Komplizierte Zeemaneffekte. 42931 ; **Koch.** 40840 ; **Risco.** 42146 : Zur Dissymmetrie der Zeemanschen Triplets.

Wendt. 43081. Zeemaneffekt mit Quecksilber in schwachen und starken Feldern.

Zeemann. 43252. Le cas général de la décomposition magnétique des raies spectrales et son application en astrophysique.

4210 INTENSITY AND DISTRIBUTION OF ENERGY. TEMPERATURE AND RADIATION. TEMPERATURE LAW OF RADIATION. RADIATION OF BLACK BODIES.

Abbot and **Fowle.** 38884. Reflecting power of clouds.

Baisch. 39055. Wien-Planeksches Strahlungsgesetz im Bereich kurzer Wellenlängen.

Bauer. 39118. Théorie du rayonnement.

Born und **Ladenburg.** 39333. Verhältnis von Emissions- und Absorptionsvermögen bei stark absorbierenden Körpern.

Buchwald. 39438. Untersuchungen von Flammenspektren mit dem Vakuumbolometer.

Buisson et **Fabry.** 39448. Mesure des intensités des diverses radiations d'un rayonnement complexe.

Coblentz. 39585, 7. A characteristic of spectral energy curves. 39588 : The elementary electrical charge. 39589 : The color of the light emitted by fire-flies. 39590 : Radiation laws of metals. 39591 : Selective radiation from various substances. 39592 : Vorläufige Mitteilung über die selektive Strahlung der Azetylenflamme.

David. 39696. Radiation in explosions of coal-gas and air.

Du Bois und **Rubens.** 39813. Polarisation langwelliger Wärmestrahlung durch Hertzsche Drahtgitter.

Féry et **Drecq.** 39990. La constante du rayonnement.

Foix. 40025. Rayonnement des corps amorphes.

Gibson. 40184. Eine monochromatische Temperaturstrahlung des Thalliumdampfes.

Grebe. 40287. Strahlung der Quecksilberbogenlampe.

Gross. 40314. Lambertsches Kosinusgesetz.

Gruner. 40333. Die neueren Anschauungen über die Strahlungserscheinungen. [Ref.]

Harkányi. 40426 ; **Hnatek.** 40533. Strahlung und Temperatur der Sterne.

Hess. 40507. Absorption der γ-Strahlen in der Atmosphäre.

Hyde. 40598. Selective radiation from tantalum.

Ishiwara. 40627. Thermodynamisches Verhalten einer Strahlung in einem bewegten diathermanen Medium.

Kamerlingh Onnes. 40718. A heliumcryostat. (English, Dutch.)

Koch. 40839. Messung der Intensitätsverteilung in Spektrallinien.

Kurlbaum. 40947. Messung der Sonnentemperatur.

Kyll. 40949. Intensitätsmessungen im positiven Bandenspektrum des Stickstoffs.

Ladenburg. 40971. Das Verhältnis von Emissions- und Absorptionsvermögen des leuchtenden Wasserstoffs.

La Rosa e **Muglia.** 41010. La potenza specifica e la struttura spettrale nell' arco di piccola intensità.

Le Bel. 41041. L'échauffement singulier des fils minces de platine.

Mendenhall. 41397. Emissive power of wedge-shaped cavities and their use in temperature measurements.

Natanson. 41569. Statistical theory of radiation.

Nordmann. 41643. Les diamètres effectifs des étoiles.

Parmentier. 41750. Vérification de la loi de Stefan-Boltzmann au moyen d'un four Memker.

Peddie. 41782. Problem of partition of energy in radiation.

Planck. 41884. Gesetz der schwarzen Strahlung.

Pokrovskij. 41917. Détermination spectrophotométrique de la température du corps noir et la sensibilité chromatique de l'œil. (Russ.)

Schaum und **Wüstenfeld.** 42355. Selektive Absorption und Emission.

Schidlof. 42373. Aufklärung der universellen elektrodynamischen Bedeutung der Planckschen Strahlungskonstanten h.

Schneider. 42403. Energie der aus glühendem CaO entweichenden Elektronen.

Schröder. 42419. Absorptionsvermögen des Natrium-Dampfes.

Voigt. 42935. Emission und Absorption in Zusammenhang mit der Frage der Intensitätsmessungen beim Zeeman-Effekt.

Wamsler. 43001. Wärmeabgabe geheizter Körper an Luft.

Weyl. 43107. Das asymptotische Verteilungsgesetz der Eigenwerte linearer partieller Differentialgleichungen. Theorie der Hohlraumstrahlung.

4215 RADIATION-PRESSURE.

Biernacki. 39250. Strahlungsdruck.

Lémeray. 41091. Pression de radiation.

Myśkin. 41547; **Lebedev.** 41035. Forces pondéromotrices dans le champ de la lumière. (Russ.)

Poincaré. 41915. Les hypothèses cosmogoniques.

Rizhi. 42140. Kometen und Elektronen.

Waals, *Jr.*, van der. 42962. Energy and mass. (English, Dutch.)

4220 CHEMICAL LUMINESCENCE. (*See also* 6840.)

Broglie et **Brizard.** 39407. La radiation du sulfate de quinine, ionisation et luminescence.

Delépine. 39727. Nouveaux cas d'oxydabilité spontanée avec phosphorescence.

Eck, van. 39869. Luminiscence par pression. (Hollandais.)

Richter. 42104. Fluorescenz in der p-Benzochinon-Reihe.

Vanino und **Zumbusch.** 42888. Bologneser Leuchtsteine.

4225 PHOTOCHEMISTRY AND PHOTOGRAPHY.

Jahresbericht über die Fortschritte der Photographie und Reproduktionstechnik. Jahrb. Phot. Halle **25** 1911 (263-650).

Angewandte Photographie v. C **10** p. 310. Hrsg. von **Wolf-Czapek.** Berlin (Union) 1911. [6030].

Agulhon. 38907. Action des rayons ultraviolets sur les diastases.

Albert. 38914. Proiezioni ordinarie e cinematografiche a luce fredda.

Bakunin. 39057-61. Reazioni fotochimiche.

Becker. 39148.

Benoist. 39183. Application de l'harmonica chimique à la chronophotographie.

Berthelot et Gaudechon. 39212–8. Les effets chimiques des rayons ultraviolets.

Bierry, Henri et Ranc. 39250A. Action des rayons ultraviolets sur la glycérine.

—— et Larguier des Bancels. 39251. Action de la lumière émise par la lampe à mercure sur les solutions de chlorophylle.

Boll. 39314. Application de l'électromètre à l'étude des réactions chimiques dans les électrolytes.

Byk. 39458. Fortschritte der Photochemie 1909 und 1910.

Chanoz. 39530. Développement physique d'une image radiographique après fixage par l'hyposulfite de soude et lavage prolongé de la plaque sensible irradiée. 39531. Des images révélées physiquement après fixage de la plaque au gélatinobromure d'argent irradiée. Actions isolées ou successives de la lumière et des rayons X.

Chapman and Petrie. 39533. Action of the latex of *Euphorbia peplus* on a photographic plate.

Ciamician e Silber. 39561. Azioni chimiche della luce.

Costanzo. 39642. Effetti foto-elettrici con i raggi β.

Courmont. 39654. Stérilisation de l'eau potable par les rayons ultraviolets.

Dangeard. 39681. L'action de la lumière sur la chlorophylle.

David. 39695. Lehrbuch der Photographie.

Defregger. 39718. Untersuchung orthochromatischer Platten.

Demeler. 39737; Forster. 40036; Schuller. 42427. Das „Weiss" auf Autochromplatten.

Eder. 39862. Relative Aktinität.

—— und Valenta. 39864. Photographie.

Ermen and Gamble. 39930. Modification in the sulphide toning of bromide tints.

Fontenay. 40028. Reproduction photographique des documents par réflexion (cataphotographie).

Frederking. 40071. Naturfarbige mikrophotographische Aufnahmen auf „Autochromplatten" bei künstlichem Licht.

Gaedicke. 40104. Intermittierende Entwicklung.

Geiger. 40166. Schwärzung und Photometrie photographischer Platten.

Gleichen. 40222. Die Optik in der Photographie.

Goldberg. 40240. Herstellung neutral-grauer Keile und verlaufender Filter für Photographie. 40241: Detailwiedergabe in der Photographie.

—— Luther und Weigert. 40242. Automatische Herstellung der charakteristischen Kurve.

Goldschmidt. 40247. La photographie des couleurs.

Grész. 40300. Luminographie. (Ungar.)

Guntz et Minguin. 40368. Radiations ultraviolettes.

Hübl. 40583. Ist eine farblose Dunkelkammerbeleuchtung möglich ?

Inghilleri. 40620. Sintesi fotochimica degli idrati di carbonio. 40621: Azione della luce sulle soluzioni di formaldeide. 40622: Azione chimica della luce.

Jaeger. 40648. Photochemical transformations of ferri-trichloro-acetate solutions. (English, Dutch.)

Jones. 40679. Relationship between size of particle and colour of image.

Keil. 40753. Beziehung der Sensibilisierenden Wirkung des Uranylsulfates zu seiner Fluorescenz. Diss.

Koch. 40841. Zahl der Zentren von Lichtemission und Intensitätsverhältnis verschiedener Interferenzordnungen.

Landau. 40994. Action des rayons ultraviolets sur l'acide lactique.

Lasareff. 41019. Ausbleichen von Farbstoffen im sichtbaren Spektrum.

Lewin et alii. 41115. Sensibilisierung von photographischen Platten für das Infrarot.

Lüppo-Cramer. 41220. Natur des latenten Röntgenstrahlenbildes. 41221: Mikroskopische Beobachtungen über den Reifungsvorgang. 41222 : Photographie mit unsichtbaren Strahlen. 41223 : Kolloidchemie und Photographie. 41224 : Das latente Bild.

Lumière, A. et **Lumière, L.** 41230. Fotografia dei colori e tricromia.

——— ——— et **Seyewetz.** 41231. Différenciation par voie de développement chimique des images latentes obtenues au moyen des émulsions au chlorure et au bromure d'argent. 41232 : Développement des images photographiques après fixage.

Marmier. 41336. Action des rayons ultraviolets sur l'hyposultite de sodium.

Mascarelli. 41351. Contegno delle aldeidi benzoica e paratoluica in presenza di iodio e sotto l'azione della luce.

Mebes. 41387. Farbenphotographie mit Farbrasterplatten.

Mees and **Piper.** 41389. Fogging powers of developers.

Meyer. 41426. Zerstreuung des Lichts im Negativ.

Miethe. 41452. Farbenphotographie. 41453 : Neuer Schwärzungsmesser für Negative. 41454 : Chemische Wirkung des Lichtes.

Namias. 41558. Ottenimento d'imagini dei più svariati colori. 41559 : Fotografia dei colori e tricromia. 41560 : Influenza dello spessore e rapidità delle lastre fotografiche sulla ricchezza del chiaroscuro dell' imagine negativa. 41561 : Uno strano fenomeno fotografico. 41562 : La fotografia ordinaria e ortocromatica.

Novak. 41646. Gelbfilter für Autochromblitzlichtaufnahmen.

Padoa. 41723. 6. Relazioni fra fototropia e costituzione chimica.

Paternò et alii. 41770-1. Sintesi per mezzo della luce.

Pioro. 41847. Zusammenhang zwischen Sensibilisierung und Fluoreszenz.

Pizzighelli. 41872. Fotografia con raggi invisibili di R. W. Wood.

Plotnikow. 41893. Klassifikation der Lichtreaktionen. 41894 : Photochemische Versuchstechnik.

Popoff. 41937. Une cause qui peut influer sur l'estimation de la grandeur des étoiles.

Pritzsche. 41959. Verwendung der Lumière'schen Farbenplatten in der Mikrophotographie.

Proszyński. 41961, 4. La prise des vues cinématographiques.

Purcell. 41976. Kopierbare farbige photographische Aufnahmen. (Ungar.)

Puxeddu. 41979. Azione chimica della luce.

Reboul. 42039. Impressions photographiques sur cuivre.

Recoura et **Colin.** 42045. Action des rayons émis par la lampe à quartz à vapeurs de mercure sur la colorabilité des bacilles acidorésistants.

Reinders. 42065. Konstitution der Photohaloiden. (Holländisch.)

Santoponte. 42316. Annuario della fotografia.

Schall. 42348. Demonstration photochemischer Wirkungen im ultravioletten Licht mittels sensibler Schichten.

Schaum. 42350. Sogenannte „dunkle" Funken. 42351-2 : Photographische Probleme.

Scheffer. 42365. Lichthöfe.

Schell. 42367. Photographischphotometrische Absorptionsmessungen an Jodsilber im ultravioletten Spektrum.

Shepherd. 42503. Cause of reversal and its remedy : the photographic process.

Stark. 42602, 5, 11 ; **Leimbach.** 41081. Schwärzungsgesetz der Normalbelichtung.

Steiner. 42631. Farbige Photographien. (Ungarisch.)

Stenger. 42635. Nachreifen panchromatischer Platten. 42636 : Gradation von Bromsilbergelatineschichten im Ultraviolett.

——— ——— und **Heller.** 42637. Intensitätsunterschied des Schleiers auf belichteten und nicht belichteten Trockenplatten.

Sterry. 42645. Reversal and rereversal. 42646 : Light and development.

Stolze. 42672. Handbuch des Vergrösserns.

Strecker. 42677. Ein neues Druckverfahren : Stagmatypie.

Tian. 42790. Décomposition de l'eau oxygénée produite par la lumière. 42791 : Sur les radiations qui décomposent l'eau et sur le spectre ultraviolet extrême de l'arc au mercure.

Trivelli. 42827. Konstitution der Photohaloïden. II. III. 42828 : Expositionsunterschied bei physikalischer und chemischer Entwicklung. (Holländisch.) 42829 : Theorien der photochemischen Vorgänge in der Bromsilbergelatine - Platte. 42830 : Ostwald's Gesetz der Umwandlungsstufen und die photochemische hersetzung der Silberhaloïde. 42831 : Natur der Schaumschen Substanz B.

Tsvett. 42844. Mechanismus der photosynthetischen Energieübertragung.

Valenta. 42873. Fortschritte der Photochemie und Photographie 1910.

Wall. 42995. Die Farbe photographischer Bilder.

Weigert. 43041. Konstruktion von Schwärzungskurven photographischer Platten. 43042 : Chemische Wirkungen des Lichts. 43043 : Einteilung der photochemischen Reaktionen.

Winther. 43163. Optische Sensibilisierung. 43164 : Theorie der Farbenempfindlichkeit.

Worel. 43201. Farbenphotographie.

Yvon. 43230. Cataphotographie.

4230 PHOSPHORESCENCE PRODUCED BY IMPACT OF RADIATION, HEAT, ELECTRIC DISCHARGE, Etc. FLUORESCENCE.

(*See also* 6840.)

Barkla. 39077, 39078. The spectra of the fluorescent Röntgen radiations.

Becquerel. 39151–5. L'effet magnéto-optique présenté par les bandes de phosphorescence du rubis. 39157 : La propagation de la lumière dans les corps fluorescents. 39156 : La durée de la phosphorescence des sels d'uranyle.

————— *et alii.* 39152A. Phosphorescence des sels d'uranyle aux très basses températures.

Boutaric. 39369. Phénomènes présentés par les grains d'amidon en lumière polarisée.

Brüninghaus. 39424–5. Loi de Stokes et une relation générale entre l'absorption et la phosphorescence.

Dickson. 39758. Ultraviolette Fluoreszenz des Benzols.

du Bois. 39809. L'effet Zeeman généralisé dans les absorbants sélectifs.

Dunoyer. 39832. Fluorescence des vapeurs des métaux alcalins.

Franck and Wood. 40054. Influence upon the fluorescence of iodine and mercury of gases with different affinities for electrons.

Gernez. 40173. Un moyen de restituer aux sulfures alcalino-terreux leurs propriétés phosphorescentes.

Goldstein. 40254. Untersuchung der Emissionsspektra fester aromatischer Substanzen mit dem Ultraviolettfilter. 40258 : Emissionsspektra aromatischer Verbindungen in ultraviolettem Licht, in Kathodenstrahlen, Radiumstrahlen und Kanalstrahlen.

Grotowski. 40317. L'effet photoélectrique et la phosphorescence.

Ives and **Luckiesh.** 40640. Effect of red and infra-red on the decay of phosphorescence in zinc sulphide.

Kaempf. 40708. Lambertsches Absorptionsgesetz beim Fluoreszein.

Kamerlingh Onnes. 40722.

Koenigsberger und **Küpferer.** 40864. Absorption des Lichtes in festen und gasförmigen Körpern.

Kowalski. 40901. Phosphoreszenz organischer Verbindungen bei tiefen Temperaturen.

————— **et Dzierzbicki.** 40902. Influence des groupements fonctionnels sur le spectre de phosphorescence progressive.

Lehmann. 41070, 2. Lumineszenzanalyse mittels der UV-Filterlampe.

Nichols. 41601. Effects of temperature on phosphorescence and fluorescence. 41602 : Fluorescence and phosphorescence.

————— and **Merritt.** 41603. Fluorescence and phosphorescence between + 20° and − 190°.

Duculot. 39822. Propriétés des rayons.

Droż. 39798. Rationelles Verfahren mit Röntgenröhren. (Čechisch.)

Foveau de Courmelles. 40042. Identification par les rayons X de cadavres carbonisés.

Freund. 40080. Fortschritte auf dem Gebiete der Röntgenstrahlen.

Fürstenau. 40095. Röntgenstrahlendosierung.

Guilleminot. 40354. Les rayons de Sagnac. 40355 ; Le rendement en rayons secondaires des rayons X de qualité différente.

Haret. 40424. Mesures en radiologie.

Holzknecht. 40552. Dosimeter für Röntgen-Strahlen.

Katz. 40740. Röntgenaufnahmen auf Bromsilberpapier.

Klingelfuss. 40814. Exakte Dosierung therapeutischer Voll- und Teildosen und praktische Eichung einer Röntgenröhre.

Kunz. 40946. Positive potential of metals in the photoelectric effect and the determination of the wavelength equivalent of Roentgen rays.

Lindemann und **Lindemann.** 41146. Abhängigkeit des Durchdringungsvermögens der Röntgenstrahlen von Druck und Gasinhalt.

Lüppo-Cramer. 41220. Natur des latenten Röntgenstrahlenbildes.

Marx. 41347–8 ; **Franck u. Pohl.** 40049. Geschwindigkeit der Röntgenstrahlen.

Morton. 41510. Les rayons X.

Owen. 41714. Scattering of Röntgen radiation.

Sadler. 42289. Transformation of the energy of homogeneous Röntgen radiation into energy of corpuscular radiation.

————— and Steven. 42290. Apparent softening of Röntgen rays in transmission through matter.

Schiller und **O'Donnell.** 42376. Induzierte Radioaktivität durch Röntgenstrahlen.

Szilárd. 42730. Apparat zur Messung der Röntgenstrahlen in absoluten Einheiten. (Ungar.)

Tschugaeff. 42841. Neuer Typus der anomalen Rotationsdispersion.

Vaillant. 42871. Nouvelle méthode permettant de constater par la radiographie si un enfant déclaré né mort a vécu.

Walter. 42998. Bauersches Qualimeter.

Weiss. 43071. Spectres de bandes.

Wendt. 43081. Quecksilberlinien.

Wertheimer. 43092. Strom- und Spannungsverlauf (Charakteristik) an Röntgenröhren.

Wetterer. 43104. Instrumente zur qualitativen und quantitativen Messung der X-Strahlen : Radiosklerometer und Quantitometer.

Whiddington. 43110. Production of characteristic Röntgen radiations. 43111 : Production and properties of soft Röntgen radiation.

Whittaker. 43117. Dynamical nature of the molecular systems which emit spectra of the banded type.

Zemplén. 43269. Relativitätsprinzip.

4250 ELECTRIC RADIATIONS. GENERAL.

Grotowski. 40317. L'effet photoélectrique et la phosphorescence. Diss.

Horton. 40561. Spectroscopic investigation of the nature of the carriers of positive electricity from heated aluminium.

Kamerlingh Onnes. 40718. A helium-cryostat. (English, Dutch.)

Thomson. 42778. New method of investigating the positive rays. 42779, 42781 : Rays of positive electricity.

4270 VARIOUS RADIATIONS.

Fulcher. 40009. The production of light by canal rays.

Haber. 40378. Elektronenemission bei chemischen Reaktionen.

————— und **Just.** 40379. Aussendung von Elektronenstrahlen bei chemischen Reaktionen.

Krause. 40908. Pseudoradioaktivität des Zinkperoxyds. Diss.

Kristensen. 40916. Colouring of surfaces when struck by a Bunsenflame. (Danish.)

Matuschek und Nenning. 41369. Auftreten von chemisch wirksamen Strahlen bei chemischen Reaktionen.

Remele. 42082. Dunkle Strahlungen [des Borstickstoffs].

Schidlof. 42374. Théorie du rayonnement.

Steubing. 42648. Neue strahlende Emission seitens des Funkens.

4275 RADIOACTIVITY (RADIUM, Etc.).

Intorno alla determinazione di radioattività delle acque. [Sunto.] Riv. ing. san. Torino 5 1909 (365-368); 6 1910 (365-368).

Preparazione del radio metallico. [Sunto.] Ind. chim. Torino 10 1910 (327).

Allen. 38930. Secondary β radiation from solids and liquids. 38931-2 : Absorption of the γ rays of radium by solids and liquids.

Ammon. 38954. Radioaktive Substanzen in Bayern.

Antonoff. 38971. Disintegration products of uranium.

Accquino. 38998. Le emanazioni radioattive nell' aria di Napoli.

Artmann. 38997. Radioaktivität des Meerwassers.

Auer von Welsbach. 39012. Chemische Untersuchung der Aktinium enthaltenden Rückstände der Radiumgewinnung.

Baborovský. 39036. Radioaktivität: Fortschritte i. J. 1908. (Čechisch.)

Baeyer, Hahn und Meitner. 39045-7. β-Strahlen.

Baillehache (De). 39054. Battelli, Occhialini e Chella "La radioactivité et la constitution de la matière."

Barduzzi. 39073; Monti. 41488; Murani. 41538. Radioattività delle sorgenti minerali.

Battelli, Occhialini e Chella. 39113. La radioattività.

Baxmann. 39131. Absorption und Geschwindigkeitsverlust der β-Strahlen des Radiums.

Bennewitz. 39182. Messmethoden der Radioaktivität.

Bernini. 39205. Radioattività dei gaz emananti dalle sorgenti termali.

Boltwood. 39315. Séparation de l'ionium et de l'actinium de certains résidus et production de l'hélium par l'ionium.

————— et Rutherford. 39316. Production de l'hélium par le radium.

Boyer and Wherry. 39373. Radioactive minerals.

Boyle. 39374. Behaviour of radium emanation at low temperatures.

Bragg. 39378. Radio-activity as a kinetic theory of a fourth state of matter.

Braun. 39389. Ursachen der Färbung dilut gefärbter Mineralien und Einfluss von Radiumstrahlen auf die Färbung.

Budig. 39443; Lindemann. 41151. Messungen der Radioaktivität der atmosphärischen Luft.

Buchner. 39444. Radiumgehalt der Erdrinde. (Holländisch.) 39445 : Radium content of rocks. (English, Dutch.)

Caan. 39460. Radioaktivität menschlicher Organe.

Callendar. 39465. The radiobalance. A thermoelectric balance for the absolute measurement of radiation, with applications to radium and its emanation.

Campbell. 39473. Delta rays.

Chaspoul et Jaubert de Beaujeu. 39539. Radioactivité des eaux de Vals-les-Bains.

Clo. 39583. Effect of temperature on the ionization of a gas.

Costanzo. 39841. Misure di radioattività sull' acque di Fiuggi.

Curie. 39669, 73. Traité de radioactivité. 39671 : Variation avec le temps de l'activité de quelques substances radioactives. 39670 : Distribution des intervalles d'émission des particules α du polonium.

————— e Debierne. 39674. Radio metallico.

des lumières brèves à la limite de leur portée.

Delemer. 39735. La correspondente delle impressioni sulla retina prodotte sui due occhi nell' atto della visione.

Estanave. 39944. Synthèse des couleurs complémentaires par les réseaux lignés.

Hylla. 40599. Binokulares Sehen.

Pigeon. 41839. Stéréoscope à coulisses.

Poppelreuter. 41938. Quantitativer Vergleich der binokularen und monokularen empirischen Raumwahrnehmung.

Pultrich. 41973. Stereoskopisches Sehen und Messen.

Quidor. 41985. Vision binoculaire.

Stöhr. 42666. Monokulare Plastik.

4450 COLOUR VISION. SUBJECTIVE COLOURS. COLOUR BLINDNESS.

Abney. 38887. Colour-blindness and the trichromatic theory of colour vision.

Baroncz. 39083 : **Exner.** 39062. Metakontrast.

Blondel et **Rey.** 39293 : **Hoorweg.** 40556. Perception des lumières brèves.

Brücke und **Inouye.** 39421A. Anordnung der homogenen Lichter auf der Mischlinie des Rotgrünblinden mit unverkürztem Spektrum.

Cady. 39462. Color dispersion in the astigmatic eye.

Höfler. 40536. Modelle schematischer Farbenkörper und die vermutliche Gestalt des psychologischen Farbenkörpers.

Ives. 40639. Spectral luminosity curves obtained by the equality of brightness and flicker photometers.

Katz. 40738. Erscheinungsweisen der Farben und ihre Beeinflussung durch die individuelle Erfahrung.

Kollner. 40851. Erworbene Farbensinnstörungen.

Liebermann. 41124. Verschmelzungsfrequenzen von Farbenpaaren.

────── und **Marx.** 41125. Empfindlichkeit des normalen und des protanopischen Sehorgans für Unterschiede des Farbentons.

Lummer. 41233. Helligkeitsempfindlichkeitskurve des Auges und ihre Benutzung zur Temperaturbestimmung.

Nutting. 41651. Visibility of radiation. A recalculation of König's data.

Pauli. 41772. Beurteilung der Zeitordnung von optischen Reizen.

Pfenninger. 41824. Kinematographische Lichtränder.

Pizzighelli. 41871. Alcuni fenomeni anormali [fotografia].

Pokrovskij. 41917. Détermination spectrophotométrique de la température du corps noir et la sensibilité chromatique de l'œil. (Russ.)

Pokrowsky. 41922. Spektrophotometrisches Verschiebungsgesetz.

Rayleigh. 42021. Sensibility of the eye to variations of wave-length in the yellow region of the spectrum.

Révész. 42090. Bestimmung der Helligkeitswerte der Farben durch Kontrast.

Rosenstiehl. 42189. L'harmonie des couleurs réalisée par l'emploi des camaïeux complémentaires.

Zeeman und **Weve.** 43257. Spektralapparat zur Untersuchung des Farbensinnes.

4470 INSTRUMENTS CONNECTED WITH PHYSIOLOGICAL OPTICS.

Baum. 39123. Ophthalmo-Fundoskop. 39124 : Corneal-Mikroskop für grösste Vergrösserungen.

Bourcart. 39357. Appareil rotatif pour observer les nuances données par un mélange de couleurs.

Blondel et **Rey.** 39292, 3. Application aux signaux de la loi de perception des lumières brèves à la limite de leur portée.

Fraenkel. 40046. Über binokulare Ophthalmoskopie.

Gallenga. 40119. Stereoscopio a corsoio per esercizii di visione binoculare.

Golowin. 40259. Ophthalmoskop ohne Zentralöffnung.

Inouye und Oinuma. 40623. Untersuchung der Dunkeladaptation des einen Auges mit Hilfe des helladaptierten andern.

Langenhan. 40990. Diasklerale Augendurchleuchtung mit starker Lichtquelle.

Lasareff. 41017. Einfluss der Grösse des Gesichtsfeldes auf den Schwellenwert der Gesichtsempfindung.

Löhlein und Gebb. 41173. Sehprüfung.

Lummer. 41233. Helligkeitsempfindlichkeitskurve des Auges und die Benutzung zur Temperaturbestimmung.

Perlia. 41799. Ein vereinfachtes Stereoskopometer.

Thorner. 42784. Stereoskopische Photographie des Augenhintergrundes.

Zeeman und Weve. 43257. Spektralapparat zur Untersuchung des Farbensinnes.

ELECTRICITY AND MAGNETISM.

4900   GENERAL.

Fortschritte der Elektrotechnik. Jg 24. H. 2, 3, 4. 1910. Berlin 1911. [0032].

Ministero della Guerra. Corso di telefonia. Roma (Tip. coop. sociale) 1910 (90 con 8 tav.). 31 cm.

Barni. 39082; Gaisberg. 40111. Il montatore elettricista.

Barreca. 39089. Correnti alternate.

Białobrzeski. 39239. Le principe du relativisme et ses applications. (Polish.)

Biffi. 39252. Elettricità all' esposizione di Torino 1911.

Borino. 39329; Bracchi. 39375; Cantani. 39485; Pesenti. 41811. Telegrafia.

Calzecchi Onesti. 39469. Conduttività elettrica delle limature metalliche.

Fletcher. 40018. Vérification de la théorie du mouvement brownien et détermination de la valeur de N pour l'ionisation des gaz.

Grassi. 40276; Jervis. 40664; Marchi. 41319; Versi. 42904. Elettrotecnica.

Farkas. 39973. Kontinuitätstheorie der Elektrizität und des Magnetismus. (Ungar.)

Föppl. 40021. Maxwellsche Theorie der Elektrizität.

Foveau de Courmelles. 40043. L'année électrique. 1911.

Gaglio. 40109. Il telefono.

Garbasso e Vacca. 40138. Una esperienza di Bennet e Volta.

Ghersi. 40178. Galvanostegia.

Gibson. 40182; Gruner. 40334. Wesen der Elektrizität.

Laguna. 40982. L'elettrochimica. 40983; Pila e correnti elettriche. 40984 5; Correnti variabili ed alternate e loro applicazioni.

Lenard. 41096. Äther und Materie.

Lombardi. 41186. Unità elettriche.

Marconi. 41327; Barreca. 39090. Telegrafia e telefonia senza fili.

Martinelli. 41342. Pile elettriche.

Mašek. 41358. Elektrizität und Magnetismus 1908. (Čechisch.)

Montù. 41491. Elettricità alla esposizione di Bruxelles 1910.

Piazzali. 41829. Illuminazione elettrica.

Righi. 42139. La materia radiante e i raggi magnetici.

Schincaglia. 42381. I raggi X.

Silberstein. 42518. Quaternionenform der Relativitätstheorie. (Polish.)

Staffieri. 42591; Majorana. 41286. Telegrafia e telefonia.

Tommasina. 42811. Nature de l'électricité et dynamique de l'électron.

Vieweger. 42909. Gleich- und Wechselstromtechnik.

Weiler. 43017. Galvanische Induktionsapparate.

Werth. 43091. La galvanoplastica.

Záviška. 43249. Elektrizität und Magnetismus 1908. (Čechisch.)

Zomparelli. 43286.

GENERAL DYNAMICAL THEORY AND RELATIONS. UNITS.

4940 EQUATIONS OF THE ELECTRODYNAMIC FIELD.

Bateman. 39104. Transformation of a particular type of electromagnetic field, and its physical interpretation. 39105 : Certain vectors associated with an electromagnetic field, and the reflexion of a disturbance at the surface of a perfect conductor.

Bjerknes. 39272. Einfachste hydrodynamische Kraftfelderscheinungen.

Born. 39332 : **Gehrcke.** 40152 : **Ignatowsky.** 40611 : **Herglotz.** 40488 : **Laue.** 41029, 6 : **Mizuno.** 41470 : **Riebesell.** 42107 : **de Sitter.** 42528 : **Wiechert.** 43122 : **Zemplén.** 43269. Relativitätsprinzip.

Conway. 39618. Application of quaternions to some recent developments of electrical theory.

Cunningham. 39668. Application of the mathematical theory of relativity to the electron theory of matter.

Daniele. 39683. Induzione magnetica di un involucro ellisoidico.

Farkas. 39973. Kontinuitätstheorie der Elektrizität und des Magnetismus. (Ungar.)

Frank. 40064. Verhalten der elektromagnetischen Feldgleichungen gegenüber linearen Transformationen der Raumzeitkoordinaten.

Gerber. 40171. Gravitation und Elektrizität.

Ishivara. 40634. Elektromagnetische Impulsgleichungen in der Relativitätstheorie.

Kármán. 40732. Mechanismus des Widerstandes, den ein bewegter Körper in einer Flüssigkeit erfährt.

Korn. 40890. Weiterführung eines mechanischen Bildes der elektromagnetischen Erscheinungen.

Kraft. 40903. Vierdimensionale Vektoranalysis und deren Anwendung in der Elktrodynamik. 40904 : Direkte Integration der typischen Differentialausdrücke von Raum-Zeit-Vektoren. 40905 : Problem der Integraldarstellung der elektromagnetischen Vektoren in bewegten Körpern nach Minkowski's „Grundgleichungen".

Mie. 41450. Grundlagen einer Theorie der Materie.

Tamaki. 42739. Electric and magnetic force due to a moving electric charge. 42740 : General equations for electromagnetic fields in a moving system. 42741 : Fundamental equations for an electromagnetic field in a moving medium.

Witte. 43167. Behaupteter inverser Kräftezusammenhang zwischen Elektro- und Hydrodynamik.

4960 ELECTRONS. MOVING MEDIA.

Allen. 38929. Path of an electron in combined radial magnetic and electric fields.

Babcock. 39032. Grouping of triplet separations produced by a magnetic field.

Billiter. 39257. Atomtheorie.

Birkeland. 39265. Les anneaux de Saturne sont-ils dus à une radiation électrique de la planète ? 39266 : Le Soleil et ses taches.

Blake. 39280. Is energy atomic in structure ?

Bordoni. 39325. Teoria degli elettroni.

Cisotti. 39568. Deformazione di una sfera elastica dovuta al suo moto in seno al un liquido. (Modello meccanico di un elettrone.)

Coblentz. 39588. Determinations of the elementary electrical charge.

Collodi. 39604. Misura della carica portata dai raggi magnetici.

Davisson. 39697-8. Positive thermions from salts.

Decombe. 39715. Théorie électronique des phénomènes diélectriques résiduels.

Deslandres. 39739. Explication simple des protubérances solaires et d'autres phénomènes par des champs magnétiques très faibles. 39740 : Champs magnétiques faibles de l'atmosphère solaire.

Ehrenhaft. 39876. Elementarquantum der Elektrizität. 39875 : **Joffé.** 40667 : Atomistische Konstitution der Elektrizität.

Tamaki. 42744. Motion of an electron in the neighbourhood of a negatively charged sphere.

Tommasina. 42811. Nature de l'électricité et dynamique de l'électron.

Varicak. 42894. Zum Ehrenfestschen Paradoxon.

Waals, jr., van der. 42962. Energy and mass. (English, Dutch.)

Wassmuth. 43005. Bewegungsgleichungen des Elektrons und das Prinzip der kleinsten Aktion.

Wertheimer. 43094. Die Plancksche Konstante h und der Ausdruck h ν.

Wilson. 43149. A method of making visible the paths of ionising particles through a gas.

Wolff. 43179. Kräfte, welche die Ladung eines Elektrons zusammenhalten.

4980 TRANSFER OF ENERGY, MOMENTUM, Etc.

Belluzzo. 39168. Le centrali termoelettriche ed il consumo di carbone per KW-ora.

Douglas. 39790. A simple proof of Poynting's theorem.

Farkas. 39973. Grundlegung zur Kontinuitätstheorie der Elektrizität und des Magnetismus. (Ungar.)

Ignatowsky. 40611: **Laue.** 41020, 3, 6. Relativitätsprinzip.

Livens. 41163. Initial accelerated motion of a perfectly conducting electrified sphere. 41164: The initial accelerated motion of a rigidly charged dielectric sphere.

McLaren. 41265. Emission and absorption of energy by electrons.

Nordström. 41644. Relativitätsmechanik deformierbarer Körper.

Timiriazev. 42795. Elektromagnetische Theorie der Wärmestrahlung. (Russ.)

5000 ELECTRIC AND MAGNETIC UNITS.

Laboratoire central d'Électricité. Communication du L. C. E. au sujet des unités électriques. J. phys. Paris (sér. 5) 1 1911 (131).

Gehrcke und **Wogau.** 40455. Absolute Messung des Ampère.

Guillaume. 40351. La définition des unités électriques pratiques.

Lombardi. 41183. Standardizzazione elettrica.

Roiti. 42170. Conferenza per le unità e i campioni elettrici, Londra 1908.

Strecker. 42679. Einheiten und Formelgrössen.

ELECTROSTATICS.

5200 GENERAL.

Drumaux. 39803. Théorie corpusculaire de l'électricité.

Hoffmann. 40544. Experimentelle Prüfung der durch verschiedene Messungsanordnungen in einem homogenen elektrischen Felde hervorgerufenen Störungen der Niveauflächen.

Langevin. 41001. Exposé expérimental des phénomènes fondamentaux de l'électrostatique au moyen de l'électromètre à quadrants.

Pasquier. 41767. Équilibre statique dynamique.

Robinson. 42153, 42154. Electric dust figures.

Schaffers. 42346. Loi de Coulomb.

Witkowski. 43165. L'intensité du champ électrique. (Polish.)

5210 ELECTRIFICATION BY CONTACT OR FRICTION. VARIOUS SOURCES OF ELECTRIFICATION.

Calzecchi. 39468. Modo semplice di caricare l'elettroscopio protetto dalla camera di Faraday.

Christiansen. 39555. Origin of electricity produced by friction. (Danish.)

Czudnochowski. 39678. Quecksilber-Elektrisiermaschine.

Gramatzki. 40272. Lamellar-Elektrizität.

Heissner. 40172. Elektrizitätserregung durch Reibung.

Immisch. 40618. Elektrizitätsträger an der Grenze von Gasen und Flüssigkeiten.

Kunz. 40946. The positive potential of metals in the photo-electric effect and the determination of the wavelength equivalent of Roentgen rays.

Schneckenberg. 42462. Scheinbare Kontaktpotentialdifferenzen zwischen einem Metall und elektrolytischen Lösungen.

Szilárd. 42729. Ausströmung elektrischer Wellen aus Metallen. (Ungar.)

Szivessy. 42734. Voltaeffekt bei Kristallen.

Wiesent. 43132. Quecksilber-Reibungselektrisiermaschine.

Wommelsdorf. 43187. Bau von Influenzmaschinen.

Wright. 43211-2. Photo-electric effects in aluminium as a function of the wave-length of the incident light.

Zemplén. 43268. Anwendung der Sonnenstrahlen zur Erregung des elektrischen Stroms. (Ungar.)

5220 ELECTRIC CHARGE AND DISTRIBUTION; QUANTITY; DENSITY; INDUCTION; CONDENSERS.

Almansi. 38934. Distribuzione dell' elettricità in equilibrio nei conduttori.

Bernini. 39204. Macchina idroelettrica ad influenza di R. W. Thomson.

Colard. 39600. Efforts mécaniques dans les champs électriques ou magnétiques.

De Heen. 39721. L'analyse du phénomène de l'induction électrostatique.

Drexnowski. 39795. Condensateurs de M. Mościcki et leur application. (Polish.)

Ellis. 39903. Ölemulsionen; elektrische Ladung.

Ferroux. 39986. Les applications des condensateurs industriels.

Fischer. 40003. Verwendung von Kondensatoren in Starkstromanlagen.

Grover. 40320. Capacity and phase difference of paraffined paper condensers as functions of temperature and frequency.

Leduc. 41057. Application du principe de Lenz aux phénomènes qui accompagnent la charge des condensateurs.

Mallik. 41296. Lines of force due to given static charges.

Russell. 42267. Capacity coefficients of spherical electrodes.

Weiss. 43059. Ladungsbestimmungen an Silbertedchen.

Zipp. 43281. Theorie der Oberflächenentladungen.

5240 POTENTIAL DIFFERENCE.

Baborovský. 39034. Elektrochemischer Potential des Metallmagnesiums in Aethylalkohollösungen von Magnesiumchlorid. (Čechisch.)

Broglie. 39403. L'abaissement des différences de potentiel de contact apparent entre métaux par suite de l'enlèvement des couches d'humidité adhérentes.

De Heen. 39723. Signification physique du potentiel électrique.

Kuhn. 40935. Spannungsgefahren an geerdeten, eisernen Masten.

Piouchon. 41846. Un effet électrique du déplacement relatif d'un métal et d'un électrolyte au contact.

Riety. 42149. Force électromotrice produite par l'écoulement d'une solution de sulfate de cuivre dans un tube capillaire.

Spath. 42583. Absolutes und relatives elektrisches Potential.

Turnwald. 42846. Zusammenhang zwischen Potentialdifferenz und Stromstärke in einem metallischen Leiter.

5250 THEORY OF THE DIELECTRIC. STRESS, ENERGY, Etc.

Białobrzeski. 39238. L'ionisation des carbures d'hydrogène liquides. 39249: L'ionisation des diélectriques. (Polish.)

Debye. 39701. Eine kinetische Theorie der Isolatoren.

Decombe. 39714. La chaleur de Siemens et la notion de capacité. 39716: Théorie des diélectriques.

Giurgea. 40204. Phénomène de Kerr dans les vapeurs et les gaz.

Grumbach. 40330. L'électricité de contact.

Ryan. 42277. Luft und Öl als Hochspannungsisolatoren.

Schiller. 42377. Aenderung der Dielektrizitätskonstante des Kautschuks bei Zug senkrecht zu den Kraftlinien.

Schulze. 42436. Dielektrizitätskonstante und langwelliges Refraktionsvermögen binärer Gemische.

5252 MEASUREMENT OF DIELECTRIC CONSTANTS. DIELECTRIC HYSTERESIS.

Addenbrooke. 38901. Electrical properties of celluloid.

Arndt. 38982. Methoden zur Bestimmung von Dielektrizitätskonstanten.

Bates. 39106. Effet de la lumière sur l'isolement par le soufre.

Böhm. 39303. Dielektrizitätskonstante von Isomeren.

Décombe. 39715. Théorie électronique des phénomènes diélectriques résiduels.

Fleming and Dyke. 40014. Measurement of energy losses in condensers traversed by high-frequency electric oscillations.

German und Hills. 40172. Prüfung von Isoliermitteln.

Hovda. 40575. Effect of distance upon the electrical discharge between a point and a plane.

Jordan. 40686. Messung dielektrischer Verluste an faserigen Isolierstoffen.

Kousleff. 40899. Conductibilité thermique et électrique des principales matières obturatrices.

Lowy. 41177. Dielektrizitätskonstante und Leitfähigkeit der Gesteine.

Malclès. 41292. L'effet dit " de pénétration " dans les diélectriques.

Monti. 41486. Vernici isolanti.

Niven. 41633. Measurement of specific inductive capacity.

Ortvay. 41700. Dielektrizitätskonstante einiger Flüssigkeiten bei hohem Druck.

Rohmann. 42162. Messung von Kapazitätsänderungen mit schnellen Schwingungen, angewandt auf die Vergleichung der Dielektrizitätskonstanten von Gasen.

Rudolph. 42245. Erzeugung kurzer elektrischer Wellen mit Gleichstrom und ihre Verwendung zur Bestimmung von Dielektrizitätskonstanten und Absorptionen.

Schiller. 42377. Aenderung der Dielektrizitätskonstante des Kautschuks bei Zug senkrecht zu den Kraftlinien.

Schulze. 42436. Dielektrizitätskonstante und langwelliges Refraktionsvermögen binärer Gemische.

Tobey. 42806. Rigidità dielettrica dell' olio.

Vallauri. 42878. Misure sopra un condensatore a celluloide.

Vaupel. 42897. Dielektrizitätskonstante flüssiger Kristalle.

Verain. 42902. La constante diélectrique de l'anhydride carbonique au voisinage du point critique.

Wagner. 42984. Messung dielektrischer Verluste mit der Wechselstrombrücke.

Wallot. 42996. Einfluss von Hüllen und Schirmen auf elektromagnetische Drahtwellen. 42997: Elektrische Drahtwellen.

5253 ELECTROSTRICTION.

Nikolaev. 41627. Elektrostriktion und Funkenbildung in Elektrolyten. (Russ.)

5260 PYRO- AND PIEZO-ELECTRICITY. OTHER SOURCES.

Dike. 39766. Photo-electric potentials of thin cathode films.

Stuhlmann. 42694. Difference in the photoelectric effect caused by incident and emergent light.

Veen, van der. 42898. Recherches physico-chimiques et crystallographiques sur la symétrie du diamant. 42899: Recherches piézo- et pyroélectriques sur le diamant. (Hollandais.)

5270 ATMOSPHERIC ELECTRICITY.

L'origine de l'électricité atmosphérique. J. d'A. Rev. technique 1906 (279-289). [5270].

Protokoll über die Sitzung der luftelektrischen Kommission der kartellierten deutschen Akademien zu Leipzig am 30. Oktober 1910. Leipzig Ber. Ges. Wiss. math.-phys. Kl. 63 1911 (3-13).

Angenheister. 38969. Luftelektrische Beobachtungen am Samoa-Observatorium 1906, 1907, 1908.

Ballet. 39062. Les mesures récentes d'électricité atmosphérique en ballon libre. 39063; **Chauveau.** 39543: Observations sur les charges électriques de la pluie en 1910 au Puy-en-Velay.

Chauveau. 39544. Mesures récentes du courant vertical de conductibilité entre l'atmosphère et le sol.

Carie. 39669. Radioaktivität.

Gockel. 40231. Messungen der durchdringenden Strahlung bei Ballonfahrten.

Guarini. 40342; **Lagrange.** 40978; **Ludeling.** 41213; **Marcillac.** 41321. L'électricité atmosphérique.

Kotelow. 40898. Ionisation der Atmosphäre während des Durchganges des Halleyschen Kometen.

Lagrange. 40977. L'électricité atmosphérique dans les régions antarctiques.

Le Cadet. 41047. L'origine des manifestations électriques des orages.

Lindemann. 41151. Radioaktivität der Atmosphäre und ihre Abhängigkeit von meteorologischen Faktoren.

Nordmann. 41642. Diverses recherches relatives au magnétisme terrestre, à l'ionisation atmosphérique et au champ électrique de la Terre, exécutées notamment à l'occasion de l'éclipse totale de Soleil du 30 août 1905.

Pavlow. 41775. Anwendung der thermodynamischen Theorie der dispersen Systeme auf Hydrometeore.

Radge. 42240. Electrification of the air near the Zambesi falls.

Schünemann. 42424. Elektrischer Zustand der Luft in Höhlen und Kellern. Diss.

Simpson and **Wright.** 42526. Atmospheric electricity over the ocean.

Thornton. 42785. Thunderbolts.

Turpain. 42847. Effets d'un coup de foudre sur une antenne réceptrice d'ondes électriques. 42849, 50: Appareils enregistreurs et préviseurs des orages. 42851: La protection contre l'orage.

Unruh. 42863. Methodik luftelektrischer Messungen.

Vallot. 42884. Protection contre la foudre des observatoires de grande altitude.

Weiler. 43046. Ursprung der Luftelektrizität.

MAGNETISM.

5400 GENERAL.

Bauer. 39121. Broader aspects of research in terrestrial magnetism.

Bidwell. 39242A. Magnetism.

Weiss. 43064. Razionalità dei rapporti magnetici molecolari; il magneton.

Williams. 43141. Comparison of the influence of planes of transverse section on the magnetic properties of iron and of nickel bars.

Zahn. 43235. Magnetischer Skineffekt von Metallscheiben in hochfrequenten Wechselfeldern.

5410 NATURAL AND ARTIFICIAL MAGNETS.

(See also 6030.)

Bestelmeyer. 39230. Berechnung, Herstellung und Messung eines homogenen Magnetfeldes.

Colard. 39600. Les efforts mécaniques dans les champs électriques ou magnétiques.

Drysdale. 39804. Propagation of magnetic waves in an iron bar.

Grotrian. 40318. Eisenzylinder im homogenen Magnetfelde.

Müller. 41528. Pole gerader Drahtmagneten.

Oxen. 41713. Corpi magnetici composti di elementi non magnetici.

Morris and **Langford**. 41506. The method of constant rate of change of flux as a standard for determining magnetisation curves of iron.

Murdoch. 41544. A friction permeameter.

Oxen. 41748. Thermomagnetische Eigenschaften der Elemente.

Panebianco. 41738. Suscettibilità magnetica dei metalli ferromagnetici in campi deboli.

Peirce. 41789. Effects of sudden changes in the inductances of electric circuits as illustrative of the absence of magnetic lag and of the Von Waltenhofen phenomenon in finely divided cores.

Roop. 42176. Methode für Untersuchungen über die magnetische Permeabilität der Gase. 42177 : Magnetische Eigenschaften der Flammen.

Sève. 42496. Mesure des champs magnétiques en valeur absolue.

Siegbahn. 42597. Magnetische Feldmessung.

Stern. 42643. Determinazione dei campi magnetici di un motore monofase a repulsione sistema Déri.

Stüler. 42655. Magnetization of cobalt as a function of the temperature and the determination of its intrinsic magnetic field. 42657 : Saturation value of the specific intensity of magnetization of cobalt at various temperatures.

Takamine, **Ōba** and **Matsumoto**. 42735. Induced magnetism in an elliptic toroid.

Wild. 43136. La prova magnetica del ferro per trasformatori.

5450 MEASUREMENT OF HYSTERESIS. ENERGY LOSSES.

Alexanderson. 38924. Magnetische Eigenschaften des Eisens bei Hochfrequenz bis zu 200000 Per Sek.

Beattie e **Gerrard**. 39133. L'isteresi magnetica alla temperatura dell' aria liquida.

Epstein. 39924. Magnetische Prüfung von Eisenblech.

Kummer. 40945. Magnetisierung des Eisens bei sehr kleinen Feldstärken.

La Rosa. 41605. Due regole semplici per l'interpolazione grafica tra due curve particolari di magnetizzazione.

Ollivier. 41675. Aimantation hystérétique des électro-aimants droits.

Perrier. 41807. Les variations thermiques de l'hystérèse tournants et l'hystérèse alternative.

Radt. 41989, 41990. Die Eisenverluste in elliptischen Drehfeldern.

Steiner. 42630. Hysteresisverluste der ferromagnetischen Manganaluminiumbronzen in Abhängigkeit von der Frequenz des Wechselfeldes.

Weiss. 43068. La grandeur du magnéton déduite des coefficients d'aimantation des sels de fer.

Wild. 43135. Zusätzliche Eisenverluste in umlaufenden glatten Ringankern. Drehende Hysterese.

Wild. 43136. Testing of transformer iron.

Thompson. 42771. Ciclo di isteresi e figure di Lissajous ; energia dissipata in un ciclo di isteresi.

Vallauri. 42880. Isteresi del ferro nei cicli asimmetrici di magnetizzazione alternativa.

5460 RELATIONS BETWEEN THERMAL, ELASTIC AND MAGNETIC PROPERTIES OF BODIES. EFFECT OF TEMPERATURE.

Behnsen. 39462. Einfluss von thermischer Behandlung auf den Magnetismus des Kupfers.

Brown. 39421. Mechanical stress and magnetisation of nickel (Part II), and the subsidence of torsional oscillations in nickel and iron wires when subjected to the influence of longitudinal magnetic fields.

Ercolini. 39925, 7. Variazioni magnetiche prodotte nel ferro e nel nichel dalla deformazione. 39926 : Alcuni fenomeni magneto-elastici del ferro e del nichel.

Gnesotto e **Binghinotto**. 40348. Costanti magnetiche di leghe debolmente magnetiche.

———— e **Breda**. 40349. Il fenomeno Wiedemann in fili sottili di acciaio al silicio.

Hilpert und Mathesius. 40524.
Magnetische Eigenschaften von Mangan- und Nickelstählen.

Holtz. 40551. Einfluss von Fremdstoffen auf Elektrolyteisen und seine magnetischen Eigenschaften.

Kamerlingh Onnes. 40722. Die im cryogenen Laboratorium zu Leyden ausgeführten Untersuchungen.

———— and Perrier. 40725-6. Para- and diamagnetism at very low temperatures. The initial susceptibility of nickel at very low temperatures. (English, Dutch.)

Leduc. 41053. Sur le travail d'aimantation.

Moir. 41478. Influence of temperature upon the magnetic properties of a graded series of carbon steels.

Owen. 41715. Change of resistance of nickel and iron wires placed longitudinally in strong magnetic fields.

Owen. 41718. Thermomagnetische Eigenschaften der Elemente.

Piola. 41845. Magnetizzazione, temperatura e campo magnetico nel ferro.

Ross. 42193. Propriétés de certains alliages ternaires de cuivre.

Stifler. 42655. Magnetization of cobalt as a function of the temperature and the determination of its intrinsic magnetic field.

Vallauri. 42882. Perdite per magnetizzazione alternativa e rotante nelle macchine elettriche.

Weiss et Fœx. 43073. L'aimantation des corps ferromagnétiques au-dessus du point de Curie.

Wilson and Budd. 43151. Previous magnetic history as affected by temperature.

5462 MAGNETOSTRICTION.

Houstoun. 40571 : Leduc. 41052 : Nikolaev. 41623.

Williams. 43145. Joule and Wiedemann magnetostrictive effects in steel tubes.

5466 MAGNETIC PROPERTIES OF ALLOYS OF IRON AND OF OTHER FERROMAGNETIC SUBSTANCES.

Alexanderson. 38924. Magnetische Eigenschaften des Eisens bei Hochfrequenz.

Behnsen. 39162. Einfluss von Oxydbildung und thermischer Behandlung auf den Magnetismus des Kupfers.

Bloch. 39287. Magnetische Eigenschaften der Nickel-Kobalt-Legierungen.

Epstein. 39923. Determinazione delle proprietà magnetiche della lamiera di ferro.

Gnesotto e Binghinotto. 40347. Costanti magnetiche di leghe debolmente magnetiche.

Griffiths. 40303. Magnetic properties of some manganese steels.

Hadfield and Hopkinson. 40386. Magnetic properties of iron and its alloys in intense fields.

Hamley and Rossiter. 40406. Magnetic properties of stalloy.

Hilpert et alii. 40520-1, 4 ; Mathesius. 41363. Magnetische Eigenschaften von Nickel- und Manganstählen.

———— und Dieckmann. 40522. Eisen- und Manganarsenide. 40523 : Ferromagnetische Verbindungen des Mangans mit Phosphor, Arsen, Antimon und Wismut.

Ihde. 40615. Magnetisierbarkeit von Mangan, Mangankupfer und Chrom.

Kaufmann und Meier. 40742 ; Gans. 40129, 40130. Magnetische Eigenschaften elektrolytischer Eisenschichten.

Knowlton. 40825. Heusler alloys.

Lahrs. 40986. Einfluss der thermischen Behandlung auf die magnetischen Eisensiliciumlegierungen.

Lang. 40996. Einfluss des Mangans auf die Eigenschaften des Flusseisens.

Martens. 41349. Metalle und Legierungen.

Mendenhall and Lent. 41399. A method of measuring the susceptibility of weakly magnetic substances and a study of the susceptibility of alloys of bismuth with tellurium and thallium.

Owen. 41718. Thermomagnetische Eigenschaften der Elemente.

Pascal. 41758, 41759. Recherche magnétochimiques sur la structure atomique des halogènes.

Richarz. 42103. Magnetismus von Legierungen.

Ross and Gray. 42194. Magnetism of the copper-manganese tin alloys under varying thermal treatment.

Steiner. 42630. Hysteresisverluste der ferromagnetischen Manganaluminiumbronzen in Abhängigkeit von der Frequenz des Wechselfeldes.

Take. 42736. Alterungs- und Umwandlungs-Studien an Heuslerschen ferromagnetisierbaren Aluminium-Manganbronzen ; Schmiedeproben.

Viscidi. 42918. Le proprietà magnetiche del ferro e leghe relative in campi intensi.

Wedekind. 43023. Beziehungen zwischen magnetischen Eigenschaften und chemischer Natur.

———— und Veit. 43025. Ferromagnetische Verbindungen des Mangans.

Weiss et Bloch. 43072. L'aimantation du nickel, du cobalt et des alliages de nickel et de cobalt.

5467 MAGNETIC PROPERTIES OF SALTS AND SOLUTIONS.

Bahr und Koenigsberger. 39049. Farbe anorganischer Salze und Berechnung der schwingenden Teile.

Bose. 39336. Schwarmtheorie der anisotropen Flüssigkeiten. [Klärung durch magnetische Kräfte.]

du Bois. 39809. L'effet Zeeman généralisé dans les absorbants sélectifs.

Feytis. 39993. Magnétisme de quelques sels complexes. 39995 : Étude magnétique du rôle de l'eau dans la constitution de quelques hydrates solides.

Heydweiller. 40512. Magnetonentheorie. [Lösungen paramagnetischer Salze.]

Oxley. 41719. Magnetic susceptibilities of certain compounds.

Pascal. 41756.

Statescu. 42617. Solutions de sels magnétoptes hétérogènes dans un champ magnétique hétérogène.

Weber. 43019. Magnetisierbarkeit der Oxyd- und Oxydulsalze der Eisengruppe.

Wedekind. 43023. Beziehungen zwischen magnetischen Eigenschaften und chemischer Natur.

———— und Horst. 43024. Magnetisierbarkeit und Magnetonenzahlen der Oxyde und Sulfide des Vanadiums.

5470 DIAMAGNETISM.

Behnsen. 39162. Einfluss von Oxydbildung und thermischer Behandlung auf den Magnetismus des Kupfers.

Owen. 41718.

5480 PHYSICAL THEORIES OF THE NATURE OF MAGNETISM.

Belot. 39170. Expériences de Weyber sur les tourbillons.

Gans. 40126. Elektronentheorie des Ferromagnetismus. 40129 : Magnetische Eigenschaften elektrolytischer Eisenschichten.

Harckmae. 40423. Le magnétisme et l'électricité d'après De Heen.

Heydweiller. 40512. Magnetonentheorie. [Lösungen paramagnetischer Salze.]

Pascal. 41757. Mode de contrôle optique des analyses magnétochimiques. 41758 : Recherches magnétochimiques. 41759 : Recherches magnétochimiques sur la structure atomique des halogènes.

Richarz. 42101. Anwendung der Elektronentheorie auf den Magnetismus.

Weiss. 43064-5. Rationalité des rapports des moments magnétiques moléculaires et le magnéton. 43066 : Une propriété nouvelle de la molécule magnétique. 43067 : Rationalité des rapports des moments magnétiques des atomes et un nouveau constituant universel de la matière. 43070 : Le magnéton dans les corps solides paramagnétiques.

5490 THEORIES CONCERNING THE TERRESTRIAL MAGNETIC FIELD.

Bauer. 39122. Allgemeine Gesichtspunkte für die erdmagnetischen Untersuchungen. (Ungar.)

Bidlingmaier. 39242 : **Bauer.** 39120. Säkulare Variation des Erdmagnetismus.

Bosler. 39340. Les relations des courants telluriques avec les perturbations magnétiques.

Chree. 39553A.

Maunder. 41373. L'origine solaire des perturbations du magnétisme terrestre.

Nodon. 41637–S. Variations de l'intensité du magnétisme terrestre.

Ricco. 42094. Anomalies de la pesanteur et du champ magnétique terrestre en Calabre et en Sicile mises en rapport avec la constitution du sol.

Schmidt. 42386. Zerlegung des erdmagnetischen Feldes.

Weiler. 43046. Ursprung des Erdmagnetismus und der Luftelektrizität.

THE ELECTRIC CURRENT AND CONDUCTION.

5600 GENERAL.

Report of the British Association Committee of practical standards for electrical measurements. Elect. London **67** 1911 (895).

Günther. 40346. Der elektrische Strom. Bd 1.

Jonas. 40678. Mathematische Zeichen [für Phasenverschiebung].

Mayer. 41381. Elektrotechnische Messkunde.

Nowak. 41649. Maschine zum Berechnen elektrischer Leitungsnetze.

Occhialini. 41656. Definizione di intensità di corrente elettrica.

Szilárd. 42729. Ausströmung elektrischer Wellen aus Metallen. (Ungar.)

5610 THEORY AND CONSTRUCTION OF PRIMARY CELLS.

Abegg :, Auerbach und **Luther.** 38885. Messungen elektromotorischer Kräfte galvanischer Ketten mit wässerigen Elektrolyten.

Auerbach. 39011. Potentiale der wichtigsten Bezugselektroden.

Bechterew. 39136. Untersuchung einiger galvanischer Elemente mit Kohlenanoden.

Beutner. 39235. Versuche mit Gaselementen unter Strom bei hohen Temperaturen.

Bjerrum. 39274. Elimination des Flüssigkeitspotentials bei Messungen von Elektrolenpotentialen.

Brandt. 39384. Herstellung von Kohlenelektroden.

Bronson and **Sha v.** 39414. Clark and Weston standard cells.

Capart. 39487. Les caractéristiques des piles.

Cohen. 39596. Berechnung elektromotorischer Kräfte aus thermischen Grössen. 39597 : Thermodynamik der Normalelemente.

Cooper. 39619. Benkö primary battery.

Ehrhardt. 39879. Hydromechanischer Apparat zur Erläuterung einiger beim galvanischen Element auftretenden Erscheinungen.

Ginneken und **Kruyt.** 40192. Theorie der Normalelemente.

Glazebrook. 40214. Electromotive force of standard cells.

Halla. 40400. Thermodynamische Berechnung elektromotorischer Kräfte.

Heidenreich. 40466. Photo-elektromotorische Untersuchungen von Chlorsilber und Bromsilber.

Heyl. 40514. Conversion of the energy of carbon into electrical energy on solution in iron.

Hulett. 40588. Construction of standard cells.

——— 40589 : **Ginneken.** 40191. Merkurosulfat als Depolarisator in Normalelementen.

Kanevskij. 40727. Piles thermiques. (Russ.)

Landis. 40995. Laws concerning voltaic cells.

Le Blanc. 41044. Chemisch-passive unpolarisierbare Elektrode.

Nylén. 41654. Trockenelement " RR." (Schwedisch.)

Palma (Di). 41736; **Pezzini.** 41821. Nuovo generatore di corrente elettrica primaria.

Peller. 41794. Neuerungen an galvanischen Elementen.

Pfeiffer. 41822. Chemische Theorie galvanischer Ketten vom Typus des Daniell-Elementes.

Pollitzer. 41929. Bestimmung spezifischer Wärmen bei tiefen Temperaturen und ihre Verwertung zur Berechnung elektromotorischer Kräfte. 41930; Thermodynamik des Clark-elements.

Ramsey. 42006. Polarization of cadmium cells.

Reichinstein. 42059. Belastungsfähigkeit der galvanischen Elemente. 42060; Chemische Polarisation der umkehrbaren elektrolytischen Elektrode.

Rosa, Dorsey and **Miller.** 42181. The Bureau of standards' current balances.

Sichling. 42504. Natur der Photochloride des Silbers und deren Lichtpotentiale.

Spencer. 42584. Elektrode dritter Art zur Messung der Potentiale des Thalliumions.

Timofejew. 42799. Einfluss des Druckes auf die Affinität.

Zacharias. 43232. Erzeugung elektrischer Kraft auf elektrochemischem Wege.

5620 THEORY AND CONSTRUCTION OF SECONDARY CELLS.

Ancora sull' Accumulatore Edison. [Trad. Sunto.] Industria Milano 24 1910 (370–372).

Beckmann. 39150. Tecnica degli accumulatori stazionari e trasportabili.

Cerati. 39528. Acido solforico per accumulatori.

(c-1388)

Coppadoro. 39620. L'accumulatore Edison 1910.

Fredenhagen. 40068. Fortschritte im Akkumulatorenbau. Edison-Akkumulator.

Goldschmidt. 40248. Accumulateur léger.

Herrmann. 40491; **Holzt.** 40553. Elektrotechnik.

Hobel. 40535. Volumenänderungen von Sammelelektroden.

Kretzschmar. 40911. Krankheiten des stationären elektrischen Blei-Akkumulators.

Lucchini. 41211. Elettroliti nuovi ed usati d'elementi secondari al piombo.

Montpellier. 41489. L'accumulatore alcalino a ferro-nichel.

Morse. 41508. Storage batteries.

——— and **Sargent.** 41509. Internal resistance of the lead accumulator.

Raimondi. 41994. Procedimento anoditico per determinare la capacità di alcuni tipi di condensatori.

Rebora. 42038. Raffreddamento ed isolamento dei trasformatori.

Š. apošnikov]. 42317. Hochspannungsakkumulatorenbatterie. (Russ.)

Stauffer. 42619. Verunreinigungen der Akkumulatorensäure.

Reiffer. 42061. Un dispositivo di carica per batterie di accumulatori.

Schleicher. 42384. Schnellformation von Bleiakkumulatoren mit Lösungen von Schwefelsäure und Chlorat bezw. Perchlorat.

Winther. 43162. Elektrischer Lichtakkumulator.

5630 OHM'S LAW. DIVIDED CURRENTS AND NETWORKS OF LINEAR CONDUCTORS.

Arlitewicz. 38981. Méthode qui peut servir au calcul simplifié de la distribution des courants dans les circuits fermés complexes. (Polish.)

Dittmann. 39772. Berechnung elektrischer Leitungsnetze.

Donati. 39782. Distribuzione del potenziale nelle reti di fili conduttori.

2 A

Holzt. 40553. Die Schule des Elektrotechnikers.

Mattausch. 41368. Die Verlegungs-oder Reductionsmethode von Frick zur Ermittelung der Stromverteilung in Leitungsnetzen.

Nowak. 41649. Maschine zum Berechnen elektrischer Leitungsnetze.

Searle. 42467. Resistances with current and potential terminals.

5640 METHODS OF COMPARISON OF RESISTANCE.

Brown and Clark. 39420. A method of measuring the fluctuations in a rapidly varying resistance.

Bruger. 39426. Messapparate.

Feussner. 39992. Neuer Kompensationsapparat.

Lichtenecker. 41122. Poggendorfsche Kompensationsmethode.

Schlee. 42383. Methoden und Apparate zur Widerstandsmessung.

Streintz und Wellik. 42681 ; Koenigsberger et alii. 40872. Widerstand zwischen Metall und Kristall an ebenen Grenzflächen.

Wurm. 43228. Messbrücke zur Untersuchung von Blitzableiteranlagen.

5650 STANDARDS OF RESISTANCE. ABSOLUTE DETERMINATION.

Curtis and Grover. 39675. Resistance coils for alternating current work.

Glazebrook, Bonefield and Smith. 40215. Heating effect of the currents in precise measurements of electrical resistance.

Wolff et alii. 43178. Construction of primary mercurial resistance standards.

5660 SPECIFIC RESISTANCE· RELATIONS TO TEMPERATURE, TORSION, MAGNETISM, LIGHT, Etc.

Addenbrooke. 38962. Selenium.

Amaduzzi. 38939, 38940. L'effetto Hallwachs nel selenio cristallino. 38941 : Der innere Hallwachs-Effekt im Selen.

Aten. 39005. Spezifische Leitfähigkeit des geschmolzenen Kaliumnitrats.

Aust. 39014, 39015. A variable high resistance of India ink on paper.

Bates. 39106. Effet de la lumière sur l'isolement par le soufre.

Beckman. 39149. Einfluss des Druckes auf die elektrische Leitfähigkeit bei Pyrit, Eisenglanz und Metalllegierungen.

Berndt und Wirtz. 39200 ; Müller. 41533. Elektrischer Widerstand von unbewehrtem Beton.

Boll. 39314. Application de l'électromètre à l'étude des réactions chimiques dans les électrolytes.

Boudouard. 39350. Résistivité électrique des aciers spéciaux.

Broniewski. 39410, 3. Propriétés électriques des alliages aluminium-magnésium, des métaux alcalins, du rhodium et de l'iridium.

Brown. 39417-9. Electric properties of light-positive and light-negative selenium.

Bruni und Meneghini. 39432. Bildung metallischer fester Lösungen durch Diffusion im festen Zustande.

Byk und Borck. 39459. Einfluss des Lichtes auf das Leitvermögen von Anthracenlösungen.

Carvallo. 39509. Conductibilité de l'éther pur.

Clay. 39577, 9. Change with temperature of the electrical resistance of metals and alloys at very low temperatures. 39578 : Influence of electric waves upon platinum mirrors. (Coherer action.)

Corbino. 39623, 31. Variazioni periodiche di resistenza dei filamenti sottili percorsi da correnti alternate e deduzione delle loro proprietà termiche a temperatura elevata.

Dellinger. 39731. Temperature coefficient of resistance of copper. 39729 : The expression of resistivity of electrical conductors. 39730 : A variable low resistance.

Edler. 39867. Specifische elektrische Leitfähigkeit und ihre Abhängigkeit vom Widerstands-Temperatur-Koeffizienten und vom Wärme-Ausdehnungs-Koeffizienten.

Edwards. 39868. Distribution of current and variation of resistance in linear conductors of square and rectangular cross-section when carrying alternating currents of high frequency.

Eucken und **Gehlhoff.** 39950. Elektrisches, thermisches Leitvermögen und Wiedemann-Franzsche Zahl der Antimon-Cadmiumlegierungen zwischen 0° und 190° C.

Geibel. 40158. Elektrische und mechanische Eigenschaften von Edelmetall-Legierungen. II.

Glatzel. 40209. Die Trägheit von Selenzellen.

Goldmann u. **Kalandyk.** 40243. Lichtelektrische Untersuchungen an festen Dielektriken.

Gripenberg. 40305. Kristallisation dünner Selenplatten.

Guntz et **Broniewski.** 40366. Résistance électrique des métaux alcalins, du gallium et du tellure. (Polish.)

Hayes. 40457. Electrical conductivity of argentic sulphide.

Huber-Stockar. 40582. L'alluminio per le condutture elettriche.

Immisch. 40617. Leitfähigkeit der Selenpräparate im Lichte.

Kamerlingh Onnes. 40716, 17, 20. Change of electric resistance of pure metals of very low temperatures, etc. Disappearance of the resistance of mercury. (English, Dutch.)

Korber. 40876. Widerstandsmaterial mit variablem Temperaturkoeffizienten.

Korolikov et **Bartoŝević.** 40895. Les lampes à incandescence de zirconium. (Russ.)

Lafay. 40974. Mesure des pressions élevées déduite des variations de résistivité des inducteurs soumis à leur action.

Lang. 40996. Einfluss des Mangans auf die Eigenschaften des Flusseisens.

Lindeck. 41143. Beziehung zwischen dem Temperaturkoeffizienten und dem spezifischen Widerstand einiger Metalle, insbesondere von Kupfer.

(c-4388)

Loessuer. 41174. Unterphosphorige Säure und Wasserstoffverbindungen der Schwermetalle.

Lowy. 41177. Dielektrizitätskonstante und Leitfähigkeit der Gesteine.

Lutke. 41228. Gesetz von Wiedemann und Franz an Metalllegierungen.

Martin geb. **Landschütz.** 41341. Metallische Leiter von sehr hohem Widerstand und elektronentheoretische Folgerungen.

Meyer. 41425. Änderung des elektrischen Widerstandes reinen Eisens mit der Temperatur in dem Bereiche 0 bis 1000° C. Diss.

Muller. 41526. Absorption von Gasen durch Metalle.

Muller. 41532. Elektrische Leitfähigkeit der Metalllegierungen im flüssigen Zustande.

Nernst. 41581. Spezifische Wärme bei tiefen Temperaturen.

Nienhaus. 41610. Lichtelektrisches Verhalten von Lösungen. Diss.

Olie, jr. and **Kruyt.** 41672. Photoelectric phenomena with antimony sulphide (antimonite). (English, Dutch.)

Pecheux. 41779. Résistivité et thermoélectricité du tantale.

Pelabon. 41790. Résistivité des séléniures d'antimoine.

Pirani. 41852. Darstellungsweise für den Temperaturkoeffizienten des elektrischen Widerstandes.

———— und **Meyer.** 41854. Schmelzpunkt und Temperaturkoeffizient des spezifischen Widerstandes des Tantals.

Pochettino. 41895. Sensibilità alla luce dei preparati di selenio.

Polara. 41926. Conducibilità elettrica della saliva mista dell' uomo.

Raus. 42016. Galvanische Widerstandsänderung des Quecksilbers im Magnetfelde. (Čechisch.)

Ries. 42115. Spannungseffekt am Selen und Antimonit. 42116: Ursache der Lichtempfindlichkeit des Selens.

Rossi. 42290. Variazione di resistenza del mercurio e delle amalgame di bismuto nel campo magnetico.

2 A 2

Schulze. 42440. Wärmeleitfähigkeit einiger Edelmetallegierungen. 42416 : Bildung schlechtleitender Schichten bei der Elektrolyse des Glases.

Smith. 42539. Hall effect and some allied effects in alloys.

Somerville. 42571. Temperature coefficients of electrical resistance.

Steinberg. 42628–9. Halleffekt und Widerstandsänderung im Magnetfelde bei jodhaltigem Kupferjodür. Diss.

Streintz und **Wellik.** 42681 : **Koenigsberger** *et alii.* 40872. Widerstand zwischen Metall und Kristall an ebenen Grenzflächen.

Suchý. 42702. Aenderung des elektrischen Widerstandes der Stahl- und Eisendrähte bei mechanischer Spannung. (Čechisch.)

Szivessy und **Schäfer.** 42732. Erhöhung des elektrischen Leitvermögens bei flüssigen Dielektrika durch Bestrahlung mit ultraviolettem Lichte.

Uller. 42860. Elektrische Leitfähigkeiten von Meer und Land.

Urasow. 42864. Leitfähigkeit und Härte der Magnesium-Cadmiumlegierungen.

Vaillant. 42872. Variations de la conductibilité d'un corps phosphorescent sous l'action de la lumière.

Weidig. 43038. Legierungen.

Wolff and **Dellinger.** 43177. Electrical conductivity of commercial copper.

Zâvada. 43247. Anordnung zur Beseitigung der störenden Wirkungen der Trägheit von Selenzellen für telephotographische Zwecke.

Zomparelli. 43289. Le proprietà elettriche del selenio.

5675 NATURE OF METALLIC CONDUCTION. FREE ELECTRONS.

Achalme. 38897. Rôle des électrons intra-atomiques dans la catalyse.

Baedeker. 39042. Elektronentheorie der Thermoelektrizität.

Behr. 39311. Theory of electrons for metals. (Danish.)

Bernoulli. 39207–8. Elektronentheorie der metallischen Mischkristalle. 39209 : Das Nernstsche Wärmetheorem und die Thermodynamik der thermoelektrischen Erscheinungen.

Cermak. 39524. Theorien der Thermoelektrizität.

Clay. 39579. Der galvanische Widerstand von Metallen und Legierungen bei tiefen Temperaturen.

Corbino. 39625. Il fenomeno di Hall e la teoria elettronica dei metalli. 39627 : Effetti elettromagnetici dovuti alla distorsione che un campo produce sulla traiettoria degli ioni nei metalli.

Ishiwara. 40631. Elektronenbewegung in Metallen. 40632 : Berechnung der elektrischen Leitfähigkeit für oszillirende elektrische Kraft aus der Elektronentheorie.

Koenigsberger. 40858. Physikalische Messungen der chemischen Affinität durch Elektrizitätsleitung und Kanalstrahlen.

——————— und **Weiss.** 40873. Thermoelektrische Effekte (Thermokräfte, Thomsonwärme) und Wärmeleitung in einigen Elementen und Verbindungen. Experimentelle Prüfung der Elektronentheorie.

Krüger. 40919. Anwendung der Thermodynamik auf die Elektronentheorie der Thermoelektrizität.

Lama (De). 40987. Concetto di resistenza elettrica.

Lindemann. 41148. Beziehungen zwischen der elektrischen Leitfähigkeit der Metalle und ihrem Energiegehalt.

Martin geb. **Landschütz.** 41341. Beobachtungen an metallischen Leitern von sehr hohem Widerstand und elektronentheoretische Folgerungen.

Nernst. 41581. Spezifische Wärme bei tiefen Temperaturen. 41582 : Ein allgemeines Gesetz, das Verhalten fester Stoffe bei sehr tiefen Temperaturen betreffend.

Nicholson. 41607. Number of electrons concerned in metallic conduction.

Reinganum. 42067. Elektronentheorie der Metalle.

Weiss. 43062. Elektronentheorie der Thermoelektrizität.

Werner. 43087. Permanente Dehnung und elektrische und thermische Leitfähigkeit der Metalle.

Zakrzewski. 43236. Optische Eigenschaften der Metalle.

5680 CONDUCTION IN CONTINUOUS MEDIA OF TWO OR THREE DIMENSIONS.

Broniewski. 39442. Propriétés électriques des alliages d'aluminium.

Guertler. 40347. Electrical conductivity and constitution of alloys.

Härdén. 40388. A curious coherer phenomenon.

Huber-Stockar. 40582. L'alluminio per le condutture elettriche.

Léauté. 41033. Certaines difficultés que présente l'emploi des développements exponentiels.

Lees. 41063. Effect of a narrow saw cut in the edge of a conducting strip on the potential and stream lines in the strip and on the resistance of the strip.

Nicholson. 41608. Optical properties of fused metals.

Rusch. 42264. Plattenförmige Leiter in zylinderischem Wechselfeld.

5685 CONDUCTION IN GASES AND VAPOURS. (See 6805.)

Andrade. 38960. Eine neue Methode, die Flammengeschwindigkeit zu bestimmen.

Beatty. 39134. Ionisation of heavy gases by X-rays.

Becker. 39144. Elektrizitätsträger in Gasen.

Bloch. 39285. Les actions chimiques et l'ionisation par barbotage.

Bonacini e Nicolis. 39319. Conducibilità elettrica dell' aria.

Bouty. 39371. Cohésion diélectrique des gaz monoatomiques.

Bragg. 39379. Mode of ionization by X-rays.

Broglie. 39404. Couche superficielle très mince contenant des ions des deux signes. 39405: Les petits ions dans les gaz issus des flammes.

────── et Brizard. 39409. Effets d'ionisation des gaz observés

en présence de corps non radioactifs. Activité et luminescence du sulfate de quinine.

Chassy. 39540. Conductibilité des gaz sous la pression atmosphérique sous l'influence d'une haute tension alternative.

Clo. 39583. Effet de la température sur l'ionisation d'un gaz.

Franck und Pringsheim. 40050. Elektrisches und optisches Verhalten der Chlorflamme.

Fredenhagen. 40069. Abgabe negativer Elektronen von erhitztem Kalium und Natrium und Leitfähigkeit der Dämpfe dieser Metalle.

Füchtbauer. 40093. Elektrizitätsleitung in gesättigtem Alkalimetalldampf.

Greinacher. 40298. Stromkurve für gleichförmig ionisierte Luft.

Hauser. 40447. Untersuchung von Bronsonwiderständen.

Hoffmann. 40544. Experimentelle Prüfung der durch verschiedene Messungsanordnungen in einem homogenen elektrischen Felde hervorgerufenen Störungen (Deformationen) der Niveauflächen. Diss.

Ichinohe and Kinoshita. 40605. Unilateral electric conductivity in a vacuum bulb containing an incandescent metallic filament.

────── ────── and Kimura. 40606. Electrical conductivity of the air.

Jacot. 40646. Effect of the electric discharge in water vapour.

Kinoshita and Ichinohe. 40990. Ionization due to an incandescent metallic filament in a vacuum tube.

Leineweber. 41086. Elektrische Leitfähigkeit von Salzdämpfen.

Lenard. 41095. Elektrizitätsleitung und Lichtemission metallhaltiger Flammen.

────── et Ramsauer. 41099. L'action de la lumière ultraviolette de très courte longueur d'onde sur les gaz.

Lusby. 41247. Mobility of the positive flame ion.

Moreau. 41497. Conductibilité électrique des fluorures et rayonnements corpusculaires.

Owen and **Pealing.** 41717. Condensation nuclei produced by the action of light on iodine vapour.

Przibram. 41967. Ladungsbestimmungen an Nebelteilchen.

Reboul. 42040–1. Conductibilité accompagnant des réactions chimiques.

Reinganum. 42068. Ionenbeweglichkeit in Gasen.

Righi. 42131. L'action ionisante probable du champ magnétique. 42133, 42136. Influenza del campo magnetico sull'intensità di corrente nell'aria rarefatta.

Salles. 42301. La diffusion des ions gazeux.

Schmidt. 42389. Elektrizitätsleitung von Salzdämpfen.

Thieme. 42762. Elektrische Abscheidung von Kohlenstoff aus Flammen. 42763 : Abscheidungen aus Flammen durch Elektrizität.

Todd. 42807. Mobility of the positive ion in gases at low pressures.

Townsend. 42814. Charges on ions in gases. 42815 : The mode of conduction in gases.

Unruh. 42863. Methodik luftelektrischer Messungen.

Wilson. 43153. Velocity of the ions of alkali salt vapours.

5695 MEASUREMENT OF ELECTROMOTIVE FORCE.

Baillehache. 39053. Force électromotrice de l'élément Weston normal.

Guglielmo. 40348. Sede della forza elettromotrice delle coppie voltaiche. 40349 : Valore delle componenti la forza elettromotrice della coppia Daniell.

Orlov. 41694. Deux nouvelles méthodes potentiométriques. (Russ.)

5700 MEASUREMENTS OF CONTINUOUS CURRENTS (STRENGTH, CONSUMPTION OF ENERGY, Etc.).

Brooks. 39415. Deflection potentiometer considered as a generalized null instrument.

Chopin. 39552. La mesure absolue des courants de grande intensité.

Kučera. 40932. Messung sehr hoher Potentiale. (Čechisch.)

Tietze. 42793. Untersuchungen über die Brauchbarkeit des Thermoelementes zu energetischen Messungen.

Turnwald. 42846. Zusammenhang zwischen Potentialdifferenz und Stromstärke in einem metallischen Leiter.

5705 MEASUREMENTS OF ALTERNATING CURRENTS (PERIODICITY, AMPLITUDE, CONSUMPTION OF ENERGY, WORK, Etc.).

Il rendimento delle lampade elettriche a incandescenza. [Sunto. Trad.] Roma Ann. Soc. ing. 26 1911 (282–283).

Arnò. 38983. Nuovi metodi di misura industriale. 38986 : Voltamperometro, voltcoulombometro, fasometro.

Barbagelata. 39068, 39071. Prova indiretta dei trasformatori di misura per forti intensità di corrente.

Corbino. 39626. Variazioni periodiche di resistenza dei filamenti metallici sottili resi incandescenti con correnti alternate e deduzione delle loro proprietà termiche a temperatura elevata.

Curtis and **Grover.** 39675. Resistance coils for alternating current work.

Edler. 39866. Ein Wattmeter-Umschalter für Drehstrom-Leistungs-Messungen.

Edwards. 39868. Distribution of current and variation of resistance in linear conductors of square and rectangular cross-section when carrying alternating currents of high frequency.

Forssblad. 40035 Berechnung des Spannungsabfalles in Freileitungen.

Glatzel. 40210. Maschine zur Demonstration von Wechselstromvorgängen.

Glatzel. 40213. Demonstrationsversuch über die Energieaufnahme in Wechselstromkreisen.

Görges, Weidig und **Jaensch.** 40236. Bestimmung der Koronaverluste auf Freileitungen.

Guillot. 40361. Application du polygone de Fresnel à la composition des forces électromotrices d'induction.

Hausrath. 40452. Darstellung periodischer Hochfrequenzkurven mit der Braunschen Röhre.

Kapp. 40730. Elektrische Wechselströme.

Leprince-Ringuet. 41106. Propriétés géométriques du point représentant la terre dans le diagramme des voltages d'un réseau polyphasé.

Motta. 41499. La calcolazione di massimo tornaconto delle linee per trasmissione elettrica di energia.

Orlich. 41693. Die Theorie der Wechselströme.

Pichelmayer und Schrutka. 41834. Analyse von Wechselstromkurven.

Steinhaus. 42632. Angaben von Hitzdrahtinstrumenten bei schnellen Schwingungen.

Tietze. 42793. Brauchbarkeit des Thermoelementes zu energetischen Messungen.

Wittmann. 43168. Experimentaluntersuchungen ungedämpfter und gedämpfter Oszillationsphänomene. (Ungarisch.)

Zahn. 43233. Scheinbarer Halleffekt bei hochfrequenten Wechselströmen und ein hierauf beruhendes empfindliches Nullinstrument.

Ziegenberg. 43276. Wechselstrom-Präzisions-Messmethoden.

5710 THERMOELECTRICITY. PELTIER AND THOMSON EFFECT.

Altenkirch. 38935. Elektrothermische Kälteerzeugung und reversible elektrische Heizung.

Baedeker. 39042. Elektronentheorie der Thermoelektrizität.

Beck. 39138. Absolute Messungen über den Peltier-Effekt.

Bernoulli. 39207-8. Elektronentheorie der metallischen Mischkristalle. 39209: Thermodynamik der thermoelektrischen Erscheinungen.

Bordoni. 39326. Influenza dello stato magnetico sopra i fenomeni termoelettrici.

Broniewski. 39440, 2. Propriétés électriques des alliages d'aluminium.

——— et Hackspill. 39413. Propriétés électriques des métaux alcalins, du rhodium et de l'iridium.

Cermak. 39524. Theorien der Thermoelektrizität.

——— und Schmidt. 39525. Die thermoelektrischen Kräfte beim Übergang vom festen zum flüssigen Aggregatzustande.

Coblentz. 39590. Thermoelectric properties of molybdenum.

Dickson. 39759. Thermo-electric diagram from — 200° C. to 100° C.

Eucken und Gehlhoff. 39959. Elektrisches, thermisches Leitvermögen und Wiedemann-Franzsche Zahl der Antimon-Cadmiumlegierungen zwischen 0° und 190° C.

Geibel. 40158. Elektrische und mechanische Eigenschaften von Edelmetall-Legierungen.

Grober. 40310. Verwendung von Barretter und Thermoelement zu Messzwecken.

Jordan. 40684. The Thomson and Peltier effects. 40685: Direct measurement of the Peltier effect.

Kanevskij. 40727. Les piles thermiques. (Russ.)

Kimura et alii. 40784. Thermoelectric properties of minerals.

Koenigsberger und Weiss. 40873. Thermoelektrische Effekte und Wärmeleitung in einigen Elementen und Verbindungen.

Krüger. 40949. Anwendung der Thermodynamik auf die Elektronentheorie der Thermoelektrizität.

Liebisch. 41126. Schichtenbau und elektrische Eigenschaften des Zinnerzes.

Nernst. 41586. Thermodynamik und spezifische Wärme.

Oosterhuis. 41683A. Méthode pour la détermination de l'effet Peltier. 41684A: Le phénomène de Peltier et la pile thermo-électrique fer-mereure. (Hollandais.)

Pécheux. 41779. Résistivité et thermoélectricité du tantale.

Smith. 42539. Hall effect and some allied effects in alloys.

Starling. 42616. Demonstration of Peltier and Thomson effects.

Weiss. 43060-2.

Wunder. 43226. Thermoelemente.

5720 MEASUREMENTS RELATING TO ENERGY OF THE CURRENT. HEATING EFFECT.

Alexanderson. 38924. Magnetische Eigenschaften des Eisens bei Hochfrequenz.

Arnò. 38984. Misura industriale per la tariffazione dell'energia elettrica nei sistemi di distribuzione a corrente alternata.

Cegielskij. 39522. Sieden von Elektrolyten bei Stromdurchgang.

Corbino. 39626. Variazioni periodiche di resistenza dei filamenti metallici sottili resi incandescenti con correnti alternate.

Grober und **Zollich.** 40311. Theorie des Barretters.

Günther. 40345. Energie von Oeffnungs- und Schliessungsfunken.

Korolikov et **Bartošević.** 40895. Les lampes à incandescence de zirconium. (Russ.)

La Rosa. 41008. Schmelzen des Kohlenstoffs mittels des Jouleschen Effektes.

Lupi. 41246. Fattore di potenza dei circuiti trifasi.

Malloux. 41299. Determinazione della corrente costante che produce lo stesso riscaldamento di una corrente variabile.

Meyer. 41430. Theorie der Abschmelzsicherungen. 41431A: Kurzschlüsse in Wechselstromnetzen, ihre Rückwirkung auf die Generatoren, insbesondere bei Turbodynamos.

Norsa. 41645. Fattore di potenza e sistemi polifasi non equilibrati.

Ponzini. 41935. Apparecchio ad induzione per trasformare industrialmente in calore l'energia elettrica.

Squier and **Crehore.** 42587. Oscillatory interference bands and some practical applications.

5740 MEASUREMENT OF CAPACITY. (See 6005.)

Campbell. 39472. Method of determining capacities in measurements of ionization.

Geiger. 40164. Bestimmung der Kapazität eines Elektrometers.

Rohmann. 42162. Messung von Kapazitätsänderungen mit schnellen Schwingungen, angewandt auf die Vergleichung der Dielektrizitätskonstanten von Gasen.

Seibt. 42481. Präzisionsdrehplattenkondensator und eine Methode zum Vergleichen von Kapazitäten.

Squier and **Crehore.** 42587.

Wagner. 42984. Messung dielektrischer Verluste mit der Wechselstrombrücke.

5770 DETERMINATION OF RESISTANCE OF INSULATION. LOCATION OF FAULTS IN CONDUCTORS.

La porcellana per materiale elettrotecnico. Mon. tecn. Milano **16** 1910 (252-254).

Dina. 39768. Misura delle resistenze di isolamento in un impianto a corrente alternativa durante l'esercizio.

Giersing. 40186. Fehlerortsbestimmung in Fernsprechkabeln ohne gute Rückleitung.

Kulmann. 40944. Isolatori per alta tensione.

Monti. 41487. Materiali isolanti adoperati in elettrotecnica.

Osten. 41702. Phasophon, ein Instrument für die Betriebskontrolle in Drehstromwerken.

Planer. 41887. Methode für Fehlermessungen an Drehstromkabeln mit unterbrochener Ader und gleichzeitigem Erdschluss.

Raphael. 42012. Isolationsmessungen und Fehlerbestimmungen an elektrischen Starkstromleitungen.

Rebora. 42035. Isolatori di vetro e di porcellana.

Soleri. 42570. Sostegni per cavi ad alta tensione.

Stifler. 42656. Tests on certain electrical insulators at high temperatures.

Weicker. 43133. Comportamento elettrico degli isolatori delle linee aeree ad alta tensione.

Zeeman. 43253. Insulating power of liquid air for high potentials. (English, Dutch.)

5900 PHYSIOLOGICAL ELECTRICITY.

Handbuch der gesamten medizinischen Anwendungen der Elektrizität einschliesslich der Röntgenlehre. In drei Bdn bearb. v. A. Alexander [u. a. . . . .]. Hrsg. v. H. Boruttau und L. Mann . . . Bd 2. 1. Hälfte. Leipzig (W. Klinkhardt) 1911 (VII + 409 mit 1 Taf.). 28 cm. 20 M. [5900].

Albrecht. 38916. Methode zur Untersuchung elektrischer Vorgänge am menschlichen Körper.

Cardot et **Laugier.** 39494. Localisation des excitations de fermeture dans la méthode unipolaire.

Carnevale Arella. 39499. L'azione dei raggi X a dosi minime. 39500: Azione dei raggi Röntgen sul timo.

Doumer. 39791. D'Arsonvalisation.

Galeotti e **Porcelli.** 40115. Influenza della temperatura sulle correnti di demarcazione dei nervi.

Ghilarducci. 40179. Azione biologica e curativa della folgorazione.

Gildemeister. 40189.

Groedel und **Meyer-Lierheim.** 40313. Vergleich des Saitengalvanometers und des Oscillographen - Elektrocardiogramms.

Göcke. 40234. Schwankungen der Erfolge untermaximaler Reize.

Hoke. 40545; **Kahn.** 40711; **Rehfisch.** 42052; **Seemann** u. **Victoroff.** 42476; **Winterberg.** 43160. Elektrokardiogrammstudien.

Hoorweg. 40556. Perception des lumières brèves.

Kahane. 40710. Hochfrequenzströme und ihre Indikationen.

Kinoshita. 40792. Einfluss mehrerer aufeinanderfolgender wirksamer Reize auf den Ablauf der Reaktionsbewegungen bei Wirbellosen.

Lampe. 40990. Faradokutane Sensibilität. Diss.

Leduc. 41058. Der elektrische Widerstand des menschlichen Körpers.

Lenz. 41100. Kombination von Hochfrequenzströmen und Röntgenstrahlen. (A. d'Arsonvalströme. B. Diathermie.)

Moravcsik. 41495. Psychogalvanisches Reflexphänomen.

Muller. 41529. Induzierte elektrische Phänomene am menschlichen Körper und darauf beruhendes Tönen der Haut.

Nassauer. 41567. Wirksamkeit des Schutzes durch Isolierschemel und die Kapazität des menschlichen Körpers.

Piper. 41849. Aktionsströme der Krebsscherenmuskeln.

Reiss. 42074. Entartungsreaktion.

Rumpf. 42260. Physikalische Erscheinungen der oszillierenden Ströme.

Schwartz. 42449. Beeinflussung der Leistungsfähigkeit des polarisierten Nerven.

Simon. 42521. Physik und Technik der Thermopenetration.

Simons und **Hoffmann.** 42524. Aktionsströme der Muskeln während des Crampus.

Wertheim-Salomonson. 43095. Aktions-Ströme der willkürlichen und reflektorischen Kontraktionen der menschlichen Muskeln.

Wiener. 43056. Umkehr des Zuckungsgesetzes bei der Entartungsreaktion.

Wildermuth. 43137. Leitungswiderstand der Gewebe.

Wilke und **Atzler.** 43139. Versuche, die Reizwellen im Nerven durch Interferenz sichtbar zu machen.

Zanietowski. 43241. Kondensatorversuche. 43242: Berechnung der modernen Erregungskoeffizienten.

Zipp. 43284. Unter welchen Umständen ist die Berührung einer elektrischen Anlage gefährlich?

ELECTRICAL INSTRUMENTS AND MACHINES.

6000 GENERAL.

Elektromotor. Süddeutsche Monatsschrift für Elektrizitäts-Verwendung und -Verbreitung in Haus und Gemeinde. . . . Hrsg. v. Greeff. Jg 1. Berlin (U. Meyer) 1911. 26 cm. Der Jg zu 12 Nrn. 3,00 M. [0020 6000].

Fortschritte der Elektrotechnik. Hrsg. von **Strecker.** Jg 24 c. 0032.

6005 ELECTROMETERS.

6010 GALVANOMETERS, RESISTANCE COMPARATORS, VOLTMETERS. WATTMETERS, Etc. REGISTERING INSTRUMENTS.

Volkmann. 42937-8. Die beste Gestalt für die Spulen eines Nadelgalvanometers. 42941 : Die zweckmässige Grösse des Galvanometerspiegels. 42945 : Verbesserungen an Schieberwiderständen.

Walker. 42993. An electrostatic voltmeter for photographic recording of atmospheric potential.

Wenner. 43084. Method for eliminating the effect of all connecting resistances in the Thomson bridge.

Wilson. 43150. High-tension electrostatic wattmeters.

Wurm. 43228. Eine neue Messbrücke zur Untersuchung von Blitzableiteranlagen.

Žáček. 43231. Theorie des Saitengalvanometers von Einthoven. (Čechisch.)

Zahn. 43234. Empfindliches Drehspulgalvanometer von kleinem Widerstande.

Zâvada. 43248. Neue Form von Elektrodynamometer.

Zeleny. 43261. The causes of zero displacement and deflection hysteresis in moving-coil galvanometers.

Ziegenberg. 43277. Der Elektrolytzähler.

Zipp. 43280. Indicatori di alte tensioni.

6015 APPARATUS FOR DETERMINING THE CHARACTER OF VARIABLE CURRENTS. (See 5705.)

Angermann. 38970. Schlupfmessung.

Görner. 40237. Neue Ferraris-Messgeräte.

Gossen. 40263. Drehspul-Messinstrument.

Gradenwitz. 40269. Ondometro a lettura diretta.

Hausrath. 40452. Darstellung periodischer Hochfrequenzkurven mit der Braunschen Röhre.

Kock. 40846. Aufnahme von Resonanzkurven unter Anwendung eines Kurvenzeichners.

Scherbing. 42369. Nuovo sistema per regolare la velocità dei motori a corrente trifase.

Wittmann. 43168. Ungedämpfte und gedämpfte Oszillationsphänomene. (Ungarisch.)

6020 APPARATUS FOR STARTING AND REGULATING CURRENTS.

Il regolatore automatico di tensione "Tirrill." Elettricità Milano 37 1911 (260-264 279-284 291-296).

Edler. 39865. Schaltungstheorie.

Gerstmeyer. 40175 : Philippi. 41828. Das Ausschalten von Wechselstrom.

Léauté. 41034. Développement d'une fonction en série d'exponentielles ; application au transport de force à 100,000 volts.

Lippmann. 41160. Contacts électriques efficaces sans pression.

Ragonot. 41993. Interruttori automatici.

Rixon. 42149. Regulierwiderstand für das Laboratorium.

Schmidt. 42394. Anfertigung einer Stark- oder Schwachstromschalttafel.

Thierry (De). 42765. Limitatore per corrente alternata e continua.

Zevi. 43275. Impiego di batterie di accumulatori per regolare le reti a corrente alternata.

6025 FRICTIONAL ELECTROSTATIC MACHINES.

Villard et Abraham. 42914. Une grande machine électrostatique.

6030 ELECTROMAGNETS.

(See also 5410.)

Electro-aimants de laboratoire, système P. Weiss. Electro Bruxelles 1910 (68).

Elettromagneti per laboratorio. Mon. tecn. Milano 17 1911 (177-179).

Bestelmeyer. 39239. Berechnung, Herstellung und Messung eines homogenen Magnetfeldes.

du Bois. 39808. Neue Halbring-Elektromagnete.

Euler. 39951. Zugmagnet für Gleichstrom.

Liska. 41162. Berechnung von Wechselstrom-Hubmagneten.

Pfiffner. 41825; **Schulz.** 42129. Lasthebemagnete.

Rusch. 42265. Berechnung der Magnetisierungskurve bei Mehrlochwicklungen.

Steil. 42626. Solenoide und ihre Verwendbarkeit für Strassenbahnbremsen.

Voss. 42954. Der Elektromagnet. Schwachstromtechnik.

Voss. 42953. Berechnung von Elektromagnet- und Widerstandsrollen.

Weichsel. 43032. Berechnung der Magnetisierungskurve bei Mehrlochwicklungen.

6040 INDUCTION COILS. TRANSFORMERS. INTERRUPTERS FOR INDUCTION COILS.

Barbagelata. 39071. Prova indiretta dei trasformatori di misura per forti intensità di corrente.

Benischke. 39179. Experimentelle Bestimmung des Streufaktors von Transformatoren und Drehstrommotoren.

Bunet. 39451. Il problema della trasformazione della frequenza.

Dessauer. 39745. Versuche mit Funkeninduktoren und Röntgenröhren.

Goldstein. 40257. Erzeugung von Kanalstrahlen in Kalium, Rubidium und Cäsium.

Guillet. 40357. Trieur par synchronisation. 40358 ; Interrupteur de la bobine d'induction constitué par l'arc primaire.

Joly. 40676. Des transformateurs statiques de fréquence. 40677 ; Un tripleur statique de fréquence.

Hunzinger. 40592. Bestimmung des Spannungsabfalles bei verschiedenen Phasenverschiebungen an Transformatoren.

Klingelfuss. 40815. Zeitschalter. Zwangläufige Steuerung eines Induktoriums zur vollständigen Ausschaltung der Schliessungsinduktion.

La Rosa e **Pasta.** 41011. Distribuzione del flusso d'induzione concatenato lungo il secondario ; scelta delle dimensioni più convenienti per gli organi più importanti di un rocchetto d'induzione.

Lenz. 41102. Elektromagnetisches Wechselfeld der Spulen und deren Wechselstrom-Widerstand, Selbstinduktion und Kapazität.

Lignana. 41135. Trasformatori di misura.

Lori. 41196. Le dimensioni più opportune dei rocchetti di auto-induzione senza ferro per ottenere fenomeni di risonanza elettromagnetica.

Ludewig. 41214. Unregelmässigkeiten beim Wehneltunterbrecher.

Mollinger und **Gewecke.** 41474. Diagramm des Spannungswandlers.

Niethammer. 41612. Piccoli antitrasformatori per lampade ad incandescenza.

Salomonson. 42303. Induction coil.

Schultze. 42428. Untersuchung von Spannungstransformatoren mittels des Quadrantelektrometers.

Stone. 42673. Maximum current in the secondary of a transformer.

Talsch. 42737. Gekoppelte elektrische Schwingungskreise.

Thieme. 42764. Der Selbstinduktionsversuch von Lodge.

Vallauri. 42881. Raddoppiatore statico di frequenza.

[**Viscidi.**] 42919. Generatore di corrente alternata ad alta frequenza.

Wertheim-Salomonson. 43096. Die günstigste Unterbrechungsfrequenz bei dem Induktorbetrieb.

Wilson and **Wilson.** 43152. New method for producing high-tension discharges.

6043 WIRELESS TELEGRAPH APPARATUS. COHERERS.

Registratori di tempeste. [Sunto.] Riv. maritt. Roma **1910** 4. trim. (578–579).

Il radiotelegrafo Hovland a scrittura segreta. Riv. maritt. Roma **1910** 3. trim. (201–203).

Austin. 39018. The sliding contact rectifying detector. 39019: Resistance of radio-telegraphic antennas. 39022: Thermo-elements for experiments with high frequency currents.

Bartoli. 39095. Alternatore per telegrafia senza fili.

Bettineschi. 39231. Comportamento del coherer a limatura metallica.

Braun. 39387. Electrische Schwingungen und drahtlose Telegraphie.

Clay. 39578. Influence of electrical waves upon platinum mirrors. (Coherer action.) (English, Dutch.)

Dieckmann. 39760. Thermischer Indikator zur Resonanzbestimmung nach der Nullmethode.

Eales. 39847. Patentschau.

Ganzlin. 40132. Bleiglanz-Graphit-detektor.

Geronimi. 40174. Telegrafo Hughes.

Glatzel. 40207. Excitation par choes dans la télégraphie sans fil.

Goldschmidt. 40249. An alternator for direct production of electric waves for wireless telegraphy. 40251-2: Maschinelle Erzeugung von elektrischen Wellen für die drahtlose Telegraphie.

Grober. 40310-1. Verwendung von Barretter und Thermoelement zu Messzwecken.

Härden. 40388. A curious coherer phenomenon.

Hartmann-Kempf. 40440. Hitzdrahtamperemeter ohne Nebenschluss für drahtlose Telegraphie.

Hirsch. 40531; **Huth.** 40594. Wellenmesser.

Hoerschelmann. 40537. Wirkungsweise des geknickten Marconischen Senders in der drahtlosen Telegraphie.

Howe. 40577. Brown telephone relay in wireless telegraphy.

Isakow. 40625. Thermischer Indikator zur Resonanzabstimmung nach der Nullmethode.

Jégou. 40658. Réception d'un signal horaire hertzien de la Tour Eiffel. 40659: Empfang der Zeit und Pendelsignale.

Kalahne. 40714. Frequenz- und Dämpfungsberechnung gekoppelter Schwingungskreise nach der Cohenschen Methode.

Kann. 40728. Apparat zur Bestimmung der konstanten elektrischen Schwingungskreise mittels Nullmethoden.

Kiebitz. 40779. Aperiodische Detektorkreise.

Kimura and **Samaki.** 40780. Oscilloscopic study of condenser discharge with the application to crystal-contact detector for electric oscillation.

—— and **Yamamoto.** 40783. Crystals and crystal-metal contact detectors.

Klock. 40846. Aufnahme von Resonanzkurven unter Anwendung eines Kurvenzeichners.

Leimbach. 41084. Unipolares Leitvermögen von Kontaktdetektoren und ihre Gleichrichterwirkung.

Levitsky. 41113. Resonator zur Messung der Dämpfung kurzer elektrischer Wellen.

Ludewig. 41216. Dämpfungsmesser für drahtlose Telegraphie.

Marconi. 41330. Wireless telegraphy.

Merritt. 41410. Silicon detector used with short electric waves; theory of contact rectifiers.

Mosler. 41517. Tickerempfang mit aperiodischem Kreis.

Nasmyth. 41566. Impact excitation. Characteristics of short arcs between metal electrodes.

Nesper. 41589. Frequenzmesser und Messung der Wellenlänge in der drahtlosen Telegraphie und Telephonie. 41590: Entwickelung der Apparatur in der drahtlosen Telegraphie. 41591: Vielton-Stationen für drahtlose Nachrichten-Übermittlung. 41592: Ungesteuerte und gesteuerte Stossender für drahtlose Telephonie. 41593: Detektoren der drahtlosen Telegraphie und Telephonie.

Rein. 42064. Der radiotelegraphische Gleichstrom-Tonsender.

[**Rossi.**] 42199. Il convector.

Seibt. 42479. Ein Instrumentarium zur Untersuchung von Mineralien auf Empfindlichkeit gegen elektrische Schwingungen.

Niethammer. 41614. Quecksilberdampf-Gleichrichter als Periodenwandler.

Pohl. 41905. Zusatzpole für Umformer.

Rasch. 42014. Umwandlung von
Drei- in Zweiphasenstrom.

Schäfer. 42339. Ein neuer Quecksilberdampf-Gleichrichter für grosse
Leistungen.

Schulze. 42444. Einfluss der Elektrolyte auf die Maximalspannung der
elektrolytischen Ventilwirkung.

Thompson. 42772. Relazione sui
motori generatori, convertitori e raddrizzatori.

6050 MAGNETO-ELECTRIC MACHINES.

Wright. 43209. Electric-magnetic
brake.

6060 DYNAMOS.

Binder. 39262. Äussere Wärmeleitung und Erwärmung elektrischer
Maschinen.

Biscan. 39269; **Schulz.** 42430.
Dynamos.

Dreyfus. 39795A. Vektordiagramm
der mehrphasigen Einankerumformer
und Doppelmaschinen.

Dyk. 39844. Messung der Voreilung
parallel arbeitender Wechselstrommaschinen.

Eschenburg. 39940. Caratteristiche
elettriche e meccaniche dei generatori
elettrici moderni.

Firth. 39998. Measurement of
relative angular displacement in synchronous machines.

Hawkins. 40455. The principle
of the static balancer.

Hinlein. 40525. Erwärmung der
elektrischen Maschinen.

Kinzbrunner. 40794. Die Gleichstrommaschine.

Marchand. 41317. L'avenir des
stations centrales d'électricité.

Meyer. 41431A. Kurzschlüsse in
Wechselstromnetzen, ihre Rückwirkung auf die Generatoren.

Mises. 41467. Dynamische Probleme der Maschinenlehre.

Moser. 41516. Synchronmaschinen
zur selbsttätigen Spannungs- oder
Stromregelung.

Neubauer. 41594. Theorie des
Dreiphasenstromes und seines Generators.

Niethammer. 41613. Pendeln von
Synchronmaschinen.

Noeggerath. 41639. Stromabnahme.

Pichelmayer. 41833. Zur Theorie
der Stromwendung.

Punga. 41974. Versuche über das
kritische GD² von Drehstromgeneratoren.

Radt. 41990. Eisenverluste in
elliptischen Drehfeldern.

Rebora. 42037. Rotore delle
macchine a corrente continua.

Rogowski. 42160; **Schouten.** 42409;
Sumec. 42707. Gegen- und Querwindungen eines Drehstromgenerators.

Rüdenberg. 42247. Selbsterregende
Drehstromgeneratoren für veränderliche Frequenz.

Rusch. 42265. Berechnung der
Magnetisierungskurve bei Mehrlochwicklungen.

Sartori. 42321. Macchine a corrente
alternata a collettore.

Schüler. 42423. Parallelbetrieb.

Sumec. 42708. Spannungsabfall
von Drehstromgeneratoren.

Ugrimoff. 42857. Die unipolare
Gleichstrommaschine.

Weber. 43013. Gleichstromwick-
lungen.

Weichsel. 43032. Berechnung der
Magnetisierungskurve bei Mehrlochwicklungen.

Wengner. 43082. Synchrone Einphasenmaschine.

Wolf. 43172. Entwicklung der
Gleichstrommaschine.

Wolf. 43173. Neuere Anordnungen
zur Aufhebung von Wellenspannungen
und Lagerströmen.

6070 MOTORS.

Abraham. 38888. Principe de nouveaux appareils pour courants alternatifs. 38889 : Les relais et les servomoteurs électriques.

Auerbach. 39009. Formel für die Überlastbarkeit des Asynchronmotors.

Benischke. 39177. Leistungssprung asynchroner Drehfeldmotoren beim Durchgang durch den Synchronismus. 39179 : Experimentelle Bestimmung des Streufaktors von Transformatoren und Drehstrommotoren.

Brückmann. 39422. Stroboskopischer Schlüpfungsmesser. 39423 : Wechselstrom-Kollektormotoren.

Firth. 39998. Measurement of relative angular displacement in synchronous machines.

Gerstmeyer. 40176 : **Marguerre.** 41334. Wechselstrom-Kommutatormotoren.

Heather. 40459. A new method of determining the efficiency of slipring induction motors. 40460 : The Heyland diagram for induction motors and reverse current operation.

Herrmann. 40491. Gleichstromtechnik.

Hoock. 40555. Der maximale Leistungsfaktor und die Baulänge der Induktionsmotoren.

Kesseldorfer. 40774. Theorie und Konstruktion der Quecksilber-Motorzähler.

Krug. 40927. Kreisdiagramm der Induktionsmotoren.

Legouez. 41064. Motori a collettore.

Linker. 41155. Bestimmung des Wirkungsgrades elektr. Maschinen nach der Hilfsmotormethode.

Marchand. 41317. L'avenir des stations centrales d'électricité.

Meyer. 41431. Verwendung verlustlos regelbarer Drehstrommotoren.

Meyer-Wülting. 41438. Die doppelt verkettete Streuung beim Zweiphasenmotor.

Milch. 41456. I motori monofasi a eccitazione in serie.

Moser. 41514. Bestimmung der Hauptabmessungen elektrischer Maschinen : Drehstrommotor. 41515 :

Einfacher graphischer Beweis des genauen Diagramms des Drehstrommotors.

Müller. 41531. Gegenstrom- und Kurzschlussbremsung bei Reihenschluss-Kommutator-Motoren.

Niethammer. 41616. Formel für die Überlastbarkeit des Asynchronmotors. 41617 : Wirbelstrombremsen.

——— und **Siegel.** 41620. Doppelt verkettete Streuung von Drehstrommotoren.

Ossanna. 41701. Dimensionierung der einphasigen Kommutatormotoren : schwere Zugförderung.

Rajz. 41906. Kaskadenschaltung von dreiphasigen Induktionsmotoren und Kommutatormotoren.

Rezelman. 42091. Reactance of asynchronous motors. 42092 : Reactance of asynchronous motors with squirrel-cage rotors.

Richter. 42105. Zur Funkenunterdrückung bei Wechselstrom-Kommutatormotoren.

Righini. 42141. Metodo per calcolare i reostati d'avviamento dei motori a corrente continua.

Robertson. 42151. Rotor hysteresis in polyphase induction motors.

Rosenberg. 42183. Hunting of direct current interpole motors.

Rüdenberg. 42246. Stabilität, Kompensierung und Selbsterregung von Drehstrom-Serienmaschinen.

Rusch. 42263. Repulsionsmotor.

Schenkel. 42368. Elektrische Bremsung mit Wechselstrom-Kommutatormotoren.

Schneckenberg. 42491. Schlupfzähler für Induktionsmotoren.

Silberberg. 42513. Ableitung des Ossannakreises.

Smith. 42544. Irregularities in the rotating field of the polyphase induction motor.

Stern. 42644. Untersuchung der Statorfelder eines Einphasenmotors.

Thomälen. 42767. Die Ableitung des Ossannaschen Kreises. 42768 : Das Stromdiagramm des Drehstrom-Serienmotors. 42769 : Streuung im Diagramm des Drehstrom-Serienmotors.

Verhoeckx. 42903. Essai d'une
théorie du champ magnétique tournant.
(Hollandais.)

Wolf. 43171. Experimentelle Bestätigung des Vektorendiagramms für
den Motor nach Winter-Eichberg-
Latour.

6080 ELECTRIC LAMPS.

Una nuova lampada a mercurio-
quarzo. [Sunto.] Mon. tecn. Milano
17 1911 (400).

Lampade al tantalio e correnti alternative. Mon. tecn. Milano 17 1911
(298).

Lampade a luminescenza Moore.
Elettricità Milano 36 1911 (102-106
121-124).

Lampade elettriche a filamenti metallici. Riv. Artig. Genio Roma I. trim.
1910 (128-138); Industria Milano
25 1911 (42-43); Elettricista Roma
(Ser. 2) 10 1911 (136-138); Riv.
marit. Roma 1910 I. trim. (618-620).

Röntgen-Taschenbuch. (Röntgen-
kalender.) Begr. und hrsg. von Ernst
Sommer. Bd 3. Leipzig (O. Nemnich)
1911 (VIII + 290). 18 cm.

Barnes. 39080. An enclosed arc
for spectroscopic work.

Bauer. 39119; Walter. 42998.
Das Qualimeter.

Baumbauer. 39128. I filamenti di
wolframio per le lampade elettriche ad
incandescenza. 39129; Escard. 39938;
Fabbricazione dei filamenti per lampadine elettriche.

Beez. 39160. Ein direkt zeigendes
elektrisches Röntgenstrahlen-Energiemeter.

Bertarelli. 39211. L'evoluzione
dell' illuminazione elettrica.

Berthier. 39219. Lampade elettriche
a filamento metallico.

Boas. 39295. Methode zur Erzeugung hochgespannter, gleichgerichteter
Stromstösse für Röntgentechnik.

Börnstein. 39306. Beleuchtung und
Lichtmessung.

Chevallier. 39548. Le fonctionnement des lampes à incandescence à
filament de carbone et filament métallique.

Classen. 39570; Krüss. 40926.
Universalbogenlampe mit festem Lichtpunkt.

Claude. 39573; Marchesini. 41318;
Zamparelli. 43287. L'illuminazione
al neon.

Darmois e Leblanc. 39694. L'arco
a mercurio a luce bianca.

Dessauer. 39746. Neuerungen.

Dussaud. 39836. Nouvelles applications des ampoules à bas voltage.

Escard. 39939. Les lampes électriques à arc, à incandescence et à luminescence.

Fürstenau. 40095; Klingelfuss.
40814. Röntgenstrahlendosierung.

Gage. 40108. Radiant efficiency of
arc lamps.

Grande. 40273. Le lampade da
10 candele.

Hyde. 40598. Selective radiation
from tantalum.

Korolikov et Bartoŝeviĉ. 40895.
Lampes à incandescence de zirconium.

Leblanc. 41043. Lampada di
quarzo a vapore di mercurio.

Legrand. 41065. Résistance au
choc du filament des lampes métalliques.

Leimbach. 41083. Strahlungseigenschaften der elektrischen Glühlampen.

Lloyd. 41166. Effect of wave form
upon incandescent lamps.

Loose. 41190. Die Luft-Fern-
regulierung der Röntgenröhren nach
Bauer.

Monasch. 41479. Sviluppo delle
lampade ad incandescenza al tungsteno. 41480; Entwicklung der
Glühlampentechnik.

[Moore.] 41492. Luce Moore.

Pecheux. 41778, 80. Proprietà
elettriche dei filamenti delle lampade
elettriche ad incandescenza.

Peri. 41797. Le moderne lampade
ad arco metallico in serie su corrente
continua costante con apparecchi raddrizzatori a mercurio.

Pole. 41928. Photometrische
Untersuchungen an Quecksilberdampflampen.

Righi. 42123. Lampada ad arco trifase a quattro carboni.

Rossi (De). 42204. Lampade a filamento metallico e trasformatori.

Russner. 42271. Strahlungseigenschaften elektrischer Glühlampen.

Schäffer. 42345. Hintereinanderschaltung von Bogenlampen und Glühlampen.

Schwenckenbecher. 42454. Der Quecksilberdampf-Lichtbogen.

Stöckl. 42665. Vakuum-Röhren-Licht.

Tiersot. 42792. Vérification du vide dans les lampes à incandescence.

Wertheimer. 43092. Strom- und Spannungsverlauf an Röntgenröhren.

Willcox. 43140. Effect of alternating current on drawn tungsten wire.

6090 ELECTRIC FURNACES AND HEATING.

Arsem. 38996. Electric vacuum furnace installations.

Bölling. 39304. Widerstandsmaterial für elektrische Oefen.

Borchers. 39324. Elektrischer Tiegelofen zum Schmelzen.

Carcano. 39490. Forno elettrico quale produttore di ghise.

Catani. 39515–6 : Devoto. 39754 ; Zomparelli. 43290–1. Forni elettrici.

Fischer und Tiede. 40002. Elektrischer Woltram-Widerstandsofen.

Goecke. 40235. Der elektrische Vakuumofen.

Heraeus. 40486 : Uobelohde. 42855. Elektrische Laboratoriumsöfen mit Wicklung aus unedlem Metall.

Herzog. 40504 : Rossander. 42495. Apparecchi elettrici per riscaldamento e per cucina.

Ponzini. 41934. Apparecchio ad induzione per convertire industrialmente in calore l'energia elettrica anche ad alto potenziale.

Seibert. 42477. Elektrischer Widerstandsofen mit Heizwiderstand aus unedlen Metallen.

Vondráček. 42950. Elektrischer Ofen in der Eisenindustrie. (Čechisch.)

(c-1388)

ELECTROLYSIS.

6200 GENERAL. (See also Physical Chemistry, D 7255, etc.)

Jahrbuch der Elektrochemie. Hrsg. von J. Meyer. Jg 15 u. 14. c. 4020.

Baborovský. 39034. Elektrochemischer Potential des Metallmagnesiums in Aethylalkohollösungen von Magnesiumchlorid. (Čechisch.)

Borns. 39334. Elektrochemie 1910.

Cegielskij. 39522. Sieden von Elektrolyten bei Stromdurchgang.

Danneel. 39687 : Le Blanc. 41045. Elektrochemie.

Heilenreich. 40466. Photo- elektromotorische Untersuchungen von Chlorsilber und Bromsilber.

Hertz. 40497. Abhängigkeit des Leitvermögens von der Konzentration.

Kohlrausch. 40877. Gesammelte Abhandlungen.

Kruger. 40921. Wesen der elektrolytischen Dissoziation und Lösungstension.

Nikolaev. 41624. (Russ.)

Revessi. 42089. Le correnti tramviarie di ritorno.

Sanford. 42311. Positive atomic charges.

Schulze. 42444. Einfluss der Elektrolyte auf die Maximalspannung der elektrolytischen Ventilwirkung. 42446 : Bildung schlechtleitender Schichten bei der Elektrolyse des Glases. 42447 : Kapazitäten der elektrolytischen Ventilwirkung in geschmolzenen Salzen und in absoluter Schwefelsäure.

Timoleew. 42799. Einfluss des Druckes auf die Affinität.

Winther. 43162. Elektrischer Lichtakkumulator.

Wright. 43211–2. The positive potential of aluminium as a function of the wave length of the incident light.

6210 ELECTROCHEMICAL SERIES AND EQUIVALENTS. VOLTAIC POTENTIAL DIFFERENCES.

Abegg et alii. 38885. Messungen elektromotorischer Kräfte galvanischer Ketten mit wässerigen Elektrolyten.

2 B 2

Anderson and **Bowen.** 38956. Measurement of contact differences of potential.

Bechterew. 39136. Untersuchung einiger galvanischer Elemente mit Kohlenanoden.

Bedeau. 39159. Variation de force électromotrice des piles avec la température.

Broniewski. 39412. Propriétés électriques des alliages d'aluminium.

Deventer, van. 39753. Selbstveredlung mit einem Semi-Isolator in Bezug auf Konzentrationszellen. (Holländisch.)

Ducelliez. 39816. Les alliages de cobalt et d'argent. 39817 : Forces électromotrices des alliages de cobalt et de zinc.

Eisenreich. 39898. Verwendung von Silberfluoridlösungen im Silbercoulometer.

Freedericksz. 40073. Beziehungen zwischen den optischen Konstanten und dem Eigenpotential der Metalle.

Früh. 40090. Abscheidung von Eisen und Nickel aus komplexen Oxalat- und Laktatlösungen.

Guyot. 40375. Différences de potentiel de contact apparentes entre un métal et des solutions électrolytiques.

Halla. 40400. Thermodynamische Berechnung elektromotorischer Kräfte.

Janet et alii. 40654. Détermination de la force électromotrice en valeur absolue de l'élément Weston normal.

Mareš. 41333. Konzentrationsmessung der Wasserstoffionen. (Čechisch.)

Schneckenberg. 42402. Scheinbare Kontaktpotentialdifferenzen zwischen einem Metall und elektrolytischen Lösungen.

Szivessy. 42731. Voltaeffekt bei Kristallen.

Vigouroux. 42912. Le système nickel-argent.

6220 MIXED ELECTROLYTES AND SECONDARY ACTIONS.

Böeseken et **Rossem,** van. 39301. Études sur la configuration des systèmes annulaires [par la détermination de la conductibilité des mélanges d'alcools et de phénols].

Euklaar. 39920. La courbe de neutralisation de l'acide sulfurique. [Concentration des ions.] (Hollandais.)

Hobel. 40535. Volumenänderungen von Sammelelektroden.

Schulze. 42444. Einfluss der Elektrolyte auf die Maximalspannung der elektrolytischen Ventilwirkung. 42445 : Maximalspannung der elektrolytischen Ventilwirkung in geschmolzenen Salzen. 42447 : Kapazitäten der elektrolytischen Ventilwirkung in geschmolzenen Salzen und in absoluter Schwefelsäure.

6230 POLARIZATION AND PASSIVITY.

Bechterew. 39136. Untersuchung einiger galvanischer Elemente mit Kohlenanoden.

Dolch. 39780. Verhalten von Zinnanoden in Natronlauge.

Flade. 40008-9 ; **Grave.** 40281-2. Passivität.

Foerster. 40022. Elektrochemisches Verhalten der Metalle. (Sammelreferat über 1909-1910.)

Haber und **Zawadzki.** 40380. Polarisierbarkeit fester Elektrolyte.

Le Blanc. 41044. Eine chemischpassive unpolarisierbare Elektrode.

Limb. 41139. Compoundage des alternateurs au moyen des soupapes électrolytiques.

Reichinstein. 42060. Chemische Polarisation der umkehrbaren elektrolytischen Elektrode.

6235 ELECTROCAPILLARY PHENOMENA.

Fichter. 39996. Kapillarelektrische Fällung positiver Kolloide.

Gouy. 40264. Tension de vapeur d'un liquide électrisé.

6240 CONDUCTIVITY. MIGRATION OF THE IONS.

Aten. 39005. Spezifische Leitfähigkeit des geschmolzenen Kaliumnitrats.

Baborovský et **Voženílek.** 39039.
Ueberführungszahlen von Magnesiumchlorid in Aethylalkohollösungen. (Čechisch.)

Benrath und **Wainoff.** 39184 :
Wainoff. 42989. Elektrische Leitfähigkeit von Salzen und Salzgemischen.

Brochet. 39400 : **Delvalez.** 39732.
Figuration des lignes équipotentielles
dans un électrolyseur.

Clausen. 39576. Temperatureein-
fluss auf Dichte und elektrische Leitfähigkeit wässeriger Salzlösungen.

Dutoit. 39839-40. Volumétrie
physico-chimique.

Ellis. 39903. Elektrische Ladung
der Ölemulsionen.

Hamacher. 40404. Elektrolytische
Leitfähigkeit und Hydratation in ihrer
Beziehung zur Temperatur.

Hertz. 40497. Abhängigkeit des
Leitvermögens binärer normaler Elektrolyte von der Konzentration.

Jaffé. 40653. Fall von elektrolytischem Sättigungsstrom.

Jellinek. 40660. Leitfähigkeit und
Dissociation von Natriumhydrosulfit
und hydroschwefliger Säure im Vergleich zu analogen Schwefelsauerstoffverbindungen.

Johnson. 40669. Dissolution of a
metal in a binary solution, one component acid.

Kalischer. 40715. Wanderung der
Ionen bei der Elektrolyse.

Klemenc. 40807. Messung der
elektrischen Leitfähigkeit.

Körber. 40875. Einfluss von Druck
und Temperatur auf das elektrolytische
Leitvermögen von Lösungen.

Kohlrausch. 40877. Abhandlungen.

Mameli. 41303. Conducibilità
elettrica degli acidi cloroacetici in soluzione acquosa.

Mazzucchelli. 41385. Numeri di
trasporto e complessità molecolare.

Scarpa. 42336. Calcolo dei numeri
di trasporto reali.

Schmidt. 42391. Leitvermögen
des Oberflächenwassers der Nordsee.

Sérkov. 42494. Leitfähigkeit einiger
Salze in binären Gemischen von Wasser,
Alkoholen und Aceton.

Stubbs. 42693. Conductivity of
aqueous solutions of carbon-dioxide
prepared under pressure at various
temperatures.

Uller. 42860. Elektrische Leitfähigkeiten von Meer und Land.

Walden. 42992. Zusammenhang
zwischen dem Grenzwert der molekularen Leitfähigkeit und der innern
Reibung.

Weitzel. 43075. Temperaturkoeffizienten der Leitfähigkeit einiger
Elektrolyten in nichtwässrigen Lösungsmitteln. Diss.

6242 PROPERTIES OF ELEC-
TROLYTIC DEPOSITS.

Baborovský et **Kuźma.** 39037.
Sog. elektrolytischer Silbersuperoxyd.
(Čechisch.)

Horák u. **Šebor.** 40557. Aluminium
als Kathodenmaterial. (Čechisch.)

6245 ELECTRICAL OSMOSE.
DIAPHRAGM CURRENT.

Donnan. 39787. Theorie der Membrangleichgewichte und Membran-
potentiale bei Vorhandensein von nicht
dialysierenden Elektrolyten.

6250 THEORIES OF ELECTRO-
LYSIS. DISSOCIATION OF
ELECTROLYTES.

Colson. 39608-9. Théorie des
solutions.

Drucker. 39860. Dissoziationsschema der Schwefelsäure und die
Beweglichkeit des Hydrosulfations.

Fouard. 40040. L'osmométrie des
solutions salines et la théorie des ions
d'Arrhenius.

Heydweiller. 40513. Die Ionenmoduln der Dichte im Wasser.

Jaffé. 40653. Fall von elektrolytischem Sättigungsstrom.

Kjellin†. 40799. Die elektrolytische
Dissociationstheorie.

Lundén. 41237. Influence de la
température sur l'énergie interne et
l'énergie libre des dissociations électrolytiques des acides et bases faibles.

Michaelis. 41441. Bestimmung der
Wasserstoffionenkonzentration durch
Gasketten.

Rolla. 42173. Dissociazione dei sali idrati.

Sérkov. 42494. Leitfähigkeit einiger Salze in binären Gemischen von Wasser, Alkoholen und Azeton.

Vanzetti. 42890. Idrolisi di sali in soluzione.

6255 CONCENTRATION CELLS. THEORIES RELATING TO DIFFUSION.

Bjerrum. 39273. Gültigkeit der Planckschen Formel für das Diffusionspotential. 39274: Elimination des Flüssigkeitspotentials bei Messungen von Elektrodenpotentialen.

Fedotieff. 39980. Fall des heterogenen Gleichgewichts.

Geissler. 40167. Konzentrationsketten mit ternären Elektrolyten.

Kanevskij. 40727. Piles thermiques.

Michaelis. 41441. Bestimmung der Wasserstoffionenkonzentration durch Gasketten.

Nikolaev. 41625. Diffusion de la paire eau-alcohol sous l'influence du courant électrique. (Russ.)

Vanzetti. 42893. Diffusione di elettroliti in soluzione acquosa.

ELECTRODYNAMICS, SPECIAL PHENOMENA.

6400 GENERAL.

Accolla. 38895. Rotazione magnetica delle scariche elettriche del rocchetto d'induzione.

Colombo. 39605. Trasporto dell'energia.

Corbino. 39622. Anello di Pacinotti. 39627: Elektromagnetische Effekte, die von der Verzerrung herrühren, welche ein Feld an der Bahn der Ionen in Metallen hervorbringt.

Donati. 39783. Relazioni fondamentali dell' elettromagnetismo.

Herrmann. 40494 : **Simons.** 42525. Elektrotechnik.

Lampa. 40989. Wechselstromversuche.

Loit. 41182. Induzierte Ströme in einem ruhenden Netze linearer Leiter und das Prinzip der kleinsten Aktion.

Neumann. 41595. Werke.

Peirce. 41789. Effects of sudden changes in the inductances of electric circuits as illustrative of the absence of magnetic lag and of the Von Waltenhofen phenomenon in finely divided cores.

Rebora. 42036. La temperatura delle macchine elettriche rilevata col termometro a mercurio.

Tamaki. 42740. A four dimensional vector treatment of the electromagnetic field in a moving body. 42741: On fundamental equations for an electromagnetic field in a moving medium.

Wagner. 42980. Kabelprobleme und ähnliche Randwertaufgaben, die auf Reihenentwicklungen nach nicht orthogonalen Eigenfunktionen führen.

Zahn. 43235. Magnetischer Skineffekt von Metallscheiben in hochfrequenten Wechselfeldern.

6410 THEORIES OF ELECTRODYNAMICS. (See 4940.)

Bateman. 39104. Transformation of a particular type of electromagnetic field, and its physical interpretation. 39105 : On certain vectors associated with an electromagnetic field and the reflexion of a disturbance at the surface of a perfect conductor.

Brunelli. 39428. Moti pendolari delle macchine sincrone.

Cunningham. 39668. Application of the mathematical theory of relativity to the electron theory of matter.

Daniele. 39683. Induzione magnetica di un involucro ellissoidico.

Fesch. 39991. Nouvelles démonstrations des deux formules fondamentales de l'électromagnétisme.

Gans. 40128. Das Biot-Savartsche Gesetz.

Grover. 40321. Wirbelströme in einem Blech oder Zylinder mit Rücksicht auf die Theorie der Induktionswage untersucht. Diss.

Korn. 40892. L'état hélicoïdal de la matière électrique ; hypothèses nouvelles.

Kraft. 40903. Eine Identität in der vierdimensionalen Vektoranalysis und deren Anwendung in der Elektrodynamik. 40904 : Direkte Integration der typischen Differentialausdrücke von Raum-Zeit-Vektoren. 40905 : Integraldarstellung der elektromagnetischen Vektoren in bewegten Körpern nach Minkowski's „Grundgleichungen".

Müller. 41527. Feldstärke innerhalb eines Kreisstromes.

Pirro (Di). 41857. Problemi della telegrafia e telefonia.

Tamaki. 42740. A four dimensional vector treatment of the electromagnetic field in a moving body. 42741 : On fundamental equations for an electromagnetic field in a moving medium.

6420 MUTUAL ACTIONS OF STEADY CURRENTS, AND OF CURRENTS AND MAGNETS.

Corbino. 39632. Azione elettromagnetica di un disco percorso da corrente radiale e disposto in un campo.

Ehrhardt. 39878. Magnetische Kraftlinien.

Gans. 40128. Biot-Savartsches Gesetz.

Gehrcke und **Wogau.** 40156. Magnetische Messungen.

Jans. 40656. Liaison entre la loi de Coulomb et la loi de Biot et Savart.

Kolbe. 40884. Versuche mit dem elektrodynamischen Pendel.

Niethammer und **Czepek.** 41619. Mechanische Kräfte zwischen Stromleitern.

Wenner. 43083. Stretching of a conductor by its own current.

6435 ELECTRIC CONVECTION. ROWLAND EFFECT.

Eichenwald. 39883. Magnetische Wirkung der elektrischen Konvektion. (Russ.)

Guillet. 40356. Courant continu et courant alternatif de convection.

Swann. 42722. Magnetic field produced by a charged condenser moving through space.

6440 SELF INDUCTION AND MUTUAL INDUCTION. EDDY CURRENTS. COEFFICIENTS OF INDUCTION. MEASUREMENTS OF INDUCTION.

L'induttanza per correnti alternate di un circuito comprendente ferro. Elettricista Roma (Ser. 2) 10 1911 (154-155).

Una disposizione del campo magnetico per dinamo e motori a correnti continue. [Trad.] Industria Milano 24 1910 (129-131).

Adams. 38900. Propagation of long electric waves along wires.

Alexanderson. 38924. Die magnetischen Eigenschaften des Eisens bei Hochfrequenz.

Anderson. 38955. The comparison of two self-inductions.

Bergansius. 39187-8. Formule nouvelle pour le calcul exact du coefficient de self-induction dans le cas de longs solénoïdes à nombreuses couches de fil. (Hollandais.)

Boucherot. 39348. Fenomeni elettromagnetici che risultano dalla brusca chiusura di un alternatore in corto circuito.

Campos. 39481. Propagazione delle sovratensioni oscillatorie.

Collis. 39602. L'influenza dell'apertura di corti circuiti sulla tensione.

Creighton. 39657. Condizioni per la protezione di apparecchi elettrici in America.

Dina. 39769. Metodi di prevenzione delle sovratensioni interne.

Emanueli. 39915. L'autoinduzione e le perdite di energia nei cavi trifasi.

Esau. 39933-5. Widerstand und Selbstinduktion von Spulen für Wechselstrom. 39936 : Selbstinduktionskoeffizient von Flachspulen.

Giebe. 40185. Präzisionsmessungen an Selbstinduktionsnormalen.

Grover. 40321. Wirbelströme in einem Blech oder Zylinder.

————— and **Curtis.** 40322. Measurement of inductances with very small time constant.

Guillet. 40359. Machine à plan de référence électrique, propre à répéter une même translation donnée.

primary and secondary currents of a transformer by means of simple apparatus.

Wagner. 42980. Kabelprobleme und ähnliche Randwertaufgaben, die auf Reihenentwicklungen nach nicht orthogonalen Eigenfunktionen führen. 42983 : Elektromagnetische Ausgleichsvorgänge in Freileitungen und Kabeln.

6455 EFFECTS OF A MAGNETIC FIELD ON ELECTRIC FLOW. HALL EFFECT.

Aubel. 39006. Le phénomène de Hall et l'effet thermomagnétique transversal dans le graphite.

Corbino. 39624. Azione elettromagnetica degli ioni dei metalli, deviati dalla traiettoria normale per effetto di un campo magnetico. 39625, 8 : Fenomeno di Hall e teoria elettronica dei metalli. 39633 : Forze elettromotrici radiali indotte in un disco metallico da un campo magnetico variabile. 39634 : Rotazione nel campo magnetico di un disco di bismuto riscaldato al centro o alla periferia. 39635 : Rotazione in un campo di un disco metallico percorso da una corrente elettrica radiale.

Hall and **Campbell.** 40399. Electromagnetic and thermomagnetic transverse and longitudinal effects in soft iron.

Macků. 41262. Einwirkung des magnetischen Feldes auf den Volta-Effekt. (Čechisch.)

Raus. 42016. Galvanische Widerstandsänderung des Quecksilbers im Magnetfelde. 42017 : Messung des Hall-Effekts ; dessen Assymmetrie. Methode von Koláček mit der Modifikation von Kučera. (Čechisch.)

Righi. 42130. Potenziale di scarica nel campo magnetico.

Smith. 42539. Hall effect and some allied effects in alloys. 42540 : The transverse thermomagnetic effect in nickel and cobalt.

Steinberg. 42628-9. Halleffekt bei jodhaltigem Kupferjodür.

Zahn. 43233. Scheinbarer Halleffekt bei hochfrequenten Wechselströmen.

6460 ALTERNATING AND POLYPHASE CURRENTS IN WIRES.

Bierlein. 39249. Elektrische gekoppelte Schwingungssysteme.

Breitfeld. 39392. Berechnung von Wechselstrom-Fernleitungen.

Bonazzi. 39320. L'induttanza per correnti alternate di un circuito comprendente ferro.

Campos. 39480. Propagazione e smorzamento delle sovratensioni. Nuovi dispositivi di protezione.

Cohn. 39598. Kraftübertragung mittels Wechselstroms auf weite Entfernungen.

Deutsch. 39749. Das Blondel-Le Roysche Annäherungsverfahren zur Berechnung von Hochspannungs-Kraftübertragungen. 39750 : Die elektrische Festigkeit der Kabel.

Dick. 39757. Abnormal pressure rises on H.T. alternating circuits.

Donati. 39784. Effetti delle alte frequenze nelle trasmissioni di correnti alternate.

Edwards. 39868. Distribution of current and the variation of resistance in linear conductors of square and rectangular cross-section when carrying alternating currents of high frequency.

Esau. 39933-5. Widerstand und Selbstinduktion von Spulen für Wechselstrom.

Faccioli. 39968. Misura delle perdite nelle linee ad alta tensione.

Ferroux. 39986. Applications récentes des condensateurs industriels.

Girousse. 40290. Protection des installations à courant faible contre les perturbations par les courants alternatifs.

Gorges et alii. 40236. Koronaverluste auf Freileitungen.

Grassi. 40274. Raddoppiamento della frequenza di una corrente per mezzo di lampade a filo metallico. 40275 : Oscillazioni prodotte in una corrente alternata per mezzo di lampade a filamento metallico.

Hay. 40456. A graphical treatment of the skin effect.

Herrmann. 40492. Widerstandszunahme von Spulen bei Wechselstrom.

Kennelly. 40760. Vector-diagrams of oscillating-current circuits.

Lampa. 40989 : **Orlich.** 41693. Wechselströme.

Lenz. 41101. Effektiver Widerstand einer Spule.

Lindemann. 41152. Widerstandszunahme von Drahtlitzen bei schnellen elektrischen Schwingungen.

Möller. 41471. Widerstandszunahme unterteilter Leiter bei schnellen Schwingungen.

Olper. 41676. La trasformazione della frequenza.

Peek. 41787. Leggi del fenomeno della corona e rigidità dielettrica dell' aria.

Pomey. 41932. Ondes cylindriques périodiques dans un conducteur.

Vallauri. 42879. Tentativi di trasformazione statica della frequenza di correnti alternate.

Wagner. 42982. Fortpflanzung von Strömen in Kabeln mit unvollkommenem Dielektrikum. 42983 : Elektromagnetische Ausgleichsvorgänge in Freileitungen und Kabeln.

Wittmann. 43168. Ungedämpfte und gedämpfte Oszillationsphänomene. (Ungar.)

Zomparelli. 43288. Il fenomeno della " corona " nelle linee aeree ad alta tensione.

Zipp. 43285. Elektrische Hochspannungstechnik.

6470 CURRENTS OF HIGH FREQUENCY.

Fleming. 40012. Measurement of the high frequency resistance of wires.

———— and **Dyke.** 40014. Measurement of energy losses in condensers traversed by high-frequency electric oscillations. 40015 : Resonance curves taken with impact and spark ball-dischargers.

Glatzel. 40208. Methode zur Erzeugung von Hochfrequenzströmen nach dem Prinzip der Stosserregung.

Goldschmidt. 40252. Hochfrequenzmaschine für die direkte Erzeugung von elektrischen Wellen für die drahtlose Telegraphie.

Guidi. 40350. Fenomeni ottenuti con correnti ad alta frequenza e ad alto potenziale.

Howe. 40576. Oscillatory currents in coupled circuits.

Lindemann. 41152. Widerstandszunahme von Drahtlitzen bei schnellen elektrischen Schwingungen.

Lüdtke. 41219. Behandlung der electromagnetischen Lichttheorie und der Lehre von den elektrischen Schwingungen. Geschwindigkeit der Elektrizität.

Macků. 41260 : **Rusch.** 42262. Theorie der Goldschmidtschen Hochfrequenzmaschine.

Paillat et alii. 41730A. Déselectrisation des matières textiles au moyen des courants électriques de haute fréquence.

Stone-Stone. 42674. Schwingungszahlen und Dämpfungskoeffizienten gekoppelter Oszillatoren.

Talsch. 42737. Gekoppelte elektrische Schwingungskreise.

Zomparelli. 43292. Nuove invenzioni di Tesla.

6480 TELEGRAPHY.

Il sistema multiplo di telefonia e telegrafia del Maggiore Squier. Riv. Artig. Genio Roma 3. trim. 1911 (141–145).

La frequenza delle correnti telefoniche. Riv. Leg. Stat. com. Roma 2 1909 (548–555).

Ministero della Guerra. Istruzione sull' apparato microtelefonico da campo, mod. Anzalone. Roma (E. Voghera) 1909 (11 con 1 tav.). 15 cm.

Ambrosius. 38948. Neuere Simultanschaltungen. 38949 : Beeinflussung von Telegraphenleitungen durch eine Hochspannungsanlage. 38950 : Einzelanruf in Ruhestromleitungen.

[**Andreini.**] 38963. Nuovo sistema di telegrafia multipla armonica.

Angelini. 38968. Microtelegrafia.

Barkhausen. 39074. Probleme der Schwachstromtechnik.

Battaglia. 39110. Telegrafia duplice. 39112 : Nuovo scatto meccanico per il controllo del telegrafo Hughes.

6485 TELEPHONY.

Liebisch. 41126. Elektrische Eigenschaften des Zinnerzes.

Lowy. 41177. Dielektrizitätskonstante und Leitfähigkeit der Gesteine. 41178: Eine elektrodynamische Methode zur Erforschung des Erdinnern.

Lüdtke. 41219. Behandlung der elektromagnetischen Lichttheorie und der Lehre von den elektrischen Schwingungen. Geschwindigkeit der Elektrizität.

Mie. 41448.

Nasmyth. 41566. Impact excitation. 1. Characteristics of short arcs between metal electrodes. 41566; 2. Intensity of the Lepel arc oscillations as a function of the arc current, capacity and inductance. 41566; 3. Frequency of the Lepel oscillations.

Nicholson. 41605. Bending of electric waves round a large sphere.

Pedersen. 41783. La ricerca della segretezza nelle comunicazioni radiotelegrafiche.

Rudolph. 42245. Erzeugung kurzer elektrischer Wellen mit Gleichstrom und ihre Verwendung zur Bestimmung von Dielektrizitätskonstanten und Absorptionen.

Schaefer. 42340. Beugung elektromagnetischer Wellen an isolierenden zylindrischen Hindernissen.

Schicht. 42372. Der Fritter im Hertzspiegel.

Seibt. 42479. Instrumentarium zur Untersuchung und Demonstration von Mineralien auf Empfindlichkeit gegen elektrische Schwingungen.

Stone-Stone. 42764. Schwingungszahlen und Dämpfungskoeffizienten gekoppelter Oszillatoren.

Talsch. 42737. Untersuchungen über gekoppelte elektrische Schwingungskreise.

Tamaki. 42738. Electric field due to Hertzian doublet oscillators. 42742: Energy radiated by a damped Hertzian oscillator.

Tissot. 42803. Détermination des périodes des oscillations électriques.

Uljanin. v. 42859. Die Zehndersche Röhre als Indikator für elektrische Schwingungen.

Vogler. 42927. Die elektrischen Wellen.

Wagner. 42983. Elektromagnetische Ausgleichsvorgänge in Freileitungen und Kabeln.

Wallot. 42996. Einfluss von Wellen und Schirmen auf elektromagnetische Drahtwellen. 42997: Elektrische Drahtwellen.

6615 WIRELESS TELEGRAPHY AND TELEPHONY.

Bureau des Longitudes. L'éclipse de Soleil du 17 avril 1912. Paris 1912 (16 av. 1 carte). 23 cm.

Detector elettrolitico impiegabile senza forza elettromotrice ausiliara. Riv. Artig. Genio Roma 3. trim. 1910 (235–238).

Il sistema Balsillie di telegrafia senza fili. Riv. Artig. Genio Roma 3. trim. 1910 (230–234).

La radiotelegrafia a bordo dei dirigibili e degli aeroplani. Riv. Artig. Genio Roma 1. trim. 1911 (205–214).

Adda (D'). 38899. Trasmissione delle immagini senza fili.

Arco. 38977; **Bredon.** 39390; **Eichhorn.** 39884-5; **Goldschmidt.** 40244; **Reithoffer.** 42073; **Ohlsberg.** 41669; **Pedersen.** 41786; **Schulze.** 42437. Drahtlose Telegraphie.

Austin. 39017. Quantitative Versuche über drahtlose Telegraphie auf lange Strecken. 39019: Widerstand von Antennen für drahtlose Telegraphie. 39020: Hohe Funkenfrequenz in der drahtlosen Telegraphie. 39023: Measurement of electrical oscillations in the receiving antenna. 39024: Coupled high frequency circuits.

Bardeloni. 39072; **Bouju.** 39352; **Hess.** 40505; **Mascart.** 41356; **Murani.** 41539; **Nicastro.** 41699. La radiotelegrafia. Telegrafia senza fili.

Barkhausen. 39075. Theorie der gleichzeitigen Messung vom Sende- und Empfangsstrom.

Barreca. 39088. Strahlungsfähigkeiten der Antennen.

Bellini and Tosi. 39167. Wireless telegraph working in relation to interferences and perturbations.

Bierlein. 39249. Elektrische gekoppelte Schwingungssysteme.

Blondel. 39289x. Méthodes de mesure de l'orientation en radiotélégraphie dans le cas d'ondes entretenues. 39290 : Influence de l'amortissement des ondes dans l'emploi des cadres d'orientation en radiotélégraphie. 39291 : Utilisation des cadres d'orientation en radiotélégraphie pour la réception des trains périodiques d'ondes amorties.

Bourgeois. 39359, 60 : **Claude** et alii. 39571 : **Tissot.** 42802 : **Renan.** 42083. Détermination des coordonnées géographiques en employant la télégraphie sans fil.

Branly. 39385 : **Girardeau.** 40198. Télégraphie sans fil.

Braun. 39387. Electrische Schwingungen und drahtlose Telegraphie.

Chambers. 39529. Impact excitation.

Deguisne. 39719. Messmethoden in Stationen für drahtlose Telegraphie.

Dieckmann. 39761-2. Drahtlos telegraphischer Orientierungs- und meteorologischer Beratungsdienst für die Luftschiffahrt.

Dubilier. 39806. An improved wireless telegraph transmitter.

Eccles und **Makower.** 39859. Wirkungsgrad der Löschfunkenmethoden zur Erzeugung elektrischer Schwingungen. 39858 : **Galletti.** 40120-1 : Syntony of a quenched spark.

[**Elliot.**] 39904. I brevetti Jacovello.

Erskine-Murray. 39932. Ursprung der atmosphärischen Störungen in der Radiotelegraphie.

Esau. 39937. Einfluss der Atmosphäre auf die Dämpfung funkentelegraphischer Sender und Empfänger.

Fischer. 39999. Strahlung von Antennen.

Fischer. 40005. Wahrscheinlichkeit eines Einflusses meteorologischer Verhältnisse auf funkentelegraphische Reichweiten.

Garbasso. 40137. Strahlung einer geneigten Antenne.

Goldschmidt. 40249. Alternator for direct production of electric waves for wireless telegraphy.

Guldenpfennig. 40343. Empfangssystem mit abgestimmtem Indikatorkreise. Einfluss der Atmosphäre auf die Intensität und Dämpfung der sie durchlaufenden elektrischen Wellen.

Hoerschelmann. 40537. Wirkungsweise des geknickten Marconischen Senders.

Howe. 40576. Oscillatory currents in coupled circuits. 40577 : The Brown telephone relay in wireless telegraphy. 40578 : Recent developments in radio-telegraphy.

Ives. 40644. Eine Näherungstheorie für die Antenne mit grossem Widerstande.

Jégou. 40658-9. Zeit und Pendelsignale.

Jentsch. 40663. Der deutsche Anteil an der Entwicklung der drahtlosen Telegraphie.

Kalähne. 40714. Frequenz- und Dämpfungsberechnung gekoppelter Schwingungskreise nach der Cohenschen Methode.

Kiebitz. 40776-7. Erdantennen. 40779 : Aperiodische Detektorkreise. 40778 : **Zehnder.** 43258. Gerichtete drahtlose Telegraphie mit Erdströmen.

Kimura. 40785. 1000-Funkenfrequenz.

Leimbach. 41082. Drahtlose Telegraphie im Erdinnern.

Loxy. 41179. Die Fizeausche Methode zur Erforschung des Erdinnern.

Luboxsky. 41210 : **Ludewig.** 41217. Drahtlose Telegraphie und Luftschiffahrt.

Ludewig. 41215. Freiballon als Empfangsstation für drahtlose Telegraphie. 41216 : Dämpfungsmesser für drahtlose Telegraphie.

Mackû. 41261. Dämpfung bei Hertzschen Wellen.

Majorana. 41285. Le radiazioni come mezzo di segnalazione a distanza.

Mandelstam und **Papalexi.** 41307. Methode zur Messung von logarithmischen Dekrementen und Schwingungszahlen elektromagnetischer Schwingungssysteme.

March. 41345. Ausbreitung der Wellen der drahtlosen Telegraphie auf der Erdkugel.

Marconi. 41327-30. Telegrafia senza fili.

Meslin. 41448. Application de la télégraphie sans fil à la mesure des coefficients de self-induction.

Monckton. 41481. Prevention of interference in wireless telegraph working.

Mosler. 41518; **Rinkel.** 42144. Radiotelegraphische Empfangsversuche im Freiballon.

Nicastro. 41598. Nuovo sistema di dirigibilità delle onde elettromagnetiche utilizzate per la radiotelegrafia.

Petrowsky. 41819. Strahlungsdekrement, wirksame Kapazität und Selbstinduktion einer Antenne.

Pierce. 41837. Theory of coupled circuits, under the action of an impressed electromotive force, with applications to radiotelegraphy.

Poulsen. 41948-50; **Majorana.** 41284. Telefonia elettrica senza fili.

Reich. 42053. Dämpfender Einfluss der Erde auf Antennenschwingungen.

Rein. 42064. Radiotelegraphischer Gleichstrom-Tonsender.

Rothe. 42214. Réception des radiotélégrammes météorologiques avec antennes réduites.

Schwarzhaupt. 42453. Sonnenlicht, Gebirge und Wellentelegraphie.

Seibt. 42480. Radiotelegraphischer Gleichstrom-Tonsender.

Senouque. 42493. Télégraphie sans fil en aéroplane.

Settnik. 42495; **Seibt.** 42478. Entstehung von sehr wenig gedämpften Wellen mit rein metallischer Leitungsbahn bei Nebenschaltung von Antennen an die Funkenstrecke eines Oszillators.

Sommerfeld. 42576. Ausbreitung der Wellen in der drahtlosen Telegraphie. Einfluss der Bodenbeschaffenheit auf gerichtete und ungerichtete Wellenzüge.

Taylor. 42752. Wireless telegraphy in relation to interference and perturbation.

Thurn. 42789. Demonstrationsapparat für drahtlose Telephonie mittels elektrischer Wellen.

True. 42839. Erdströme in der Nähe einer Sendeantenne für drahtlose Telegraphie.

Turpain. 42851. La protection de nos hôtels des postes contre l'orage. 42852; Enregistrement des télégrammes sans fil.

Walter. 43000. Accuracy of the Bellini-Tosi wireless compass for navagational purposes.

Werner-Bleines. 43088. Tönende Telefunken.

Zehnder. 43259. Beseitigung der Antennen bei der drahtlosen Telegraphie. 43260; Beruht die drahtlose Telegraphie auf der Ausstrahlung Hertzscher Wellen in der Erde?

6620 GENERAL THEORY OF ELECTRO-MAGNETIC RADIATIONS.

Abraham. 38891. Velocità di gruppo in un mezzo dispersivo.

Cisotti. 39566. La ereditarietà lineare e i fenomeni dispersivi. 39567; Dispersività in relazione ad una assegnata frequenza.

Laue. 41025. Conception of the current of energy. (Theory of relativity.) (English, German.)

Livens. 41163. Initial accelerated motion of a perfectly conducting electrified sphere. 41165; Motion of charged spheres.

Macdonald. 41255. Integration of the equation of propagation of electric waves.

Maclaren. 41267. Emission and absorption of energy by electrons.

Reiche. 42055. Berechnung einer einfachen Brechungserscheinung mittels des Huygensschen Prinzips.

Stark. 42614. Elementare Strahlung.

Stewart. 42654. Second postulate of relativity and the electromagnetic emission theory of light.

6650 MAGNETIC ACTION ON POLARIZED LIGHT.

du Bois. 39312, 39809. L'effet Zeeman généralisé dans les absorbants sélectifs.

Heurung. 40509; **Wood.** 13191. Magneto-optische Effekte bei Chlor und Jod.

Loria. 41199. Magneto-optic Kerr effect in ferromagnetic compounds and alloys. (English, German.)

Scarpa. 42331. Diffusione.

Ubisch. 42856. Schwingungszahl und Dämpfung im leuchtenden und nichtleuchtenden Na-Dampfe.

Wartenberg. 43002. Kristalline Flüssigkeiten.

6660 INFLUENCE OF MAGNETISM ON THE EMISSION AND ABSORPTION OF LIGHT.

(See also 4208.)

Becquerel. 39154-5. L'effet magnéto-optique présenté par les bandes de phosphorescence du rubis et de l'émeraude; relations entre l'émission et l'absorption dans un champ magnétique.

Cotton. 39648-9. La théorie de Ritz du phénomène de Zeeman. 39650; Mesures sur le phénomène de Zeeman. Changements magnétiques des raies d'émission des corps gazeux.

du Bois. 39312, 39809. Der verallgemeinerte Zeemaneffekt in selektiv absorbierenden Körpern.

———— und **Elias.** 39810. Einfluss von Temperatur und Magnetisierung bei selektiven Absorptions- und Fluoreszenzspektren.

Dufour. 39824. Mesures du phénomène de Zeeman présenté par quelques bandes d'émission de molécules de corps à l'état gazeux. 39826; Phénomène de Zeeman présenté par les groupes de raies des spectres du type II.

Graftdijk. 40270. Le phénomène de Zeeman dans les spectres du nickel, du cobalt et du fer de λ = 4400 jusqu'à λ = 6500. (Hollandais.)

Gaudet. 40339. Une méthode d'observation et d'étude du phénomène de Zeemann.

Heurung. 40509. Magneto-optische Effekte bei Chlor und Jod.

Ubisch. 42856. Schwingungszahl und Dämpfung im leuchtenden und nichtleuchtenden Na-Dampfe.

Voigt. 42935. Emission und Absorption in Zusammenhang mit der Frage der Intensitätsmessungen beim Zeeman-Effekt. 42931; **Koch.** 40840: Dissymmetrie der Zeemanschen Triplets.

Wilke. 43138. Einfluss des magnetischen Feldes auf die Emission des Lichtes.

Zeeman. 43251. Light radiation under the simultaneous influence of electric and magnetic forces. (English, Dutch.) 43252; Le cas général de la décomposition magnétique des raies spectrales et son application en astrophysique.

ELECTRIC DISCHARGE.

6800 GENERAL.

Cottrell. 39652. Electrical precipitation of suspended particles.

Davisson. 39697. Positive thermions from salts of alkali earths. 39698; Rôle played by gases in the emission of positive thermions from salts.

Franck und **Hertz.** 40047. Zusammenhang zwischen Quantenhypothese und Ionisierungsspannung.

Haber. 40378-9. Elektronenemission bei chemischen Reaktionen.

Hoffmann. 40544.

Klemensiewicz. 40808-10. Entstehung positiver Ionen an erhitzten Metallen.

Kirkby. 40797. Theory of the chemical action of the electric discharge in electrolytic gas.

Kock. 40845. Apparat zur Aufnahme von Resonanzkurven.

Koenigsberger. 40858. Physikalische Messungen der chemischen Affinität durch Elektrizitätsleitung und Kanalstrahlen.

Lenard und **Ramsauer.** 41098; **Ramsauer.** 42002. Wirkungen sehr kurzwelligen ultravioletten Lichtes auf Gase; sehr reiche Quelle dieses Lichtes.

Nipher. 41629–30. Electrical discharge. 41631 : Phenomena of forked lightning.

Platania. 41889. Effetti magnetici del fulmine sulle lave di Stromboli.

Schneider. 42403. Die Energie der aus glühendem CaO entweichenden Elektronen.

Schofield. 42405. The anti-kathodes of X-ray tubes.

Stark. 42614. Atomdynamik. Elementare Strahlung.

Zeleny. 43263. Presence in point discharge of ions of opposite sign.

6805 IONISATION OF GASES.

Becker. 39144. Elektrizitätsträger in Gasen.

Bernini. 39206. Velocità degli ioni di fiamma.

Besson. 39226. Dissymétrie des ions positifs et négatifs relativement à la condensation de la vapeur d'eau. 39227 : Condensation de la vapeur d'eau par détente dans une atmosphère de gaz carbonique.

Białobrzeski. 39240. L'ionisation des diélectriques. (Polish.)

Bieber. 39243. Kondensation von Wasserdampf in Gegenwart von Ozon, Stickstoffoxyden und Wasserstoffsuperoxyd. Kerne des blauen Nebels.

Birkeland. 39267. Constitution électrique du Soleil.

Bishop. 39270. Eine absolute Bestimmung der kleinsten Ionisierungsenergie eines Elektrons und die Anwendung der Theorie der Ionisierung durch Stoss auf Gasgemische.

Bloch. 39285. Actions chimiques et ionisation par barbotage.

Bouty. 39371. Cohésion diélectrique des gaz monoatomiques.

Broglie. 39404. L'ionisation dans un gaz. Couche superficielle très mince contenant des ions des deux signes. 39405 : Les petits ions dans les gaz issus des flammes.

———— et **Brizard.** 39408. Mobilité des ions produits dans l'air par le sulfate de quinine en voie d'hydratation. 39409 : Activité et luminescence du sulfate de quinine.

Campetti. 39478. Mobilità degli ioni positivi prodotti nell'ossidazione del rame.

Cannegieter. 39482. Ionisation of gases by light emitted from Geissler tubes. Research after the existence of selective effects on the ionisation. (English. Dutch.) 39484 : L'ionisation des gaz par la lumière émise par des gaz rayonnants. (Hollandais.)

CIo. 39583. Effect of temperature on the ionization of a gas.

Deslandres. 39711. Ionisation des gaz solaires. Relations entre le rayonnement et la rotation des corps célestes. 39742 : Mouvements des protubérances solaires.

Duane. 39805. Sur la masse des ions gazeux.

Erikson. 39929. Coefficient of recombination of ions in carbondioxid and hydrogen.

Eve. 39956. L'ionisation de l'atmosphère par les substances radioactives. 39957 : Number of ions produced by the beta rays and the gamma rays from radium C.

Franck und **Hertz.** 40047. Zusammenhang zwischen Quantenhypothese und Ionisierungsspannung.

———— und **Pringsheim.** 40050. Elektrisches und optisches Verhalten der Chlorflamme.

———— and **Westphal.** 40051. Question of valency in gaseous ionization. 40052 : Beeinflussung der Stossionisation durch Fluoreszenz.

Fredenhagen. 40069. Abgabe negativer Elektronen von erhitztem Kalium und Natrium und die Leitfähigkeit der Dämpfe dieser Metalle.

Garbasso e **Vacca.** 40139. Diffusione del potenziale elettrostatico nell'aria.

Greinacher. 40296. Ionisierungsgefäss zur Messung von Radium- und Röntgenstrahlen. 40298 : Stromkurve für gleichförmig ionisierte Luft.

Hauser. 40417. Untersuchung von Bronsonwiderständen.

Immisch. 40618. Elektrizitätsträger an der Grenze von Gasen und Flüssigkeiten.

6810 CONVECTIVE LOSS. POINTS. LEAKAGE.

Marsh and **Nottage.** 41337. Formation of dust striations by an electric spark.

Metzner. 41421. ,,Dunkle" Funken.

Nikolaev. 41627. Elektrostriktion und Funkenbildung in Elektrolyten. (Russ.)

Riegger. 42112. Gekoppelte Kondensatorkreise bei sehr kurzer Funkenstrecke.

Riesenfeld. 42117–8. Stille elektrische Entladungen in Gasen bei Atmosphärendruck.

Robinson. 42154. Electric dust figures.

Rohmann. 42163. Stosserregung bei zahlreichen Partialentladungen.

Roschansky. 42182. Einfluss des Funkens auf die oszillatorische Kondensatorentladung.

Rother. 42215. Elektrizitätsübergang bei sehr kleinen Kontaktabständen.

Rottgardt. 42216. Entstehung und Vermeidung von Lichtbögen bei Verwendung von Resonanztransformatoren. 42217: Einfluss von Elektrodenmaterial und Medium der Funkenstrecke auf die Bildung von Lichtbögen bei Verwendung von Resonanztransformatoren.

Ryan. 42277. Luft und Öl als Hochspannungsisolatoren. Glimmen von Freileitungen.

Seibt. 42478; **Settnik.** 42495. Entstehung von sehr wenig gedämpften Wellen mit rein metallischer Leitungsbahn bei Nebenschaltung von Antennen an die Funkenstrecke eines Oszillators.

Stone-Stone. 42674. Schwingungszahlen und Dämpfungskoeffizienten gekoppelter Oszillatoren.

Subkis. 42701. Einfluss der Kopplung bei langsamen ungedämpften Schwingungen.

Valentin. 42874. Messungen der Funkenkonstanten in Luft, Chlor, Brom- und Joddämpfen bei verschiedenen Drucken.

Weicker. 43035, 7. Funkenspannung.

Williams. 43142. Spark discharge at very small distances.

Wood. 43195; **Steubing.** 42648. Strahlende Emission seitens des Funkens.

Zorn. 43295. Abhängigkeit der Dämpfung in Kondensatorkreisen mit Funkenstrecke von der Gestalt und dem Material der Elektroden sowie von dem Dielektrikum in der Funkenstrecke.

6825 MECHANICAL ACTION OF THE DISCHARGE (DISINTEGRATION OF METALS, Etc.).

Donau. 39785. Herstellung kolloider Färbungen des Glases und anderer Stoffe durch elektrische Zerstäubung im 18. Jahrhundert.

Drago. 39793. Influenza delle scariche oscillatorie sulla rapidità di smorzamento delle oscillazioni torsionali di fili di terro.

Svedberg. 42712. Bildung disperser Systeme durch Bestrahlung von Metallen mit ultraviolettem Licht und Röntgenstrahlen.

6830 THE VOLTAIC ARC.

La temperatura dell' arco voltaico. [Sunto.] Mon. tecn. Milano **17** 1911 (498).

Battaglia. 39111. Arco voltaico in globo chiuso.

Elliot. 39995. Arco Duddell alimentato da corrente alternativa.

Elliott and **Parsons.** 39908. A mercury arc converter.

Fabry et **Buisson.** 39966. Propriétés spectroscopiques et électriques de l'arc entre métaux.

Hagenbach. 40392. Verschiedene Formen des Kupfer- und Eisenbogens.

Kerbaker. 40763. L'avvenire dell'arco voltaico.

Kimura and **Yamamoto.** 40781. Arc characteristics in gases and vapours.

Kock. 40844. Lichtbogengenerator für Laboratorium-zwecke.

La Rosa. 41008. Schmelzen des Kohlenstoffs mittels des Jouleschen Effektes.

Matthies. 41366. Findet im Quecksilber-Vakuumlichtbogen ein elektrischer Massentransport statt?

Occhialini. 41655. Arco elettrico. 41657 : Scintille a basso potenziale. 41658 : Condizioni di esistenza dell'arco fra carboni. 41659, 61 : Come si stabiliscono fenomeni luminosi all'inizio dell' arco.

Pflüger. 41826. Ist der elektrische Lichtbogen ein „Geschosshagel" oder ein „Pumpenstrahl" ?

Pugliese. 41971. La nuova lampada a fiamma a lunga accensione di T. L. Carbone.

Putscher. 41978. Elektrischer Lichtbogen in Alkalidämpfen.

[**Righi.**] 42123. Lampada ad arco trifase a quattro carboni.

Rihl. 42142. Schallintensität des tönenden Lichtbogens.

Rudolph. 42245. Erzeugung kurzer elektrischer Wellen mit Gleichstrom.

Sabatier. 42282 ; **Salmon.** 42302. Procédé pour faire réagir deux corps dans l'arc électrique.

Schulze. 42443. Metallzerstäubung durch ultra-violettes Licht.

Siegbahn. 42506. Elektrische Schwingungen dritter Art in einem Lichtbogen.

Simon. 42522. Der elektrische Lichtbogen.

Strutt. 42690. The flame arising from the nitrogen-burning arc.

Zenneck. 43272. Energiemessung an Hochbogenspannungslichtbögen.

6840 DISCHARGE IN RAREFIED GASES.

Aston. 39004. Distribution of electric force in the Crookes dark space.

Berndt und **Wirtz.** 39200. Elektrischer Widerstand von unbewehrtem Beton.

Birkeland. 39268. Phénomènes célestes et analogies expérimentales.

Bishop. 39270. Anwendung der Theorie der Ionisierung durch Stoss auf Gasgemische.

Bloch. 39283 I. Le potentiel de décharge dans le champ magnétique.

Bouty. 39372. Potentiel d'effluve et potentiel en décharge dans les gaz très raréfiés.

Broglie et **Brizard.** 39407. La radiation du sulfate de quinine, ionisation et luminescence.

Claude. 39572, 4. Les tubes luminescents au néon.

Collodi. 39603. Scarica intermittente attraverso i gas rarefatti posti nel campo magnetico.

Dechend, von und **Hammer.** 39703. Positive Strahlen. 39704 : Spezifische chemische Wirkungen von Kanalstrahlen verschiedener Elemente.

Dember. 39734. Methode zur Erzeugung sehr weicher Röntgenstrahlen im äussersten Vakuum.

Dorn. 39788. Erzeugung kathodenstrahlartiger Sekundärstrahlen durch Röntgenstrahlen.

Gehlhoff. 40149. Glimmentladung und Emission der Alkalimetalldämpfe.

Gill. 40190. Intensity of the ultra-violet light emitted by an electrical discharge at low pressures.

Kinoshita and **Ichinohe.** 40789. A glow phenomenon in vacuum bulbs.

Koenigsberger und **Kutschewski.** 40865. Gerade Dispersion von Kanalstrahlen.

Kyll. 40949. Intensitätsmessungen im positiven Bandenspektrum des Stickstoffs.

Lilienfeld. 41136. Elektrizitätsleitung im extremen Vakuum.

Matthies. 41365. Methode zur Bestimmung des Potentialgradienten bei der Glimm- und Bogenentladung in zylindrischen Gas- und Quarzröhren.

———— und **Struck.** 41367. Potentialgradienten auf der ungeschichteten positiven Säule des Glimm- bzw. Bogenstromes in N_2 und H_2 bei hohen Strom- u. Gasdichten.

Merservey. 41411. Potentials required to produce discharges in gases at low pressures.

Perot. 41801. Luminescence de l'arc au mercure dans le vide.

Raisch. 41995. Anoden- und Kathodengefälle und Minimumpotential in Chlor.

Reiger. 42063. Die unselbständige Strömung bei der Ionisation durch die leuchtende Entladung.

Reboul et Grégoire de Bollemont. 42042. L'émission des charges positives par les métaux chauffés.

Regener. 42049. Einfluss der Kondensatorform auf den Verlauf der α - Strahlen - Sättigungsstromkurven. 42050: Die Strahlen der radioaktiven Substanzen. I. II.

Righi. 42129. Les rayons magnétiques. 42130: Potenziale di scarica nel campo magnetico. 42135: Due nuove esperienze sui raggi magnetici. 42136: Influenza del campo magnetico sull'intensità di corrente nell'aria rarefatta.

Schneider. 42403. Energie der aus glühendem CaO entweichenden Elektronen.

Seeliger. 42474. Bremsung eines Elektrons in einem verdünnten Gase. 42475: Gasionisation durch Kanalstrahlen.

Stark. 42614. Prinzipien der Atomdynamik.

Stormer. 42668-9. La structure de la couronne du Soleil.

Swinne. 42724. Einige zwischen den radioaktiven Elementen bestehende Beziehungen.

Thomson. 42778. A new method of investigating the positive rays. 42781: Rays of positive electricity.

Weiss. 43059. Ladungsbestimmungen an Silberteilchen.

Wellisch. 43076. Vorgänge beim Transport des aktiven Niederschlages.

Wertheim-Salomonson. 43098. Milliampèremeter und Röntgenlicht.

Wien. 43130. Bestimmung der mittleren freien Weglänge der Kanalstrahlen.

Wilsar. 43148. Ursprung der Träger der bewegten und der ruhenden Intensität der Kanalstrahlen.

6850 EFFECTS OF LIGHT, RÖNTGEN RAYS, &c., ON THE DISCHARGE.

Amaduzzi. 38939-41. L'effetto Hallwachs nel selenio cristallino.

Baeyer und Fool. 39044. Anfangsgeschwindigkeit lichtelektrisch ausgelöster Elektronen.

Costanzo. 39642. Effetti fotoelettrici con i raggi β.

Dember. 39733. Einfluss von Radiumstrahlen auf die lichtelektrische Empfindlichkeit der Metalle. 39734: Methode zur Erzeugung sehr weicher Röntgenstrahlen im äussersten Vakuum.

Elster und Geitel. 39940. Lichtelektrischer Effekt im Ultrarot und einige Anwendungen hochempfindlicher Kaliumzellen. 39941: Photoelektrische Zellen mit gefärbten Kaliumkathoden.

Franck et alii. 40047. Zusammenhang zwischen Quantenhypothese und Ionisierungsspannung. 40052: Beeinflussung der Stossionisation durch Fluoreszenz.

Freund. 40080. Röntgenstrahlen.

Gehrts. 40157. Reflexion und Sekundärstrahlung lichtelektrisch ausgelöster Kathodenstrahlen.

Goldmann und Kalandyk. 40243. Lichtelektrische Untersuchungen an festen Dielektriken.

Heidenreich. 40466. Photoelektromotorische Untersuchungen von Chlorsilber und Bromsilber.

Lebedinskij. 41037. Action de la lumière sur la décharge électrique. 41038: Variation du potentiel de décharge sous l'influence des radiations. (Russ.)

Lindemann. 41149. Berechnung der Eigenfrequenzen der Elektronen im selektiven Photoeffekt. 41150: Beziehungen zwischen chemischer Affinität und Elektronenfrequenzen.

Martin qb. Landschutz. 41341. Beobachtungen an metallischen Leitern von sehr hohem Widerstand und elektronentheoretische Folgerungen.

Nienhaus. 41610. Lichtelektrisches Verhalten von Lösungen.

Partzsch. 41754. Theorie des Lichtelektrischen Stromes in Gasen.

Pohl. 41904. Beziehung zwischen dem selektiven Photoeffekt und der Phosphoreszenz.

———— und Pringsheim. 41907. Lichtelektrische Effekte an kolloidalen Alkalimetallen. 41908: Selektiver Photoeffekt ausserhalb der Alkaligruppe. 41909 : Selektiver Photoeffekt des Lithiums und Natriums. 41910 : The normal and selective photoelectric effect.

Ramsauer und **Hausser.** 42003. Aktinodielektrische Wirkung bei den Erdalkaliphosphoren.

Raymond. 42031. Mesures photoélectriques faites à Antibes pendant 1911.

Ries. 42116. Ursache der Lichtempfindlichkeit des Selens.

Righi. 42128. Potenziale necessario a provocare la scarica in un gas posto nel campo magnetico.

Sichling. 42504. Natur der Photochloride des Silbers und deren Lichtpotentiale.

Sommerfeld. 42574. Das Plancksche Wirkungsquantum und seine allgemeine Bedeutung für die Molekularphysik.

Szivessy und **Schäfer.** 42732. Erhöhung des elektrischen Leitvermögens bei flüssigen Dielektrika durch Bestrahlung mit ultraviolettem Lichte.

Williams. 43142. Spark discharge at very small distances.

Winther. 43162. Ein elektrischer Lichtakkumulator.

Wright. 43211-2. Photo-electric effects in aluminium as a function of the wave-length of the incident light.

VIBRATION AND SOUND.

8990 GENERAL.

Nachtikal. 41551. Fortschritte der Akustik 1908. (Čechisch.)

Poynting. 41952. Sound.

Waetzmann. 42973A. Die Resonanztheorie des Hörens.

KINEMATICS OF VIBRATIONS AND WAVE-MOTIONS.

9000 GENERAL.

Delemer. 39736. Rôle véritable de la vibration pendulaire en acoustique.

9020 METHODS OF MAINTAINING, OBSERVING, AND MEASURING VIBRATIONS.

Garten. 40141. Verwendung der Seifenmembran zur Schallregistrierung.

Hartmann. 40436. A simple generator for waves of sound. (Danish.)

Litchiz. 41134. Ecartement des particules dans les mouvements browniens à l'aide des chocs sonores très rapides.

Wittmann. 43168. Ungedämpfte und gedämpfte Oszillationsphänomene. (Ungar.)

9030 METHODS OF EXHIBITING AND ILLUSTRATING THE PHENOMENA OF WAVE-MOTION.

Bahrdt. 39050. Wellenmaschine zur Demonstration der Interferenz zweier gegeneinander laufender Wellen.

Dörge. 39777. Schulversuche.

Hartmann-Kempf. 40441. Resonanzerscheinungen und deren experimentelle Vorführung.

Magin. 41274. Optische Darstellung schwingender Vorgänge.

Pfund. 41827. A new method of producing ripples.

Waetzmann. 42970. Akustisches Interferenzrohr. 42972 : Demonstration von Wasserwellen.

9040 REFLEXION AND REFRACTION OF WAVES.

Benndorf. 39181. Bestimmung der Geschwindigkeit transversaler Wellen in der äussersten Erdkruste.

9050 INTERFERENCE, DIFFRACTION AND SCATTERING OF WAVES. HUYGENS' PRINCIPLE.

Réthy. 42087. Anstrengungslinien der Metalle.

Stewart. 42653. The acoustic shadow of a rigid sphere.

VIBRATIONS.

9100 GENERAL.

Budde. 39439. Zur Theorie des Mitschwingens.

Caras-Wilson. 39506. Musical sands of Eigg.

Frank. 40057 : **Schaefer.** 42341. Manometer.

Griveau. 40307. Le pendule et l'oscillation mélodique.

Kneser. 40817. Die Integral gleichungen.

Reinstein. 42072. Transversalschwingungen der gleichförmig gespann ten elliptisch oder kreisförmig begrenzten Vollmembran und Kreismembran.

9105 MECHANICAL ACTION OF VIBRATIONS. (ACOUSTIC ATTRACTION.)

Raman. 42600. Phenomena observed in connection with Melde's experiment.

9110 VIBRATIONS OF STRINGS AND RODS. CURVED RODS.

Hartmann-Kempf. 40439. Resonanzverlauf abgestimmter Klangkörper.

Herbst. 40487. Schwingungsbewegungen.

Ives. 40643. An approximate theory of an elastic string vibrating, in its fundamental mode, in a viscous medium.

Kneser. 40817. Die Integralgleichungen.

Le Heux. 41066. Lissajoussche Stimmgabelkurven in stereoskopischer Darstellung.

Nikolai. 41622. Oscillations d'un cylindre à mur mince (vibrations des tubes). (Russ.)

Raman. 42001. The small motion at the nodes of a vibrating string.

Robin. 42152. Hauteur du son dans les alliages et ses variations en fonction de la température.

Roy. 42219. De la viscosité dans le mouvement des fils flexibles.

Tamarkine. 42745. Problème des vibrations transversales d'une verge élastique homogène.

Timoschenko. 42800. Erzwungene Schwingungen prismatischer Stäbe.

Wittmann. 43168. Ungedämpfte und gedämpfte Oszillationsphänomene. (Ungar.)

9120 VIBRATIONS OF MEMBRANES AND PLATES. CURVED PLATES. BELLS.

Blessing. 39282. Klang der Kirchenglocken.

Garten. 40444. Seitenmembran zur Schallregistrierung.

Lifchitz. 41133. La reproduction sonore d'une courbe périodique.

Rayleigh. 42023. Bessel's functions as applied to the vibrations of a circular membrane. 42025: Calculation of Chladni's figures for a square plate.

Reinstein. 42071-2. Untersuchung der Schwingungen gleichförmig gespannter elliptisch begrenzter Membranen.

Roy. 42218. Viscosité dans le mouvement des membranes flexibles. 42220: Les équations générales des membranes flexibles.

Sizes. 42529. Résonance multiple des cloches.

Weyl. 43106. Abhängigkeit der Eigenschwingungen einer Membran von deren Begrenzung. 43107: Das asymptotische Verteilungsgesetz der Eigenwerte linearer partieller Differentialgleichungen (Theorie der Hohlraumstrahlung).

9130 VIBRATIONS OF GASES IN TUBES AND OTHER CAVITIES. EFFECTS OF APERTURES.

Campbell and **Dye.** 39471: **Wertheim-Salomonson.** 43097. Very high sound vibrations produced by electric sparks.

König. 40854. Theorie der Kundtschen Staubfiguren.

Mather. 41362. Sound vibrations produced by electric sparks.

Melchissédec et **Frossard.** 41395. Théorie mécanique de quelques tuyaux sonores.

Weyl. 43107.

9135 FORCED VIBRATIONS.

Broemser. 39404. Theorie der registrierenden Apparate.

Budde. 39439. Mitschwingen.

Frank. 40059 ; **Malmström.** 41300.
Erzwungene Schwingung.

Kneser. 40817.

Mackŭ. 41261 ; **Grober.** 40309.
Zur Theorie der Dämpfung bei Hertzschen Wellen.

Oosting. 41688. Démonstration des vibrations forcées de fils et de verges. (Hollandais.)

Timoschenko. 42800. Erzwungene Schwingungen prismatischer Stäbe.

9140 RESONANCE. RESONATORS. OBJECTIVE COMBINATION-TONES.

Budde. 39439. Mitschwingen.

Garten. 40141. Verwendung der Seifenmembran zur Schallregistrierung.

Giesswein. 40187. „Resonanz" der Mundhöhle und der Nasenräume.

Hansing. 40416 ; **Hermann.** 40490 ; **Schulze.** 42439 : **Waetzmann.** 42969.
Kombinationstöne.

Hartmann-Kempf. 40439. Resonanzverlauf abgestimmter Klangkörper.
40441 : Resonanzerscheinungen und deren experimentelle Vorführung.

Waetzmann. 42971. Zusammenklang zweier einfacher Töne. 42973A.
Resonanztheorie des Hörens.

Zimmermann. 43279. Vibrationen des Schädels beim Singen.

PROPAGATION OF SOUND.

9200 GENERAL.

Hoesslin. 40538.

Krüse. 40922. Schallfortpflanzung in einer Flüssigkeit.

Lebedew. 41036. Grenzwerte der kürzesten akustischen Wellen.

Reko. 42081.

Wunder. 43225. Bildung stehender Wellen in den Wandungen explodierender Gefässe.

9210 VELOCITY OF SOUND.

Berger. 39191. Schalldurchlässigkeit. Diss.

Fujiwara. 40097. Anomalous propagation of sound rays in the atmosphere.

Hoesslin. 40538. Schallgeschwindigkeit als Funktion der Verteilung der molekularen Geschwindigkeiten.

Martini. 41344. Velocità del suono nei liquidi.

Omori. 41683. Velocity of sound waves of the noon gun of Tokyo observed on Mt. Tsukuba.

Stevens. 42651. Vitesse du son.

9220 REFLEXION AND REFRACTION OF SOUND.

Gallé. 40118. Echo of sound-signals in mist, diffraction and reflection of sound waves. (Dutch.)

Mahillon. 41280. Stéthoscopes au points de vue acoustique.

Watson. 43006. Echoes in an auditorium. 43007 : Musical echoes.

9230 INTERFERENCE AND DIFFRACTION OF SOUND. BEATS.

Neuscheler. 41596. Untersuchung stehender Schallschwingungen mit Hilfe des Widerstandsthermometers.

Waetzmann. 42970. Neues akustisches Interferenzrohr. 42971 : Zusammenklang zweier einfacher Töne.

9240 DAMPING OF SOUND-WAVES BY VISCOSITY AND HEAT CONDUCTION.

Mallock. 41297. The damping of sound by frothy liquids.

Zwaardemaker. 43300. Camera silenta.

9250 ACOUSTIC TRANSPARENCY.

Berger. 39190-1. Durchlässigkeit gegen Luftschall.

Neklepajew. 41576. Absorption kurzer akustischer Wellen in der Luft.

McGinnis and **Harkins.** 41256. Transmission of sound through porous and non-porous materials.

9255 ACOUSTICS OF BUILDINGS.

Heger. 40464 Raumakustik.

Van der Noot. 42886. L'acoustique des salles.

Watson. 43006. Echoes in an auditorium.

Zwaardemaker. 43304. Akustik der
öffentlichen Gebäude. (Holländisch.)

9310 METHODS OF ILLUSTRA-
TING AND OBSERVING AIR-
WAVES.

Dorge. 39777. Schulversuche.

Hartmann Kempf. 40441. Experimentelle Vorführung wichtigere Resonanzerscheinungen.

Kruse. 40922. Schallfortpflanzung
in einer Flüssigkeit.

Litchitz. 41132. La photographie
d'une courbe sonore.

Raman. 41998. Photographs of
vibration curves.

9320 MEASUREMENT OF THE
VELOCITY, AMPLITUDE,
ENERGY AND FREQUENCY
OF SOUND-WAVES.

Berger. 39490–1. Schalldurchlässigkeit.

Elsässer. 39909. Bestimmung der
Schwingungszahl eines Tones mit der
Sirene.

Heindlhofer. 40470. Eine absolute
Messung der Schallintensität.

Konig. 40854. Theorie der Kundtschen Staubfiguren.

McGinnis and Harkins. 41256. Transmission of sound through porous and
non-porous materials.

Neuscheler. 41597. Untersuchung
stehender Schallschwingungen mit Hilfe
des Widerstandsthermometers. Diss.

Ritter. 42147. Einrichtung zum
Messen von Knallstärken.

Robinson. 42153–4. Electric dust
figures.

Schaefer. 42344. Methode der
Schwingungszahlenbestimmung.

Zemplen. 43265. Nachweis des
Wärmeeffektes der Schallwellen. (Ungar.)

9340 ANALYSIS OF COMPOUND
SOUND-WAVES.

Edwards. 39869. Quantitative analysis of musical tone.

Gutzmann. 40374. Die Analyse
künstlicher Vokale.

Waetzmann. 42971. Zusammenklang zweier einfacher Töne.

THE PHYSICAL BASIS OF MUSIC
AND THE SENSATION OF
SOUND.

9400 GENERAL.

Auerbach. 39010. Die Grundlagen
der Musik.

Knosp. 40823. La musique indo-
chinoise.

Peterson. 41817. Combination
tones and related auditory phenomena.

Stumpf. 42697. Die Anfänge der
Musik.

9410 MUSICAL INSTRUMENTS.

Berry. 39240. Pianoforte bridges.

Biehle. 39245. Theorie der pneumatischen Orgeltraktur und die Stellung des Spieltisches.

Blessing. 39282. Klang der Kirchenglocken.

Buschmann. 39454. Glasmaterial
für Musikinstrumente.

Kellermann. 40756. Blechinstrumentenbau.

Riemann. 42114. Wesen des Klavierklanges und seine Beziehungen zum
Anschlag.

Thomas. 42770. Die Stimmgabel.

Volker. 42923. Die Lackierkunst
der alten Meister.

9420 THE VOICE. SPEAKING
MACHINES.

Grégoire. 40293. Machines parlantes (dans l'enseignement des langues).

Gutzmann. 40374. Die Analyse
künstlicher Vokale.

Hermann. 40489. Einfluss der
Drehgeschwindigkeit auf die Vokale bei
der Reproduktion derselben am Edison-
schen Phonographen.

McKendrick. 41258: Parsons.
41752. Experiments with the gramophone.

Reko. 42077. Tonempfindliche
Kunststoffe. 42078: Klanggefässe.
42079: Geschichte von der doppelt
wirkenden Schalldose.

Reko. 42080. Geschichte der Sprechmaschinen.

Zimmermann. 43279. Vibrationen
des Schädels beim Singen.

9430 LIMITS OF AUDITION AS DEPENDENT ON INTENSITY AND PITCH.

Muraoka. 41542. Unterschiedsschwellen der Tonhöhe.

Schulze. 42441. Bestimmung der oberen Hörgrenze mit der Zahnradsirene.

Streit. 42682. Endophonoskop.

Struycken. 42692. Obere Hörgrenze für Luft- und Knochenleitung.

Zoth. 43296. Fallphonometer.

9450 QUALITY OF MUSICAL TONES. CONSONANCE AND DISSONANCE. CHORDS. PHYSICAL EXPLANATION OF HARMONY.

Artom. 38999. Successione dei suoni spiegata col fenomeno dell'attrazione melodica tetracordale.

Bielschowsky. 39246. Objektive Wertung von Dissonanz und Geräusch.

Brauer. 39386. Die harmonischen Obertöne und ihre Bedeutung für Harmonie und Stimmkunst.

Edwards. 39869. Quantitative analysis of musical tone.

Goebel. 40233. Ursache der Einklangsempfindung bei Einwirkung von Tönen, die im Oktavenverhältnis zueinander stehen.

Hansing. 40416. Kombinationstöne und ihre hohe Bedeutung für die Musik.

Riemann. 42113A. Tonhöhenbewusstsein und Intervallurteil.

Stumpf. 42695. Differenztöne und Konsonanz. 42696 : Konsonanz und Konkordanz. Wohlklang musikalischer Zusammenklänge.

Weigle. 43044. Natürliche und künstliche Obertöne, einfache Töne, Mixturen.

Wesendonk. 43099. Zur Theorie der Klangfarbe.

PHYSIOLOGICAL ACOUSTICS.

9500 GENERAL.

Auerbach. 39010. Die Grundlagen der Musik.

Edelmann. 39861. Leitfaden der Akustik für Ohrenärzte.

Stefanini e **Tonietti.** 42624. Un fonometro per la voce afona.

9510 ARRANGEMENT AND ACTION OF THE VOCAL ORGANS.

Barth. 39093. Physiologie der menschlichen Stimme.

Handek und **Fröschels.** 40409. Röntgenaufnahmen der Form des Ansatzrohres bei den Sprachlauten.

Goebel. 40232. Ueber die tonverstärkende Wirkung des über den Stimmlippen befindlichen Ansatzrohres.

Poirot. 41916. Die Phonetik.

Zwaardemaker. 43299. Effusion of acoustic energy from the head. (English, Dutch.)

9520 ARRANGEMENT AND ACTION OF THE EAR.

Bocci. 39298. Teoria dell' audizione più consentanea alla complessa morfologia dell' organo del Corti.

Frey. 40082. Bedeutung der Hammer-Ambossverbindung.

Quix. 41987. Le phénomène de Hensen et l'accommodation des oreilles. (Hollandais.)

Schulze. 42442. Ermüdung des Ohres.

Shambaugh. 42497. Tonempfindung.

Waetzmann. 42973. Die [durch den Bau der Basilarmembran bedingte] ...Ausdehnung der Tonempfindungen. 42973A : Die Resonanztheorie des Hörens.

ERRATUM IN NINTH ISSUE.

p. 363. Transfer entry under **Kempe** *in* 6045 *to* 6043.

ERRATA IN TENTH ISSUE.

p. 92. Entries 35818 *and* 35819 *should be assigned to* **Doelter.**

p. 223. Entry 38585 *should be assigned to* **Waals, J[ohannes] D[iderik] van der. Jr.**

p. 256. Add an entry **Lorenz.** 37114.

LIST OF JOURNALS WITH ABBREVIATED TITLES

*The numbers at end of full Title are those used in the
General List of Journals.*

Aachen, Mitt. eisenhüttenmänn. Inst.—Mitteilungen aus dem eisenhüttenmännischen Institut der königl. techn. Hochschule Aachen, hrsg. v. G. Müller. Berlin. [¼ jährl.] — Ger.

Abh. Didakt. Natw., Berlin.—Abhandlungen zur Didaktik und Philosophie der Naturwissenschaft, hrsg. v. F. Poske, A. Höfler und E. Grimsehl. Berlin. [zwangl.] — Ger.

Acireale, Atti Acc. Zelanti.—Atti e Rendiconti della R. Accademia degli Zelanti. Acireale. 1 It.

Agricoltore, Catania.—L'Agricoltore calabro-siculo. Catania. 3 It.

Akad. afhandl., Upsala.—Akademisk afhandling [Dissertatio academica — Inaugural-Dissertation] at the University of Upsala. 62 Swe.

Allg. Ztg Judentum, Berlin.—Allgemeine Zeitung des Judentums. Ein unparteiisches Organ für alles jüdische Interesse. Berlin. [wöch.] — Ger.

Amer. Chem. J., Baltimore, Md.—American Chemical Journal (Johns Hopkins University), Baltimore, Md. 12 U.S.

Amsterdam, Chem. Weekbl.—Chemisch Weekblad, Orgaan van de Nederlandsche Chemische Vereeniging, Amsterdam. — Hol.

Amsterdam, Proc. Sci. K. Akad. Wet.—Proceedings of the Sections of Sciences, Koninklijke Akademie van Wetenschappen, Amsterdam. 8vo. 3 Hol.

Amsterdam, Versl. Wis. Nat. Afd. K. Akad. Wet.—Verslagen der Vergaderingen van de Wis- en Natuurkundige Afdeeling der Koninklijke Akademie van Wetenschappen, Amsterdam. 8vo. 7 Hol.

Ann. bur. longit., Paris.—Annales du Bureau des longitudes. Paris. [annuel.] 41 Fr.

Ann. chim. phys., Paris.—Annales de chimie et de physique, réd. MM. Berthelot, Friedel, Mascart, Moissan. Paris. [mensuel.] 44 Fr.

Ann. Gew., Berlin.—Annalen für Gewerbe und Bauwesen, hrsg. v. Glaser. Berlin. [½ monatl.] 42 Ger.

Ann. Hydrogr., Berlin.—Annalen der Hydrographie und maritimen Meteorologie, hrsg. v. d. deutschen Seewarte. Nebst Beiheften. Berlin. [monatl.] 43 Ger.

Ann. Natphilos., Leipzig.—Annalen der Naturphilosophie. Leipzig. 1285 Ger.

Ann. Obs. Bordeaux.—Annales de l'Observatoire de Bordeaux (Gironde). 70 Fr.

Ann. Pharm., Louvain.—Annales de pharmacie. Pharmacie pratique, pharmacognosie, denrées alimentaires, chimie toxicologie, microscopie, hygiène, intérêts professionnels, législation. Louvain. [mensuel.] 4 Bel.

Ann. Physik, Leipzig.—Annalen der Physik, hrsg. v. Drude. Leipzig. [monatl.] 44 Ger.

Arch. ges. Physiol., Bonn.—Archiv für die gesammte Physiologie des Menschen und der Thiere, hrsg. v. Pflüger. Bonn. [48 H. jährl.] 63 Ger.

Arch. Laryng., Berlin.—Archiv für Laryngologie und Rhinologie, hrsg. v. Fränkel. Berlin. [3—4 H. jährl.] 74 Ger.

Arch. ophtalm., Paris.—Archives d'ophtalmologie. Paris. [mensuel.] 12 Bel.

Arch. physik. Med., Leipzig.—Archiv für physikalische Medizin und medizinische Technik nebst Beiblatt, hrsg. v. H. Kraft etc. Leipzig. [¼ jährl.] — Ger.

Arch. Post, Berlin. Archiv für Post und Telegraphie, hrsg. im Auftrag des Reichs-Postamts. Berlin. 84 Ger.

Ark. Kemi, Stockholm.—Arkiv för kemi, mineralogi och geologi utgifvet af K. Svenska Vetenskapsakademien i Stockholm. 8vo. — Swe.

Ark. Mat., Stockholm.—Arkiv för matematik, astronomi och fysik, utgifvet af K. Svenska Vetenskapsakademien i Stockholm. 8vo. — Swe.

Armiert. Beton, Berlin.—Armierter Beton. Monatsschrift für Theorie und Praxis des gesamten Betonbaues, hrsg. v. E. Probst und M. Foerster. Berlin. — Ger.

Artill. Monatshefte, Berlin.—Artilleristische Monatshefte, red. v. H. Rohn. Berlin. — Ger.

Astr. Nachr., Kiel.—Astronomische Nachrichten, hrsg. v. Kreutz. Kiel, Hamburg. [72 Nrn jährl.] 94 Ger.

Astroph. J., Chicago. Ill.—Astrophysical Journal (University of Chicago) Chicago, Ill. 27 U.S.

Atel. Phot., Halle.—Das Atelier des Photographen, red. v. Miethe. Halle. [monatl.] Nebst Beibl.: Photographische Chronik. [wöch.] 95 Ger.

Atti Ass. Elettrotecn. ital., Milano.—Atti dell'Associazione Elettrotecnica italiana, Milano. — It.

Aus d. Natur, Stuttgart.—Aus der Natur. Zeitschrift für alle Naturfreunde, hrsg. v. W. Schoenichen. Stuttgart. [½ monatl.] — Ger.

Balneol. Ztg, Berlin.—Balneologische Zeitung, hrsg. v. Petzold. Berlin. [36 H. jährl.] 109 Ger.

Bayr. IndBl., München.—Bayrisches Industrie- und Gewerbeblatt, hrsg. v. Ausschuss des polytechnischen Vereins München. München. [wöch.] 119 Ger.

Beitr. Akustik, Leipzig.—Beiträge zur Akustik und Musikwissenschaft, hrsg. v. Carl Strumpf. Leipzig. [zwangl.] — Ger.

Beitr. Anat. Ohr., Berlin.—Beiträge zur Anatomie, Physiologie, Pathologie u. Therapie des Ohres, der Nase u. des Halses, hrsg. v. A. Passow u. K. L. Schaffer. Berlin. [zwangl.] — Ger.

Beitr. Geophysik, Leipzig.—Beiträge zur Geophysik, hrsg. v. Gerland. Leipzig. [1-2 H. jährl.] 129 Ger.

Berlin, SitzBer. Ak. Wiss.—Sitzungsberichte der kgl. preussischen Akademie der Wissenschaften. Berlin. [wöch.] 182 Ger.

Berlin, Verh. D. physik. Ges.—Verhandlungen der deutschen physikalischen Gesellschaft. Leipzig. [½ monatl.] 186 Ger.

Berlin, Verh. Kol.-techn.Komm.—Verhandlungen der Kolonial-Technischen Kommission des Kolonial-Wirtschaftlichen Komitees E. K. wirtschaftlicher ausschuss der Deutschen Kolonialgesellschaft. Berlin. [zwangl.] — Ger.

Berlin, Veröff. Hufeland. Ges. Balneol.—Veröffentlichungen der Hufelandischen Gesellschaft zu Berlin. Oeffentliche Versammlung der balneologischen Gesellschaft. Berlin. [jährl.] 193 Ger.

Berlin, Veröff. met. Inst.—Veröffentlichungen des kgl. preussischen meteorologischen Institutes. Zugleich Deutsches meteorologisches Jahrbuch, Beobachtungssystem des Kgr. Preussen. Ergebnisse d. Beobacht. a. d. Stationen 2. u. 3. Ordn. Ergebnisse d. Gewitterbeobacht. Ergebnisse d. Niederschlagsbeobacht. Ergebnisse d. magnet. Beobacht. in Potsdam. Ergebnisse d. meteorolog. Beobacht. in Potsdam. Berlin. [jährl. in zwangl. H.] 195 Ger.

Berlin, Verh. Ver. Gewerbfl. Verhandlungen des Vereins zur Beförderung des Gewerbfleisses. Berlin. [10 H. jährl.] 190 Ger.

Berlin, Zs. Ver. D. Ing. Zeitschrift des Vereins deutscher Ingenieure. Berlin. [wöch.] 202 Ger.

Ber. intern. Kongr. Thalassother., Berlin. Bericht über den internationalen Kongress für Thalassotherapie. Berlin. [zwangl.] — Ger.

Ber. Kongr. exp. Psych., Leipzig. — Bericht über den Kongress für experimentelle Psychologie. Im Auftrage des Vorstandes hrsg. Leipzig. — Ger.

Ber. Lehrersem., Frankenberg. Bericht über das königl. Lehrerseminar zu Frankenberg i. Sa. [zwangl.] — Ger.

Berliner Klinik. — Berliner Klinik. Sammlung klinischer Vorträge. Berlin. [16 H. jährl.] 210 Ger.

Berliner klin. Wochenschr. — Berliner klinische Wochenschrift. red. v. Ewald u. Posner. Berlin. 209 Ger.

Ber. Ver. D. Fabr. feuerfester Produkte, Berlin. — Bericht über die Hauptversammlung des Vereins deutscher Fabriken feuerfester Produkte. Berlin. [jährl.] — Ger.

Bibl. math., Leipzig. - Bibliotheca mathematica, hrsg. v. Eneström. Leipzig. [1 jährl.] 217 Ger.

Bl. Fortbildg Lehrer, Berlin. — Blätter für die Fortbildung des Lehrers und der Lehrerin. Halbmonatsschrift mit besonderer Berücksichtigung der Bedürfnisse der jüngeren Lehrerwelt, hrsg. von Wolfgarten, T. Meyer, A. Potbag. Berlin. — Ger.

Bl. GymnSchulw., München. — Blätter für das Gymnasial-Schulwesen. München. 1282 Ger.

Bologna, Mem. Acc. sc. Memorie dell' Academia delle scienze dell' Istituto, Bologna. 42 It.

Bordeaux, Proc.-verb. soc. sci. phys. nat. — Procès-verbaux de la société des sciences physiques et naturelles de Bordeaux (Gironde). — Fr.

Boston, Mass., Proc. Amer. Acad. Arts Sci. — Proceedings of the American Academy of Arts and Sciences, Boston, Mass. 60 U.S.

Bot. Gaz., Chicago, Ill., Univ. Chic. — Botanical Gazette (University of Chicago), Chicago, Ill. 64 U.S.

Bruxelles, Ann. Soc. scient. — Annales de la Société scientifique de Bruxelles. Louvain. [trimestr.] 26 Bel.

Bruxelles, Bul. Acad. roy. — Bulletin de la classe des sciences de l'Académie royale des sciences, des lettres et des beaux arts de Belgique. Bruxelles. [mensuel.] 27 Bel.

Bruxelles, Bul. Soc. astron. — Bulletin de la Société belge d'astronomie. Comptes-rendus des séances mensuelles de la Société, et revue des sciences d'observation. Bruxelles. [mensuel.] 37 Bel.

Bruxelles, Bul. Soc. belge électr. — Bulletin de la Société belge d'électriciens. Bruxelles. [trimestr.] 38 Bel.

Bruxelles, Bul. Soc. belge ophtalm. — Bulletin de la Société belge d'ophtalmologie. Bruxelles. 39 Bel.

Bruxelles, Bul. Soc. roy. sci. méd. nat. — Bulletin de la Société royale des sciences médicales et naturelles de Bruxelles. Bruxelles. [mensuel.] 51 Bel.

Bruxelles, Bul. Techn. Ass. ing. — Bulletin Technique de l'association des ingénieurs sortis de l'école polytechnique de Bruxelles. Bruxelles. [mensuel.] — Bel.

Bul. astr., Paris. — Bulletin astronomique, publié sous les auspices de l'Observatoire de Paris par Lœwy. Paris. [mensuel.] 205 Fr.

Bul. Commis. intern. chem. de fer, Bruxelles.—Bulletin de la Commission internationale du Congrès des chemins de fer Bruxelles. [mensuel.] 62 Bel.

Cambridge, Mass., Ann. Obs. Harvard Coll.—Annals of the Harvard College Observatory, Cambridge, Mass. 69 U.S.

Cambridge, Proc. Phil. Soc.—Proceedings of the Cambridge Philosophical Society, Cambridge. 48 U.K.

Carinthia II, Klagenfurt.—Carinthia II, Mitteilungen des Naturhistorischen Landesmuseums für Kärnten, red. v. Karl Frauscher. Klagenfurt. [2 monatl.] 67 Aus.

Cas. Lékar̆. Cesk., Prag.—Casopis Lékar̆ů Ceských. Praha. [Zeitschrift der Tschechischen Ärzte. Prag. [wöch.] 72 Aus.

Catania, Bul. Acc. Gioenia.—Bullettino delle sedute dell' Accademia Gioenia di scienze naturali, Catania. 49 It.

Catania, Mem. Soc. spettroscop. ital.—Memorie della Società degli spettroscopisti italiani, Catania. 96 It.

Centralbl. Min., Stuttgart.—Centralblatt für Mineralogie, Geologie und Paläontologie, hrsg. v. Bauer etc. Stuttgart. [½ monatl.] 285 Ger.

Centralztg Opt., Berlin.—Centralzeitung für Optik und Mechanik. Berlin. [½ monatl.] 294 Ger.

Chapel Hill, N.C., J. Elisha Mitchell Sci. Soc.—Journal of the Elisha Mitchell Scientific Society, Chapel Hill, N.C. 88 U.S.

Chem. Ind., Berlin.—Die chemische Industrie, red. v. Witt. Berlin. [½ monatl.] 297 Ger.

Chem. News, London.—Chemical News and Journal of Science, London. 58 U.K.

Chem. pols., Warszawa.—Chemik Polski, czasopismo poświęcone wszystkim gałęziom chemii teoretycznej i stosowanej, red. Br. Znatowicz. Warszawa. 8vo. [weekly.] 2 Pol.

ChemZtg, Cöthen.—Chemikerzeitung. Centralorgan für Chemiker, Techniker etc. Cöthen. Nebst Supplement : Chemisches Repertorium. [½ wöch.] 301 Ger.

Ciel et Terre, Bruxelles.—Ciel et Terre. Revue populaire d'astronomie, de météorologie et de physique du globe. Bruxelles. [bimensuel.] 78 Bel.

Clin. ocul., Roma.—La clinica oculistica, Roma. — It.

D. landw. Wochenschr., Berlin.—Deutsche landwirthschaftliche Wochenschrift, hrsg. v. Vogel. Berlin. 349 Ger.

D. MechZtg, Berlin.—Deutsche Mechaniker-Zeitung. Beiblatt zur Zeitschrift für Instrumentenkunde. Berlin. [½ monatl.] 1264 Ger.

D. med. Wochenschr., Leipzig.—Deutsche medicinische Wochenschrift, red. v. Eulenburg u. Schwalbe. Leipzig. 352 Ger.

D. Mus. Vortr., München.—Deutsches Museum. Vorträge und Berichte. München. [zwangl.] — Ger.

D. Thierfreund, Leipzig.—Deutscher Thierfreund. Illustrirte Monatsschrift, hrsg. v. Klee u. Marshall. Leipzig. 374 Ger.

Denver, Proc. Colo. Sci. Soc.—Proceedings of the Colorado Scientific Society, Denver. 134 U.S.

Dinglers polyt. J., Stuttgart.—Dinglers polytechnisches Journal, hrsg. v. Pickersgill. Stuttgart. [wöch.] 403 Ger.

Dublin, Proc. R. Irish Acad.—Proceedings of the Royal Irish Academy, Dublin. 74 U.K.

Echo indust., Bruxelles.—L'Echo de l'industrie. Publication hebdomadaire, industrielle, commerciale et économique. Bruxelles. — Bel.

Edinburgh, Proc. R. Soc. —Proceedings of the Royal Society of Edinburgh. 96 U.K.

Elect., London. Electrician, London. 112 U.K.

Electro, Bruxelles. Electro. Revue internationale de l'électricité et industries annexes. Bruxelles. — Bel.

Elektr. Betr., Leipzig. —Elektrische und maschinelle Betriebe. Zeitschrift für Bau, Betrieb und Bewirtschaftung, hrsg. v. A. Plumecke. Leipzig. [½ monatl.] Ger.

Elektr. Kraftbetriebe, München. —Elektrische Kraftbetriebe und Bahnen. Zeitschrift für das gesamte Anwendungsgebiet elektrischer Triebkraft, hrsg. v. W. Reichel. München. [36 H. jährl.] — Ger.

Elektroch. Zs., Berlin. —Elektrochemische Zeitschrift, red. v. Neuburger. Berlin. [monatl.] 427 Ger.

Elektrot. Anz., Berlin. —Elektrotechnischer Anzeiger, hrsg. v. Grünwald. Berlin. [½ wöch.] 429 Ger.

Elektrot. Zs., Berlin. — Elektrotechnische Zeitschrift (Centralblatt für Elektrotechnik), red. v. Kapp v. West. Berlin, München. [wöch.] 434 Ger.

Elettricista, Roma. — L'Elettricista, Roma. 58 It.

Ergebn. wiss. Med., Leipzig. —Ergebniss der wissenschaftlichen Medizin, hrsg. von C. Lewin. Leipzig. [monatl.] — Ger.

Ferrara, Atti Acc. med. nat. — Atti dell'Accademia di scienze mediche e naturali, Ferrara. 60 It.

Firenze, Bol. Soc. fot. —Bollettino mensile della Società fotografica italiana, Firenze. 39 It.

Fördertechnik, Berlin. —Die Fördertechnik. Zeitschrift für den Bau und Betrieb der Pumpen etc., hrsg. v. M. Wille. Berlin. [monatl.] — Ger.

Fortschr. Min., Jena. —Fortschritte der Mineralogie. Kristallographie und Petrographie. Stuttgart. [jährl.] Ger.

Fortschr. natw. Forschg, Berlin. —Fortschritte der naturwissenschaftlichen Forschung, hrsg. v. E. Abderhalden. Berlin. [zwangl.] — Ger.

Fortschr. Röntgenstr., Hamburg. —Fortschritte auf dem Gebiete der Röntgenstrahlen, hrsg. v. Deycke u. Albers-Schönberg. Hamburg. [2 monatl.] 471 Ger.

Frankfurt a. M., Jahresber. physik. Ver. —Jahresbericht des physikalischen Vereins zu Frankfurt a. M. [jährl.] 477 Ger.

Freiburg i. B., Ber. natf. Ges. —Berichte der naturforschenden Gesellschaft zu Freiburg i. B. Freiburg i. B. [jährl. in zwangl. H.] 485 Ger.

Fribourg, Mém. Soc. Sci. Nat. —Memoires de la Société Fribourgeoise des Sciences naturelles. [4 Séries.] [I. Série.] Botanique. [II. Série.] Chimie. [III. Série.] Geologie et Géographie. [IV. Série.] Mathématique et Physique. Fribourg. 8vo. — Swi.

Gasmotorentechnik, Berlin. —Die Gasmotorentechnik. Monatsschau hrsg. v. Neuberg. Berlin. 1291 Ger.

Gas, Venezia. —Rivista mensile delle industrie gas, elettricità acquedotti della municipalizzazione, Venezia. — It.

Gazz. chim. ital., Roma. Gazzetta chimica italiana, Roma. 68 It.

Genève, Bul. Inst. Nat. —Bulletin de l'Institut national genevois. Genève. 8vo. 39 Swi.

Genève, C. R. Soc. Phys. Hist. Nat. —Compte rendu des séances de la Société de physique et d'histoire naturelle de Genève. 8vo. Genève. — Swi.

Geogn. Jahreshefte, München. Geognostische Jahreshefte, hrsg. v. d. geognostischen Abtheilung des kgl. bayerischen Oberbergamts in München. München. [jährl.] 507 Ger.

Gesundhtslng., München. Gesundheits-Ingenieur, hrsg. v. Anklam. München. [½ monatl.] 517 Ger.

Giorn. Genio Civ., Roma. Giornale del Genio Civile, Roma. 81 It.

Göttingen, Abh. Ges. Wiss. Abhandlungen der kgl. Gesellschaft der Wissenschaften zu Göttingen. Berlin. [jährl. in zwangl. H.] 529 Ger.

Göttingen, Nachr. Ges. Wiss. Nachrichten von der kgl. Gesellschaft der Wissenschaften zu Göttingen. Göttingen. [jährl. in zwangl. H.] 531 Ger.

Graefes Arch. Ophthalm., Leipzig. Graefes Archiv für Ophthalmologie, red. v. Leber u. Wagenmann. Leipzig. [5-6 H. jährl.] 533 Ger.

Granville, Ohio, Bul. Sci. Lab. Denison Univ. Bulletin of the Scientific Laboratories of Denison University, Granville, Ohio. 160 U.S.

Haarlem, Arch. Néerl. Sci. Soc. Holl. Archives Néerlandaises des Sciences exactes et naturelles publiées par la Société Hollandaise des Sciences, Haarlem. 8vo. 22 Hol.

Halle, Leopoldina. Leopoldina. Amtl. Organ der kais. Leopoldinisch-Carolinischen deutschen Akademie der Naturforscher. Halle. Leipzig. [15 Nrn jährl.] 546 Ger.

Handl. Ned. Nat. Geneesk. Congres. Handelingen van het Nederlandsch Natuur en Geneeskundig Congres. 8vo. 26 Hol.

Hansische GeschBl., Leipzig. Hansische Geschichtsblätter, hrsg. v. Verein für hansische Geschichte. Leipzig. [½ jährl.] — Ger.

Heidelberg, SitzBer. Ak. Wiss. Sitzungsberichte der Heidelberger Akademie der Wissenschaften. Heidelberg. [zwangl.] — Ger.

Helios, Leipzig. Helios. Abhandlungen und Mittheilungen aus dem Gesammtgebiete der Naturwissenschaften. Organ des naturwissenschaftlichen Vereins des Reg.-Bez. Frankfurt a. O. Berlin. [jährl.] 579 Ger.

Hermes, Berlin. Hermes. Zeitschrift für classische Philologie hrsg. v. G. Kaibel und C. Robert. Berlin. — Ger.

Himmel u. Erde, Leipzig. Himmel und Erde. Illustrirte naturwissenschaftliche Monatsschrift red. v. Schwahn. Leipzig. 585 Ger.

Hochland, München. Hochland. Monatsschrift für alle Gebiete des Wissens, der Literatur und Kunst, hrsg. v. K. Muth. München u. Kempten. — Ger.

Indianapolis, Ind., Proc. Acad. Sci. Proceedings of the Indiana Academy of Science, Indianapolis. 169 U.S.

Industrie, Bruxelles. L'Industrie. Revue scientifique, industrielle et financière. Bruxelles. [hebdomad.] 166 Bel.

Industria, Milano. Industria, Milano. Rivista tecnica ed economica illustrata. — It.

J. Amer. Chem. Soc., Easton, Pa. Journal of the American Chemical Society, Easton, Pa. 182 U.S.

J. Chim. Phys., Genève. Journal de Chimie physique. Electrochimie, Thermochimie, Radiochimie, Mécanique chimique, Stoechiométrie. Publié par M. Philippe A. Guye. Genève. 8vo. — Swi.

J. éc. polytech., Paris. Journal de l'école polytechnique. (Parait par volume.) Paris. [annuel.] 395 Fr.

J. Gasbeleucht., München. Journal für Gasbeleuchtung und verwandte Beleuchtungsarten, sowie für Wasserversorgung. Organ des deutschen Vereins von Gas- und Wasserfachmännern, hrsg. v. Bunte. München. [wöch.] 983 Ger.

J. pharm., Liége. Journal de pharmacie de Liége. Revue scientifique et professionnelle. Organe de la Fédération pharmaceutique de Liége. Liége. [mensuel.] 108 Bel.

J. phys., Paris. Journal de physique théorique et appliquée, publié par Bouty, Cornu, Lippmann, Mascart, Potier. Paris. [mensuel.] 411 Fr.

J. prakt. Chem., Leipzig. Journal für praktische Chemie, hrsg. v. v. Meyer. Leipzig. [½ monatl.] 598 Ger.

J. Psychol., Leipzig. Journal für Psychologie und neurologie. Zugleich Zeitschrift für Hypnotismus, red. v. K. Brodmann. Leipzig. [zwangl.] — Ger.

Jahrb. Chem., Braunschweig. Jahrbuch der Chemie, hrsg. v. Meyer. Braunschweig. 605 Ger.

Jahrb. drahtlos. Telegr., Leipzig. Jahrbuch der drahtlosen Telegraphie und Telephonie sowie des Gesamtgebietes der elektromagnetischen Schwingungen, hrsg. v. G. Eichhorn. Leipzig. [4 H. jährl.] — Ger.

Jahrb. Radioakt., Leipzig. Jahrbuch der Radioaktivität und Elektronik. Unter . . . besonderer Mitwirkung v. H. Becquerel und William Ramsay hrsg. v. Johannes Stark. Leipzig. — Ger.

Jahrb. schiffsbaut. Ges., Berlin. Jahrbuch der schiffsbautechnischen Gesellschaft. Berlin. 617 Ger.

Jahresber. D. MathVer., Leipzig. Jahresbericht der deutschen Mathematiker-Vereinigung, hrsg. v. Hauck u. Gutzmer. Leipzig. [2–4 H. jährl.] 625 Ger.

Janus, Leyde. Janus, Archives internationales pour l'historie de la Médecine et la Géographie médicale, Leyde. 8vo. 30 Hol.

Kälte-Ind., Hamburg. Die Kälte-Industrie. Offizielles Organ des Verbands Deutscher Eis-Händler und Fabrikanten. Hamburg. [monatl.] — Ger.

Kali, Halle. Kali. Zeitschrift für Gewinnung, Verarbeitung und Verwertung der Kalisalze, hrsg. v. Verein der deutschen Kali-Interessenten. Halle. [½ monatl.] — Ger.

Karlsruhe, Arb. bakt. Inst. Arbeiten aus dem bakteriologischen Institut der technischen Hochschule zu Karlsruhe. Karlsruhe, Wiesbaden. [jährl.] 677 Ger.

Kattowitz, Mitt. BezVer. D. Ing. Mitteilungen des Oberschlesischen Bezirksvereins Deutscher Ingenieure und des Oberschlesischen Elektrotechnischen Vereins. Kattowitz. [½ monatl.] — Ger.

Kiel, Schr. natw. Ver. Schriften des naturwissenschaftlichen Vereins für Schleswig Holstein. Kiel. [jährl.] 691 Ger.

Kjöbenhavn, Forsikr. Tid. Dansk Forsikringstidende, Kjöbenhavn. 28 Den.

Kjöbenhavn, Vid. Selsk. Oars. Oversigt over det kongelige danske Videnskabernes Selskabs Forhandlinger, Kjöbenhavn. 19 Den.

Klin. Monatsbl. Augenheilk., Stuttgart. Klinische Monatsblätter für Augenheilkunde, hrsg. v. Zehender. Stuttgart. 695 Ger.

Kolloidchem. Beih., Dresden. Kolloidchemische Beihefte. Ergänzungshefte zur Kolloidzeitschrift, hrsg. F. V. Oswald. Dresden. [zwangl.] — Ger.

Kosmos, Lwów. Kosmos, czasopismo Polskiego Towarzystwa przyrodników im. Kopernika, red. B. Radziszewski. Lwów. 8vo. [monthly.] 21 Pol.

Kraków, Bul. Inter. Acad. Bulletin International de l'Académie des Sciences de Cracovie, classe des Sciences mathématiques et naturelles, red. J. Rostafiński, Cracovie. 8vo. [monthly.] 11 Pol.

Kraków, Rozpr. Akad. A. Rozprawy Wydziału Matematyczno-Przyrodniczego Akademii Umiejętności. Dział A. nauki matematyczofizyczne. Kraków. 8vo. [monthly.] 14 Pol.

Kunststoffe, München. Kunststoffe. Zeitschrift für Erzeugung und Verwendung veredelter oder chemisch hergestellter Stoffe, hrsg. v. R. Escales. München. [½ monatl.] — Ger.

Math. Phys. L., Budapest. Mathematikai és Physikai Lapok, Budapest. [Mathe
matische und physikalische Blätter, Budapest.] 10 Hun.

Math. Terml. Ért., Budapest.— Mathematikai és Természettudományi Értesitö,
Budapest. [Mathematischer und naturwissenschaftlicher Anzeiger, Budapest.] 11 Hun.

Mechaniker, Berlin. Der Mechaniker. Zeitschrift zur Förderung der Präcisions-
Mechanik und Optik sowie verwandter Gebiete, hrsg. v. Harrwitz. Berlin.
[½ monatl.] 778 Ger.

Med. Klinik, Berlin.— Medizinische Klinik. Wochenschrift für praktische Ärzte,
hrsg. v. Th. Axenfeld etc. Berlin. — Ger.

Metallurgie, Halle.—Metallurgie. Zeitschrift für die gesamte metallurgische
Technik, Aufbereitung, Metallgewinnung, Metallverwertung unter Ausschluss
des Eisenhüttenwesens, hrsg. v. W. Borchers. Halle. [14 tägig.] — Ger.

Milano, Atti fondaz. Cagnola (Ist. lomb.). Atti della fondazione Cagnola presso
l'Istituto lombardo di scienze e lettere, Milano. 101 It.

Milano, Rend. Ist. lomb.—Rendiconti dell'Istituto lombardo di scienze e lettere,
Milano. 105 It.

Mitt. Grenzgeb. Med. Chir., Jena.—Mittheilungen aus den Grenzgebieten der Medicin
und Chirurgie, hrsg. v. Angerer etc. Jena. [jährl. in zwangl. H.] 806 Ger.

Min. Petr. Mitt., Wien.—Tschermaks Mineralogische und Petrographische Mitteilungen, hrsg. v. F[riedrich] Becke. Wien. [2 monatl.] 193 Aus.

Mitt. Forsch.Arb. Ingenieurw., Berlin.—Mitteilungen über Forschungsarbeiten auf
dem Gebiete des Ingenieurwesens, hrsg. vom Vereine deutscher Ingenieure.
Berlin. J. Springer in Komm. [zwangl.] 1273 Ger.

Mitt. Gesch. Med., Hamburg. — Mitteilungen zur Geschichte der Medizin und der
Naturwissenschaften, hrsg. unter red. v. W. A. Kahlbaum, M. Neuburg u.
K. Sudhoff. Hamburg. [¼ jährl.] — Ger.

Monatshefte natw. Unterr., Leipzig. — Monatshefte für den naturwissenschaftlichen Unterricht aller Schulgattungen, hrsg. B. Landsberg u. B. Schmid.
Leipzig. — Ger.

Mon. tecn., Milano.—Il Monitore tecnico, Milano. 108 It.

Mülhausen, Bul. Soc. ind. - Bulletin de la Société industrielle de Mulhouse. Mülhausen. [monatl.] 831 Ger.

Münchener med. Wochenschr.— Münchener medicinische Wochenschrift, red. v.
Spatz. München. 847 Ger.

München, SitzBer. Ak. Wiss. Sitzungsberichte der kgl. bayerischen Akademie
der Wissenschaften zu München. München. [jährl. in zwangl. H.] 839 Ger.

Musikinstrumentenztg, Berlin.—Musik-Instrumentenzeitung, red. v. P. Berger,
Berlin. [wöch.] — Ger.

N. Jahrb. Min., Stuttgart.—Neues Jahrbuch für Mineralogie, Geologie und
Paliontologie, hrsg. v. Bauer. Stuttgart. Nebst Beilage-Bänden. [2 monatl.]
854 Ger.

N. Weltanschaung, Leipzig. -Neue Weltanschauung. Monatschrift für Kulturfort-
schritt auf naturwissenschaftlicher Grundlage, red. v. W. Breitenbach. Leipzig.
— Ger.

Napoli, Atti Ist. Incoragg. sc. nat.—Atti dell'Istituto d'incoraggiamento delle
scienze naturali, Napoli. 113 It.

Napoli, Rend. Soc. sc.—Rendiconti della Società Reale delle scienze fisiche e
matematiche, Napoli. — It.

Nature, London.—Nature, London. 337 U.K.

Natur u. Unterr., Stuttgart. Natur und Unterricht. Monatschrift für den elementaren naturwissenschaftlichen Unterricht, red. v. J. F. Herding. Stuttgart. Ger.

Natw. Rdsch., Braunschweig.—Naturwissenschaftliche Rundschau, hrsg. v. Sklarek. Braunschweig. [wöch.] 867 Ger.

Natw. Wochenschr., Jena.—Naturwissenschaftliche Wochenschrift, red. v. Potonié. Jena. 868 Ger.

Ned. Tijdschr. Geneesk., Amsterdam.—Nederlandsch Tijdschrift voor Geneeskunde, tevens Orgaan der Nederlandsche Maatschappij ter bevordering van Geneeskunst, Amsterdam. 8vo. 39 Hol.

Neuchâtel, Bul. Soc. Sci. Nat.—Bulletin de la Société neuchâteloise des sciences naturelles. Neuchâtel. 8vo. 73 Swi.

Nuovo Cimento, Pisa.—Il Nuovo Cimento, Pisa. 123 It.

Organ Eisenbahnw., Wiesbaden.—Organ für die Fortschritte des Eisenbahnwesens in technischer Beziehung, hrsg. v. Barkhausen. Nebst Ergänzungs-Heften. Wiesbaden. [monatl.] 891 Ger.

Öst. ChemZtg, Wien.—Österreichische Chemiker-Zeitung (vormals Zeitschrift für Nahrungsmittel-Untersuchung. Hygiene und Waarenkunde), hrsg. v. Hans Heger u. Eduard Stiassny. Wien. [! monatl.] 233 Aus.

Öst. Zs. BergHüttWes., Wien.—Österreichische Zeitschrift für Berg- und Hüttenwesen, red. v. Friedrich Toldt und Karl [Ritter] v. Ernst. Wien. [wöch.] 253 Aus.

Padova, Atti Mem. Acc.—Atti e Memorie dell'Accademia di scienze, lettere ed arti, Padova. 120 It.

Paris, C. R. Acad. sci.—Comptes-rendus hebdomadaires des séances de l'Académie des sciences. Paris. 612 Fr.

Petermanns geogr. Mitt., Gotha.—Petermanns geographische Mittheilungen aus Perthes' geographischer Anstalt. Gotha. Nebst Ergänzungs-Heften. [monatl.] 904 Ger.

Petroleum, Berlin.—Petroleum. Zeitschrift für die gesamten Interessen der Petroleum-Industrie und des Petroleum-Handels, hrsg. v. Geo. Springer. Dresden. [wöch.] — Ger.

Pharm. Centralhalle, Dresden.—Pharmaceutische Centralhalle für Deutschland, hrsg. v. Schneider. Dresden. Berlin. [wöch.] 908 Ger.

Pharm. Weekbl., Amsterdam.—Pharmaceutisch Weekblad voor Nederland, Amsterdam. 8vo. 45 Hol.

Philadelphia, Pa., J. Franklin Inst.—Journal of the Franklin Institute, Philadelphia, Pa. 369 U.S.

Philadelphia, Pa., Proc. Amer. Phil. Soc.—Proceedings of the American Philosophical Society. Philadelphia, Pa. 372 U.S.

Philadelphia, Pa., Trans. Wagner Free Inst. Sci.—Transactions of the Wagner Free Institute of Science, Philadelphia, Pa. 376 U.S.

Philippine J. Sci., Manila.—The Philippine Journal of Science, Bureau of Science of the Philippine Islands, Manila. — U.S.

Phil. Mag., London.—London, Edinburgh and Dublin Philosophical Magazine and Journal of Science. 372 U.K.

Phot. Zs., Berlin.—Photographische Zeitschrift, red. v. G. Rothgiesser. Berlin. [wöch.] — Ger.

Phot. Ind., Berlin.—Die photographische Industrie. Fachblatt für Fabrikation und Handel sämtlicher photographischen Belarfsartikel, hrsg. v. Geo. Springer. Dresden. [wöch.] — Ger.

Phot. J., London. Photographic Journal, including Transactions of the Royal Photographic Society, London. 373 U.K.

Physic. Rev., New York, N.Y. Physical Review, (Cornell University), New York, N.Y. [Includes: Ithaca, N.Y., Proc. Amer. Physic. Soc.] 386 U.S.

Physik. Zs., Leipzig. Physikalische Zeitschrift, hrsg. v. Riecke u. Simon. Leipzig. [½ monatl.] 920 Ger.

Pittsburg Pa., Pub. Allegheny Obs. Univ. Pittsburg. Publications of the Allegheny Observatory of the University of Pittsburg [formerly Western University of Pennsylvania]. Pittsburg. U.S.

Politecn., Milano. Il Politecnico, Milano. 151 It.

Pop. Sci. Mon., New York, N.Y. Popular Science Monthly, New York, N.Y. 392 U.S.

Potf. Termt. Kozl., Budapest. Pótfüzetek a Természettudományi Közlonyhöz, Budapest. [Beiblätter zu den naturwissenschaftlichen Mittheilungen, Budapest.] 13 Hun.

Prace mat.-fiz., Warszawa. Prace matematyczno-fizyczne, Warszawa. 8vo. [annual.] 37 Pol.

Prag, Vestn. Ceske Ak. Frant. Jos. Vestnik České Akademie Cisaře Františka Josefa pro Vedy, Slovesnost a Umeni. Praha. [Anzeiger der Čechischen Kaiser Franz Josefs Akademie für Wissenschaft, Literatur und Kunst.] [9 H. jährl.] 312 Aus.

Presse med. belge, Bruxelles. La Presse médicale belge. Bruxelles. [hebdomad.] 142 Bel.

Przegl. techn., Warszawa. Przegląd techniczny, tygodnik poświęcony sprawom techniki i przemysłu, red. J. Heilpern, Warszawa. fol. [weekly.] 44 Pol.

Psych. Rev. Monogr. Suppl., Baltimore, Md. The Psychological Review. Series of Monograph Supplements. New York and London. — U.S.

Radium, Paris. Le Radium, Paris. — Fr.

Rec. Trav. chim., Leiden. Recueil des Travaux chimiques des Pays-Bas et de la Belgique, Leiden. 8vo. 47 Hol.

Rev. gén. sci., Paris. Revue générale des sciences pures et appliquées, dir. L. Olivier. Paris. [bi-mensuel.] 693 Fr.

Rev. quest. scient., Bruxelles. Revue des questions scientifiques. Bruxelles. [trimestr.] 153 Bel.

Rev. sci., Paris. Revue scientifique de la France et de l'étranger, dir. Ch. Richet. Paris. [hebdomad.] 749 Fr.

Rev. univ. intern. illustr. Bruxelles. Revue universelle internationale illustrée. Science, industrie, finance. Bruxelles. 4to. [trimensuel.] — Bel.

Rev. univ. mines, Liège. Revue universelle des mines, de la métallurgie, des travaux publics, des sciences et des arts appliqués à l'industrie. Liège. [mensuel.] 159 Bel.

Riv. Artig. Genio, Roma. Rivista di Artiglieria e Genio, Roma. 162 It.

Riv. geogr. ital., Roma. Rivista geografica italiana, Roma. 165 It.

Riv. ligure sc. lett. ar., Genova. Rivista ligure di scienze, lettere ed arti, organo della Società di letture e conversazioni scientifiche, Genova. 169 It.

Riv. maritt., Roma. Rivista marittima, Roma. 170 It.

Riv. music., Torino. Rivista musicale italiana, Torino. 174 It.

Roma, Bul. Acc. med. Bullettino dell'Accademia medica, Roma. 201 It.

Roma, Mem. Acc. Nuovi Lincei. Memorie dell'Accademia pontificia dei Nuovi Lincei, Roma. 204 It.

Rostock, SitzBer. natf. Ges. — Sitzungsberichte der naturforschenden Gesellschaft zu Rostock. Anhang zum Archiv des Vereins der Freunde der Naturgeschichte in Mecklenburg. Rostock. 1293 Ger.

Sammelbde intern. Musikges., Leipzig. — Sammelbände der internationalen Musikgesellschaft. Leipzig. [⅟ jährl.] — Ger.

Samml. chem. Vortr., Stuttgart. — Sammlung chemischer und chemisch-technischer Vorträge, hrsg. v. Ahrens. Stuttgart. [monatl.] 970 Ger.

Schuss u. Waffe, Neudamm. — Schuss und Waffe, illustrierte gemeinverständliche Zeitschrift für jagdliches, militärisches und sportliches Schiesswesen, Schiessplatz-Anlagen, Waffentechnik, Minen- und Torpedowesen. — Ger.

Schweiz. Vierteljahrschr. Zahnheilk., Zürich. — Schweizerische Vierteljahrschrift für Zahnheilkunde. Revue trimestrielle suisse d'odontologie. Zürich. 8vo. 103 Swi.

Schweiz. Wochenschr. Chem., Zürich. — Schweizerische Wochenschrift für Chemie und Pharmacie. Journal suisse de chimie et de pharmacie. Zürich. 8vo. 104 Swi.

Scientia, Bologna. — "Scientia" Rivista di Scienza, Bologna. — It.

Siena, Atti Acc. fisiocritici. — Atti dell'Accademia dei fisiocritici. Siena. 212 It.

Sperimentale, Firenze. — Lo Sperimentale. Firenze. 215 It.

Stadt. Tiefbau, Heidelberg. — Der städtische Tiefbau. Zeitschrift für neuzeitlichen Ausbau, technisch-, gesundheitliche und wirtschaftliche Entwicklung der Städte. Heidelberg. [⅟ monatl.] — Ger.

Stahl u. Eisen, Düsseldorf. — Stahl und Eisen. Zeitschrift für das deutsche Eisenhüttenwesen, red. v. Schrödter u. Beumer. Düsseldorf. [½ monatl.] 1010 Ger.

Steinbruch, Berlin. — Der Steinbruch. Zeitschrift für die Kenntnis und Verwertung natürlicher Gesteine. Berlin. [⅟ monatl.] — Ger.

Stimme, Berlin. — Die Stimme. Centralblatt für Stimme- und Tonbildung, Gesangunterricht und Stimmhygiene, hrsg. v. T. S. Flatau etc. Berlin. [monatl.] — Ger.

Stockholm Medd. Vet. Ak. Nobelinst. — Meddelanden fran K. Vetenskasakademiens Nobelinstitut. Uppsala, Stockholm. 8vo. — Swe.

Stockholm, Vet.-Ak. Handl. — Kongl. Svenska Vetenskaps-Akademiens Handlingar. Stockholm. 4to. 40 Swe.

Strassenbau, Halle. — Der Strassenbau. Zeitschrift für Tiefbau im Stadt- und Gemeindewesen. Organ für Strassenbau, Bewässerung, Entwässerung und Stadtreinigung. Halle. [10 tägig.] — Ger.

Strassburg, Monatsber. Ges. Wiss. — Monatsbericht der Gesellschaft zur Förderung der Wissenschaften, des Ackerbaues und der Künste im Unterelsass. Bulletins mensuels de la Société des sciences, agriculture et arts de la Basse-Alsace. Strassburg. [2 monatl.] 1020 Ger.

Südd. ApothZtg, Stuttgart. — Süddeutsche Apothekerzeitung, hrsg. v. Kober. Stuttgart. [½ wöch.] 1024 Ger.

Sv. Kem. Tidskr., Stockholm. — Svensk Kemisk Tidskrift. Organ för Kemistsamfundet i Stockholm, Kemiska sektionerna i Upsala och Lund samt Kemistföreningen vid Stockholms högskola, utgifven af A. G. Ekstrand. Stockholm. 8vo. 46 Swe.

Taschenbuch f. Präzisionsmechaniker, Nikolassee. — Taschenbuch für Prazisionsmechaniker, Optiker, Elektromechaniker und Glasinstrumentenmacher, hrsg. v. F. Harrwitz. Berlin—Nikolassee. [jährl.] — Ger.

Taschenbuch Math., Leipzig. — Taschenbuch für Mathematiker und Physiker, hrsg. F. Auerbach. Leipzig u. Berlin. [jährl.] — Ger.

Techn. Monatshefte, Stuttgart. Technische Monatshefte. Zeitschrift für Technik, Kultur und Leben, hrsg. v. F. Kuhl etc. Stuttgart. — Ger.

Tekn. Tidskr., Stockholm. Teknisk Tidskrift. Utgifven af Svenska Teknologföreningen med understöd af Letterstedtska Föreningen. Stockholm. 4to. 50 Swe.

Termt. Közl., Budapest. Természettudományi Közlöny. Budapest. [Naturwissenschaftliche Mittheilungen, Budapest.] 16 Hun.

Textil, Berlin.— Textil. Tageszeitung für die gesamte Textil Industrie. Berlin. — Ger.

ThonindZtg, Berlin. Thonindustrie-Zeitung, red. v. Cramer etc. Berlin. [120 Nrn jährl.] 1047 Ger.

Tokyo, Bul. Cent. Met. Obs. Bulletin of the Central Meteorological Observatory. *English Language.* Tokyo. — Jap.

Tōkyō, Buts. Z. Tōkyō Butsuri gakkō Zasshi. [Journal of the Tōkyō School of Physics.] 22 Jap.

Tōkyō, Kishō Sh. Kishō Shūshi. [Journal of the Meteorological Society.] Tōkyō. 31 Jap.

Tōkyō, Su. Buts. Kw. K. Tōkyō Sūgaku Butsurigaku Kwai Kiji. [Proceedings of the Tōkyō Mathematical and Physical Society.] *Japanese and European languages.* 38 Jap.

Torino, Giorn. Acc. med. — Giornale della R. Accademia di medicina, Torino. 226 It.

Torino, Mem. Acc. sc. — Memorie della R. Accademia delle scienze, Torino. 228 It.

Turbine, Berlin. Die Turbine. Zeitschrift für modernen Schnellbetrieb, für Dampf-, Gas-, Wind und Wasserturbinen, hrsg. v. R. Mewes. Berlin. [½ monatl.] — Ger.

Uhlands Wochenschr. Ind., Leipzig. Uhlands Wochenschrift für Industrie und Technik. Leipzig. 1065 Ger.

Umschau, Frankfurt a. M. Die Umschau. Uebersicht über die Fortschritte und Bewegungen auf dem Gesammtgebiet der Wissenschaft, Technik, Litteratur und Kunst, hrsg. v. Bechhold. Frankfurt a. M. [wöch.] 1068 Ger.

Union ing., Louvain.— Union des ingénieurs sortis des écoles spéciales de Louvain. Louvain. [trimestr.] 168 Bel.

Uns. Welt, Godesberg.—Unsere Welt. Illustrierte Monatschrift zur Förderung der Naturerkenntnis, hrsg. v. Keplerbund. Godesberg. — Ger.

Unterrichtsbl. Math., Berlin. Unterrichtsblätter für Mathematik und Naturwissenschaften, hrsg. v. Schwalbe u. Pietzker. Berlin. [2 monatl.] 1071 Ger.

Upsala, Univ. Arsskr.— Upsala Universitets Arsskrift. Upsala. 8vo. 59 Swe.

Utrecht, Onderz. Physiol. Lab. Onderzoekingen gedaan in het physiologisch Laboratorium der Utrechtsche Hoogeschool, Utrecht. 8vo. 54 Hol.

Venezia, Ateneo Veneto.—Ateneo Veneto, Venezia. 234 It.

Venezia, Atti Ist. ven. Atti del R. Istituto veneto di scienze, lettere ed arti, Venezia. 235 It.

Verh. D. otol. Ges., Jena. Verhandlungen der deutschen otologischen Gesellschaft. Jena. [jährl.] 1080 Ger.

Verh. D. Röntgenges., Hamburg. Verhandlungen der deutschen Röntgen-Gesellschaft, red. v. Albers-Schönberg. Hamburg. [zwangl.] — Ger.

Verh. Ges. D. Natf., Leipzig. Verhandlungen der Gesellschaft deutscher Naturforscher und Aerzte. Leipzig. [jährl.] 1083 Ger.

Verh. Schweiz. Natf. Ges.—Verhandlungen der schweizerischen naturforschenden Gesellschaft. Aarau, Basel etc. 8vo. 116 Swi.

Verh. Ver. D. Laryng. Würzburg — Verhandlungen der deutschen laryngologischen Gesellschaft, hrsg. i. Auftrage des Vorstandes. Würzburg. [2 jährl.] — Ger.

Verkehrstechn. Woche, Berlin. — Verkehrstechnische Woche. Technische Rundschau über das Gebiet des gesamten Verkehrswesens, red. v. G. Braun. Berlin. [wöch.] — Ger.

Vopr. fiziki, St. Peterburg. — Вопросы физики. С.-Петербургъ [Questions physiques. St. Pétersbourg]. — Russ.

Warszawa, Spraw. Tow. Nauk. — Sprawozdania Towarzystwa Naukowego Warszawskiego. [Proceedings of the Scientific Society in Warsaw. Warsaw.] — Pol.

Washington, D.C., Dept. Comm. Lab. Bul. Bur. Stand. — Department of Commerce and Labor. Bulletin of the Bureau of Standards, Washington, D.C. — U.S.

Washington, D.C., Proc. Biol. Soc. — Proceedings of the Biological Society of Washington, Washington, D.C. 488 U.S.

Washington, D.C., Smithsonian Inst. Cont. Knowl. — Smithsonian Institution. Smithsonian Contributions to Knowledge, Washington, D.C. 496 U.S.

Washington, D.C., Smithsonian Inst. Misc. Collect. — Smithsonian Institution. Smithsonian Miscellaneous Collections, Washington, D.C. 497 U.S.

Washington, D.C., Smithsonian Inst. Rep. — Smithsonian Institution. Annual Report of the Board of Regents, Washington, D.C. 502 U.S.

Washington, D.C., U. S. Dept. Agric. Bul. Mt. Weather Obs. — U. S. Department of Agriculture. Weather Bureau. Bulletin of the Mount Weather Observatory, Washington. — U.S.

Washington, D.C., U. S. Dept. Agric. Month. Weath. Rev. — U. S. Department of Agriculture. Monthly Weather Review. Washington, D.C. 509 U.S.

Wasser u. Gas, Oldenburg. — Wasser und Gas. Halbmonatsschrift für die Gesamtinteressen städtischer Wasser- und Gaswerke. hrsg. v. E. Stein. Oldenburg. — Ger.

Wellington, Trans. and Proc. N. Zeal. Inst. — Transactions and Proceedings of the New Zealand Institute. Wellington. — N.Z.

Weltall, Berlin. — Das Weltall. Illustrierte Zeitschrift für Astronomie und verwandte Gebiete. Berlin. 1287 Ger.

Wiad. mat., Warszawa. — Wiadomości matematyczne, red. S. Dickstein, Warszawa. 8vo. [once in two months.] 54 Pol.

Wien, Schr. Ver. Verbr. Natw. Kenntn. — Schriften des Vereins zur Verbreitung Naturwissenschaftlicher Kenntnisse in Wien. [Nebentitel:] Populäre Vorträge aus allen Fächern der Naturwissenschaft, hrsg. vom Vereine zur Verbreitung Naturwissenschaftlicher Kenntnisse in Wien. Wien. [jährl. bezw. in zwangl. H.] 471 Aus.

Wien, SitzBer. Ak. Wiss. — Sitzungsberichte der Kaiserlichen Akademie der Wissenschaften. Mathematisch-Naturwissenschaftliche Klasse. Wien. [4 Abt. zwangl.] 472 Aus.

Wien, Verh. ZoolBot. Ges. — Verhandlungen der k. k. Zoologisch-Botanischen Gesellschaft in Wien, red. v. A[nton] Handlirsch. Wien. [10 H. jährl.] 479 Aus.

Wien, VierteljBer. Phys. Chem. Unterr. — Vierteljahrsberichte des Wiener Vereines zur Förderung des Physikalischen und Chemischen Unterrichtes. Zugleich Organ der Chemisch-Physikalischen Gesellschaft, red. v. Karl Haas. Wien. 480 Aus.

Wiesbaden, Amtsbl. LandwKammer. — Amtsblatt der Landwirtschaft-Kammer für den Regierungsbezirk Wiesbaden und Zeitschrift des Vereins nassauischer Land- und Forstwirte. Wiesbaden. [wöch.] Ger.

Wiss. Rdsch., Leipzig. Wissenschaftliche Rundschau. Zeitschrift für die allgemeinwissenschaftliche Fortbildung des Lehrers, hrsg. H. Baege.   Leipzig. [½ monatl.] — Ger.

Wr. Med. WochSchr., Wien. Wiener Medizinische Wochenschrift, red. v. Heinrich Adler. Wien. 199 Aus.

Wszechswiat, Warszawa. Wszechświat, tygodnik poświęcony naukom przyrodniczym, red. Br. Znatowicz. Warszawa. 4to. [weekly.] 57 Pol.

Zs. angew. Chem., Berlin. Zeitschrift für angewandte Chemie, hrsg. v. Fischer u. Wenghöffer. Berlin. [wöch.] 1156 Ger.

Zs. anorg. Chem., Hamburg. Zeitschrift für anorganische Chemie, hrsg. v. Lorenz u. Küster. Hamburg. [12–18 H. jährl.] 1158 Ger.

Zs. Archit., Wiesbaden. — Zeitschrift für Architektur und Ingenieurwesen, hrsg. von dem Vorstande des Architektur- und Ingenieur-Vereins zu Hannover. Schriftleiter C. Wolff [von 1901 an]. Wiesbaden. 1159 Ger.

Zs. Augenheilk., Berlin. Zeitschrift für Augenheilkunde, red. v. Kuhnt u. v. Michel. Berlin. [monatl.] 1160 Ger.

Zs. Balneol., Berlin. — Zeitschrift für Balneologie, Klimatologie und Kurort-Hygiene, hrsg. v. Graefner und Kaminer. Berlin. [½ monatl.] — Ger.

Zs. Beleuchtungsw., Berlin. —Zeitschrift für Beleuchtungswesen, Heiz und Lüftungs-Technik, hrsg. v. Lux. Berlin. [36 H. jährl.] 1165 Ger.

Zs. Biol., München. — Zeitschrift für Biologie, hrsg. v. Kühne u. Voit.   München. [1 jährl.] 1168 Ger.

Zs. biol. Techn., Leipzig. —Zeitschrift für biologische Technik und Methodik, hrsg. v. M. Gildemeister. Leipzig. — Ger.

Zs. Dampfkessel, Berlin. —Zeitschrift für Dampfkessel- und Maschinenbetrieb. Mitteilungen aus der Praxis des Dampfkessel- und Dampfmaschinen-Betriebes sowie des Feuerungs- und allgemeinen motorischen Betriebes, hrsg. v. H. Minssen etc. Berlin. [wöch.] — Ger.

Zs. Elektroch., Halle. —Zeitschrift für Elektrochemie, hrsg. v. Nernst u. Borchers. Halle. [wöch.] 1177 Ger.

Zs. Elektrot., Potsdam. —Zeitschrift für Elektrotechnik und Maschinenbau. red. v. Bauch. Potsdam. [½ monatl.] 1178 Ger.

Zs. Flugtechnik, München. — Zeitschrift für Flugtechnik und Motorluftschiffahrt, hrsg. u. Schriftl. A. Vorreiter. München. [½ monatl.] — Ger.

Zs. ges. Neurol., Berlin. —Zeitschrift für die gesamte Neurologie und Psychiatrie, hrsg. v. A. Alzheimer etc. Berlin und Leipzig. [zwangl.] — Ger.

Zs. Hyg., Leipzig. — Zeitschrift für Hygiene und Infektionskrankheiten, hrsg. v. Koch u. Flügge. Leipzig. [8 H. jährl.] 1193 Ger.

Zs. InstrBau, Leipzig. — Zeitschrift für Instrumentenbau. Offizielles Organ der Berufsgenossenschaft der Musikinstrumentenindustrie etc., hrsg. v. de Wit. Leipzig. [36 H. jährl.] 1196 Ger.

Zs. Instrumentenk., Berlin. —Zeitschrift für Instrumentenkunde, red. v. Lindeck. Berlin. Nebst Beiblatt: Deutsche Mechaniker-Zeitung. Vereinsblatt der deutschen Gesellschaft für Mechanik und Optik. [monatl.] 1197 Ger.

Zs. Kältelnd., München. Zeitschrift für die gesammte Kälte-Industrie, hrsg. v. Lorenz. München. [monatl.] 1198 Ger.

Zs. Kolloide, Dresden. —Zeitschrift für Chemie und Industrie der Kolloide, hrsg. v. R. Ditmar. Dresden. [monatl.] — Ger.

Zs. komprim. Gase, Weimar. — Zeitschrift für komprimirte und flüssige Gase sowie für die Presshuft-Industrie, hrsg. v. M. Altschul und C. Heinel. Weimar. [monatl.] 1281 Ger.

Zs. Krystallogr., Leipzig. —Zeitschrift für Krystallographie und Mineralogie, hrsg. v. Groth. Leipzig. [12–18 H. jährl.] 1203 Ger.

Zs. math., Leipzig. —Zeitschrift für Mathematik und Physik, begründet v. Schlömilch, hrsg. v. Mehmke u. Cantor. Leipzig. [2 monatl.] 1210 Ger.

Zs. öff. Chem., Plauen. —Zeitschrift für öffentliche Chemie, red. v. Riechelmann. Plauen. [½ monatl.] 1216 Ger.

Zs. physik. Chem., Leipzig. —Zeitschrift für physikalische Chemie, hrsg. v. Ostwald u. van't Hoff. Leipzig. [½ monatl.] 1225 Ger.

Zs. physik. Ther., Leipzig. —Zeitschrift für physikalische und diätätische Therapie, hrsg. v. v. Leyden u. A. Goldscheider. Leipzig. [monatl.] — Ger.

Zs. physik. Unterr., Berlin. —Zeitschrift für den physikalischen und chemischen Unterricht, hrsg. v. Poske. Berlin. [2 monatl.] 1226 Ger.

Zs. Psychol., Leipzig. —Zeitschrift für Psychologie und Physiologie der Sinnesorgane, hrsg. v. Ebbinghaus und König. Leipzig. [18 H. jährl.] 1229 Ger.

Zs. Röntgenkunde, Leipzig. —Zeitschrift für Röntgenkunde und Radiumforschung, red. v. P. Krause. Leipzig. [monatl.] — Ger.

Zs. Sauerstoffind., Berlin. —Zeitschrift für Sauerstoff- u. Stickstoff-Industrie und damit zusammenhängende Gebiete, hrsg. v. R. Mewes. Berlin. [monatl.] — Ger.

Zs. Schiesswesen, München. —Zeitschrift für das gesamte Schiess- und Sprengstoffwesen, hrsg. v. R. Escales. München. [½ monatl.] — Ger.

Zs. Schulgesundhtspfl., Hamburg. —Zeitschrift für Schulgesundheitspflege, red. v. Erismann. Hamburg. [monatl.] 1231 Ger.

Zs. Schwachstromtechn., München. —Zeitschrift für Schwachstromtechnik. Zentralblatt für Telegraphie, Telephonie, elektr. Apparaten- und Messkunde und verwandte Gebiete, hrsg. v. J. Baumann. München. [½ monatl.] — Ger.

Zs. Turbinenwesen, München. —Zeitschrift für das gesamte Turbinenwesen, Wasserturbinen, Dampfturbinen mit Einschluss der Turbodynamos und der Turbinenschiffe sowie der Kreisel, Pumpen und Gebläse, hrsg. v. W. A. Müller. München. [36 H. jährl.] — Ger.

Zs. Urol., Berlin. —Zeitschrift für Urologie (Fortsetzung des Zentralblattes für die Krankheiten der Harn- und Sexualorgane und der Monatsberichte für Urologie), hrsg. v. L. Casper etc. Berlin. [monatl.] — Ger.

Zs. wiss. Phot., Leipzig. —Zeitschrift für wissenschaftliche Photographie, Photophysik und Photochemie. Leipzig. 1368 Ger.

Zee, Tijdschr. Ned. Stoomv., Rotterdam. —De Zee, Tijdschrift gewijd aan de belangen der Nederlandsche Stoom- en Zeilvaart, Rotterdam. 8vo. 60 Hol.

Lightning Source UK Ltd.
Milton Keynes UK
UKHW040029260920
370514UK00002BA/514

9 789354 048678